RICHARD MASTERS stu
(with Computing) at the
since spent over 30 yea
devoted to financing projects which are socially and
environmentally constructive. He also spends a number
of hours each week looking after adults with learning
disabilities.

RUDOLF STEINER AND
SOCIAL REFORM

Threefolding and other proposals

RICHARD MASTERS

RUDOLF STEINER PRESS

Rudolf Steiner Press
Hillside House, The Square
Forest Row, East Sussex RH18 5ES

www.rudolfsteinerpress.com

Published by Rudolf Steiner Press in 2022
© Richard Masters 2022

A catalogue record for this book is available from the British Library

ISBN 978 1 85584 598 5

Cover by SI-EM Designs
Typeset by Symbiosys Technologies, Visakhapatnam, India
Printed and bound by 4Edge Ltd., Essex

For those who are suffering
who deserve better.

Contents

1. Preliminary Remarks

1.1   Aim of the book

In the face of profound environmental degradation, and with heartbreaking news stories overwhelming us more or less daily, stories of crushing life circumstances tormenting people not only overseas but also closer to home, this book is offered as a contribution to the debate about how society could improve the ways it organises itself, how we might coexist in a more dignified manner.

Rudolf Steiner (1861—1925) is not especially known for his thoughts on public affairs, but he wrote and spoke at some length on the subject over a number of years, and indeed in Germany enjoyed something like fame on account of his writings and campaigning on the topic at the end of the Great War.

In the following pages the attempt is made to bring together the various threads of his suggestions in a structured and accessible way that clarifies what, on the one hand, was in effect his main thesis, and what, on the other, amount to more ancillary suggestions and examples. It is an attempt to distil the essentials from some fifteen English books of source material, plus dozens of lectures untranslated from the German, without inappropriately over-simplifying anything. As well as his writings on the subject, Steiner gave a hundred or so related lectures and discussion evenings across Europe—his audiences ranging from 'the great and good' to illiterate, dispossessed factory workers.

The hope is that readers, by the end of the book, will feel they have a reasonable overview and understanding of Steiner's main observations on the matter without having to read all the primary literature.

Here and there, reflections are also offered on the extent to which his proposals relate—or don't relate—to current practice.

1.2   Format

The book is essentially a guided tour through a collection of Steiner's more salient observations regarding societal health—observations which are quoted verbatim. The book started out as a collection of these quotes, and as it progressed it continued to seem fitting to retain them. This unabashed regurgitating of passages by Steiner will not please every palate. But in the end I have tried to write a book that I myself would have found helpful when looking to get a foothold into the subject.

Misunderstanding, misinterpreting and even misrepresenting Steiner's social ideas are easy mistakes to make, and an advantage of the inclusion of so much from 'the horse's mouth' is that it both removes any ambiguity as to what Steiner actually said, as well as greatly reduces the danger of any second-hand misinterpretation. Another advantage of original quotes is that these provide more points of reference for anyone wanting to investigate the original material.

Throughout, quotes by Steiner are in shaded boxes. They are accompanied by a 'CW' reference followed, where relevant, by a page number or date.[1]

I should apologise in advance that these quotations are peppered throughout with the male 'he / his / him' etc. which are taken verbatim from the English translations of his works, and which, in turn, are simply a direct translation of the German of the time, not any indication of gender bias on Steiner's part.[2]

The book assumes no prior knowledge of Steiner's works, so anyone well-versed in the subject may find the going a bit repetitive and elementary. Hopefully, though, even *they* may find it useful at times, since the various topics and sub-topics are presented in a systematic way which should allow easy return to areas of particular interest. It is hoped there will be something here for all readers.

1.3   Why Steiner ?

Steiner is better known today as an educationalist and esotericist than as a social reformer. His 'biodynamic' agriculture also increasingly

---

[1] CW (collected works) reference numbers are synonymous with the German GA (*Gesamtausgabe*) numbers used by the Rudolf Steiner archive. The works referenced are listed at the back of the book.

[2] Steiner was relatively ahead of his time in being un-sexist, as illustrated for example by the fact that the executive council he appointed when he founded the Anthroposophical Society included women, or by the fact that the Christian Community / Movement for Religious Renewal (a Christian denomination set up by clerics who had asked Steiner for advice) accepted women priests at all levels from the outset.

catches people's attention. Amongst other things, this produces award-winning wines, and consistently outperforms both conventional and organic agriculture in long-term soil fertility tests[3]—something of critical concern when the UN has suggested there may only be sixty harvests left in conventionally-farmed soil.[4] Notable, also, is that Steiner predicted future bee colony problems and, long before the outbreak of BSE[5], he warned that if you fed meat to cows, they would go mad.[6] In 2017 HRH Prince Charles noted: 'It is truly remarkable that so many of the farming principles and practices highlighted in Steiner's 1924 agricultural lectures are still so pertinent today. If only the visionary advice he gave had been more widely recognized and adopted, perhaps much of the damage that intensive farming has inflicted on our long-suffering planet ... could have been prevented'.[7]

During Steiner's life, however, it was for his suggestions concerning public affairs that he was probably most widely known, even though these amounted to under 5% of his mammoth output. The attention these views attracted is outlined briefly in Section 4.1 ('Public exposure').

Although Steiner's first degree was in the sciences and his PhD was in philosophy and mathematics, and although as a 21-year-old graduate he was commissioned to edit Goethe's *scientific* writings, a key phenomenon behind Steiner and his work—indeed *the* key phenomenon, perhaps—is his claim to a wide-ranging clairvoyance that could observe in full, alert, waking consciousness an 'other' world, a spiritual world that he asserted had objective reality. This capability was very different from what he referred to as 'vague mysticism', for which he had no time. Remarkably, he described the increase in awareness between a normal waking consciousness and a

---

[3] See, for example, the findings of 20-year field trials at https:www.fibl.org/en/Switzerland/research/soil-sciences/bw-projekte.dok-trial.html#c29084.

[4] Susan Cosier, 'The world needs topsoil to grow 95% of its food—but it's rapidly disappearing', *The Guardian*, 30 May 2019.

[5] Bovine spongiform encephalopathy—or 'mad cow disease'—when over 4 million head of cattle were slaughtered during the eradication programme and over 200 people died from contracting the variant Kreutzfeldt-Jacob disease.

[6] Mark Watts, 'The birth of BSE', *The Independent*, 31 March 1996.

[7] HRH Prince Charles addressing the 2017 biodynamic conference, https://youtu.be/MImiGhM92_I.

heightened clairvoyance as being equivalent in magnitude to the increase in awareness when one wakes up from a dreaming sleep. A further assertion he made was that everyone has latent faculties which can, over a long period of sustained mental / meditative practice, slowly become more sensitive to the esoteric phenomena he described. This study of spirit based on honed faculties of soul (thinking / feeling / willing) he called anthroposophy or spiritual science.

[People] have lost faith in the strength of spiritual life. They do not believe that there can be any kind of spiritual life able to overcome the remoteness and unreality that has characterised it during the last few centuries.

It is a kind of spiritual life such as this, nevertheless, that is the goal of anthroposophy. The sources it would draw from are the sources of reality itself. Those forces that hold sway in our inner-most being are the same forces that are at work in external reality. Scientific thinking cannot penetrate down to these sources when it merely elaborates natural law intellectually out of external experience. Yet the world views that are founded on a more religious basis are no longer in touch with these forces either. They accept the traditions that have been handed down without penetrating to their fountainhead ... The spiritual science of anthroposophy, however, seeks to penetrate to this fountainhead. [...] The insights of spiritual science ... shape themselves into ideas that are not mere mental concepts, but rather something saturated with the forces of reality. Hence such ideas are able to carry within them the force of reality when they offer themselves as guides to social action. One can well understand that, at first, a spiritual science such as this should meet with mistrust. Such mistrust will not last when people come to recognise the essential difference that exists between this spiritual science and modern natural science, which is assumed today to be the only kind of science possible. If one can struggle through to a recognition of the difference, then one will cease to believe that one must avoid social ideas when one is intent upon the practical work of shaping social reality. One will begin to see, instead, that practical social ideas can be had only from a spiritual life that can find its way to the roots of human nature. One will see clearly that in modern times social events have fallen into disorder because people have tried to master them with thoughts from which reality constantly struggled free. (CW24, pp. 31-32)

... the anthroposophical spiritual movement should not be regarded as something which gives you the opportunity to listen to Sunday afternoon sermons, which caress the soul because they speak of an everlasting life, and so forth; but [it] should be taken as a path which enables us to cope in a real, concrete way with the modern problems of life, the burning problems of the present. (CW188 [ii], 1 February 1919)

Kindle a deeper social feeling, a deeper understanding between one person and another when social matters are being discussed, and you will be discharging in a truly social manner one of the living tasks coming into being through anthroposophical spiritual science. (CW193, p.16)

Whilst the possibility of esoteric phenomena that have objective reality may be inspiring to some, it is appreciated that, to others (possibly, most), claims of such seem eccentric and implausible. Speaking for myself: without the sort of mind and self-discipline required to attain any of the extra-sensory faculties mentioned, I can't claim to know from direct experience the rightness—or otherwise—of Steiner's claims. But having read dozens of his books over some 30 years, I am convinced he was a man of integrity.

Whether the other-worldly aspect of Steiner's work intrigues you or sends you running for the hills, it is problematic either way insofar as the existence of a divine world is difficult to prove or disprove. Archbishop Dr Rowan Williams and arch-atheist Dr Richard Dawkins didn't manage when they sat down together in 2012![8] So, for reasons of unverifiability, much of what Steiner describes is, perhaps understandably, avoided by academia.

But given that we still seem to be getting an awful lot wrong in public life, even in countries with a good standard of living, an approach from a less conventional quarter seems deserving of consideration. So many burning issues remain to be solved despite (a) politicians, econ-

---

[8] 'Nature of human beings and the question of their ultimate origin'—debate held at the Sheldonian Theatre, Oxford.

omists and social scientists the world over having chewed on the subject of societal health for centuries, (b) thousands (possibly millions) of degrees—including doctorates—devoted to these and other relevant subjects having been completed, (c) a range of political approaches having been tried, and (d) many thousands of progressive, devoted groupings of ordinary people trying to improve matters by doing things differently / more thoughtfully (and these often achieve wonderful, positive results, as we know). There remains a gnawing undercurrent in society, a lingering malaise, an open wound which badly needs attention—although it should be pointed out at the outset that Steiner does not claim his suggestions are any sort of utopian solution that will fix everything. Yet the on-going relevance of some of them is striking.

His ideas about public life can be considered on their own merits, without reference to anything other-worldly. In this book, references to anything esoteric are almost entirely avoided. Steiner's observations are taken at face value, and the book proceeds on the basis that his articulating of what he saw as occult realities no more disqualifies his political ideas from consideration than, say, Isaac Newton's or Marie Curie's religious views disqualify their scientific works from analysis. His yearning to alleviate human distress is without doubt a laudable goal; readers can make up their own minds whether any of the suggestions he makes might be useful.

1.4   Limitations of a book on a limitless subject

... the conditions of human life have grown so complicated that it is extremely difficult to survey them ... (CW332a, p. 25)

What can we make of the social question nowadays? If we look squarely at human life as it is today we certainly do not find a clear picture with any obvious solutions. What we see is a huge number of differentiated conditions of life spread across the face of the earth, conditions that have created great gulfs and abysses within humanity between internal human experiences and the external life of commerce and industry. [...] Compared with the complicated facts of social, economic life, what we see under the microscope or in the sky through the telescope is exceedingly simple. (CW305(ii), p. 107)

Infinitely more complicated, variable and unstable are the phenomena in economics than in nature—more fluctuating, less capable of being grasped with any defined or hard and fast concepts. (CW340, p. 28)

... in economics [...] one is dealing with something alive and changing and one has always to be prepared, therefore, to modify one's concepts. Economics does not deal with substances, which one can shape, but with living human beings. [...] You will readily appreciate ... that it is difficult to work in economics. (CW341, p. 182)

As well as acknowledging the extreme complexity of social life, and notwithstanding his claims to unusual insight, Steiner was also at pains to emphasise (a) that any attempt to improve the body social was only ever likely to constitute a partial fix, and (b) that an approach to improving things that might seem desirable and appropriate for the peoples in one part of the world may be less so elsewhere. On many occasions he pointed out it was an improved direction of travel that he was describing, not any detailed solution, and certainly neither a one-size-fits-all nor a once-and-for-all solution. Social forms that may be suitable in one age or place may well not be so in others. This will be covered in more detail later.

No one should cherish the illusion that any social institution could ever create an 'ideal situation'. What can be attained, however, is a viable, healthy social organism. (CW24, p. 14)

... we must not ask whether human beings have been created by circumstances or circumstances by human beings. It is essential to understand that each is both cause and effect, that everything affects everything else. The foremost question to ask is: 'What social arrangements will enable people to have the right thoughts on matters of social concern, and what kind of thoughts must exist so that these right social arrangements can arise?'

In practical life people tend to think in terms of doing one thing after another. But this leads nowhere. We can only make progress if we think in circles, but many people do not feel up to doing this ... It is essential to think in circles. Looking at external circumstances we must admit that they have been created by people but also that

*people are affected by them. And looking at the things people do
we must realise that these actions bring about the external circumstances but also that they are sustained by these same external
circumstances. To arrive at reality we must skip back and forth in
our thoughts, but people do not like doing this. (CW305(ii), p. 153)*

Although this book sets out to leave the reader with some idea of Steiner's take on what can make the social organism healthy, or at the very least, healthier, the occasional references to other authors come nowhere near close to a thorough survey of related literature. Personally, I am only aware of a fraction of all the innovative and painstaking efforts being made by progressive projects and thinkers to alleviate social torment. So, apologies in advance to all those who are already working or campaigning for anything along the lines of what is contained herein, but of whose efforts I am ignorant—efforts which are consequently not referenced as examples.

Where I *have* referenced current practice, this usually relates to the Anglo-Saxon West; but these references will hopefully find some resonance with readers elsewhere, too, and so have relevance to people in most countries.

2. What's the Problem ?

As alluded to above, categorising societal problems into causes and effects is not always straightforward. A broken shop window might be a societal problem that one sees as an end result, an effect, a symptom, 'damage'. Behind this there might be a miscreant who threw a stone, so one might conclude: miscreants are the cause of broken windows. Digging deeper, one might ask: why did the person throw the stone? What were the root causes? Unhappiness with life? Yes, perhaps. And the cause of this? Parents who are drunks? Poor education? Growing up with no beauty in one's surroundings, e.g. in an area where there are lots of broken windows? And we are back at the beginning again.

This circularity need not always apply, of course. Another end result / symptom / effect / damage might be poor global oxygen levels. The cause of this might be deforestation. The cause of this might be the greed of logging companies, or the corruptability of the government where the trees are felled. But to complete the circle by claiming that the greed of the logging companies or the corruptability of the government was caused by poor levels of oxygen in the air might be taking things a bit far!

2.1 Today

It is of course recognised that most of us in the so-called 'developed world' have an enormous amount to be thankful for. We have made phenomenal advances to provide for our comfort, health and fulfilment. But as we know, even the most cursory of glances over the fence reveals all manner of issues, issues that betray acute societal dysfunction which can make us, as a species with extraordinary learning, feel repulsion and deepest shame. The most self-absorbed amongst us may be blind to these issues; but for anyone who has taken the trouble to buy a book such as this, it would hardly seem necessary to enumerate the challenges we currently face—the tragic effects, the symptoms, the damage. These are, after all, well-rehearsed. Rather, a number of these disorders are looked at through the course of the book, particularly later—for example in Chapter 12 ('Relevant to Now?').

Crucially though, there are strong signs that our problems will pro-liferate if we do not get our act together: ' ... the serious impacts of climate change, demographic ageing and population growth kick in around the year 2050. If we can't create a sustainable global order and restore economic dynamism, the decades after 2050 will be chaos'.[9] To this perfect storm one could add things like the ever-growing con-centrations of wealth in the hands of an ever-shrinking proportion of the world's population.

2.2   In Steiner's day

General sociological changes witnessed by the 'developed world' since Steiner's day are touched on in Chapter 12. But as far as social *problems* go—i.e. end results, symptoms—many of those we have today are of course as nothing compared to a hundred years ago. Environmental destruction may not have been a big concern back then, and the absence of drug-fuelled gang warfare probably meant less knife crime. But the horrors of international conflict were fresh in the minds of all. And, war aside, general poverty and struggle were unsurprisingly both more profound and more widespread. The blue collar working class comprised over 75% of the population[10], and had a militancy that, in Germany for example (in Britain too, but to a lesser extent), threatened revolution and clamoured for socialism / communism—something Steiner, like so many others, thought would be a thoroughgoing disaster. However, whilst he considered socialism[11] a grave error, his sympathy for those who campaigned for it was unequivocal.

> *... we must look at the deep, virtually unbridgeable cleft between the working and non-working classes. The civilisation enjoyed by the latter has been highly praised as a sign of progress in modern times. Commonplace technologies now quickly deliver people and*

---

[9] Paul Mason, *Postcapitalism: A Guide to Our Future* (London: Allen Lane, 2015), p. x.

[10] Selina Todd, *The Rise and Fall of the Working Class*, (UK: John Murray, 2014), Introduction.

[11] In the traditional sense of widespread economic planning and state-owned / state-run industry.

thoughts around the globe in ways that would once have been derided as utopian visions. We never tire of glorifying this progress. But today we must also add another perspective: we must ask how this progress came about. It is based entirely on an underlying structure made up of broad masses of humanity, of countless individuals whose work makes possible the culture of the few. Now these masses have grown up; they have come to their senses and are demanding their rightful share. (CW333, p. 3)

... what we call the class struggle of the working class. Underlying this struggle is nothing more or less than the great and justified demand for a humanly worthy existence for all people. (CW333, p. 9)

... all they [the workers] could see was that their work produced the profits that supported upper class lifestyles. That is why the words of the Communist Manifesto resonated so deeply with them and made them conscious of their situation. (CW333, p. 10)

What have the upper classes done in this field? Admittedly they have poked their noses into proletarian misery and created works of art from it ... made it into what present-day poets, sculptors and painters have created out of it: art with a social conscience. (CW305, p.38)

And, reflecting on the material hardships that existed during his youth:

It's enough to make your heart bleed to think about how members of the upper classes gathered to talk about 'brotherly' love and all such Christian virtues in rooms heated with coal mined by children as young as nine. In the mid 1800s, these poor children literally never saw daylight on weekdays because they went down into the mines before sunrise and came up only after sundown. Credit for later improvements in these conditions is due to proletarian demands, not to any effort on the part of the upper classes. (CW333, p. 51)

Ring any bells? Today it would perhaps be more relevant to refer, instead of to upper and lower classes, to those in the 'developed world' and those in the 'developing world'—who make our shirts, grow our bananas and assemble our laptops, often living in conditions that have not been experienced where I live possibly since medieval times. Nonetheless, we still have our own profound hardships at home, too: people living in fear and so on; although the scale of these difficulties is perhaps dwarfed when one considers the hardships experienced by the world's 80 million refugees and others with no safe home to return to.[12]

Of course, by the time Steiner made these comments, Bismarck and others had already introduced various measures to improve the lot of the lowest in European society (most notably, with health insurance and some pension provision.). But Steiner insisted very much more could be achieved, as we shall see presently.

Apart from the *material* hardship and exploitation experienced by great swathes of the population, there was also a psychological burden resulting from industrial mechanisation. Decades earlier, Karl Marx (many of whose observations Steiner admired highly) had spoken of the alienation of the worker, of how, by being little more than a cog in a world of mechanised production, the worker had become estranged from the production process, from their product, from other people (e.g. customers), and thus from their humanity. Cut off from one's creativity one ultimately experiences loss of self. In the *Communist Manifesto* (1848) we have: 'Owing to the extensive use of machinery and to division of labour, the work of the proletarians has lost all individual character, and, consequently, all charm for the workman. He becomes an appendage of the machine, and it is only the most simple, most monotonous, and most easily acquired knack, that is required of him'.[13] Steiner echoed these concerns:

> *Men were called away from their old handiwork and placed at machines, crowded together in a factory. The machines at which they stand, the factories in which they are crowded together with their fellows, these, governed only by mechanical laws, have nothing to give a man that has any direct relationship to himself as a man. Out of his old handicraft something flowed to him that gave answer to his query regarding human worth and human dignity.*

[12] https://www.unhcr.org/uk/figures-at-a-glance.html (accessed 26 June 2021).
[13] Karl Marx & Friedrich Engels, *The Communist Manifesto* (London: Penguin Classics, 2015), p. 12.

The dead machine gives no answer. Modern industrialism is like a mechanical network spun about the man, in the midst of which he stands; it has nothing to give him that he can joyfully share, as did the work at his old handicraft. (CW332a, p. 10)

The old connection between the workman and his work is no longer possible, but man needs a relationship to his work. It is necessary that he should feel joy in his work, that he should feel a certain devotion to it. The old devotion, the immediate companionship with the thing he has made, exists no longer; yet it must be replaced by something else. (CW332a, p. 70)

What happened is that through modern economic life, which has been permeated by technology, the human being has been separated from his product so that no real love can any longer connect him with what he produces. (CW339)

The peasant was linked with the soil. A trader in his commercial dealings was linked with other human beings. We no longer appreciate properly how one individual valued another when he bought something from him or sold him something he had made himself and which therefore meant something to him. [...] Human beings who are now immersed in the world of machines have been wrested from all earlier links. They are no longer bound to the land and the soil; they no longer live in the interplay that existed between one individual and another during the age when trade and the crafts dominated society. (CW305(ii), p. 137)

... division of society has reached its zenith ... once we recognise it, we realise the imperative demand of the age: to find and follow the path that leads to reunion. (CW24, p. 49)

The following pages describe the ways in which Steiner suggested these divisions and other societal issues could be addressed.

3. Pre-threefold Comments

Before moving on to Steiner's main ideas for societal reform, ideas that were disseminated widely at the end of the Great War, and which have come to be known as 'threefolding' or 'social threefolding', we shall first consider some related comments he made more than a decade earlier.

Prior to 1898 it seems Steiner said little—publicly at least—about the health of the social organism. He had of course had a great deal to say about the human being per se, and at times this would have a direct bearing on social matters.

In his philosophical work *The Philosophy of Freedom*—published in 1894—he traced, for example, the different levels of motive prompting a person to action. At one end of the spectrum we have basic drives like hunger and so on, drives we have in common with the animal world and which, therefore, he suggests have little to do with our unique self, our (divine) spirit. We submit to these in a more or less un-free way. Further along the spectrum of motives, we have social norms which we may follow simply because it is the done thing. Here again, such actions are not strictly 'us'. When we are subservient to such things, we may also not be acting out of freedom. Then there is submission to some outer moral authority: we act in a particular way because the Church says so, or the law, or someone we respect. Here too, such actions are perhaps not fully our own. Steiner points out that we can even act out of a kind of un-freedom when we submit to rules that we ourselves have pre-determined prior to the action. We might have decided at some point in the past that doing things in such-and-such a way is best, even perhaps the most morally justifiable. But by acting in this way once again, there might still be something of the automaton in our action. Ultimately Steiner points to a higher state where a person has followed a path of inner development, inner work, to the extent that he or she has awakened what otherwise slumbers, i.e. that part of the human being which he calls the 'real self'. Here, a person has so refined their being that they no longer act out of compulsion from these external promptings (external, that is, to their unique self), but rather, rising above these, becomes a 'free individual' acting out of clear insight, complete freedom from externalities, and a fully independent recognition of the rightfulness of an action and love for the moral consequences that will follow. Steiner asserts that at this point a human being can become properly 'free', a true 'self', a true individual. He terms this 'ethical individualism'.

One might wonder how on earth people could live together peacefully if we were all to freely follow our true individuality. In answer to this, Steiner says something that can seem paradoxical:

> *This objection is indicative of a wrongly understood moralism. This moralism believes that a community of people is possible only when they are all united through a communally established moral order. This moralism does not, in fact, understand the unity of the world of ideas. It does not comprehend that the world of ideas active within me is no other than that within my fellow man. (CW4, p. 153)*
>
> *The free person lives in the confidence that any other free person belongs with him to one spiritual world and will concur with him in his intentions. (CW4, p. 154)*

That is, the person who has freed themselves from compulsions unconnected to their unique self, and instead acts purely out of this unique self, ultimately draws on universally objective ideas, on a universal spirit that is the same universal spirit that others can share in.

The numerous mental / meditative exercises for self-development which Steiner shares also have a bearing on social life inasmuch as they can simply help one to become a more thoughtful citizen.

To any reader concerned that this is going to be a book full of spiritual philosophy: fear not; it isn't!

3.1 1898

In July 1898 Steiner writes an article (in three instalments) in *Das Magazin fur Literature* entitled 'The Social Question'. This is in response to *The Social Question in the Light of Philosophy*—a book by philosopher Dr Ludwig Stein that had been published the year before. Steiner commends the author for what he regards as accurate observations of the main aspects of social evolution, but he does not share Stein's conclusions. The main theme of the article concerns the progression of humanity from primitive times when the social grouping is prominent and the individual is not (nothing is owned by anyone, etc.), to more modern times where the concerns of the individual begin to come to the fore.

What better illustration that there was once a time when it was experienced as right to sacrifice the individual to the interests of the community than that during a certain period of time the Spartans used to cast weak individuals out into the wilderness, where they were left to die so that they would not be a burden to the community. Another confirmation can be found in the fact that it did not occur to philosophers in earlier times, such as Aristotle, to regard slavery as barbaric. To Aristotle, for example, it seems quite natural that a certain sector of humankind has to serve another as slaves. One can only hold such a view if one is mainly concerned about the interests of the totality and not about those of the individual. It can easily be demonstrated that the forms of all social institutions at the beginning of cultural evolution were such that the interests of the individual were sacrificed for the sake of the community. However, it is equally true that in the further course of evolution the individual attempts to assert his needs over against those of the community. If we observe closely, a good deal of human history is encompassed in the self-assertion of the individual over against the communities that arose of necessity at the beginning of cultural evolution and that developed at the expense of the individual.

Common sense compels us to acknowledge that social institutions were necessary and that they could only come about through priority being given to common interests. However, it is equally obvious that it is necessary for the individual to resist the sacrifice of his own particular interests. In this way a situation has come about in the course of time, in which social institutions have taken on forms in which the interests of individuals are given more scope than was the case in earlier times. If one rightly understands the nature of our times one might well say that the most advanced members of our society endeavour to develop social forms in such a way that through the forms of human interaction any restrictions on the individual are reduced to a minimum. The idea that a community could be an end in itself is gradually disappearing, and it is seen more and more as providing for the development of the individual. The state, for example, should be constituted in a way that will give the greatest scope to the unrestricted development of the individual. All general arrangements should be made in such a way that they serve the individual rather than the state as such. J.G. Fichte expressed this tendency in an apparently paradoxical yet pertinent way when he said: 'It is the task of the state gradually to make itself redundant.' Underlying this expression is the important truth that initially the individual needs community, for only on the basis of the community can he develop his capacities; however, as soon as these capacities have been developed, the tutelage of the community becomes unbearable to him. He then says to himself: I will constitute the community in such a way that it best serves the development of my individual qualities. (CW30, pp. 29-31)

Steiner cites examples given by Ludwig Stein that bear out this trend, but then observes that Stein fails to go one step further and arrive at what he (Steiner) calls a 'fundamental sociological law':

... it seems to me that, having stated all these facts, it would have been the task of the sociological philosopher to proceed to describe the fundamental sociological law governing the development of mankind that follows from the above with logical necessity, and that I would like to express as follows: in the early stages of cultural evolution, mankind tends towards the formation of social units; initially the interests of individuals are sacrificed to the interests of those groupings; the further course of development leads to the emancipation of the individual from the interests of the groupings and to the unrestricted development of the needs and capacities of the individual.

Now the point is to draw the logical conclusions from these historical facts. Which social forms can be the only acceptable ones if all social development is tending towards individualisation? The answer cannot be too difficult. Any state or society that regards itself as an end in itself has to aim for control over the individual, regardless of the way in which such control is exercised, whether it be an absolutist, constitutional or republican manner. As soon as the state no longer considers itself an end in itself, but as a means towards an end, the principle of state control will no longer be emphasized. All arrangements will be made in such a way that the individual receives the greatest scope. The greatest ideal of the state will be not to control anything. It will be a community that wants nothing for itself, everything for the individual. If one wishes to further developments in this direction, one is bound to oppose everything that tends towards a socialization[14] of social institutions. Ludwig Stein does not do that. He proceeds from the observation of a certain fact, from which he is not able to deduce the right law, to a conclusion that represents a poor compromise between socialism and individualism, between communism and anarchism ... The evidence of sociological observation should have forced Stein to represent anarchistic individualism as the social ideal, but for that Stein was not a courageous enough thinker. He seems to know anarchism only in that completely idiotic form in which it is being propagated by bomb-throwing gangs. (CW30, pp. 32-34)

Thus Steiner describes a simple, historical progression—away from a more or less group consciousness towards ever greater individual expression. And he concludes that political institutions ought to increasingly respect this trend, ought to step back from the controlling of individuals. He then goes on to single out socialist regimes as being particularly poor at observing this need (despite their worthy maxim 'To each according to his need; from each according to his abilities').

No socialist or communist form of government or social order is capable of taking adequate account of the natural diversity of human beings. Any organisation that is in any way predetermined in its nature by any principles must of necessity suppress the full and unhindered development of the individual in order to maintain its own integrity as an organism. (CW30, p. 36)

... he who can read the development of mankind rightly can only support a social order that has as its aim the unrestricted, all-round development of individuals, and that abhors the domination of any one person by another. The question that then remains is how

---

[14] E.g. nationalisation

each individual is to cope with himself. Each individual will solve this problem for himself if all sorts of communities do not get in the way.

The worst of all forms of government is that propagated by the Social Democrats.[15] [...] Those who can think know that the realisation of the ideals of social democracy would mean the suppression of all individuality. However, because it is impossible to suppress—for human evolution has set its sight on human individuality once and for all—the victory of social democracy would at the same time be its downfall. (CW30, pp. 37-38)

Read in isolation, these passages might make one wonder whether Steiner then goes on to advocate some sort of laissez-faire, free-for-all neo-liberalism where the weak are simply left to fall by the wayside. But this is very far from the case.

3.2   1905–1908

Between 1898 and 1905, Steiner writes and lectures extensively on philosophy, religion and esotericism, and is also invited to become General Secretary of the German-speaking section of the Theosophical Society. He holds this position until 1913 when the Society's leader Annie Besant declares an Indian boy, Krishnamurti, to be the reincarnation of Christ—something Steiner regards as a falsehood.

From 1899 until 1904, he also teaches history and a range of scientific and literary subjects at the Berlin Workers College founded by Marxist, Karl Liebknecht.[16] Despite his classes being by far the most popular in the college, he is eventually relieved of his position by the college directors for refusing to toe their Marxist line.

In 1905 (still twelve years before he shares his key 'threefold' analysis), Steiner briefly returns to the theme of the social organism

---

[15] Since 1891, this had essentially been Marxist, although based on Marx's later ideas which, amongst other things, accepted the possibility of the socialisation of the means of production via peaceful means as opposed to violent revolution.

[16] With Rosa Luxemberg and others, lawyer Karl Liebknecht later founded both the Spartacist League and the Communist Party of Germany. He and Luxemberg were both assassinated in 1919.

in three lectures he gives in Berlin, as well as in an essay for the theosophical magazine *Lucifer Gnosis*. In these, a number of themes emerge which complement the individualism of which he had spoken seven years earlier.

3.2.1   Brotherhood

Having previously brought people's attention to the gradual emergence, over long epochs, of the human individuality, and having then concluded that any prescriptive political construct (especially Communism) is something that inappropriately hinders this emergence, Steiner relates how this emergence of the human individuality does *not* imply that human evolution is heading towards a self-centred, 'me, me, me' culture. Rather, he considers how vital the role of brotherhood has been as humanity advances.

> *What has brotherhood achieved for human development? We have only to look at our own ancestors. One could easily gain the impression that it was the hunt and warfare that advanced them, that primarily moulded their character. But when one delves deeper, it will be found that this first impression is not correct, that precisely those early Teutonic tribes prospered most that had developed the principle of brotherhood to an extraordinary degree ...*
>
> *There was a great movement towards freedom throughout Europe in the middle of the Middle Ages. This movement towards freedom grew out of a spirit of the brotherhood of man, and from it arose a general culture, the city culture of the middle Middle Ages. Those who could not endure servitude on the land fled their masters and sought their freedom in the growing cities. People came down from Scotland, France, and Russia; from everywhere they came together and built the free cities. Thus the principle of brotherhood developed and furthered culture to a high degree. Men of similar occupations joined in societies called oath-brotherhoods,[17] which later grew into the guilds. These oath-brotherhoods were far more than mere societies of crafts or tradespeople. Born of the practical, everyday life, these associations developed to moral*

---

[17] Or 'confraternities'—see Wikipedia, under 'Guilds'.

> *heights. Mutual aid was the fundamental concern of these broth-*
> *erhoods, and many aspects of life that are of nobody's concern*
> *today were occasions for such support. For example, members*
> *of such a brotherhood would help each other in case of illness.*
> *Two brothers were appointed to keep daily vigil at the bedside of a*
> *sick brother. Members who were ill received food, and the fraternal*
> *spirit prevailed even beyond death: the responsibility for burying a*
> *brother member in proper fashion was considered a special hon-*
> *our. Finally, the care of widows and orphans was a duty of the*
> *oath-brotherhood. You can see from these examples how there*
> *grew up an understanding of the moral life of the community that*
> *modern man can hardly imagine. (CW54, pp. 3-5)*

Steiner goes on to relate how the development of the individual does not hinder 'brotherliness'—the consideration of others. Instead, it strengthens it and so assists humanity's healthy development.

> *In a sense, the words of Rusckerts hold here: when the rose beau-*
> *tifies itself, it also beautifies the garden. If we do not make our-*
> *selves capable of helping our fellow men, we shall be poor helpers.*
> *If we do not see to it that all our talents are developed, we shall be*
> *poor helpers. If we do not see to it that all our talents are devel-*
> *oped, we shall have little success in helping our brothers. In order*
> *to develop these talents, a certain egoism is necessary, because*
> *egoism is connected with initiative. The person who understands*
> *how not to be led, how not to be influenced by everything in his*
> *surroundings, but who descends into his own, inner being where*
> *the sources of strength are to be found will develop into a strong*
> *and able person, in whom there will be a greater ability to serve*
> *others than in the one who conforms to all kinds of influences that*
> *come from his surroundings. (CW54, pp. 7-8)*
>
> *The people who join with others and who put their strength at the*
> *disposal of all are those who will provide the foundation for healthy*
> *development in the future. (CW54, pp. 10-11)*

In the past—in Greece, Egypt and further back—the sacrificing of the concerns of the individual for the sake of the community may have found expression even in slavery. But here Steiner talks of the individual joining with others out of *free choice*—community arising between free individuals.

Within the same lecture, he refers to how the Theosophical Society (where he remained General Secretary of its German Branch until 1913), has the principle of brotherhood at its core:

> *Those of you who have occupied yourselves even a little with the aims of our spiritual-scientific movement know our main principle: to create the heart, the kernel, of a brotherhood based on all-embracing human love that transcends race, sex, profession, religion, and so on. Thus, the Theosophical Society has placed this principle of general brotherhood foremost, made it the most important of its ideals. Of all these cultural endeavours that we need most at present, the society considers this great ethical striving towards brotherhood to be most closely connected with the ultimate aim of human development. (CW54, p. 1)*

The following (in fact, from 1912) relates how this 'all-embracing human love' can be stimulated:

> *... if, as anthroposophists, we set ourselves the task of extending our interests more and more and of widening our mental horizon, this will promote the universal brotherhood of mankind. Progress is not gained by the mere preaching of universal love, but by the extension of our interests further and further, so that we come to interest ourselves increasingly in souls with widely different characters, racial and national peculiarities, with widely different temperaments, and holding widely different religious and philosophical views, and approach them with understanding. Right interest, right understanding, calls forth from the soul the right moral action. (CW155)*

3.2.2   Root causes of societal ills

Steiner acknowledges the self-evident: that much of the misery and suffering in the world is down to the poor conditions in which so many people have to live, and that the wellbeing of these people is improved when the conditions in which they live are improved. And he commends the effective attempts at social policy which address this. He is also particularly complimentary about the efforts of individual social reformers, citing Robert Owen and political theorist Henri de Saint-Simon as notable examples (as, indeed, had Marx half a century earlier).

However, he stresses that improving people's living conditions in these ways is only a partial fix and doesn't really get to the root of the problem.

We can agree without hesitation … that much can be achieved with the means that have been suggested by many for the improvement of man's social condition. One party wants one thing, others something else. To a clear-thinking person, some of the demands which such parties make prove to be devoid of any real substance; on the other hand, some of it certainly contains the making of something really substantial.

Robert Owen, who lived from 1771 to 1858 and who certainly was one of the noblest social reformers, emphasized again and again that the human being is moulded by his environment in which he grows up, that his character is not formed by himself, but by the conditions in which he lives. What is obviously so right in such a statement should not be disputed. But neither should it be treated with a disdainful shrug of the shoulders, even if on the surface it appears to be more or less self-evident. Rather, it should be readily admitted that much in public life can be improved by working according to such ideas. The science of the spirit, therefore, will never prevent anyone from doing anything for human progress which sets out to produce a better lot for the oppressed and suffering classes of humanity.

The science of the spirit must go deeper. Really effective progress cannot be achieved by such means any longer. If we do not admit this we have not recognised how conditions come about in which people live. For inasmuch as the life of man is dependent on these conditions, the latter themselves are brought about by man. Or who has arranged it that one person is poor and another rich? Other people, of course … A thorough knowledge of things teaches us that all evils connected with social life originate in human actions. In this respect it is not the individual human being but the whole of humanity that is the 'fashioner of individual fortune'. (CW34)

… what needs to be taken up first as the social question, are the souls of today which produce the environment of tomorrow. (CW88, p. 57)

Yes, misery may be caused by poor living conditions; but poor living conditions are caused by people, by thoughts, by the way society organises itself. An obvious point perhaps, but possibly directed at any Communist who preferred to deny the mind had any importance (believing, instead, that surplus value was created solely by the workers, not by ingenuity).

3.2.3   Exploitation

Steiner goes on to consider the nature of exploitation, a theme uppermost in the minds of a great many at the time. With damp houses and squalor and families living eight-to-a-room at one end of social life, and landed barons and others enjoying capital at the other, the class struggle was a pressing issue of the day. Indeed, it had been for a long time, and was the widespread soil in which Marxist ideas had taken hold.

... if in our emotions and perceptions we are able to feel a certain pain over the fact that the clothes we have on have been produced for a starvation wage, then we are looking deep into the heart of the question. (CW88, p. 49)

... it is also true that by and large no part of humanity, no caste or class, maliciously causes the suffering of another part ... Those who exploit their fellow men would naturally not want the victims of their exploitation to suffer. We would make considerable progress if people not only found this self-evident, but also adapted their feelings to it. (CW34)

A person who maintains a home in grand style, who can travel first class on the railway, may easily appear on the surface to be an oppressor. And a person who wears a threadbare coat and who travels fourth class will appear to be the oppressed. But one does not have to be an incompassionate individual nor a reactionary in order to understand the following clearly. Nobody is oppressed or exploited because I wear a particular coat, but only because I pay the man who made the coat for me too little. The poor worker who has acquired his inferior coat for little money is, in relation to his fellow human beings in this respect, in exactly the same position as the rich man who had a better coat made. Whether I am poor or rich, I exploit if I acquire things for which insufficient payment is made. Actually today nobody ought to call someone else an oppressor; he ought first to look at himself. If he does this carefully he will soon discover the 'oppressor' in himself. Is the work which you have to deliver to the well-to-do delivered only to them at the price of bad wages? No, the person who sits next to you and complains about oppression enjoys the work of your hands on exactly the same conditions as the well-to-do whom you have both turned against ...

Thinking things over in this way makes it clear that the concepts 'rich' and 'exploiter' must be completely separated. It depends on individual ability or on the ability of our forefathers, or on quite different things, whether we are now rich or poor. The fact that we exploit the work of others has absolutely nothing to do with these things. At least not directly. But it is very much connected with something else. And that is, that our social situation and environment are built upon personal self-interest. We have to think very clearly for otherwise we shall arrive at a quite wrong idea of what is said. If I acquire a coat today it appears quite natural, according to the conditions which exist, that I acquire it as cheaply as possible. This means: I have only myself in mind. Here, however, we touch the point of view that governs our whole life. Of course, it is easy to raise an objection. We can say: do not the socially-minded parties and personalities try to do something about this evil? Is there not an effort to protect 'work'? Do not working classes and their representatives demand higher wages and shorter working hours? It has already been said above that the present-day view can have absolutely nothing against such demands and measures. Nor is there any intention here for agitating for one or the other of the existing party demands. From the present point of view, we are not concerned with taking sides on particular points, 'for' or 'against'. This, in the first place, lies quite outside the approach of the science of spirit.

However many improvements are introduced to protect a particular class of worker, and that would certainly contribute much to the raising of conditions of one or the other group of people, the actual nature of exploitation will not be mitigated. For this depends on a person acquiring the products of another person's work from the point of view of self-interest ... (CW34)

A poor person can exploit another just as a rich person can. Wealth as such is not a cause of the exploitation (although it may, indeed, be the result). Rather, Steiner points out, exploitation lies in self-interest. Whilst, again, this may be self-evident, it is nonetheless helpful to have it stated. It is probably also true to say that whilst 'by and large no part of humanity' wishes to exploit (as Steiner states) there are—surely nowadays—far too many exploiting corporate leaders who would appear to know full well what they are doing, be that pushing their pharmaceuticals onto a largely unsuspecting public when other drugs would be more effective and cheaper,[18] or pushing their baby milk onto impoverished African mothers whose children would be greatly better-off if breastfed, or whatever.[19]

3.2.4   Self-interest

Following the great success of his New Lanark project, where Robert Owen made sure all the workers in his mills had decent living conditions, and where he integrated wasters and drunkards from Glasgow with those who could act as good examples, Robert Owen went on to buy a village in Indiana, USA and attempted to set up something similar, inviting all and sundry to join him. The project failed after two years, however, following strife and disagreement, not least because a number of the members were, quite simply, work-shy.

> *Through this experience, Owen was able to be completely cured of the belief that all human misery comes about through bad 'conditions' in which people live, and that the goodness of human nature would come to life of itself if these conditions were improved. He was forced to the conviction that good conditions can be maintained only if the human beings who live in them are naturally inclined to maintain them, and when they do this with enthusiasm ... We have to advance from merely a belief in the goodness of human nature that deceived Owen, to a real knowledge of man ... (CW34)*

---

[18] Richard Smith, 'Foregone Conclusions', *The Guardian*, 14 January 2004.
[19] Mike Muller, 'Nestlé baby milk scandal has grown up but not gone away', *The Guardian*, 13 February 2013.

Again, the point that is perhaps obvious: misery is born not just of external conditions but also of human attitudes and behaviour.

> ... egotism happens to be part of human nature. And this means that it stirs in the feelings of the human being when he lives together with others and has to work within a community. This necessarily leads to the fact that in practice most people think the best social conditions to be those where the individual can best satisfy his needs. Thus under the influence of egotistical feelings the social question comes to be formulated quite naturally as follows: what must be done in society in order that each person can have the returns of his work for himself? ... How often does one hear it accepted as a matter of course that a social order based on goodwill and feeling for one's fellow human beings is an absurdity. Rather it is assumed that the totality of a human community can prosper best when the individual can pocket the 'full' or greatest possible yield of his work.
>
> Exactly the opposite of this is taught by the science of spirit, which is founded on a deeper knowledge of the human being and of the world. It shows that all human misery is simply a consequence of egotism, and that misery, poverty and distress must necessarily arise at a particular time in the human community if this community is based on egotism in any way. (CW34)

This sentiment is also expressed in 1908:

> ... need, misery and grief are nothing else than the results of egoism. Like a physical law we have to understand this sentence, not in such a way that possibly with a single human being need and grief happen if he is always selfish, but that this grief is connected with this egoism—maybe at another place. Like cause and effect, egoism is connected with the need and grief. (CW54(ii), 2 March 1908)

So, Steiner (who, of course, is not alone) turns on its head the idea that self-interest ultimately leads to the greatest prosperity for all, that 'greed is good' (a claim for which 'The inevitable consequence is a decline in public integrity and a new carelessness about others', as

Will Hutton observes).[20] The logic of 'greed is good' is simple enough: people generally want to be able to afford more for themselves; so they work harder; thus more is produced; and there is therefore more available to go round.

But:

> *If I buy a factory in order to earn as much as possible for myself, I shall see that I acquire labour as cheaply as possible, etc. Everything that happens will be done from the point of view of self-interest. If, on the other hand, I buy a factory from the point of view of looking after 200 people as well as possible, all my actions will take on a different character...*
>
> *All our interests, and therefore all our social conditions, change when in acquiring something we no longer have ourselves in mind but others. What does a person have to look to who only looks after his own well-being? To seeing that he earns as much as possible ... If I do not consider myself but hold the point of view: how does my own work serve others? everything changes. Nothing then forces me to undertake anything prejudicial to someone else. I then place my powers not at my own disposal, but at someone else's. The consequence of this is a quite different unfolding of the powers and capacities of the human being. (CW34)*

It is clear: exploitation arises from self-interest; distress arises from self-interest; George Soros betting against sterling and creating phenomenal problems in the process arises from self-interest.[21] If it were true that a system based on self-interest leads to a healthy state of affairs, would we read that, in the 1980s, 60% of the income gains went to the wealthiest 1% of the population?[22] Or, indeed, would Bernie Sanders have observed in 2015: 'people are looking out and seeing ... since the

---

[20] Will Hutton, 'Inequality has become a challenge to us as moral beings', *The Guardian,* 25 January 2015.

[21] Andrew Beattie, 'How did George Soros break the Bank of England?', https://www.investopedia.com/ask/answers/08/george-soros-bank-of-england.asp (accessed 10 May 2020).

[22] Anthony Giddens, *The Third Way: The Renewal of Social Democracy* (Cambridge: Polity Press, 2008), p. 104.

Great Recession of 2008, 99 per cent of all new income going to the top 1 per cent. So you're seeing people working in my state, all over this country, two jobs, they're working three jobs, and they're getting nowhere in a hurry. They're working hard. They can't afford to send their kids to college in many instances. They can't afford childcare for their little babies. They're worried to death about retirement. [...] ... we're living in a rigged economy—where it doesn't matter how hard you worked, the result will be all the income goes to the people at the very top'.[23] The idea that the wealth of the billionaire trickles down to the pauper, would appear questionable. Our system—based on self-interest—is wanting.

Be that as it may, the final sentence of Steiner's, above, takes us somewhere altogether subtler—uplifting, even—remarking that, if a person stops only thinking about themselves, there follows 'a quite different unfolding of the powers and capacities of the human being'.

3.2.5 A fundamental social law

People say it is quite natural that the human being is paid for his work, that he receives the proceeds of his work personally. Nevertheless, that is nothing but the implementation of egoism in economic life. Egoism controls us as soon as we live by the principle: I have to be paid personally for my work. [...] Real social progress is only possible if I do that which I work for in the service of the community, and if the community gives me what I need, if, in other words, what I work for does not serve me. [...] Absurd as this is for many people today, it is also true. The opposite fact influences our life today: the claim of the worker to get the full yield of his work more and more. As long as the thinking moves in this direction, one comes into worse and worse situations. (CW54(ii), 2 March 1908)

---

[23] Jim and Tankersley, 'Bernie Sanders on America's "grotesquely unfair" society', *The Washington Post*, 16 July 2015.

In contradistinction to the view that greed is good, that self-interest and profit maximisation raise the quality of life for all, Steiner offers the following:

> *There is, then, a fundamental social law which the science of spirit teaches us and which is as follows: In a community of human beings working together, the well-being of the community will be the greater, the less the individual claims for himself the proceeds of the work he has himself done; i.e. the more of these proceeds he makes over to his fellow workers, and the more his own requirements are satisfied, not out of his own work done, but out of the work done by the others. All conditions in a community of human beings that are contrary to this law will inevitably engender in some part of it, after a while, suffering and want. It is a fundamental law which holds good for all social life with the same absoluteness and necessity as any law of nature within a particular field of natural causation. (CW34)*

Instead of saying society is best off when each pursues their own self-interest, when we all compete with one another and just work for the sake of ourselves, Steiner instead conveys the above which he says is a fundamental social law. One might be tempted to rejoinder: here in the West we have lived almost entirely under competition over the last century, and conditions have improved hugely. As Michael Portillo pointed out, one would not have seen the worst off in 19th century society suffering from obesity as we do now, so capitalism surely *has* worked.[24] Well, yes, conditions have indeed improved greatly, but the acute levels of hardship that persist in many quarters are nonetheless still evident to all but the most cloth-eared. Not everyone has benefited from the increase in living standards to the same extent. Also, Steiner isn't saying competitive self-interest will put a stop to progress. He is saying: it 'will inevitably engender in some part of it, after a while, suffering and want'. And so it does, big time—however much some may like to turn a blind eye.

Reading the previous quote, one might wonder what Steiner means exactly by a *'community of human beings working together'*. If one

---

[24] Former (Conservative) UK Secretary of State for Defence, Michael Portillo on *This Week*, BBC1.

takes 'working together' in its most literal sense, then one would have to conclude he means a single enterprise such as a company or partnership. But if one interprets 'working together' more broadly, one could deduce he is implying all those, say, in a particular geographical region such as a village or country. The former seems more likely. Perhaps it doesn't matter.

He goes on:

> *Wherever this law manifests, wherever someone works in accordance with it to the extent possible in the position he occupies within the human community, good will follow, even if in very small measure in individual cases. And it is only by means of such isolated examples of work which arise in this way that beneficial progress [throughout society] will come about. (CW34)*

Further:

> *How can the law be carried out in real life? It is clear that it says nothing less than this: the smaller the egotism is, the greater the human well-being. Thus in putting the law into practice, our concern is with people who extricate themselves from the path of egotism. This is in practice, however, quite impossible if the well-being of the individual is measured according to his work. Whoever works for himself is bound gradually to succumb to egotism. Only someone who works for others can gradually become an unegotistical worker. (CW34)*

The last sentence in this passage seems noteworthy. Instead of saying one needs to be unegotistical to work for others, it claims the reverse: one needs to work for others to become unegotistical. Whilst, undoubtedly, there are people who are exceptions to this rule (i.e. there are people who manage to be completely unegotistical from the outset), Steiner seems to be suggesting that only by working within some structure whereby one doesn't work for oneself, i.e. for one's pay, can one *gradually* become an un-egotistical worker. He seems to be implying that only by living in this way, concretely, will one's feelings develop in an un-egotistical direction.

3.2.6   Separation of work and income

> *It must not be supposed, however, that it is sufficient to acknowl-edge this law as one for general moral conduct, or to try and inter-pret it into the sentiment that everyone should work for the good of his fellow men. No, this law only finds its living, fitting expression in actual reality when a community of human beings succeeds in creating conditions of such a kind that no one can ever claim the results of his own labour for himself, but that they all, to the last fraction, go wholly to the benefit of the community. And he, again, must himself be supported in return by the labours of his fellow men. The important thing is to see that working for one's fellow human beings and aiming at a particular income are two quite sep-arate things. (CW34)*

So, this fundamental social law is not to be seen as a law in the sense of 'thou shalt', but rather in the sense of $e = mc^2$, in the sense that if one thing applies (self-interest), the other (misery) will follow somewhere down the line. And, conversely, the more it *can* be observed, the greater will social health turn out to be.

By suggesting that people not simply adopt an *attitude* of service to others, but ideally also *forego the proceeds* of their own work, and instead live from the proceeds of others, Steiner is airing an idea that is both novel and radical—probably, for most, uncomfortably so: the idea of separating work and income.

In reality, under the division of labour, the things we make or ser-vices we provide when we go to work are, to all intents and purposes, entirely for consumers other than ourselves. The work we do serves others. And yet, if we do more overtime, *we ourselves* receive more pay. In one sense, then, there is a peculiar disconnect between what happens (work for others) and money flows (which come to us). Plus, if our *attitude* is that we are working only in order to better our own lot, there is also perhaps a strange disconnect between our thoughts (working for ourselves) and our actions (working for others).

> *And what is the labour of the present time? It is based on self-in-terest, on the compulsion that egoism exerts on us. Because we want to exist, we want labour to be paid for. We work for our own*

> *sake, for the sake of our pay. In the future we will work for our fellow human beings, because they need what we can provide. That is what we will work for. We will clothe our fellow human beings, we will give them what they need—in completely free activity. Compensation [i.e. remuneration] must be completely separated from this. Labour in the past was tribute, in the future it will be sacrifice. It has nothing to do with self-interest, nothing to do with compensation [remuneration]. If I base my labour on consumer demand with regard to what humanity needs, I stand in a free relation to labour and my work is a sacrifice for humanity. Then I will work with all my powers, because I love humanity and want to place my capacities at its disposal. That has to be possible, and is possible only when one's livelihood is separated from one's labour. And that is going to happen in the future ... (CW88, p. 61)*

Comments like this remind one of the idea of a Universal Basic Income[25], of course, as might the following:

> *... the course of evolution is in the direction of completely voluntary work. This path no one will change or reject. Just as the Greek labourer did his work under the compulsion of his master and modern workers are compelled to work for pay, in the future all work will be performed freely. Work and income will be completely separated. (CW88, p. 61)*

When reading these words, one can wonder whether Steiner may indeed be talking of a rather distant future, of some utopia, even! Work being voluntarily offered whilst one's livelihood is else-how underwritten? What about the work-shy? What about all those who would rather spend their life on the golf course, or on some foreign beach, or working in the garden? Who would volunteer to do the unappealing night shift, or to be a janitor?

Whilst it is recognised that many are happy to work even when they don't need to for income reasons (as evidenced by the number of pensioners and others 'of independent means', for example, who happily engage in voluntary work), and whilst it is recognised that, with

---

[25] A system where all are given an income by the state, regardless of any work they perform.

increasing automation, the need for a 40-hour week may very well lessen, it is notable that, when Steiner develops his threefold analysis for broad public consumption (twelve years after these comments), he certainly does not appear to be implying a Universal Basic Income when he talks further of the separation of work and income. All will become clear!

However, at this juncture—in 1905—he makes a suggestion as to how people could experiment with separating work and income. His audience at this point in time is tiny compared to the tens or even hundreds of thousands who consider his threefolding ideas when he develops these at the end of the Great War. Moreover, his current audience is also largely made up of members and friends of the Theosophical Society. So the following should perhaps be read with this in mind; these comments were not made to anything resembling a typical audience, and certainly not a large one. And I would venture to suggest they may not have been made with any expectation of widespread public take-up.

> People must be educated for voluntary[26] work, one for all and all for one. Everyone has to act accordingly. If he were to found a small community today in which everyone throws all their income into a common bank account and everyone works at whatever they can do, then one's livelihood is not dependent on what work one can do, but rather this livelihood is effected out of the common consumption. This brings about a greater freedom than the coordination of pay with production does. If that happens, we will gain a direction which corresponds to needs ... Even today one can organize factories in the right way. But that demands healthy,

---

[26] The German word Steiner uses here is *'frei'*—free. There is no compulsion by one's owner, as in slavery; no compulsion by the lord of the manor, as in serfdom; and no compulsion from one's need to make a living. The word 'voluntary' is possibly not the most helpful translation as it suggests one receives no income at all. The point is that one is not un-freely pushed by external drivers into doing work. Rather, the motivator is uncompelled—and thus 'free'—volition to work in order to provide for others.

If personal income comes from a common pot and is determined by our needs, not by our pay grade, then our attitude to our work changes. We don't seek promotion, for example, to earn more money. Rather, we might do so if we feel we can offer the necessary experience and skill to take on more responsibility.

clear, sober thinking in the spirit of theosophy ... And just as the one determines the other, so this life of the human soul will also determine that the outer arrangements will be a mirror image of it, so that our labour will be a sacrificial offering and no longer self-interest—so that what controls the relationship with the outer world is not compensation [remuneration] but rather what is in us. We offer to humanity what we have in our power to do. If we cannot do much then we cannot offer much; if we have a lot, then we offer a lot ... Thus labour becomes anything but a burden. It becomes something into which we place what is most sacred for us, our compassion for humanity, and then we can say: labour is sacred because it is a sacrifice for humankind. (CW88, p. 61)

Let us bring about what should happen as much as we can in ourselves. The reshaping of labour, not working for pay, is a sacrifice. Then we will have done our duty, then we will have regarded life in a healthy way. (CW88, p. 65)

For any readers sceptical, at this juncture, about what might seem like very idealistic notions, it should be stressed, again, that Steiner's ideas regarding personal income are significantly modified when, twelve years later, he embarks on widespread public campaigning for social reform. The 'communal pot' / 'income community' idea evolves significantly.

Many 'income communities'—where everyone's income is thrown into a common pot—have been tried around the world with, no doubt, varying degrees of success. The three I know something about all sprang from members or friends of the anthroposophical movement, although there are many examples unconnected to anthroposophy, of course. Saint Simon germinated similar ideas back in the early 1800s, for example, and indeed the Acts of the Apostles and related anthropological evidence suggest such practice was not uncommon among early Christians.[27]

One of the three examples I am aware of was almost entirely populated by people on low incomes and did not last many years. When there is barely enough income to go round, the discussions around what is a basic need can become rather ponderous and painful. Another of

---

[27] See 'Christian Communism' in Wikipedia.

the examples I know about contained a high proportion of highly paid lawyers and, in the absence of strife, was very successful. The third example is that seen in the Camphill movement founded by Dr Karl König. This is slightly different from the first two inasmuch as it is workplace based—that is, all those working *in the same setting* draw their income from a communal pot. Camphill centres are life-sharing communities which look after people with learning disabilities. Originally, all or most staff would live on site and pool resources. People would then draw on the communal pot to cover their financial needs. People with children would take more, for example, on account of needing to buy more food, clothing, and so on. In the face of regulatory pressure, many of these establishments have switched to a conventional employment model in recent years.

For the avoidance of doubt, it should perhaps be added that Steiner is not talking about communities attempting self-sufficiency, attempting to cut themselves off from the rest of the world. He is simply speaking of communities which can put to one side the bond between work and income. The following observations, made many years later, make clear his view of little enclaves detached from the rest of the world.

> *Many years ago, when Oppenheimer was already a housing man, he said: 'Now I have the capital, we can found a new cultural colony.' I replied: 'Doctor, let's talk about this project when it has perished.' For it has to perish. It is not possible to create a little area within the general economy, based on privileges derived from something different, without its becoming a parasite within the economic life as a whole. Such enterprises are always parasites. They last until they have taken enough from others; but then they perish.* (CW341, p. 181)

> *... or whether someone founds a little settlement like an economic parasite which can only exist because the rest of the world is there around it, which can only exist so long as it can maintain itself as a parasite on the commercial world and then perishes.* (CW305(ii), p. 109)

3.2.7 Shared ideals

That Steiner does not have widespread public take-up in mind at this juncture (1905) is perhaps confirmed by the following:

> *For this [i.e. not claiming the proceeds of one's work for oneself, and so gradually becoming an un-egotistical worker], one prerequisite is necessary. If a person works for another he must find in this other person the reason for his work; and if someone is supposed to work for the community he must be able to feel the value, the being and the significance of this community. He can do this only if the community is something quite different from a more or less undefined collection of individuals. It has to be permeated by a real spirit in which each person can partake. It has to be such that everyone says: it is right, and I want it to be like that. The total community must have a spiritual mission; and each individual must wish to contribute to the fulfilment of this mission ... The spirit of the total community must be alive and right down into each individual. (CW34)*

In other words, he is not talking about any loose grouping of individuals but about people joined together under common aims or ideals, people who are all pulling in the same direction: an *intentional* community. But what does he mean by the community having a shared *spiritual* mission? The German word '*Geist*' can mean 'spirit' in a more everyday sense: shared ideals and so on. Or it can have more other-worldly connotations. A group of secular humanists[28], say, might fall within the first meaning—within the everyday sense of a shared spirit; but they would not fall under the latter—the more other-worldly sense. I assume the first meaning applies here. However, since Steiner considered his spirituality as very much 'of the world' he might have considered the former—shared ideals—as being included in the latter. Both are, after all, metaphysical.

Be that as it may, he goes further still and suggests that, ultimately, the most effective way to deal with distress and poverty is

---

[28] 'Secular humanism is a philosophy or life stance that embraces human reason, secular ethics, and philosophical naturalism while specifically rejecting religious dogma, supernaturalism, and superstition as the basis of morality and decision-making' (Wikipedia).

by the inspiration from a spiritual understanding of the world, in the more other-worldly, esoteric sense. Of course, if one bears in mind the carnage and strife perpetrated throughout history in the name of religion, then this can seem a highly controversial assertion. In relation to this, however, Steiner would almost certainly have opined that the behaviour of believers through the ages, as well as the claims of many clerics and, in a number of cases, Scripture, were distortions of great occult truths. His body of work regarding the various religions—particularly Christianity—is a vast subject in its own right, however.

> *A bald economic theory can never act as a force to counteract the powers of egoism. For a while, such an economic theory may sweep the masses along with a kind of impetus that, to all out-ward appearance, resembles the enthusiasm of an ideal. But in the long run it helps nobody. Anyone who inoculates such a theory into a mass of human beings, without giving them some real spiritual substance along with it, is sinning against the real meaning of human evolution.*
>
> *There is only one thing which can be of any use; and that is a spiritual world-conception, which, of its own self, through that which it has to offer, can make a living home in the thoughts, in the feelings, in the will—in a man's whole soul ... With people who have no world-conception centred in the spirit it is inevitable that just those institutions which promote men's material well-being will have the effect of also enhancing egoism, and therewith, little by little, will engender want, poverty and suffering. (CW34)*

So, the 'catchment area' wherein Steiner's proposals might fruitfully take root appears to be shrinking yet further! It is important to note, however, that he is not imagining these are ideas that can be taken up with ease. Having narrowed one's hopes for proper societal health such that this can ultimately only spring from a spiritual view of the world, Steiner also adds that one can only make extremely modest progress with regards to these ideas—just a few small steps here and there. He is certainly not suggesting society at large will be persuaded to go down this route.

Knowledge of these fundamentals [the need for a spiritual view of the world] removes several illusions from those who set themselves up to be bringers of happiness to the people. For it makes work designed to improve the social well-being a really difficult matter. And it means too that the overall success of such work can, in certain conditions, only be pieced together out of very small individual successes ... it is only by means of such isolated examples of work which arise in this way, that beneficial progress in the whole social sphere will come about ... What anyone can do, however, is to work in conformity with the above law [namely the 'fundamental social law'] in his own particular sphere. There is no position which a person might have in the world where this is not possible, however insignificant or without influence it may appear to be. (CW34)

One can be left doubting whether such modest steps can really be better than the efforts of other reformers—with their ideas for the improvement of outer conditions, their welfare state ideas, etc. But two things should be emphasised: (a) the limited applicability of these ideas contrasts significantly with the threefold ideas Steiner introduces twelve years later, as shall be seen in the following chapters; and (b) Steiner by no means wishes to discourage reform from other quarters 'some of [which] contains the making of something really substantial' (CW34).

In summary, from 1898 to 1908, Steiner makes the following observations concerning social affairs:

- In ancient times, the concerns of the individual are sacrificed for the sake of the community.
- As humanity evolves, this is reversed, and the concerns of the individual come to the fore.
- Individual liberty is of central importance for the future direction of humanity and social affairs.
- Socialist / communist governments can be among the worst at respecting individuality.
- Alongside this cornerstone of individualism, a further, complementing cornerstone of brotherhood is also held up as key to future social health. (These two principles—liberty and

brotherhood—come to have central importance in the threefold approach that Steiner elucidates over a decade later.)

- People's wellbeing is, naturally, improved by the conditions in which they live; but …
- an improvement in conditions alone won't necessarily make people more social, as Robert Owen discovered.
- Conditions are created by people, so one needs to start with people if one wants to create lasting social reform or, at least, address both conditions *and* people by 'thinking in circles' (i.e. by considering how each affects the other).
- Those who exploit others do not, on the whole, wish suffering on the victims of their exploitation.
- Exploitation is not carried out only by the rich; it occurs whenever insufficient is paid for a commodity.
- A fundamental cause of poverty and misery is work / action based on egotism / self-interest.
- The health of a group of people working together is greater, the less each claims the proceeds of his/her work for him/herself (a 'fundamental social law').
- This principle will better succeed if practical arrangements are in place such that people are literally unable to claim the proceeds of their own work.
- Such arrangements will only succeed if the community in question is made up of individuals with shared ideals / mission.
- Steiner suggests groups of people could experiment by (a) putting all their income into a common bank account, and then (b) drawing on these funds more in accordance with need.
- The future direction of humanity will see a separation of work and pay.
- Ultimately, only a spiritual world-view can be the impetus to bring about lasting change that overcomes egotism.
- Social improvement of the type Steiner outlines is only likely to come about in small steps.

It is perhaps not unreasonable to experience these last two points as a somewhat unsatisfying and even depressing prognosis. However, the widespread strife that obtains to this day perhaps bears out what Steiner is saying.

The offerings he has made up to this point which specifically concern societal health amount to a few droplets in a veritable ocean of other matter he covers. And it is not until 1917 that he begins to share his far more substantive conclusions as to a healthier way of structuring society more generally.

4. The Threefold Social Organism

At the end of the Great War, social conditions are chaotic and combustible in varying degrees across Europe, with inflation here, strikes there, and a general shortage of basic necessities. In Italy, for example, worker dissatisfaction brings repeated, drawn-out strikes and thus a further decline in economic output resulting in yet greater hardship. In Germany, workers, soldiers and sailors begin electing their own councils which seize military and civil powers in several cities. Rival groupings proclaim supremacy. The country appears to be on the verge of a communist revolution. A volunteer force is used to suppress the Spartacist Uprising in Berlin. The monarchy falls.

In this atmosphere, Steiner introduces his observations about the threefold nature of society.

> *After having been busily engaged for some 20 or 30 years past in working at what I call spiritual science, it was really not any personal attraction that led me to extend into [... politics and economics ...], but simply the urgent necessity imposed on a man by the present times [...] I neither wished, nor in a way was I able, to bring this thing to public notice until close upon my 60th year of life. (CW330(ii), 31 May 1919)*

4.1   Public exposure

Whilst this book is more about Steiner's *recommendations* concerning public life than the history of these ideas in the public domain, a few milestones are briefly related here to give a flavour of events at the time. For those interested in the historical detail, excellent accounts are available elsewhere.[29]

It is towards the end of the war that Steiner first talks about a threefold analysis of public affairs—threefolding, as it has come to

---

[29] See, for example, Edward Udell (Chapter 6) in Martin Large and Steve Briault (Eds), *Free, Equal and Mutual: Rebalancing Society for the Common Good* (Stroud: Hawthorn Press, 2018), and Albert Schmelzer, *The Threefold Movement, 1919: A History* (Forest Row: Rudolf Steiner Press, 2017).

be known. His ideas are initially outlined in 1917 in two Memoranda for consideration by the Austrian and German governments.[30] Both the Austro-Hungarian emperor, Kaiser Karl 1, and his Prime Minister Ernst Seidler show considerable interest,[31] the Kaiser asking for further details. Steiner also has meetings[32] with the German Foreign Secretary Richard von Kühlmann[33] as well as with the soon-to-become Chancellor of the German Empire, Prince Max von Baden (who reportedly referred to Steiner as 'such a significant man').[34] But, despite this interest among some of the most senior political figures in the region, these threefolding efforts hit something of a brick wall the following year—on 11 November 1918—when the Armistice ends fighting between the Central and the Allied Powers. The Austrian Kaiser falls from power on the same day, two days after the German Kaiser.

In these Memoranda presented to the German and Austrian leaders, the threefold approach is described only in very broad-brush terms. But over the next five years, Steiner returns to the subject and elaborates on it in over a hundred lectures and discussion sessions across Europe, in dozens of essays and articles, in meetings with political figures (from proletarian activists at one end of the spectrum to royalty and senior ministers[35] at the other), and in a book *Kernpunkte der Sozialen Frage* ('The Main Aspects of the Social Question'[36]), published in April 1919. Most of these offerings have been translated into English and are contained in some fifteen books. However, there remain about fifty lectures / seminars that are, as yet, only available in German.

---

[30] See CW24 (ii).

[31] Edward Udell in Martin Large and Steve Briault (Eds), *Free, Equal and Mutual: Rebalancing Society for the Common Good* (Stroud: Hawthorn Press, 2018), p. 79.

[32] Ibid.

[33] Thomas Meyer, 'The birth of threefolding in June 1917', *The Present Age,* Vol. 3 / No. 4, July 2017.

[34] Albert Schmelzer, *The Threefold Movement, 1919: A History* (Forest Row: Rudolf Steiner Press, 2017), p. 80.

[35] Such as Kurt Eisner, Prime Minster of Bavaria from 8 November 1918 (Schmelzer, 2017).

[36] Published in English at different times under the titles *The Threefold Commonwealth; The Threefold State; The Tri-organic Social Order; The Threefold Social Order; Towards Social Renewal.*

At the start of 1919, matters are particularly volatile in Germany; revolution is in the air. Communists, workers' council members, right-wing paramilitary groups, militant, striking proletarians, and a weak government backed by what is left of the army engage in armed clashes.[37] Thousands die.[38] In March—just before his *Kernpunkte* book comes out—Steiner pens an appeal *To the German People and the Civilised World* advocating a threefold approach. This is signed by over 300 notable Germans including Kurt Wolzendorf—a member of the German delegation at the Versailles peace negotiations, Hugo Sinzheimer of the Weimar national assembly, and the writer Herman Hesse. This appeal is distributed as an insert in what is estimated to have been hundreds of thousands of newspapers.[39] The DDP-backing[40] newspaper *Stuttgarter Neues Tagblatt* runs a front page explanation of the appeal and an editorial suggesting that to pay attention to threefolding is 'the duty of everyone who, thinking progressively, has recognised that we must at last exit stagnation. [...] in our time's tremendous poverty of ideas, a poverty that has left us helpless between the concepts of Wilson and those of bolshevism'.[41]

In April, *Kernpunkte* comes out and becomes something of a bestseller, selling up to 80,000 copies in its first year.[42] When English translations are published, a *New York Times* book review says it has 'novelty and bigness as a contribution to sociological literature—the most original contribution in a generation'.[43] In the *London Quarterly Review* it is cited as 'perhaps the most widely read of all books on politics appearing since the war'.[44] The *Daily News* (later incorporated into *The Daily Mail*) reports: 'On the Continent everyone who thinks is discussing a remarkable book ... Dr. Simons, the German Foreign

---

[37] Albert Schmelzer, *The Threefold Movement, 1919: A History* (Forest Row: Rudolf Steiner Press, 2017) p. 157.

[38] Edward Udell in Martin Large and Steve Briault (Eds), *Free, Equal and Mutual: Rebalancing Society for the Common Good* (Stroud: Hawthorn Press, 2018), p. 82.

[39] Ibid.

[40] German Democratic Party.

[41] *Stuttgarter Neues Tagblatt,* 11 March 1919 (see Schmelzer, 2017, p.101).

[42] Ilya Zilberberg, 'The Genesis and Understanding of the Threefold Social Order', *New View,* 4th Quarter, Autumn 2014, p. 7.

[43] Raymond G. Fuller (a pseudonym of Genevieve May Fox), 'New scheme of social organization', *New York Times*, book review, 14 January 1923.

[44] W.F. Lofthouse, *London Quarterly Review,* January 1923.

Secretary, has spoken of the plan it outlines as the one practical alternative to bolshevism. Dr. Benes, the Foreign Minister of Czecho-Slovakia, and one of the ablest and most effective of the builders of small States, had it on his table at Spa. Mr. Venizelos has been reading it. Everybody who is anybody has been reading it. Here, oddly enough, it has passed almost unnoticed. [...] But a living and arresting idea runs through the book ...'.[45]

During 1919, Steiner gives dozens of 'threefold' lectures in Germany in halls that are full to bursting. Some of these lectures are for the general public, others are to raucous crowds of smoking, beer-swilling, illiterate factory workers (at Daimler, Bosch and Delmonte, for example). He engages intensively with the works' councils movement over a prolonged period. At one point, over 10,000 workers adopt a resolution petitioning the Württemberg government 'that Dr Rudolf Steiner immediately be appointed in order that social threefolding, which appears to be the only rescue from looming collapse, may be undertaken at once'.[46] Little resulted from the latter. Steiner was not prepared to take up such a position unless the incumbent administration was prepared to consider significant structural changes which, it seems, it wasn't.[47] And the Prime Minister of the region, Wilhelm Blos declared in his memoirs: 'I was sure that a man who operated with esoteric sciences, with theosophy and anthroposophy, with astral bodies and lotus flowers, who also claimed inner vision, was not qualified to collaborate in the shaping of the foundation of a new democratic state'.[48] A further issue also may have been that Steiner was an Austrian, not a German. Nonetheless, threefold ideas were being considered to such an extent that Steiner was seriously contemplating turning the newspaper *Threefolding of the Social Organism* into a daily.[49]

---

[45] Crispian Villeneuve, *Rudolf Steiner in Britain: A Documentation of his Ten Visits* (Forest Row: Temple Lodge, 2004), p. 613.

[46] Albert Schmelzer, *The Threefold Movement, 1919: A History* (Forest Row: Rudolf Steiner Press, 2017), p. 118.

[47] Ibid.

[48] W. Blos, 'Von der Monarchie zum Volkstaat: Zur Geschichte der Revolution in Deutschland, insbesondere in Würtemberg' (Stuttgart: 1922/23 2nd edition), p.72. (from Schmelzer p.88).

[49] CW337b [also Albert Schmelzer, *The Threefold Movement, 1919: A History* (Forest Row: Rudolf Steiner Press, 2017) p. 163].

In his phenomenally well-researched book *The Threefolding Move-ment, 1919* Albert Schmelzer catalogues in great detail the frenetic activity within the movement in that year. However, by the autumn of 1919 it appears to have become apparent to Steiner that enthusiasm for a threefold approach, although widespread, was not extensive enough for it to have any realistic prospect of being adopted. So he and his many collaborators wound down the campaigning. Threefold thinking was probably too libertarian and inclusive for many of the vocifer-ous communist factions, steeped as they were in smouldering class grievances and dreaming of the dictatorship of the proletariat, and too lefty for most well-connected capitalists and industrialists (well connected, that is, to the former ruling classes and other reactionaries, and to the new government, backed, as it was, by the army). And the vast majority of the public was probably too attached to their familiar party slogans.[50] Plus, threefold ideas were in all likelihood just a bit too novel for a worn-out populace aching for some semblance of calm, order and familiarity as quickly as possible after the devastation at the end of the Great War. Certainly, as Count Otto Lerchenfeld observed, many within the political class seemed much too overworked, drained and devoid of the energy needed to entertain innovation.[51]

All the same, Steiner continues to lecture on the subject, albeit more intermittently, in venues across Europe including Basel, Oslo, Oxford, Stuttgart, Zurich. This continues until 1922. The following rant written by Adolf Hitler in 1921 serves as a somewhat oblique and uncomfortable illustration of the extent to which threefold ideas had permeated public awareness during this period.

> It is straight-on monstrous impudence when this Mr Simons, who is not a reactionary man but, on the contrary, an employee of the German people, presumes to announce that the German people cannot correctly value their own capacity for work. It is possible that Simons can actually value it

---

[50] Albert Schmelzer, *The Threefold Movement, 1919: A History* (Forest Row: Rudolf Steiner Press, 2017), p. 158.

[51] Count Otto Lerchenfeld (German aristocrat with a seat in the Bavarian Royal Council, admirer of Steiner, childhood friend of Richard von Kühlmann who became Secretary of State for Foreign Affairs in 2017) quoted in Thomas Meyer, 'The birth of threefolding in June 1917', *The Present Age*, Vol. 3 / No. 4, July 2017, p. 9.

better; the man appears to have exactly valued the capacity for work of the German people. In the course of the London affair there now rises to the surface, by degree, such mysterious accompanying circumstances that it is not only appropriate but also necessary to inspect somewhat closer this Mr Minister—the intimate friend of the gnostic anthroposophist Rudolf Steiner, himself the adherent of the Threefold Social Order which is one of the many completely Jewish[52] methods of destroying the people's normal state of mind—to see whether his mindless face, mindless according to the opinion of Lloyd George, is really only the result of the lack of spirit or whether it is the larva behind which something else is concealed …

Poland will occupy Upper Silesia. Germany will rebel. France rumbles occupation of the Ruhr in the event of German opposition, and then Mr Simons with his mindless, stupid face, as Mr Lloyd George said, will again represent the German people. Then this friend of Germany and of Rudolf Steiner will again make us observe that, in order to keep the Ruhr, we could trade off Upper Silesia more quickly because Upper Silesia dispatches 43 million tons of coal and the Ruhr 115 million tons. So will he persuade us, a God-and-reason-forsaken people, only yes, in God's heavenly will no real opposition, only peace and prudence, the recognised war cry of the German newspaper Lion and the Levite. We will for the sake of peace, of quiet, and of the Ruhr region renounce Upper Silesia and six months later, due to some other cause, will lose the Ruhr region anyway to the amusement of the whole world. Mr Simons will still have his stupid gaze. As Lloyd George says, he has no mind.

And this is one of the chief reasons for the disarmament of the German people. It is the intention to make the German people defenceless and this does not apply only to the Bavarian militia. And therefore we protest against it and not from a narrow-minded, bird-brained perspective. And what is the driving force behind all this devilishness? The Jews, friends of Dr. Rudolf Steiner, who is friend of the mindless Simons.[53]

The following year, on 15 May 1922, during a lecture Steiner is giving in the concert hall of the Four Seasons Hotel in Munich, the lighting is mysteriously cut. He continues lecturing in the near-darkness, and after

---

[52] Steiner was not Jewish—see Edward Udell in Martin Large and Steve Briault (Eds), *Free, Equal and Mutual: Rebalancing Society for the Common Good* (Stroud: Hawthorn Press, 2018), p. 75.

[53] Printed on 15 March 1921 in the National Socialist newspaper *Völkischer Beobachter*.

some time the lights are restored. At the end of the lecture there is rapturous applause, but just as he is leaving the hall, three or four thugs make a dash for him. Audience members are able to prevent them from reaching Steiner, however. (With delicious restraint, Edward Udell refrains from speculating that Hitler's presence there in Munich on the same day might have had anything to do with this.) The following morning a posse of shady characters turns up at the station when Steiner is due to depart, only to discover he has slipped away on an earlier train.[54]

But that is by the by.

In the decades following, public awareness of Steiner's threefold approach to public life is very patchy, unlike the much greater interest, for example, in his educational or agricultural ideas.

In 1937, as further world tragedy threatens, King Leopold of Belgium writes to his Prime Minister, van Zeeland, urging him to consider certain threefold measures. Reflecting on 'the state of disorganisation in which society is plunged' he argues it is 'necessary to encourage vigorously and with conviction every attempt at organisation, the pursuit of which may lift minds up towards an ideal of human solidarity'.[55]

In 1945, after the second, cataclysmic world war has come to an end, Field Marshal Jan Smuts[56] observes whilst in Ottawa: 'There are many people who ... think that the creation of the Threefold Commonwealth should be delayed until humanity is more ripe for it. However, the ordering of human society was certainly not meant to wait until mankind should have grown more mature. Its introduction will bring about the maturity we desire'.[57] (I am not sure, however, how he proposed to square his support of racial segregation in South Africa with threefolding's requirement for democracy!)

---

[54] Edward Udell in Martin Large and Steve Briault (Eds), *Free, Equal and Mutual: Rebalancing Society for the Common Good* (Stroud: Hawthorn Press, 2018), p. 75.
[55] Walter Johannes Stein, 'King Leopold's Plan', *The Present Age*, Volume 2, Sept—Oct. 1937, p.1.
[56] Amongst other things, Prime Minster of South Africa and founder of the League of Nations. He was also the first non-British Chancellor of Cambridge University, and, in 1940, on account of his centrality in the Imperial war effort, there was one plan afoot to install him as UK Prime Minster should anything happen to Winston Churchill.
[57] Joanna Scott, *Death in Europe—Why?* (London: Simpkin Marshall, 1941), p. 39.

In the 1980s, Otto Schily[58] talks of Steiner's ideas in the German parliament when addressing the German political party donations scandal. And Rolf Henrich recommends Steiner's approach in his book *Der Vormundschaftliche Staat* ('the Custodial State'). 'Henrich's book was a devastating critique of the East German communist state, where he had grown up and become a lawyer. His book was one of the factors that led to the end of that state, in 1990'.[59] More recently still, founding member of the German Greens (and anthroposophist) Gerald Häfner[60] has been a significant adherent.[61]

4.2 Shortcomings of other societal constructs, as observed by Steiner

Believing as men do today that they can continue their economic life in the way that has brought the world to this catastrophe is simply refusing to think. (CW189, 7 March 1919)

4.2.1 Capitalism

By capitalism we simply mean ... the private ownership of the means of production. (CW330(ii), 31 May 1919)

Although Steiner has no desire to do away with mass production and turn the clock back to medieval times, he does note how mass production and capitalism had brought with them the alienation of the worker, mentioned earlier—alienation from both product and customer.

---

[58] Lawyer, founder member of the Green Party in Germany, Interior Minister 1998—2005.
[59] Edward Udell, translator of Albert Schmelzer, *The Threefold Movement, 1919: A History* (Forest Row: Rudolf Steiner Press, 2017) p. 7.
[60] Also a Bundestag member three times between 1987 and 2002, and MEP 2009-2014.
[61] See for example Gerald Häfner in Martin Large and Steve Briault (Eds), *Free, Equal and Mutual: Rebalancing Society for the Common Good* (Stroud: Hawthorn Press, 2018), p. 127.

> *... technology and capitalism were not able to provide the worker with the human dignity his soul needed. This dignity was available to the medieval artisan through his craft, to which he felt humanly related—a situation which allowed him to consider life in society as worth living. (CW23, p. 34)*

And he notes how the pursuit of profit, over and above what one needs to cover one's living costs, sooner or later takes on a life of its own, and the economy takes a further step away from the personal, from the human being:

> *If we consider the development of humanity during the past three or four centuries, if we study above all the development of what has been designated as capitalism, another standpoint must be borne in mind, as well as the one that smaller industrial concerns were swallowed up by the gigantic industries of modern times [...] Things can only be judged in the right way if we compare modern capitalist production to the craftsmanship of past times, and if we make this comparison from a certain definite standpoint. The artisan of olden times produced goods and delivered them to the consumer, and the money which he thus earned enabled him to live, provided the foundation for his existence. [...] In a certain sense, this economic life was a restricted one, but it was closely linked up with the individual human being ... every form of production was therefore linked up with personal skill, personal diligence, and the personal ambition to do something as well as possible, and so forth. Significant moral impulses were connected with the economic life in those days of simple craftsmanship. [...]*
>
> *After a period of transition, which went from the 15th century to about the 16th/17th century, a complete change took place ... For, what may be designated as capitalist production, capitalist industry, only developed during the past three to four centuries. If we wish to understand that which really lies at the foundation of the social question, ... the following characteristic must be borne in mind: For a capitalist, insofar as he is a member of the capitalist economic order, the essential point is not that of providing for his own existence, or forming a life foundation through his capital, but the essential point is for him that of increasing his capital, of seeing to it that it grows. This increase in capital constitutes the profit.*

Consequently the aim of the capitalist economic order is not that of earning money enabling capitalists to meet their cost of living, but its aim is that of making profits, of increasing the capital ... When the process of production or the industrial process grows in the course of the years through the accumulation of capital, when this industrial process grows and forms the incentive of accumulating capital, then the chief element in this economic process really becomes separated from the individual human being, from every personal element. If we wish to understand the social question, we must bear in mind above all the following standpoint: that the economic process becomes emancipated from the personal element, from the individual human being. [...] if people were to occupy themselves with such matters they would see that the human being has, as it were, become separated from everything which constitutes the economic process. Tell me, where can we find today genuine pleasure in the production of goods, and with the exception of a few restricted circles, where do people find true enjoyment in the production of goods? The decisive element of past economic orders, that, for instance, a man felt the keenest pleasure in every key made by his own hands, and that he saw a point of honour in making it as perfect as possible—this belongs to the past. Human beings have become separated, as it were, from the economic process as such. Only in the artistic field or that which is related to the sphere of art, we may still come across that element which once permeated craftsmanship. (CW188(ii), 1 February 1919)

Thus, under capitalism, the economic process becomes divorced from the human, from the personal. Money-making and money itself take on a life of their own. Nonetheless, Steiner does appreciate that capitalism has brought many great things ...

It is not right when it is said that today's misery, even if we could portray it in its direst colours, is greater than it was in former centuries. That is not the case. (CW88, p. 49)

... but he does not mince his words when expressing his more acute misgivings about it (capitalism)—in its familiar form.

We have seen, as it is easy to see, that under the private capitalist order of the last few centuries, certain evils have arisen. (CW332a, p. 30)

> *In the modern economic process, evils have arisen through control of the means of production by private capital. (CW24, p. 125)*
>
> *What have we, exactly, in capitalism? We have something that fundamentally has become a terrible oppressor of the great mass of human beings. (CW189(ii), 15 March 1919)*
>
> *... path of healing, that leads us out of the cataclysms of capitalism, out of the indignity of seeing human beings only as a workforce, and so on. (CW24(ii), p. 98)*
>
> *... regulating themselves, that is, according to profit, according to the most sordid competition, the blindest human egoism, which leads every man to try and earn as much as ever he can squeeze out of the social system. [...] ... based upon the war of competition, upon profit, upon economic coercion in the tug of war between capital and wages. (CW330(ii), 31 May 1919)*
>
> *Just as it is true that modern technology and capitalism have moulded our society in recent times, it is also imperative that the wounds necessarily inflicted on human society by them be thoroughly healed ... (CW23, p. 59)*

Capitalism had entailed the oppression of great masses of people. Furthermore, the encroachment of its power into the political domain, on account of great concentrations of wealth, had already been a problem for some time:

> *With a deep feeling for the social conditions of America in their development since the War of Cessation in the sixties of last century, Woodrow Wilson perceived a relationship between the political and legal conditions and those of the economic life. With a considerable amount of unbiased judgment he watched how the great accumulations of capital have grown in consequence of the complication of modern economic life. He saw the formation of trusts[62] and of the great financial companies. He saw how, even in a democratic state, the principle of democracy has tended more and more to disappear before the secret operations of those*

---

[62] In the sense of a corporate trust, a holding company, a conglomerate of different businesses.

companies whose interest was served by secrecy, those companies that with their massed capital acquired great power and obtained influence over enormous numbers of people. [...] He has declared that the fundamental evil of modern development lies in the fact that, notwithstanding the progress in economic matters, the latter have been controlled by the secret machinations of certain persons, and the idea of justice, of the political life of the community, has not kept pace with economic progress, but has lingered behind at an earlier stage. (CW332a, p. 14)

Steiner pinpoints the financial world as an aspect of capitalism with a lot to answer for. On a separate occasion he cites the behaviour of some 30 banks in America which in 1907 had speculatively bought futures to an extent that created an economic crisis in Europe.

Such a thing as was done by the Morgan Group in 1907, by which any number of human existences in Europe were flung into ruin ... How has it come about that such a thing is possible? It has come about through the separation of the money market from the goods market. This separation dates from about the years 1810 to 1815 ... It was at this period first, that the earlier, purely economic conditions controlling public life gave place to a control of public life by the money market. It was the time when the bank system first really became the dominant factor in economic life. (CW335, 15 September 1920)

Although he commends Woodrow Wilson's awakeness to many of the social problems of the time, Steiner also notices that he (Wilson) is sadly unable to come up with much to address the issues in question.

These issues, of course, are painfully familiar to us today. As George Monbiot observes of capitalism's neo-liberal fairy tale:

We were promised unending growth on a finite planet. We were told that a vastly unequal system would remove all differences. Social peace would be delivered by a system based on competition and envy. Democracy would be secured by the power of money. The contradictions were crushingly obvious. The whole package relied on magic. [...]

Pankaj Mishra in his book *Age of Anger*, explains the current crises as new manifestations of one long disruption that has been ripping up society for 200 years or more. Our sanitised histories of Europe and America allow us to forget that bedlam and carnage, civil and international war, colonialism and overseas slaughter, racism and genocide, were the norms of this project, not exceptions.

Now the rest of the world is confronting the same disruptive forces, as industrial capitalism is globalised. It destroys old forms of authority while promising universal freedom, autonomy and prosperity. Those promises collide with massive disparities of power, status and property ownership. The result is the global spread of the 19th century European diseases of humiliation, envy and a sense of impotence. Frustrated expectations, rage and self-disgust have driven support for movements as diverse as Isis, resurgent Indian nationalism and stomping demagoguery in Britain, the U.S., France and Hungary.[63]

Or, whilst talking of capitalism, New Zealand's Prime Minister Jacinda Ardern despairs: 'If you have hundreds of thousands of children … without enough to survive, that's a blatant failure. What else could you describe it as?'[64]

Or, Ann Pettifor: 'the failed system of capitalism that now threatens to collapse our life support systems and with them, human civilisation'.[65]

And a penetrating article by Tanya Kerssen and Eric Holt-Giménez reflects on how the blight of unrestrained capitalist expansion infects the developing world and becomes economic imperialism. The resultant, creeping, winners-and-losers paradigm is aided by the World Bank, for example, whose head is chosen by the President of the USA, and whose …

purpose—then as now—is to spread capitalism across the globe. […] Critics, however, point to the Bank's complicity in a new feverish wave of global land grabs. […]

---

[63] George Monbiot, 'The case for despair is made. Now let's start to get out of the mess we're in', *The Guardian*, 13 December 2016.

[64] Chris Baynes, 'New Zealand's new prime minister calls capitalism a "blatant failure"', *The Independent*, 1 April 2019—https://www.independent.co.uk/news/world/australasia/new-zealand-new-prime-minister-jacinda-ardern-capitalism-blatant-failure-a8012656.html.

[65] Ann Pettifor, *The Case For the Green New Deal* (Verso: London, 2019), p. xv.

By the late 1980s ... the Bank enthusiastically supported the idea that poor countries should buy food from transnational corporations on the global market rather than grow it themselves.

It is difficult to overstate the degree to which the International Monetary Fund and World Bank-promoted cocktail of liberalisation, deregulation, and privatisation contributed to extreme vulnerability for farmers and peasants. [...]

... a global wave of largely speculative investments and dispossession has affected upwards of 86 million hectares of land worldwide (with some estimates as high as 227 million hectares). The Bank facilitates these land grabs in a number of interrelated ways: low-interest loans to agribusiness and other land-based industries; investment guarantees and insurance; loans to governments for investor-friendly infrastructure like roads and dams; *and technical advice on how to reform regulatory regimes to attract foreign investment.* [my emphasis, RM]

Beyond agriculture, these activities support a whole slew of industries that restructure the countryside as a site of dirty extraction and capital accumulation instead of community health and wellbeing. These include timber, mining, fisheries, tourism, energy, and plantation agriculture (including agrofuels)—industries that either expel peasants from their territories or contaminate the land and water they depend on. Of course, once rendered poor and landless, former peasants are enlisted as cheap labour for the very industries that uprooted them. This, for the World Bank, is what constitutes 'job creation' and 'development'. [...]

Perhaps the most egregious cases of World Bank-facilitated land grabbing have occurred under the auspices of the Bank's private sector lending arm, the International Finance Corporation (IFC). The IFC recently came under fire for a US$30 million loan package to the Dinant Corporation in Honduras, associated with the illegitimate acquisition of peasant lands for palm oil production and the killing of local community members. Half of the loan was dispersed to Dinant only four months after a military coup, supported by the country's land owning and business elite, threw the country into political turmoil which included heavy repression targeting peasant communities.

Further, a new report by Oxfam details the IFC's increasing use of third parties, such as banks or private equity funds, to channel development money that amounted to US$36 billion between 2009 and 2013, or 62 percent of IFC spending. This allows the IFC to distance itself from development outcomes such as human rights abuses, environmental impacts, and displacement.

Remarkably, the Bank doesn't keep even basic statistics on the number of people displaced by its projects. A review of the Bank's 'Involuntary Resettlement' programme completed in mid-2014 revealed that the status of displaced people was unknown for 61 percent of sampled Bank-funded projects. Based on this inadequate data, the Bank estimates that half a million people have been displaced due to its 218 active projects—with no clear idea of how many of those received compensation or new land. A separate 11-month investigation by the International Consortium and of Investigative Journalists found that 1,000 World Bank projects approved between 2004 and 2013 forced 3.4 million people from their homes, grabbed their land, or damaged their livelihood.

While Bank president Jim Yong Kim stated that 'additional efforts must be made to build capacity and safeguards related to land rights,' a leaked draft of new World Bank social and environmental safeguards showed just the opposite. Most shockingly, a statement endorsed by over 100 human rights organizations and experts notes: 'The draft framework provides an opt-out option for governments who do not wish to provide essential land and natural resource rights protections to Indigenous Peoples within their States'.[66]

It may reassure the reader to know there are no more quotes of this length in the book!

As we know, capitalism is in a sorry state, but activities like the above show its wider implications—in those distant lands that fewer people are aware of.

The pill becomes especially bitter when the way is enthusiastically cleared for private capital, only for the taxpayer to be left picking up the pieces when everything goes wrong. Such privatisation of gains and socialisation of losses revealed themselves in stark relief when the UK taxpayer had to bail out the Royal Bank of Scotland after it had become overexposed to US sub-prime mortgages in 2008. (Intriguingly, one rarely hears anything about the economic prosperity in Iceland following their government's decision to just let their banks go bust.)

---

[66] Tanya Kerssen and Eric Holt-Giménez of Food First, 'The World Bank's Long War on Peasants', 20 April 2015, http://www.telesurtv.net/english/opinion/The-World-Banks-Long-War-on-Peasants-20150417-0003.html.

4.2.2 Socialism

Steiner's views of socialism (in the traditional, nationalisation-of-the-means-of-production, state-planned economy sense) are also highly critical, possibly more so.

As the Great War ends, vast swathes of the 'proletariat' are on manoeuvres, agitating for an expansion of communism into parts of Central and even Western Europe. On the one hand, Steiner is sympathetic to their grievances:

> ... yoked to the factory, yoked to the technical processes, to the soul-blighting capitalist system were the working classes, who turned with all their spiritual fervour to the doctrine of Marx; for they saw in this Marxian doctrine the most brilliant, the most grandiose criticism, which they themselves felt in their own hearts towards the social order: a social order on which they could only wage war, because it was one that allowed them no share in its material and spiritual possessions. (CW330(ii), 31 May 1919)

And he also wholeheartedly endorses the famous socialist maxim (a maxim that predates Marx): 'From each according to his abilities, to each according to his needs' ...

> ... which should not only be a socialist but also a universal ideal ... (CW329, 11 March 1919)

But he is unimpressed by the impractical ways in which the likes of Marx and Lenin envisage such an ideal can be followed.

The following speak for themselves:

> ... industry, especially in our complicated life, is based on the initiative of the individual. If we try to substitute for individual initiative the abstract community at large, we give the death blow to economic life. Eastern Europe will prove this if it remains much longer under its present rule. This means extinction and death to the economic body when we deprive the individual his initiative which must proceed from his intellect and take part in the ordering of the means of production purely for the benefit of human society. (CW332a, p. 36)

The great mistake of current socialism is its belief that a healthy social structure can be brought about by State regulation, and particularly by socialising the means of production. (CW188(iii), 24 January 1919)

One may perhaps have good intentions toward the proletariat today, yet one is not dealing with them objectively and honestly if one does not make it clear to them that the programmes to which their faith is pinned are leading them not to the welfare they desire but to the downfall of European civilisation, which seals their own downfall. (CW24, p. 54)

Establishing a world bureaucracy—the Leninist and Trotskyite ideal—is out of the question. It would most certainly eliminate independent intellectual initiatives and cause the starvation of the social organism. (CW190, p. 60)

A great portion of Europe wants to sail into a community, a social community politics, in which the freedom of the individual, each person's distinct powers, will go under. [...] Let us hypothetically assume that Europe were to achieve the ideals of Bolshevism ... all powers of freedom would necessarily drain away to free America ... Terrible competition would develop between Europe and America, and this would inevitably lead to Europe's impoverishment and the enrichment of America: not because of injustice but due to the idiocy of socialist politics in Europe. (CW189, p. 14)

In February 1919 Steiner elucidates what he regards as one of the central absurdities of Marxist and Leninist doctrine: the two-phase progression from capitalism to communism where, firstly, the proletariat take over the state—the 'dictatorship of the proletariat' (itself fraught with all manner of questions)—which then, secondly, at some future date, magically gives rise to a completely different type of human race where no state is needed at all, and everyone lives in harmony, each contributing according to their ability, and taking according their need. Steiner despairs how this noble idea becomes such an abstraction when in the heads of these socialist thinkers. He describes as superstition the idea that human beings would become this enlightened, ethical race purely on the strength of living within a particular economic framework with no cultural input. (CW189, pp. 41-49)

And he takes an especially grave view of Lenin's Communism which had made Marxism into ideological dogma (not something Marx advocated) and stripped it of the human liberty that Marx in fact cherished.[67]

In a nutshell ...

The horrendous beliefs of Lenin and Trotsky ... (CW333, p. 40)

... Lenin and Trotsky, the gravediggers of modern civilisation. (CW332a, p. 16)

... the infinite human suffering caused by failed so-called social movements such as Leninism, Trotskyism, and the like, which are nothing more than intellectual poison. (CW333, p. 105)

The experiment [of communism] will ... fail miserably and bring unimaginable disaster to humanity. (CW79, 30 November 1921)

The lack of scope for individual initiative, the grim shortage of basic necessities: we saw all this with the USSR and its inefficient Gosplan.[68] 'Centralized planning had destroyed freedom without the compensation of material benefits', as Edmund Dell observed.[69]

And, of course, it was not only the economy that suffered under Soviet totalitarianism:

In Russia ... one can no longer read anything which is not sold by the Soviet state. At the most one might be able to sneak in a book here or there. (CW341, p. 188)

It is clear, Steiner sees as a dead end the idea of a state that is based on, and that directs, economic life.

With the same sincerity as those who make such demands, one can hold the view, from a deeper reading of social impulses, that nothing special is achieved with the conversion of private property

---

[67] Bettany Hughes, 'Genius of the Modern World', BBC4, 2018.
[68] Gosplan (1921—1991) was the Soviet Union's State Planning Committee responsible for central economic planning.
[69] Edmund Dell, *A Strange Eventful History: Democratic Socialism in Britain* (London: Harper Collins, 1999), p. 89.

into common property. On the contrary, it would replace a devastating capitalism with a no less devastating bureaucracy. (CW329, 9 April 1919)

4.2.3 The unitary state

In addition to his criticisms of both capitalism and socialism (in their traditional forms), Steiner also took issue with the idea of the state as being something to look up to as the be-all-and-end-all of public life, an all-encompassing body that oversees not only politics but also much of culture and industry too (in a free market economy, unlike communism). He described the Switzerland of the time as such a state (CW339). Civil society barely gets a look-in; daddy presides over everything. He calls this the unitary or unified state—something that most countries are to some degree, perhaps.

What has been the fundamental character of the central European states? Their essential character consisted in a state structure based upon very old, traditional forms. In Central Europe, and even in Russia the ideas which influenced the mentality which was connected with the state had been handed down from very ancient times. These ideas had been preserved—no matter whether they were monarchical or non-monarchical, for this is not so important—but they had been preserved in such a way that the old corporations developed into the so called modern states. These modern states of Central Europe, stretching as far as Russia, are in reality remnants of medieval thoughts and feelings. Their structure is in keeping with medieval elements. But life does not adapt itself to obsolete ideas. In the countries where such obsolete structures arose, something else appeared as well, out of a necessity which was far stronger than that which had been transplanted from the Middle Ages: the economic structure, the economic body arose. And this economic body has laws of its own, it demands its own laws.

The thoroughly pathological process now arose that modern economic life and its requirements turned to the old government structures; people thought that economic life could be permeated with these old state structures. Economic life which was, or rather is, a completely new element was to be incorporated with the body of the state, although this had grown out of entirely different conditions. (CW188(iv), 31 January 1919)

... the old social orientation of the unified state is what has brought the world into its present catastrophic situation ... one must therefore decide to rebuild from the ground up [...]

To admit to themselves candidly that the evils they now see around them are the result of this idea is, for many today, like being asked to stand with no ground beneath their feet. The ground these people want to stand on is the unified state. They want to take it as given, and build upon it institutions they hope will lead to an improved state of affairs. However, what is necessary is to create new ground ... (CW24, p. 141)

Whoever thinks today of the historical facts will not ask: what should states do? On the contrary, he will perhaps be compelled to ask: what should states refrain from doing? Since what they do, and thereby bring about, is what we have experienced in the killing of ten million people and what has left a further eighteen million crippled. [...] The unnatural coupling of economic matters with the rights realm is what gobbled up the so-called Austrian state like a cancer. (CW329, 17 March 1919)

... political states are not merely the products of economic forces, and the attempt to transform them into economic communities is the cause of the social chaos of modern times. (CW23, p. 17)

Clearly, Steiner saw the close involvement between state and industry as being a significant contributor to the horrific hostilities that had just been experienced.

Noting this close involvement between state and industry in Central Europe (and also Japan) Paul Mason observes: 'By 1913, for example, most industrial countries were protecting their domestic industries with double-digit import taxes on manufactured goods. The monopolies, in return, placed key personnel inside government. The ideology of state as "nightwatchman", standing aloof from economic life, was dead'.[70] He does point out, however, that economic

---

[70] Paul Mason, *Postcapitalism: A Guide to Our Future* (London: Allen Lane, 2015), p. 57.

advances under the system were frequently significant. Economic historian P. A. Toninelli also includes Germany and France amongst the countries which 'shared the belief that the state could and should form a primary role in catching up with the nation that led world industrialization: Great Britain' and notes the 'continental pattern leaned towards more and more massive government intervention in the economy'.[71]

Also inappropriate, in Steiner's eyes, was that this closeness between state and economy was leaving its mark on cultural endeavour:

> ... it becomes ever more evident that the manner in which the business of a nation is carried on determines, in reality, the cultural and political life of the people. It becomes ever more evident that the commercial and industrial magnates, by their position alone, have acquired the monopoly of culture. The economically weak remain the uneducated. A certain connection has become apparent between the economic and the cultural, and between the cultural and political organizations. The cultural life has gradually become one that does not evolve out of its own inner needs and does not follow its own impulses, but, especially when it is under public administration, as in schools and educational institutions, it receives the form most useful to the political authority. The human being can no longer be judged according to his capacities; he can no longer be developed as his inborn talents demand. Rather it is asked, 'What does the state want? What talents are needed for business? How many men are wanted for a particular training?' The teaching, the schools, the examinations are all directed to this end. The cultural life cannot follow its own laws of development; it is adapted to the political and the economic life. (CW332a, p. 19)

With the vast range of study options available and life paths to choose from in the 'developed world' nowadays, this is perhaps somewhat less of an issue now than when Steiner is talking.

---

[71] Pier Angelo Toninelli, *The Rise and Fall of State-Owned Enterprise in the Western World* (New York: Cambridge University Press, 2008), p.11.

4.3　Introduction to the threefold approach

One knows, of course, that union life, co-operative life, party-political life have achieved a great deal in recent times, and that much is due to them. On the other hand, one needs to say that despite all of these achievements, there remains something unsatisfactory, unfinished. We don't really have the conviction that new facts are in front of us. (CW329, 19 March 1919)

The essence of the threefold social order is that it looks at social relations without party or class prejudice and poses the question: what must be done at this juncture of human evolution in order to create viable social forms? (CW24, p. 128)

If we do not want to perish under a cultural life and a life of rights that are degenerate in the extreme, we have no choice but to organize society in a threefold way. (CW194, p. 48)

As already mentioned, Steiner initially introduces his threefold ideas in two Memoranda in 1917 written for the German and Austrian governments. In these Memoranda, he addresses some of the causes of the Great War and then proposes Central Europe adopt a threefold approach—an approach which he considers the best way forward for peaceful coexistence. At this point, this threefold approach is outlined only in the broadest terms. His concern at this stage seems primarily to illustrate a way forward whereby the different nationalities of Austria-Hungary (Austrians, Hungarians, Czechs, Slovaks, Germans, etc.) can live side by side, around and amongst each other, as they had been doing hitherto—a fact US President Woodrow Wilson's proposed 'self-determination of nations' takes little account of.

... the realization of Wilson's programme will bring the European peoples to ruin. (CW24(ii), p. 108)

The way forward that Steiner proposes is also highly pertinent to the different nationalities within Russia being able to coexist peacefully too (Latvians, Lithuanians, Poles, Estonians, Ukranians, etc.).

How society 'carries on' falls into a number of academic disciplines (politics, economics, philosophy, sociology, international relations, anthropology, law, etc.) and into all manner of cultural pursuits, from jousting to journalism. However, Steiner outlines how society comprises three *basic* aspects, and how these three aspects each need to take their own particular approach in order for the beginnings of a healthier, more civilised and peaceful state of affairs to take root. He emphasises how these proposals come from no abstract ideology or theory but amount to organising, in a healthy way, what exists already. They describe, he says, what he sees as living just under the surface of Central European society, namely a regeneration that could bring greater societal health if only given the opportunity to get a proper foothold. He cites the example of philosopher Eduard von Hartmann who had already made suggestions in a somewhat similar direction. Indeed, the Prussian government functionary and philosopher Wilhelm von Humboldt had already advocated something slightly similar as far back as in 1792.[72]

> ... it must be said that the threefold order of the social organism is not an idea conceived out of personal inclinations by one or more persons; it is an impulse resulting from an impartial observation of the historical development of humanity in modern times. We may say that actually the most important impulses of humanity have been tending unconsciously in the direction of this threefold membering for centuries, only they have never garnered sufficient force to carry it through. The failure to develop this force is the cause of the present state of things and of the misery in our surroundings. (CW332a, p. 107)
>
> I believe the thoughts expressed here are not merely the private thoughts of one individual: they voice the unconscious will of Europe as a whole. (CW24, p. xx)

The two Memoranda penned by Steiner herald the beginning of a five-year period during which he describes the three aspects of social life and how these need to be administered in three different ways instead of being bundled together under the collective concerns of a single state umbrella.

Broadly speaking, the three aspects of society he is referring to are the familiar ones of (a) politics, (b) economics, and (c) culture.

---

[72] Wilhelm von Humboldt, *Towards an Attempt to Determine the Limits of State Action*, first published (posthumously) in 1851.

However, Steiner's definitions of these realms are very particular, as we shall see. Frequently he refers to the political realm as the rights realm or the legal realm. And the cultural realm is more often called the spiritual realm, that is to say, the realm of '*Geist*' which covers both the spirit in its more other-worldly sense as well as the life of thought generally—the mind. Exactly what does and does not constitute these three realms of society is clarified when Steiner's definitions of them are considered in the next chapter.

In the previous section, his misgivings about the 'unitary state' were introduced, and even with no knowledge of Central Europe's political history, one can deduce from the following that the bundling together of the three realms of society was a prominent feature of life at the time:

> *At present, a single administrative body embraces these three elements of life in our states ... (CW332a, p. 27)*
>
> *... the unnatural mixing of political, economic and general human interests. (CW24(ii), p. 97)*
>
> *For example, the government organises the education system, while the economy determines who can make his or her way into this sphere. (CW334, p. 98)*

... that is, (a) the government is running the educational part of the cultural realm, and (b) educational advancement is largely determined by the economic position of one's parents. (Education is a particular hobby horse that Steiner returns to repeatedly, as we shall see.)

As well as addressing this 'unnatural mixing' of public affairs within the 'unitary state', the threefold approach also addresses—with interest—the iniquities that result under capitalism as well as what Steiner sees as the disaster of communism. Albert Schmelzer notes: 'within the modern history of ideas, threefolding can be classified as a concept that reconciles libertarian and democratic thinking with socialistic approaches'.[73]

---

[73] Albert Schmelzer, *The Threefold Movement, 1919: A History* (Forest Row: Rudolf Steiner Press, 2017), p. 67.

In the modern economic process, evils have arisen through control of the means of production by private capital. If one tries to eliminate these evils by an economic measure, such as the communal control of the means of production [as in socialism, communism or nationalisation, RM], one undermines modern industry. One can, however, work against these evils, by creating alongside the economy an independent legal system and a free life of the spirit. In this way, the evils that result—and result continually—from the economic life will be removed as they arise. It will not be a case of the evils arriving first and people having to suffer under them before they disappear; rather, the other organic systems that exist alongside economic institutions will, in each instance, turn aside the mischief. (CW24, p. 125)

Just as it is true that modern technology and capitalism have moulded our society in recent times, it is also imperative that the wounds necessarily inflicted on human society by them be thoroughly healed by correctly relating man and the human community to the three members of the social organism. (CW23, p. 59)

While in wide socialist circles the belief is current that the economic system must first be changed and everything else will follow of itself, the truth is that each one must ask himself the question: what conditions within the sphere of equity and of culture must first be created in order that a new cultural and a new legal system may give birth to economic conditions that will satisfy the demands of an existence worthy of human beings? (CW332a, p. 57)

The above passages air some of the broad issues which need to be overcome. The following introduce the alternative approach he advocates:

... society should be seen as a trinity, composed of three members. (CW188(iii), 24 January 1919)

... if the social organism is to be sound it must be divided into these three branches. (CW193, p. 77)

The health of the social organism can be brought about only when economic matters are regulated by one member, democratic rights discussed in another, and all cultural, spiritual relations arranged by the third. (CW189(ii), 7 March 1919)

> *... I should like to show how, out of the circumstances of modern life, the social question must be felt in its three aspects, a cultural, legal-political, and economic. (CW332a, p. 14)*

This threefoldness, however, is not as simple as there being three *sectors*, where we either belong to one or the other.

> *The health of the social organism depends upon its articulation into three independent spheres: a spiritual-cultural sphere [Geistes-glied], a legal or rights-sphere, and an economic sphere. Far from dividing people up into three social strata, the articulation will allow them to participate in all three spheres according to their interests ... (CW24, p. 13)*

Further:

> *When I speak of threefolding, ladies and gentlemen, I do not mean that there is at present a beautiful unity in social life which we are to cut into three pieces so that three elements can evolve side by side. I mean that a threefoldness already exists, just as it does in the human being who has a system of head and nerves, a rhythmic system [heart / lung, RM], and a system of metabolism. The three must function properly together, however, and to each must be assigned what belongs to it. If the digestive system works too little, leaving too much for the head to do, the result is all kinds of migraine-like disorders. (CW305(ii), 26 August 1922)*

Steiner uses this analogy of the human body on a number of occasions when characterising the threefold structure of society.

> *The arrangement meant ... is not a spatial delimitation of the bodily members, but is according to the activities (functions) of the organism. The term 'head-organism' is only to be used in that one is aware that the nerve-sense faculty is principally centralised in the head. Of course the rhythmic and metabolic functions are also present in the head, as is the nerve-sense faculty in the other bodily members. Nevertheless, the three functional types are, according to their natures, sharply separated. (CW23, p. 54)*

As we shall see, this absence of spatial delineation is important to recognise. The three societal realms are intermingled; they interpenetrate.

Precisely (a) what, in Steiner's analysis, does and does not constitute these three aspects of society, and (b) what guiding principles he proposed they should each observe will be the subject of a multitude of quotes and comments over the coming chapters, as will (c) many of his operational suggestions for the three realms.

The three aspects of society elaborated by Steiner are variously referred to by him and other authors / translators as 'realms', 'spheres', 'domains', 'members', 'elements', 'dimensions', 'aspects', 'systems', or 'life' (as in 'the rights life', 'the economic life', the 'cultural life') etc. Sometimes the word 'sector' is used, although this can be misleading since the word is already used so much in public life to denote either the three divisions of public sector, private sector and third sector, which are not the same as Steiner's three realms, or to denote specific areas of work such as the energy sector, the hospitality sector, the education sector, etc. They also suggest a spatial demarcation which does not fit well with Steiner's analysis.

In summary:

- The three realms in the threefold social organism are (a) the political / rights realm, (b) the economic, and (c) the spiritual / cultural.
- They should be administered separately, not all together under one state roof.

4.4   Not a fixed programme

> *... it is impossible to speak at all of an absolutely complete solution of the social problem ... But this need not lead anyone to say that, if the social problem is simply not to be solved, we should permit the old nonsense to continue on its course. (CW186, pp. 72-73)*

In contrast to what Steiner (amongst others) regards as the utopian and impractical dogmas of the socialists / communists, he emphasises that, instead, he is indicating a direction of travel via which social affairs might be shaped in *many different* ways, although in each case, more healthily. By observing the threefold nature inherent in society, and by being mindful of the guiding principles most fitting to each aspect (all this to be covered presently), he asserts that a foundation can then be created which, perhaps paradoxically, is highly flexible but on which sound social decisions can be based that will lead to an improved state of affairs. The more this threefold basis is respected, he asserts, the more healthily will matters be organised over time.

A number of passages are quoted here which illustrate Steiner's thoughts in this regard. Quite a few are given, partly to emphasise the importance he gave to this flexible and non-dogmatic aspect of his suggestions, and partly because this non-fixedness supports the idea that threefolding has longer-term relevance; it was not imagined as being applicable only to the time in which he was speaking. (In the following, the spellings 'programs' and 'programmes' both appear, as translations from both sides of the Atlantic are quoted.)

... within a threefold order of the social organism, human beings will find it possible to work together in such a way that out of this co-operation, *they shall create what cannot be brought about by any programmatic theory.*

Anyone who is unwilling to see the distinction in principle between the threefold idea and the usual programs will refuse to be convinced that it could bear fruit. The idea is one attuned to reality; it does not try to tyrannise life with a program, but aims at creating a basis that allows the life from which social impulses spring to develop freely. (CW24, p. 130)

The threefold commonwealth ... seeks, not to set up an artificial programme, but to find how men must meet one another ... in order to find out for themselves what is necessary. It goes straight to reality. (CW192, 21 April 1919)

... we need a three-fold division of the social organism [...] How that is organised in detail must be left to each person to work out for himself. Because I only want to indicate here the direction in which we need to move. (CW338, p. 185)

What will happen in detail always shows itself in such things when they are on the way to being realized. (CW24(ii), p. 110)

... a living thing may realise itself in a variety of ways. By the act of grasping it livingly, you give it the possibility to realise itself in the most varied ways ... This is the essence of a non-dogmatic concept. (CW340, p. 174)

... one should always at least evoke this feeling: the threefold order of the social organism is nothing which can be 'made' in the sense that state constitutions can be made in a parliament—of the kind, for example, that the Weimar National Assembly was. These are made! But one cannot speak in the same sense of making the threefold social organism. Just as little can one speak of 'organising' in order to produce the threefold order. That which is an organism, this one does not organise; this grows. It is just in the nature of an organism that one does not have to organise it, that it organises itself. That which can be organised is no organism. We must approach things from the start with these feelings ... (CW339(ii), 12 October 1921)

Today, there is no shortage of idealistic programmes [...] Supporters of these various political, cultural, ethical, or social programmes always think that their idea of what is right for humanity needs to be implemented immediately and universally—in America, Europe, Asia, and all over the globe. Very often they also think that whatever they have dreamed up will remain the absolute salvation of the whole world for all time to come. This absolutist thinking is both the fate and the cardinal sin of our modern intellectualism, which prefers not to look at the concrete human condition or how it differs between East and West, to give an example. (CW333, p. 85)

If we think realistically we know that particular ends appear in diverse forms. Only when we think in abstractions does everything appear to us in clearly defined outlines. (CW23, p. 22)

Utopian programmes are based on the idea that they must be realized as formulated, and that things will go badly otherwise. But this is not my aim in the slightest. [...] I could also imagine that nothing ... might remain of what I have said here ... Everything might develop in a different way—I want to make clear that this is absolutely possible ... Rather than an abstract ideal, some programme, these proposals encompass forces of reality, as far removed as possible from all fantasy, and equally all dry theory. (CW189, p. 15)

It has certainly not been invented as programmes are invented today [...] but it is asserted on the basis of those forces that can be observed if we enter into the reality of evolution. (CW186, p. 79)

This last quote conveys a point Steiner often makes: that his three-fold 'take' on society is not something he has dreamt up but rather is something that is there already and which, if brought to people's awareness, can be factored into—and thus support—social repair.

Whilst he clearly deems it important for people to understand that his proposals contain a flexibility that can accommodate the 'living' nature of the social organism, it should perhaps also be noted here that this does not necessarily mean he is proposing only subtle tweaking. Indeed, any widespread heeding of these principles implies considerable adjustment to a number of the ways society goes about its business.

> *We should not be thinking about minor adjustments. Significant re-learning and significant changes in thinking are required. (CW333, p. 46)*

For Steiner to say his suggestions do not amount to a programme of specific measures can at times seem contradictory when one goes on to consider the various operational indications he gives, some of which are very concrete. However, once one reads that the operational details simply amount to *examples and illustrations* of practice to *characterise* how a threefold approach could manifest, then his claim of it not amounting to a fixed programme is borne out.

As we shall see, these operational illustrations are extremely useful in not only helping one picture how his recommendations might be implemented, but also at times helping one understand the underlying principles.

In summary:

- The threefold approach does not propose a fixed set of measures for a society to implement.
- It constitutes a disentanglement of three aspects of society that are inherently different …
- … in order to provide a sound, 'hygienic' structure on which healthy reform can build.
- The operational examples he gives are simply by way of illustration.

4.5   Not forever

Not particularly with reference to social reform, Steiner delivered
many a lecture on the development of human consciousness through
the epochs. To a Darwinist or materialist it would perhaps be obvious
that consciousness has evolved over time if, after all, we were once
apes, and before that, slugs, and before that, mud. But for Steiner too
(who in other contexts frequently speaks of weighty spiritual origins
and purposes of humanity), human consciousness is by no means
a constant. In view of this, it is perhaps no surprise that he does not
consider threefolding as an answer for all time. Humanity evolves and
threefolding will not be relevant forever:

> The 'social question' is not something which has suddenly appeared
> at this stage of human evolution and which can be resolved by a
> few individuals or by some parliamentary body, and stay resolved.
> It is an integral part of modern civilisation which has come to stay,
> and as such will have to be resolved anew for each moment in the
> world's historical development ... A food which permanently stills
> hunger does not exist; neither does a universal social panacea.
> (CW23, p. 15)
>
> To attempt to give it [the social organism] a supposedly best form,
> in which it is expected to remain, is to undermine its vitality. (CW23,
> p. 97)
>
> A socialist in Western or Central or Eastern Europe is likely to have
> certain, quite specific socialist ideals, founded on the fundamental
> belief that because they satisfy him they will also satisfy all other
> human beings anywhere on the earth, and that they will remain
> eternally valid for the whole of the earth's future.
>
> Since people fail to understand that ideals for social life have to be
> born out of the fundamental tenor of an age and of a place, they
> do not easily realise how necessary it is to introduce the threefold
> ordering of the social organism with varying nuances ... (CW194,
> p. 38)
>
> ... the best institutions that can be devised for a particular period
> can never remain valid beyond that period [...] If organisms are to
> flourish and to develop their powers from within themselves, they
> must also be capable of ageing and of dying off. [...] You can only

comprehend the social organism when you know that, even if you put into practice the wisest designs and establish, in a given area of social life, something that has been learnt from conditions as they really are, it will after a time reveal moribund forces, forces of decline, because men with their individual personalities are active in it. (CW83, p. 167)

Threefolding is necessary because the times demand it. Later— not now, but three or four centuries from now—a time will come when threefoldness will have to be overcome, and people will have to think about how to undo it. This reality is in stark contrast to millennial thinking, such as the idea of a thousand-year kingdom, a state of blessedness that (once established) will allow humanity to remain in that state forever. In the real world, however, things are not that convenient—they are always right for specific places and times. (CW192(ii), p. 67)

In summary:

- Societal constructs that may be appropriate in one era may not be in another, and threefolding is no exception.

5. The Three Realms—Defined

Consideration will now be given to how Steiner defines the three realms of society. These definitions are quite easy to misinterpret, and indeed have been on many an occasion.

5.1   Not classes or sectors

First of all, let's be clear about what these three aspects are *not*:

> ... the exposition of these views does not constitute an attempt to revive the three estates—food producers, military, and scholastics—as some have mistakenly assumed upon hearing my lectures on the subject. (CW23, p. 126)

> ... the ancient Greek classification into husbandmen, soldiers and teachers must be superseded ... (CW186, p. 4)

> ... for those who understand what I mean by a threefolding of social life it will be obvious that it is the opposite of what Plato meant by his three orders, for Plato lived a good many years prior to the Mystery of Golgotha.[74] His three orders were appropriate in his time, but to bring them back to life now would be absurd. The idea of a threefold organism is not concerned with dividing individuals into groups with some being producers, others soldiers and yet others statesman. What we want to do now is create arrangements, institutions in which every individual can partake in turn; for today we are concerned with human individuals not with orders or categories. (CW305(ii), p. 155)

> ... not a division into three of the social organism, as in Montesquieu,[75] but a threefold articulation of it, which yet comes together in the unity of the social organism as a whole, by virtue of the fact that, after all, every individual belongs to all three realms. (CW83, p. 180)

---

[74] I.e. the incarnation of Christ.

[75] Charles-Louis de Secondat, Baron de La Brède et de Montesquieu, French political philosopher, 1689-1755. As well as the three separate functions within a state administration (executive, legislative, judicial), Montesquieu also spoke of three classes within society (monarchy, aristocracy, commons).

> *It is the differentiation according to classes that brings chaos into our contemporary social structure. This differentiation will be superseded by the fact that human beings will not be divided in any way according to classes ... In the very nature of things, these classes will completely disappear. It is in this direction that historic necessity moves. Man ... shall bring about the connections among the three spheres of society ... he himself forms the connecting link among the different elements ... There will not be a separate economic class, a separate class of producers, but a structure of economic relationships. (CW186, pp. 4-5)*

Despite Steiner pointing out that 'every individual belongs to all three realms', it is nonetheless also the case that, *in their work life*, individuals will more often than not *predominantly* be concerned with one realm in particular. And in the case of organisations, these too would generally 'belong' to one or the other realm. This is explored particularly in Chapter 8.

In summary, the threefold approach is:

- not about dividing up society / people into categories, sectors, classes;
- it is about three *aspects* of society in which all partake.

* * *

So, to the respective definitions of the three realms. Throughout these, and also throughout the subsequent chapters on guiding principles and operational examples, some of Steiner's remarks are considered first, followed by a handful of bullet points by way of summary. Where opportune, these bullet points are followed by further comments that compare Steiner's suggestions with current practice.

We will begin with the political / rights realm. It is perhaps the simplest to grasp despite, in some respects, being different from what one is used to.

5.2   Definition of Rights Aspect

The rights element is, moreover, that of the political domain, of the state. (CW23, p. 64)

Human rights and obligations are to be determined within this member of the social organism. (CW23, p. 21)

... where the individual faces the other human being in such a way that this encounter is a purely human one, a relationship from man to man. And this realm includes all relationships in which the individual human being directly encounters the individual human being, not as an economically active being but as man, where he also has nothing to do with the capabilities with which one was born or which one has learnt, but where he is concerned with what he is allowed to do within the social organism or what his duties are, what his rights are, with that which he signifies within the social organism by his pure human relationship with the other man despite his capacities, despite his economic position. (CW79)

Nothing unusual about this: the rights realm concerns rights and responsibilities. However, as demonstrated by the following, that's pretty much it, as far as Steiner is concerned.

In the sphere of law and equity [...] the only thing to be considered is the making of laws that shall regulate the rights of the public ... [my emphasis, RM] (332a, p. 66)

... the field of political life, where the only consideration will be what are the rights of the matter. [my emphasis, RM] (CW24, p. 26)

In Steiner's analysis, the political domain is limited to rights, responsibilities, legislation. Running elements within the economy is not included. Neither is overseeing any elements of cultural life:

What should states stop doing? They should before all things stop mixing themselves up in spiritual and economic life ... Today the question cannot be: What should the state do? but: What should the state give up doing? Only that is appropriate for the present time. (CW192, 21 April 1919)

> *What should the state refrain from? From a consideration of this comes the answer: it should refrain from meddling in the functions of spiritual and economic life. It should limit itself to the purely political, the purely rights realm. (CW329, 11 March 1919)*
>
> *The endeavours which have already begun to be realized by those in authority to turn certain economic functions (post office, railroads, etc.) over to the state must be reversed; the state must be relieved of all economic functions. (CW23, p. 71)*

The political / rights realm is simply about rights and responsibilities, about legislation, about the rules we wish to live by—the rules that help us coexist in peace. The creation of these rules, that is, plus also the upholding of them:

> *... the object of a democratic representation of the people can only be political, military and police matters. (CW24(ii), p. 79)*
>
> *Strictly speaking the life of the state is the sum total of common[76] law, together with the sum total of everything that affords society a certain outer protection. (CW193, p. 49)*
>
> *What we need, however, is for government to retain the initiative only in the centre—that is, to retain oversight of security services, public hygiene, and the like ... (CW333, p. 20)*

Although Steiner's definition of the political realm is one that excludes the running of industrial concerns (even natural monopolies like postal and railway services), the security services *are* included—as upholders of the rights and rules we live by, including those rules protecting us from harm. So, too, would be the likes of the UK's Health and Safety Executive, for example. In view of this, it is interesting to then ask what other public services might or might not properly fall under the responsibility of the rights domain. Council housing? Health services? We shall return to this. But a rule of thumb would be: the more the rights domain focuses purely on rights and responsibilities and the less it manages the provision of goods and services, the closer will it be to threefold principles.

---

[76] *Öffentlich* = public.

Interestingly, Steiner excludes the judiciary from the rights realm and, as we shall see in due course, includes it as part of the cultural realm instead. This might at first seem counter-intuitive since the job of the judiciary is also to uphold the law, just as it is the job of the police. But there is a difference, and when we come to consider the guiding principles that apply to each of the three societal aspects, the reasons for the judiciary's exclusion from the rights domain will become clear.

Steiner's advocacy of a judiciary independent of politics was of course nothing new. Montesquieu's 'separation of powers'[77] had enshrined this principle in 1748, a principle that safeguards against political power interfering in cases coming before the court, a safeguard, in essence, against political favouritism or prejudice (i.e. corruption). A defendant who is at odds with the incumbent legislature, who is against the government of the day, has a much greater chance of being treated fairly and of not being victimised if the presiding judge is not overseen by the political realm. However, as we shall come to see, this is not the only angle Steiner is coming from when he states the judiciary does not 'belong' to the political / rights realm.

The likes of prison services, however, *do* fall under the auspices of this realm:

> *The execution of sentences is the responsibility of the rights-state.*
> *(CW23, p. 126)*

So far, so good. The establishing of rights and responsibilities, the making and upholding of law / rules to protect people, are the main tasks of the political / rights realm. It should not concern itself with either overseeing culture or with running economic activity.

However, whilst economic and cultural functions are *not* part of this aspect of the threefold social organism, there are other things that, perhaps surprisingly, are. Steiner includes both land and also the means of production (factories, plant and the like) within the scope of this rights realm, explicitly excluding them from his (yet to be introduced) definition of the economic realm. Use of land or

---

[77] Charles-Louis de Secondat Baron de Montesquieu, *The Spirit of the Laws* (CreateSpace Independent Publishing Platform, 2015).

the means of production is a matter of right. More exactly, it is a concern of both the rights and cultural realms, as we shall discover. Steiner posits land, unlike consumer goods, ideally should not be something that is bought and sold. Instead, it should be something over which people are simply *granted* a right of use. Just how such rights are bestowed and transferred, with assistance from the cultural realm, will be covered amongst the more detailed, operational aspects of threefolding (see Sections 7.3.7 and 7.5.6). For now we are just concerned with being clear about the main things the three realms include and the main things they exclude. Operational detail is addressed later.

As with land, so too with the means of production. These are also something over which people should ideally only be *granted* (not sold) rights of use. They also, ultimately, are excluded from Steiner's definition of the economic realm. Again, they become a matter for a combination of the rights life and the cultural. I say 'ultimately' as the means of production have a lifecycle, as is explained (in Sections 7.3.7 and 7.5.6).

> *The legal provisions by which these transfers are to take place are the province of the rights state. It will also have to see to their execution and administration. (CW23, p. 103)*

Importantly, though, this does not mean the rights state takes either land or the means of production under its own management:

> *... it will remain a rights-state in regard to private property, never making private property its own, but ensuring that the rights of dispossession are transferred at the right moment ... (CW23, p. 101)*

Also worth noting at this point is the special mention labour issues frequently get when Steiner talks of the rights realm. He emphasises that 'labour' should fall squarely within the remit of this realm and not the economic. Not labour in the sense of work per se, but in the sense of employment—people being taken on / working together within an enterprise. Working *relationships* are a concern of the rights realm. (Naturally, he does not mean the rights state should be telling workers how to go about their actual work.)

> *The proper relationship between the employee and the employer cannot belong in the sphere of the economic process at all but only in the sphere of the political state as a rights relationship. (CW189, p. 82)*
>
> *Labour must lie quite outside the economic circuit; it belongs to the department of equity ... (CW332a, p. 43)*
>
> *Human labour must be recognized as separate and independent from the economy ... If it is transferred to the sphere of rights, where it belongs ... (CW333, p. 11)*
>
> *The correct relation between contractor or employer and the worker cannot be brought about in the sphere of economic processes, but only in the sphere of the political state as a relation of rights. (CW189(iii), 2 March 1919)*

For Steiner, the relationship between two or more people working together (e.g. manager and worker) should not be seen as economic, as one of purchase; it is a legal / rights relationship. The various implications of this principle are explored in Section 7.3.3. The aim at this stage is to delineate the three realms in simple terms.

In summary, the political / rights aspect concerns:

- protecting people;
- rights and responsibilities / the rules society lives by;
- enshrining these rules in legislation;
- the upholding of these rules (inspectorates, police, military, prison service);
- the right to use land;
- the right to operate the means of production;
- labour relations;
- running economic enterprise (see following sections) does not belong to this realm;
- cultural endeavours (see following sections) are not a concern of this realm;
- the judiciary is also excluded.

Reflections in relation to the present

Since the 1980s, the privatisation programme in the UK has seen the state divest itself of British Airways, British Telecom, British Gas, British Rail, British Leyland, the Royal Mail and so on. The argument for nationalisation is generally strongest where natural monopolies exist, that is, in sectors where it would be highly impractical to have competing firms. It makes little sense, for example, having competing firms digging up the roads to lay competing gas pipes. With industries of this kind, it seems eminently sensible to have a single provider, as overlap of function and duplication of effort would mean waste. This generally leads people to think the state should run such enterprise since, otherwise, in private hands, monopolistic behaviour will exploit the absence of any undercutting competitor.

But nationalisation can also come with problems. Not only can it distract the state from its main function of considering what is just, of establishing rights and responsibilities; it can also bring ponderous bureaucracy to business. Working in the rights domain and running enterprise require different skill sets. Also, complacent inefficiency can set in. If those managing a nationalised industry are aware the government can never let them fail, they can become lazy, inefficient, sloppy, complacent, unmotivated to innovate, and so forth. The state will always pick up the tab! Collective bargaining laws permitting, nationalised industries can also hold the government to ransom by striking for ever higher pay.

The removal from UK state ownership of the aforementioned industrial concerns conforms with the threefold principle of the rights state just focusing on rights and responsibilities. The subsequent ownership structure of these firms, however, i.e. privatisation, *does not* conform with threefold principles. Just how such economic concerns would be owned and managed under threefolding, to ensure they worked for the common good, is considered in Chapter 7.

There are various other economic activities that remain within the responsibility of the UK government. These include public services like Council Housing and refuse collection, the road network, some of the railways, Cardiff Airport and so on. In order for the state to further its focus on rights, responsibilities, on what is just, on equity, and be less compromised or distracted from this function by acting as provider, more of these things could be de-nationalised—which, it must be emphasised, is *not* the same as saying privatised. If, like me, you find it eminently sensible—comforting, even—to have, say, a single, stable rail or postal service throughout the land, then the idea of removing this from the political system can at first sound unsettling. But under Steiner's suggestions, it can remain a single, stable rail or postal service; it is simply removed from the hands of politicians and instead run in a rational way for the common good, by those who know the industry. More on this anon.

Prior to 2020, Jeremy Corbyn's Labour Party (in opposition in the UK parliament) was proposing to bring energy companies and more of the railways into public ownership which, whilst bringing the UK more in line with the likes of France and Germany, would not have been in keeping with threefolding. But it must be repeated: neither is it in keeping with threefold principles when these industries are owned by private, profit-maximising investors.

Concerning the exclusion of cultural endeavours from the rights realm's remit, Steiner had the following to say when visiting England in 1922:

> In Germany you feel that cultural life is so interwoven with the life of the state that it will need a good deal of help before being able to stand on its own feet. Here in England, on the other hand, cultural life is so independent that it takes no notice at all of the other two strands. (CW305(ii), p. 127)

Despite this observation, the UK state still has a number of formal links to cultural life. Yes, our colleges and universities are largely independent of the state. So, too, are most of our arts, sciences and also religious life. But the Church of England, for example, is still the state church (of England), notwithstanding that it does appear to be slowly but surely heading for disestablishment. The General Synod replaced parliamentary authority over the church in 1970, and, more recently, parliamentary involvement in the appointment of senior clergy was ended under Gordon Brown.[78] A number of MPs and clerics are reportedly keen to complete the separation.

---

[78] Prime Minister of the UK, 2007–2010.

Under a threefold approach, promoters of the arts would also be independent. So the Department for Culture, Media and Sport would ideally be 'disestablished'.

A particularly persistent mismatch with threefolding is the state's ongoing involvement in schools. Whilst there is also an independent school sector in the UK, and even state schools nowadays are encouraged, to an extent, to follow their own paths (as free schools or academies), the comprehensive and grammar school system continues to be characterised by state oversight (meddling). Indeed, in recent decades, the sector has too often been treated like a political football—with one Education Secretary after the next (seemingly with little understanding of pedagogy or child development) each feeling the need to make their mark and introduce some new nationwide regime. The result? Incessant testing of children is enforced, which has resulted in increasing mental health problems among pupils, and one of the most demoralised teaching professions in the world. 'Physically exhausted and mentally broken', despaired the general secretary of the NEU teaching union in 2019.[79] These politicians might be driven by a wish for better educational outcomes, but they then ignore all the evidence demonstrating, for example, the advantages to child development of delayed formal learning. And so on. Under a threefold approach, the state might enshrine the *right* of every child to an education and uphold such right by ensuring all had access with no financial barriers; but that's where its involvement would stop. Education per se would not be its business.

Lastly, a word about the UK prison service which is somewhat at odds with Steiner's definition of the rights realm. At the time of writing, most of the prisons in the UK are state-run. But we have the strange situation that there are 14 privately managed ones (in England and Wales) that are shared between three companies: G4S, the French firm Sodexo, and outsourcing firm Serco. Quite apart from the fact that Steiner recommends the running of prisons be a matter for the state, common sense would suggest that leaving such matters of security in private hands must come with risks, especially when the companies concerned are likely to be looking to cut corners in order to increase profit.

---

[79] Amy Gibbons, 'Exhausted teachers terrorised by nonsensical OFSTED', *TES*, 5 November 2019.

5.3   Definition of Economic Aspect

It is quite easy to be confused by what Steiner says about the economy. Some passages can appear to contradict others—at first, at least. A basic definition is:

> The economy is concerned with all aspects of the production, circulation and consumption of commodities. (CW23, p. 58)

This quote seems straightforward enough. But there is plenty to qualify.

To start with, it should be noted the word 'commodities' is here used in its everyday sense (meaning goods, consumables, wares) and not in the more limited sense in which economists and the financial sector use it (meaning unrefined, unmodified crops and raw materials like metals etc.). The German is '*Waren*'.

But what is meant by '*all* aspects' in this quote? As we saw above, and shall return to presently, there are certain factors of production (i.e. labour, land and the means of production) that Steiner explicitly excludes from the ambit of the economic domain.

We also have the following:

> Whereas the economy is concerned with all aspects of what man needs from nature and the production, circulation and consumption of commodities ... (CW23, p. 58)

This is an amended translation. The published translation is: 'Whereas the economy is concerned with all aspects of man's natural needs ...' which is not consistent with the original German[80] as it suggests Steiner's definition of the economy amounts to what a person needs for their physical existence, what a person needs on account of their bodily nature. If this were the case, a loaf of bread, being a thing a person needs for their bodily maintenance, would qualify as a commodity, but not a book. However, the original German would include the book too which, whilst maybe not needed by a person for their natural / bodily needs, is nonetheless made from paper, from the products of nature,

---

[80] '*... mit alldem zu tun hat, was der Mensch braucht aus der Natur ...*'.

and so falls within this definition of the economic realm as per the original German. The following also confirm this: publication of books and other physical things that satisfy metaphysical needs fall within Steiner's definition of the economy:

> *In economic life one person works for another. People do this because each one finds it to his advantage. Economic life arises from needs, and consists in the satisfying of needs through working on all those things on the physical plane which can satisfy both the ordinary natural needs of human beings as well as those more delicate needs of the soul which are still of an instinctive kind. (CW193, p. 77)*
>
> *... human need which comes from the natural foundations of physical and psychological life, and which must find satisfaction in the cycle of economic life, by production, by circulation and consumption. (CW329, 11 March 1919)*

Economic life consists in satisfying needs—both physical and psychological—via work on physical matter. But does Steiner's definition of the economic realm *only* encompass those commodities that derive from physical matter? The following might also suggest this:

> *Just think for a moment of the kind of relation we have to the world through the economic sphere. You will easily understand what this relation is if you make yourselves imagine the possibility of our becoming totally submerged in purely external, economic life. If that were to happen, what should we be like? We should be nothing else but thinking animals. What prevents us from this is that, apart from the economic life, we have the life of rights—a political life, a sphere of the state—and a ... spiritual / cultural life. Economic life pushes us more or less down onto a subhuman level. (CW193, p. 50)*
>
> *... because we are people of flesh and therefore connected with the earthly animals, we must submerge ourselves in the life of plain economy. (CW193, p. 39)*
>
> *The entire homogeneous entity consisting of processes which begin with man's relation to nature and continue through his activities in transforming the products of nature into consumable goods, all these processes, and only these, comprise the economic member of healthy social organism. (CW23, p. 61)*

These passages suggest that what Steiner deems the economic realm is the system where we work on the products of nature—on material things—to meet needs, be those physical or metaphysical needs. So a book or a purchased bunch of flowers would qualify, i.e. things not strictly necessary for our physical existence, but nonetheless things that come from physical nature.

However, the shaping of physical matter may not necessarily result in physical goods that one can take home and touch. A train journey, say, or a postal service, or a haircut are such services rather than goods to take home. But they nonetheless constitute working on the products of nature—steel, wood, hair, etc.—to satisfy needs.

But what about services that barely seem to touch the physical world at all, such as an accountant's audit, say, or what (before the Internet) used to be called directory enquiries? Auditors and people on the end of a phone might *use* physical tools like pens, phones, computers, but the comments quoted above could suggest that unless matter is being *worked on*, then Steiner does not consider the activity part of the economic realm.

This question could be solved by interpreting these passages as meaning simply *all* the processes involved in production. Then an audit would be included, since one part of the 'entire homogeneous entity' of, say, car manufacture is the audit of the manufacturer's accounts. And one can also imagine that at various times (before the Internet, at least) manufacturing firms would make use of directory enquiry services too.

But this interpretation can feel somewhat tenuous and unsatisfactory. Thankfully, the following remarks address the question more squarely:

> ... *where spiritual and intellectual products are concerned—and these are often inseparable from the sphere of the material, physical goods ... (CW332a, p. 105)*
>
> ... *even spiritual services are consumable goods for the economic life ... (CW340, p. 176)*
>
> *With what does the economic system provide us? With commodities for our consumption. We need not pause today to distinguish between mental [geistig] and physical commodities, for the former may also be included in the economic system and used for human consumption. (CW332a, p. 21)*

So now the definition of the economic realm has broadened out. The earlier quotes suggested it might have covered only *physical* products, but from the latter it appears that, after all, there is a spectrum of commodities from physical products at one end to services at the other, which 'may also be included ...'. Thus, Steiner's definition of the economy comprises not only physical things, trade and industry if you like, but also non-physical things. It comprises goods *and services*.

An example of a 'mental commodity' might be a concert or a medical diagnosis. In the case of a concert, the concert ticket, the physical piece of paper is of rather less interest to us than the metaphysical experience of the music; we are buying the experience which is not a physical commodity but a metaphysical one. Similarly with a visit to a doctor. Whilst the tablets he or she prescribes may be physical commodities, the all-important diagnosis is not the physical, paper / computer record that it might be written on, nor indeed the prescription, but the conclusion the doctor has come to, which is metaphysical.

It may seem surprising to include a concert as part of economic life, when it must surely fall within the (yet-to-be-defined) cultural. But the words quoted above 'even spiritual services are consumable goods for the economic life' are instructive. As shall be explored in more detail in Chapter 8, there is continuous overlap between the three realms.

We also have:

> Activities which originate in the spiritual or state organizations also take on a commodity character for this [economic] sector. A teacher's activity with respect to his pupils is, for the economic process, of a commodity nature. (CW23, p. 117)

> As far as the economic process is concerned the spiritual organisation, in respect of its economic requirements, and also the state, are simply commodity producers. What they produce within their own sectors are not commodities however; they only become such once they enter into the economic process. Their activities are not commercial within their own sectors; the economic organism's management carries on its commercial activities using the achievements of the other sectors. (CW23, p. 118)

Cultural endeavour or state activity, insofar as they meet the needs of others, also amount to goods and services, to commodities. They are also part of economic life, they have an economic *dimension*. Again, it is a question of overlap. (This aside, education does of course also lead to all manner of economic value in the long term, as those being educated enter the realm of work and are more productive on account of their educated capacities. But that is a different matter and not what we are concerned with here.)

One does not wish to labour these things unnecessarily. On the other hand, there is a need to arrive at some clarity, since an understanding of Steiner's entire thesis regarding society does rest on his definitions of the three realms. If, for example, one were to just read a passage where he relates the economic realm to physical matter only, then one could end up with a very incomplete impression. Some of Steiner's comments on the matter can appear to contradict one another, and it seems prudent to address this head-on. Misunderstandings in connection with the definitions of the three realms are all too common, as are misunderstandings in connection with how they interrelate.

From the latter passages quoted, we can feel confident that both products *and services* fall within the threefold definition of the economic aspect of society. As Charles Waterman says: 'The picture we ought to form of the economic sphere is rather the entire community in its economic aspect'.[81]

So far, so good.

But then we come on to what Steiner specifically excludes from his basic definition 'all aspects of the production, circulation and consumption of commodities'. This is where things get more interesting and, some might say, radical (although Steiner would doubtless contend: more valid).

5.3.1   Not Labour

As was alluded to in the previous section—where the rights realm was defined, Steiner is emphatic that labour should not be treated like a commodity, not be something that is bought and sold, or allowed to be

---

[81] Charles Waterman, *The Three Spheres of Society* (London: Faber and Faber, 1946), p. 71.

subject to laws of supply and demand. In short, it should not fall under the heading of the economic realm; it is a matter for the rights realm. He is categorical about this, on every occasion, without exception. Labour is not something the economic realm should have control over. But what does he mean by this, exactly?

It is not just a sin against the social order but a sin against truth itself if—and I have often said this—we assume human labour can be a commodity. In outer apparent reality it can be made to seem so, but this illusion of reality will cause suffering in the human social order and set the stage for upheavals and revolutions ... (CW193, p. 71)

The point here is that human labour cannot be compared in price to a commodity of any sort. The labour of human beings is something very different from manufactured goods, and as such it must be removed from the economy. (CW330, p. 58)

It is not possible to divest human labour power of its commodity character without first finding a means of extracting it from the economic process. Efforts should therefore not be directed towards transforming the economic process so that human labour power is justly treated within it, but towards extracting labour power from the economic process and integrating it with social forces which will relieve it of its commodity character. (CW23, p. 50)

... the idea of the threefold order of the social organism is to detach labour completely from the economic process. (CW332a, p. 42)

That work per se does not automatically have economic value is perhaps obvious, as Steiner reminds us:

Let us suppose that a man gives himself up to sport from morning till evening ...[82] He expends exactly the same labour force as one who chops wood ... What is important is to use one's strength in working for the community at large. The sportsman does not do this; the most that can be said of him is that he makes himself strong, only, as a rule, he does not turn his strength to account. Generally,

---

[82] English translations have suggested someone engaged in sport professionally, but Steiner's original German does not imply this, and so the translation above has been altered accordingly. It is here presumed he means an amateur sportsman whose exploits are not watched / enjoyed by the public.

it is of no importance to the community that a man engages in sport by which he tires himself as much as by chopping wood. Chopping wood is of some use. That is to say, the use of labour power has no importance socially, but what results from such use has a meaning in social life. We must look at the result of the application of labour [...] Hence, the only thing that can be of value in economic life is the product *of labour power, and the only thing with which the administration of the economic life can have any concern is the regulation of the comparative values of products. Labour must lie quite outside the economic circuit. It belongs to the department of equity ... Labour will lie entirely outside the sphere to be regulated in the economic process ... (CW332a, p. 43)*

Labour per se has no value; that is easy to see. If someone digs holes all day and then fills them up again, they may have expended a lot of work but achieved no value, no commodity. So, from this point of view, one can understand the removal of labour, as such, from Steiner's definition of the economy.

Obviously, though, had you removed the labour from a coal mine in 1919, you would not have ended up with much coal. Steiner is of course not saying that commodities can somehow magically arise without labour. It is simply that, whilst labour *feeds into* the commodity production process, it is not itself a commodity. The economic domain, whilst being concerned with the production, distribution and consumption of commodities, should not also have labour within its remit. The worker / manager relationship is not a purchase relationship; it is a rights relationship. Labour conditions, labour laws, industrial relations, should not fall within the remit of the economy, within the whims of business. It is not for the economic domain to decide how much it can squeeze out of workers and how little it can pay them. This may seem more obvious to us today, but when Steiner was speaking, the eight-hour day, for example, was a relatively new idea.

The damage will be undone only by eliminating the ability to regulate the type, scope, and duration of labour—whether intellectual or manual—from the economic cycle. Regulating labour does not belong in the economy, where wealthier individuals and groups have the power to impose terms of work on the economically dis-advantaged. (CW333, p. 56)

The manager who directs a business must necessarily have a legal relationship to manual workers in the same business; but this does not mean that he, as a business manager, is to have a say in determining what the relationship is to be. [...] Only when laws are made in a field where business considerations cannot in any way come into question, and where business cannot gain any power over this legal system, will the two be able to work together in such a way that our sense of justice will not be violated, nor business acumen be turned into a curse instead of a blessing for the whole community.

When the economically powerful are in a position to use that power to wrest legal privileges for themselves, among the economically weak will grow a corresponding opposition to these privileges. As soon as it has become strong enough, such opposition will lead to revolutionary disturbances. If the existence of a separate polit-ical and legal province makes it impossible for such privileges to arise, then disturbances of this sort cannot occur. What this spe-cial legal province does is to give constant orderly scope to those forces which, in its absence, accumulate until at last they vent themselves violently. Whoever wants to avoid revolutions should learn to establish a social order that shall accomplish in the steady flow of time what will otherwise try to realise itself in one historic moment. (CW24, p. 27)

No matter what kind of words we may say about them, economic contracts that are wage agreements will always result in dissatis-faction on the worker's part. A human existence for all parties will emerge only when no more labour contracts are negotiated, and when contracts cover only production, which depends on the work of both managers and labourers. Only then will workers feel they are freely part of the process in relation to managers. (CW333(ii), p. 60)

Removing control of work conditions / relations from those responsible for production not only addresses the problem of exploitation / harmful power relationships; ultimately it can prevent major social upheaval.

The approach to remuneration which Steiner recommends should replace wage contracts is covered later (in Sections 7.3.4 and 7.4.14) when we come to the operational suggestions he makes.

In the following, he makes clear that, whilst advocating state (i.e. rights realm) oversight of work *conditions* and work *relations*, he is most certainly not advocating state influence in the *management* of business and workers. As already established, Steiner considered as somewhat disastrous the sort of bureaucratic, initiative-stifling, rights-realm interference in the economy as that advocated by traditional state socialism.

> *... the combination of technological and economic activity afforded by modern life necessitates allowing the most fruitful possible development of individual initiative and personal talent within the business community. The form production must take under modern conditions makes this a necessity. The individual cannot bring his abilities to bear in a business if in his work and decision-making he is tied down to the will of the community ... collectively, society is incapable of giving birth to economic schemes that can be realized through individuals in the most desirable way. Really practical thought, therefore, will not look to find the cure for social ills in a reshaping of economic life that would substitute communal production for private management of the means of production. Rather, the endeavour should be to forestall evils that may spring up along with management by individual initiative and personal talent without impairing the management itself. (CW24, p. 25)*

Since, in this chapter, we are concerned only with Steiner's *definition* of the economic realm, we shall leave further, more detailed comments about labour until later (see Section 7.3.3). Suffice to establish for now that labour per se (as opposed to the product of work) is not a commodity to be bought and sold, and as such does not fall within his definition of the economic realm. In the same way that people are not commodities to be bought and sold—as they were in the days of slavery—so too should their labour not be regarded or treated like a commodity.

> *... labour power is paid as cheaply as possible, because, of course, there is a tendency to buy as cheaply as possible. If labour power is included in the economic process itself, it will be cheapened by capitalism. What matters now is that the worker has to get out of the economic process. Only commodities should feature in the economic process. (CW331, 22 May 1919)*

> *The correct relation between contractor or employer and the worker cannot be brought about in the sphere of economic processes, but only in the sphere of the political state as a relation of rights. (CW189(iii), 2 March 1919)*

5.3.2 Not land or the means of production

As with labour, Steiner says similar things about land and the means of production—factories and their equipment. They, too, within his threefold observations, should not be considered part of the economic domain as things to be bought and sold like commodities. Again, they *feed into* the economy; economic life is based on them, as it is on labour. But they do not *belong to* the economic realm; they do not ultimately fall within the bounds of the economic domain as Steiner defines it. His economic realm is limited to the *system* of getting goods and services to those who need them, the merry-go-round of production, distribution and consumption of commodities.

> *I call commodity everything which has been prepared by human activity for consumption and brought to a certain locality for this purpose ... The land itself ... does not act as a commodity in economic life. (CW23, p. 66)*

Note: 'which has been prepared by human activity'.

> *Economic value begins where human labour unites itself with nature. (CW340, p. 56)*
>
> *What is a commodity ... ? A piece of land is, in itself, not yet a commodity. The coal in the ground is not yet a commodity. A commodity is the result of human activity alone, something transformed by human activity or something men have moved from one place to another. [...] land, as such, is not an object belonging to the economic process. [...]*
>
> *If you acquire a piece of land by sale, that is, by exchange, what you really acquire is a right, such as is the case for example in buying a patent. There one gets a good idea of the process of fusion that has had such unfortunate results. The fusion of the purely*

political rights-state with the economic life. For this there can be no cure other than separation. (CW189(iii), 2 March 1919)

Nowadays it is not just goods that can be bought, that is, what is produced by human labour in the social organism under the division of labour, but today one can still buy something completely different, something that no-one produces but what is naturally there, that is, land. But this purchase of land and the taking of mortgages on land is only a falsification of the economic order. It is something completely different from what people imagine. One can in fact not buy land because land is only of value if you work on it. What one buys, that is, what one acquires through so-called purchase, is an exclusive right to use the land. All that matters is the exclusive rights to use ... So you do not buy a commodity by buying land, but a right. Here we have the cancerous conditions of today's social order, that within the economic process one can not only buy goods, but also labour and rights ... By being able to buy land rights, one acquires power. (CW331, 22 May 1919)

The economy has subsumed two things that really do not belong to it—human labour and capital. Only the circulation of goods actually belongs to the economy. (CW333, p. 9)

Through the independence of the cultural and legal-political spheres, the means of production, land and human labour power will be divested of their present commodity character. (CW24, p. 45)

... the management of capital, land, the means of production (which are also capital, by the way), and labour cannot remain part of the economy. The economy can be responsible only for managing the production, circulation and consumption of goods ... (CW333, p. 57)

Steiner is not saying land has no value; he is saying it has no *economic* value (within his definition of the economy). The following makes this distinction:

So long as the nature-product is untouched, at the place where it is found in nature, it has no other value than it has, for instance, for the animals. But the moment you take the very first steps to put the nature-product into the process of economic circulation, the nature-product so transformed begins to have economic value. (CW340, p. 29)

Thus, value—in its general sense—and *economic* value are not necessarily the same thing. If I am enjoying an exhilarating walk in the mountains, it is clear the land has immense value to me; it fulfils a need. I might even find a patch of wild blueberries and enjoy eating them. Yet more value! But neither the mountains nor the blueberries have *economic* value in Steiner's definition. Economic value only occurs when one person works for another. Wild blueberries that I might graze on have value in the way they have value for the animal kingdom; but they don't enter the economy.

> *Work, in the economic sense, begins when men produce for one another. (CW341, p. 209)*

Concerning the means of production—factories and their equipment, Steiner considers the various components that go towards building them up as part of the economy *initially*. But once these components have all been bought and are in place and ready to produce, they themselves cease to be commodities for purchase / sale, they cease to fall within Steiner's definition of the economy (whilst nonetheless going on to *feed into* it). Indeed, land, too, that is being prepared for production can also have this status:

> *Up to the moment when nature—or a given part of nature—has been cleared and can be handed over for use, during this period also, some labour must be expended on it. In other words, by the time this labour has been done, even a piece of land may justly be reckoned a commodity, an economic value, in the sense that it is a piece of nature combined with human labour. (CW340, p. 183)*

> *... the soil, in our future economic order, will be a means of production, and nothing more ... a means of production can only accumulate labour-value until it is ready-finished; ... from that moment on, it is nobody's property ... from that moment on, nobody has strictly speaking any right of heritage over it ... from that moment on, it goes back into circulation in the community [...] this was the position held by the soil from the very first; that all mortgaging of the soil is a thing against nature; that land and ready-finished means of production are in no way commodities, but must pass from man to man by some other means than by exchanging them for commodities [i.e. through purchase / sale, RM]. (CW330(ii), 31 May 1919)*

... the means of production cease to be commodities. They remain commodities right up until they are used to produce something. At this moment the economic flow reverses; the means of production are separated out from their circulation as commodities ... at this juncture the means of production blend into land ... They are economically equivalent to land ... (CW341, p. 217)

These [means of production] will, however, be equivalent to nature. For the moment they are finished, and thus leave the realm of commodities altogether, they are devalued inasmuch as it is no longer possible to buy or sell them. They thus become equivalent to the means of production which we have in nature directly. (CW340, p. 183)

The disposal of land, systematised in the laws relating to its ownership, and the disposal of the finished means of production (for example, a factory with its machinery and equipment), should be no matter for the economic organization. They must belong partly to the spiritual and partly to the legal. That is to say, the transfers of land from one person or group of persons to another must not be carried out by purchase or through inheritance, but by transference through legal means, on the principles of the spiritual organisation. The means of production through which something is manufactured—a process that lies at the basis of the creation of capital—can only be looked at from the point of view of its commodity costs while it is being built up. (CW332a, p. 120)

During the building of a factory, the various components involved are commodities to be purchased by the entrepreneur and paid for as normal. But once the various pieces of plant and equipment are in place as means of production, the factory ceases to be treated as a commodity. The components of the factory arise in economic life and are bought as commodities, but when the factory is finally assembled, its commodity nature ceases. Yes, from thenceforth, the means of production are used to *make* commodities, but they themselves are no longer commodities and so ideally cease to be something which those in charge of economic matters can sell. A radical idea with far-reaching implications! The one who has control over means of production has a *right* to use them for production, and when he / she finally withdraws from involvement in production, the transfer of this right of use becomes a matter for both the legal and spiritual domains (this process is elucidated in Sections 7.3.7 and 7.5.6).

A factory is of course valuable, but its value is of a different type from the value a consumer places on a consumer good. A factory's value depends on the skill of those who operate it:

> ... *land and capital cannot be considered as merchandise, for their value is dependent on human capability. (CW79, 30 November 1921)*

As the reader probably will have spotted, if the means of production cease to be things that can be bought and sold, then share ownership ultimately follows suit.

> *You can never get out of this unnatural cycle of economic life unless you get rid of the fifth wheel on the car, which is only there so that those who haven't worked can get something out of it. This fifth wheel is called capital. [...] If you do not want that, if you do not throw out this fifth wheel on the car, which only serves those who don't work, you will not get socialization. (CW331, 22 May 1919)*

In some respects, Steiner's definition of the economy is similar to what today is termed the 'real economy'. The 'real economy' can be defined as 'That part of the economy that is concerned with actually producing goods and services as opposed to the part of the economy that is concerned with buying and selling on the financial markets'.[83] This buying and selling on the financial markets is certainly something Steiner excludes from his definition, and indeed even the *possibility* to do so is ultimately precluded within his analysis. For him, as we have seen, the economy is about creating goods and services for people's consumption, creating things that people need and getting them to where they are needed. However, labour is also excluded from his definition of the economy—but not from the definition of the 'real economy'.

Having a stock market, having the ability to sell shares at some future point may certainly encourage people to invest in new concerns, since they will do so in the hope that the company will be successful,

---

[83] See for example: https://en.m.wikipedia.org/wiki/Economy.

and they will be able to sell their investment in future when they need the cash. But if Investor B buys shares from Investor A, and then sells them to Investor C, etc., all this activity (read, the entire stock market) has not produced anything. If the business is a factory making widgets, no more widgets will be made if one or another (non-executive) investor owns it. At its worst, the stock market acts like a casino—where each investor (typically, speculator) hopes to sell for more than they buy; hopes, therefore, to inflict hurt on their fellow investors; hopes, let's face it, to see them ruined if at all possible, like in some miserable game of Monopoly. Currency speculation is much the same: nothing is produced that increases society's lot. Instead, one person wins and another loses.

The tendency to see capital, nature and labour as commodities—what economist Karl Polanyi calls 'Commodity Fiction'[84]—is addressed head-on by the threefold approach which excludes them from its definition of the economic realm.

Each produces for all on the roundabout path of economic life.
(CW23, p. 117)

In summary, the economic aspect of the threefold social organism encompasses:

- the production, circulation and consumption of consumer goods;
- these consumer goods can be services as well as physical goods;
- although labour feeds into the economic process, it is not itself part of the economy; ideally labour is not bought and sold like a commodity;
- unelaborated land, although also a factor of production that feeds into the economic process, is not itself considered to be a commodity and so is excluded;
- similarly, the finished means of production are not considered commodities and so are excluded (although during the building up of the means of production, the various components involved are included).

---

[84] Karl Polanyi, *The Great Transformation* (New York: Farrar & Reinhart, inc, 1944).

Reflections in relation to the present

When land or the means of production can be bought and sold, problems of all shapes, sizes and severity can follow. For example, 'Guy Hands, the tax exile and one of Britain's top private equity investors, has emerged as the controlling party behind a property firm which has evicted dozens of families, many of whom were previously homeless. Hands runs a multibillion-pound investment house, Terra Firma, which acquired Addington, one of the UK's largest private owners of residential property, now poised to bulldoze 142 homes on Sweets Way estate in North London. They were being used by a housing association to accommodate families on Barnet Council's waiting list, but under Hands' control, Addington plans to replace them with 229 houses and flats for sale on London's booming property market and 59 "affordable homes". […] Parents and children have said the evictions have torn their lives apart. […] A 10-year-old boy, who was rehoused several miles away in Enfield last month, told the *Guardian* his family had to move again next month, but had nowhere to go. At the moment he has to rise at 5am to start school on time … Edina, a 13-year-old who was evicted, now spends three hours travelling to and from school.' This 'investment' was held offshore in the tax haven of Guernsey.[85]

Sadly, Dickensian stories like this are all too common. To posit that land is a rights issue, on the other hand, and not something to be bought and sold like a commodity can seem quite justifiable. At the same time, it is a radical idea, given that land can at present nearly always be bought and sold—unless it has been put into some Trust in perpetuity. Encouragingly, the number of Land Trusts in operation (for organic farming, for example) has grown considerably in recent years. The Land Trust model is a good example of threefolding in practice. No-one can sell the land. When the farmer of such a farm retires, another farmer with relevant skills is appointed to continue the work. They take on the *right* to farm the land; buying and selling of the land does not come into it.

The idea of the exclusion of the means of production from the buying-and-selling economic realm is an equally radical one—when so

---

[85] Robert Booth, 'Property tycoon Hands behind firm evicting families to bulldozer estate', *The Guardian,* 21 March 2015.

much of economic life is predicated on share ownership. But, again, there are innovative examples where a more threefold approach has been taken with respect to company ownership. Hundreds of thousands of co-operatives around the world typically have structures where ownership is vested in the workers. Workers cannot sell their share of the co-op, and when they leave, they lose it; their *right* to it ceases. (Other aspects of co-operative business—like democratic management—would not necessarily be in line with threefold ideas. This is covered in Section 7.4.6.)

Or take, for example, the oft-cited John Lewis Partnership (which includes the Waitrose chain of supermarkets). This has operated under a Trust model since 1950 when the then-proprietor, John Speedon Lewis ('kindness of heart is extremely desirable'), transferred ownership of the concern into a Trust for the benefit of the employees. The means of production can no longer be bought or sold. Some twenty years earlier, observing that he and his family were already receiving an income from the business far in excess of its 300 employees *combined*, he had already taken the significant step of distributing yearly profits among all staff. There are now nearly 100,000 partners working in the firm. If you work there, you are a part-owner of the Trust. If you leave, this ends.

More recent examples of this type of employee ownership[86] include Riverford Organics, a business with a £60m turnover delivering over 50,000 boxes of organic veg per week. In 2018, its founder Guy Singh-Watson, repulsed by the thought of selling the business (value over £20m) to venture capitalists whose only interest was money, gave three quarters of the business to an employee-owned Trust. Other recent examples of this approach are the Oscar-winning animators Aardman (*Wallace and Grommit*, etc.) and home-entertainment retailer Richer Sounds whose founder transferred 60% of the business into an employee Trust.[87]

Such Trusts are a good example of the means of production being managed along the lines of threefold principles. There are no absent owners for whom the business is little more than a cash-generating plaything to be steered in whatever profit-wringing direction they desire, or disposed of at the drop of a hat.

---

[86] As of 2020, the Employee Ownership Association in the UK had about 350 such firms on its books, with membership growing by some 10% per annum.

[87] James Moore, 'A Richer lesson in capitalism', the *i* newspaper,16 May 2019.

Somewhat similar effects can be achieved with two classes of share, as seen for example with Triodos Bank whose *voting* shares are held in a foundation to protect the bank's social ethos, or Novo Nordisk—a Danish healthcare company which employs over 40,000 people around the world and produces, amongst other things, 40% of the world's insulin. Its founding scientists protected its humanitarian ethos by placing most of the voting shares in a foundation.[88] Yes, you can buy shares, so the threefold proposal that the means of production ought not be sellable is not entirely satisfied. But voting power, strategic direction, control, ability to asset strip, etc. are at least not in the hands of absent, profit-maximising investors.

5.4   Definition of Cultural Aspect

We have now looked at Steiner's definitions of the rights realm and the economic, but what of the cultural?

In the original German, he talks about *'Geistesleben'* (spiritual life), *'geistige Kultur'* (spiritual culture), and the like. As mentioned previously, the German word *'Geist'* encompasses both the spirit, in its more other-worldly sense, as well as the mind, in the more everyday sense. As such it is less loaded with religiosity than the English word 'spirit'.

The terms 'spiritual' or 'cultural' might make a native English-speaker initially think of churches or art galleries, and if one were only to read one of the following lines in Steiner's works, one could be forgiven for thinking cultural pursuits like these are indeed the extent of what he meant by the spiritual / cultural part of the social organism:

> *Art, science, philosophical world-views, and all that goes with them, need just such an independent position in human society ... (CW23, p. 76)*

> *In belonging to the realm of art, religion, learning, and all the other areas of spiritual / cultural life ... (CW193, p. 33)*

> *Everything relating to the spiritual and intellectual department of life ... (CW332a, p. 104)*

---

[88] Martin Large and Steve Briault (Eds), *Free, Equal and Mutual: Rebalancing Society for the Common Good* (Stroud: Hawthorn Press, 2018), p. 110.

Clearly, Steiner's definition of society's spiritual / cultural aspect does indeed include our public life of thought, of feelings, of morality—the realms of truth, beauty, goodness. And it includes religion too. But only as these things manifest in society; he is not talking about the spiritual world per se (which he had already spent over 20 years describing in his theosophical / anthroposophical works). This is clear for example from the following:

> Let us look [...] at what we call in an earthly sense our human
> spiritual / cultural life. Human spiritual life in an earthy sense is not
> the life of spiritual beings but what we human beings experience
> in our social togetherness as spiritual life. Everything covered by
> science, art and religion belongs here. Also everything connected
> with schooling and education belongs here. Let us look first at what
> human beings in their social togetherness experience as the spiri-
> tual life of culture ... this spiritual life—everything covering school,
> education, science, art, literature, etc.—has to form a separate
> social unit. (CW193, p. 19)

The following adds a further aspect to the spiritual / cultural realm: national culture—an aspect that would have been especially pertinent to the political context in which Steiner was writing, i.e. when the Austro-Hungarian Empire still stood (it came to an end the following year). Austro-Hungary comprised a dozen or more nationalities and languages (including Czech, Romanian, Croatian, Serbian, Ukranian, Slovenian, etc.), and presumably therefore a good few flavours of national culture.

> ... and with regard to all religious and spiritual cultural relation-
> ships, to which national culture also belongs ... (CW24(ii), p. 88)

So, under Steiner's threefold analysis, society's spiritual / cultural aspect certainly includes those cultural elements that one would expect to see included. But he emphasises that it is, in fact, broader than this:

> The third member, standing autonomous alongside the other two,
> is to be apprehended in the social organism as that which per-
> tains to spiritual life. To be more precise, because the designations

> *'spiritual culture' or 'everything which pertains to spiritual life' are perhaps not sufficiently precise, one could say: everything which is based on the natural aptitudes of each human individual,* what must enter into the social organism based on the natural aptitudes, spiritual as well as physical, of each individual. The ... system is concerned with everything which must blossom forth from each human individuality and be integrated into the social organism. *[my emphasis, RM] (CW23, p. 59)*

> *When speaking of the three-folding of the social organism, I do not only include the more or less abstract life of thought or the religious life in the spiritual realm, but I include everything which depends on human spiritual or physical abilities. I have to say this explicitly, otherwise one could completely misunderstand the demarcation of the spiritual realm within the threefold social organism. (CW79, 30 November 1921)*

> *... everything flowing into the social organism which depends on the natural gift of individuals, the natural spiritual and physical talents coming from single individuals. (CW328(ii), 5 February 1919)*

> *... the spiritual organism, which is built on people's individual physical and psychological capacities ... (CW329, 11 March 1919)*

> *... everything that human beings bring into public life in the form of their particular talents and gifts—in other words, everything that constitutes public spiritual life ... (CW196, p. 117)*

So, in addition to what we might expect to see included, we also have: 'everything which is based on the natural aptitudes of each human individual'. But, surely, pretty much everything we do is based on our aptitudes. So how is this definition going to help us demarcate things in our mind? How are we going to distinguish between this, the cultural domain, and the political or the economic? Furthermore, Steiner also makes references to *physical* skills as well as intellectual. Things are becoming confusing!

At this juncture, it might be helpful to remember what was said about overlap. Just as in the human body, the nerve / sense aspect, the rhythmic heart / lung aspect, and the metabolic aspect are all intermingled, so too in the social organism are the rights aspect, the economic aspect and the spiritual aspect intermingled. Yes, the rhythmic aspect of the human body may be centred in the chest / heart / lung, but blood still circulates round the head and the metabolism. Yes, the body's nerve / sense aspect may be centred in the head, but nerves nonetheless travel throughout the other two bodily elements. Yes, the metabolism may be centred in the lower half of the body, but nutrients are still fed to the other two elements. Likewise in the social organism. The rights realm might be centred in the state, but it regulates the other two. The economic realm might be centred in business, but it feeds the other two. The spiritual realm might be centred in individuals, but it provides the spark / stimulus that ignites and drives the other two.

With the spiritual / cultural realm, then, we are indeed talking about everything that emanates (into public life) from the individual. With 'spiritual realm' sounding churchy, and 'cultural realm' a bit arty, one could be tempted to translate '*Geistesleben*' as the 'realm of the individual', or the 'realm of human flourishing', or the 'realm of human faculties', or similar; but we will stick with the terms 'spiritual' and 'cultural' for the time being. (The 'humanities realm' would not fit the bill, incidentally, since what we are talking about includes *all* that comes from human abilities—including *scientific* endeavour and *physical* talents too.)

As an aside, it is interesting to note that, in writings unrelated to social reform, Steiner describes a person's individuality—their self (or technically, in anthroposophical terms, their 'higher self')—as spirit in the more other-worldly sense.[89] Our self-ness, the core of our being, the independent centre of consciousness that we each refer to as 'I' is, he says, a piece of the divine, is spirit. (On this basis, the dogma enacted by the Catholic Church in the Ecumenical Council of 869 A.D., whereby the human being was no longer deemed to be body, soul and spirit, but just body and soul, with one or two spiritual attributes, was, according to Steiner, a falsehood. It certainly does look rather convenient for the Catholic Church if none of us can get close to the divine without the aid of a middleman, i.e. a priest!) In Steiner's anthroposophy, he describes a fourfold nature of the human being which comprises a physical element, an etheric, an astral and a spiritual. That is to say, a mineral, plant, animal, and human. One could also say it comprises matter, life, sentience, and self.

---

[89] See, for example, Rudolf Steiner, *Theosophy*, (London: Kegan Paul, Trench, Trubner & Co, 1922), Chapter 3.

Since the aspect *of society* we are talking about—the spiritual / cultural—comprises everything coming from an individual's capacities—including even our physical capacities, and since even our physical capacities are in any case largely just an expression of our psychological / metaphysical capacities[90], and since our psychological / metaphysical capacities are based on our individuality, and since (according to Steiner, at least) our individuality is indeed spiritual in the more profound sense, then the term 'spiritual realm' might not be such a bad translation, after all.

> *An unfortunate distinction between intellectual and manual work is currently being proclaimed on every street corner[91]. What is manual work? Nothing more or less than applying our bodily instruments in the service of our will. (CW333, p. 67)*
>
> *In order for this third system to have a name it will be called the spiritual system, involved with everything which is created out of the single human individuality and needing to be incorporated into the social organism. (CW328(ii), 5 February 1919)*

However, since the English 'spiritual' implies far greater other-worldliness than does the German *'Geist'*, *the term 'cultural' will instead generally be used from now on* (although the inserted quotes more often use 'spiritual').

As mentioned previously (Section 5.2), Steiner also includes the judiciary within the cultural aspect of society and not the political:

> *This [cultural] sphere will include education, instruction, art, literature, and also ... everything concerned with the administration of civil and criminal law. [my emphasis, RM] (CW193, p. 44)*
>
> *All juridical, pedagogical and spiritual concerns ... (CW24(ii), p. 80)*
>
> *The spiritual life, including the judicial (I do not mean general administration but the administration of civil and criminal law) ... (CW186(ii), p. 129)*

---

[90] We can saw a piece of wood in a straight line because of the *control* our psyche applies to our arm (admittedly, as long as our body is healthy and muscles reasonably developed).

[91] A reference, presumably, to the followers of Marx.

> *From the moment in which the individual finds himself in a posi-*
> *tion to seek justice under either civil or penal law, or in a pri-*
> *vate or any other manner, in that moment the decision passes*
> *from the purely legal to the cultural domain... Now when a case*
> *arises in which it has to be decided how an existing law can be*
> *applied to a particular person, we have to do with the exercise of*
> *an individual judgment. It must be determined whether the*
> *elected [selected, RM] judge is really qualified by his mental*
> *and spiritual capacities to understand the person in question.*
> *Administration of punishment, civil justice, cannot rest on the*
> *general basis of law. It must be removed to another sphere ...*
> *(CW332a, p. 71)*

> *One of the effects through which the triformation of the social*
> *organism will prove itself to be based on the essential nature of*
> *human society is the severance of judicial activities from state*
> *institutions. It will be incumbent on the latter to establish the*
> *rights between persons or groups of persons. Judicial deci-*
> *sions however, will depend upon facilities formed by the spiritual*
> *organisation. This judicial decision-making is, to large extent,*
> *dependent on the judge's ability to perceive and understand the*
> *defendant's situation. Such perception and understanding will be*
> *present if the confidence which men feel towards the facilities*
> *of the spiritual organisation is extended to include the courts.*
> *(CW23, p. 124)*

Including the judiciary within the cultural domain instead of the rights domain might at first seem odd. But on closer analysis it makes sense, as judgement means a decision based on the talent of the individual judge, and individual talents fall under the cultural realm. The individual capacities of the judge must weigh up the particular circumstances of the case in question, not least the individual circumstances of the defendant. With the conclusion of the judiciary needing to be so case-specific, so individual, the judiciary comes under the cultural realm, the realm of individual talents. What a judge does is very different to what the rights realm does. The rights realm establishes generic laws that apply to all, that are universal. There may be a law saying stealing is forbidden. This will apply universally. But if a starving person steals food, the judge will likely be more lenient than if a greedy opportunist does so.

As also mentioned earlier, however: whilst sentencing is a matter for the cultural realm ...

> *The execution of sentences is the responsibility of the rights-state. (CW23, p. 126)*

That is, the execution, but not the determining. The prison service, for example, is a matter for the state, the political / rights domain.

Surely, though, people working in the other two realms—rights or economic—also use those individual talents which we have been told are part of the cultural domain? Yes indeed:

> *Everything which occurs in the social organisation due to economic activity and rights awareness is influenced by what emanates from a third source: the individual abilities of each human being. This includes the greatest spiritual accomplishments as well as superior or inferior physical aptitudes. (CW23, p. 74)*

> *This third [cultural] realm at the same time encompasses the spiritual portion of the other two spheres, supplying this to them out of its own intrinsic laws and manner of administration. (CW189, p. 10)*

> *The cultural portions of the other two spheres [i.e. the economic and the political, RM] belong to this [cultural] sphere ... (CW24, p. 147)*

> *A third member of the social organism, in full autonomy and formed from within its own potentialities, must be added to these two: that of spiritual production, to which the spiritual parts of the other two sectors [sic], supplied to them by this third sector, belong. (CW23, p. 144)*

> *... spiritual culture can also include, for instance, the experience belonging to technical ideas and work in a lively way in other structures, in the rule of law for instance ... (CW328(iii), 10 February 1919)*

> *... to be counted under the heading of spiritual life: everything which involves the unfolding and development of individual abilities, from the start of the schooling system through to the university system, right into the artistic, right into the ethical life, yes, right into those branches of the spiritual life which form the foundation of practical and even economic systems. (CW218(iv), 8 March 1919)*

In the social organism, the first thing we have are these individual human abilities. And these can be traced from man's highest spiritual achievements in art, science, religious life down to however these individual abilities—whether more mental or more physical— however these individual abilities are applied in the most ordinary, material processes within the capitalist system, within the economy ... (CW329, 11 March 1919)

Again, overlap! The cultural parts of the economic aspect and of the political aspect—the application of the minds and talents of those involved—in fact 'belong' to the cultural aspect too. The realms are *intermingled*. What a person working within the political realm brings to the political realm, from within themselves, comes from their capacities, from their individuality, from the cultural domain. What a person working within the economic realm brings to the economic realm, from within themselves, comes from their capacities, from the cultural domain. The cultural domain feeds into the other two realms.

Clearly, then, in the case of the spiritual / cultural realm we are talking about more than churches and opera. Indeed, what is becoming ever clearer is that we are not talking about a spatial demarcation of the three realms at all. They are not sectors. They are *aspects*. They are *intermingled*. The cultural realm is present in the other two in the same way that one bodily system is also present in the other two. Steiner is talking about what comes out of every person and has an impact on the social organism—what comes from their inner natures, the wellspring of their capacities, their inmost core, 'everything which must blossom forth from each human individuality', as he puts it, above. The human genius or spark that wells up and expresses itself in art, science, religion ... and indeed ... within the economic or the rights systems. It is an *aspect* of public life—not something that is spatially restricted to certain activities. Steiner also includes people's physical abilities in this.

And the cultural element concerns what issues forth from the human being's capacities *into society*—we are not talking about unused capacities, or capacities only used by someone privately. The artistic abilities of a commercial pilot are of no consequence to the social organism if he or she never exibits a picture. We are only concerned with the talents of the individual insofar as they interface with society; we are not concerned with the individual in private isolation.

> ... *a spiritual life—what this means for single individuals—is another thing. We are talking here about the social organism. [...] Someone might create poems—as many as he wants, may find friends for these poems—as many as he likes; what validates spiritual life is only what he, as a single individual, shares with other people. (CW328(iii), 10 February 1919)*

Having said that the three realms are intermingled and not spatially separated, it is nonetheless also self-evident that one or other of these three realms may well *predominate* and be the *focus* in any institution. So, a manufacturer sits largely within the economic realm, a university within the cultural, and so on. And as we shall come on to see in Section 7.1, the concept of a threefold society includes a separate central administration for each realm, for co-ordination purposes, etc. Organisations would thus generally fall under the auspices of one of the three realms. But not *every* organisation. Section 8.3 looks at some of the organisations that do not fit so neatly under one or the other administration.

Of particular note is that Steiner singles out education as a special case within the cultural realm. It is that part of cultural life where the capacities and talents of one person (the teacher / lecturer) are employed to actually enhance, grow, nurture, tend, encourage, cultivate, inspire, develop the capacities of another (the pupil / student)—notwithstanding that these capacities may be based initially on heredity or what a person 'brings with them' at birth. In education, cultural work is directed back at the 'inner' life of students to nurture the cultural aspect itself, the intellectual capacities as well as the practical skills of the learner. Formal education may not be the only means by which such 'inner growth' occurs, but it is nonetheless the prime example. Yes, literature, the arts, entertainment, sport, religion, work that is rewarding, friends and acquaintances, and even a nice, squidgy doughnut may all nourish the soul to a greater or lesser degree too. 'It takes a village to raise a child', as the African proverb says. But education is possibly the most significant when it comes to *building* the capacities of a fellow human being, with the exception, perhaps, of parenting. Education is that part of the cultural sphere that actually fertilises the cultural sphere itself.

> ... think for a moment about the socially most significant branch of cultural life—schools on every level ! (CW24, p. 4)
>
> The spirit must give the answer to the question of how men can be made strong and capable ... (CW332a, p. 23)
>
> ... free spirits have the peculiar property of loosening and liberating the spirituality, the gumption of others. They make their thinking more mobile, and these are thus able to work into the material process more effectively. (CW340, pp. 81-82)

So, within the cultural realm, there is spectrum: from this special case of education at one end—the realm of learning—through other activities which are also more purely cultural like the arts and sciences, right down, at the other end of the spectrum, into the economic and legal realms where cultural activity manifests in the application of these capabilities within the legal and economic systems.

Within the economy, things like product design or R&D 'belong' to the cultural realm, as does the organising of labour, that is to say, management. Even someone picking blackberries, as Steiner points out, uses their intelligence to gather blackberries where they are abundant rather than scarce; so there is some cultural life even here. From this, one could perhaps surmise that a person's work can only be considered as being carried out *purely* in the economic domain if it is more or less mechanical, repetitive and entails little or no skill, no use of any aspect of the worker's individuality.

It might seem somewhat paradoxical that the realm that is essentially based on the *individual* is considered to be one of the realms of society. But the paradox abates when one considers that it is entirely from individuals that the values, ideas and actions of society emerge. The individuality of each person is expressed in their work, in political choices, in personal deeds and preferences, etc. And newcomers born into the world are nurtured by the prevailing culture, too. As Albert Schmelzer says: 'The task of cultural life consists as it were in nourishing social life with a supply of ever new creative forces'.[92] In any case, Steiner talks of the cultural realm, not as the realm of the individual per se, but as what *enters society* from the individual's faculties.

Within the definition of the *economic* realm, covered previously, the exclusion from it of both land and the means of production was introduced. Under the threefold approach, Steiner advocates that these should not be seen as commodities qualifying for purchase and sale, but as factors of production over which the most suitable people, on account of their talents, have a *right* of use. The most able person available to run a gas works runs the gas works; the most skilled person available to run a theatre runs the theatre, etc. The business is safeguarded by ensuring effective management succession that favours effective management skills (capacities!) and not simply the offspring of former management, say, or shareholder buying power (which might simply lead to opportunistic asset-stripping). But whilst this *right* of use may be overseen by the rights realm, the *appointing* of the most skilful people on which to bestow such rights requires individual judgement—judgement to ascertain the capabilities of those being appointed. So, Steiner advises this appointing also be a function of suitably constituted bodies within the cultural realm—if, that is, the previous proprietor of the land or means of production in question does not wish to involve themselves in this.

> *In general, it follows that it should at first be possible for someone who proposes to effect such a capital transfer under the circumstances described to freely choose his successor. He will be able to choose a person, or group of persons, or transfer the disposition rights to an establishment of the spiritual organisation. (CW23, p. 103)*
>
> *In case someone does not wish to personally select the receiver of capital accumulated by him, he will be able to delegate this function to an establishment of the spiritual organisation. (CW23, p. 105)*

---

[92] Albert Schmelzer, *The Threefold Movement, 1919: A History* (Forest Row: Rudolf Steiner Press, 2017), p. 55.

We will return to this in more detail (in Sections 7.3.7 and 7.5.6) when we look at Steiner's operational suggestions.

In summary, the cultural aspect of the social organism concerns:

- What emanates into society from the wellspring of capacities within the individual human being (including physical capacities).
- The development of these capacities through education.
- The expression of these individual capacities in cultural endeavour such as research, art, science, philosophy, religion.
- The institutions that embody these.
- The judiciary is included.
- The expression of these capacities in national culture.
- The application of these capacities in the economic domain (e.g. craftsmanship, product design or the organising forces of management).
- The application of these capacities in the rights domain (e.g. proposing legislation, voting, etc.).
- Responsibility for the means of production and land (i.e. the appointment of suitable directors / managers) is also included.

6. The Three Realms—Guiding Principles

6.1 Relative independence and autonomy

As we have seen, there is natural overlap between the three realms; they are intermingled. So it might come as a surprise to read passages like the following:

> *Anyone who studies modern evolution will find that these three elements of life, cultural, political, and economic, have intermingled gradually, until they now form a chaotic whole, and out of the amalgamation of these three elements the present evils of society have arisen. (CW332a, p. 27)*
>
> *... these three spheres of life, spiritual life, legal life and economic life, are very different, and mixing them together is not only completely impossible but also a real disaster for human development. (CW331, 24 June 1919)*

As shall become clear, however, there is overlap and there is overlap. One realm can appropriately serve another, but it can also inappropriately interfere with another. The point Steiner is making—in a sense, the central point of threefolding—is that it is harmful when co-ordination of the three realms, and of the institutions that embody them, is all under one roof in a big muddle:

> *... if everything is centralised, if everything is piled onto a chaotically jumbled social arrangement, then human beings are bound to degenerate, as in some respects they have in recent times ... (CW193, p. 53)*

Instead of being bundled together, as they were in the communist and unitary state models he considered so problematic (as discussed in Sections 4.2.2 and 4.2.3), he recommends the three realms should to a large extent be organised independently from one another:

> *Each of the three members is to be centralised within itself. (CW23, p. 81)*

> ... if society is ordered in a threefold way; if the economic life is administered separately; if in the life of rights, the state is no longer an absolute, all-embracing concept, but something which deals solely with those things that really belong to the sphere of rights; and if the spiritual cultural sphere is truly free. (CW196, p. 73)

With the three aspects having a suitable level of independence, then each can develop its own nature in a healthy way, can play to its strengths, can adhere to socially constructive principles that are the most befitting for one realm but not necessarily all three. As Steiner points out:

> ... political circumstances demand healthy conservatism in the sense of preservation and consolidation of the historically developed state systems if these circumstances are to flourish. The economic and general human interests bristle against this conservatism, which is a vital necessity for Central Europe, only so long as they have to suffer through being mixed with the conservative state systems. And the political conservatism, when it thinks of its true interests, does not have the slightest cause to continuously let itself be disturbed by being thrown together with the economic and general human interests. If this mixing is stopped, then the economic and general human interests will reconcile themselves with the political conservatism and the latter can quietly develop according to its own being.
>
> Economic relations require opportunism,[93] which manages the organization of economic relations according to its own nature, in order to flourish. It must lead to conflict if economic measures stand in a relationship to political and general human requirements that is different from their own appropriate laws and administration in their natural context. Here we do not mean only conflict within the state, but mainly conflict that discharges externally in political difficulties and explosions of war. (CW24(ii), pp. 97-98)

The three realms are characterised by altogether different mindsets. A certain conservatism is relevant and will hold sway in the rights realm—a considered, steady-as-she-goes, more incremental approach

---

[93] In the sense of responding to opportunities as they arise.

to change that builds on what is there already; whereas the mindset more suited to the economic realm will be much more responsive and boisterous, welcoming new technical developments, etc. So, the institutions representing one realm need to be independent of the institutions representing another.

However, the threefold idea is by no means that the three realms should each carry on in glorious isolation and more or less disregard each other. They would then doubtless become untamed and harmful in a different way.

For example:

> ... the life of the economy should form a relatively *independent third sphere. [my emphasis, RM] (CW193, p. 45)*
>
> ... the strong impetus towards a system of law and equity arises, capable of keeping the economic life within its proper limits. (CW332a, p. 69)

That is, *complete* separation of the three aspects is not the aim. Rather, a separation that respects the distinct qualities of each realm in a way that can enable the social organism to become healthy. It is a case of each realm having its own particular approach inherently suited to it, of developing itself strongly and in accordance with its own nature. From this, a certain hygiene can arise not only within each realm, but also within their integration with one another. If each realm can enjoy relative independence, they will then work together more healthily:

> ... these realms can work together in the right way if they are allowed to develop their intrinsic qualities relatively independently. (CW79, 30 November 1921)
>
> I do not try to distinguish spiritual life, legal life and economic life in the way that you would distinguish in man the nervous system, the respiratory system and the metabolic system, if at the same time you wanted to insist that they are three systems, each separate from one another. In itself, such a division leads nowhere; you can advance only by seeing how these three different systems function together, and how they best combine into a single whole by each operating on its own terms. The same is true of the social organism.

> *When we know how to establish spiritual life, political and legal life, and economic life on the terms that are native to each, and how to let them run off their native sources of power, then the unity of the social organism will also follow. (CW83, p. 180)*

As already hinted, Steiner ultimately sees an appropriate threefold articulation of the social organism as something that can even reduce the chance of war:

> *What is valid for Central Europe ... is a parliamentarianism in which the political, the economic and the general human relations can unfold independently of one another in legislation and administration, and thereby support one another instead of entangling themselves in their outward effects and creating conflicts. Central Europe frees itself and the world from such conflicts when it excludes such mutual interference of the three human realms in life from its state structures. (CW24(ii), p. 99)*

Each of the three realms thrives best if it takes its own approach to organising itself. And Steiner asserts each realm has its own inherent guiding principle which, if observed, improves societal health.

What are these guiding principles? They are those same fundamental ideals that found their voice in the French Revolution (and elsewhere): *liberté, égalité, fraternité*—freedom, equality, brotherliness (mutuality / fellowship).

As many before Steiner had already pointed out, these ideals are not especially compatible with one another. For example, if people are truly free, then they won't all be equal, and so on. However, within a threefold approach to public life, these potent ideals become entirely appropriate, as shall be demonstrated.

In summary:

- The three realms should not be mixed together under the umbrella of a single unitary regime.
- When responsibility for each is separated out, each can then develop according to its own inherent nature ...

- And thus prevent conflict (which can happen when, for example, the 'opportunism' of the economic realm rubs against the 'conservatism' of the political).
- The independence of each realm is a relative one, not an absolute one; there are healthy overlaps and unhealthy ones.
- Steiner posits (see next sections) that each of the three realms has a guiding principle that ideally informs it: *liberté, égalité and fraternité* respectively.

Reflections in relation to the present

In the so-called developed world of today one can observe how the demarcation between the three societal realms is often not what a threefold approach would regard as healthy. The government (rights realm) often has executive functions within, for example, education (cultural realm) and various industrial sectors (economic aspect). The UK government, for instance, comprises over one thousand different institutions (departments, agencies, public bodies) even without counting all the district, county and parish councils. Within this long list of institutions, there are many examples of inter-realm trespass.

More seriously, there are the frequent and painful examples of corporate (economic realm) encroachment into the other two realms. Examples of appropriate and inappropriate overlap are considered in some detail in Chapter 8.

6.2   Rights — *Égalité* — Democracy

> *The social relationships that every adult is competent to judge are the legal relationships between one person and another. (CW24, p. 5)*

In the realm of rights, the realm concerned with the rules that everyone within a certain state boundary lives by, every adult (bar a few) can have a sense of what is right or wrong ... the right not to be attacked in the street, say, or the right to know what is in one's food, and so on. Whatever a person's abilities, and whatever their economic standing, each adult is on a par with every other. Thus, equality rules the day in the rights realm, and this guiding principle of equality finds expression in democracy.

> *... the political system of laws—that must rest on a democratic basis ... (CW24, p. 92)*
>
> *Every adult citizen must share equally in the regulatory process. Administration and representation must provide a climate in which a healthy consciousness of rights and responsibilities is allowed to unfold. (CW24, p. 4)*
>
> *... before the law or constitution, before the government in fact, everyone is equal ... (CW186(ii), p. 145)*

Firstly, everyone above a certain age has an equal say in the political process, in the *determining* of rights and responsibilities. One person, one vote. Secondly, all are equally *subject* to the laws passed. There is no favouritism, nepotism, discrimination or victimisation. Everything that I can do to you I must accept you can do to me.

As we know, democracy comes in various guises, but the main thing is:

> *Every person who has come of age can participate—either directly in the form of a referendum, for example, or indirectly via election, or rather, via a representative body. (CW331, 24 June 1919)*

Direct democracy, via referenda, can have a certain allure; but it can also reveal significant shortcomings where an issue under consideration has such a broad and complex range of implications that it takes much conscientious study to appreciate them all. For this reason, most democracies are representational / parliamentary: we elect politicians who sit in a parliament, thrash things out (sparing us lengthy study of every issue), and take legislative decisions on our behalf, following manifesto promises, etc.

Further comments by Steiner relating to the democratic process are considered in Section 7.3.2.

There was nothing particularly revolutionary, of course, about Steiner recommending that the rights realm observe the principles of equality and democracy. Such ideas had already been honed over some centuries. Tentative democratic principles had already been introduced into the British Isles with the Magna Carta in the early 13th century. Indeed, if you want to ignore the sexism and the slaves, Socrates was discussing such principles as far back as 400 BC.

In Steiner's day, however, universal suffrage was a hot topic. The first country to adopt it was Finland in 1906; in Germany it was introduced in 1918 for all aged 20 and over; and it eventually arrived in the UK in 1928. Switzerland, incredibly, had to wait until 1971. And it was not only a women's issue. It also affected large numbers of the male population in most countries up until just a few years before women obtained the right to vote. Steiner recalls the following in connection with 19th-century Austria:

> In Austria, where my youth was spent, I could neither elect nor be elected, for the simple reason that, in those days, nobody might elect or be elected, who did not possess a yearly income amounting to a considerable figure. (CW330(ii), 31 May 1919)

As noted previously, Steiner makes a special point of emphasising that labour relations belong to the rights / political aspect of the threefold social organism, and it is not hard to picture how (a) bringing such considerations more into the administration of the rights realm, and (b) allowing all to vote in the rights realm will have led to significant improvements in the welfare of the working classes around Steiner's time, even if the measures introduced were considerably more limited than Steiner recommended. In this chapter, however, we are just looking at the guiding principles of each of the three aspects of the social organism; Steiner's more operational suggestions / illustrations will be looked at presently.

The main point at this stage is to appreciate that equality is fundamental to the rights realm. It has less relevance to the economic or cultural realms. We don't all want to wear the same kind of cardigan, so equality in the economic realm has little meaning. And it makes no sense at all to speak of equality in the cultural realm, considering how different each person's capacities are.

In summary, the rights aspect:

- Is ideally guided by the principle of equality, universal fairness.
- This equality is achieved via the democratic process—one adult, one vote.
- This equality is also expressed in all citizens being equally subject to the same laws.

Reflections in relation to the present

In 1941 there were 11 democracies around the world; there are now over 100. In your average Western democracy, more or less everyone is free to stand for election nowadays, regardless of their views, and more or less everyone is free to vote for whomsoever they wish. We have a reasonable democracy-of-sorts, and so have a lot to be thankful for, compared to a number of countries one might mention, and certainly compared to a hundred years ago when Steiner was speaking. If we don't like a politician, we can vote them out.

Nonetheless, there are a number of oft-repeated issues with our various democracies—issues which undermine the guiding principle of equality.

One such problem can be a lack of proportional representation. In the UK, the views of the public are not represented in parliament in proportion to the numbers of people subscribing to each view. In the 2015 general election, for example, the Liberal Democrats, the UK Independence Party and the Greens got 24.1% of the vote between them—just shy of a quarter of the vote. But did they end up with a quarter of the 650 seats in the House of Commons, i.e. about 160 seats? No, with our first-past-the-post system they ended up with 10. So, electoral reform is urgently needed if we want to make the process more democratic, more reflective of public opinion, if you want your vote to carry equal weight to your neighbour's.

As an unelected upper chamber, the House of Lords in the UK is of course not democratic. However, given that its ability to block legislation coming out of the House of Commons was withdrawn by the Parliament Act of 1911, its continuation is seen more as an anachronism that exercises added scrutiny than as any final obstacle against the will of the people. The Lords can delay procedure, but they cannot block it. Another anachronism is that of the royal family with the monarch being titular head of state. Curiously, though, were our head of state to be elected, there is a high chance the Queen, on account of her popularity, would be returned to the 'throne'. However, that would necessitate her not only standing for election but also delineating and broadcasting her political views.

These particular democratic deficits (first-past-the-post, lords, monarchy) are actually built into our political system itself; they are issues relating to how we do things within the rights realm itself. But there are other substantial democratic deficits caused not within the rights realm but by inappropriate interference from the economic or cultural realms.

The corruption in US politics, for example, is legendary. Abraham Lincoln's 'government of the people, by the people, for the people' seems to have fallen by the wayside a good while back. A semblance of democracy may be sustained by periodic electoral charades and a media that is largely patsy to elitist interests. But the recent findings of Prof. Martin Gilens of Princeton University and Prof. Benjamin I. Page of Northwestern University were damning. Based on an analysis of over 1,800 policy initiatives over a 20-year period, they could not escape the conclusion: the US is not a democracy.[94] Even former US President Jimmy Carter says money makes the US closer to an oligarchy—control by a relatively small number of wealthy elites—than a democracy.[95]

In 2018, the President of Bolivia also decided to call a spade a spade: 'In no way is the United States interested in upholding democracy. If such were the case, it would not have financed coups d'état and supported dictators. It would not have threatened military intervention in democratically elected governments as it's done with Venezuela. The United States could not care less about human rights, nor justice. If such were the case, it would have signed the International Conventions and Treaties for the Protection of Human Rights. It would not have threatened the investigative mechanisms of the International Criminal Court; nor would it promote the use

---

[94] https://www.bbc.co.uk/news/blogs-echochambers-27074746.

[95] Associated Press, 'Jimmy Carter says U.S. has become more an "oligarchy than a democracy" in speech critical of Trump', *The Telegraph*, 13 September 2017.

of torture; nor would it have walked away from the Human Rights Council; and nor would it have separated migrant children from their families nor put them in cages'.[96] Just one example of an undemocratic figure supported by the US was Ferdinand Marcos of the Philippines, 'a US-backed military dictator, who used the army to impose censorship and indulge in spectacular forms of torture'.[97] It would be interesting to actually ask US citizens whether they support the perpetration of these horrors!

Also in the USA, pervasive corporate lobbying and political donations have, to a greater or lesser extent, converted a one-person-one-vote electoral system into one-dollar-one-vote; policy can be more or less bought—very often at the expense of those who most need political protection. The economic realm is corrupting the political. The guiding principle of equality in the political domain is very much on the back foot.

In the UK, some 80% of the press is owned by just five billionaires which has all manner of effects on our democracy, albeit more indirectly. These and other examples of contamination between realms will be considered in more detail in Chapter 8 ('Overlap').

To what extent there might be inviolable, universal human rights that should trump the electorate and national sovereignty, so as to protect minorities from democratic yet uncharitable majority rule for example, is beyond the scope of this book. A House of Commons debate on the matter on 1 March 2013 between Conservative MPs Rory Stewart and Jacob Rees-Mogg serves as an interesting introduction to this aspect of moral philosophy, however.[98]

6.3   Economics—Fraternité—Association

The principle of equality, whilst being wholly fitting in the rights realm, cannot really apply to the economic process.

---

[96] The President of Bolivia, Evo Morales, speaking at the UN Security Council, https://www.telesurtv.net/english.

[97] Peter Pomerantsev, 'The new propaganda', *The Guardian Weekly*, 2 August 2019.

[98] https://youtu.be/VO2Ry4j79LU (Hansard link is https://publications.parliament. uk/pa/cm201213/cmhansrd/cm130301/debtext/130301-0001.htm).

> *... the manner in which business is carried on cannot be allowed to be judged democratically by every grown up person, but only by someone who is engaged in some branch of economic life, who is capable in his branch and knows the links that connect his own branch with others. Special knowledge and special capacity are the only guarantees of fruitful work in economic life. (CW332a, p. 30)*
>
> *Everything that I described yesterday in regard to the economic sphere is based on the assumption that individuals actively engaged in one or another special branch are possessed of expert knowledge and efficiency. For instance, mere maturity in age, the mere capacity of judgment possessed by every adult, can never be sufficient qualification for a good farmer or a good industrial worker. (CW332a, p. 63)*

On the production side, a fisherman won't know how to build computers, and someone who builds computers won't know the best way to grow rye. Efficient production relies on *differences* in expertise, knowledge, skill (those talents in the cultural realm), *different* raw materials (bestowed by the climate and geology of nature), and so on. Whilst these two factors of production—people and nature—may themselves need certain levels of uniform, legal protection (as per the inner and outer rings of Kate Raworth's doughnut[99]) to talk of equality has little meaning on the production side. Its vitality relies on difference. It makes no sense to let everyone of voting age equally have their say concerning the manufacture of water skis!

And on the consumption side of the economy, people have a wide range of needs and tastes, and so the concept of equality is somewhat meaningless here too. We don't all want the same things, the same commodities. We might all want to eat cabbage at some point or other, but not to the same extent. And we don't all need a trumpet or a wheelchair. And if everyone had to wear clothes that the majority had elected to wear ... and so on and so forth.

---

[99] In *Doughnut Economics: Seven Ways to Think Like a 21ˢᵗ-Century Economist* (London: Random House, 2018) Kate Raworth spells out how thresholds of protection for both nature and people must be observed in order for a sustainable and socially acceptable world to obtain.

> *... the social impulse that must live in the economic process cannot, because of its essential nature, manifest itself democratically. The aim of this social impulse is that people engaged in economic production should pay attention to the legitimate needs of their fellows. (CW24, p. 91)*

> *What each individual really needs can only be known by himself ... (CW23, p. 16)*

Whilst equality might be the guiding principle appropriate to the rights realm, Steiner emphasises that, if societal health is to advance, the leitmotif for the economic realm should be brotherliness, the consideration of the needs of our fellow human beings.

> *There must be fraternity in the economic domain. (CW186(ii), p.146)*

> *This brotherly relationship among people is an essential component of the economic realm if this is to become healthy and sound. (CW193, p. 52)*

> *Economic life will be dominated by fraternity, that fraternity which is, as it were, fraternity on a grand scale ... (CW329, 9 April 1919)*

Since we all do things for each other in the economy, a mutual interdependence is inherent in this realm in any case. We are reliant on one another for the various goods and services that we use.

> *When labour is divided and distributed, human beings grow dependent on the principle of mutuality to a far greater extent than is the case when every man not only grows his own cabbages but also makes his own hat and boots. (CW340, p. 129)*

An obvious point, perhaps. However, this interdependence, Steiner notes, is fertile soil wherein the principle of brotherliness can flourish.

> *In no other realm than that of economic life is it possible for us to develop so easily and naturally human relationships that are brotherly in the full sense of the word. (CW193, p. 51)*

He also opines that the brotherliness / sisterliness that should pervade the economic realm need not come with any preachy overtones, any decree to love thy neighbour, any 'moralic acid' as he puts it.

> There is no lack of people nowadays who say: Our economic life will be good—ever so good—if once you human beings are good; you must become good. Think of the people like Professor Foerster and his kind, who go about preaching: If men will only become selfless, if they will only fulfil the categorical imperative of selflessness, the economic life will become good. Such judgments are really of no more worth than this one: if my mother-in-law had four wheels and a [steering wheel], she would be a bus! Truly the premise and the conclusion stand in no better connection than this, except that I have expressed it rather more radically.
>
> What underlies the threefold commonwealth is none of the 'moralic acid', which can, no doubt, play a great role in another field. Rather the purpose is to show, simply out of the economic facts, how selflessness cannot help being inherent in the very circulation of the elements of economic life. (CW340, p. 133)

Within the mutual interdependence of economic life, a selflessness exists inasmuch as we all produce commodities for each other. It may not be a selflessness in an especially moral sense, but a selflessness nonetheless is there, albeit of a purely economic kind. We are all in this together, and whilst I may not wish to deny my own interests and needs, there is nonetheless considerable scope for a certain fellowship to prevail when people get down to work. A mutuality in economic life is self-evident in the fact that we all rely on each other to provide the goods and services we need, and in such seemingly pedestrian sharing of burdens as seen, for example, in …

> … that eminently practical branch of life, insurance. (CW335, 15 September 1920)

Charting the appearance of Radicalism in Britain through Owenism, Chartism, Trade Unionism, Fabianism and Marxism, Charles Waterman observes: 'If we try to sum up in a single word what these radicals were searching for—what they felt to be most bitterly and ruinously lacking in the economic life of their time—perhaps the best word is "fraternity". Fraternity is what men experience when they work together in the service of a common aim. It is an experience of fellowship not induced by common loyalty to a system or a nation or a creed but derived directly from the work itself. It is therefore an experience perfectly compatible with differences of belief, taste, education, or even of race and language. It does not demand the loyalty of the whole man; but it demands the loyalty of the worker to the work and to his fellow-workers.'[100]

Steiner's idea of economic fraternity is perhaps even broader than this as it encompasses not only the feeling amongst a group of people engaged in a particular enterprise, but also their interdependence with customers, distributors, and those up and down the supply chain. Interdependence—mutuality—spreads out far. To make this mutuality more conscious and to provide better ground in which a sense of fraternity can take root (as well as, indeed, to enable optimal economic solutions to arise), Steiner advocates the formation of associations between consumers / distributors / producers. The makeup and scope he suggests for these associations will be looked at in Section 7.4, where the various operational suggestions he made are considered.

Associations are the living embodiment of brotherhood. (CW197, p. 203)

Associations are the health bearers. Associations work ... so that the interests of the producers and the consumers are harmonized ... Today we see how out of a diseased economic body the opposite of associative life is created, we see how passive resistance, locking out, sabotage and even revolutions come about. No-one with a healthy mind can deny that all this works in the opposite direction of the associative principle and that all this: sabotage, lock-outs, revolution and so on are symptoms of disease of the social organism that must be overcome through that which works in a harmonizing way. (CW79, 30 November 1921)

The moment the life of associations enters the economic process, it is no longer a question of immediate personal interest. The wider

---

[100] Charles Waterman, *The Three Spheres of Society* (London: Faber and Faber, 1946), p. 221.

outlook over the economic process will be active; the interest of the other fellow will be actually there in the economic judgment that is formed ... Thus we are impelled to rise from the economic process to the mutuality, the give and take between man and man, and furthermore to that which will arise from this, namely the objective community spirit[101] working in the associations. This will be a community spirit, not proceeding from any 'moralic acid' but from a realisation of the necessities in the economic process itself. (CW340, p. 133)

We cannot allow the impulse to work to be placed on egotism. It must arise naturally out of a view of the totality. (CW56(ii), p. 77)

In summary:

- The economic realm is not a place where equality / democracy should be aimed for (as it is in the political realm) since, as consumers, we have different needs, and as producers we have different skills.
- Neither are freedom or competition (which are appropriate for the cultural realm—see next section) the most healthy guiding principles.
- The economic realm should be guided by the principle of *fraternité* (brotherliness / sisterliness, mutuality, fellowship).
- The vehicle via which this fraternity can find expression is association between groups of producers, distributors, consumers–where the interests of one group engage with and offset the interests of another, where the meeting of different interests informs the decision-making process and encourages mutually agreeable arrangements.

Reflections in relation to the present

As we know, competition—typically, cut-throat—is generally the order of the day in our current 'developed world' economy. And although this 'war of all against all' was distasteful to Steiner (amongst many others), one cannot deny that competitive capitalism, whilst leading to

---

[101] The German is '*Gemeinsinn*', meaning 'sense of the community'.

multiple divisions and hardships in society, has nonetheless brought an enormous range of goods and services. The incessant and perhaps rather undignified attempt of each business to out-manoeuvre its competitors has brought with it innovation on all levels. However, a *lack* of competition need not mean lack of innovation, especially if the alternative is associative, collaborative.

Although examples of brotherly behaviour between stakeholders are less common than competition, their number is by no means insignificant and includes co-ops, charities, social enterprise and plenty of other instances where producers are genuinely interested in serving their customers without constantly trying to get the better of everyone. Indeed, worldwide there are about one billion member owners of co-operatives (individual shareholders of 'normal' companies number about one third this amount), which suggests a significant appetite for collaboration. In 2012—the UN's Year of Co-operatives—the three countries with over half their population involved in co-op membership were in Europe (Ireland with 70%, Finland with 60% and Austria with 59%). The three countries with the highest *number* of employees in co-operatives, however, were India (242 million), China (160 million) and the USA (120 million).[102]

All the same, whilst a good number of co-ops might follow the associative approach Steiner recommended—an approach involving close engagement between producers, distributors and consumers, not all of them do by any means. Examples of this type of associative behaviour are less common. This approach will be considered more closely when we come to look at Steiner's operational suggestions in Section 7.4.

The idea of promoting greater fellowship and co-operation in the economic process may seem very idealistic to some, but 'Evidence from experiments in psychology and economics, to anthropology and evolutionary biology, shows that co-operation has been more important to our evolution, and so to who we are, than competition. [...] Yet most of our systems, institutions and models of public policy lock us in, unthinkingly, to a miserable, impoverished view of ourselves as untrustworthy and selfish. [...] Far from being quaint

---

[102] John Elkington, 'Rediscovering the John Lewis economy', *The Guardian*, 9 March 2012.

and worthy, co-operation could become aspirational and dynamic. […] Milton Friedman argued that self-interest is fundamental to economic growth, actuating agents. He was wrong: most people, most of the time, are motivated by co-operation and fairness, as well as self-interest. An economy that neglects co-operation and fairness will not innovate and grow. Richard Dawkins claimed that we should teach altruism and generosity because we are born selfish. He was wrong: most of us are born helpful and generous, co-operation is written into who we are.'[103]

6.4   Culture — Liberté — Competition

How often has it been repeated in recent times that man must sacrifice everything for the common good. Yes, dear friends, that man must sacrifice everything for the sake of community at first sounds very appealing, but if this were carried out in practice then it would gradually lead to the greatest destruction of community life. For nothing underpins community life better than if, within this communal life, human individualities can develop themselves in the fullest sense of the word. (CW338, 14 February 1921)

To put it plainly, to gain any kind of insight into social life today we have to investigate the way human beings are straining to extricate themselves from old social forms because they long to be free, independent human beings pure and simple. (CW305(ii), p. 148)

The cultural domain of the threefold social organism is that domain which concerns each person's individual talents, what comes from their individual nature, as opposed to (a) what everyone has in common—the rights realm—where all make decisions together, and all are subject to the same laws, and (b) the system of production / circulation / consumption—the economic realm—where what happens depends on dialogue and agreement between interested parties (between producers, distributors and consumers; between those with needs and those who are meeting these needs).

---

[103] Charles Leadbeater, 'Why co-operation will be more important than ever', *The Guardian*, 3 January 2012.

Whilst equality may be wholly applicable in the rights realm, and brotherliness / sisterliness in the economic, here in the cultural domain, freedom is the watchword, the leitmotif. Each person is a unique fount of life with a unique spiritual core of 'self-ness' which cannot fruitfully be nurtured or find expression by democratic means, majority diktat, or ideas of equality. Nor is fraternity necessarily applicable. If someone wants to be an opera singer but shows little promise in that direction, it makes little sense, out of fraternal feelings, to invite them into an opera house and let them have a go. In the cultural realm, freedom is appropriate, and a certain individualism obtains. Each person's individual nature and capacities should be allowed—indeed encouraged—to come to the fore and flourish. If each person's capacities find full expression, if everyone can fully play to their strengths, society in any case benefits. Each can offer different capacities and different services. This is optimised when freedom applies in the cultural domain.

> ... the vital element of this member of the social organism must have its centre in the free unfolding of the physical and spiritual arrangement of the human being. Everything needs to be based on the sphere of the individuality. Everything flowing into this must come from the centre of the human individuality, and the physical and spiritual faculties must have free, evolutionary possibilities ... (CW328(iii), 10 February 1919)
>
> In a healthy social organism all spiritual life must be, in respect to the state and the economy, a 'private affair'. (CW23, p. 77)
>
> Democratic sentiments can relate only to that which each adult has in common with every other adult. It is impossible to find within democratic processes a regulatory function for matters that lie entirely within the domain of the individual. If true democracy is to become a reality, then one must exclude from its province everything that belongs in the domain of the individual. Within the province of democracy and the administrative establishments growing out of it, no impulse directing the free flow of individual human talent can arise. Democracy has to declare its impotence to provide such an impulse if it wants to be a true democracy. (CW24, p. 4)
>
> Socialism must rest upon the free initiative of individual faculties. (CW189(ii), 7 March 1919)

> *... spiritual life must be based on freedom. It is not free if there is any censorship authority of any kind, if this or that can be banned in the field of human needs. You can still rant against cinemas if you are of fanatical mind; this does not affect the free spiritual life. The moment one cries out for the police, however, where one screams: that should be forbidden, one affects the free spiritual life. (CW338, 16 February 1921)*

> *The more freedom we have in* extracting and applying *our individual abilities, the better it is for the social organism. [my emphasis, RM] (CW329, 11 March 1919)*

Government / majority rule should exercise no mandate over society's cultural life, and neither should the economy.

And, as has been ascertained, society's cultural life encompasses the general life of thought and culture, plus everything that enters society from people's capacities, plus *the institutions* that concern themselves with the flourishing of these capacities. These institutions, too, must be free to follow their own path, free from state meddling. Such ideas did not arrive with Steiner, of course; they had been gaining ground since the Enlightenment when figures like John Locke advocated the separation of Church and state. US Founding Father James Madison observed, for example: 'religion and government will both exist in greater purity, unless they are mixed together'.[104]

> *The spirit can only flourish among human beings if it is dependent upon itself and if all the institutions that cultivate the spirit depend on nothing but themselves. (CW196, p. 73)*

> *The spiritual life cannot flourish unless it is free to maintain itself every day anew. But that will only be possible if it is placed on its own basis. From the lowest school position to the highest, from the established branch of science to creative works in art, in order to endure, it must be free, because it can only build on its own strength. (CW192, 21 April 1919)*

> *All juridical, pedagogical and spiritual concerns are in the free hands of the individual. In this domain the state only has the right to police, not the right to initiate. (CW24(ii), p. 80)*

---

[104] James Madison Jr. 1751—1836, fourth President of the USA.

Indeed, Steiner even cautions cultural institutions themselves against allowing themselves to become too centralised and corporate:

> Cultural or spiritual life must really be free, not just in theory but in a real, living way. The human being standing within it must feel this freedom. Cultural life becomes very tyrannical if it spreads far and wide, for it cannot do so unless some organisational form emerges; and when this happens, the organisation itself becomes tyrannical. (CW339(iii), 14 October 1921)

Steiner placed much store in quality education for the engendering of societal health, and in relation to the guiding principle of freedom, education again frequently gets a special mention:

> ... powers of our innermost nature are stunted when we are forced to develop according to patterns imposed by the state and the economic system. Such powers, deep within human nature, cannot be developed by institutions, but only through what one being calls forth in perfect freedom from another being. The effect of what arises in this way is not antisocial, but rather deeply social. The socially active inner person is stunted only when instincts originating in the prerogatives of the state or in economic advantage are ingrained or handed down.
>
> Through its cultural branch, the threefold social order will uncover perpetual springs of social initiative. These springs will imbue the legal relations that are regulated by the democratic state with a social spirit, and they will spread the same spirit into the conduct of economic life. (CW24, p. 100)
>
> ... the state shall no longer determine the matter and manner of teaching. Only those who are actually teachers, engaged in practical education, shall be its administrators. (CW332a, p. 28)
>
> If one seriously desires to transform the present order of society into one in which social attitudes prevail, then one must not be afraid to place the spiritual-cultural life (including the school and education system) under its own independent control because from such a free, independent system within the social organism men and women will go forth with joy and zeal to take an active part in all its life. (CW24, p. 73)

Alongside the freedom that applies within the cultural realm, Steiner points out that competition must also apply. For example, the one who, on account of his or her capacities, is most suited to do a particular job meritocratically does the job instead of someone enjoying special privileges (such as family connections or wealth).

> If spiritual life really stands on its own feet, then there will be no social coercion in this realm, but only the relation of free recognition. And this free recognition arises naturally within social life. Basically, it is unlikely anyone will ever be hired as a music teacher If they have never played a musical instrument ... (CW338, 16 February 1921)
>
> Not only the creation but also the reception by humanity of this spiritual life must be freely determined in accordance with the soul's necessities. Teachers, artists and such whose only direct connection with a legislature or an administration is with those which have their origin in spiritual life itself, will be able, through their actions, to inspire the development of a receptivity for their efforts and achievements amongst individuals ... (CW23, p. 78)
>
> Whoever finds it distasteful that from this perspective cultural-spiritual affairs would in future no longer be subject to special privilege must put up with it for the benefit of society. From the ever growing habituation to special privileges, people in many circles will find it difficult to accept the need to leave behind these special privileges, especially for professions like education, medicine, law and religion, and return to the venerated ancient idea of the free spiritual-cultural organization. The cultural organisations should see to it that a person becomes qualified for his profession but also that the practice of these professions should not be a matter of special privileges but rather should come about by free competition and free human choice. (CW24(ii), p. 111)

A passage like the latter certainly highlights some of the progress we have made since Steiner's day. Today, the lowly economic position of one's parents need not prevent one from becoming a brain surgeon. Family poverty may certainly represent a *degree* of hindrance by preventing one from going to some of the best schools (where these are private), but it will not act as an out-and-out barrier, since education is available for all.

As introduced earlier, it is within the *rights* life that laws are determined, but when it comes to the judgement of people who fall foul of these laws, close account needs to be taken of the individuals coming to court, of their particular circumstances. The sentence to be passed down by the courts for a particular transgression needs to vary depending on the particular circumstances of the guilty party—needs to take account of any mitigating circumstances so that it fits the individual and society best. This weighing up cannot be done by the public democratically or by the principle of equality imposing a one-size-fits-all sentencing structure on the wayward, but only by someone with keen judicial discernment, that is, by individual skill and insight. A desperately hungry or perhaps simple person, for example, might well deserve lighter punishment for a crime of theft than an embezzling, wealthy businessperson. But, democratically, we can all decide that food theft and embezzlement should be illegal.

Whether the judge only sums up at the end of a hearing, and then hands down a suitable sentence, or whether, as in some courts, he or she also comes to the final verdict (i.e. not the population at large as represented by a jury), the institution of the judiciary is not a matter for democratic oversight, but should be subject to regulation by its own free (independent) body within the cultural domain.

Remember, too, that Steiner includes national culture within the cultural realm. If freedom is the watchword within this realm, then this implies different peoples must have complete freedom to enjoy their respective, ethnic culture within any rights state.

> ... and with regard to all religious and spiritual / cultural relationships, to which national culture also belongs ... (CW24(ii), p. 88)

The Austro-Hungarian Empire (which came to an end in 1918) comprised a dozen or more nationalities and languages (including Czech, Romanian, Croatian, Serbian, Ukranian, Slovenian, etc.), and the importance of this or that people being able to freely express and celebrate their respective character and culture within the wider social unit (state) of the Austro-Hungarian Empire would have been on many a mind. Such cultural matters should not be something that democracy, a majority of the population, can interfere with so as to artificially impose a uniform culture on the entire empire. The state should not tyrannise individual choice. The distinction between state and nation is important here. In the *state* of the UK we share much of the same legislative machinery whilst the different *nations* enjoy their own cultural life. Those in Cornwall can be protected by the same *rights* as those in Argyll without having to concern themselves with Hogmanay or Tossing the Caber. And the refugee from Jordan can be a Zoroastrian if she wishes. As Steve Briault observes: 'Liberty as a social ideal means allowing others to be different.'[105] The idea of the *nation*-state, on the other hand (i.e. the state as an ethnically circumscribed entity), is problematic as minorities may feel un-catered-for, unrepresented, cowed or even threatened.

As was touched on previously, Steiner even deems the application of people's capacities within the *economic* and *rights* systems as 'belonging' to the cultural domain, and you might well wonder what relevance the guiding principle of freedom has here. If someone working in the automotive industry is designing a gearbox, what they design needs to have the correct dimensions, be efficient, and so on. Can this form of cultural life really be free? As is clear from the following, however—where Steiner refers to a 'half-free' cultural life, cultural freedom will have natural constraints in work situations:

> *Imagine the free spiritual life in the social organism really freed so that the individual faculties were always able to evolve to the full. Then the free spiritual life will be able to exert an extremely fertilising influence on the half-free spiritual life—i.e. on that spiritual life which enters into the process of material production. (CW340, p. 81)*

The designing of the gearbox will be subject to obvious constraints and so represent a 'half-free' cultural life. However, before designing the gearbox, the engineer in question will ideally have come through an education system where his or her faculties were able to develop freely, and his or her appointment to the post will have occurred in a free, competitive manner—without favouritism, nepotism, discrimination, etc.

---

[105] Martin Large and Steve Briault (Eds), *Free, Equal and Mutual: Rebalancing Society for the Common Good* (Stroud: Hawthorn Press, 2018), p. 27.

Steiner was well known for regarding personal liberty as paramount, and those interested in his more philosophical works where he makes the case for freedom may be interested in the following comment, made in 1920, on the relationship between the guiding principle of freedom in his threefold analysis of society and the principle of freedom in his work *The Philosophy of Freedom* written in 1894:

> *In fact, my book* Kernpunkte *is in a sense an enlargement of, or complementary to, my* Philosophy of Freedom. The Philosophy of Freedom *enquires into how an individual's powers can become free, and similarly* Kernpunkte *looks at what is necessary if a social organism is to be shaped in a way that enables individuals to develop freely. Basically, these are the two great questions that must occupy us today in public life. (CW334(ii), p. 165)*

In summary, the cultural aspect of society—what sprouts from the fount of the individual:

- should be imbued through and through with the principle of freedom.
- This means not only freedom of thought, expression and choice for *individuals*, but those institutions that fall within this realm (schools, universities, places of worship, etc.) should be entirely independent from any control by state or economic concerns.
- Cultural movements should even guard against becoming too established (and thus fixed) themselves.
- Alongside this freedom, competition—meritocracy—has its proper place. The one with the most suitable skills for the job gets the job (be that laying bricks or playing Pamina in The Coliseum).

Reflections in relation to the present

Today, we enjoy a relatively good amount of individual freedom in most democracies. We have extensive personal freedoms, religious freedom, freedom of expression, and so on. On the whole, the most capable person for a job gets the job, not some comrade appointed by the party, and not your old friend from school. Racial and other types of prejudice can still get in the way of this, of course.

Colleges and universities, the arts and sciences typically proceed as they will. Naturally, these freedoms are tempered in order to prevent harm, although not offence. And as was noted previously, Steiner observed how uncontaminated by the state he found the cultural realm in Britain to be.

But there is plenty of room for improvement. As already mentioned, the education of children, does not enjoy complete independence from the rights realm in the UK. And scientific research can all too often be contaminated by the interests of corporate funders (economic realm). And in the news media the problem of corporate contamination of the public's life of thought can be extreme. An example of this is where newspapers continually reinforce a narrative that suits their billionaire owners' interests instead of the common good (e.g. by implying that tax is bad). Such examples—and others—of inappropriate overlap between realms are considered in some detail in Chapter 8.

6.5   Guiding principles—a summary

Whilst certain combinations of *liberté, égalité, fraternité* may be mutually exclusive (people can't be equal if they are also free, etc.) these three fundamental principles can coexist quite comfortably and logically when society is seen from a threefold point of view:

> *... liberty in spiritual matters; equality in the state if that is what people want to continue calling this third; and fraternity in relation to the economic life. I know well written books which rightly emphasize that the three ideals of liberty, equality and fraternity contradict one another. It is true, equality decidedly contradicts liberty. Clever writers said this even in 1848 or even earlier. If we muddle everything together these things contradict one another. There must be liberty in the spiritual and judicial domain, the domain of religion, education and jurisprudence. There must be equality in administration, the government and public security. There must be fraternity in the economic domain. (CW186(ii), p. 146)*

If equality applied in the economic realm, everyone would have to wear the same cardigans. And to talk of equality in the cultural realm—the realm of people's individual capacities—is clearly a nonsense.

Similarly, freedom cannot be a guiding principle in the rights realm. Indeed, laws, rules, are often a jointly agreed *curtailment* of freedom. Freedom in the rights realm—a free-for-all where even physical attack was not legislated against—would not be attractive. Freedom in the economic life is not ideal either. It results in cut-throat competition, destructive neo-liberalism and monopolistic exploitation. It results in products being made for which there is little need, followed by advertising campaigns to drum up a perceived need. It results in shoddy goods, sharp practice, and a disregard for worker and environmental welfare. And so on.

And fraternity does not make an ideal guiding principle for the cultural realm. As described, the capacities of the individual should be able to express themselves *freely*. Then everyone can give of their best. Indeed, there is a competitive aspect in the cultural domain inasmuch as the best person for the job gets the job. It might be very nice and fraternal to allow someone to pursue a PhD in philosophy because they really want to. But if this is not where his or her strengths lie, then society is not helped.

In Chapter 8 ('Overlap') it will be shown in more detail how *liberté, égalité, fraternité* in fact *can* overlap—to the extent that the realms themselves overlap. For example, whilst equality may be the leitmotif for the political realm, freedom *does* apply here too to the extent that the cultural realm overlaps with it. That is, equality is expressed in the legislative *system* of one-person-one-vote democracy (the making of law), and in all being equal before the law. However, each individual who *feeds into* this process is free. I am free to set up the Monster Raving Loony Party. I am also free not to vote for it.

The following 'Celtic knot' image serves as a useful aid to picturing the threefold view of society (if you ignore the white-male-ness of the figures and assume they simply represent people!). The three circles represent the three realms of society, and we all, to a greater or lesser extent, operate in all three.

The outer circle represents the cultural domain, the realm of individual human flourishing, the realm that concerns the interaction between individual capacities and society. Here, no one is constrained, each person does their own thing, each person stands in a completely free relation to everyone else.

The middle circle represents the rights realm, the system of rules. Here, connections between people are all equal. We are all equally responsible for legislation. And we are all equally subject to—and protected by—this legislation. I am not allowed to steal from my neighbour to the left, and I am not allowed to steal from my neighbour to the right. A respectful, protective space is maintained between one person and the next.

In the inner circle—representing the economic system where we all provide one another with goods and services—we are connected to one another in a myriad of different ways, in a big, inter-dependent tangle. Mutuality applies.

In tabular form, we have:

	The realm concerning	More particularly	Decisions made by	Guiding principle
Cultural aspect	Human faculties ...	their cultivation, expression and application in society	Individuals	Freedom
Political realm	Rights and responsibilities ...	establishing and upholding these to protect society	All	Equality
Economic system	Goods and services ...	their production, circulation and consumption	Interested parties in association	Brotherliness

7. The Three Realms—Operational Remarks

Now that Steiner's definitions of the three societal realms have been considered, as has the guiding principle appropriate to each, attention will now be turned to organisational / operational matters—that is, the suggestions and illustrations he gave regarding how these ideas might be applied.

As already mentioned, Steiner frequently emphasised that what he was putting forward was an *approach* to social reform, a direction of travel, as opposed to fixed policy proposals, a fixed programme of measures. He considered it only realistic for reform to be a flexible, living process, and saw little merit in utopian edicts.

But notwithstanding this living, flexible nature, he nonetheless (a) was always consistent in stressing the importance and health-bestowing advantage of grounding any progress on a threefold structure—the structure that could give wings to the organising principles associated with the French Revolution, and (b) he gave many concrete suggestions / illustrations / pointers as to how some of the operational aspects of such an approach might look—both with regard to how each realm could organise itself overall, as well as with regard to some of the activities that take place within each.

But he stressed: these suggestions and illustrations were just that—suggestions and illustrations.

Perhaps imperfections are contained in what is presented here. Then let them be found. It is not the function of a way of thinking which corresponds to reality to formulate perfect 'programmes' for all time, but to point out the direction for practical work. The intention of the specific examples mentioned here is to better illustrate the indicated direction. A productive goal can still be attained as long as improvements coincide with the direction given. (CW23, p. 106)

Threefolding is not utopian! But discussions sometimes take on a terribly utopian character. It makes no sense discussing how the seamstress or the painter will fit into the threefold social organism. All these things take on a very utopian character [...]

For this reason I have only ever cited such things as an example, and this is the only way I want them to be taken. The main thing is to thoroughly understand threefolding as such. (CW338, 2 January 1921)

In many cases, for example, what I included solely to illustrate the central argument [my emphasis, RM] was taken to be my main point. In order to demonstrate how mankind could achieve social thinking and feeling and a social will, I gave as an example the way the circulation of capital might be transformed so that it would no longer be felt by many people to be oppressive, as frequently happens at present. I had to say one or two things about the price mechanism, the value of labour, and so on. All this solely by way of illustration. Anyone who seeks to influence human life as a whole must surely hearken to it at first, in order to derive from it the human remedies for its aberrations, instead of extolling a few stereotyped formulae and recommending their indiscriminate application. (CW83, p. 164)

And just in case we are in any doubt as to what the 'central argument' is that Steiner is referring to in this last passage, he then, during the course of this particular lecture he is giving in Vienna in June 1922, goes over the three aspects of culture / rights / economy with their respective guiding principles of freedom / equality / fraternity some *six or seven* times before drawing to a conclusion!

I had to condense it into general sentences which in turn are condensed in the term 'Threefolding of the social organism'. But what these words signify, had at least to be explained by some indications. One had to say how one imagines that these things should be handled. That is why I have given some examples how the development of capitalism should proceed, how for instance the labour question could be regulated and so on. There I have tried to give concrete particular indications. Well, I have attended many discussions about these 'Essentials of the social question' and I have always found that people in their utopian opinion of to-day ask: Now how will this or that be then in future? They referred to the indications which I have given about specific things but which I never meant to be anything but examples. (CW79, 30 November 1921)

So, any operational comments Steiner gives are subsidiary to his 'central argument' that the three realms should be hygienically separated out, as already indicated.

Naturally, though, the primacy of this 'central argument' by no means invalidates what he saw as possible outcomes resulting from threefold structuring. Indeed, it would seem apparent that, since at times he provides illustrations in no uncertain terms, he sees these not only as *possible* outcomes, but also desirable. At that point in time, at least. Whilst some of the operational suggestions he gave between 1917 and 1922 might be relevant today, others might not. The passages just quoted make plain that Steiner would have been the first to acknowledge this. Also, whilst many (or most) of these operational suggestions might be subsidiary to the central thesis, it will become evident that one or two of them would appear to be more integral.

Being someone with much to say on a wide range of subjects, Steiner often gave recommendations to organisations and individuals concerning their work which aren't *directly* connected to threefold reform. However, where mention of such recommendations seems warranted within this book on societal health, occasional snippets have been included; but where it doesn't, they haven't. For example, he gave all sorts of advice to farmers—how to improve soil fertility, etc. He also made a rich contribution to the understanding of child pedagogy. The former seems less relevant to social reform and is therefore not included in the book; the latter seems more relevant and therefore is, albeit only very briefly.

So, now to his operational suggestions. These take up roughly half of the book!

7.1   Three central administrations

Threefolding has relevance at different levels: (a) at the more macro level, it proposes that *society overall* organises itself into three relatively independent realms so that each can, as far as possible, observe its respective guiding principle of freedom, equality or fraternity; (b) it has implications for how each of these three realms might best organise itself and operate in order to do justice to its respective guiding principle; and (c) at the more micro level, it can inform how each individual organization—indeed even the individual person—can go about their business in a way that supports societal health.

Regarding the first of these, instead of all public matters largely being managed by one central administration—the state (whose tentacles, Steiner considered much too far-reaching in the Germany / Austria / Switzerland of the day, for example), three independent co-ordinating administrations are recommended.

For the rights realm, a democratically elected state or legislature (with suitable civil service) is the obvious arrangement. But for the other two realms, a democratically elected central administration is not appropriate.

For the economic aspect ...

> *All economic issues are [to be] organized in a specific economic parliament.* [sic] *When the latter is relieved of all political and military concerns, then it will handle its affairs purely in a way that is solely appropriate to them, namely, opportunistically. The civil service administration for these economic issues within whose domain also lies the full administration of tariff laws is directly responsible only to the economic parliament.* [sic] *(CW24(ii), p. 79)*

'Opportunistically' may seem a strange word to use. But what Steiner is pointing to is that, whilst the rights state is more suited to proceeding in that orderly, measured, conservative (with a small 'c'), steady-as-she-goes way mentioned earlier, the economic realm requires a different modus operandi. It needs to be able to respond to ever-changing possibilities and needs as these arise, and thus lives in a world of greater vibrancy.

Regarding the use of the word 'parliament' here, the following clarifies:

> *There will be no parliamentary representation at the top, but there will be a structure of associations, coalitions, cooperatives from the professions, the aggregation of production and consumption, and so on, organizing, managing themselves. And this structure will also drive to a certain peak—I would say drive to a central council. (CW337a, 30 May 1919)*

> *Associations must arise within the various professions and trades out of the mutual interests of producers and consumers, and these are to be represented within a central economic administration ... (CW24, p. 56)*

More on 'associations' will be said in due course. But note how he continues this paragraph:

> ... The same people who participate in this economic system also constitute a legal community that, regarding its administration and representation, works quite independently ...

People don't 'belong' to only one realm!

Thirdly, the cultural aspect, whilst at all times adhering to the watchword of freedom, would have a central administration simply for coordination purposes—where coordination seemed worthwhile.

> The spiritual life should have its own administration. (CW332a, p. 112)
>
> And with regard to all religious and spiritual cultural relationships, to which national culture also belongs, this individual nature dictates administration by cultural organisations to which the individual person commits himself out of free will and which will be administered in the parliament [sic] of cultural organisations as a cultural organization such that the parliament concerns itself with the cultural organisations themselves but never with the relation between this cultural organization and the individual person. [...] Such a cultural organization would be accepted into the parliament [sic] of cultural organisations when it united a specific number of people. Until then it would remain a private affair in which no administrative or representative body could interfere. (CW24(ii), p. 110)
>
> ... the cultural administrative organ of the social organism will preside only over active cultural workers. (CW333, p. 53)
>
> In the democratic administration [i.e. rights realm, RM] a parliament is absolutely in its place, but questions belonging to the departments of spiritual life, including education and teaching, can never be properly decided in such a democratic parliament ... Only those who are actually teachers, engaged in practical education, shall be its administrators ... The individual need only spend so much time in imparting instruction as will leave him leisure to collaborate in the work of education as a whole and the sphere of spiritual and cultural life in general. (CW332a, p. 28)
>
> For instance those who are teachers should also be the administrators of the education system ... All administration in the area of the spiritual realm must come directly from the spiritual realm ... (CW79, 30 November 1921)

Thus, whilst the three realms may be intermingled and serve each other, each is to a certain extent centred in its institutions, and these institutions, in turn, are centred in their respective central administrations. But these central administrations need to assume different forms:

> *I even found one person lecturing on the three parliaments! But that is to imagine an impossibility. Only the state, the rights life can have a parliament. The cultural life must be founded on the free individual, and the economy on a basis of associations. (CW341, p. 226)*

It is important to appreciate that these realms, with their separate and independent administrations, need not coincide geographically. If I live in Merthyr Tydfil, for example, my relevant rights administration might be the UK whilst my cultural administration might cover Wales, and my central economic administration might be a European common market, or whatever.

In summary:

- Instead of the state being responsible for all three realms, there should be three separate administrations.
- For the orderly, steady-as-she-goes rights realm, this would be a democratic parliament.
- For the more responsive economic, there would be a central administration made up of representatives from consumer / producer / trader associations.
- The cultural realm would have its own central administration to coordinate any matters thought deserving of coordination. This would be made up of those actively engaged in the different areas of cultural life.
- Cultural institutions above a certain size could be represented in such an administration. Smaller ones would simply be a private affair.

Reflections in relation to the present

In the UK (as with most countries), a good deal of our economic realm's 'central administration' is seated within the rights realm's central administration. That is, the government concerns itself with much that is economic.[106] True, this state involvement is often in a more regulatory capacity (and thus might fit with the threefold approach since that concerns laws, product safety standards, etc.); but by no means always. We thus have the Treasury; we have economic policy; and so on.

In addition to this central economic administration within government, we have economic umbrella bodies *un*connected to government such as the Business Network or the Confederation for British Industry (CBI). These provide arenas for producers to meet and gain overview. The CBI, for example, provides services like sector analysis, policy liaison, etc. However, they operate very much within a competitive, profit-maximising paradigm, and since, also, they are more there for business than for consumers, they cannot really be thought of as a central administration in a threefold sense. This would require consumer representation of equal weight to that of trade and industry representation, as we shall see in Section 7.4.2.

---

[106] The following are some of the UK government departments that cover economic activity:

- The Department for Environment, Food & Rural Affairs (Defra) which works with 36 Agencies and public bodies including for example the Rural Payments Agency, and the Consumer Council for Water.
- Department for Transport (DfT) which works with 20 Agencies and public bodies including for example the Highways Agency, and the Maritime and Coastguard Agency.
- Business, Innovation and Skills (BIS) which works with 51 Agencies and public bodies including for example the Industrial Development Advisory Board, and the Insolvency Service.
- Department for Energy and Climate Change (DECC) which works with 8 Agencies and public bodies including for example the Coal Authority, and the Fuel Poverty Advisory Group.
- The Chancellor's Departments (CXD) 'HM Treasury' which works with 9 Agencies and public bodies including for example National Savings and Investments, and the Royal Mint.
- The Foreign and Commonwealth Office (FCO) which works with 11 Agencies and public bodies including for example UK Trade and Investment, and the British Council.
- Department for International Development (DfID) which works with 2 Agencies and public bodies.

Concerning the cultural domain: since Steiner emphasises that freedom is crucial within this aspect of society, it might seem paradoxical that he makes mention of a central administration for this realm at all. But there are important social 'institutions' within this realm that would require coordination. These include education (school and higher), the judiciary, science, the allocation of the means of production. Whilst freedom should at all times be the overriding principle within this cultural realm, chaos need *not* be. Institutions are necessary to coordinate different functions: an education bureau to maintain a register of the various schools, universities, training centres around the country (or region) and to ensure there are enough such establishments to meet the various educational needs; a justice bureau to coordinate legal appointments and appropriate regional representation within the courts; a skills bureau to support reallocation of the means of production to suitably qualified people, and so on.

In the UK, it would not be particularly difficult to disestablish our existing cultural administrations (the Department for Education, the Department for Culture, Media and Sport, and certain bodies within the Department for Business, Innovation and Skills), and then house them within a completely independent (from both government and industry) cultural council. Disestablishing oversight of the economy, on the other hand, would involve a sizeable shift in thinking (see Section 9.3—'Economic Policy').

7.2   An upper senate

For any state or region wanting to follow a more threefold approach, Steiner proposes that an upper senate be set up where representatives of the three realms can come together to discuss issues of mutual concern.

A kind of senate—elected from the three bodies that have the task of ordering the political / military, the economic, the judicial / educational affairs—looks after the common interests, including, for example, the joint finances. (CW24(ii), p. 81)

How educational institutions are set up, for example, which in their regulations touch on the two representative bodies not concerned with education as such, would be a matter for the superior-level senate. (CW24(ii), p. 89)

The greatest possible guarantee that one sphere of the threefold organism cannot be violated by another lies in their union, effected by the total corporate body consisting of the delegates of the three central administrations and agencies. For these central administrative committees will have to deal with the actual developments within their own spheres. They would not arrive at a situation where, for instance, the rights sphere or the cultural sphere would be impinged upon by the economic, because this would place them in opposition to the developments taking place in their several spheres. Should, however, the influence of one department over another become necessary, the factual basis for such influence can lie only in the sphere of corporate interest and not in the individual group's interest. (CW24, p. 13)

In this upper senate, questions can be discussed that can't easily be addressed in just one realm. Do we build a nuclear power station? Do we offer a new, very expensive but not very effective cancer drug? Do we build the Channel Tunnel? Do we work to introduce a Green New Deal? Do we go into lockdown on account of Covid-19?

Concerning the latter, for example: (a) epidemiologists and immunologists from the independent cultural realm, from the realm of learning, need to give objective, factual advice uncontaminated by any shareholdings in pharmaceuticals or corporate funding of their agencies / university departments; (b) those with detailed knowledge of the economy need to be present to offer their objective assessment of the economic consequences of lockdown; and (c) those representing the rights domain need to be present, since lockdown involves temporary changes to rights and responsibilities.

Crucially, this upper senate is not peopled by all-powerful delegates who, between them, basically run the whole show. The independence of the three realms permeates this forum, too. For example:

The necessary contact between the responsible persons of the legal and economic bodies will ensue in a manner similar to that at present practised by the governments of sovereign states. (CW23, p. 65)

In summary:

- A senate-type body exists as a forum for discussion of areas of common concern.
- Such a body is made up of members elected from the central administrations of the three realms.
- These members do not form a unitary authority but at all times remain representatives of their respective, independent realms.

7.3   Operational Remarks—Rights Realm

The operational remarks introduced in the following sections of the book, whilst by no means constituting an exhaustive list of the various practical matters that concern each realm, nonetheless cover most of Steiner's observations of relevance, and certainly all those matters he comments on frequently. As such, some more obvious areas of practice are touched on, some less obvious areas are touched on, and many areas are not considered at all.

7.3.1   Funding

> Tax laws will provide this political state with what it needs to maintain itself. (CW23, p. 80)

There is nothing controversial about this, but it is included here for the avoidance of doubt. I once read a piece whose author implied Steiner had said the political realm should be funded by free gifts!

7.3.2   Democratic process

> In modern times the democratic principle has become the sign and seal of human social endeavour, and has grown out of the depths of human nature. The demand of modern humanity for the principle of democracy is an elemental force. [...] this principle ... consists in the fact that the persons forming a definite social organism [e.g. a country, RM] adopt resolutions approved by every individual within the community. These resolutions, of course, can only be binding if

they are adopted by a majority. The content of such majority deci-sions is democratic only if every single individual is on an equal basis with every other single individual. These resolutions can only be adopted on any matter when every single individual is in reality the equal of every other. That is, democratic resolutions can only be passed when every adult is entitled to vote because he is an adult ... (CW332a, p. 62)

Nothing unusual about this either: democratic law-making needs to be based on majority decisions (in the absence of consensus) involving every adult. As noted previously, however, this was by no means a foregone conclusion in Steiner's day. Universal suffrage had only arrived in Germany in the previous year, and in the UK, it arrived nearly a whole decade later—in 1928. Switzerland didn't allow women to vote until 1971!

Further:

... the sphere of rights may be built up democratically through the interaction (direct or representational) of people on equal terms ... (CW24, p. 86)

Steiner is not advocating democratic involvement by the entire populace in every law-making decision, but refers to the representational democracy that we are used to: the electorate chooses representatives (politicians) to research, consider, discuss and take political decisions for us in parliament. The holding of referenda for more far-reaching decisions is, naturally, not precluded.

For the avoidance of doubt, rights / responsibilities that apply to the economic system, say, are still a matter for the rights realm, whose institutions ...

... regulate the rights, inherent in the commodity exchange pro-cess, of those individuals who produce, trade and consume. These rights are essentially no different from other rights of a per-son-to-person nature which exist independently of the commodity exchange process. If I injure or benefit my fellow man through the sale of a commodity, this belongs to the same social category as an injury or benefit through an act or omission not directly related to commodity exchange. (CW23, p. 67)

As an aside, it is interesting to note how a rights state cannot pretend to foresee and legislate for every last eventuality, and how effectively 'precedent' can build case law for adjudicating on transgressions that hover on the fringes of concepts such as 'harm', 'reasonableness', etc. The formation of case law may not be especially democratic, but any attempt to enshrine in a democratically affirmed constitution laws that cover every possible eventuality would perhaps seem both futile and unnecessary.

In Section 8.1 examples are given where the democratic process can be gravely undermined by an absence of threefold separation.

Some specific areas of legislation that Steiner commented on will now be considered.

7.3.3   Labour

> ... regulation of labour belongs to the realm of rights, to the political realm. (CW79, 30 November 1921)

As was mentioned when the rights realm was defined, Steiner emphasised how labour matters are a concern of this realm too and should not be left to the economy, should not be a matter of purchase and sale. Indeed, the following passage illustrates just how key an aspect of the rights realm he considered labour questions to be.

> ... the 'social question' may be conceived of as three particular questions. The first pertains to the healthy form spiritual-cultural life should assume in the social organism, the second deals with the just integration of labour power in the life of the community, and the third concerns the way the economy should function within this community. (CW23, p. 51)

There are several aspects to this 'just integration of labour power' and much of what Steiner says is generally uncontroversial to the reader of today:

> ... the number of hours individuals must work to support themselves will be determined on a purely democratic basis. (CW333, p. 57)

> *[individuals] ... are protected by a self-reliant, independent political state from being forced to exist only for work, and which guarantees the right to a leisure ... (CW23, p. 78)*

It is for the rights state to determine the length of the working week, and some sort of minimum remuneration to protect workers from being worked to the bone for starvation wages. Today's regulations in respect of maximum working hours, and the minimum or living wage attempt to achieve this; although they don't go as far as Steiner advocated, as we shall see.

> *... hours and conditions of labour are matters to be dealt with by the political rights-state. (CW23, p. 21)*

Working *conditions* also need health and safety laws etc. to ensure these conditions are reasonable.

> *Labour must lie quite outside the economic circuit; it belongs to the department of equity ... The manner, duration, and kind of work will be determined by the legal conditions prevailing between man and man. Labour must be lifted out of the economic process. (CW332a, p. 43)*
>
> *Human labour must be recognized as separate and independent from the economy ... If it is transferred to the sphere of rights, where it belongs, true equality among individuals will develop. Real civil rights can develop only when the true character of human labour is acknowledged. The extent, type, and time of work will be determined before workers enter the economic process. (CW333, p. 11)*
>
> *All those things that make every person the equal of every other will be arranged here, on a democratic basis. For instance, all labour regulations (the manner, amount and length of work) will fall within this community's jurisdiction. (CW24, p. 56)*

Obviously, when Steiner refers to 'the manner and kind' of work he does not mean the rights realm should be determining exactly what people within the economic realm should do, how they should go about their work. He is talking about working conditions, protection from hazard, etc. It might mean: not more than so many days per week down a mine (away from sunlight), say, or no night shifts allowable in factories. Whilst Steiner is anxious to 'de-commodify' labour, to remove labour relations from the sale / purchase paradigm in the economic realm and instead relocate these within the legal realm, the task of *organising* labour so that production can meet consumption needs as far as possible is *not* a matter for the rights domain:

> *Laws determine time, extent, and type of work, while what is then to be done within the statutory working time is governed by contract within the economic body. (CW331, 24 June 1919)*

With the necessary worker protections in place, the rights realm provides the economic realm with limits that it must work within:

> *Work should be subject to regulation by the rights realm ... The amount and type of work should be something determined within democratic life, within the constitutional state. Work then becomes, like nature, the basis of economic life, and what is produced will not be used as a yardstick for remuneration. (CW332a(ii), p. 73)*
>
> *... while economic life is on the one hand dependent on natural foundations as we saw [e.g. soil fertility, rainfall, geology], on the other it is also dependent on decisions made in the rights sphere—about working hours, for instance, and the relationship between labour and the individual in matters such as his strength, his frailty, his age. There cannot be such a thing as a fixed length of the working day but in reality only an upper and lower limit. (CW189, p. 84)*
>
> *... something will come about which will be of the utmost importance: The economic life will be placed on a healthy basis by having nature with its conditions on the one side and, on the other side, man with his conditions. (CW79)*
>
> *This will be the great economic law of the future, that economic life is confined between two limits ... (CW329, 19 March 1919)*

As Kate Raworth conveys so effectively in *Doughnut Economics*, there are both sociological and natural constraints to economic activity.[107] What the economic realm can get out of the people is subject to limits, just as what it can get out of the natural world is also subject to limits.

As a result, remuneration determines the price of a good; the price of the good does not determine remuneration:

> *As the value [price] of a commodity increases in relation to another commodity due to the acquisition of the raw materials necessary for its production becoming more difficult, so must its value [price] be dependent on the kind and amount of labour which may be expended for its production in accordance with rights legislation. Such a relationship of labour to rights legislation will compel the economic associations to accept what is 'just' as a precondition. Thereby a condition will be attained in which the economic organisation is dependent on people, and not vice-versa ...*
>
> *It is evident that by managing the social organism in this way, economic prosperity will increase and decrease according to the amount of labour rights-awareness decides to expend. In a healthy social organism it is necessary that economic prosperity be dependent in this way, for only such dependence can prevent man from being so consumed by economic life that he can no longer consider his existence worthy of human dignity. And, in truth, all the turmoil in the social organism results from the feeling that existence is unworthy of human dignity.*
>
> *... if prosperity declines excessively the type and amount of labour can be modified. This modification should not emanate directly from economic circles but from the insight which can develop in a rights organisation which is independent of economic life. (CW23, pp. 73-74)*

---

[107] Kate Raworth, *Doughnut Economics: Seven Ways to Think Like a 21ˢᵗ-Century Economist* (London: Random House, 2018).

The 'economic organisation is dependent on people, and not vice-versa'!

> Today it is stressed on many sides, and rightly so, that the salvation of the world economy has to come from a heightened will to work, a will that has been diminished by the war. Anyone who understands human nature knows that this commitment to work can only come when people are convinced that in the future their work will be done under social conditions that guarantee them a dignified human existence. (CW24, p. 23)
>
> ... when the direction of economic life is continually influenced by the law, in its application to human beings as such, then an existence worthy of humanity will be introduced into economic life. (CW23, p. 111)

It is the community at large that should decide, via democracy, the maximum amount people should have to work in order to meet their needs. It is a rights issue. Workers should have a right to a safe and dignified existence, and not be exploited and worked to the bone by anyone milking unfair advantage or power they may enjoy on account, say, of ownership of the means of production.

Of course, Steiner is speaking in a time when these things are less obvious than today, when the eight-hour day is only a very recent innovation in certain parts of Europe, and when all manner of industrial disquiet prevails. Workers' rights are minimal. Paternity leave? Forget it!

Today, by contrast, few people have a problem with worker protections being enshrined in law. There are always exceptions, of course: one person's employment protections can be another person's inflexibility in the labour market (impediment to hire and fire).

> Once the legal, political sphere is able to function properly, people will notice that it will involve itself with questions of labour. Today labour is entirely enmeshed in the economic life and is not treated as something to do with how people relate to one another. (CW305(ii), p. 159)

By a political sphere that can 'function properly' Steiner presumably means a political sphere that not only functions in a democratic manner (instead of in a manner dominated by aristocratic and / or industrial interests), but also a political sphere that deals solely with rights and does not interfere with cultural tasks or try to run industrial concerns.

What is notable about this last quote, however, is that it was made in 1922 when the state had already been occupying itself with various labour laws for some years. Certainly, there was no Working Time Directive as yet.[108] And yes, back in 1900, some 1.7 million children under 16 had been in employment in the USA. And yes, in 1919, 75,000 'Red Clydesiders' came out on strike to demand a 40-hour week—action that took government tanks and one hundred lorry-loads of troops to quash. But when the German monarchy fell in 1918, for example, the new Weimar Republic brought in a number of labour reforms that related to maximum allowable working hours per day, notice and appeal rules for dismissal, and so forth.[109] Employees might not have enjoyed the rights we nowadays take for granted in the 'developed' world, but the days of a worker facing the prospect of the workhouse unless they worked 10 hours a day, six days a week for little reward were all but over.

Indeed, even back in the 1880s, Bismarck's welfare state had provided 'reforms which went far beyond anything known at that time in other countries. They included compulsory insurance for old-age, sickness, accidents and incapacity, and they were operated by the state, but financed by employees and employers. Such reforms had the effect of dampening the workers' enthusiasm for extreme socialism but, at the same time, increased their faith in the state as protector.'[110]

So, Steiner's recommendations that the state should occupy itself with the protection of labour were nothing new. However, he had rather more in mind:

> *You can tell that this is not an outdated idea by the way labour is everywhere protected and safeguarded by laws. But these regulations are not even half-measures, they are quarter-measures. No regulations will be properly effective until there is a proper three-folding of the social organism. Only when this has happened will*

---

[108] An EU provision.
[109] See Wikipedia: Weimar Republic.
[110] Translator's note by Frank Thomas Smith in CW23, p. 148.

> *human beings meet each other as equals. Only then will labour be*
> *rightly regulated when human worth meets human worth in that*
> *sphere where all are competent to speak. (CW305(ii), p. 160)*

Clearly, he envisaged workplace arrangements and protections going significantly further than they had; and, indeed, some of his recommendations are highly unconventional even by today's standards. In addition to reasonable working hours for co-workers, and other workplace protections, he is also keen, for example, for the usual power dynamics inherent in the wage system to be replaced by something more equitable.

> *In the modern capitalist economy, the utilisation of people's indi-*
> *vidual faculties is connected with taking possession of the means*
> *of production, and is thereby connected with the acquisition of a*
> *certain economic power, an economic superiority. But that which*
> *can express itself in power, in this superiority of one person over*
> *another, that is nothing else than what constitutes a legal relation-*
> *ship ... (CW329, 11 March 1919)*

If someone's capacities are such that they make a good CEO, they gain two types of power when filling this position: control over production processes (which is a good thing for the common good as it will mean good efficiency, good productivity, etc.), but also control over how the enterprise's proceeds are shared out. For Steiner, this latter is a question of rights, as we shall see in the next section.

In summary:

- The rights realm, the democratic state, determines workplace safeguards and working time limits to ensure each has leisure time to pursue other interests and live a life worthy of human dignity.
- The rights realm reduces unhealthy power dynamics in the workplace.

Reflections in relation to the present

Concerning workplace safeguards: In somewhere like the UK today, we have employment protections stipulating maximum hours per day, maximum hours per week, breaks, grievance and disciplinary procedures, anti-discrimination, paid holidays, maternity/paternity leave, sick pay, and a minimum wage which is supposed to ensure anyone working full-time can get by without reliance on state benefits. (In recognition of the fact that this has often not been the case, the non-mandatory 'living wage' concept is now spreading which, when used, should ensure the state / taxpayer is not in effect subsidising low-paying employers.) In 2019, German Chancellor Angela Merkel approved draft legislation to ensure apprentices in Germany would also be entitled to a minimum wage.

Our employment laws could no doubt go further. For example, night work could be prohibited except for essential services like hospital work. In some places we have people doing night work at present only because it improves the return on investment for shareholders, because it maximises the annual yield from capital investment / the means of production. It may be necessary for midwives to work nights, but not those on an assembly line.

In the UK, workers are considerably better protected than in some other developed countries. In 2015, Bernie Sanders observed of the USA: 'We've got to do what every other major country on earth does and have a medical and family leave programme. We have got to have sick leave for workers. We have got to do what every other industrialized nation does and that is guarantee at least 10 days of paid vacation.'[111] And economist Joseph Stiglitz recently highlighted the plight of 'those for whom the breakdown of a car or an illness starts a downward spiral from which they never recover'.[112] In 2020, over 30 million US workers did not benefit from sick leave![113] In the richest country in the world!

Those in many less developed countries, however, continue to have woeful worker protections, and we in the West continue to take advantage of these beleaguered workforces so that we can have those cheap trousers and laptops.

---

[111] Jim Tankersley, 'Bernie Sanders on America's "grotesquely unfair" society', *The Washington Post*, 16 July 2016.

[112] Joseph Stiglitz, 'The American Economy is Rigged', *Scientific American*, November 2018.

[113] Judy Stone, 'Why the US Urgently Needs Paid Leave', *Forbes*, 10 March 2020.

If the mechanisation of work, thanks to robotics and the like, continues at its current pace, then a point may come when only half, say, of the workforce need in fact work for everyone's needs and wants to be met. Under these circumstances one can imagine that the political process (i.e. the rights realm) might cap the working week at two or three days (pegging the minimum wage accordingly) in order to spread the work / leisure balance more evenly for all concerned. This would prevent much unemployment and thereby maintain many people's self-esteem / feeling of self-worth. This, in turn, would prevent additional mental health problems, crime, and other issues that seem so ubiquitous today. (Personally, I am not as optimistic as some that our need to work is going to all but vanish in the next decade or two. Just look at the worker shortages in our NHS for a start, or at the condition of the roads and some other public spaces! Besides, there is a long history of such predictions.)

7.3.4   Remuneration—Part 1

> *The correct relation between contractor or employer and the worker cannot be brought about in the sphere of economic processes, but only in the sphere of the political State as a relation of rights. (CW189, 2 March 1919)*

Steiner was insistent that labour should never be regarded as something to be bought and sold as though it were a commodity. It should never be paid for with a wage. Indeed, in the final analysis, he regards this as simply a falsehood. He contends purchase and sale belong exclusively to commodities that we consume, to goods and services, i.e. to the economic realm; but never to labour per se. Labour is different. For many of us, with our ingrained thought habits, this can seem offbeat.

> *Money and labour are not inter-changeable values as are money and the products of labour. Therefore, if I give money for labour I do something false. I create a deception. In reality, I can only give money for the products of labour. (CW23, p. 72)*
>
> *... labour cannot be priced like a commodity. Labour is something completely different, and it needs to be extricated from the economic process. (CW333, p. 11)*

There are various aspects to this.

Firstly, as alluded to in Section 5.3.1, there is the obvious fact that labour, per se, has no value—in the sense that a person could dig holes and fill them up again, all day long, without creating value.

> ... in fact labour is nowhere paid for; only the products of labour are paid for ... (CW340, p. 104)

Even with services, we are not paying for labour; we are paying for the haircut, the audit, or the train journey. And in a factory where a worker is adding a few screws to a circuit board, he or she is really paid for that service—the addition of the screws, not for their labour. Commodities belong to Steiner's definition of the economy, with its purchase and sale, but labour does not. And so it should not be bought with a wage.

Secondly, you may remember from Steiner's comments made back in 1905, long before expounding his threefold approach, that he saw the separation of work and income as a highly desirable step towards a more healthy society. He considered a particular wage for a particular type of work to be unhealthy. He considered wages as something that brought a working-for a-living, working-for-oneself mentality and were thus unhealthily egoistic. A worker who is paid a wage may go to work harbouring resentment when they know just how much profit the firm is making out of their efforts. As such they are less likely to be conscientious in their work, less likely to go to work with any feeling of service to others. The mindset will be one of: I am doing this because I have to feed myself. On the other hand, if one's work and one's income were somehow separated, one's work would then be more motivated by a social mindset, by the meeting of human needs. The suggestions he made at the time to this end were made to a small audience, probably made up largely of theosophists. As you may remember, he suggested people experiment with combining into groupings where everyone's private incomes would be thrown into a common pool and then redistributed more according to the relative needs of those in the group. But he does not, as far as I am aware, suggest this once he has introduced threefolding; his solution has evolved. However, he does again refer to the problem of 'working for oneself':

Every wage earner in the ordinary sense is a man who provides for himself ... In effect, to provide for oneself is to work for one's earnings, to work 'for a living'. To work for others is to work out of a sense of social needs.

The thing which the ordinary wage earner manufactures has after all nothing to do with the payment for his work. [...]

Thus, one of the first and most essential economic questions comes before us. How are we to eliminate from the economic process this principle of working for a living? Those who to this day are still mere wage earners—earners of a living for themselves—how are they to be placed in the whole economic process, no longer as such earners but as men who work because of social needs? Must this really be done ? Assuredly it must. (CW340, p. 44)

Everything that a person acquires in such a way that it is received in exchange for his work within the social system has an unwholesome effect. A wholesome condition results within the social system only when the human being has to support his life, not by his own work, but from other sources within society ...

The goal towards which we must work—of course, in a rational and not Bolshevistic way—must be that of separating work from the provisions of the means of existence. (CW186, pp. 59-60)

Thus, Steiner takes a dim view of any employer / employee relationship in the economic realm where the contract of employment stipulates a wage.

Again, these comments about income being separated from our work can make one wonder whether Steiner was driving at some sort of Universal Basic Income idea. However, he does not go on to suggest this. (Universal Basic Income is considered in Section 9.5.) As he elaborates his threefold approach, the rather radical idea suggested in 1905 (income communities), no doubt not without its challenges, and seemingly not something he thought of as a solution for widespread take-up, makes way, as we shall see, for an approach that is likely to have considerably broader appeal.

In addition to (a) work not being a commodity in the first place, and (b) working for oneself—for a living—being regarded as unhealthy, a third issue with wages is (c) that the wage system enables the employer to take advantage of the employee. Steiner makes mention of this frequently.

For example:

> The modern proletarian abhors instinctively, unconsciously the fact that he must sell his labour power to his employer in the same way that commodities are sold in the marketplace, and that the law of supply and demand plays its role in determining the value of his labour power just as it does in determining the value of commodities. This abhorrence of the commodity nature of labour power has a profound meaning in the social movement. (CW23, p. 48)

> ... this disgust grows because his labour is dependent on supply and demand. (CW328(v), 3 February 1919)

> When no-one is any longer recompensed for his work, then money will lose its value as a means for acquiring power over work. There is no other means for overcoming the misuse that has been perpetuated with mere money than by forming the social structure in such a way that no one be recompensed for his work, and that the provision of the means of existence shall be achieved from an entirely different source. It will then naturally be impossible to use money for the purpose of compelling anyone to work ... Money must never in future be the equivalent for human labour, but only for inanimate commodities. (CW186, pp. 59-60)

> A legal relationship between worker and entrepreneur is necessary for the production of the commodity. Capitalism, however, is capable of converting this relationship into one which is determined by the economic supremacy of the employer over the worker. (CW23, p. 72)

> To give our money to our fellow men [for work, RM] only signifies that we are able to hold our fellow men on a leash as bound slaves and that we can compel them to labour for us. (CW186, p. 56)

Steiner asserts that these unwelcome power dynamics are to be solved by seeing labour relationships not as purchase / sale relationships but as ones existing in the rights realm.

> Entering into a wage relationship means selling one's labour, and the selling of labour belongs to older times. It is a remnant of serfdom. (CW333, p. 10)

> In antiquity there were slaves. The whole man was sold like a commodity. Somewhat less of him, but a substantial part of the human

being nonetheless, was incorporated into the economic process by serfdom. Capitalism is the force which persists in giving a commodity nature to a portion of the human being: his labour power. (CW23, p. 49)

Even as the slave has ceased to be merchandise, so human labour will cease to be merchandise. But this will not be brought about by laws forbidding that human labour should be merchandise, but by keeping asunder the spiritual, the economic and the state concerns. This alone will separate goods representing an economic value, or merchandise as such, from that which has now become crystallised within the merchandise, the human labour employed in it. [...] it is essential to separate human labour from true goods, to separate it not only in thoughts, but in the real process. (CW188(v), 26 January 1919)

... that which can express itself in a violence, which can express itself in the superiority of one man over the other, is nothing other than what constitutes a legal relationship ... (CW329, 19 March 1919)

Again, Steiner was by no means the first to be concerned about the commodity nature of labour. Some seventy years earlier, Marx and Engels had observed: 'These labourers, who must sell themselves piecemeal, are a commodity, like every other article of commerce, and are constantly exposed to all the vicissitudes of competition, to all the fluctuations of the market.'[114]

It is generally accepted that an entrepreneur, on account of the good fortune he or she has had in life (by being born with particular faculties, say, or by having been nurtured by caring parents, or from having received a particularly good education, or by having favourable access to capital) can then take advantage of the natural power dynamics that may arise between him/herself and workers. That they lead their workers *workwise*, on account of greater knowledge and experience, is one thing. Efficient production relies on those 'in the know' managing the enterprise; having entrepreneurial good fortune quite naturally leads to the management of others in questions of production.

---

[114] Karl Marx & Friedrich Engels, *The Communist Manifesto,* 1848.

But Steiner (amongst many others) finds these power dynamics problematic when they are taken advantage of by management to enrich themselves at the expense of the workforce, consigning the latter, perhaps, even to significant poverty. For Steiner, co-workers at *all* levels should have a right to a reasonable and dignified existence, and he proposes an approach to remuneration which circumvents this abuse of natural power dynamics. Just as it is a matter for the rights realm to ensure people have a right to freedom from attack in the street, so should it also be a matter for the rights realm to ensure freedom from exploitation. When two or more people work together, the rules that govern the relationship between them need to protect weaker parties from exploitation by stronger parties.

Critics of the usual, competitive wage system are no doubt numerous, but two authors who were also Steiner enthusiasts touched on the problem as follows. Firstly, Owen Barfield[115]: 'What kind of contract shall we judges declare to be illegal ... ? A contract by which a workman binds himself to ruin his health and moral welfare in order to gain a livelihood? Oh, no, that's all right—but we will not allow a contract *in restraint of trade*. Trade must be free whatever else is in chains'.[116] And secondly, Charles Waterman: 'There can be nothing approaching equality of opportunity until the right of everyone to a basic minimum living standard, sufficient for health and vigour, is made a first charge on the community's resources. Or while persons are liable to have their health impaired by working conditions that are thrust upon them. Or while glaring discrepancies exist between the medical care available to rich and poor. Or while educational opportunities are largely determined by parental means.'[117]

And Steiner:

> ... *No matter how favourably we view labour contracts, so long as they establish wage relationships, workers will not be satisfied. A humanly worthy existence for all will result only when contractual*

---

[115] Who, with J.R.R. Tolkien, C.S. Lewis and others, formed *The Inklings*—a literary discussion group based at Oxford University.

[116] Owen Barfield, *Law, Association and the Trade Union Movement* (London: The Threefold Commonwealth Research Group, 1937), p. 12.

[117] Charles Waterman, *The Three Spheres of Society* (London: Faber and Faber, 1946), p. 20.

> *agreements govern the joint output of supervisors and workers but not labour itself. Then the worker-supervisor relationship will be one of voluntary partnership. (CW333, p. 11)*

The penultimate word 'voluntary' in this passage is perhaps not the best translation. The original German (*'Dann wird der Arbeiter dem Arbeitsleiter gegenüberstehen als der freie Gesellschafter.'*) more literally translates as: Then the worker will stand opposite the manager as a free partner. The worker is free in the sense that he or she is no longer being held on a leash by the manager, as expressed in the employer / employee wage relationship—where the employer has total control over the end product and the income it generates. As 'free partners', workers are no longer working *for* the manager; rather it is a collaboration (albeit one where the manager, of necessity, may well direct the job of work).

Thus, just as the slave / slave owner relationship ceased, and just as the serf / lord of the manor relationship ceased, so too does the employer / employee relationship now cease where, typically, employers who are 'close to the money' exercise one-sided remunerational power over workers, typically squeezing as much as possible out of them for as little pay as possible, and in so doing, increasing their own or their shareholders' income. If the wage system stops, labour ceases to be bought and sold, in the market, like a commodity. The disfranchised become freed from bondage to the privileged.

> *The legal relationship between management and labour will not express itself in monetary values which, after the abolition of wages [...] will only measure commodity (and service) values. [...] Through these arrangements, what is currently referred to as class struggle can be eliminated. This struggle results from wages being an integral part of the economic process. (CW23, p. 122)*
>
> *... the concept of the work giver must actually disappear through socialisation. For someone can only be a work giver if he is a work owner, and a work owner there simply may not be. There can only be a* work leader, *which means people who are active in the organization of the work, so that the manual worker knows how to apply his work power in the best way and so forth. Of course the work*

in an enterprise cannot run on in such a way that everyone simply does what he pleases. Leadership must be there, the whole company must be penetrated with spirit / intellect, but these are no work givers, they are work leaders, which means workers of another kind. The greatest value is to be placed now on grasping at last the actual concept of work. For in reality a work giver who does not himself collaborate does not belong at all to the enterprise, but is a parasite on the work. (CW331, 22 March 1919)

With no work-giver, then all workers—both white collar and blue—are co-workers working in partnership on the common project, and absent (parasitic) owners no longer feature in the picture.

But if Steiner takes such a dim view of wages and 'work givers', what does he suggest as an alternative? How would a worker make a living, if not by a wage?

Given he emphasised that one fundamentally does not buy labour, only the products of labour, one might then expect him to advocate piece rate remuneration, that is, payment per unit of output. But no:

It would be superficial to think that the realisation of the ideas presented here would result in time-wages being converted into piece-wages. A one-sided view could lead to this opinion. However, what is advocated here is not piece wages, but the abolishment of the wage system in favour of a contractual sharing system in respect of the common achievements of management and labour [...] A contractual sharing system—in no sense a wage system—expresses the value of what has been produced in a way which changes the workers' social position in relation to the other members of society. This position is completely different from the one which arose through one-sided, economically conditioned class supremacy. The need for the elimination of the class struggle is therewith satisfied. (CW23, p. 123)

Piece rate—paying a worker so much per widget—comes with its own problems in any case: (a) management can still be tempted to make the rate as low as possible in order to increase profits and their own remuneration; (b) it can tempt the worker to rush and thereby reduce quality of workmanship; (c) it still comes with the us-and-them feel (i.e. workers and management) which a *sharing* system can alleviate; (d) the worker will still feel entitled to payment for goods that are not selling, whereas if they *share* in the company proceeds, then they will fully appreciate the logic of remuneration only being possible thanks to customers buying their product.

Thus, the remuneration arrangement advocated by Steiner involves a *sharing* of company proceeds.

> Then the wage relationship can stop, then the capital relationship can stop, and all that is needed is the contractual relationship between spiritual and physical work establishing a just distribution amongst those who produce the goods. (CW331, 24 June 1919)
>
> Within the framework of the political state he [the worker] will acquire the rights which insure him his share of the commodities he produces ... (CW23, p. 79)

Wages (both time-based and piece-based) are ideally replaced with a sharing of the proceeds of the economic undertaking by all those involved—by both workers and management. This would be enshrined in contract between co-workers. Steiner suggests that such a sharing approach would ideally be a matter of right. Also, in the first of these two passages, he talks of a 'just distribution'. The following also emphasises this:

> With regard to economic life, if there are real rights, worker and manager can only be partners who distribute the proceeds of their service in a just manner among themselves. In the future, there must be no payment of labour, that is, the wage relationship must go ... A condition must be brought about—and this will then amount to a social state of affairs—in which manager and worker produce collectively, and what they produce together, as free partners, is justly shared between them in accordance with a goods contract, not an employment contract. (CW331, 22 May 1919)

So, we have sharing 'in a just manner', company proceeds being 'justly shared', and 'just distribution'. But what is meant by this? That all should have an equal share? As the leitmotif of the rights domain is equality, then one could be tempted to jump to this conclusion. But the following, for example, shows things are not quite so straightforward:

> *The right relation will come about only when the decision is not concerned about payment [wage] but about the way in which employer and employed share in the results produced. (CW189(iii), 2 March 1919)*

It is not simply a case of dividing company proceeds equally between all co-workers. A decision must be made about 'the way in which employer and employed share in the results produced'. And in what ways might results be shared? Steiner provides the following by way of example:

> *... the working head of a family will have a higher income than a single person. (CW23, p. 115)*

> *For example, the father of a family will stand quite differently within the social organism than a single person because, if the rights state really does develop as I propose, then every child will have the right to education, then the situation will not be that the father of the family has to distribute his meagre earnings over a large family, whilst a single person can consume everything for himself. The situation will be completely different. The right to necessities is a given. (CW331, 22 May 1919)*

Thus Steiner's recommendation that work and income be separated is achieved in two ways. Firstly, if I am not an employee being paid for my work by an employer, the wage relationship ceases. My income does not come directly from my work per se but from the sale of the commodities I produce. The distinction is perhaps a subtle one, but nonetheless real. Secondly, a further level of separation is achieved by the worker with children, say, taking home more than the one without. They might be doing identical work, but have different incomes. The direct relation between work and income is thus severed. Income is pegged more to their respective economic needs.

With (a) income being determined more by *economic* needs, and since (b) Steiner suggests the proceeds generated by colleagues ought to be ...

> *... justly shared between them in accordance with a* goods contract *[my emphasis, RM] ... (CW331, 22 May 1919)*

... and since (c) he also opines:

> *The blue collar worker can associate freely with the manager of a business, because only the division, on economic principles, of that which they have earned together will be allowed ... [my emphasis, RM] (CW24, p. 10)*

... the remaining considerations relating to remuneration will be found under the operational suggestions for the *economic* domain in Section 7.4.14 ('Remuneration—Part 2').

But the topic has been introduced here—under the operational suggestions for the *rights* realm—since Steiner proposes the sharing *approach* be something workers are entitled to by right. The manager / worker relationship is not a purchase / sale relationship in the economic domain; it is a rights relationship. And within this rights relationship, the right to a sharing-of-proceeds approach would ideally prevail. But the factors determining just *how* to share the proceeds relate, at least in part, to economic needs.

In summary:

- Labour is not itself a commodity and should not be bought with a wage. Personal income comes from *what* one produces, not from one's labour. With personal income being received for *goods and services*, not work, work and income become somewhat separated.
- Workers and management are collaborators / co-operators / partners, not employees / employers.
- Personal income to come from sharing the proceeds of an enterprise among all co-workers.
- Those with more dependants or other additional needs receive more income than those with fewer, for example. Work and income thus become separated further.

'Imagine if labour ceased to be the expendable outsider and became, instead, the ultimate insider, rooted in employee-owned firms ... No need only to imagine, of course: such enterprises are growing fast.'[118]

Reflections on where Steiner's remuneration ideas relate to current practice are also offered in Section 7.4.14 ('Remuneration—Part 2').

7.3.5   Social security

Just as children have the right to an education, the elderly, infirm and widows have the right to a decent maintenance. (CW23, p. 116)

Today, the upholding of such rights by the rights realm is reasonably well established. What might constitute a 'decent' maintenance will depend on the general level of prosperity, of course:

The standard for this will simply be the lives of other people. Since with our economic fundamental principle[119] we have a yardstick for a person's standard of living that accords with total current prosperity, at the same time there is also the possibility of creating a standard for the lives of those who really cannot work. (CW337a, 30 May 1919)

The following also makes clear that Steiner feels society should organise itself in such a way that it 'takes all with it' instead of leaving the needy at the mercy of individual acts of charity:

Charity has appeared on the scene, wonderful, heart-warming human compassion. Now that the social question has become a burning question all over the world we see collecting tins for the East appearing everywhere in Western Europe. It is wonderful that

---

[118] Kate Raworth, *Doughnut Economics: Seven Ways to Think Like a 21st-Century Economist* (London: Random House, 2018), p. 190.

[119] *'Urzelle'*—the principle that producers receive enough for a commodity to cover all their needs until they produce another such commodity. This is covered in section 7.4.11.

people collect and I do not wish to decry it in the least. In fact the more we are in a position to contribute to these collections the more we ought to do so. Nevertheless, what happens in consequence of these collections belongs to the past and not the future. All this compassion and charity arises out of a kind of thinking appropriate for the Middle Ages. (CW305(ii), p. 141)

In summary:

- The 'elderly, infirm and widows' have the right to a decent maintenance.

Reflections in relation to the present

Steiner's attitude to social security would appear similar to what we have today in somewhere like the UK. Welfare benefits, although never generous, provide a safety net to prevent anyone falling into destitution. They not only cover the elderly and infirm but also those who are unable to find work. To what extent they can be considered 'a decent maintenance' is a question.

The reference to widows is rather dated, of course. As we know, gender equality in the workplace, whilst perhaps not yet perfect, has greatly improved in recent years. Personal tax regimes are no longer different for men and women.

Being one of the richest nations in the world, the UK is also able to be one of the most generous when it comes to percentage of GNP donated to charity. This is a wonderful thing. However, some would say that, since we have a pretty shameful past of going round the world helping ourselves to various raw materials etc, perhaps it is only fitting that we send something back to those whose territories we might have once plundered. Some would argue that what happened a century or two ago has little relevance today to those living in either kind of country—the plunderer or the plundered. Others would argue that, had the plundering not happened, we in the West might not be quite as comfortable, and the plundered nations would be more developed.

Charity aside, it is worth remembering that we also frequently buy commodities from parts of the world that have no social security / safety net, parts of the world where absence of work can mean extreme hunger unless the person concerned can rely on extended family or charity. As a result, people in such regions will often work for pennies; and as a consequence we expect to pay very little for the provisions in question. With the laws of supply and demand, we play one supplier off against another and exploitation continues onward.

7.3.6 Taxation

Although tax concerns money (which represents commodities and so is directly connected to the economic system), it is included under the operational suggestions for the rights realm since it concerns legislation that all of us must decide on and be subject to.

One or two of the things Steiner says about tax can be challenging!

Four broad aspects of taxation to consider are: (a) who decides on tax legislation? (b) who administers the collection and application of tax? (c) who / what activities are suitable recipients of the tax collected? (d) what types of tax are thought appropriate, i.e. who pays and in what proportion?

Concerning (a)—the formation of tax law—it can be assumed that, since this is about law making, it is the rights realm that should be responsible for this. However, given that economic matters are separated off from the state in a threefold structure, then those working in the rights realm may not, on their own, have sufficient economic overview to draft meaningful tax proposals. In view of this, they would in all likelihood propose (to the voting public) tax regimes in close, upper-senate consultation with the central administration of the economic realm, since the latter would have the overview of the complexity of the multitudinous values circulating in the economy. This is confirmed by:

The tax position is a question to be regulated between the economic life and that of rights. (CW189(iii), 2 March 1919)

... contributions necessary for the upkeep of rights institutions will be arranged through agreement between the leaders of the rights sector [sic] and economic sector [sic]. (CW23, p. 114)

But the final decision falls to the rights domain. For example:

> *The essential point ... is that the income of the non-earners is not determined by the economic sector* [sic]. *(CW23, p. 116)*

With a rights realm that is legitimated democratically by the electorate then, naturally, it is ultimately voters who have the final say on tax law. On one occasion, when emphasising that the independence of the three societal realms was more important than any operational suggestions he offered, Steiner had the following to say:

> *... consider the taxation system. At present it is not a matter at all of conceiving the best possible taxation system but instead of working towards threefolding. And as this is increasingly realised, the best tax system will naturally develop via the action of this threefold social organism. We have to create the conditions under which the best social institutions can emerge. It is no good for someone to sit down and think up the best system for this will have no value in reality. Even if you were the greatest genius ... and could conceptually elaborate the best taxation system possible, it will serve no purpose if others reject it. Maybe what they want is wrong, but they do not want what you propose. That is the important thing. So it isn't a matter of conceiving the best system but of discovering what can form the soundest basis on which all humanity will do the best it can. (CW189, p. 19)*

This comment underscores the sovereignty of the electorate in matters of legislation generally, and tax specifically.

However, concerning import tariffs (admittedly different from basic taxes) Steiner opines:

> *... The civil service administration for these economic issues, within whose domain also lies the full administration of tariff laws, is directly responsible only to the economic parliament.*[120] *(CW24(ii), p. 80)*

---

[120] At a later date, Steiner confirms the word 'parliament' is not the best as it might be taken to mean a body elected by the whole population, whereas what he is talking about is a central administration peopled by representatives from economic associations.

> *Within a unified world economy, free trade offers the best way of guaranteeing that production in separate parts of the world is neither too expensive nor too cheap. A social body with independent economic management that is not surrounded by threefold organisms [countries, RM] will, of course, be forced to protect certain branches of production from economically unfeasible price reduction by raising tariffs. The management of these tariffs will then be entrusted to associations for the public's benefit. (CW24, p. 22)*

Whether the 'full administration of tariff laws' also includes the *setting* of them is not explicit in these comments, but it can probably be safely assumed that the economic realm would be very closely involved in such measures, if not entirely responsible for them.

Concerning (b)—the administration, the mechanics of tax collection, this would presumably also be the responsibility of the rights realm, a department of the Civil Service, given the universality of tax law, given the fact that all are *equally* subject to the same tax laws. But again, one imagines this might be in close co-operation with the economic domain given that, ultimately, taxation and spending concerns the redistribution of goods and services, i.e. economic values. Where, exactly, the formalities of tax collection / application fall is perhaps of no great consequence.

Concerning (c)—what tax is used for, we have already seen:

> *Tax laws will provide this political state with what it needs to maintain itself. (CW23, p. 80)*

Servants of the state also have to live, and their remuneration is achieved via taxation.

Of course, since (i) the rights and obligations of taxation are a matter for the rights realm, the legislature, and since (ii) the guiding principle of this realm is equality as expressed in democracy, then the question of what are appropriate *applications* of tax is also ultimately a matter for the people (albeit a matter that is likely to be strongly informed by information and representations produced by the economic realm).

Some examples of public spending are considered later under 'Economic Policy' (Section 9.3). But in relation to health, welfare and also education, we have:

> *Of course everything that relates to support for invalidity, sickness, etc. has to be factored in, too; everything that relates to the raising / education of children etc. (CW332a(ii), p. 75)*

Interesting, however, is that Steiner mentions these things when he is talking about commodity price, i.e. when he is talking about the economic realm. His concept of 'fair price' (Section 7.4.11) is a commodity price such that (a) all of a producer's needs are covered until he / she has again produced a like item, plus (b) an additional element is included to cover society's welfare needs.

But if an additional surcharge is to be incorporated into commodity prices in order to cover public spending, how are such surcharges to be structured and gathered up so that they can be thus applied? This question leads on to ...

(c)—*from whom* should tax be collected—did Steiner see merit in any particular *types* of tax?

Again, the broad principle of democracy applies. The obligation to pay taxes would be enshrined in laws arising out of the democratic, political process in which all adults have a say, as is current practice (more or less). But notwithstanding this primacy of the democratic process, Steiner did express views about different types of tax.

The following comments *could* be read as though he supports the idea of income tax. But that would be a misinterpretation. He is simply making the general point that those who work need to produce enough also to provide for those who don't work.

> *The necessary capital [to cover welfare spending] must be provided for in the same way that it is for the education of those who are not yet productive. [...] Those who work in an economic organism will receive that much less from the results of their work as more flows to the non-earners. However, this 'less' will be borne equally by all participants in the social organism if the social impulse described here is realized. The education and support of those who are incapable of working is something which concerns all humanity ... (CW23, p. 116)*

The more that flows to the non-earners, the less will be the income of the earners. Logical enough! But Steiner does not recommend income tax as a mechanism for this. What he *does* say about income tax is a good example of him making an observation that needs to be seen in the context of much else he has said; it is not to be taken as a recommendation that could meaningfully be adopted without other things evolving first.

During a lecture he gives in Zurich, for example, he spends about ten minutes talking about income tax and notes that, ultimately, it would make sense if this were replaced by a purchase tax. This ties in with what he has said about commodity prices needing to include an element to cover welfare spending and the like (last quote but one).

Among all those who today profess to be experts in practical life, there is not a single individual who doubts that an improvement has been made by the transition from all kinds of indirect taxation and other sources of national income to what we call the income tax, especially the graduated income tax. Everyone thinks it is unquestionably right to pay income tax and yet, however paradoxical this may sound to the modern mind, the belief that the imposition of a tax on income is a just measure, is only an illusion resulting from the modern financial system of economy. We earn money; we trade with it. By money we detach ourselves from the sound productive process itself. Money is made into an abstraction, so to speak, in the economic process [...] It is likewise impossible to bring forth by enchantment something real from money, if that money is not merely a symbol for commodities that are produced, if it is not merely a kind of bookkeeping, a currency system of bookkeeping, in which every piece of money must represent a commodity. [...] Today it must be stated that in a period that is only concerned with turning money into an economic object, incomes cannot escape being considered an object of taxation.

By imposing taxes we make ourselves responsible with others for the whole system of financial economy. Something is taxed that is not a commodity at all, but only a symbol for a commodity. We are dealing with an abstraction from the economic life. Money only becomes a reality when it is spent for something. It then takes its place in the circuit of economic life, whether I spend it on amusement, or for bodily or mental necessities, or whether I bank it to

> *be used in the economic process. Banking my money is a way of spending [using] it. This must, of course, be kept in mind. Money becomes a reality in the economic process at the moment it passes out of my possession into the process of economic life. If people would reflect, they would see that it is of no use for a man to have a large income. [...] The only thing that benefits a person is the ability to spend a great deal. [...] Hence, if a system of taxation is to be created that constitutes a real service of the economic process to the good of the general community, instead of a parasitical growth upon it, capital must be taxed at the moment it is transferred to the economic process. Strange to relate, income tax comes to be transformed into a tax on expenditure. (CW332a, pp. 48-50)*

> *... the income a person procures is of no significance for the life of society as such, for human life in the social organism. As we procure our income, we detach ourselves from the social organism, and this can be a matter of great indifference to the social organism. The income someone earns has no importance whatsoever for its functions. Instead, a person becomes a social being by spending. Only as he spends, does someone start to act with social relevance. And taxation must start precisely when we spend—I am not referring here to indirect taxation but expenditure tax, which is something quite different. (CW189, p. 85)*

If you are struggling with this, then join the club! However, the following may help.

First of all, these comments need to be seen in the context of a number of things Steiner says which will be discussed later. In view of this, any reader particularly interested in the subject may find it practical to reread the current Section (7.3.6) after having read Section 7.4 ('Operational Remarks—Economic Realm').

Ideally, in Steiner's view, commodities (products and services) would stand behind all money, and income without the production of such commodities would cease to exist (except welfare income for those unable to work). *Production* would bring an income, but not ownership (e.g. of company shares or land). As the reader will recall, his definition of the economic realm concerns the production / circulation / consumption of commodities. The ownership of land and the means of production are a concern of the rights realm; they are excluded from the economic, from the merry-go-round of buying and selling. His definition of the economic realm strictly precludes any rentier element (that element which famed economist Keynes would also argue strongly against in the 1930s).[121] Rents and income from ownership of the means of production (as opposed to actively working *with* the means of production) are therefore, in Steiner's analysis, not real *economic* transactions. To be something real and not an abstraction, money should be a symbol for commodities, a kind of bookkeeping. Otherwise it ceases to be a proper agent of the economic process, it becomes removed from economic activity.

But if the Exchequer relies on a taxing of this abstraction (of rentier income) for part of its revenue, then it too (the Exchequer) becomes complicit in perpetuating this abstraction, this money system that is removed from the threefold definition of the economic process. So, Steiner's comments regarding income tax may presuppose, in the first instance, an economy from which any rentier element has been removed. No one would be receiving an income from owning, trading or selling land or the means of production.

And if money is to be seen as a simple bookkeeping system of debits and credits which go up and down as we produce and consume, then having money (a credit) simply means we have the ability to procure a commodity, a product or service. *In reality*, any real benefit is only bestowed on us when we spend the money and can enjoy the commodity. A credit in our account is no real benefit; it is a token indicating that we can procure a benefit. The *real* economic benefit only arises when we make the purchase. And it is this real economic transaction which Steiner deems the healthy target for taxation. Then, taxation remains within the realm he regards as truly economic. That is to say, the reallocation of *values*—via tax—remains a phenomenon in the economic realm, even if the laws stipulating what tax *obligations* apply might be a rights-realm concern.

Looking at the economy overall, the goods and services produced by those who are productive need to supply not only those same who are productive but also those who are not productive. Removing

---

[121] John Maynard Keynes, *The General Theory of Employment, Interest, and Money* (London: Macmillan, 1936).

money from the picture for a moment: a baker might make ten croissants, nine of which go to people who are productive. The last one is
redistributed by the tax man (by whatever means) to an unproductive
person—be they elderly, sick or whatever. Or, bringing money back
into the picture, if I buy nine croissants, I will need to actually pay for
ten, need to pay a bit extra to cover the croissant for the unproductive
person. That is to say, in reality, the customer pays a purchase tax.

However, given that it is *producers* who collectively produce more
than they need in order to also maintain those who are not productive,
one wonders why Steiner does not talk of a sales tax to reflect the fact
that the surplus that goes to the Exchequer is in fact a contribution
from *producers*. That is to say, the baker *sells* nine croissants but also
gives one to the Exchequer (as it were). But in the end: who has provided for the baker's livelihood while he or she has baked that tenth
croissant? Paying customers! That is, purchasers need to maintain the
baker while he or she produces the surplus croissants, so purchasers
are really paying the tax. In the end, a purchase / expenditure tax and
a sales tax are perhaps not so very different inasmuch as they are a tax
imposed at the point of sale.

The thing to appreciate with all this, though, is that Steiner is certainly not saying that if we moved from an income tax to a purchase
tax tomorrow, this would be a good thing. His comments have to be
seen in the context of other things he has said, particularly those things
concerned with removing rentier elements from the economy—that is
to say, removing unearned income derived purely from ownership (of
property, stocks and shares, etc).

Income tax is generally seen as attractive because of its ability to be
a progressive tax—the *rate* of tax can become progressively higher, the
more someone earns. A better off person can pay a higher *proportion*
of their earnings than someone who is poor. On the other hand, a
purchase tax is generally regarded as a regressive tax: every customer
pays at the same rate, regardless of whether they are a care worker on
the minimum wage or a footballer receiving £250,000 per week. Yes,
one can exempt certain essentials such as food so that the worst off are
excused from most taxes, but that also benefits our footballer.

In answer to this, there is the more obvious point that, even with a
universally flat rate of purchase tax, the richer person will pay more
tax in absolute terms simply because they are likely to buy more

goods, and more expensive goods, to boot. But, perhaps more importantly, a purchase tax needn't have a flat rate in any case. It can also be
graduated; the rate of tax can increase with luxury. So, for example,
there can be one tax rate for cars costing up to £10,000, a higher rate
for cars costing between £10,000 and £20,000, a still higher rate for
cars between £20,000 and £30,000, and so on. Likewise, butter can be
exempt, but not caviar. Furthermore, a purchase tax can be structured
in order to modify consumption habits (if via taxation is the way one
wants to approach this). So, for example, in a region where fresh water
is scarce, the consumption of so many litres of water per day (enough
for drinking, working and washing, say) could carry a low rate of tax,
if any, and consumption beyond that could be taxed at a higher rate to
discourage car washing and lawn watering. Tiered pricing of this kind
applies in Durban, for example.[122]

Steiner's 'fair price' referred to earlier (where all producers receive
enough for their products / services to cover all of their needs, plus
an additional element to cover welfare, etc.—see Section 7.4.11) also
has some bearing on these considerations. Such an approach implies
a very considerable levelling out of remuneration between one person and the next. The incomes of the care worker and the footballer
would, in theory, be closer to each other. And Steiner's recommendation that the wage relationship be replaced by a sharing relationship also implies a levelling out. So, too, does his recommendation
that unearned income from rent, dividends, capital gains on shares
or currency speculation be phased out. These substantial measures
would doubtless make the need for progressive taxes substantially
less pressing.

> *... a person's surplus performance, made possible by his individual
> abilities, will be passed on to the community [after death, possibly,
> RM] just as the legitimate support for the deficit performance of
> the less capable will be drawn from the same community. 'Surplus
> value' will not be created for the enjoyment of individuals, but for
> the increased supply of intellectual or material wealth to the social
> organism ... (CW23, p. 116)*

---

[122] The Worldwatch Institute, *State of the World 2012: Moving Toward Sustainable Prosperity* (Washington DC: Island Press, 2012), p. 21.

The further complication that Steiner introduces (earlier quote)—the idea that, for tax purposes, introducing one's savings into the economic process by banking them is to be seen in the same way as expenditure on commodities—will not be tackled here, not least because I do not feel qualified to tackle it! As we will see in Section 7.4.15, Steiner does not have a problem with savings and loans; these enable entrepreneurs to build factories etc. So income arising from savings (in the form of interest) still exists within his threefold suggestions.

One thing that can be said for purchase tax is that it could, if structured well, be a good, partial solution to one of the world's most pressing problems: that of certain corporations and individuals avoiding tax by exploiting accounting loopholes and hiding their affairs away in offshore tax havens. The release of the Panama Papers in 2016 revealed what we all half knew anyway: that the wealthy (including the then-Prime Minster David Cameron's family) can afford the right accountants to ensure they avoid mountains of tax by off-shoring.[123] 'Ultra-rich are opting out of society while controlling it,' despaired Aditya Chakrabortty.[124] Any company selling commodities in a country whose Exchequer relied solely on purchase tax and no other, would not be able to escape tax by moving offshore, since tax would be levied inland, at the point of sale of their merchandise. This could, in part, address the fear governments have that, if they increase corporation tax or top-end income tax, the companies / individuals affected will simply off-shore themselves into tax exile, leading to domestic unemployment and a *drop* in tax receipts. If corporation tax and income tax were replaced by a purchase tax, then this particular headache might be reduced.

In connection with funding education, Steiner observes:

> *The right to education could be arranged in that the economic organization's administration, in accordance with general economic situation, calculates the amount of educational income possible, while the rights state, in consultation with the spiritual organisation, determines the rights of the individual in this respect. Once again,*

---

[123] Wikipedia: Panama Papers.
[124] Aditya Chakrabortty, 'Ultra-rich are opting out of society while controlling it', *The Guardian,* 11 April 2016.

> *this indication is meant as an example of the direction in which arrangements can be made. It is quite possible that quite different arrangements would be appropriate in specific cases. However they can only be found through the purposeful co-operation of the three autonomous members of the social organism. (CW23, p. 115)*

However, he also recommends:

> *Everything necessary for the maintenance of the spiritual organisation, including remuneration, will come to it through the free appreciation of the individuals who participate in the social organism. The sound basis for the spiritual organisation will result from free competition among the individuals capable of spiritual work. (CW23, p. 114)*

And on another occasion:

> *As the payment of taxes must be compulsory even in a healthy social organism, what on the other hand is given to the spiritual life can be a matter of free will alone; for the spiritual life must be built wholly upon the spirit of man and be completely emancipated from anything else. (CW189(iii), 2 March 1919)*

How is one to reconcile these comments? In the first quote we have money flows to educational establishments being calculated in dialogue between the three central administrations. In the second and third quote, maintenance of cultural institutions is to be based on 'free will alone' and 'free appreciation'? The former, although non-prescriptive, sounds centralised. The latter sounds decidedly self-directed and reiterates the vital importance of the guiding principle of freedom / personal choice in cultural matters.

A good solution to this conundrum exists perhaps in the education vouchers favoured by Margaret Thatcher and others. With these, (a) all children / students have a *right* to a certain amount of education; (b) funding for this education is made available to parents / students who are given (tax-funded) vouchers with which to procure it; (c) in freedom, parents / students spend these vouchers on the education they deem best for themselves / their children. Such an approach would fit

184   RUDOLF STEINER AND SOCIAL REFORM

with all of these three quotes. Education funding is considered further in Sections 7.4.14 and 7.5.1.

The first of the above three quotes also illustrates the level of three-fold separation Steiner considers healthy. If the rights state needs the economic administration to advise how much spare value is available in the economy, this suggests he sees many, or most, of the usual Treasury / Exchequer functions carried by governments as really belonging within the economic administration instead. In which case, deciding on rights to other 'public' services, in addition to education, would also arise after close consultation between rights and economic administrations in order to establish affordability.

Steiner's assertion that, ultimately, purchase tax is the most rational form of taxation, is further enhanced in the following passage. Here he suggests that such tax should in the end only be collected from individuals, and not in any form of corporation tax. This passage also confirms he is clear that such proposals could not be brought in overnight!

> You see, a concept will have to completely disappear in the future, the concept of the legal person, also the economic-legal person. In actual fact, what is to be paid in taxes must be paid by individuals, because in the state, in the democratic state, in the realm where law lives, the individual faces the individual. People can only be the same if one person faces the other as an individual. Corporations need to exist within the economic life and within spiritual life. But within the state, only rights exist that are the same for all and that every adult can grasp. But this means that tax is only paid by private individuals, by every single individual. This can be set up proportionately so that injustice never occurs, but this proportionality will not be necessary if any real evening-out has taken place between people. The tax question will then be something completely different. That's why matters that crop up and questions that arise today apply more to a transition stage. One often has to do things that don't endure. Of course, it is about gradually moving towards taxation of the individual, not the taxation of corporations. Of course, a purchase tax must also be created, by which I do not mean indirect taxes, that are unjust. A consumption tax must be created, that is, he who spends a lot of money will be called on to a greater extent than he who doesn't spend much. For if someone puts their money under the mattress, that has no meaning for social life. It only takes on meaning when it is spent. (CW331, 22 May 1919)

In the same lecture, Steiner makes another intriguing and undoubtedly very long-term assertion in relation to where, within a threefold societal structure, responsibility for taxation could ultimately lie:

> *... because, in the future, one person will be placed in an economically just relation to another, it will be possible to remove the state as tax collector from the economic process. (CW331, 22 May 1919)*

Presumably that is to say: the production, circulation and consumption of commodities, if placed on the more equitable footing he advocates (with 'fair price', with work being rewarded, but not ownership, etc.), would be so managed by the economic realm that all, including the unproductive, would have the commodities they needed, and the state would merely concern itself with the rights and responsibilities. Distribution of income would cover respective needs, would be equitable enough to obviate the need for *re*-distribution. But perhaps, even then, the rights realm would still collect tax to fund its own activities. Again, these are only suggestions. And he is certainly not talking about short-term objectives!

In the case of inheritance, Steiner's primary concern is that the estate of someone who dies should be passed on to enable productive work. His concern is *productivity* as this brings greatest benefit to the community. So, if a factory owner dies, or indeed simply someone with savings, for Steiner the question is then: what is best for the common good? If one was minded to allow the state to appropriate the factory or the savings, the question would be whether it (the state) would then:

> *... husband it as advantageously for the economic life as would the original legatee ... (CW340, p. 80)*

The aim is to further the standard of living for all.

> *Taxing of legacies should not be based on feeling—e.g. envying the rich heir, but the proposal should be assessed on the basis of what is more advantageous. This is the right way to look at it from an economic point of view. (CW340, pp. 80-81)*

> *... the question to be decided is not whether this ought to be done, but whether it is necessarily advantageous. Whether the individual heir alone should receive the inheritance, or whether he must share it with the state, is a question which must first be settled on economic grounds. Which is more advantageous? That is the point. (CW340, p. 81)*

If an entrepreneur built up a factory or some other business, and upon retirement their first-born was without question best placed to take over, then it would make sense for their first-born to take over. In farming, such familial succession very often applies.

One might argue that the economy would be equally well promoted if the first-born were to simply own the legacy, and appoint a good manager to advantageously husband the factory. But Steiner did not sympathise with the idea of inheritance being passed on from generation to generation unless the heir also became the hands-on manager of the business:

> *After the death of the earner, or at a certain time thereafter, assets acquired ... go to a spiritually or materially productive person or group—but only to such a person or group and not to an unproductive person in whose hands it would constitute a private pension— to be chosen by the earner and specified in his will. Here again, if a person or group cannot be chosen directly, the transfer of disposition rights to an establishment of the spiritual organism will come into consideration. Only if someone does not himself effect a disposition will the rights-state step in and, through the spiritual organisation, make the disposition for him. (CW23, p. 105)*

But, if such rules were to exist, wouldn't people, before they died, make a gift of their wealth to their children? Steiner closes this loophole in a simple manner:

> *It is of course possible to point out that there will be a strong temptation to pass on property to one or more descendants during the original owner's lifetime. Also, that although descendants could be made to look like producers, they would nevertheless be*

inefficient compared to others who should replace them. This temptation could be reduced to a minimum ... The rights-state has only to require that under all circumstances property transferred from one family member to another must, upon the lapse of a certain period of time after the death of the former, devolve upon an establishment of the spiritual organisation. Or evasion of the rule can be prevented in some other way through the law. The rights-state will only insure that the transfer takes place; a facility of the spiritual organisation should determine who is to receive the inheritance. Through the fulfilment of these principles an awareness will develop of the necessity for offspring being made qualified for the social organism through education and training, and of the socially harmful results of transferring capital to unproductive persons. (CW23, p. 107)

Clearly, Steiner objects to heirs receiving a private pension that enables them to stop contributing to society before retirement age.

Few people today have the sense that they must give back to the social organism everything they gained from it. (CW189, p. 65)

In summary:

- Societal support (via whatever means) is a given for sickness, invalidity, education.
- Tax decisions to be made via the political (rights) process as usual, albeit in consultation with the economic and cultural domains, as appropriate.
- A purchase tax would, ultimately, conform more closely to economic facts than income tax. However, this could not simply be imposed without other changes—in particular, changes that curtailed the rewarding of ownership (as opposed to the rewarding of work).
- At some (possibly rather distant) future date, the economic realm could function in such an equitable way that it obviated the need for the state to act as tax collector for the economic realm (i.e. for redistribution).

- A deceased's estate (including any substantial gifts made during their lifetime) ideally passed on in full so many years after death to someone who is culturally or materially productive (this *could* be an heir).

Reflections in relation to the present

Income tax became a permanent feature of British life in 1842. Prior to that, a window tax was payable that increased relative to prosperity (i.e. increased with the number of windows in your home). What was known as the 'purchase tax' between 1940 and 1973 was in fact applied at the point of manufacture and / or distribution, not at the point of sale. As such, it was less purchase tax and more excise duty (payable regardless of any end sale). It was graduated according to luxury. When the UK joined the European Economic Area in 1973, this 'purchase tax' was replaced by VAT which is also payable along all points of a supply chain, and therefore also payable (at least in part) regardless of end sale. What Steiner appears to advocate, however, is a tax such that any liability only arises when the eventual consumer makes the purchase. At the time of writing the UK Exchequer's annual tax income of circa £600 billion comprises: income tax (25% of total tax receipts), national insurance contributions (19%), VAT (18%), property taxes (9%), corporation tax (8%), capital taxes (5%), fuel duties (4%), and other taxes / duties (12%).

Currently, the first £325,000 of the estate of a UK resident who dies is tax free, and the remainder is taxed at 40%. Under Steiner's suggestion, the tax rate could in effect be as much as 100% at the time of death, or, to cater for dependants, a number of years thereafter. This would also apply to gifts made before the benefactor died. In their *Land for the Many* proposals, proffered to the UK's Labour Party in 2019, George Monbiot and others also proposed a lifetime gifts tax.[125] Vince Cable, former leader of the UK's Liberal Democrats, also proposed such a tax.[126] In Ireland, lifetime gifts above a certain amount are taxed at 33%.

---

[125] https://landforthemany.uk.

[126] Vince Cable on *The Andrew Marr Show*, BBC1, 16 September 2018.

7.3.7   Land and the means of production

Whilst Karl Marx advocated that the means of production, and also land, be owned and managed communally, Steiner agreed with those who thought this would be disastrous and insisted that, for the sake of productivity and advantage to the community at large, the means of production and manufacturing should be left entirely in the hands of individuals with the necessary expertise. The most competent should have the means of production at their disposal, and a ponderous collective or state apparatus (bureaucracy) would suck the vibrancy out of the economy by killing the initiative and innovation that comes from individuals. (It would also distract the state away from its main function of focusing on rights and responsibilities under the guiding principle of equality.)

So, Steiner is sanguine about concentrations of capital / means of production in the hands of individuals:

> *In the living social realm we can never prevent capital arising as a self-evident phenomenon that accompanies the work of individual human capacities, as the development of property, of private property. If someone directs a branch of production ... the social organism simply could not survive without capital as an accompanying phenomenon: capital owned by the individual just as he owns what he needs for his own use. [...] Instead we should think only about how this capital must be transformed in turn at a different moment in time, what should become of it. You cannot wish to prevent the accumulation of capital without undermining the whole social organism and its capacity for life. All you can try to do is ensure that the capital which is created does not become harmful ... (CW189, p. 111)*

> *It is obvious that one does not have to elaborate on the fact that in to-day's economic life nothing can be achieved without capital and that polemics against capitalism is economically amateurish. (CW79, 30 November 1921)*

> *... those who simply say that capital should be abolished or transformed into common property have no idea how capital works in the economic system, especially under the present conditions of production. They do not know that accumulations of capital are needed in order that through the control of capital men may work for the public good. (CW332a, p. 118)*

> *... social life is just as unthinkable without the continual building-up of capital; without the constant building-up of the means of production which, strictly speaking, is nothing more and nothing less than capital. (CW189(iv), 15 March 1919)*

However, whilst being happy with sizeable concentrations of capital in the hands of individuals, Steiner's approach is far from capitalist in the ordinary sense.

> *Whilst the economy depended on traders and industrialists until around 1810, in the nineteenth century traders and industrialists ... essentially became dependent on the national and international money economy, on bankers. You can only be completely driven into economic egoism by this kind of money economy. But this kind of money economy should not be confused with mere capitalism, as is often done today. Mere capitalism ... should make it possible that only he who is capable and can manage production, can have in his hands large amounts of capital—be that means of production or money. [...] This mere capitalism is absolutely necessary for the modern economy, and to rage against it is nonsense. To abolish it would mean to undermine the entire modern economy. (CW337a, 3 March 1920)*

> *Contemporary socialism is thoroughly justified when it demands that the modern facilities which produce for the profit of individuals be replaced by others which produce for the consumption of all. However, the person who fully recognizes this demand cannot come to modern socialism's conclusion: that the means of production must pass from private ownership to common ownership. Rather, he will come to a quite different conclusion: that what is privately produced through individual competence must be made available to the community in the correct way. (CW23, p. 112)*

> *[The means of production] cannot be administered by a private individual for his private interests to the detriment of the community; but neither will the community be able to administer them bureaucratically to the detriment of the individual; rather will the suitable individual have access to them in order therewith to serve the community. (CW23, p. 113)*

As was seen in Chapter 5, Steiner defines the economy as the production / circulation / consumption of commodities, and he excludes from this the owning of land and the finished means of production—two things which, he explains, hold a certain equivalence for the purposes of current considerations. He describes how the plant and machinery—the components—that go to make up the means of production should be seen as part of the economy up until the point when the means of production are in place and ready for use. Whoever manufactures or distributes these components needs to be paid for them; they are a concern of the economic system until such time as the means of production are assembled and ready for production themselves.

The owning of these *finished* means of production (either by an entrepreneur or subsequent manager) and the owning of land (by, say, a forester or farmer) is acceptable, but the ability to buy and sell them presents a problem. For Steiner, buying and selling should be for commodities only. Commodities are goods and services that meet the needs of a consumer (or an entrepreneur building up means of production). But land and the finished means of production are not consumed in this way; they fall into a different category: things that *themselves* produce. Instead of consuming them (economic realm), people have a *right* to operate them. As such, they fall under the remit of the rights realm. And Steiner recommends this right be granted / gifted, not sold, once the factory or whatever has been set up.

Also, this right of use should always remain vested in the hands of experts; ideally, land and the means of production should not be managed by the state or controlled by anyone not fully engaged in the business. Steiner is keen for these rights to be held by an individual (or group) until such time as they stop managing the enterprise to the advantage of the common good. (This could be seen as at odds with the American economist Henry George's submission that 'The equal right for all men to the use of land is as clear as their equal right to breathe the air.'[127] Were this statement to be interpreted to mean the land is seen as a free-for-all commons, this would have less chance of benefiting the common good. If there is a spare plot of land going, somewhere, it is better if it is put at the disposal of someone who can husband it carefully for the community.)

---

[127] George, H. *Progress and Poverty* (New York: Modern Library, 1879) Book VII, Chapter 1.

> *The rights-state will not have to prevent the formation and administration of privately owned capital as long as individual abilities remain bound to the capital base in a way that constitutes a service to the whole of the social organism. Furthermore, it will remain a rights-state in regard to private property, never making private property its own, but ensuring that rights of disposition are transferred at the right moment to a person or a group of persons capable of restoring the appropriate individual relationship to the property. [...] The democratic rights-state, which is concerned with what affects all men in equal manner, will guard against property rights becoming property wrongs. (CW23, p. 101)*

> *... the means must be found whereby this private property loses all meaning, so that the so-called private owner is only the temporary leader because he has the abilities to best manage the means of production for the common good. (CW329, 2 April 1919)*

But how does Steiner justify the rights realm making the means of production its business when it is surely *individuals* who have built them (the means of production) up? He cites the example of intellectual property which passes over to the community after a certain time:

> *The possibility of free disposition over the capital base through individual abilities must exist; it must be possible to change the related property rights as soon as they become a means for the unjustified acquisition of power. We do have a facility in our times which partially fulfils this requirement in respect of so-called intellectual property. At a certain time after its creator's death it becomes community property. This corresponds to a truly social way of thinking. Closely as the creation of a purely intellectual property is bound to an individual's talents, it is at the same time a product of human society and must, at the right moment, be handed over to this society. It is in no way different with respect to other property. That which the individual produces in the service of the community is only possible in co-operation with this community. So the right of disposition over a property cannot be administered separate from the community's interests. A means of eliminating the ownership of the capital base is not to be sought, but rather a means of administering this property so that it best serves the community. (CW23, p. 100)*

This seems a cogent argument: the formation of capital has only been possible with the assistance of others in society (whether as co-workers, or makers of the means of production, or paying customers, or educators, or even as donors[128]), so should also return to society eventually.

And again …

> The basic principle seems least difficult to grasp with regard to spiritual [i.e. intellectual] property. In this regard, our thinking is already somewhat socially responsible. We recognise that no matter how clever or talented individuals may be … they would not be able to produce socially valuable innovations—whether practical or cultural—in isolation from society. Although patent and copyright periods vary from place to place and individuals are allowed to benefit from their intellectual property, we recognise at least in principle that, in the cultural domain, individual benefit ceases a certain number of years after the innovator's death. Intellectual property eventually enters the public domain; it cannot be passed down indefinitely to heirs who had nothing to do with its creation.
>
> History demands similar treatment of capital in the future … In the future, capital will still have to be raised to fund the means of production for any branch of the economy or any cultural purpose … In the future the means of production— that is, capital—will circulate freely in the social body just as blood circulates in the healthy human body. Blood must flow throughout the entire body and cannot be allowed to stagnate anywhere. Similarly, capital will not be allowed to accumulate in the form of private property. When it has served its purpose in one place, it must pass to those who will manage it best. It will thus be relieved of a function that has caused great social damage. (CW333, p. 12)

---

[128] As former Greek Finance Minister, Yanis Varoufakis, and others point out: there will be technologies in, say, an iPhone that have arisen thanks to state grants to educational establishments, etc. These grants were enabled by our taxes, and so the technologies should really be held in common. But, instead, they become appropriated by private capital. https://yanisvaroufakis.eu/2016/05/12/techni-cal–change-turns-basic-income-into-a-necessity/ (wherein he argues for a Basic Income—something that is addressed later in this book).

The right of ownership is not a problem as such; but Steiner opines this right should only endure for as long as the owner continues to manage the means of production in a capable way to serve the common good. Charles Waterman calls this *conditional ownership*— ownership rights that also come with obligations.[129] The question is one of ensuring prudent succession from one expert to the next. When the person running an enterprise or the person with rights of use over a piece of land no longer wishes to exercise that right, or is no longer able to use it fruitfully, or stops for whatever other reason, the right of use is ideally transferred to another person with the relevant expertise so that production can continue in the most efficacious manner possible, and society continues to get what it needs. The means of production are not bought and sold. This eventually overcomes the power relationship problem—and its concomitant resentment—where non-working owners gain from the work of others. However, this is to be achieved without a state bureaucracy (socialist or any other) taking over the means of production itself and thereby stifling initiative.

> Legal arrangements will ensure that a productive enterprise remains connected to a person or group only as long as the connection is justified by their individual abilities. Instead of common ownership of the means of production, a circulation of these means—continually putting them at the disposal of the persons whose individual abilities can best employ them for the benefit of the community— will be introduced into the social organism. (CW23, p. 112)

In this connection, one can distinguish three principal ways in which someone might have capital at their disposal: (a) a CEO has means of production at their disposal thanks to capital built up by others (i.e. either he / she had the finished means of production bestowed on them when a previous CEO stopped, or he / she borrowed money capital from others to then build up the means of production), (b) this CEO has additional capital at their disposal thanks to profits generated under

---

[129] Charles Waterman, *The Three Spheres of Society* (London: Faber and Faber, 1946), p. 26.

their watch, and (c) someone has built up capital from scratch from their own efforts and not benefited either from means of production being 'circulated' to them from others, or from borrowing money that has been built up by others.

Steiner suggests that the CEO in scenario (a) (means of production at their disposal thanks to capital built up by others) should relinquish the business as soon as they stop running it, and ...

> *The only thing personally owned by the individual who operates an enterprise should be what he draws in accordance with the terms agreed to when he takes over responsibility for production ... (CW23, p. 102)*
>
> *When the first administrator [of capital built up by another, RM] no longer can or will manage an enterprise, the capital with which it was established will either be transferred to a new administrator, along with all obligations or, depending on the wishes of the original owners, be returned to them [i.e. to the original builders-up of the capital].* Such arrangements concern the transference of rights. *The legal provisions by which these transfers are to take place are the province of the rights-state. It will also have to see to their execution and administration. [my emphasis, RM] (CW23, p. 103)*

The accumulated profits in scenario (b), if not used for expansion of the business, would not be returned to the owners of the original capital but be passed on:

> *... this capital accumulation should pass to another person, or group of persons, to be utilised for the same or some other type of production which serves the social organism. (CW23, p. 102)*
>
> *Settlements of this kind will pertain to capital accumulations exceeding a certain amount which are acquired by a person or group through the use of the means of production (to which land also belongs), and which are not included in what is originally agreed upon as remuneration for the activities of individual abilities. (CW23, p. 104)*

The capital built up in scenario (c), i.e. built up entirely from scratch by someone's own efforts, without any reliance on capital (loans / means of production) that others in society have built up previously, would, Steiner suggests, remain in their possession as follows:

> *Such earnings, acquisitions and savings which result from the individual's own work will remain in his personal possession until his death, or in his descendants' possession until a later date. Until this date interest (the amount of which is to be determined from rights-awareness and set by the right-state) will be paid by whoever receives such savings for the procurement of means of production. (CW23, p. 104)*

That is, if the original entrepreneur (i.e. an entrepreneur not benefiting from capital built up by others) were to retire from the business they had built up, he or she would still be entitled to receive income from the venture, post-retirement, just like the owner of intellectual property.

However, as the following passages confirm, once the means of production are in place, they ought not be sellable thereafter:

> *In a healthy social organism, capital goods and other means of production will have a one-time cost at the time of delivery. The producer will then be able to manage them, but only for as long as he can contribute to production by his management. The business will then have to be transferred to another, not by sale nor by inheritance, but rather as a free gift to the one best able to manage it. It will have no sale value, and thus no value in the hands of an heir who does not work. Capital with independent economic power will work in the establishment of the means of production; it will dissolve itself instantly when the creation of the means of production is finished. (CW24, p. 12)*

> *Money lent for production does not return, it stays there. But we insist on selling the means of production ... However, if one imagines the means of production as something one does not sell, then the money stays in ... (CW341, p. 221)*

If the means of production cannot be sold, outside share ownership ceases (along with the ancillary obsessions with share price and all the other unproductive business related to the stock market), and the complaint one so often hears—that our current way of doing things rewards ownership more than work—is addressed.

> There is no longer any possession [of the means of production], only an administration. (CW329, 19 March 1919)
>
> Through the fulfilment of these principles an awareness will develop ... of the socially harmful results of transferring capital to unproductive persons. (CW23, p. 107)
>
> The beneficial social structure will always prevent capital assets from being isolated from the management of the means of production [i.e. no external owners / shareholders, RM]. It will also put a stop to the attempts of those who strive only for capital assets, but shirk participation in the economic process ... The harmfulness of the nonworking recipient of dividends is not that to a small degree they diminish the working man's earnings, but that the sheer possibility of someone being able to have an income without working for it lends an antisocial aspect to the whole economic body. (CW24, p. 11)

Only those involved with the production process would control the undertaking, not ineffectual heirs and not shareholders simply because they have financial wherewithal. Steiner's suggested approach creates a context for good, long-term *productivity* compared to the destructive short-termism that one sometimes sees when management wants to impress shareholders by getting short-term profits and the share price up, regardless of wider implications (e.g. environmental damage, deterioration in product quality, mistreatment of workers).

It should be pointed out, however, that Steiner is not interested in small fry when he is discussing ownership of the means of production:

> If you want to be practical about these things, it is no good to ask: At what point does a device become a means of production, for example a sewing machine? Is it when I no longer use it only for personal use, and am I then no longer allowed to put it to personal use? Ladies and gentlemen, when considering the great questions of the day, it will not do to look for answers within such limited horizons. I guarantee, under threefolding, you will still have a relationship with your sewing machine that is perfectly satisfactory! ... One should not reduce the term 'means of production' in this way. It is important not to think within such narrow confines. (CW337b, 19 July 1920)

He also emphasises, as elsewhere, that these suggestions are just that—suggestions. If something falls within the remit of the state, it should be the democratic process that ultimately decides how to proceed.

> One can imagine that the representatives in the rights state will, at different times, enact completely different laws concerning the transfer of property from one person, or groups of persons, to others. (CW23, p. 101)
>
> One can safely assume that the detailed determinations which regulate such rights transfers will vary according to what rights-awareness considers correct. A realistic way of thinking will never desire more than to point out the direction that such regulation can take. If this direction is taken with understanding, the appropriate action for specific individual cases can always be found. The correct solution will always have to be in accordance with the spirit of the thing as well as whatever special conditions practical considerations may impose. (CW23, p. 103)

Interestingly, Steiner's contemporary, Henry Ford, who went to great lengths to provide a quality car for the customer as cheaply as possible, conveyed similar sentiments in 1922 about capital serving society instead of absent shareholders: 'Capital that a business makes for itself, that is employed to expand the workmen's opportunity and increase comfort and prosperity, and that is used to give more and more men work, at the same time reducing the cost of service to the public—that sort of capital, even though it be under single control, is not a menace to humanity. It is a working surplus held in trust and daily use for the benefit of all. The holder of such capital can scarcely regard it as a personal reward. No man can view such a surplus as his own, for he did not create it alone. It is the joint product of his whole organisation. The owner's idea may have released all the energy and direction, but certainly it did not supply all the energy and direction. Every workman was a partner in the creation. No business can possibly be considered only with reference to today and to the individuals engaged in it. It must have the means to carry on. The best wages ought to be paid. A proper living ought to be assured every participant in the business—no matter what his part. But for the sake of that business's ability to support those who work in it, a surplus has to be held somewhere. The truly honest manufacturer holds his surplus profits in that trust. Ultimately it does not matter where this surplus be held nor who controls it; it is its use that matters. Capital that is not constantly creating more and better jobs is more useless than sand. Capital that is not constantly making conditions of daily labour better and the reward of daily labour more just, is not fulfilling its highest function. The highest use of capital is not to make more money, but to make money do more service for the betterment of life. Unless we in our industries are helping to solve the social problem, we are not doing our principal work. We are not fully serving.'[130] Also: ' ... we have no place for the non-working stockholders. The working stockholder is more anxious to increase his opportunity to serve than to bank dividends.'[131]

With the guiding principle of the rights sphere being equality, where all, democratically, make decisions about rights (and these rights then apply to all, too), there is a universality about this sphere. As far as the allocation of land or the means of production is concerned, this universality would find expression in the fact that (a) all (via democracy) could decide on the *rules* for ownership succession, and (b) all those owning / managing land or means of production above a certain size would then be subject to the same rules of succession.

However, whilst it would be a rights-realm matter to ensure *that* the transfer of the means of production took place, based on what the democratic process considered appropriate, it would not be this realm's job to determine *to whom* the transfer should be made. Such a decision clearly cannot be made by a democratic process where all have a say; it is a question of people with relevant experience and insight identifying suitable successors:

> *... the rights-state will never take over the disposition of capital through its administration of transfer rights. It has only to provide for the transfer to a person or group of persons whose individual abilities seem to warrant it. In general, it follows that it should at first be possible for someone who proposes to effect such a capital transfer under the circumstances described to freely choose his*

---

[130] Henry Ford, *My Life and Work* (Hawthorne, CA: BN Publishing, 2008), p. 132.
[131] Ibid., p. 112.

successor. He will be able to choose a person, or group of per-
sons, or transfer the disposition rights to an establishment of the
spiritual organisation. (CW23, p. 103)

The rights-state has only to determine that the transference of the
capital in question takes place in the manner indicated; it will not
be incumbent upon it to decide which material or spiritual produc-
tion is to have disposition over transferred capital or other savings.
That would lead to a tyranny of the state over spiritual and material
production—which is best administered through individual human
abilities. In case someone does not wish to personally select the
receiver of capital accumulated by him, he will be able to dele-
gate this function to an establishment of the spiritual organisation.
(CW23, p. 105)

The disposal of land, systematised in the laws relating to its own-
ership, and the disposal of the finished means of production (for
example, a factory with its machinery and equipment), should be
no matter for the economic organization. They must belong partly
to the spiritual and partly to the legal. That is to say, the transfers
of land from one person or group of persons to another must not be
carried out by purchase or through inheritance, but by transference
through legal means, on the principles of the spiritual organisation.
The means of production through which something is manufac-
tured—a process that lies at the basis of the creation of capital—
can only be looked at from the point of view of its commodity costs
while it is being built up. (CW332a, p. 120)

So, the overall responsibility of 'stewarding' the means of production
(and land) would fall to the cultural domain (covered later). Thus,
whilst those managing factories would not have shareholders breathing
down their necks, there might still, if considered appropriate in certain
corporations, be some form of arm's length scrutiny—but from a body
within the cultural realm which could intermittently check that those
in charge of a business they had been entrusted with were still making
good use of the means of production to society's advantage.

Steiner notes how imbalance and unfairness in economic relations are stoked when perpetual-ownership structures apply instead
of structures where land and the means of production pass from the
capable to the capable:

It is impossible to reach a just determination of price as long as the means of production and land function as they now do within the economic system. (CW332a, p. 120)

You see, the conditions under which the price of land originates are not those of a mature economy. To take an extreme instance, we may consider how a piece of land may have come under the control of particular persons by conquest, that is, by the exercise of force. Even here, no doubt, the element of exchange will enter in to some extent; the invader will have granted certain portions of the conquered territory to those who helped him to victory. Here, then, at the starting point of an economic process we have something that is not properly economic. The process is not really economic; it is a process to which we can only apply the word 'power' or 'right' [...] But what is it that takes place under the influence of such relationships of rights and power? This is what happens continually: the man who has the free right of disposal over land looks after himself better than those others whom he attaches to himself as labourers—who deliver products to him by labour. I'm speaking now not of the labour, but of the products of the labour; it is the products of labour with which we are concerned. The others have to deliver more to him than he delivers to them. This, indeed, is only the prolongation of his relationship to them of conquest or right. Now, what is this excess of what they give him over what he gives them? What is it, in other words, that falsifies the price relationship in this case? It is none other than compulsory gift. (CW340, pp. 86-87)

The following passage describes how such 'compulsory gifts' could, in theory (only), be removed and prices thereby brought into what Steiner terms a 'just relation'. It must be emphasised this is not something he was actually advocating but just a hypothetical illustration.

Assume 35 million inhabitants at a given time, and that the problem is to bring these 35 million people economically into an economically just relation. [...] What would you have to do if you wished such a condition to prevail among these 35 million as would bring about feasible prices? The moment you begin to lead ... the economic life of the region into a healthy condition, you would have

> *to give each one of them an amount of land corresponding to one*
> *35-millionth of the entire area available for production, adjusted*
> *according to fertility and ease of cultivation. Suppose that every*
> *child were to receive such an area of land at birth, to be worked*
> *by him in perpetuity. The prices which would thus arise would be*
> *feasible prices for such an area, for things would then have their*
> *natural exchange values. (CW340, p. 180)*

To repeat, Steiner is only conveying this by way of example; it is certainly not something he is suggesting. (And in any case, it would go against the principle that land and means of production are best given to those best able to manage / husband them for the community.) But the comment does illustrate his disapproval of the very varying ownership rights that exist which lead to rentier influences undermining price fairness.

In the following, he considers private ownership from the opposite angle: not out of a disapproval of the inequitable ownership patterns that prevail under capitalism, but out of a disapproval of the disfranchisement and disempowerment of the individual under socialism.

> *One of the fundamental demands of the materialism of the prole-*
> *tariat with its Marxist colouring is the nationalisation of the means*
> *of production. The means of production are to be given over to*
> *common ownership and this would only represent the first move*
> *towards common ownership of property in general, of land and*
> *so forth. It is part of the programme of the Russian Soviet Repub-*
> *lic, which I explained to you, to nationalise, or better said, social-*
> *ise the means of production and land. This in turn points to the*
> *most important subsidiary social question of the present. This*
> *can be formulated as follows: is social action in our current cul-*
> *ture or, indeed, the current chaos if we consider the Central Pow-*
> *ers and the countries of the East, to happen in such a way that*
> *there is a trend towards individuals becoming owners or should*
> *the development be such that the community becomes the owner?*
> *You understand what I mean—should it be the individual who has*
> *ownership or should those things which can be owned, such as*
> *land, means of production and so on, become communal prop-*
> *erty to avoid injustice? That is a very important subsidiary social*

question. Today the tendency of proletarian thinking is to make things communal property. But for the most important social impulses, it makes no difference at all whether an individual or an association or the community as such is the owner. To anyone who is able to study the realities, this is clearly revealed. In relation to the individual worker, the community will be no different from, no less bad as an employer than an individual entrepreneur. This lies in the nature of the case, it is like a law of nature, people only fail to see it, and hence they are misled. For the real question is this: should all people become owners of property? That would happen if, instead of having communal property ... individuals—every one of them—owned property in a just way according to the given opportunities in any territory. Should everyone become a property owner or should everyone join the proletariat? That is the alternative. The present thinking of the proletariat wants to make everyone join the proletariat so that the community alone would be the entrepreneur. But if we can see the reality, the very opposite will be the outcome. The threefold nature of the social structure can never be attained by making everyone into the proletariat. The tendency of the threefold structure must really be to attain the freedom of the individual in respect of body, soul and spirit. That will not be attained by everyone joining the proletariat, but it will be achieved for every individual if everyone possess a certain basis of property. (CW186(ii), pp. 144-145)

Just prior to these comments, Steiner had been talking about the proletariat's resentment of having to sell their labour, that the commoditisation of their labour was only one or two steps better than being sold as slaves themselves, and that the threefold approach addresses this by not treating labour as commodity, but instead by replacing wages with a sharing of the proceeds of the enterprise.

If I am not a slave owned by another, as in Ancient Greece or the New World plantations, and if I am not a serf beholden to the lord of the manor, and if I am not a wage labourer employed by a capitalist who has power over me on account of their ownership superiority, then I am in a freer relationship to those I work with. And if all have a certain equivalence, capital-wise, instead of being proletarian subordinates to either a capitalist employer or a state bureaucracy, then rentier factors are removed from commodity pricing; prices become more equitable.

This gives me a much freer sphere of action to pursue my calling (even if that is quite menial) without feeling downtrodden. All being well, I may no longer need to slave away quite as much as before in order to get by.

Although giving all 35 million inhabitants in a region one 35-millionth of the land in that region might be equitable on paper, it is of course not practical for a variety of reasons. But if land and the means of production are continually recycled back into the service of society, instead of becoming cash cows for heirs or investors, then the potentially harmful power of capital is greatly reduced.

In summary (concerning land):

- Land ideally not buyable or sellable.
- Land not to be passed on to heirs indefinitely.
- Instead, rights of use attaching to land to be bestowed by way of gift on those who can use it meaningfully for society, for the common good.
- As these are not transfers of consumer goods, they occur outside the economic realm. Instead, they are a concern of the rights realm—which should ensure that such transfers occur as appropriate. However, *to whom* the land is to be passed is a matter for the *cultural* realm if the previous owner is unable or unwilling to nominate.
- Such an approach moves society forward from hereditary entitlements that may even have arisen from historic military conquest.
- Such an approach reduces rentier elements in commodity pricing.

Concerning the means of production, one can deduce the following as a possible lifecycle for such capital:

- An entrepreneur builds up an enterprise and means of production ('MOP') from scratch, i.e. without the use of capital from elsewhere.
- Whilst the individual components of the MOP must be bought and so are initially considered part of the economic realm, once the MOP are in place and ready for production, they are ideally no longer bought or sold. They are something over which a person has right of *use* (but not right of sale).
- This right is passed on by way of gift.

- When the entrepreneur stops acting as such, the MOP are passed to another person or group with the requisite capacities so that production can continue in such a way that best serves the community. They must have 'free disposition' over the capital (i.e. no one else is directing them). They have exclusive *rights* of use.
- If the original entrepreneur doesn't want to choose the successor, a specially constituted organisation within the cultural realm does this for them.
- Whilst the cultural realm might choose the successor, it is the rights realm which a) ensures *that* the transference takes place in the appropriate manner, b) provides the necessary ownership laws, and c) determines at what point the original entrepreneur or their heirs cease to benefit financially from the business.
- The rights state never owns or manages the MOP, as this undermines initiative and innovation in the economy (and also distracts the rights state from its central function of being concerned with rights and responsibilities, with what is just, as well as distracts it from its guiding principle of equality).
- The original entrepreneur can receive income from their capital after they have withdrawn from running the business.
- When the entrepreneur's successors in the business stop acting as such, the MOP are either (a) passed to new managers, by way of gift, or (b) returned to the original entrepreneur if he / she wants this. (However, this is only justified if the entrepreneur had set up the MOP from scratch. If, on the other hand, they had borrowed money capital to procure the plant, or had themselves been gifted MOP originally set up by others, then, on withdrawal from the business, their ownership and income rights would also cease at this point.)
- When the original entrepreneur dies, their estate (including savings and any MOP they own) can perhaps benefit dependants for so many years after death, but are eventually handed over in full to enterprise that is materially or culturally productive.
- Such enterprise to be specified in the deceased's will, or otherwise an establishment within the cultural realm to allocate such capital in accordance with the principle of service to the community. At this point also, any capital passed to family members during the entrepreneur's lifetime is to be handed over too (see previous 'Taxation' section). This pre-empts any temptation

the entrepreneur might have to gift ownership of capital to heirs before death.

- Unearned income adds an anti-social element to society.
- As elsewhere, Steiner emphasises that these are *suggestions*, and that the main point is the hygienic separation of the three realms.

Reflections in relation to the present

As mentioned in the previous section, the inheritance tax laws we currently have in the UK allow anyone's estate (including house, valuables, savings and investments) to be inherited tax free up to a value of £325,000, and any value over and above that is taxed at 40%. Any part of the estate given to the spouse or to charity escapes tax altogether, as does any part given away to non-charity (e.g. to the benefactor's children) seven or more years before death. Steiner, on the other hand, suggests the *entire* estate—including anything given away before death—could be made over to the common good either upon death, or so many years thereafter— allowing dependants to enjoy it for however many years people's 'rights awareness' deemed appropriate. One imagines such rights awareness would always allow at least something to 'pass to the children'. Who else would appreciate the family photo album in any case!

Labour's erstwhile President of the Board of Trade, Lord Douglas Jay also once observed: 'It is not the ownership of the means of production as such, but ownership of large inherited incomes, which ought to be eliminated.'[132] However, when inheritance tax is collected, it goes into the government's coffers. By contrast, Steiner suggests that the estate of the deceased go to a culturally or materially productive individual / venture (a research institute or a manufacturer, for example), either specified by the deceased in their will or, in the absence of this, chosen by an institution of the cultural realm specially constituted for the purpose. Such a process would presumably need to include safeguards to prevent an estate being left to an enterprise planned by the first-born, say, that had little chance of success, or to an enterprise that would allow the new CEO to draw remuneration incommensurate with their productivity for the community.

---

[132] Douglas Jay, *The Socialist Case* (London: Faber & Faber, 1947) p. 195.

It is conceivable that a Western-style democracy might, over time, change inheritance rules in the direction Steiner suggests, whereby heirs could no longer live off the work of others without working themselves. But, contrary to his recommendations, the more likely destination of the estates in question would be the rights realm itself—the Exchequer—in the first instance. UK-based assets owned by a trust or a non-domiciled individual would present a problem, however, regardless of whether or not the rights realm was so minded to treat a deceased's estate as Steiner suggests. If an Italian billionaire owned 10,000 acres of UK grouse moor, no UK inheritance laws would return this land to the common good without further measures being enacted in the rights domain.

One can therefore imagine that a national audit of land might be attractive to the electorate if it prompted a reallocation that enabled land to be used for the public benefit. Grouse moor owners cut and burn vegetation to create a relatively barren landscape that serves the amusement of a handful of grouse shooters ('The places that should be our wildlife reservoirs are in fact wildlife deserts').[133] Instead, the woodlands that once graced such hills could be slowly reintroduced which would absorb carbon and put badly-needed oxygen back into the air. For that matter, it might even be preferable to use such hills for sheep grazing if that would obviate the need to ship thousands of tonnes of lamb from New Zealand each year—with all the ecological implications which that entails. In view of such broader considerations, some form of compulsory purchase might be deemed equitable such that the land could then be used according to society's needs. All three realms would have a part to play in such an exercise. The rights state would establish the rules, institutions of the economic realm would ascertain society's needs, and agents working in the cultural domain would contribute research findings—as well as identify those individuals best suited to steward any land thus reallocated.

Remember, though: Steiner is not advocating these things in any prescriptive manner. What he is saying is that land is a matter for the rights realm; and it is the rights realm, via the democratic process, that should decide exactly what measures would appear sensible. The

---

[133] George Monbiot: 'Why are Britain's conservation groups so lacking in ambition?', *The Guardian*, 18 Oct 2013.

population as a whole ultimately would decide. So, the fondness that many in the UK have for their monarchy, for example, might translate into special dispensations for certain royal estates.

But what about the idea of land and the means of production becoming unsellable altogether?

Taking land first ...

If land were a matter for the rights realm and, in addition to not being inheritable, was also neither buyable nor sellable, then, for one, housing costs would reduce significantly over time. This would reverse the substantial difficulty most first-time buyers face in the UK where there is an acute shortage of housing, especially housing that is affordable to the less well-off. Staggeringly, home ownership among the 25-34 age group has fallen from 65% to 27% over a twenty-year period.[134] In Scotland, the price of land has risen from 2% of the cost of a house in the 1930s to 70% today.[135] Further South, 'an acre of rural land worth £5,000 becomes an acre of development land worth between £500,000 and £1m once planning permission is obtained. Moreover, most land granted planning consent is registered offshore and is thus tax free, or virtually so'.[136] With development land kept scarce, 'UK homes are both the smallest in Europe and the most expensive'.

We also have builders sitting on undeveloped building land that has planning permission for the erection of 600,000 homes, that is, homes for well over a million people.[137] As we know, builders often hold this land for years, either with the aim of building on it at some later date when the fancy takes them, or with the aim of selling it or building on it when house prices have risen even higher. Under a threefold approach, one can imagine this land could not be owned by builders

---

[134] Cribb, J., Hood, A. and Hoyle, J., 'Just 1 in 4 middle-income young adults own their own home—down from 2 in 3 twenty years ago' (London: IFS press release, 16 February 2018).

[135] The Land Reform Review Group, 'The land of Scotland and the common good: report' (Edinburgh: Scottish Government, 23 May 2014), http://wwwscotland.gov.uk/About/Review/land-reform/events/FinalReport23May2014.

[136] Kevin Cahill, 'The great property swindle: why do so few people in Britain own so much of our land?', *The New Statesman*, 11 March 2011.

[137] Graham Ruddick, 'Revealed: housebuilders sitting on 600,000 plots of land', *The Guardian,* 31 December 2015.

(or anyone else) to do with as they pleased. If it was designated as land for housing, then it would be given to someone intending to build a home on it (builder or otherwise). If the recipient did not use it as agreed, it would be passed to someone else. The former leader of the Labour Party Ed Miliband took a similar view with his 'use it or lose it' proposal.[138]

Whilst houses themselves (being nature modified by labour to form consumer goods—and thus falling within Steiner's definition of the economy) would be bought and sold, the land on which houses sit would not. One can imagine a sensible and equitable way forward could be such that everyone would have the automatic *right* to a piece of housing land—since everyone needs to live somewhere. And if the law said this right to exclusive use of the land could only be passed (not sold) to someone needing somewhere to live, then the house would only be sellable to such a person or persons, and perhaps not to investors (the land itself would come free, so to speak, with the house).

There would be related matters for the political realm to settle, such as: what level of multiple home ownership to allow? For many people, home ownership is not suitable. They may be an Aberdonian with a two-year work contract in London, or a Londoner with a two-year work contract in Aberdeen. For this short period, they are unlikely to want to go through all the hassle of buying and selling a house twice in two years. Renting will suit them very well for those two years. So the rights to land for rental housing would still need to exist for landlords. These landlords could be housing enterprises / associations; or perhaps individuals could be granted the right to two housing plots, or three, or whatever, depending on the need for rental property in the area. And this right could be held on condition that these additional houses were not only let out, but also only let out at a rent level to cover the cost of the building, not one that included any rental element relating to the land. Multiple home ownership could be limited to two or three dwellings, say. That is, no one would have the right of dispensation over more than two or three housing plots of land, and would thus simply not be able—in law—to purchase

---

[138] Patrick Wintour, 'Ed Miliband issues warning to developers over "hoarding" of land', *The Guardian*, 20 June 2013.

more than two or three dwellings (because they would not have the right to the land *under* dwellings). The number of multiple homes allowable could be worked out such that just enough rental properties were available for (a) those not wishing or able to buy, and (b) holiday makers. These rules would be for the rights realm to establish, acting partly on advice from the economic realm re levels of housing need. It would not be a case of houses being available ad infinitum to those who could afford to buy them. The President of the United Arab Emirates might then not be able to buy over a billion pounds-worth of property in London.[139] Many empty properties would also be brought back into circulation. Capital would not be able to snap up real estate and increase housing costs in the process—on account of demand outstripping supply. Land would be allocated in a way that best served all. Home ownership would rise (and more people would then doubtless take more care of where they lived). Renting would fall. Social justice would advance.

If such an approach were taken, this would also solve the socially unhelpful practice of agricultural land being purchased speculatively in the hope that one day it might be granted planning permission for dwellings. Companies specialising in buying fields near built-up areas, and then dividing these up into multiple plots which they sell on at a premium (to people who hope that one day planning permission for dwellings will be granted) leads to the nonsensical situation where there are many agricultural fields around the country which are not used for agriculture. At the same time, we are importing basic, home-producible foodstuffs from overseas. Under threefolding, such companies would simply not be able to buy the land; land would not be buyable or sellable. Dispensation over land would be granted to those who would use it for its intended purpose, in this case someone with the appropriate farming skills. If that person happened to be a builder successfully masquerading as a farmer, but who had the intention of putting houses on the land at a later date, his or her scheming could be circumvented since, if planning permission were granted at a later date, the land could simply be *given* to people in need of housing who had no plot of their own. Special rules would presumably also

---

[139] Vickie Oliphant, 'UAE president developed £1.2 billion UK property empire with help of the offshore businesses', *The Express*, 7 April 2016.

need to exist to allow building companies to develop larger housing schemes in such a way that they could sell the finished houses without being able to profit from the land itself.

In 2019 in their *Land for the Many* policy suggestions submitted to the UK Labour Party, George Monbiot et al proposed a number of reforms along threefold lines that would make significant inroads into the UK land problem.[140] These would steer land away from the economic system, from being available to the highest bidder, and instead in the direction of the rights system which would ensure the land be used where needed. Amongst other things, the report proposed: (a) the Land Registry revert to being a government agency; (b) a Common Ground Trust be set up to procure land for affordable housing for first-time buyers; (c) more Community Land Trusts to promote community ownership of land; (d) a review of tax exemptions to ensure farmland is used for farming not speculation and tax avoidance; (e) reform of the Land Compensation Act to enable affordable housing projects to buy development land at current use value instead of future residential value (reducing the cost of affordable housing by up to 50%); (f) measures to ensure Local Authorities sell land for affordable housing instead of to the highest bidder; (g) firmer regulation of buy-to-let mortgages.

As with housing land, commercial and other land would ideally not be tradable under Steiner's proposals either. It would be passed in effect by way of gift to the next available person / group most capable of managing it for the common good, for the meeting of people's needs.

Whilst one can perhaps imagine such ownership laws relating to *land* appealing to the electorate, what seems unlikely any time soon is any sort of legislation to enshrine the principle that the *means of production* become unsellable. In a world where the economy is predicated largely on share ownership, share trading, share price, such ideas can seem particularly bold—eccentric, even. It is hard to imagine, in the short or medium term, any political party convincing the populace to do away with the internationally established paradigm of capital markets and of shares retaining sellability and value in

---

[140] See https://landforthemany.uk.

perpetuity (if, that is, the company continues to thrive). For a start, the largely right-wing press (owned, as they generally are, by billionaires who have managed to do very well by having things just as they are), would defend the status quo to the last. More on that in Section 8.1.8.

But if one reflects on the collateral damage inflicted by share ownership—and its twin, profit maximisation—the case for an alternative approach to business ownership can become compelling. Unbridled profit maximisation is exacerbated by share ownership, by people investing in something with no interest in the activity, only in the profit, indeed often in the short term profit at that. Short term profit may lift share price and make for a fast buck, but this relentless pursuit of profit puts pressure on management to cut corners, to keep wages low, to turn a blind eye to the environment, to engage in underhand geo-political machination, to exploit and disfranchise indigenous tribes, and to generally act irresponsibly. (Of course, it can be difficult not to be a player in this destructive cycle oneself. If one's savings are not with an ethical bank, or one's car battery is not fair-trade, then one is probably encouraging the continuation of the problem!) Steiner's ownership suggestions may be novel, but they are arguably a lot less controversial than much that goes on in 'the market', a lot less controversial than, for example, the asset-stripping raid on the ailing Comet electronics chain by financier Henry Jackson and his mates which 'cost 1,000 workers their jobs, left staff and taxpayers out of pocket, and yet private equity bankers walked away with £114m ... the total compensation bill to the public purse could hit £70m'.[141] If it were not possible to buy the means of production, such behaviour would not occur.

Steiner did not mince his words regarding the need for our treatment of capital to be overhauled:

> *I have been told that some of my audience at a recent lecture in Bern, capitalists apparently, were livid when I asked why a law couldn't be passed obliging owners of capital, a certain number of years after their death, to relinquish their capital to the free governance of a body, a spiritual-cultural organization, in the spiritual*

---

[141] Simon Neville, 'Comet's legacy: lost jobs, out-of-pocket taxpayers—and a windfall for banker', *The Independent*, 2 August 2014.

sphere of the social organism. There are of course many different ways of establishing a specific law. [...] And what is the outcome of their outrage? That over the last four-and-a-half years human-kind has killed ten million people and made eighteen million into cripples, and is now embarking on much more such devastation. (CW189, p. 113)

Whilst it might not be out of the question for inheritance laws to move more in the direction Steiner advocates, any measures to effectively put an end to (saleable) share ownership seem fairly unlikely in the near future. Nonetheless, if inheritance laws did move in the direction Steiner suggests, then share portfolios in people's estates could gradually be transferred into some kind of Trust for the common good, some kind of commons, some kind of socially responsible 'spiritual-cultural organisation' (instead of simply being sold onward to other investors). Whether this would have much impact on the typical capitalist practices of the companies in question, though (i.e. on those companies whose shares such spiritual-cultural organisation would increasingly own), is perhaps questionable.

In the absence of macro, legislative solutions to what Steiner regards as the inappropriate ability individuals have to buy and sell land and the means of production (e.g. shares), to amass capital, and amass ever-increasing amounts of capital without even working or adding value, might there be micro solutions that fit the bill? Comments like the following offer encouragement in this direction:

The threefold idea is not a program or system ... requiring the old system to cease suddenly and everything to be 'set up' anew. The threefold idea can make a start with individual undertakings in society. (CW24, p. 47)

Concerning land: in the absence of blanket laws addressing land ownership, the Land Trust model achieves a very similar outcome on a project-by-project basis. The last two or three decades have seen a marked increase in the number of Land Trusts being set up—especially in the USA. Thousands of organic farms, for example, have been placed into Land Trusts for farming organically in perpetuity. Instead of being something for which rent is due to an owner, the land is held in trust as a commons for community benefit. When the farmer retires, the land is made available to another farmer. As per Steiner's recommendations, the land is transferred without financial consideration. The *right* to farm the land, and the transfer of this right, is a purely legal matter; the right is bestowed on a new farmer by a specially constituted body of the cultural realm (i.e. the Trustees) which can identify (possibly with the assistance of the previous farmer) someone with the appropriate skills to take over. However, whilst Steiner proposes this newcomer be given entirely unfettered disposition over the means of production, with Land Trusts the Trustees are generally more hands-on. All the same, this model offers a good way to more incrementally adopt the principle of land being a matter of *right*, not something to buy and sell. In *Common Wealth*[142], Martin Large writes at length about such Land Trusts as a way of converting land to the status of a commons, not a commons in a free-for-all sense where all and sundry can come and graze their sheep, but in the sense that it has to be managed for the common good and not for private profiteering—much in the same way that sites of great beauty are stewarded by the National Trust in the UK (and similar in other countries), enabling all to visit them.[143]

In the case of land, therefore, the prospects are good for the adoption of more threefold ownership approaches. Not only can one imagine voters being amenable to at least *some* adjustment to nationwide ownership laws, but also the grass-roots Land Trust approach provides an effective mechanism if one wants to remove individual plots / tracts of land from the economic realm's buying and selling process.

But what of the means of production; what of shares?

Given that a virtual bedrock of business in somewhere like the UK, and indeed in most of the 'developed world' with whom we trade, revolves around share ownership, one might well ask how realistic it is to suppose this familiar, capitalist way of doing things could ever change. The ramifications of this would be incredibly far-reaching.

---

[142] Martin Large, *Common Wealth: For a Free, Equal, Mutual and Sustainable Society* (Stroud: Hawthorn Press, 2010).

[143] The National Trust holds and preserves in perpetuity over 600,000 acres of land which include castles, farms, nature reserves, historic houses, gardens, commons, wild parkland, 775 miles of coastline, etc. so that these can be enjoyed by the public.

Well, clearly, it is not realistic to think this could change from one approach to another overnight, or even in the medium term. Indeed, one can't help feeling that an approach where the means of production circulated only by way of gift rather than purchase might well first be adopted in some far-flung corner of the earth (unless the CIA or IMF get in there with some 'freedom' first!), with the rest of us then waking up one day and noticing that their crime rate is very low and their gross national happiness is very high. Then we will have a look to see how they have managed it.

When Steiner was addressing these issues, things were of course very different, and it was by no means a foregone conclusion in which direction politics would go. A substantial German landowner of the time reportedly remarked: 'had the Republic confiscated half our property in 1918, we would have considered the other half a gift from heaven'.[144] And influential entrepreneur Robert Bosch observed, for example, that there probably 'are no really serious objections' to an orderly 'transition of the capitalist economic system into the socialistic'.[145] By contrast, Steiner's proposals were moderate. He was not promoting ownership / management by the state, neither was he proposing that ownership change overnight. What he suggested was a transfer of ownership of the means of production upon the death of the owner (or some time thereafter).

Whilst the thought of doing away with stocks and shares in their entirety may be unrealistic today, one appealing aspect of such an idea is that, ultimately, it would make redundant the need for casino-like stock markets where ludicrously vast sums are transacted each day within a system that has limited benefit to the real economy. Not a lot is achieved by this daily scramble other than one group of shareholders (typically, speculators) makes a capital gain on their investment and another (also speculators) makes a loss. A vast industry—comprising analysts, traders, back office, advisers, investment managers, and so on and so forth—deals in shares, options, swaps, futures, currency, etc. whilst making a rather questionable net contribution. 'Of the tril-

---

[144] Albert Schmelzer, *The Threefold Movement, 1919: A History* (Forest Row: Rudolf Steiner Press, 2017), p. 33.
[145] Ibid., pp. 83-84.

lion U.S. dollars' worth of currencies exchanged every day, only 5 per cent relate to trade and other substantive economic transactions. The other 95 per cent is made up of speculations and arbitrages, as traders wielding huge sums look for rapid profits on exchange rate fluctuations and interest rate differentials.'[146] One of the more famous speculations occurred when George Soros made in excess of $1 billion of profit as the pound sterling was forced out of the European Exchange Rate Mechanism in 1992. Whether he was very pleased with himself, or concerned about the devastating effect this might have on the lives of many others, I don't know. He did at least direct a good portion of his winnings to philanthropic causes.

Another appealing aspect of Steiner's ownership model (in this Rights Realm section we are just concerned with ownership / the way in which the means of production are held) is that, as already alluded to, CEOs would no longer be answerable to shareholders, most of whom have little interest in the business beyond demanding the maximum possible profit. Ownership without work would not be rewarded (save for interest on loans). Non-working heirs could not wield power over the concern, nor benefit financially beyond a certain time frame. Ultimately, the wider community would benefit from cheaper goods, and workers would earn more since not only would there be no sleeping partners / non-working shareholders expecting a dividend, but any new management's income could be within some range pre-agreed at the time of management succession, or even, in the case of new start-ups, at the time of borrowing money (capital built up by others), pre-agreed within the loan terms, perhaps. In the words of Bernie Sanders: 'If Rob Walton, a key owner of Walmart, can afford an estimated $226 million for an antique car collection that includes 12 Ferraris, 6 Porsches … [etc.] … you know what? Walmart can afford to pay at least $15/hour to all of its workers.' And: 'While Walmart refuses to raise its $11 minimum wage, Alice Walton had no problem purchasing a $500 million private art collection.'[147] Neither Rob nor Alice set Walmart up, it should be added. They inherited it, or part of it at least, and so now enjoy a combined wealth of some $140 billion.

---

[146] Anthony Giddens, *The Third Way: The Renewal of Social Democracy* (Cambridge: Polity Press, 2008), p. 148.

[147] @SenSanders, 27 and 28 February 2021.

If a blanket 'ban' on being able to buy or sell the finished means of production *were* achievable (speaking hypothetically for a moment), one significant issue to address—among many—would be the resultant reluctance budding entrepreneurs might have to start up new businesses. If someone had a hunch that they could make a go of setting up a new facility to produce some new kind of widget, they might nonetheless be very wary if they knew they would not be able to sell the plant and machinery on again, were the business to fail. Steiner suggests these means of production would be passed on 'with all obligations', e.g. with any loans taken out when the means of production were initially bought etc. But if the business proposition had appeared risky, would the entrepreneur even have been able to borrow in the first place (as opposed to attracting risk capital)? And if not, would the entrepreneur want to use their own money to set up means of production, if there was no chance of selling them on if the business failed? Perhaps businesses below a certain size could have special dispensation allowing the means of production to be sold (remember the sewing machine quote!). Also, something that would make business failure much less likely in the first place is Steiner's recommendation (which we shall come on to in Section 7.4.3), that, instead of taking a punt, businesses manufacture in a much more rational way that corresponds with identified need.

In the same way that an inability to sell the finished means of production might dissuade entrepreneurs from risking their savings on some new venture, it would also dissuade outside investors. The existence of a secondary market for shares makes people willing to invest in the first place, since they know in advance that if they need the cash back at some point in the future, they will be able to sell the shares. Presumably, however, in our hypothetical society where shares (as we know them) did not exist, then the only options open to someone with savings would be either (a) to put them under the mattress, or (b) to lend, either individually or via an agent such as a bank. Lending would then be the accepted norm for those seeking a return on their savings.

Something of a halfway house between shares and loans can exist where a company issues both voting shares and preference shares—the latter having stronger dividend rights but no voting rights. Whilst still being buyable and sellable and thus not entirely removed from what Steiner regards as the economic domain, preference shares do at least (since they preclude voting) prevent wealthy—but unskilled—people from being able to meddle in operational matters, or insist on profit maximisation at all costs, or engage in asset stripping, etc. And since such shares can be bought and sold on the stock market, they are likely to be a faster way of attracting large amounts of capital into a business than borrowing. Furthermore, if, like famed economist Keynes and others propose, return to shareholders were capped in some way such that shareholders were not entitled to every last drop of value created, then this would also perhaps not be too far from the 'lending only' rule Steiner seems to favour.[148]

And were our hypothetical blanket ban on selling the finished means of production to actually be considered desirable, what would be the fate of existing businesses? How could these be chaperoned into the new ownership conditions?

It would of course be technically possible for a government, with funds to spare (!), to buy up any publicly quoted, *domestic* company, as happens with nationalisation. Such appropriated companies could then be directly transferred straight back out of the state's remit (in true threefold fashion) and into a legal form that excluded sellable means of production. (Karl Marx proposes nationalisation as a tactical, intermediate step prior to socialisation; but his socialisation involves control of the means of production by the community, something Steiner rails against as highly impractical. Community control can work in simple businesses—as confirmed by the successful community buyouts of pubs and village shops; but where complex know-how is crucial to effective management, the community management model can rather quickly fall apart.) Such government would need to make the case for all this in their manifesto, and it might be a tall order to convince a public unversed in the advantages of a threefold approach!

The argument for nationalisation is of course easier to make when the industry is a natural monopoly such as the national rail network or electricity grid. With these, it is easier for the electorate to see

---

[148] Christopher Houghton Budd explores this in *The Right On Corporation: Transforming the Corporation, a Micro Response to a Macro Problem* (Canterbury: New Economy Publications, 2004).

the point in placing the means of production under the management of a single body and having them run on the principle of service rather than return for shareholders / competition / profit maximisation (with perhaps some contrived, duplicative attempt at competition thrown in, and all policed by an industry regulator to prevent naughty behaviour!). With natural monopolies it would be relatively easy to implement the threefold principles of (a) removing outside (shareholder) ownership of the means of production (with its obsession with profit maximisation), and (b) removing government involvement in economic activity, too.

But other than via such an intermediate stage of nationalisation, how else could one transfer a publicly quoted company into an unsellable ownership model consistent with threefolding if, indeed, our hypothetical ban on saleability *were* deemed desirable? A country could, in theory, pass a law stating that, in 20 years' time all shares in *domestic* companies be converted into loan stock without voting rights. Share values would adjust themselves over the 20-year period as analysts got their teeth into the implications, and on the 20th anniversary they could crystallise into a loan of same value. What the likes of the World Trade Organisation would think of this is just one of the many questions one would need to consider. Plus, affected companies might simply be tempted to jump ship and register offshore.

So much for publicly quoted companies—that is, ones quoted on the stock market. But how could privately owned businesses be transitioned into a more threefold ownership model? This transitioning could be via the adoption of inheritance laws along the lines Steiner suggests. That is, so many years after the death of the proprietor, ownership of the means of production in question would be passed on by way of gift in such a way that was of benefit to the common good, that efficiently met the needs of consumers. Again, there would be a plethora of things to consider, not least what to do about business owned by those who have registered their affairs offshore.

However possible these things are in thought, though, it seems rather pie-in-the-sky to think any sort of macro, blanket ban on reselling the finished means of production would make it through parliament any time soon. And one can safely assume that, in the absence of legislation, most shareholders of publicly quoted companies would be unlikely to vote in favour of converting their shares to unsellable loan stock or similar. In view of this, what more piecemeal, micro ways might there be for business to move more in the direction Steiner suggests?

First of all, there is that substantial array of enterprises whose founders saw the point in a less rentier-type structure from the outset. These include a great many producer co-ops, Housing Associations, and so on. In all these cases, the means of production are relieved of their saleability. Their capital value has little relevance; *the raison d'être* of most of these organisations is service, not return for investors. To the extent that many charities are predominantly active in the economic realm, these are examples, too. For example, the Royal National Life-boat Institute (RNLI) provides sea rescue services, and its life boats and boathouses are means of production which have been removed from the economic realm in true threefold fashion. They are simply not available for sale; no one, however wealthy, could come along and snap them up. (Although not related to the ownership structure of the RNLI, one can also note that its *management* structure is somewhat in keeping with Steiner's suggestions too. He advises that management has full, unfettered dispensation over the means of production until such time as they no longer wish to exercise such rights in the manner originally intended, whereupon they—or some specially constituted body within the cultural domain—choose a successor. The Trustees of the RNLI are in effect such a cultural-realm body. They make sure the assets are used in the intended field of service, and will oversee smooth managerial succession when needed. However, it is also possible they have more executive power than Steiner seems to recommend when he talks of management's unfettered disposition over the means of production.)

Apart from these businesses that have more threefold ownership structures from the outset—with asset locks, etc.—there are inspiring examples of initially *private* business where an enlightened proprietor has seen the advantages of breaking the cycle of ownership being rewarded at the expense of work, has seen the social health inherent in co-workers sharing the proceeds of the business rather than absent owners. As a deed for humanity, if you like, these entrepreneurs have then voluntarily passed all or part of their business over to its workers. As cited earlier (Section 5.3.2), the John Lewis Partnership (which includes the Waitrose chain of supermarkets), Riverford Organics,

Aardman Animations and Richer Sounds are good examples of this. Employee ownership is a key part of these businesses.

But what of an entrepreneur who had no interest in setting up an unsellable venture? One might well wonder whether *anyone* would want to sink all their savings into getting a venture going if it was not going to be possible to sell the means of production later on, when they had had enough! Without our hypothetical law preventing such sale, then new private ventures following a more threefold course would presumably only arise where a more equitable approach simply appealed to the entrepreneur(s), or because they had identified a body of customers interested in supporting alternative ownership models. The interest, particularly of the younger generations, in social justice and more ethical ways of doing things appears to be a growing force to be reckoned with after all. The sizeable support for politicians like Jeremy Corbyn and Bernie Sanders in recent years, despite scathing media coverage, has shown that many—especially amongst the young—are fed up with the old ways. What's the point of smooth talkers and slick dressers when all they will do is deliver more of the same, perpetuate a system that serves investors more than the needy … and it will still be impossible to buy a house?! Political discourse can in fact change quickly when the will—and heart—is there. Who would have thought that a Swedish schoolgirl (who shared that she was initially sitting around at home with 'no friends' and 'an eating disorder')[149] would so quickly become an eco-activist inspiring millions?! More equitable business propositions already have a significant, waiting market, surely! And of course, from this very pool of individuals with a more active conscience, new businesses are likely to enter the landscape, businesses which have been founded by those wanting to proceed in more equitable ways.

An enthusiast of threefold ideas could be discouraged by the rather incremental ways in which such an approach is likely to unfold, discouraged at the potential irrelevance of it all. The huge multinationals, through which the lion's share of business operates, would no doubt just carry on as usual. And because of their significant economies of scale, would continue to provide the cheapest goods and services long into

---

[149] https://www.google.com/amp/s/amp.the.guardian.com/environment/2019/sep/02/greta-thunberg-responds-to-aspergers-critics-its-a-superpower.

the future. But remember, Steiner's supposition was a societal improvement that developed organically, that was in keeping with reality at all times. 'Dreaming big' has little value where it is unrealistic. And you never know, Jeff Bezos of Amazon might wake up one morning and decide that, after all, addressing more of the profound and urgent needs of humanity here on earth is more worthwhile than squandering billions on ecologically irresponsible joy rides into space and excruciatingly impractical space cities! (Jeff, if you are reading this, we know you do a lot of good things too; but this stuff pains us deeply!)

7.3.8   The police and the armed forces

> *Militarisation, the fundamental evil of our time ... (CW192(iii), 8 June 1919)*

Notwithstanding his friendship with Germany's pre-war Chief of Staff, General Helmuth von Moltke, Steiner unsurprisingly had little to say about how the army or the police should be run, other than that internal and national security fell properly under the auspices of the democratically elected state. Although based in neutral Switzerland during 1914–1918, he was naturally profoundly aware of the horrors of the war, and said on more than one occasion how the possibility of such dreadful conflicts could be greatly reduced in future under a proper 'threefolding' of society.

Although perhaps obvious, it should be noted that, whilst the security services fall under the auspices of the rights sphere, and whilst the leitmotif of the rights sphere is democracy, this does not mean that the democratic principle would apply to the *internal workings* of the police or armed forces. Whilst the democratic principle—the will of the people—determines the general remit of the security services, this does not mean a democratic principle applies *within* these bodies. If an enemy's tactics changed during battle, say, it would be inadvisable for your regiment to promptly down rifles and convene a meeting to discuss, and vote on, what to do next! The democratic part applies to the political, legislative realm as a whole, not to the internal workings of every organisation that might be working within it.

* * *

This concludes Steiner's operational suggestions / illustrations for the rights domain.

7.4   Operational Remarks — Economic Realm

In the summer of 1922, Steiner gives a course of lectures on economics which form a more in-depth supplement to what he has said thus far about the economic realm. These lectures are primarily for students of economics, and are not only quite specialised but also, at times, borderline impenetrable! Indeed, as can be ascertained from the questions and answers at the end of some of the lectures, even his economics-reading listeners found them hard-going. In these talks, he frequently departs from accepted economic theory to make original observations about economic life, referencing various economic thinkers in the process.

He also acknowledges that the subject is a complex and challenging one.

> *Infinitely more complicated, variable and unstable are the phenomena in economics than in nature—more fluctuating, less capable of being grasped with any defined or hard and fast concepts.*
> *(CW540, p. 28)*

That many of the comments made during this lecture course are not aimed at the general public is further affirmed by the fact that they are only made during this fortnight, unlike his more general threefold comments which he repeats a great many times both in written material placed before the public, as well as in a multitude of lectures as he criss-crosses Europe to address all types of audience.

Building on the economic domain's overriding principles of fraternity, mutuality, interdependence we will now look at the operational observations and approaches that Steiner suggested for this realm both in those more specialised lectures delivered in 1922 as well as in his more general threefold works. His operational suggestions / illustrations for the economic realm greatly outnumber those he gave for either the cultural or rights domains, so this section of the book is correspondingly longer. Some of these suggestions relate more directly to the threefold nature of society, others less so.

Remember two things, though: firstly, his definition of the economy as the system of production, circulation and consumption of commodities (i.e. goods and services—which exclude virgin land, the finished means of production, and labour); and secondly his emphasis on not wishing to be prescriptive beyond the main principle of separate administrative regimes for the three realms—realms which can then gain strength and health by working according to their appropriate guiding principles.

Again, after the main points of each section have been summarised in a few bullet points, some additional comments are added, where this seems appropriate, that reflect how the suggestions made might apply today.

7.4.1   Competition or co-operation ?

As we have seen, the economic realm is a very different beast from the rights realm. In the rights realm all adults, via democracy, can *equally* make decisions (about rights / obligations / rules / laws), and all are then *equally* bound by these rules too. Equality rules the day.

But in the economy, only those with the relevant technical expertise are suitable to make decisions about the production and circulation of goods. And whilst all can make decisions about their *own* needs, any democratic approach whereby consumption for the whole population was determined by majority decision would come at the (not insubstantial) expense of minority needs and tastes not being met. We don't all want to wear the same types of cardigan. Equality does not apply within the economic realm. Different citizens have different production expertise and so produce different commodities. No equality there. And they also want to consume different commodities. No equality there either.

For Steiner, like many others, the idea of an economy run by a socialist state bureaucracy was anathema that would spell economic disaster. It would all but strangle the ability of the boundless, creative potential of human initiative to express itself, to continually invigorate and reinvigorate enterprise. And it would in all probability mean tyranny over consumption by the state.

So, in his view, state socialism was out. The idea of equality in the economic realm made little sense. But what did he recommend instead? A traditional, crush-thy-neighbour, competitive form of capitalism? Some sort of neo-liberal free-for-all? Not this either, unsurprisingly, as becomes evident when, for example, he talks about companies of this sort proceeding ...

> ... *according to profit, according to the most sordid competition, the blindest human egoism, which leads every man to try and earn as much as ever he can squeeze out of the social system. [...] based upon the war of competition, upon profit, upon economic coercion in the tug of war between capital and wages. (CW330[ii])*
>
> *Purely outward advances in the development of work would lead to the dissolution of all ties within humanity. People would become increasingly unable to understand each other or to develop relationships that satisfy the requirements of human nature. Individuals would increasingly pass each other by, safeguarding only their own interests, and would be incapable of relating to each other except as competitors. This must not be allowed to happen, or the human race will fall into complete decadence. [...] It would be hell if the human race were controlled entirely by competition and addiction to acquisition. (CW172, p. 75)*

In such remarks, his feelings about traditional capitalism are clear.

But before looking at his alternative, let's remind ourselves of one or two of the characteristics of competition.

Broadly speaking, in the competitive markets that we are used to, prices find something of an equilibrium. If there is only one seller of a particular good, they might take advantage of their unique position as a monopoly and set a high price which delivers them a large profit. But other producers will eventually notice this, assuming that what economists call 'perfect information' exists—which is often not the case.[150] Having noticed the profit, or the high selling price, another producer will also start to make the same commodity, but undercut the first producer, thereby forcing the latter to also reduce price lest all their customers are lost to the second producer. In theory, this process continues until no further undercutting can be done without a

---

[150] 'Perfect information' applies when all buyers in a market are fully informed of prices and quantities available, and producers have equal knowledge of production techniques and costs.

loss being made on the sale. Therefore, in theory, the price will settle here—at the cheapest possible level for the customer. That's the theory, and it's a pretty neat one. Supply and demand (the willingness of producers to produce and the willingness of buyers to buy) eventually lead to an equilibrium price—the best price a customer can expect, since any lower and the producer would not cover their costs. And for this reason, of course, producers only ever make tiny profits!

But, as we know, there are problems with this competitive approach. One is that it can encourage business leaders to pay ever lower wages, especially when there is unemployment and cheap labour is available. This might continue until a national minimum wage is reached (if this exists), which can then go hand in hand with employees claiming in-work state benefits. In other words, the taxpayer starts to subsidise the business (or its customers). The next stage after this sees production outsourced abroad to where there may be no national minimum wage at all, and more-or-less starvation wages can be paid instead. This may all signify cheap products for the home market, but at the cost of home job losses and the exploitation of, typically, distant, faceless Asians.

In the further quest to undercut the competition, producers may start to cut corners from a product quality point of view, and we then end up with shoddy goods—screwdrivers from the pound shop, perhaps, that are nigh useless after turning just a few screws.

Further corner cutting might lead to irresponsible treatment of the environment, disregard for people's health, mistreatment of indigenous tribes, and so on.

Another problem can be that the 'perfect information' assumption does not hold good. It may take other manufacturers some time to notice that the first producer, having no competition initially, is taking advantage of its sole-producer, monopoly status (not to mention its customers) by charging high prices and thereby making an inflated profit on the commodity. With this time delay, the first producer can have such a head start before other producers get in on the act, that, with the greater experience under its belt, it will have honed the operation to such an extent that the second producer's operating cost may be higher on account of their relative lack of experience in producing the item. The second operator's entry into the market may well provoke the first producer to reduce prices in order to maintain its advantage—which benefits the consumer. But with significant reserves under its belt, the first producer may well be able to reduce the price to such an extent that it represents a loss-making price for the second producer. A naive or undercapitalised second producer is then forced out of business. And then up go the prices again as the first producer returns to its old, profiteering ways once the competition has been seen off.

If two or more producers do survive this game, however, which is typically the case eventually, especially if everyone's industrial espionage has got a handle on the new technologies, and anti-monopoly laws have taken effect (don't hold your breath!), we then bear witness to the competitive behaviour we are used to—whereby each company spends thousands on PR, then hundreds of thousands, and so on, to raise the profile of their particular widget and maintain / increase market share. Marketing specialists are taken on, junk mail starts to land on the doorstep, teams of rival sales reps begin roaming the country, and your TV night gets interrupted with adverts telling you which particular widget is, without question, the best. Oh, and in some countries, teams of cold callers (one of the most demoralising jobs imaginable?) phone hordes of uninterested victims, achieving very little apart from annoying thousands and disproportionately hoodwinking the elderly and the gullible. The cost of all this scheming, of course, has to be passed on to the consumer. The additional PR and 'bullshit jobs' (David Graeber) add little or nothing to overall productivity.[151]

As mentioned, however, competition *can* have its advantages for the customer. Not only can it bring prices down to their lowest price possible, but manufacturers may (repeat, *may*) improve quality to give their particular widget the edge. The motivation can arise—driven by the self-interest of making a higher profit—to innovate in order to outsmart the competition.

Nonetheless, if taken to its logical conclusion, this seems inevitably to lead to ugly neo-liberal extremes, as Paul Mason reminds us (whilst also acknowledging that capitalism has brought many benefits): 'Neoliberalism is the doctrine of uncontrolled markets: it says that the best route to prosperity is individuals pursuing their own self-interest, and the market is the only way to express that self-interest. It says the state should be

---

[151] David Graeber, *Bullshit Jobs: A Theory* (2018). D. Graeber argues that, unlike 'shit jobs' (blue collar jobs that are unpleasant but necessary), 'bullshit jobs' (white collar jobs that are largely pointless) are a 'scar across our collective soul'.

small (except for its riot squad and secret police); that financial speculation is good; that inequality is good; that the natural state of humankind is
to be a bunch of ruthless individuals, competing with each other.'[152] But
also: 'Neoliberalism's guiding principle is not free markets, nor fiscal
discipline, nor sound money, nor privatisation and offshoring—not even
globalization. All these things were byproducts or weapons of its main
endeavour: to remove organized labour from the equation.'[153]

There are plenty of studies, though, that have disproved the idea
that humanity is naturally this ruthlessly and selfishly inclined.[154]
Yes, some may be like this, and competitive capitalism is a breeding
ground wherein the bearers of these possibly psychopathic tendencies are allowed (encouraged, even) to rise to elite power. 'Among the
1 per cent, neoliberalism has the power of a religion: the more you
practise it, the better you feel—and the richer you become.'[155] But
with unending problems in its wake, this conventional approach will
sooner or later have surely run its course. No doubt its proponents will
cling on to their power for however long they can, like the monarchs
of old; but it seems the world will eventually decide their ideology has
come to the end of whatever usefulness it may have once had. Referring to the Davos address of one such proponent (Prudential CEO
Tidjane Thiam) in 2012, Mason winces: 'Workers' rights and decent
wages stand in the way of capitalism's revival and, says the million-
aire finance guy without embarrassment, must go'.[156]

There is certainly a strange logic behind this capitalist 'religion':
'the extraordinary belief that the nastiest of men for the nastiest of
motives will somehow work together for the benefit of all'.[157]

---

[152] Paul Mason, *Postcapitalism: A Guide to Our Future* (London: Allen Lane,
2015), p. xi.
[153] Ibid., p. 91.
[154] See, for example, Owen Jones, 'Grotesque inequality is not a natural part of
being human', *The Guardian*, 24 November 2014.
[155] Paul Mason, *Postcapitalism: A Guide to Our Future* (London: Allen Lane,
2015), p. 12.
[156] Ibid., p. 4.
[157] Attributed to John Maynard Keynes, with some uncertainty. See Martin Large
and Steve Briault (Eds), *Free, Equal and Mutual: Rebalancing Society for the
Common Good* (Stroud: Hawthorn Press, 2018), p. 19.

Instead of what he calls 'sordid competition', Steiner advocates co-operation in the economic realm to reflect the guiding principle of brotherliness / sisterliness that is fitting for this aspect of society. But he is not necessarily talking about the co-operation seen in co-operatives, or not, at least, as seen in those co-operatives where collective bargaining is used simply to get better deals for co-op members.

> ... neither by nationalisation or communalisation, nor by the founding of co-operative societies by people who all need the same kind of articles, can any fruitful result be attained. (CW332a, p. 31)
>
> ... newer kinds of communities (cooperatives, for example), which are not fully in harmony with these new requirements, having been copied from the old forms using traditional thought habits. (CW23, p. 143)
>
> It must be shown how neither producer co-operatives nor consumer co-operatives can work prosperously for the future. Producer co-operatives are not ideal because experience shows that people with real personal initiative do not get involved ... Consumer co-operatives are not ideal even though they are among the best, especially when they pass into self-production. But they cannot reach the necessary goal for the future for the simple reason that they don't arise out of an association with what is there but instead stand inside ordinary capitalism, at least in a corner where they first one-sidedly organize consumption and then simply integrate production into the consumer organization, if they do it at all. Less helpful still for real progress are co-operatives such as the raw materials co-operatives and the like. Such co-operatives have no feel for associative life whatsoever; what they do amounts to activity in one corner of economic life, whilst the question of raw materials is in fact closely connected to the issue of consumption. (CW337b, 10 October 1920)

There are of course a great many co-operatives which embody noble, brotherly principles. But where people join together in a co-op principally in order to gain bargaining power, or bulk discounts, or similar, which is essentially in order to look after themselves, this does not really encompass the extent of the co-operation Steiner is advocating. His approach is broader.

The original Rochdale co-operative principles set out in 1844 were, it is true, somewhat more limited in scope compared to the significantly more outward-looking ones adopted in 1995 (i.e. seventy years after Steiner died). The original principles were: (1) Open membership (i.e. non-discriminatory); (2) Democratic control (one person, one vote); (3) Distribution of surplus in proportion to trade (if you buy more stuff, you receive more of the profit); (4) Payment of limited interest on capital (to those co-operators investing); (5) Political and religious neutrality; (6) Cash trading (no credit extended); (7) Promotion of education. The principles adopted in 1995, on the other hand, are: (1) Voluntary and Open Membership; (2) Democratic Member Control; (3) Member Economic Participation; (4) Autonomy and Independence; (5) Education, Training and Information (to enable effective member engagement as well as public understanding); (6) Co-operation among co-operatives; (7) Concern for Community.

As is clear in new rules (6) and (7), the principles observed by modern co-operatives have broadened out appreciably: other co-operatives and the community at large are taken into consideration. This can mean considerably closer alignment between newer co-operative models and Steiner's idea of collaboration. Indeed, in the UK we now have an enhanced legal form for co-ops (the Community Benefit Society) which, for example, can include an asset lock as strong as any charity's. However, it is doubtful even these more recent principles would have been regarded by Steiner as appropriate in all circumstances. The idea of democratic control, for example, was not something he advocated for all forms of business. The most successful co-ops of today, in the main, operate businesses where there is limited differentiation of function. That is to say, the businesses are not especially complex, and so all the co-workers can understand what all the other co-workers are doing. A typical example is the wholesale food co-op. With such a simple business, all co-workers can have a reasonably good understanding of what everyone is doing and, with this common understanding, it would not seem inappropriate for decisions to be taken democratically—if that is how they want to operate. Group decision-making is unlikely to undermine efficiency when all can have a clear idea of the whole operation.

But what about Network Rail, say, or Air France? It would clearly be highly impractical (and costly to passengers) for such companies to hold whole-company meetings that included the thousands of ticket inspectors (Network Rail) or the stewards / stewardesses (Air France) each time the former was considering building a new bridge in Lancashire or the latter exploiting a new time slot to the Seychelles.

Henry Ford summed up the issue thus: 'We expect the men to do what they are told. The organisation is so highly specialized and one part is so dependent on another that we could not for a moment consider allowing men to have their own way. Without the most rigid discipline we would have the utmost confusion.'[158] With his colleagues, he had built up a highly efficient operation that, by 1921, was employing over 40,000 workers making the relatively inexpensive but high quality Model-T at a rate of 5,000 cars per day. If the cost of each single part rose by a mere one cent (not one *per* cent, but one *cent*), this represented an additional cost to the company of $50m per annum! All staff were encouraged to always consider whether there was a better way of doing things, and this culture of efficiency enabled the company to not only sell the cheapest (and also most durable) cars, but also to pay its workers a minimum of $5 per day when the rest of the industry was paying between $2 and $3 per day.

Instead of group decision-making, Steiner insists those with the most suitable abilities manage the business in question. His concern is efficiency and productivity, an optimal ability to meet society's needs. In larger, more complex businesses, this would not come with group decision-making. (However, as discussed in Sections 7.3.4 and 7.4.14, he recommends remuneration structures such that decision-makers cannot exploit non-decision-makers.)

So, the co-operation seen in co-operatives, certainly those co-operatives active in Steiner's day, is not really what he is talking about. Neither is he interested in that co-operation seen, for example, in trade unions.

Take ... the union movement [...] People join together without regard for any concrete shaping of economic life; they merged into ... the Metalworkers' Federation, the Printers' Associations, and so on, only to pursue collective bargaining and wage battles. What do such associations do? They play politics in the economic realm. They bring the state principle into the economic realm. Just as producer cooperatives—associations formed by producers—conflict

---

[158] Henry Ford, *My Life and Work* (Hawthorne, CA: BN Publishing, 2008), p. 78.

> *with the principle of association [see next section, RM], so, too, do*
> *trade unions. (CW337b, 12 October 1920)*
>
> *... such connections, which have emerged purely from the capital-*
> *ist economic order, like the unions, must, above all, disappear as*
> *quickly as possible. (CW337b, 12 October 1920)*
>
> *... they must disappear, because only by the disappearance of the*
> *trade unions, which are pure labour unions, will association take*
> *place ... That is what matters, above all, to eradicate what tears*
> *people apart. (CW337b, 12 October 1920)*

It should be stressed (if it isn't clear already) that Steiner was by no means unsympathetic to the plight of workers, blind to the poor industrial relations that lay behind the formation of trade unions. But these exist to 'fight our corner', to advocate for workers' rights, and as such were more concerned with rights than economics. As shall become clear, Steiner's approach squarely aims to remove the *need* for trade unions.

So, what precisely *does* Steiner envisage when he talks of co-operation / collaboration in economic matters? He recommends ...

> *... associations that will create through economic co-operation what*
> *has been brought about hitherto by the egotistical competition of*
> *individuals. It is a question of free social coordination between the*
> *various complexes of production and consumption ... (CW24, p. 89)*

fraternité; co-operation; coordination; associations. Such associations will be considered in the next section. But note, this collaboration is not only a collaboration between those with the same interests. A collaboration only between producers, say, can easily lead to collusion, cartels, monopolistic profiteering. No, the economic collaboration he is talking about extends beyond the narrow confines of one's immediate 'tribe', beyond the interests of one side only. Instead, it is one where the interests of all parties—producer, distributor and consumer—have a voice. These different stakeholders—or their representatives—associate, engage with each other, with all the (opposing) interests relevant to the trade in question, in order to arrive at mutually satisfactory solutions, solutions that all interest groups can sign up to.

> *One should not think so narrowly that one only considers a company; one must be clear of the effects on the whole economic life. That's what matters. (CW337b, 30 August 1920)*

In summary:

- State-run economy is out.
- Competition-based economy is out.
- Co-operation is in.
- But not simply co-operation in furtherance of one's own advantage on *one* side of an otherwise adversarial system.
- Instead, this co-operation is to exist between producers, distributors and consumers.

Reflections in relation to the present

Apart from the co-ops and trade unions mentioned above, one can always find plenty of other instances of co-operation today that simply perpetuate the competitive paradigm, perpetuate co-operation that is not particularly brotherly / sisterly in any wider sense. We have syndicates where several individuals or companies take on larger projects which they would not be able to undertake on their own. We have the likes of OPEC (in fact, a group of oil-producing *nations* rather than companies) which meets twice per year to look at capacity, demand, prices, output and so on. Their decision-making is based on their own interests; it is not really modified by the interests of consumers being represented 'from the other side'. Their main concern is the balancing of over-production against under-production. Over-production leads to low prices and poor profit levels. Under-production leads to high prices which they realise will encourage industrialised nations (us, their customers) to accelerate research into and take-up of alternative power types such as nuclear and renewables. Essentially, they are a cartel.

As we know, though, there are a great many encouraging examples today of businesses that, without entering into any formal collaboration, voluntarily take account of 'the other' instead of pursuing out-and-out competition and self-interest. These would include all those companies which take social responsibility or environmental protection seriously (and not simply because the law requires it or because it makes them 'look good'). Or, for example, all those endeavours that fall under the general heading of 'social enterprise'—because they put certain ideals and consideration of 'the other', the common good, or the planet before their own profit. They have moved on from profit maximisation. The 1995 co-operative rules mentioned earlier, which include the additional principles of co-operation with other co-operatives and concern for the community, are also a case in point. So, too, is Fair Trade. As is much of the multi-billion pound ethical investment sector. And so on. Happily, recognition of 'the other' and 'the other's needs' is frequently to be found.

The assumption that everyone is out to outdo everyone else is disproved by so many examples of social enterprise, collaborative business, good old-fashioned charity, volunteering, creative commons licensing[159], and more besides. As Paul Mason says: 'According to standard economics a person like Richard Stallman[160] should not exist: he is not following his self-interest but suppressing it in favour of a collective interest that is not just economic but moral.'[161] Indeed, a study by political scientist Peter Hall found that nearly 20% of UK citizens do some form of voluntary work in an average year, with 10% doing so on a weekly basis.[162] An example Kate Raworth gives of the 'generous design' she advocates is the launch of the Open Source Circular Economy, whose 'worldwide network of innovators, designers and activists aims to follow in the footsteps of open-source software by creating the knowledge commons needed to unleash the full potential of circular manufacturing. Why a knowledge commons? Because, as those in the OSCE movement point out, the full regenerative potential of circular

---

[159] Creative commons licensing, covering almost 1.5 billion works worldwide, allows more flexible copyright approaches, including complete copyright waiver. The most well-known example of creative commons is Wikipedia with 8.5 billion page views per month and over 100,000 contributors who give their services for free.

[160] Pioneer of free software that lead to the likes of the open-source operating system Linux.

[161] Paul Mason, *Postcapitalism: A Guide to Our Future* (London: Allen Lane, 2015), p. 122.

[162] PA Hall 'Social Capital in Britain', Mimeo, Centre for European Studies, Harvard University, 1997.

production cannot be reached by individual companies seeking to make it happen all within their own factory walls: it is an illogical and unfeasible basis for creating a circular economy'.[163] When freely sharing things like experience and design specifications, circular economy principles (e.g. easy reuse of components because of common shape and size) become much easier to follow. The OSVehicle—the electric car born in Silicon Valley is one product of this collaborative, open source approach. Whilst Steiner is by no means suggesting the economic realm becomes an arena based on gift, what is abundantly clear is that the human being can find significant meaning in mutuality and altruism. And a conclusion to be drawn from this is that the idea of a more collaborative economy is by no means eccentric.

In her bestselling *Doughnut Economics*, Raworth bemoans the inadequacy of 'rational economic man'—the self-seeking and insatiable image of ourselves on which most economic thinking has been based. Noting that, were it true, our chances of survival as a species would be poor, Raworth proposes 'taking his cartoon depiction out of the economic gallery and painting, in its place, a new portrait of humanity. It will turn out to be the most important portrait commissioned in the twenty-first century, mattering not just to economists but to us all. [...] The preliminary sketches for this updated self-portrait are underway, revealing five broad shifts in how we can best depict our economic selves. First, rather than narrowly self-interested we are social and reciprocating. Second, in place of fixed preferences, we have fluid values. Third, instead of isolated we are interdependent. Fourth, rather than calculate, we usually approximate. And fifth, far from having dominion over nature, we are deeply embedded in the web of life. [...] It is time to redraw ourselves as people who thrive by connecting with each other and with this living home of ours that is not ours alone'.[164]

That's not to say greed doesn't exist! One date can very adequately remind us of this: 2008. What was behind the financial crash if not the obsessive drive to try and wring just that bit more out of the system?

---

[163] Kate Raworth, *Doughnut Economics: Seven Ways to Think Like a 21st-Century Economist* (London: Random House, 2018), pp. 229-231.
[164] Ibid., pp. 95-127.

Frustratingly, as Raworth points out, various studies have demonstrated how, if one is presented with an image of what people are supposed to be like, one can start to behave the same way. The cartoon of rational economic man has a lot to answer for![165]

All the same, a question one could ask is: has the growth in community benefit models, social enterprise, ethical investment, etc. to some extent reduced the need for the more formal association of which Steiner speaks? With most ethical practice in business, 'others' are generally taken into consideration without their necessarily being in the room or otherwise voicing their needs. Their needs are simply anticipated by the more socially minded business. Steiner would no doubt be highly appreciative of such sincere consideration for the needs of others, but one imagines he would nonetheless still encourage the wider economy to become more associative along the lines we shall see in the next section. For one, these inspiring, ethical ventures are still very much in the minority, whilst rapacious corporatism with its playground-bully mentality of indifference to the plight of its victims has been allowed to run riot with some truly shocking consequences. (Sooner or later the school bell is surely gonna have to ring for everyone to go back into the classroom and continue the business of growing up! There are more dignified ways of approaching life than constantly going about like a bunch of spivs 'on the make'!) Also, as will be seen in the following section, Steiner's idea of association involves a more formal collaboration between parties, where this is possible: a more formal collaboration between producers, distributors and consumers such that production becomes a more organised response to need.

7.4.2   Associations

> ... human co-operation in economic life must be based on the fraternity which is inherent in associations. (CW23, p. 81)

As noted previously, in the rights realm, decisions are ideally reached by all adults via an equal, democratic process. In the economic domain, however, Steiner encourages association such that decisions

---

[165] Kate Raworth, *Doughnut Economics: Seven Ways to Think Like a 21ˢᵗ-Century Economist* (London: Random House, 2018), p. 100

are reached neither by all, via democracy, nor by the individual in isolation, but between *interested parties* in negotiation. Decisions about the production / distribution / consumption process are ideally arrived at within groupings of individuals, within associations between those affected.

> ... when I was speaking in Germany to a fairly small group of working men about associations, they said to me: we have heard of very many things, but we don't really know what associations are; we haven't really heard anything about them. An association is not an organisation and not a consortium ['Koalition']. It comes into being through the conflux of the individuals within the economy. The individual does not have to adopt something handed out from a central body, but is able to contribute the knowledge and ability he has in his own field. From a collaboration in which each gives of his best, and where what is done springs from the agreement of many—only from such associations does economic life in general derive. Associations of this kind [...] will link together those engaged in production and commerce, and the consumers. Only production, distribution and consumption will have any part in them. (CW83, pp. 178-179)
>
> The economic process can only be sound when such a wise self-active intelligence is working within it. And this can only happen if human beings are united together—human beings who have the economic process within them as pictures, piece by piece, and being united in the associations, they complement and correct one another so the right circulation can take place in the whole economic process. (CW340, p. 132)

Whilst consumption might be based on *individual* tastes, and production might be based on *individual* competence and expertise in one field or another, Steiner nonetheless stresses that it is unhealthy for the economic realm in general—for the production / circulation / consumption continuum—to be based on the decisions of individuals working in isolation. What to produce, and in what quantity, is no matter for individuals to decide, even though it may be individuals who decide *how* to make the commodities needed.

> *... as far as economic life is concerned, the* individual *cannot reach valid judgments at all. Judgment here can only be arrived at collectively, through co-operation of many people in very different walks of life. It is not just theory, but something that will have to become practical wisdom, that truly valid judgments here can arise only from the consonance of many voices. (CW83, p. 172)*
>
> *... economic life can in no way be circumscribed by the consideration of the individual, because economic experience, economic perception can only come to valid judgement by the agreement between persons interested in economic life in various ways. The individual can never gain a valid judgement, also not through statistics, how economy should be conducted, but only by agreement say of consumers and producers who form associations, where the one tells the other what the needs are and, conversely, the other tells the one what possibilities there are for production. Only when a collective decision comes about by agreement within the associations of economic life, can a valid decision for economic life be found.*
>
> *[...] a real economic judgement can only result from the agreement[166] of those who participate in the economic life from the knowledge which individuals gather as partial knowledge and which only becomes valid[167] judgement when the individual knowledge of the one is modified[168] by the individual knowledge of the other. Only discussion[169] can lead to a valid judgement in economic life. (CW79, 30 November 1921)*

Former Labour leader Hugh Gaitskell once observed that: 'So long as production is left to the uncontrolled decisions of private individuals, conducted, guided and inspired by the motives of profit, so long will Poverty, Insecurity and Injustice continue.'[170] But, as Edmund Dell noted in relation to this: 'There remained the question how all-wise and all-seeing would be the governmental calculations with which the

---

[166] *Verständigung* also means communication.

[167] *adäquaten* = adequate.

[168] *abschleift* = smoothed out, rubbed down.

[169] *Auseinandersetzung* = debate, dispute, intense engagement, argument.

[170] Edmund Dell, *A Strange Eventful History: Democratic Socialism in Britain* (London: Harper Collins, 1999), p.13.

market was to be replaced. The rationality that was to govern society was the rationality of certain high priests—politicians, economists, civil servants. The explicit assumption was that they would know what was good for the congregation.'[171] Steiner opines the economic system should be left neither to individual decisions, nor to political bureaucracy. Instead, producers, distributors and consumers ideally talk to one another, associate.

And different producers should talk to each other too, where they have mutual concern:

> ... people in different trades working in related industries and suppliers and consumers in a particular industry should form associations so that the resulting structure of the economy allows each person to see how his or her job fits into in the circulation of goods and services. (CW334, p.104)

> ... associations in the various trades and professions as well as associations of consumers and manufacturers; the structure of our economy will be based on what one person can learn from another. (CW334, p.130)

> Persons who belong to the same branch of the economy will have to unite with each other; they will have to form associations with those from other economic sectors. Through a lively intercourse between such associations and cooperatives the interests of producers and consumers will be able to organize themselves. In this way, economic impulses[172] alone will be able to work within the economy. (CW24, p. 10)

> ... persons with similar professional or consumer interests, or with similar needs of other kinds, to unite in co-operative associations which, through reciprocal activities, will underlie the entire economy. This organisation will structure itself on an associative foundation and on the interrelations between associations. The associations will engage in purely economic activities. (CW23, p. 68)

---

[171] Edmund Dell, *A Strange Eventful History: Democratic Socialism in Britain* (London: Harper Collins, 1999), p.14.

[172] 'Economic impulses' meaning production, circulation and consumption of commodities, in contradistinction to any engagement with workers' rights and working conditions.

> So, what's the point of these associations in economic life? The purpose of these associations is to first of all connect professional circles which are somehow related, which have to cooperate in a practical way, which attend to their business and get together completely independently of any state interference. And then these associations of professional circles should in turn associate with their consumers, so that that which arises as reciprocal exchange first happens between the related professional circles, and then also within the associations between producer and consumer circles. (CW337a, 3 March 1920)

On one occasion, a machine operator listening to one of Steiner's factory talks asked whether associative working could reduce the sort of duplication and waste of capital evident in several factories which had all invested in similar plant even though none was working to capacity. In response ...

> ... what the gentleman has just said really confirms the principle of association. If the work is carried out in a completely individualistic way, and without the producers associating, that is to say working together, then naturally the situation that you describe will happen—which is that the machine is only partly used. The complete use of the machine however can only happen if those involved associate together. Therefore what you have said is very clearly along the lines of the principle of association. (CW332a(ii), p. 63)

However, whilst Steiner talks of people with similar interests or needs needing to unite, one such grouping on its own would perhaps not amount to an association in his sense of being a place where dialogue with 'the other' can happen, where the different parties in one or another area of trade can negotiate. The following clarifies:

> To believe that one can set up associations simply between producers within the same industry—that is not association. (CW337b, 10 October 1920)
>
> Associations within an industry really do not exist, these are not associations. Rather, associations live between one industry

and the next, and above all, between producers and consumers. Associations are the exact opposite of what results in trusts[173] or syndicates, and the like. We will still see how certain connections between the manufacturers of a particular type of commodity are necessary; but then they have a completely different function. (CW337b, 10 October 1920)

... there has always been a need for people within the same industries to join forces, but this lacks economic value because it's about not having to compete on the open market, about not needing to undercut prices and the like. As a result, you will find that such associations—that are essentially single-industry associations—will, on the whole, be bodies that resemble co-operatives. These no longer need have any actual economic significance, however; they will tend to fall away from economic life. If those who manufacture the same product do connect with each other, that's all well and good, but it will be a good opportunity for more spiritual interests to unfold, for those people to get to know each other who are preferably working out of a common mind-set, who have a certain moral connection. (CW337b, 10 October 1920)

Steiner also emphasises that associations do not rely on new kinds of business being created; he encourages any already-existing producer etc. to enter into association with the others they do business with.

Within the economic sphere of the social organism there will be associations in which consumers, producers and distributors will together reach an associative judgment based on practical experience—not an individual judgment that can only be irrelevant in this sphere. The small beginnings being tried today shows that this is not yet possible, but the fact that these small beginnings are being tried shows that unconsciously humanity does have the intention to form associations. Cooperatives, trade unions, all kinds of communities show that this intention exists. But when cooperatives are founded side by side with ordinary social life as it exists today they will perish unless they conform to this social life by charging the same prices and using the same marketing practices. In working

---

[173] In the US sense of a corporate trust, a holding company, a conglomerate of different businesses.

towards a threefold social organism we should not be trying to cre-
ate new realities based on Utopian concepts; we should be coming
to grips with what is already there. Institutions already in existence,
consumers, producers, the entrepreneur, everything already in
existence needs to come together in associations. There is no
need to ask how to create associations. The question to ask is:
how can existing economic organizations and institutions be inte-
grated in associations? (CW305(ii), p. 161)

The following comments demonstrate how Steiner sees little merit in being prescriptive about economic associations, beyond simply saying different stakeholders should talk and negotiate with each other.

... what is needed is that people observe the social currents from
their economic viewpoint and, through associations, in which alone
an economic judgement can be formed, bring the economic life
into the right streams, not by laws but out of immediate life by
direct human negotiation. The social life must be based practically
on the human condition. Therefore the 'Essentials of the Social
Question' [i.e. CW23] is not concerned with describing some social
structure, but with indicating how people can be brought into a
relationship in which they can, by their working together, do from
time to time what is needed for the social question.

The point is not to state how institutions should be that the socially
right thing happens, but to bring people into such a social connec-
tion that from the collaboration of the people the social question
can gradually be solved. (CW79, 30 November 1921)

... it is of no great fruitfulness to speak of associations in general,
and so on, and not much comes of it when one wants to get an idea
how one association really has to be connected to another. Just let
associations arise ... because then the right questions will arise ...
(CW337b, 12 October 1920)

Once we have understood how human beings can once again find
one another we shall be able to tackle the social question along the
right lines. (CW305(ii), p. 142)

We must bridge the chasms that have opened up between us.
(CW305(ii), p. 140)

So, the idea is to bring people together, to get people talking to one another from their various standpoints. And then out of this dialogue and transparency, out of these joint considerations and negotiations, decisions are made about goods and services. Such association brings a more brotherly / sisterly flavour into the economy.

Notwithstanding Steiner's assertion that the main thing is to get stakeholders talking to one another and that, from there, they will sort themselves out as well as can be expected, he does also at times mention particular aspects of the economy that such associations might mull over and be responsible for. These aspects are identified through the next few sections of the book.

At least as consumers, *everyone* has an interest in economic life:

> *Every individual will belong to the associations of the economic sphere, including representatives of the cultural sphere, for they, too, have to eat, as do the representatives of the legal, political sphere. Conversely, too, every individual also belongs to each of the other spheres as well. (CW305(ii), p. 163)*

However, this does not mean that every last consumer needs to be closely involved:

> *... associations which arise within the social sphere, where everyone can see what is going on—either as a member or because his representative sits on the association, or he is told what is going on, or he sees it for himself and realises what is required—this is what we must aim at. (CW340, p. 71)*

Size and reach of such associations were not something to be prescriptive about either:

> *In practical economic life there is no other effective way of knowing what is going on in a trade, for example, except to be engaged in trade oneself. You must be in the midst of it. You must be trading. There is no other way. There are no theories about it. Theories may be interesting, but [...] the point is not that you should know how trade goes on in general, but that you should know how the products circulate in the process of trade*

in Basel and its immediate surrounds. And if you know that, you do not thereby know how they circulate in the Lugano district. [A comment that no doubt has less relevance today in many sectors, RM]. The point is not that we should know about things in general, but that we should know something in a particular region. Likewise if you can form an effective judgment as to the higher or lower prices at which scythes [!] or other agricultural implements can be manufactured, you do not thereby know the prices at which screws can be manufactured or the like.

The judgments that have to be formed in economic life must be formed out of immediate concrete situations. And that is only possible in this way: for definite domains or regions (whose magnitude, as we have seen, will be determined by the economic process itself) associations must be formed in which all three types of representatives will be present alike. From the most varied branches of economic life, there must be representatives of the three things that occur in it—production, consumption and circulation.

It is really tragic that no understanding should be formed in our time for what is, after all, so simple and so sensible. [...] it is not a question of radical changes but of seeking for the proper associative union and co-operation in each case. [....] This is the thing that touches one so painfully for, at this point after all, economic thinking does to some extent coincide with moral and religious thinking. (CW340, pp. 106-107)

If they [associations] are too small they would be too costly; if they are too large they would become economically unmanageable. Practical necessity would indicate how inter-associational relations should develop. (CW23, p. 17)

The mention of scythe prices in different parts of Switzerland might make one wonder what relevance any of these ideas can have today when trade is so international. We shall come on to this presently. But a general picture is beginning to emerge of an economic realm where the mood is more one of co-operative mutuality than everyone trying to get the better of each other. Instead of so many individualistic spiders or giant clams waiting to ambush unsuspecting passers-by, the image is perhaps more that of ants or bees—all working collaboratively, or of different species working in symbiotic relationship.

Concerning the attitude with which people would ideally enter into association:

> *You may even found associations, associations whose members have a great deal of economic insight, yet if something else is not contained within the associations, all their insight will be of little avail. Something else must be contained in the associations and will be contained in them once the necessity of such associations is recognized. There must be in them the* community spirit[174], *the sense for the economic processes as a whole. [not just one's own narrow wishes, RM] (CW340, p. 132)*

Around the same time, Henry Ford wrote: 'We leave for private interest too many things we ought to do for ourselves as a collective interest. We need more constructive thinking in public service. We need a kind of "universal training" in economic facts. The over-reaching ambitions of speculative capital, as well as the unreasonable demands of irresponsible labour, are due to ignorance of the economic basis of life. Nobody can get more out of life than life can produce—yet nearly everybody thinks he can. Speculative capital wants more; labour wants more; the source of raw material wants more; and the purchasing public wants more. A family knows that it cannot live beyond its income; even the children know that. But the public never seems to learn that it cannot live beyond its income—have more than it produces.'[175]

It is also important to note Steiner's mention of 'partial solutions' in the following. By no means are grand claims being made that associative working is some silver bullet to fix everything.

> *In the associations the social judgment would not come from individuals but from all that lives in the communal life of the associations of consumers, producers and traders. Then we should have new social groups in which judgements would be formed in full consciousness, judgements of a kind that individuals would be incapable of forming in isolation. However long you spend trying to work out a solution to the social question, your efforts will be*

---

[174] *Gemeinsinn*—a sense of community.
[175] Henry Ford, *My Life and Work* (Hawthorne, CA: BN Publishing, 2008), p. 149.

> *fruitless. The only sensible thing to do is form social groups which can be expected to come up with partial solutions to the social question, groups in which people who form judgements in common create something that is a partial solution to the social question for a particular place at a particular time ... [my emphasis, RM] (CW305(ii), p. 131)*
>
> *Such associations will be able to formulate the [social question] in a realistic way and—partially, I have to say—find some solutions to it. (CW305(ii), p. 140)*

Nonetheless, he still considers the associative approach to have a substantial role:

> *... the principle of association in economic life means nothing other than that which must necessarily come to pass against the degeneration of economic liberalism. (CW338, 17 February 1921)*

To illustrate how associative working could take shape, Steiner gives two small examples from the anthroposophical movement of the time.[176] Whilst these may have existed in a rather particular context, they nonetheless act as a useful aid to understand what he is driving at:

> *How do associations form? ... Of course, the association idea does not mean that commissions are set up to form associations and the like, but that these associations are formed out of economic life itself. I would like to give two examples ... Some time before the*

---

[176] Separate from these, a conglomeration of businesses in Germany also formed in 1920 under the name *Der Kommende Tag* (literally, The Coming Day), as did a sister corporation, *Futurum*, in Switzerland. But although these were set up by supporters of Steiner's work, they were not associations in Steiner's sense; they were more to form a basis of financial solidarity for cultural initiatives based on anthroposophy such as schools and medical research. They comprised a range of largely unconnected businesses, including the Jose del Monte cardboard packaging company, the Waldorf-Astoria cigarette factory, a farm / timber mill, an anthroposophic publishing house in Stuttgart, an engineering works, the natural remedies and toiletries maker Weleda, and so on. The *Kommende Tag* experienced various difficulties, however, and disbanded in 1924 following the crippling hyperinflation that led to one US dollar being worth over four trillion German marks!

war, one of our members was a baker ... he made bread along with everything that goes with that. Now, an approach was taken that can act as an example. We had the Anthroposophical Society; anthroposophists also eat bread. They were already united, and nothing was easier than to pair the bread producer with the anthroposophists. He had his consumers, and there was a ready-made association. Of course, if such a thing stands on its own, it can have all manner of shortcomings. In this case it had shortcomings in that the producer also had his quirks and so the whole thing hit the rocks. But in the final analysis that doesn't matter. An association arises by itself out of an organic pairing between consumers and producers, whereby of course the producer usually has to take the initiative ...

And then I often give an example from a different type of work, the one created by the Philosophic-Anthroposophic Publishing House in Berlin. This does not work the way other publishers work. How do other publishers work? They sign as many authors as possible, good or bad, and then print their books. But to print books, you need paper, you need typesetters and so on. Now try to imagine how many books are printed every year—let's just say in Germany—that don't get sold, for which there are simply no consumers. Just compare how much poetry is printed in Germany and how much poetry is bought, and you then have an idea how much human labour is spent on producing paper that is thrown to the wind, how many typesetters are needed, etc., all for nothing. That's what matters. We need to enter economic life by thinking economically, that is, by thinking in a way that avoids unnecessary work, wasted work. This is not possible in an association such as that between the Anthroposophical Society and the Philosophic-Anthroposophic Publishing House since the latter does not print books that are not sold ...

And just what one sees in these two examples can be achieved in all fields. Above everything else, when the association is properly conceived, unnecessary work will be avoided. That's what matters. The point is to create an appropriate relationship between production and consumption across the board. (CW337b, 30 August 1920)

Of course, not every publisher—especially those taking on new authors—can have the luxury of only printing books they know for sure they can sell. But the example illustrates a point: that of production being an organized response to demand, not a speculative endeavour necessitating pushy salespeople trying to shift the merchandise, which, if they fail, leads to waste. Thankfully, today, the ability to 'print on demand' can mean smaller print runs can now be more viable.

These two examples convey a very direct link between producer and consumer. However, within a few sentences, Steiner also goes on to add:

> *It doesn't really come down to making so many items and shipping them from one place to another; what matters is that there are living people in the association who have the overview to mediate between consumption and production. (CW337b, 30 August 1920)*

On a different scale to these small examples, Steiner suggested for example, during his extensive discussions with the Works Councils movement of the time, that the Works Councils in the Württemberg region of Southern Germany form a central council where around one thousand delegates from the various companies represented could more closely co-ordinate economic activity.[177]

Once or twice he also points out that a firm is going to be rather better placed to work associatively if, in the first instance, it has progressed beyond the old adversarial white-versus-blue-collar antagonisms and adopted collaborative, associative principles *within* the organisation itself first. For example:

> *Associations are the health bearers. Associations work towards the harmonizing of interests, so that the interests of the producers and the consumers are harmonized by the working together in the association, [so] that other interests are harmonized, [so] that above all the interests between employers and workers are harmonized. Today we see how out of a diseased economic body the opposite of associative life is created, we see how passive resistance, locking out, sabotage and even revolutions come about. No-one with a healthy mind can deny that all this works in the opposite direction of the associative principle and that all*

---

[177] Albert Schmelzer, *The Threefold Movement, 1919: A History* (Forest Row: Rudolf Steiner Press, 2017), p. 127.

this: sabotage, lock-outs, revolution and so on are symptoms of disease of the social organism that must be overcome through that which works in a harmonizing way. [my emphasis, RM] (CW79, 30 November 1921)

The old misguided ways need to be abandoned where entrepreneurs sit up on high and, at best, behave paternalistically, while on the other side there are workers organized into trade unions ... This gap must first be bridged, and this cannot be done otherwise than by preparing real associations, real associations which consist in associating people from one side—from the entrepreneurial side, the management side, the spiritual worker side—and from the other side, the workers. In the first instance, an economic, a really social, economic association which embodies co-operation between consumers and producers cannot be formed. (CW337b, 11 October 1920)

Note, in particular, this last sentence. There are associations and associations!

One imagines that the associative reform needed within an organisation in order to remove the 'us and them' mentality between workers and management might include the introduction of a sharing approach to remuneration to replace the wage system (as discussed in Sections 7.3.4 and 7.4.14).

Be that as it may, Steiner is clearly eager to bring a renewed sense of goodwill and fellowship into corporate life and ...

... do everything we can to dissolve union life and create associations between business leaders and workers. If we can work towards the dissolution of trade union life, we can do many other things. (CW337b, 12 October 1920)

Whilst many or even most of Steiner's *operational* suggestions are simply illustrations of how he imagines matters *could* proceed if the threefold approach were adopted, his comments regarding economic associations are perhaps rather more than this. It seems clear from the above that he sees associative working as a more fundamental medium via which the economy's guiding principle of mutuality / *fraternité* can prosper.

Some of the other tasks that Steiner envisages associations would occupy themselves with will be looked at in the coming sections of the book.

In summary:

- Whilst it might be the expert knowledge and skill of *individuals* (cultural realm) that manages *production* ...
- and whilst it might be the needs and desires of *individuals* that drive *consumption* ...
- an economic life—*as a whole*—that is based on the decisions of individuals in isolation is not healthy; neither is economic activity based on decisions made by all / the state.
- Instead, producers, distributors and consumers—or their respective representatives—to join together in interest groups and form associations with each other where the viewpoint of each can inform healthy economic decisions / solutions, where transparency is the norm, where consumers can express their needs and producers / distributors can convey what is possible. Decisions are arrived at via the interaction of the (possibly opposing) interests of stakeholders.
- Makeup of associations, and their ways of working, is not prescribed. The various players enter into dialogue and proceed as circumstances suggest is practical.
- Existing producers, distributors and consumers can associate; new enterprises not essential.
- Local knowledge is all important; general knowledge less so (in Steiner's day, at least).
- Associations that are too small will be too costly; ones that are too large will be too unwieldy. Circumstances will determine size in each case.
- A 'community spirit' is necessary.
- One can only expect partial solutions, not to solve everything.
- Best if relations between 'employer' and 'employed' become more associative / less adversarial first.
- Functions of associations covered in subsequent sections of book.

Reflections in relation to the present

So, Steiner holds that co-operation should ideally replace competition, and he recommends an associative approach via which producers, distributors, and consumers can achieve this.

The reader may, at this juncture, be starting to lose heart and think this all sounds very ponderous, clunky and unsuited to the efficient, modern-day production methods and the international, internet-driven distribution networks enjoyed in the developed world. We have such an abundance of affordable products that can be delivered to our door within a day or two of a few mouse clicks. If it ain't broke, what is there to fix?

We are very used to the idea of equality—the guiding principle of the rights realm which finds expression in the mechanism of democracy. And we are very used to the idea of freedom—the guiding principle of the cultural realm which finds expression in the *absence* of mechanism. But Steiner's description of associations and collaborative, inter-associational dialogue as the mechanism by which the guiding principle of *fraternité* should find expression in economic life is one of the harder aspects of his analysis to grasp, and certainly one of the harder aspects to relate to the present.

Steiner certainly had no interest in making anything inefficient, encouraging, as he did …

> ... *facilities in the social organism which [...] have the exclusive function of activating the circulation of commodities in the most expedient manner ... (CW23, p. 67)*

One can imagine that in his time, at the end of the First World War, when there was widespread devastation and want, when the range of products available was significantly smaller than today, and the number of imported goods significantly lower, the prevailing circumstances may have constituted particularly fertile soil in which an associative approach within the economic realm could have taken root. One can imagine, with the economy in a depressed state, a collaborative, we're-all-in-this-together, satisfying (joyful, even) mood existing while the population clawed its way out of the disaster of war: a camaraderie whilst everyone focused on the common problem—that of trying to get commodities to where they were needed. (Ironically, a camaraderie not dissimilar to that often recollected by soldiers when reminiscing about life in the trenches!)

One can imagine a body of consumers in one geographic area ascertaining their most pressing needs, a similar body of consumers in another area, a guild of tailors and haberdashers, a confederation of farmers, another of house builders, another of blacksmiths and so on. One can imagine these (or their delegates, at least) holding both internal as well as associational meetings, in the town hall perhaps, to exchange information regarding needs, shortages, prices, production possibilities, output capacity, workforce requirements and so on, and that this collaborative process would sooner or later enable needs to be met at realistic prices acceptable to producers / distributors / consumers alike. And then, once everyone's basic needs had been properly met, spare capacity among the workforce might soon have become evident that could have gone toward producing more luxurious items again, or towards expanding the railway or the local school, etc. It is not too difficult to imagine a camaraderie that could have been experienced by the community pulling together and working out effective ways of meeting one another's needs. And once things had been set up in this way, one can imagine they would have continued in a similar vein, albeit with frequent modifications to adapt to circumstances. Who knows what the economic landscape would have looked like by now, had this approach been properly established a hundred years ago, and then expanded. A society far more at peace with itself, perhaps?

But is this approach at all realistic nowadays when, at the drop of a hat, we can go online and buy a rug today, a pyrex dish tomorrow, and a holiday in Corsica the day after? And, typically, all at very affordable prices (for Westerners, at least). Is it really possible that the associative approach Steiner outlined a century ago would be an improvement today, or even work? Could people really be bothered? Wouldn't the extra hassle only add to costs? Why rock a reasonably serviceable boat? Is it at all realistic to imagine hitherto competitive supermarkets or different car battery manufacturers sitting down and deciding how best to serve their customers?

It is indeed hard to imagine a *fully* associative approach coming about any time soon throughout an economy as developed and differentiated as ours in the West. The observation attributed to Oscar Wilde

'The trouble with socialism is that it takes up too many evenings' might also apply to association.

Firstly, though, it is worth noting that getting together in groups is not the preserve of war-torn regions by any means. Indeed, a study by sociologist Robert Wuthnow found that 40% of US citizens were members of at least one group that met regularly in pursuit of mutual interests and support.[178]

Secondly, whilst the economy might seem to be working terribly well for those of us with nice work, regular paycheques, good health, a pleasant place to live, fulfilled lives and general good fortune, it may well not be for those having to wait in freezing, dark bus stops at 5:30 in the morning to go and toil in grimy, hated jobs (if they have one), only to return exhausted in the evening to unmaintained, mould-infested homes in ugly, threatening neighbourhoods, and then possibly have a poor night's sleep on account of noise from anti-social neighbours on the other side of paper-thin walls. And all for what? To pay the rent! Indeed, some of these unfortunates may be the very people (together with those veritable armies of faceless brown people living on the breadline overseas) who make it possible for those internet-ordered niceties to so effortlessly (it seems) waft onto our doormats. Further, with the internet's ability to bring a plethora of competing, virtual shop windows to our smartphone screens, we—the generally fickle consumer—can choose a CD from this seller rather than that because it is 10p cheaper. Rather than collaborative consumers taking producers' needs into account, we end up fuelling that cut-throat competition which means paltry wages for those very workers in their mould-infested nightmares.

Not everyone's needs are being met! At the same time, though, many are being over-met.

Although the regeneration of a deprived neighbourhood (one of the many areas where rampant capitalism can rather painfully demonstrate its shortcomings) is often led by local government, from a threefold

---

[178] Robert Wuthnow, *Sharing the Journey: Support Groups and America's New Quest for Community* (New York: Free Press, 1994), p. 45. About half of these groups were connected to religion, and the rest were split more or less evenly between self-help groups, book / discussion groups, sports / hobby groups and political / current events (p.76).

point of view (which considers the state's remit essentially to be the establishing of rights and responsibilities), the actions taken to regenerate an area are principally economic. Local residents have needs (not to forever be looking at derelict buildings, say) and these needs need to be met by providers of goods and services (builders of new buildings, say). True, the local residents in such an area are unlikely to be able to afford any rebuilding programme themselves, so it may be that the rights realm has to have a role with its tax-raising powers. (In some highly community-minded, threefold region, profitable businesses in the surrounding areas might voluntarily stump up the cash for this, but for now let's assume this is not the case.) The point is, where local residents join together to establish and voice their needs, then this shows at least one side of the associative working Steiner talks about.

There are inspiring examples of how people living within significant urban decay have done just this, have become inspired by more public engagement, often with noteworthy results. Community involvement in the municipal budgeting of Porto Alegre in Brazil, for example, led to city money actually going to where it was most needed, to significant regeneration, and to the mafia disappearing! When people appreciated what needed to be done, they even demonstrated for their taxes to be raised so that the necessary measures could be afforded![179]

At the other end of Brazil, in the state of Ceara, it wasn't only local residents (consumers with needs) who got involved in reviving marginalised neighbourhoods. 'Normal' businesses could also see the point of a more public-spirited approach. Sociologist Anthony Giddens notes: 'The reforms in the area were initiated by a group of young business leaders, working in such sectors as television, retail marketing and services. The traditional elites in Ceara exported agricultural products abroad, and were interested more in keeping the wages down than in local development. The reformers subsequently joined with government agencies, using participatory planning techniques and meeting community organisations. In order to promote indigenous development, schemes were set up to introduce new enterprises into the area. Families with the greatest need were allocated one

---

[179] George Monbiot, 'Out of the wreckage: a new politics for an age of crisis', public talk in Nailsworth, Gloucestershire, 14 March 2018.

minimum-wage job per household. Day-care centres were set up, run not by the government but by volunteers guaranteed at least the minimum wage. Neighbourhood groups and community organisations were given resources to lend on a small scale—for example, lending a woman money to buy a sewing machine so she can earn a living on her own. Between 1987 and 1994 Ceara's economy grew at a rate of 4 per cent, compared with 1.4 per cent for Brazil as a whole.'[180] Needs were better met by parties talking to one another, by association.

Or in Cleveland, Ohio, the population shrank by nearly 60% between 1950 and 2008 with 27% of inhabitants living in poverty (fully 40% in the poorest Glenville area) compared to the U.S. national average of 12.5%. In response to this, worker-owned producer co-operatives were set up in collaboration with the city government to serve the biggest spenders in the city, for example to provide laundry services to universities and hospitals. These co-operatives are jointly owned and operated by members for their mutual benefit, and members include the poorly educated as well as those with criminal convictions.

Again, you may wonder: how is this related to Steiner's idea of *economic* associations if the measures were guided by local government? It is related because certain consumers (universities, hospitals, etc.) and certain producers (laundry co-ops, etc.) entered into dialogue. They associated. If one thinks away the term 'city government', and in its place substitutes the term 'city association' or similar, then the confusion abates.

The success in Cleveland inspired what has come to be known as the 'Preston Model' in the UK. With one in three school children living in poverty in Preston, Lancashire, the city council committed to a co-operative initiative for economic development in 2011. Under this approach, more of the spending by the city and county council (e.g. the university, the police, the hospital) now goes to local businesses. (After Brexit this may be easier since, under European procurement law, contracts are often required to be tendered widely.) The council is considering setting up a local bank to provide loans to small businesses, and is also considering becoming a municipal energy provider to facilitate the retention of wealth in the locale. A co-operative

---

[180] Anthony Giddens, *The Third Way: The Renewal of Social Democracy* (Cambridge: Polity Press, 2008), p. 82.

network has also been set up to include food and growers' co-operatives and even an educational psychologists' co-operative! Undergraduates at the local university are being educated about co-operative models. As a result, Preston saw 'the joint second biggest improvement in its position on the multiple deprivation index between 2010 and 2015. [...] The changes are profound enough that the former shadow chancellor, John McDonnell, has used Preston as an example of how Labour councils can cope with hefty budget cuts'.[181] Other councils have taken notice, with Manchester City council, for example, increasing its spending in the local economy from 51.5% in 2008-9 to 73.6% in 2015-16. That a collaborative, associative, mutually supportive model such as this can give those involved a meaningful, 'warm' feeling instead of a cynical, everyone's-out-to-rip-me-off feeling isn't hard to see. 'I feel like I'm involved in a new movement that's building,' a member of one of the community farms is quoted as saying.

Here too, readers may wonder whether the involvement of local government makes this a poor example of economic association. But the approach being taken in Preston is highly associative. Again, if one replaces the words 'city council' with 'city association', then hey presto (or hey Preston)!

In a somewhat similar vein, when public and private sector organisations engage with one another in order to inform local or regional industrial strategies, this can often have little to do with the rights realm. If such forums are not only collaborative but also include end-user (not just producer) representation, then this is certainly a process with an associative flavour.

But regional industrial strategies are a bit removed from everyday economic activity; and solving urban decay or environmental damage are also rather special cases. So, what examples of association might there be nowadays that sit within the more normal, everyday producer / distributor / customer relations of the economic realm?

Community supported agriculture is often cited as a good example of associative behaviour. The CSA movement has grown considerably in the West since the 1980s, and so has the parallel Teikei movement

---

[181] Hazel Sheffield, 'The Preston model: UK takes lessons in recovery from rust-belt Cleveland', *The Guardian*, 11 April 2017.

in Japan which took off in the 1960s. There are now some 13,000 farms using this model in the USA and Canada, for example. Typically, such a farm will work out what level of income it needs to maintain itself and convey this to a circle of customers needing produce. Between producer and customer (and distributor, where there is a delivery service) an agreement is made whereby the customers get the weekly (typically organic) produce they need, and in return pay regular amounts such that the farm gets the income it needs. There is dialogue. Human being meets human being. The predictable income gives the farm stability. The farm is not out to maximise profit. Customers do not go out and buy other eggs because they are 10p cheaper. The uncertainties resulting from competition are reduced or even removed.

A situation perhaps even closer to Steiner's associative approach can arise where a number of such farms form a grouping where, between them, they work out who is best placed to grow peaches, who is best placed to graze sheep and so on; customers then have access to a fuller range of produce. The coming together of the producers and the customers would constitute the association proper, however, in Steiner's sense.

Given that some of the most acute problems in the world concern food (e.g. poor distribution between regions; extreme soil erosion as a result of non-organic farming; bee colony collapse as a result of non-organic farming; poor quality of product; unwanted GM crops being pushed by multinationals; increasing risk of drought and heat extremes because of climate change), and given that association is well suited to the regular provision of fresh, local produce, it is perhaps not surprising that examples of associative economics are most often to be found in the food sector. The appearance of meals-on-wheels providers serving vulnerable groups during the Covid-19 outbreak was another instance of food-related association.

Fair Trade is another good example of associative engagement with the counterparty's needs. Here, as is now well known, customers are willing to pay an amount for their imported produce that reduces exploitation, i.e. gives producers a bit more income and thereby a more dignified existence. Customers in the importing country maintain dialogue, via agents (e.g. a Fair Trade Association), with their producing counterparties, and between them they ascertain what is realistic and proceed accordingly. *The parties talk to one another.* Prices are aimed for that (a) are closer to meeting the needs of the producer, and (b) are not so high that customers will be deterred. When I buy Fair Trade, I might not be a formal member of an association in the sense of having my name on some list somewhere. But, through my purchase, I am nonetheless engaging with the broader Fair Trade Association and ultimately with those producers in warmer climes. I am happy to let the Fair Trade Association represent me as agent; I am willing to trust that they will be making a difference to producers.

As Gerald Häfner writes: 'With every item that I purchase there is a long chain extending from me via the salesman and a manufacturer of the final product to the originator, whether this be a cotton gatherer in India, a cocoa farmer in Nicaragua or a miner in the Congo. These chains, which for the most part embrace half the globe, need to be perceived in their totality and warmed through in a human way. A task in the coming years will be to form them in accordance with the viewpoint of brotherhood. Ultimately it means that I cannot take pleasure in rejoicing either about the product that I have acquired or the price that I paid for it until I am certain that not only I but all the people connected through this chain of value creation have been treated fairly and are able to live adequately from their work. In this way a revolution of brotherhood comes about.'[182]

Another example of working along associative lines can be seen in the affordable housing sector, where housing associations build homes which those on lower incomes can rent or part own. Such house building is not done in a profiteering or speculative way, that is to say, in the blind hope of enticing residents. It is carried out in response to need. And, indeed, engagement with 'customers' does not stop once the homes are built and occupied. On-going, collaborative dialogue is maintained between producer and consumer by significant customer involvement, for example with tenant representation on housing association boards. A single housing association might manage one building or several sites. Together, these separate providers manage homes for some five million people in England alone. The National Housing

---

[182] Gerald Häfner in Martin Large and Steve Briault (Eds), *Free, Equal and Mutual: Rebalancing Society for the Common Good* (Stroud: Hawthorn Press, 2018), p. 132.

Federation is the umbrella body for the sector to which individual housing associations belong as members. It is the central hub through which individual housing associations (service providers / 'producers') can enter into dialogue with one another and then act in an organized and rational way that investigates and responds to demand / needs within the sector. It is also the central hub via which best practice can be shared (with regard to dealing with local authorities, builders, tenants' rights, etc.). At the more local level, there can be a tenants' (i.e. consumers') association in dialogue with the landlord housing association. Again, the coming together of housing providers and tenants constitutes the association proper, in Steiner's sense.

Some readers might wonder whether renting a property is in fact part of the economic realm at all. Is the *right* to occupy a dwelling not in fact part of the rights realm? The answer to this is layered. The economic realm of course has a rights dimension to it. If I buy a suit (commodity, so economic realm), I also then enjoy exclusive *right of use* to this suit (assuming, that is, that the democratic, legislative process in the state where I live has deemed it desirable that a person's belongings are not fair game for anyone who can lay their hands on them). But what if I *hire* a morning suit for some function which has stipulated a dress code which I may only ever need to observe once or twice in my life? It will not be hard to find some enterprising individual who, noticing that most people have little interest in buying morning suits they will hardly ever use, will buy several in various sizes and then be happy for me to hire one for the day. Yes, the rights realm plays its part inasmuch as I will have exclusive *right* of use in relation to the suit for the day. But we are nonetheless primarily still in the economic domain. The suit itself is a commodity, of course; it is nature modified by labour to make a consumer good. The hire firm is perhaps a special case of distributor. It is providing a service that meets my need. The commodity I am paying for is the 'amenity' of the clean, pressed suit for the day, and the money I pay will pay for the service provider's running / living costs, including a portion of the cost of the suit (one hundredth of the suit, perhaps, if it will last a hundred days of hiring).

Renting a house or flat is, in many respects, no different to renting a morning suit. The rights realm plays its part and ensures my exclusive enjoyment of the commodity, be that dwelling or suit. But we are nonetheless primarily in the economic realm. As with the suit, the house is nature modified by labour making a consumer good, and the rent I pay must cover the living expenses of (in this case) the housing association's staff, plus any plumbers, electricians, etc. needed to maintain it, plus a proportion of the cost of the house (one hundredth of its build cost per annum, say, if the house will last a century). The commodity I pay for is the amenity of the dwelling space. In a proper threefold context, however, one would not pay for renting the land—ground rent; here, in all likelihood, everyone would simply have the right to live on a piece of housing land.

Even if the rights state I live in has decided every person within its boundary will have a right to housing, the rights realm's involvement is to establish and legislate for this *right*, and maybe even to inspect or police its observance. This does not mean the *provision* of such housing is part of the rights realm. The provider exists in the economic realm, albeit in likely dialogue with a rights domain that might wish to pass favourable laws that mean money and land are freed to enable a good supply of Housing Association dwellings and what we in the UK call Council Housing. And it is important to appreciate: whilst a threefold approach might deem the provision of housing to be part of the economic realm, this does *not* mean such activity becomes a privatised, profit-maximising activity.

A natural monopoly such as the road network could very easily be structured on an associative basis, were it to be removed from state management. If one were to take seriously the recommendation that the political state should only concern itself with rights and not be responsible for economic activity, then the provision of a road network might be 'disestablished'. Again, this is by no means the same as saying privatised, i.e. made available for purchase by private capital. Under threefolding, responsibility for it could simply be hived off from government. At present, the larger roads around the UK are the responsibility of the national highways agencies (Highways England, Transport Scotland, etc.) and the smaller roads are the responsibility of County Councils. These local and national road management bodies could simply be removed from the political process by the rights state conferring on regional road-maintaining / road-building bodies the *right* to manage the means of production—the roads, the signs, the bridges, the land on which roads sit, etc. Such rights could be

conferred on condition that these bodies had a not-for-profit structure and continued to provide highways that were of satisfaction to
road users. These de-politicised, regional bodies could perhaps join
together in a road providers confederation (a de-politicised Highways
Agency or Highways Association) through which they could continue
to enjoy professional dialogue, compare notes on best traffic calming
practice and signage, jointly commission research into improved sur-
facing, coordinate road maintenance to reduce disruption, coordinate
the collection of subscription income ('road tax'), etc. And they could
be required to continue fruitful dialogue in association with hauliers'
and motorists' groups such as the AA, RAC, Green Flag, etc. which,
whilst being predominantly about breakdown services, nonetheless
also represent the general interests of motorists, conducting online
surveys, relaying our needs, etc.

Where there are natural monopolies such as this, it is generally
recognised that competition makes little sense. We don't want or need
a rival road provider building a second motorway parallel to the M1,
we don't need more than one set of gas pipes going to each house, or
more than one set of telephone wires or railway lines. We probably
don't even need more than one set of postmen and women, with their
delivery vans; although in recent years, with our internet shopping,
we seem to have decided otherwise. When a number of these services
were de-nationalised in the UK in the latter part of the 20th century,
a good opportunity momentarily existed to vest these businesses into
associative business structures. But, alas, the government of the day
preferred the short-term prize of large sums of capital for the Exchequer, and the 'family silver' was sold off. Instead of sensible, healthy
associative working, instead of Steiner's safeguards against inappropriate ownership, profit maximisation, silly salaries, and so on, these
utility providers were opened up to private capital. And then industry
regulators Ofgas, Ofcom, etc. were set up to make sure the providers
of these utilities didn't exploit their monopolistic position, were set
up to guard against the damaging excesses of capitalism. And then,
alongside this, we also have to have the rather contrived competition
amongst, for example, a number of gas providers which many would
argue amounts to wasteful duplication. And we then have 'energy
switching', with numerous call-centres hosting hives of life-wasting
activity that enables us to switch from one provider to another, and

then in all likelihood back again a year or two later, all in order to save a few pounds a year—which in all likelihood could have been saved twice over, had there not been those armies of call centres, and the concomitant publicity campaigns that try to convince you that this gas is so much better than that gas! Similarly, with 7-day switching between banks now possible in the UK, about one million people per annum are doing just that: moving their current account from one bank to another. And all for what? Such competition means different players are forever out to outsmart and undermine their competitors and make up some story to convince the customer to switch. Association—à la Steiner—would have introduced a more social, grown-up and less duplicative / wasteful approach.

Most producers, however, do not fall under the heading of natural monopolies (or food growers, or housing providers), and it is often harder to imagine association working in sectors where an extensive choice of similar product is of interest to the consumer. If I want to drive the few miles from Prussia Cove to Marazion, I don't need a choice of roads. Here, therefore, scope for association between provider and consumer (the Highways Agency and motorist) is good. If I want an organic cabbage, I don't especially need a choice of different organic cabbages; I just want one that is reasonably fresh. Here too, therefore, scope for association between producer and consumer is also good (in the form of Community Supported Agriculture, say). But if I need a bicycle or some soap, then a range of options becomes of interest. My neighbour might also need a bike, but with different features. And so bikes, as we know, come to us from dozens of companies in a multitude of countries. And these companies are all competing with one another, all hoping you will buy their particular product.

The diverse innovation and choice arising from these different manufacturers undoubtedly brings benefits, and it can be quite hard to imagine how—or why—the millions of such trans-national businesses might choose to begin to associate with their customers. Goodness, I might only ever buy one or two bikes in my life in any case; so to have some direct, associative link to Raleigh, Trek or Canondale would seem absurd. With the efficiencies we have in 'developed' economies—computerised order processing and stock control, just-in-time production, manufacturing robotics, etc.—it is hard to imagine much slicker ways of getting certain commodities to where they are needed. So it is perhaps difficult to imagine associations arising around certain product categories. From a meeting-of-needs point of view, would association really lead to improvement? Would it not simply be cumbersome, unwieldy, impractical?

But even in such industries, there will always be plenty of scope for a more associative approach to prevail. Indeed, there will without doubt already be many examples of associative dialogue in traditional manufacturing industries, where one particular set of businesses will be in close and regular contact with other sets of businesses, up and down their supply chains, such that the parties' needs are met in a somewhat collaborative and predictable manner. Our bike factory may reach medium-term agreements with its inner tube or gear shift suppliers, and perhaps even with certain of its distributors—the shops we all visit. Even if these enterprises can associate in this way, they give each other a measure of business stability and reduce competitive waste.

A less traditional example of an international business working associatively is the Swiss-based trading company, Remei AG, which 'has developed a supply chain of associated businesses based on co-operation and transparency, beginning with several thousand small organic cotton farmers in India and Tanzania. Remei AG markets organic cotton thread, yarn, and clothing worldwide, including clothing for the Naturaline eco-label of Coop Swiss, a Swiss consumer co-operative network with over two million member consumers'.[183]

However, with so many established businesses being so set in their competitive ways, and with so many of us appreciating wide choice within many product categories, one can imagine closer collaboration in economic life being of little interest in many sectors. Nonetheless, there is probably a 'market' for more brotherly trade even within some of these less likely sectors. In the same way that ethical investment services grew from a niche concept in the 1970s into the multi-billion-pound 'industry' they are today, one can imagine associations arising around more equitable remuneration models, for example: an association between a group of distributors (e.g. shops) and producers

---

[183] Gary Lamb, *Associative Economics: Spiritual Activity for the Common Good* (Ghent, NY: The Association of Waldorf Schools of North America, 2010), p. 82.

(of different products) using slavery-free components, or with non-ex-ploitative remuneration ratios (that prevent management enriching themselves on the back of workforce impoverishment). So, not just fairtrade coffee, but fairtrade car batteries, too (especially relevant when the mining of cobalt for the batteries of electric cars appears to be creating a whole new class of severely exploited workers). Or a network of distributors which only sell products from 'green' pro-ducers providing commodities with exemplary ecological credentials, etc. Some form of online retail platform could be well suited to this. However, it might also be optimistic to think this could grow very quickly. After all, *The Ethical Consumer* has been doing its sterling work for over three decades, but still these issues only seem to hover on the periphery of people's awareness and purchasing patterns—not, of course, everyone's, but probably still the majority of the public's.

But, things can also change remarkably quickly. Who in the 1980s would have dreamed it would be possible to ban smoking in all public places—even in pubs?! Who would have thought it would be possible to force shops to charge for plastic bags? Who would have thought, prior to August 2017, that the Tories would propose that (some) salary ratios be published? Who would have thought that the proportion of homes in rural America would drop from 90% to 10% in the 15 years between 1935 and 1950?[184] Who would have thought a single Swedish schoolgirl with Asperger's could become as famous for highlighting the plight of the Earth as some of her compatriots became for singing *Dancing Queen*? Public sentiment can change quickly. I remember being pleasantly astonished in the 1990s when the café on one of the platforms at Clapham Junction[185] was adorned with a large sign saying something like 'Fairtrade coffee sold here'. This seems commonplace now—wonderfully so. But at the time it almost felt subversive—an act of defiance against the status quo.

One can also imagine that a version of associative working could be sensibly employed among some of the more local trades and services. Some kind of associative body could maintain a real-time awareness of regional activity levels amongst one-man-bands, etc. If there was a greater consciousness, with perhaps an on-line presence, that plumbers

---

[184] Ann Pettifor, *The Case For the Green New Deal* (Verso: London, 2019), p. 164.
[185] The busiest railway station in the UK.

and restauranteurs, say, were always run off their feet (and therefore might overcharge) in a particular area, whereas hairdressers and
psychotherapists were forever sitting around waiting for customers,
this could be a useful tool, amongst other things, for school leavers
wondering in what direction to apply themselves. Something akin to
the local Chambers of Commerce, perhaps, but with a broader, more
community-spirited portfolio. Certain levels of best practice could be
a condition of entry on a list of approved providers, say, in order to
protect customer and meet their needs.

Whilst not all co-ops might be in keeping with the associative
approach that Steiner advocates, where these do embody a broader
approach (e.g. opposing interests engaging with one another such that
each takes 'the other' into account, and decisions are taken that seem
as fair as possible to all concerned), then these can demonstrate strong
associative traits; where they are only focused on the small microcosm of themselves, then less so. The former is perhaps epitomised
by the Mondragon federation of worker co-operatives in the Basque
region of Spain that was founded in the 1950s. Based around the ideals of social responsibility and participation, some 75,000 people are
now involved in this vibrant undertaking.

As has been ascertained, a grouping of similar producers or distributors is not really what Steiner has in mind when he talks of economic
associations. His associations are more about producers in collaborative dialogue with consumers, or producers in collaborative dialogue
with producers of different goods in their supply chain, or producers
in collaborative dialogue with distributors, or distributors in collaborative dialogue with consumers. And where, say, there was an association between a set of consumers and a larger grouping of producers
in one particular industry, this grouping would, of course, need to take
care not to collude and fall foul of monopoly / antitrust laws. The fact
that consumers were represented in the association should perhaps
prevent this. Not that the prevailing antitrust regimes are always very
good at keeping up with developments! The domination of digital
music sales by iTunes with around 75% of the global market is a case
in point.[186] As is the colossus that is Amazon with their 'systematic

---

[186] Paul Mason, *Postcapitalism: A Guide to Our Future* (London: Allen Lane,
2015), p. 119.

annihilation of retail competitors'.[187] But, naturally, laws from time to time need updating, and if a new associative approach was seen to display sensible, practical solutions to economic issues, laws might then need to be refined to accommodate such developments. A large number of *profit-maximising* businesses collaborating together would more likely be seen as collusion that risked monopoly / monopsony (sole buyer) behaviour that could pose a threat to fair, non-exploitative trade. But collaboration between businesses whose structures entailed no motivation to exploit would be a different matter. Any motivation to exploit would be all but removed where (a) there was an absence of shareholders demanding higher profits, (b) locks were in place to prevent extortionate remuneration, and (c) the association contained consumers. The producer would be focused on creating quality products as efficiently as possible. The culture would be one of producing decent commodities for one's fellows.

In this connection, it is also interesting to note that, in Steiner's day, cartels were not uncommon by any means. Paul Mason notes: 'In Germany, where price fixing cartels were politically encouraged and legally registered, their number more than doubled between 1901 and 1911. Just one of these cartels, the Rhine-Westphalia Coal Syndicate, involved sixty-seven companies, had the power to set 1,400 different prices and controlled 95 per cent of the region's energy market. To be absolutely clear, because it's difficult to comprehend today, this was a system where supply and demand did not set prices: millionaires did.'[188] Government-endorsed collusion of this sort illustrates just how cosy the relationship was between the economic realm and the political in the 'unitary state' model bemoaned by Steiner (not to mention those instances where industry was simply government-run).

In addition to Housing Associations, Community Supported Agriculture, Fair Trade and the other types of associative behaviour cited above, there will undoubtedly be many other significant examples both at home and around the world of enterprises—especially smaller ones—that employ wonderful, collaborative, fraternal principles

---

[187] Mark O'Connell, 'A managerial Mephistopheles: inside the mind of Jeff Bezos', *The Guardian*, 3 Feb 2021.

[188] Paul Mason, *Postcapitalism: A Guide to Our Future* (London: Allen Lane, 2015), p. 56.

which take into account the needs of all stakeholders; and I can only apologise to them and to the reader for my ignorance of these.

The organisations registered with Social Enterprise UK, for example, demonstrate that a lot of people are keen to approach business in less self-centred ways.[189] And indeed, where an enterprise unilaterally undertakes to operate in such a way that it takes others fully into consideration (that is to say, without those others being in the room to voice their own interests), then in a sense they have already gone further than Steiner suggests. All he recommends is that the interests of all parties to a trade are represented and factored into that trade. Are represented—in dialogue—not imagined from one side.

The idea of associative economics offers an alternative to Adam Smith's 'invisible hand'—based, as that is, on competitive markets and self-interest. The associative approach is more collaborative, more conscious, more considerate, more dignified perhaps.

But if competition were reduced, one might wonder where the incentive to innovate would come from when there were fewer rivals to try and get the better of. The short answer to this is possibly that, within a culture of service, human nature will surely be keen to innovate in any case. Indeed, where *all* players in a particular industry, instead of competing, adopted a more associative approach, things like R&D, production engineering tips, and other useful experience gained during the course of business would be likely to become more open-source—shared between them in such a way that, to a degree, they acted together. (This closer contact between producers could occur with minimal temptation to behave monopolistically if (a) management were subject to sensible, pre-appointment agreements regarding remuneration, and (b) there were no shareholders pushing for profit maximisation—because the means of production had been removed from the economic realm, and were thus no longer buyable or sellable but, instead, fell under the remit of the rights and cultural realms, as covered previously.)

Innovation / R&D can at times be underfunded in conventional business in any case, when management instead use profits to pay dividends so as to achieve the short-term goal of getting the share

---

[189] The biggest network of social enterprises in the UK (www.socialenterprise.org.uk).

price up. Also, as it happens, even in conventional, profit-maximising and unconnected business, a degree of collaboration can demonstrate significant advantages for all concerned as seen, for example,
in the Frauenhofer-Gesellschaft in Germany ('a part publicly-funded
research organisation that provides applied science for companies that
would otherwise find the cost prohibitive').[190] Over 25,000 staff work
here—mainly scientists and engineers—enabling much R&D effort
to be pooled.

The fact that, in an association, the voice of customers is as important as the voice of producers would also act as an important guard
against innovation giving way to complacency by producers. Where
consumers, via their representatives, or via some innovative online
platform for association, voiced a wish for greater product reliability
(or faster delivery, or a wider choice of colours, or less grotty trains,
or improved functionality, or whatever), but this request for a better
product was unreasonably ignored by the producers in question, this
might be at their peril. An associative relationship between buyer and
seller need not imply unquestioning loyalty for all time!

It is doubtless easier for consumers to organise themselves into a
negotiating body when their concern is a local one, such as with a
typical community-supported farm. Nonetheless, the various consumer associations we have today (associations in the everyday sense)
demonstrate that these things can also operate reasonably satisfactorily
across much wider geographical areas, even without paying attention to
national boundaries. Writing on threefolding in 1946, Charles Waterman
observed: 'The representation of consumers might become a distinc-
tive profession with its own standards of qualification and professional
Institute. Its practitioners—let us call them consumers' advocates [...]
would often be able to use the argument, "in that event I shall advise my
clients to deal elsewhere".'[191] And: 'They would command, in theory,
two effective weapons—purchasing power and publicity.'[192]

---

[190] Larry Elliott, 'The UK could learn a lot from Germany's long-term industrial
strategy', *The Guardian*, 30 March 2016.
[191] Charles Waterman, *The Three Spheres of Society* (London: Faber & Faber,
1946), p. 94.
[192] Ibid., p. 117.

The latter—publicity—is nowadays used to good effect by consumer magazines, TV programmes, etc. that expose dishonest service, substandard manufacture and so on. And Waterman's use of the word 'weapons' well reflects the fact that the brotherliness of which Steiner speaks need not always imply blissful harmony. It often exists, after all, in opposing interests rubbing against one another (e.g. customers may hope for a lower price, producers for a higher). This reminder complements nicely the altogether more genial idea that, with association, business becomes 'warmed through' (Gerald Häfner) with human contact and conscientious service—an image that, encouragingly, one generally finds within already existing associations (like CSAs), an image that Gary Lamb also conveys: 'Associations of individuals and groups—the actual stakeholders in the various sectors of production, distribution, and consumption—who share perspectives and information will organize economic activity. Such associations, formed in freedom, will foster conscious collaboration and fellowship rather than instinctual self-interest and competition.'[193]

Those who are still feeling sceptical about the whole idea of association (which I would think is a perfectly natural reaction) may be pacified to some extent by Steiner's comments that these ideas can provide *partial* solutions, here and there. He is not imagining an overnight, root-and-branch conversion to some new type of economy. And it is always worth remembering that these partial solutions will come in very different guises depending on whether the goods and services you are thinking about are locally provided—like cabbages or refuse collection—or from another continent—like bikes, perhaps, or CDs. And perhaps one can take encouragement from Ann Pettifor who declares in *The Case For the Green New Deal* the intention to build 'an economy based on social and economic justice, one that celebrates the altruism, co-operation and collective responsibility that is characteristic of human nature'.[194] With *Jubilee 2000*, remember, Pettifor forced powerful institutions—including the IMF and World Bank, to cancel some $100 billion of poor-country debt.[195] She also predicted the 2008 crash. Perhaps she knows which way the wind is blowing!

[193] Gary Lamb, *Associative Economics: Spiritual Activity for the Common Good* (Ghent, NY: The Association of Waldorf Schools of North America, 2010), p. 58.
[194] Ann Pettifor, *The Case For the Green New Deal* (Verso: London, 2019), p. 171.
[195] Ibid., p. 166.

Having looked at some of Steiner's general comments about associations—their makeup and modus operandi—some of the specific tasks he deemed suitable for these associations will now be considered, as will some other operational aspects of the economic realm.

7.4.3   Production according to need

The task of the future will be to find, through associations, the kind of production which most accords with the needs of consumption ... (CW23, p. 112)

The institutions and provisions of a healthy economy ... can only be created through a network of corporations that regulate production by considering consumption ... The issue is the mediation between consumption and production based on economic experience and real economic relationships. (CW24, p. 12)

... rather will the associations adapt the production of goods to actual need. (CW23, p. 119)

Although there may have been fewer products available in Steiner's day, it was certainly not a case of food, shelter and clothing, and nothing else. So, ascertaining need was not simply a question of multiplication: so many thousand women will need so many thousand cardigans in the year, etc. There was already a vast array of goods available. Indeed, Steiner bemoaned the likes of the 'cri-cri' that had been a fad some years earlier and made the maker a wealthy man. This was a gadget you could keep in your pocket and make it shriek such that, for a time ...

... the streets were made quite intolerable ... [...] ... as regards human existence, the manufacture of cri-cris might well have been dispensed with. (CW337a, 15 September 1920)

Steiner's contemporary, the industrialist Henry Ford, also observed:

'There is more gear, more wrought material, in the average American backyard than in the whole domain of an African king. The average American boy has more paraphernalia around him than a whole Eskimo community ... There is no adequate realization of the large proportion of the labour and material of industry that is used in furnishing the world with its trumpery and trinkets, which are made only to be sold, and are bought merely to be owned—that perform no service in the world and are at last mere rubbish as at first they were mere waste.'[196]

So, how did Steiner imagine needs would be ascertained in practice? Surely, needs reveal themselves perfectly well in the traditional supply and demand arena of a market economy? If an article is flying off a shop's shelves, more will be produced. If it is gathering dust, production will cease. But Steiner had reservations concerning how well the traditional interplay between supply and demand can respond to actual need:

> *The remodelling of the market ... will follow as soon as a real principle of association finds a place in our social life. Then it will no longer be the impersonal supply and demand ... that will determine whether a commodity shall be produced or not. [...] demand in our present social conditions is extremely doubtful because there is always the question whether there are sufficient means available to make the demand possible. We may want things; if we do not possess the means to satisfy our wants, we shall not be able to create a demand. (CW332a, p. 45)*

If a hard-up family badly needs to replace a broken washing machine or would dearly love to buy a pram for their newborn, but can't afford to, no demand will be registered in the first place; no demand will be there to stimulate supply. *But despite no demand, there is need.*

> *Between these two—consumption governed by egotism, and production in which love is the ruling principle—there is the distribution of commodities, holding the balance between them. Today this is brought about through the rise and fall of the market, through supply and demand, but in future times an association of men will substitute intelligence for the fluctuation of the market. Men will be there who will make it their task to regulate production in conformity with their observation of the needs of the consumer. So that the market will consist in commodities that the associations,*

---

[196] Henry Ford, *My Life and Work* (Hawthorne, CA: BN Publishing, 2008), p. 180.

already mentioned, will be able to produce, these associations having first studied and observed intelligently the needs of consumption. (CW332a, p. 134)

... following the principle of association, it will be possible to produce a supply of commodities corresponding to the needs that have been investigated. That is, arrangements must exist with persons who can study the wants of consumers. Statistics can only give the present state of affairs. They can never be authoritative about the future. The needs for the time being must be studied, and, in accordance with these, measures must be taken to produce what is needed. (CW332a, p. 45)

The statistics that reveal so-and-so many thousand washing machines were bought last year cannot reveal the overall need for them this year, or next, especially if some who needed them were unable to afford to buy them in the first place. The alternative Steiner proposes—where real need is investigated more consciously—may sound rather idealistic; but it also sounds very civilised: there is a greater chance that everyone gets taken into consideration so we can then all move forward together. Even today, one often sees unmet needs in somewhere as supposedly advanced as the UK. In Steiner's day, despite Bismarck's significant welfare reforms in the second half of the 19th century, many a need was undoubtedly left unquenched, especially just after the Great War and during the hyper-inflation that followed (1921-1923).

As has been described already, the crucial difference between state socialism and what Steiner is advocating is that, in his threefold approach, the state—the rights domain—has little to do with these things. That is, it would have little to do with ascertaining *where* needs lay or with organising production to suit. All this belongs to the economic realm and its guiding principle of *fraternité*—fellowship, collaboration, association. The rights realm might establish *which* needs were so basic that, given the general prosperity of the region / state in question, the fulfilment of these needs ought to be seen as a right. In such cases, it might enshrine in law people's *right* to sufficient food or healthcare, say. (That's not to say that the right to food is necessarily a *universal* human right. If a shipwrecked sailor is washed up on some barren rock thousands of miles from civilisation, he or she may have no right to fresh water if it doesn't rain.) However, we are not concerned here with rights, but with needs.

And how exactly does Steiner propose such needs be ascertained, if not by statistics, if not by counting the number of washing machines sold last year, and then extrapolating forward? This is addressed in rather general terms:

> *That is fundamental and vital in the economy: that it starts from the satisfaction of needs … What we are dealing with, because it is a living process, cannot be determined by statistics, but only by people from associations going out into a particular territory and becoming humanly acquainted with those who have this or that need, humanly getting to know the sum of needs, and then from a purely human, living point of view, not from statistics, ascertain the number of people needed to produce an article. (CW338, 16 February 1921)*

> *The association must include people who cover a certain territory (with its boundaries determined on an economic basis) to inform themselves about existing needs and initiate negotiations about how many people must be involved in production in a particular branch of industry in order to meet those needs. [...]*

> *… the associations will need objective agents who cannot be exclusively interested in selling the greatest possible quantities of the commodities they represent, but must rather ask: what are the needs? These agents, who make up one element of the associations, must also be experts in determining how to organize production to meet these needs. The second element enlists transport providers who ship products and initiate negotiations to ensure those products get to where they are needed. The associations need consumption experts, distribution experts, and—as the third element—production experts. (CW338, 16 February 1921)*

> *[The situation] will only be improved by enabling the economic process to be clearly and transparently observed at every place, assuming always that those who make the observations are in a position to follow them out to their logical conclusion. (CW340, p. 71)*

It is up to our intelligence (perhaps even common sense) to work out ways of ascertaining where the needs are. Those working in associations—the people 'on the ground'—determine this in whatever way seems practicable; and this human attention replaces impersonal supply and demand. Needs can be established by producers in close association with networks of consumer groups, for example.

But how would needs even be ascertained by networks of consumer groups? Simply observing that such-and-such is selling well takes us straight back to those very statistics which Steiner cautions against. Is he proposing the population literally be canvassed for what they see as their needs? Focus groups to estimate interest in a new iPhone 25? Door-to-door enquiries to estimate interest in rocking horses? What about those things one largely buys on a whim? You see a table cloth that looks nice and you put it in your trolley. Not every purchase can be predicted.

With the efficient, largely internet-driven markets of nowadays circulating millions of products and services, these ideas of Steiner's can seem very dated and possibly even irrelevant to a modern-day citizen of the 'developed world'. In an undeveloped or war-ravaged country, seeking to take itself to sunnier, more equitable climes, one can imagine these ideas being effective, even highly effective. But in somewhere like Britain? Or Norway? Or Japan? What an almighty palaver it would be, surely, to reorganise matters in the way Steiner is suggesting? We shall return to this question shortly, bearing in mind Steiner's repeated insistence that threefolding should never be seen as some utopian, inflexible blueprint, but rather that human beings active in the three realms at all times adapt it to the prevailing conditions of their work.

But one thing is clear, the driver behind economic activity is ideally need, not greed (or, as socialist literature generally puts it, production should be 'for use' and not 'for profit'):

> *When it is a question of starting a factory, people will not consider it merely from the point of view of how much profit it will yield under the existing conjuncture; but they will start from a collective insight into what is needed. It requires no government regulations; that would only tie the whole thing up in red tape. What it requires is the practical knowledge of the people actually engaged in various businesses and the various branches of business; and this gives the means of finding out whether a particular business works is needed. If it is needed, then one may go on to production, and the people can make their earnings by it. It will be done by way of the associations ... (CW337a, 15 September 1920)*

Again, Henry Ford sees things somewhat similarly: 'It is the function of business to produce for consumption and not for money or speculation. Producing for consumption implies that the quality of the article produced will be high and the price will be low—that the article is one which serves the people and not merely the producer. If the money feature is twisted out of its proper perspective, then the production will be twisted to serve the producer.'[197]

Having bemoaned manufacture of the likes of the cri-cri that 'might well have been dispensed with', Steiner nonetheless insists that, whilst the economic domain should ascertain and meet needs, it should not judge them:

> ... 'market' relationship must be superseded by associations that regulate the exchange and production of goods through an intelligent consideration of human needs. Such associations can replace mere supply and demand by contracts and negotiations between groups of producers and consumers, and between different groups of producers. Excluding on principle one person's making himself a judge of another's legitimate needs, these negotiations will be based solely on the possibilities afforded by natural resources and by human abilities. (CW24, p. 41)

> It is important that the people assigned to this task allow needs to emerge freely, without in any way imposing their opinions as to whether some need is justified or not. They must limit themselves to objectively confirming needs as people perceive them. Fighting pointless, luxurious, or harmful needs is not the concern of associative, economic life; these are subject only to the influence of the cultural sphere. Pointless or damaging needs ought to be removed from the world via education in the spiritual realm whereby desires and feeling are ennobled. An independent cultural life will certainly be able to do that ... That is the only healthy way to combat harmful influences in society. When either the government or the economy passes judgment on needs as such, we are dealing with a chaotic and confusing mix of cultural, economic and other interests, not with the threefolding of the social body. Threefolding is a profoundly serious matter. Cultural affairs [what comes from each individual, RM] really must be allowed their independence. They are not free when any type of censoring agency can forbid anything that falls into the realm of human needs ... (CW338, 16 February 1921)

---

[197] Henry Ford, *My Life and Work* (Hawthorne, CA: BN Publishing, 2008), p. 13.

It is for the individual to decide what he or she needs or wants. Matters concerning the individual are part of the cultural domain, and the guiding principle of the cultural domain is freedom. The individual should be able to express him- / herself freely at all times (subject, naturally, to not encroaching on another's freedom and rights). So, associative working within the economic realm should ascertain what people see as their needs, not decide for people what their needs ought to be. Clearly, there will always be a spectrum of needs, with basic needs at one end and more luxurious ones at the other. And in a world of finite resources, one imagines that lively association between producers, distributors and consumers might, at times, prioritise.

Although Steiner advises against judging needs, the following comment concerning the fabricating of needs via advertising is noteworthy:

> ... an economic process should never give rise to demands, but demands should instead come from outside, through some other cultural process, through an ethical process, or something similar. During unsound times, demands arise through purely economic processes, and people who cannot think soundly rejoice over this. [...] Advertising has come out of the purely economic sphere. It does not give rise to real demands. To produce demands in such a way as to arouse an artificial interest in certain goods, is unsound and a source of illness in the social organism. (CW188(v), 26 January 1919)

Whilst advertising might be a rather small detail, it can create significant problems. The elderly and gullible are always the most likely to buckle under more direct sales techniques—like cold calling and so on. I have known elderly people who have been taken in by smooth-talking salespeople and spent thousands of pounds on things they didn't need. Within hours they have regretted the purchase. Even seemingly harmless advertising techniques—where you are not pressured face-to-face by a pushy seller—can be highly problematic, and it is always the poor, young, elderly or uneducated who succumb the most. A seemingly innocuous TV advert for some foodstuff that is blatantly unhealthy can easily—and often does—make these more vulnerable members of society think it is just normal to consume it. Indeed, it seems even people who think of themselves as not at all vulnerable can be far more susceptible to this normalising (a kind of low-level brainwashing) than they realise. Otherwise, why is it that so many overweight people fall for refined sugars or dubious 'diet' products instead of sating their craving for sweetness with a few dried dates or figs, or simply eating less? Dried dates and figs cannot be mass produced on an industrial scale in the same way that certain 'diet' items can, so there is little profit in them, and no one advertises them. As a result, dates and figs end up being seen as rather fringe and alternative (even though just two figs represent one of the five fruit and vegetable portions the UK government has recommended everyone eat each day), whilst foodstuffs containing a plethora of additives from chemistry labs, become seen as normal. Bingo, the advertisers have done their job!

In the following, Steiner touches on the relationship between 'production according to need' and price.

We can easily understand that some reply to these arguments: 'What is the point of it all? When all is said and done, it is human need that rules over production, and no one can give or receive credit unless there is a demand somewhere or other to justify it.' Someone might even say, 'After all, these social institutions and methods you have in mind amount to nothing more than a conscious arrangement of the very things that "supply and demand" will surely regulate automatically.' It will be clear to one who looks more closely that this is not the point. The social thoughts that originate in the threefold idea do not aim at replacing the free business dealings governed by supply and demand with a command [i.e. planned, RM] economy. Their aim is to realise the true relative values of commodities, with the underlying idea that the product of an individual's labour should be of a value equal to all the other commodities consumed in the time spent producing it.

Under the capitalist system, demand may determine whether someone will undertake the production of a certain commodity. Yet demand alone can never determine whether it will be possible to produce it at a price corresponding to its value in the sense defined above. This can be determined only through methods and institutions whereby society, in all its aspects, will bring about a sensible valuation of the different commodities. Anyone who doubts that such methods and institutions are worth striving for lacks vision; he does not see that, under the exclusive rule of supply and demand, needs whose satisfaction would upgrade the life of the community are being starved. He has no feeling for the necessity of trying to include the satisfaction of such needs among the practical incentives of an organized community. The essential aim of the threefold social order is to create a just balance between human needs and the value of the products of human work. (CW24, pp. 50-51)

A truly social order must be guided by the fact that those who quite justifiably must have commodities must be able to pay for them ... Instead of the present chaotic market, there must be an arrangement by which the tyrannizing over human needs and the interference with consumption is eradicated. [...] research [must] be made into the scope of consumption, and decisions reached on how consumption needs can be met. (CW332a, p. 45)

The subject of price will be returned to in Sections 7.4.10 and 7.4.11. Suffice to say for now, however, that, with respect to 'producing to need', Steiner is not advocating that a family which cannot afford to buy a washing machine is simply given one by some association that has worked out how many washing machines need to be produced. Instead, it is a question of aiming for realistic prices such that the washing machine is affordable. But, you might exclaim, these days one can buy washing machines for £200, which seems almost criminally cheap; there is no way all the association in the world is going to get prices any lower! Well, this may very well be true, but then the solution to the un-affordability problem will lie in the remuneration the hard-up family is bringing home. Clearly, the prices of the services *they* provide are too low.

The general approach of equitably trying to meet everyone's needs was proposed by Scottish lawyer James Steuart in 1767, when contemplating the discipline of 'political economy': 'The principal object of this science is to secure a certain fund of subsistence for all the inhabitants, to obviate every circumstance which may render it precarious; to provide every thing necessary for supplying the wants of the society, and to employ the inhabitants (supposing them to be free-men) in such a manner as naturally to create reciprocal relations and dependencies between them, so as to make their several interests lead them to supply one another with their reciprocal wants.'[198]

---

[198] Steuart, J., 'An Inquiry into the Principles of Political Economy', https://www.marxists.org/reference/subject/economics/steuart/.

Clearly, Steiner closely concurs with these sentiments; although, as we have seen, he insists that economic considerations are best co-ordinated by an administration that is quite separate from the political system.

In summary:

- Production according to need is the aim, rather than production that makes the highest profit.
- Such needs to include those which don't find expression in traditional demand, for lack of funds.
- Associations to ascertain needs as best they can.
- Ascertaining such needs not to be based on past statistics (or, not only).
- Those ascertaining needs are not to judge what others perceive to be their needs (pointless / luxurious / damaging needs only to be addressed via education—i.e. in the cultural domain).
- It is unhealthy when the economic realm 'creates needs' via advertising.
- The proposal is not to replace free dealings governed by supply and demand with a command economy, but ...
- organise production such that prices are brought into a just relation.

Reflections in relation to the present

As with associations, one can well imagine that 'production according to need' could have had considerable appeal and potential in somewhere like Germany immediately after the horrors of the Great War. Once industrial concerns had stopped making weaponry, there would have been an urgent need to get them back to making things to meet the people's basic needs, not luxuries for the lucky few, or random articles to sit in shops for months or years until someone happened to want to buy them. If communicated well, one can imagine an all-hands-to-the-pump atmosphere arising from the satisfaction of knowing that within one year, say, every household would have the use of electric lighting or whatever. One can imagine the wider community gaining a deep satisfaction in this 'working to meet needs' in an organised and conscious way, a way that would raise the standard of living for all.

As we have seen, Steiner is categorically not advocating govern-
ment-directed production, a 'command economy', a centrally planned,
communistic bureaucracy (like the USSR's Gosplan) which can result
in (i) items being produced that not everyone wants (you can have any
colour curtains you like, as long as they're dark green); (ii) little interest in work as you are often producing stuff people don't want; (iii) no
responsibility for work as you get paid anyway (grain pouring off the
back of a lorry in transit as no one can be bothered to adjust the tail-
gate); (iv) low levels of innovation as a sluggish state apparatus may
take years to adopt your idea, if at all (what's the point suggesting an
improvement to the method of production if no-one's listening?). No,
under threefolding, a consumer would still be free to buy a new dining
table on a whim, and a producer would be perfectly free to bring out a
razor with three blades instead of two if they so wished. But, it would
be to the advantage of both producers and consumers to be in (or, at
least, represented in) associations, and one of the functions of these
associations would be to ascertain need, as far as possible, and thence
tweak production to suit.

As mentioned earlier in the book, Steiner's 'third way' soon had
tens of thousands of supporters, if not more, including a number of
influential advocates in high places. But once it became clear, after
two or three years, that it was not going to attract enough followers
to unseat other political traditions, he ceased campaigning for it. So,
his threefold ideas probably only inspired a few isolated examples of
attempts to produce according to need at the time. There will no doubt
have been small, more domestic endeavours in this direction, like the
baker and publisher examples Steiner gives, but the most notable effort
was probably the inauguration of the World Energy Council (originally, World Power Conference), the now UN-accredited energy body
where 92 countries are currently represented. This 'principal impartial
network of leaders and practitioners promoting an affordable, stable
and environmentally sensitive energy system for the greatest benefit
of all'[199] was set up by Scotsman, anthroposophist, and indeed friend
of Steiner, Daniel Dunlop (who also founded BEAMA—the British Electrotechnical and Allied Manufacturers Association), to keep
abreast of both energy needs and energy sources worldwide with a

---

[199] https://www.worldenergy.org.

view to ensuring rational distribution along associative lines, according to need. To what extent the World Energy Council has been able to stand up to the flood of economic neo-liberalism in the energy market is of course a question, but the original intentions were, without doubt, along Steiner's lines.

Again, it may be tempting to think that trying to consciously attune production according to need in the associative way Steiner recommended is perhaps rather pointless today given how established markets have become, and how effective. Not only can (a) information (e.g. re what is selling or what is not selling) fly round the world in a split second, but also (b) this transmission now costs next to nothing, and (c) humans barely need be involved. As already alluded to, we have computerised order processing and stock control, just-in-time production, highly automated manufacturing and shipping robotics— it is hard to imagine much slicker ways of needs being met, of getting commodities to where they are needed. In so many sectors, advanced logistics enable supply to adjust to demand almost automatically, minimising overproduction, underproduction, waste, and storage costs. So, one could conclude the meeting of needs and profit maximisation are not mutually exclusive. If things are needed, there will be money to be made in producing them. Therefore, people will produce them … and needs will be met.

And yet … there are still those needs Steiner talks about which remain unquenched, for want of funds.

And as Grace Blakely observes: 'We produce endless amounts of data about our habits, behaviours, and preferences that can be agglomerated and used by firms like Amazon to determine how much they should be producing, and of what. But the revolutionary power of these technologies is limited because they are concentrated in the hands of a tiny elite, which is using them to maximize their profits.'[200] Much of the electronic wizardry that has brought remarkable efficiency to the economy is used in the pursuit of profit for a shrinking few rather than in the pursuit of meeting people's needs. Indeed, the incidence of traditional, supply-and-demand, competitive, neo-liberal behaviour showing little ability in catering for needs is so high in

---

[200] Grace Blakeley, *Stolen: How to Save the World from Financialisation* (London: Repeater Books, 2019), p. 21.

some sectors of the economy that other, more enlightened approaches
are more or less pleading to be adopted.

Take what we in the UK call 'directory enquiries'. When there was
one telecoms provider—British Telecom—there was one 'directory
enquiries' service. If you wanted someone's phone number, you would
phone directory enquiries, and for a minimal charge, you would either
be given the number or be connected, depending on what you wanted.
Then came that blissful answer to everything, the free market and
deregulation! A number of competing companies set themselves up
to provide the service, and each service had its own number. One had
118 500, another 118 118 and so on. The latter decided to spend many
millions of pounds on a TV advertising campaign to smother the competition. But of course the only way to recoup the huge cost of their
TV campaign was to pass it on to customers. And so the charge for
being given the number you need went up to £8.98 and the cost if you
were connected for a ten-minute call shot up to £49.39—the cost of a
good quality jumper or pair of trousers! And who falls for this, in the
main? Once again, the vulnerable and elderly—who often don't have
access to online services. And who are the perpetrators of this pain?
Grown men (and they usually *are* men) who in all likelihood think of
themselves as respectable members of the community.

Or take the infamous example of Nestlé trying to convince African
women, with their extremely limited resources, to buy artificially produced baby formula, when breast milk is not only free but far more
healthy.[201] Nestlé had no interest in need.

Or take the 2008 financial crash when banks, which had been putting profit before needs, were excruciatingly bailed out by taxpayers.
(When, not long after the crash, banks were up to no good again,
fixing the LIBOR rate, and once more awarding themselves odiously
unwarranted bonuses, you could almost feel the entire nation collectively wanting to hug the telly as Channel 4's Economics Editor, Paul
Mason, seethed over this on the evening news.)

Or think of the tool you buy from the local Pound Shop which
breaks soon after. Throwing it away can be a rather sad as well as
frustrating experience: not sadness at having lost a pound, but at the

---

[201] Mike Muller, 'Nestlé baby milk scandal has grown up but not gone away', *The
Guardian*, 13 February 2013.

thought of (probably) Chinese workers (possibly children) wasting their lives producing things that are not very useful. And frustration, as you now need to go back to the shops for another screwdriver. No one *needs* shoddy goods (although, granted, a cheap, poorly-made item can be a godsend to someone with little money).

Or take the fact that my local town (population circa 25,000) had, until recently, five biggish supermarkets that by all accounts appeared (along with a number of smaller food shops) to be providing everyone with the food they needed. The arrival of two further supermarkets does not represent supply according to need; it is supply according to the 'war of competition', and it means duplication and waste. The builders involved in putting up the new buildings might have been better employed building affordable housing or repairing the dreadful roads in the area. If one were to add up all the instances of such duplication, it would doubtless come to a depressing total. And this duplication is ultimately likely to lead to goods that are *more* expensive; although, in the short term, customers will quite possibly see that a cabbage in the new Aldi or Lidl is cheaper than in the existing Sainsbury's / Tesco / Iceland / Waitrose / Co-op.

Or take all those junk foods that are not produced to meet people's need for sustenance but because they are cheap to mass produce and so can wring large profits out of the poorly educated.

Or take 'big pharma' which has come under severe criticism for repeatedly designing clinical trials that give corporations the green light to market drugs that are *worse* than existing treatments.[202] Why do they do this? Because when the patent on an existing treatment runs out, large profits are harder to come by. Production according to need? Production in order to heal the afflicted? Or production according to sociopathic, corporate greed? Indeed, a friend of mine managed to increase her bone density—and so reverse her osteoporosis—with a natural remedy. Under an associative approach, any company making less effective pills would, instead of perpetrating propaganda for the sake of profit, move production to the more affective natural remedy, which would better correspond to need. A body like the FDA in the USA should really be something that facilitates such progress.

---

[202] Richard Smith 'Foregone Conclusions', *The Guardian*, 14 January 2004.

Or take the fact that in the UK, with knife crime rampant, the acute need for an expansion of youth services is overlooked while vast wealth is allowed to slink off into tax exile.

Or look at the pharmacy, Boots. In 2016, *The Guardian* published anonymous concerns by the staff of Boots that, having been taken over by private equity firm KKR and billionaire Monaco tax exile Stefano Pessina, the safety of its pharmacy customers was dropping fast.[203]

Or take the fact that there are millions of people in the UK alone who would dearly love to own their own home, but cannot afford to buy one and are thus forced to rent from someone else until their dying day.

Or take GM foods which bio-tech producers tell us are the only way to feed the world, and which have purportedly led to a harrowing 250,000 farmer suicides in India as a result of debt.[204] Lest we forget, it was one or two of those self-same producers who, a few years back, were developing the 'terminator gene' to remove plant fertility and so remove the ability of farmers to keep useful seed for the following year's crop. Hardly a solution to world hunger!

Within some services at least, there is growing recognition that the profit motive has no place. As noted by Zoe Williams: 'Every care home scandal you read about—from Southern Cross nearing bankruptcy in 2011 to Care UK workers going on strike last month—springs from the attempt to wring profit out of this business at the expense of the lowest paid within it. The companionship of care work, the longevity of the relationship between the care worker and the cared-for, the living standards and career progressions of the workers—it is all hollowed out or tainted.

'I have argued in the past that a social enterprise could do this work, and pay workers better, treat them better, and create an entirely different dynamic of mutualism, permanence and participation. Keeping the money in the local community isn't the half of it, though clearly that would be a huge improvement on siphoning it all off to a guy in Guernsey. I have seen social enterprise companies—asset-locked, copper-bottomed—doing exactly that.'[205]

---

[203] Aditya Chakrabortty, 'Profit seems to matter more than the health and safety of customers', *The Guardian*, 18 April 2016.

[204] Arundhati Roy on *Desert Island Discs*, BBC Radio 4, 31 March 2017.

[205] Zoe Williams, 'Going beyond left and right could save the public sector', *The Guardian*, 8 September 2014.

Clearly, in some sectors at the very least, the need for 'production according to need' is acute.

In 2016, reports of a severe shortage of care home places for the elderly were in the news—places for the very people who had helped make the UK a relatively well-off country. If we produced according to need—and care homes are unquestionably a need—their provision would be a priority. Indeed, the rights realm might even decide that *all* should have a care home place if required. It would then be incumbent on those working within an associative economy to work out ways of providing more care homes and perhaps, if necessary, less of something else. No doubt news of such bed shortages will have prompted a number of care home providers to embark on a period of expansion and construction to be the first to capitalise on the 'investment opportunity'. But it would not be difficult for an umbrella body of care homes to associate with the ageing population and maintain an overview of capacity in the sector as well as projected demand based on the country's demographics. This information, complete with regional variances and so on, could be passed on to care home providers well in advance to prevent shortages arising.

But whilst, in *certain* sectors, production according to need seems an obvious approach, could it be meaningfully replicated in others?

What about chocolate bars? Currently, a confectioner might think: with one or two million dollars-worth of advertising it could steal competitors' trade by making a new chocolate bar—one with chocolate and vanilla stripes, perhaps, called the Tiger Bar or the Zebra! Under production-according-to-need, the question might be: are there enough chocolate bars on the shelves already? The latter approach would seem aesthetically more pleasing and somehow more grown-up. But changing our approach in the case of such trifles might not seem a priority. For certain goods (e.g. loft insulation to encourage everyone to make their homes more energy efficient), ascertaining need and then organising production accordingly would seem to make perfect sense. Indeed this is not uncommon, albeit typically with coordination coming from those working in the rights realm rather than the economic.

With the natural monopolies mentioned previously (gas, rail, etc.), adopting a needs-based approach is certainly possible. We don't want two rail networks covering the same area, or two sets of water pipes. Instead, we allow profit-maximising companies to manage such monopolies, and then set up industry regulators like Ofwat etc. to make sure they don't exploit their position as sole provider. The likes of Ofwat in a sense represent the consumer interests in what is an association-of-sorts. However, inasmuch as private capital underpins such industries, profit maximisation remains the *raison d'être* instead of meeting need.

In 2019, the UK's Labour Party indicated it would nationalise some of the country's natural monopolies, if elected, and this was undoubtedly with a view to basing production on need, not on maximising return on investment. (Having the rights state run these concerns is, of course, not in keeping with the threefold approach. But this issue is covered elsewhere.) Again, free market fundamentalists would doubtless argue that nationalisation / lack of competition brings those inefficiencies mentioned earlier and removes any incentive for innovation because the provider knows they don't need to worry about competition. But this complaint is likely only to be a reflection of the fact that they themselves might not bother to innovate if there was nothing in it for them. Plus, they will only make the complaint if they have not used French or Japanese trains which operate very well without competition. Even the UK Conservative Party (as of 2021) has decided to nationalise a significant swathe of the rail network in Britain because of poor performance in private hands.[206]

That the British have an affinity for the idea of replacing the profit motive with a meeting-of-need motive is demonstrated by their almost religious loyalty towards the National Health Service. Indeed, traditionally, any neo-liberal politician in the UK has been only too aware that an attempt to privatise the NHS would probably be tantamount to political suicide (notwithstanding that privatisation of one or two aspects has been achieved in the past—a sizeable part of dental services, for example). At the time of writing, however, it has emerged that 59 GP practices have been taken over by an American health insurance company Operose Health.[207] Whether this becomes enough

---

[206] See, for example, Tanya Powley and Jim Pickard, 'Northern rail franchise to be nationalised, says UK government', *The Financial Times*, 30 January 2020, or Dominic O'Connell, 'Better rail services in huge shake up', BBC News, 20 May 2021.
[207] Sarah Wilson, '37 NHS GP practices have been sold to a private US health company—here's what it means', *Edinburgh Evening News*, 19 March 2021.

to eventually bring down the Conservative government led by Boris Johnson remains to be seen. In the USA it is only more recently that access to healthcare has become more universal—in the form of Obamacare (which former president Trump and others were then keen to abolish on account of the cost).

Rudolf Steiner had no time for abstractions, but let's indulge momentarily to illustrate a point. Imagine if some hypothetical, ocean-going liner full of a perfectly diverse range of passengers covering all the professions and trades were, a month after engine failure in the middle of nowhere, to run aground on some hypothetically off-the-radar, fertile island, never to be heard of again. The passengers could, if they wanted, found their society on a neo-liberal model with each unto themselves. All the strong, young men would run off the ship at first mooring and go and fence off and defend the most fertile portions of land for themselves, and the struggle of all against all would ensue. Or, in the period before landfall, the passengers could all sit down and discuss how to proceed in a more orderly manner. They could decide to ascertain needs and then proceed with production accordingly: so many farm workers needed to produce food for all; houses to be built firstly for the elderly and infirm, etc. As this associative, needs-observing society evolved over the years it would doubtless end up looking somewhat different to the one we currently 'enjoy'!

By the same token, if, one hundred years ago, public life in Central Europe had been organised more along the lines Steiner and his threefold campaigners advocated, it would have been interesting to see what sort of society we would now be looking at. If production had proceeded more according to needs, objectively ascertained, perhaps we would now also see, not only an effective and efficient economic system, but also one that was much more equitable, peaceful and inspiring. And perhaps some of those many thousands of people engaged in stock broking, currency speculation and the like would instead be concerned with the 'real economy', doing useful things, producing actual goods (with some, no doubt, in positions facilitating the consumer / producer dialogue that a needs-based approach would entail).

But it is all very well to say: If I was aiming for such-and-such a destination, I wouldn't start from here! We are where we are, and where we are is very different to where Steiner was a hundred years ago. As Steiner insisted, ideas for social reform must always adapt to circumstances.

One thing seems clear, though: existing, profit-maximising firms with shareholders who invested with profit-maximising motives are unlikely to change the way they go about business. Production more according to need instead of profit can therefore mainly be expected to arise either in new start-ups, in social enterprises such as certain co-ops, in unquoted businesses whose owners wish to take their business in this direction, or in quangos or nationalised industries.

That said, there will without doubt also be many examples of associative dialogue in traditional industries, where one particular set of businesses will be in close and regular contact with other sets of businesses in their supply chains, such that the parties' needs are met in a more or less collaborative manner. The more of this, the better, in Steiner's view.

Concerning advertising (that tries to stimulate artificial 'need'), it would certainly be very welcome to see less of it. Junk emails in the inbox are a nuisance; junk mail on the doormat is wasteful; cold calling is maddening and exploits the vulnerable; unhealthy foods etc. become normalised; sales targets are predatory; and the interruption of TV programmes can be in extremely poor taste (e.g. when a harrowing account of war or starvation is interrupted, perhaps, by some cheery breakfast cereal or package holiday advert). A more dignified economy would be very welcome.

7.4.4   Contracts as basis of trading relationships

Steiner proposes that, once producers, distributors and consumers (or representatives of these three) have associated, have established need, collaborated, negotiated and reached agreement on matters of mutual trade, such agreement would best then be formalised:

> Within the economic circuit ... associations must be formed. Representatives of the different occupations should meet; producer and consumer should come together. The purely business operations and measures that take place should be based on contracts entered into by the associations. In the economic world, everything should rest on contracts, everything should depend upon mutual service rendered. (CW332a, p. 66)

... associations of the various branches of production with the consumers will be called into existence in the sphere of economic life, so that everywhere there will be a combination of the producers with the consumers. These associations will enter into contracts with other associations. A kind of collective will then arises within larger or smaller groups. This collective will is an ideal for which many socialists yearn, but they visualise the matter in a confused, by no means reasonable manner. (CW332a, p. 124)

This 'collective will' could be seen, perhaps, as a more conscious expression of our de facto interdependence, our mutuality, our we're-all-in-this-together-ness. As well as being distinct from state socialism, Steiner's approach is, of course, very different to traditional capitalism too:

... the [threefold] commonwealth is the social order in which production will be carried on by associations through contracts with other associations [...] If this should really come about, where would the real difference lie between such a community and the mere trading system of society, the ruling system of today?

The difference shows itself in the fact that in the trading system the individual or the single group has, for the most part, to do with another individual or another group. What are the common interests of individuals or groups in their mutual relations? At present whether they are producers or consumers, their production and consumption are divided from one another, as if by a chasm, by the chances of the market. The chances of the market are the means of bringing about the distribution of commodities and of facilitating commerce. [...] Distribution is the link between production and consumption; when these are sundered from each other by the abyss of the market, there is no means of communication between them through the exercise of intelligence.

What, in the [threefold] commonwealth, will take the place of the system of distribution now prevailing? The whole domain of economic life will be drawn into the sphere of interest of every producer. Whereas it is now the interest of the producer to find out how he can procure and dispose of his products, which, however, he does out of self-interest, it will be necessary for every producer in the commonwealth to have a full interest in consumption, distribution, and production. (CW332a, pp. 135-136)

Clearly, Steiner did not much like the idea of people / factories making goods simply in the *hope* of selling them. He felt it was important that producers make things for which there is a definite, pre-established need. This not only creates business certainty, it also gives people enhanced feelings of human purpose perhaps, gives them stronger connections with others, with their fellow human beings—something he stressed was important.

Again, these suggestions would undoubtedly work better in some scenarios than others. In the example he gives of the bakery associating with a definite set of customers (see Section 7.4.2), one can see this would work well. Bread and cakes are regular purchases a customer can predict with reasonable certainty. So, just as Community Supported Agriculture today—box schemes and the like—can be based on pre-dictable, *contracted*, on-going custom, so too could his bakery.

But what about that dining table? What about the lampshade some-one wants to buy on a whim? What about windows? Naturally, no cus-tomer can predict in 1919 that they will want to replace their dining table in 1934. And even less will they *contract* in 1919 to purchase one fifteen years later. Yes, they might be prepared to place an order (contract) and wait four weeks for it. For a nice oak table this might work. But, for most commodities, bespoke production to order undoes the normal benefits of mass production. Not even in Steiner's day would anyone have been prepared to place an order for a toothbrush and then wait four weeks for it to arrive! Likewise (and thankfully), it is unlikely any toothbrush manufacturer would have considered ship-ping toothbrushes out one at a time! Such an interpretation of Stein-er's advice is ruled out, of course; he was not an impractical man. However, the *shop* selling dining tables, or an alliance of chemists in a particular region could have entered into contracts with suppliers (perhaps even sole-supplier or sole-distributor contracts) to buy their wares for the following twelve months, or whatever, such that produc-ers would feel reasonably confident in setting their output levels.

As Steiner points out, contracts will generally be time-limited:

> ... *everything in economic life needs to be based on the contract principle. In the future we should have cooperatives, economic associations, which base their mutual services and reciprocal*

services on the contract principle, on the contracts they conclude with each other. This contract principle must govern everywhere, especially life within consumer cooperatives, producer cooperatives and professional associations. A contract is always limited in some way. If no more services are provided, then it loses its meaning. All of economic life is based on this. (CW331, 24 June 1919)

Suppose that, in 1919 when Steiner is speaking, windows are not generally made onsite by builders but are bought in from manufacturers and then incorporated into the building of houses. And suppose there are, say, ten window manufacturers in a certain area—a large county, perhaps, or a small country (although remember that the boundaries of administrative areas in the rights realm and the economic need not coincide). And, for the sake of simplicity, suppose these factories all make the same range of window styles and sizes that are popular in the area. These window makers could form a window makers' alliance and enter into contracts such that:

a. They collectively (via this alliance) enter into dialogue with the regional builders' trade confederation (this coming together of the window makers with the builders would constitute an association in Steiner's sense), and conclude an exclusive-supplier contract with same such that (i) the members of the builders' confederation agree to only buy windows from this window makers' alliance, and (ii) the window makers agree to always keep a ready supply of windows to meet these needs and not increase price or reduce quality over the period of the contract—a year or whatever. This way, the manufacturers will have greater certainty about the number of windows they will be able to sell, and so perhaps be more confident about taking on a particular number of workers or investing in / developing more efficient machinery, etc.

b. If another factory starts up in the area and can for some reason make windows more cheaply, the builders will not buy from them until the end of the contract already in place and, even then, there might be stipulation within the contract that the builders must first negotiate with the existing manufacturers alliance (e.g. to see if they can offer better terms) before switching to the new supplier. The contract might even be longer term such that the new, more efficient factory will have the incentive to join the alliance since, without doing so, sales will be limited to domestic customers and the few builders who are not part of the builders' confederation.

c. The window makers might, as members of the window makers' alliance, contract with each other not to leave the alliance during the period of the contract and also not to cut / raise prices for other customers, or engage in underhand sales techniques, or whatever.

d. Conversely, there might be a condition of membership stating that, should one of them be found to be consistently making substandard windows, their membership of the alliance would cease.

e. On the strength of the contract with their customers (the builders' trade confederation), the window makers might calculate that they need so many thousand tons of oak per annum and contract with particular timber merchants (belonging to some timber merchants' co-op, perhaps) that they will buy an amount of oak between x and y thousand tons per annum at a certain price (possibly subject to certain all-else-being-equal clauses, or with a certain percentage of scope for price variation in the event of living costs changing). They could enter into an exclusive-supplier contract whereby they guarantee not to go off buying timber from elsewhere, provided the quality and availability of the timber from the current suppliers remains stable.

f. The window makers might even enter into an agreement amongst themselves that, should any one of them discover / invent a more efficient production process, this gets shared amongst the others in some pre-agreed way.

g. They might enter into an agreement amongst themselves to jointly develop new machinery for more accurate planing, faster mortising, or whatever else seemed within reach.

h. In order to develop this machinery, they might enter into a contract with a supplier of loan capital[208] on condition, say, that 75% of the eventual cost savings arising from the new machinery be passed on to the consumer.

---

[208] A threefold supplier of capital would neither own nor control the business, but just lend, as we shall see.

Going about business in this way would lend a certain stability to things and reduce the 'accidents of the market' which Steiner considers unhealthy in economic life. By bringing people into dialogue, it would close up the 'chasm' between them that he finds so damaging. No longer would different economic players hunker down in their bunkers in order to scheme and try and outwit their competitors. Competitive, speculative randomness would give way to a more organised, conscious, stable, collaborative sense of togetherness.

With the more usual way of proceeding, two competing window manufacturers might employ sales reps and send them off to shops and builders' merchants around the region with the remit of selling as many as possible. And they would probably also keep their workers' wages at rock bottom to remain competitive. They might also spend considerable energy on a marketing campaign saying how splendid their particular windows were. Under Steiner's approach, some of these reps would instead work on collaboratively associating with the other parties in the process. The danger of these window makers colluding in order to behave monopolistically is addressed in part by the fact that customers (in this case, builders) represent one half of the association (between customers and suppliers).

What other safeguards might be needed to prevent unwelcome collusion would depend on the extent to which other suggestions of Steiner's had been observed. If the window makers had not been financed by profit maximising shareholders, and if a condition of their joining was a commitment to 'fair price' (covered presently), then the system might be self-regulating. If this was not the case, and particularly if the ten window manufacturers were the only ones in the area, then safeguards to prevent profiteering might need to be considered. In all likelihood, however, the builders would simply not enter into association with these window makers but, instead, elect to buy from further afield.

In connection with what role the state should have in such matters, Christoph Strawe observes: 'associations are contracting bodies; and contracts create a right freely agreed by the parties. How much competition and how much co-operation obtains is a matter of contract design. Attempts to allow only competitive relations to exist between the business partners are, in effect, a serious interference with the freedom to contract. The state would merely have to ensure that no

contractual agreements are made at the expense of third parties. This
is the only way to get a cartel law which is conformable with the freedom of contract.'[209]

Also, state *boundaries* have minimal relevance to associative economic activity:

> The preservation of free initiative in management is possible only if
> the leadership is not yoked to a central administration[210], but rather
> is permitted to combine into associations. The result of this is that
> a central administration does not control management operations;
> management retains freedom, and the social orientation of the
> economic body is based upon agreements [i.e. contracts] between
> independent management operations. A management responsible
> for export will be able to act completely out of its own free initiative
> in its commercial dealings with foreign countries; and domestically
> it will maintain relations with those associations that will help the
> most with the supply of raw materials and the like, to satisfy for-
> eign demands. The same will be possible for import management.
> (CW24, p. 20)

Lastly, the following is a reminder that the association of which Steiner
speaks is a very un-prescribed affair. The contracts in question can just
as well involve single individuals associating and forming contracts with
each other as they can involve larger alliances associating. The point is
the dialogue, the mutually-arrived-at agreement, and the formalising of
this mutuality in contract.

> ... with person-to-person, association-to-association agreements,
> work would go on as usual. Of course it is necessary that all agree-
> ments reflect the workers' insights and the consumers' interests.
> (CW23, p. 18)

---

[209] Christoph Strawe in Martin Large and Steve Briault (Eds), *Free, Equal and
Mutual: Rebalancing Society for the Common Good* (Stroud: Hawthorn Press,
2018), p. 246.

[210] I.e. the state. Much of what Steiner says about public life can be read as a manifesto which, whilst highly social, is against state socialism.

In summary:

- Production based on 'accidents of the market' to be reduced.
- Production based on contracts to be increased.
- Such contracts to be entered into within and between associations (comprising producers and consumers, or producers and distributors, or producers and other producers in their supply chain, or distributors and consumers, etc.).
- Both business certainty and human connection are thereby enhanced.

Reflections in relation to the present

No doubt, today, a good proportion of production will be based on contractual relationships. Manufacturers will have all manner of supply-chain agreements whereby production is tailored to definite orders and pre-agreed, repeat business. Conventionally structured firms that do this will, of course, lack many of the other features Steiner recommends; but such supply-chain agreements could be considered by threefold analysis to have at least *some* healthy effect, even where they have arisen following competitive tender initially.

Clearly, *ongoing* business relationships between one party and another lend themselves to Steiner's recommendation that production be based on contract. However, whilst such repeat business between one manufacturer and another, or between a manufacturer and a distributor (e.g. a shop) may be common, repeat business with end-users—us—is less common.

As mentioned previously, food purchase is a relatively predictable and regular thing that we all do, and so contracts involving end-users can work well here, as seen with Community Supporting Agriculture. CSA customers contract with a farm to purchase so much veg per month. This seems to work particularly well for *organic* food—possibly because those who eat organic food often think along more progressive lines and don't just accept the status quo, swallow the latest TV ad … and the additive-packed, snack being extolled.

However, even in more traditional business models we do see contractual relationships that involve the end-consumer and also extend over time. The most common of these are probably phone contracts or those for utilities like electricity or water. But, as we know, such business is very often accompanied by that unedifying game of cat and mouse, where the provider tries to nudge up prices without consumers noticing. New customers are enticed on board with attractive deals, and the most loyal customers often end up paying the most. The game also then involves consumers wasting part of their lives (not to mention the lives of all those in the accompanying, soul-destroying call centres) reciprocally trying to outsmart the supplier by switching from one provider to the next—which removes the business certainty Steiner is hoping for. If contracts can be abandoned at the drop of a hat, they are not really what he is proposing. This only highlights that trade contracts can be less than satisfactory if business is not functioning within an associative ethos where customer interests and provider interests enjoy both good representation and a sympathetic ear. Official industry regulators help, no doubt, but an overall air of collaboration, generally, there ain't.

The above is a reminder that exploitation is not always in one direction. Customers or distributors (e.g. shops) are perfectly capable of tyrannising producers, too—like we do when we buy a book on Amazon from one supplier instead of another because it is 10p cheaper. Or the price that farmers get for milk, for example, has at times been pared down so ruthlessly that many farms have had to give up producing milk, or have only been able to continue under ever-decreasing standards of environmental and animal welfare. And all for what? Most customers could afford to pay a few pence more per litre of milk. So the main driving force behind such practices may not necessarily be customer inability—or unwillingness—to pay a tiny bit more, but simply the obsession distributors (i.e. shops) have with minimising costs / maximising profit, or with undercutting the competition purely so they can broadcast that their milk is cheaper than elsewhere.

Also broached earlier: an argument in favour of the status quo with its 'accidents of the market' can be that its competitive nature encourages innovation, and this brings greater choice and improved products for the customer. On the other hand, if shops only enter into long-term, exclusive-supplier contracts, new producers with improved products might be unlikely to enter the market at all. Again, Steiner would presumably have argued that, in an economy acting associatively / fraternally, existing producers would be inspired, out of their focus on service, to have bustling R&D departments and find satisfaction in making production processes more efficient and in improving their products. Also, an innovative newcomer, rather than setting up a brand new production facility, could simply talk to the relevant associations and thence be taken on by an existing manufacturer and be responsible for the various design and manufacturing changes that would bring about the product improvements in question. Existing manufacturers might even have to accept such progress as a condition of remaining in the association and being one of the preferential providers of the product in question to the outlets in question. That is to say, if existing manufacturers were closed to innovation of this type, their contracts with distributers / customers would risk not being renewed. It is important to constantly remind oneself that the dialogue of Steiner's associative approach involves consumer groups just as much as producers and distributors. It is also important to remind oneself that the type of economy he promotes is not only associative, but also one constantly reinvigorated by the vibrancy of entrepreneurial flair (see next section).

> *... associations ... can and must make the economy self-managing in a way that preserves individual initiative to the greatest possible extent. (CW333, p. 58)*

In our 21st-century world, though, economies are rarely very local. If a car plant in Country A is buying tyres from a manufacturer in Country B, and then one day wants to start buying them from a manufacturer in Country C instead (because of lower price, perhaps, or superior wear), where would that leave Steiner's idea of production based on contracts? Presumably it would simply be a case of any contract being such that the existing supplier, in associative discussion, would be given sufficient notice to either improve or risk being dropped in favour of the new supplier—which is possibly what usually happens in any case. And where this does happen, one imagines Steiner would be *partly* satisfied. Partly—because a conventional maker of tyres would also need to change a number of other aspects of its practice before being able to demonstrate broader threefold credentials.

With internet shopping being so prevalent today, people are used to looking at hundreds of cushion covers before deciding which one will go best with that lampshade. And since customers can buy online from a huge multitude of outlets, it is hard to imagine to what extent the contracts of which Steiner speaks might have relevance in certain sectors. Whilst our repeat purchases (e.g. food, phone minutes, utilities) might lend themselves to contractual relationships, the things we buy on a whim don't.

If I need a new watch, I might buy a Casio that has been made in Japan. Would it be remotely practical to try to imagine being a member of some consumers' association in the Cotswolds having, ultimately, some rational, predetermined *contractual* relationship with a factory in Japan? Via some network of linked associations, this might not have been completely out of the question had Steiner's ideas been taken up widely a hundred years ago. But it is hard to imagine existing multinationals signing up to such ideas unless my purchasing power has first become very (associatively) organised and pooled into extensive consumer networks. Even though my online purchase of this watch might be from a British online outlet, not direct from Japan, this outlet will in all likelihood be happy to sell me a hundred different watches of varying brands. Any exclusive-supplier contracts it had with just one or two manufacturers would in all likelihood lead to customers going off to another website, seeking more choice, and thus to business failure of the first outlet. In many business sectors, therefore, extensive associational contracts involving end-consumers, or even retail outlets, are hard to imagine. However, given how my online order can in theory be clocked by Casio in Japan more or less in real time, one could perhaps argue that they will in any case be producing more 'to order' nowadays, more in response to predetermined contract. And remember, Casio could—and probably does—have good, stable, contractual relationships with its own suppliers. Japanese industry has a long tradition of business loyalty, after all.

In conclusion, one probably has to simply say: the more the idea of working to contract can be observed, the healthier will social life be, in Steiner's eyes.

7.4.5   Entrepreneurial abilities

As we have seen, the idea of a state-run or community-run business, à la Trotsky or Lenin, was something Steiner considered profoundly impractical:

> The threefold order must start from facts. Hence, taking its stand on the realities of life, it must recognise that industry, especially in our complicated life, is based on the initiative of the individual. If we try to substitute for individual initiative the abstract community at large, we give the death-blow to economic life. Eastern Europe will prove this, if it remains much longer under its present rule. It means extinction and death to the economic body when we deprive the individual of his initiative, which must proceed from his intellect and take part in the ordering of the means of production purely for the benefit of human society. (CW332a, p. 36)
>
> ... a vibrant economy demands that competent people be given full scope ... (CW24, p. 29)

For the sake of productivity and advantage to all, production should be left to those with the relevant nous and expertise. And these should be given 'full scope', as Steiner puts it. If the political realm runs the economy, this can deprive the latter of the invigorating innovation of individual initiative. Also, it can distract the state from its key role of focusing on rights and responsibilities, on what is equitable, on what is just, as well as on its guiding principle of equality. There is nothing equal about production. This comes down to personal abilities—both latent and trained. The best person for the job should do the job. That is, those skills coming from the cultural domain are allowed to freely feed into the economic domain.

> It is to the advantage of economic life that individuals or groups who have special qualifications for a particular business of production are able to accumulate capital for their business. [At present], the best services can be rendered to the community as a whole only by qualified persons through the control of large sums of capital. However, the nature of economics dictates that such services can only consist of the most efficient production of the goods that the

community needs. A certain amount of economic power flows into the hands of the people who produce such goods. It cannot be otherwise, and the threefold social order recognizes this. Accordingly, it aims to bring about a society in which this economic power will still arise, but out of which no social evils can grow. The threefold idea does not propose to hinder the accumulation of large sums of capital in individual hands; it recognizes that to do so would be to lose the possibility of employing socially the abilities of these private individuals in the service of the general public. It proposes, however, that the moment an individual can no longer attend to the management of the means of production within his sphere of power, these means of production should be transferred to another capable person. The latter will not be able to obtain these means of production through any economic power he may possess, but solely because he is the most capable person. (CW24, pp. 103-104)

The acute inadequacies of Communist models of community-run industry were plain to see. In relation to the Hungarian workers' republic in 1919, for example, Paul Mason notes: 'Factories needed managing, but the workers could not manage.'[211]

Despite promoting individual initiative in industry, however, Steiner is keenly aware of the iniquities arising from unbridled capitalism:

... the endeavour should be to forestall evils that may spring up alongside management by individual initiative and personal talent, without impairing the management itself. (CW24, p. 26)

The suggestions he makes to this end—of forestalling the evils that can spring up alongside management by individuals—have been dealt with in other sections of the book. You may recall the following, for example: (a) sensible remuneration limits imposed on management when they take over the means of production; (b) remuneration by sharing of business proceeds (thereby preventing management paying ever lower salaries to workers so as to pocket

---

[211] Paul Mason, *Postcapitalism: A Guide to Our Future* (London: Allen Lane, 2015), p. 65.

more for themselves); (c) the finished means of production not to be available by purchase (and so become cash-cows for idle shareholders); (d) the means of production not to be inherited ad infinitum (and so become cash-cows for idle heirs). Instead, the means of production are allocated to management to the best advantage of the common good.

The entrepreneurial talent working in industry is an example of the cultural realm serving the economic. This will be looked at further in Chapter 8 ('Overlap').

In summary:

- Community-run or state-run economy, à la communism / socialism, is ruinous as it stifles the free individual initiative that invigorates enterprise.
- It is advantageous for all when the most capable *individuals* run industry and have sufficiently large sums of capital at their disposal to this end.

Reflections in relation to the present

Today, in the 'free world', there is a high incidence of individual abilities being able to freely assert themselves in business. People get promoted on merit. By and large, the best person for the job *does* get the job, provided no prejudice such as racism is in evidence. Yes, the whole paradigm of competition and maximising profit for shareholders etc. may be inconsistent with societal health, but that is a separate issue.

7.4.6   Management / workforce relationship

As has been established, Steiner was no fan of the typical, shareholder-owned, profit-maximising, labour-buying company. But neither was he an advocate of that type of co-operative model where all workers democratically take decisions together. Whilst such group decision-making might work well in simpler ventures (as seen in the many very successful wholesale food co-ops), in a large multinational where there is extensive task differentiation needing a wide range of abilities and experience, group decision-making would clearly be highly inefficient, if not impossible. Steiner by no means wishes to see efficiency compromised:

> To work socially requires ... an economic life that produces in the most efficient fashion the goods required for actual needs. (CW24, p. 33)

Instead, he is keen for the workforce to see the point of and indeed value management—an attitude which did not always prevail in the labour movement of the day:

> Were the demands of the social organism widely understood the worker would say: It is a question of having confidence in the director of the undertaking, for unless he takes responsibility for it I cannot do my work. (CW189(iv), 15 March 1919)

But, for Steiner, the old master / servant culture ought ideally give way to one with a greater sense of joint enterprise, of partnership. Yes, workers might labour and managers might direct; but the latter feathering their nests off the toil of the former is superseded.

> ... a new order of society ... that shall no longer be based on relations of coercion, of economic coercion, but based upon reciprocal services, justly exchanged;—based, that is, in this respect upon a really unegoistic and social way of thinking amongst the human community. [...] The old privileged rights, and the old system of capital and wages, must give place to the system of mutual services. (CW330(ii), 31 May 1919)
>
> ... there must come a free communal association of the manual worker and the spiritual worker in the non-capitalist order of the economy. A free communal association, which makes the manual worker the free partner of the spiritual worker, who is no longer a capitalist, will do away with the wage principle, with the wage relation; and, with the wage relation, will do away with the capital relation ... (CW330(ii), 31 May 1919)

If, on the one hand, workers' rights are regulated in the political state, and on the other hand, ownership becomes, in the true sense of the word, a possession-cycle, then a free contractual relationship over the joint output from worker and work leader will be possible. Workers and managers will be there, entrepreneurs and employees no longer. (CW329, 2 April 1919)

Considering each institution as being, in reality, a partnership is perhaps not that strange. Whilst with most organisations—certainly larger ones—a degree of hierarchy is practical (as it enables those with good knowledge of the operation to manage / direct without interference from those who have little knowledge or who may only concentrate on one or two small details), all co-workers are nonetheless dependent on one another. Henry Ford, who was one of the most prolific entrepreneurs of the time, recognised this too: 'It is not usual to speak of an employee as a partner, and yet what else is he? Whenever a man finds the management of a business too much for his own time or strength, he calls in assistants to share the management with him. Why, then, if a man finds the production part of a business too much for his own two hands should he deny the title of partner to those who come in and help him produce? Every business that employs more than one man is a kind of partnership. The moment a man calls for assistance in his business— even though the assistant be but a boy—that moment he has taken a partner. He may himself be sole owner of the resources of the business and sole director of its operations, but only while he remains sole manager and sole producer can he claim complete independence. No man is independent as long as he has to depend on another man to help him. It is a reciprocal relation—the boss is the partner of his worker, the worker is partner of his boss. And such being the case, it is useless for one group or the other to assume that it is the one indispensable unit. Both are indispensable. The one can become unduly assertive only at the expense of the other—and eventually at his own expense as well. It is utterly foolish for Capital or for Labour to think of themselves as groups. They are partners.'[212]

---

[212] Henry Ford, *My Life and Work* (Hawthorne, CA: BN Publishing, 2008), p. 81.

In keeping with this principle of partnership, interdependence, reciprocity between white and blue collar, Steiner makes a special point of management keeping the 'lower echelons' constantly informed about the business (something Ford was less interested in!). As we have seen, a significant concern of Steiner's is the alienation of the worker both from the customer and end product. Repeatedly turning maybe just a few screws without having much overview either of what one's efforts are contributing towards, or indeed even in which country those few screws might end up, can make for a rather mind-numbing and soulless existence. To help alleviate this, Steiner recommends as follows (which good management would hopefully recognise today):

> In a healthy social organism the proletarian worker should not merely stand at his machine, concerned with nothing but its operation, while the capitalist alone knows the fate of the produced commodities in economic circulation. Through fully active participation the worker should be able to develop a clear idea of his own involvement in society through his work on the production of commodities. Regular discussions, which must be considered to be as much a part of the operation as the work itself, should be arranged by management with a view to developing ideas which circumscribe employer and employees alike. A healthy activity of this kind will result in an understanding by the worker that correct management of capital benefits the social organism and therewith the worker himself. By means of such openness, based on free mutual understanding, the entrepreneur will be induced to conduct his business in an irreproachable manner. (CW23, p. 88)

> It is important that, in the healthy social organism, the relationship between, let's say, the manual worker and the person or group that organises this work with the aid of capital, is seen as one of mutual trust only, founded upon reciprocal understanding ... In the healthy social organism, the employer or entrepreneur can no longer live in a world apart from the employee. [...] Just as important as the worker's labour is that business matters are discussed at regular meetings between the employer and employee, so that the latter continually has an overview of what is happening. [...] The employer should be required at any moment to tell the employee exactly what is happening, and discuss all its details with him, so that the factory or company is embedded in a shared culture.

That's the important thing. Only then is it possible to establish the kind of relationship which will enable the worker to say, 'yes, he is as necessary as I am, without him my labour would get nowhere in the social organism ...'. [...] A healthy relationship between work and capital cannot be established by some kind of social bureaucracy [e.g. communism, RM] but only through a shared culture in which someone who has the individual gifts and capacities to do so in this field, that is to work as a capitalist, can also be really productive, can make his individual skills fruitful for the healthy social organism, in the process eliciting the free understanding of the manual labourer. (CW189, pp. 102-104)

Think how different it would be if in any establishment the individual workers were involved also in terms of soul and spirit in the whole process which the commodity they make undergoes in the world, if they understood how they stand within the social structure through the fact that they produce the specific commodity. (CW186(ii), p. 155)

... a great deal nowadays depends on whether the man who has to run a business, for instance, is able to bring his whole personality to bear, either directly or through assistants, on his work-people, so that he comes close to them by really discussing with them, as man to man, everything that goes on in the business, from the purchase of the raw material to the marketing of the finished product and the means by which it reaches the consumer. If you repeatedly discuss this chain of production with your employees, in a way that is attuned to human considerations, you establish a basis on which you can build the other things that are socially desirable and worth striving for. (CW83, p. 149)

Whether the business is making copper piping or nappies, pianos or aircraft, Steiner is keen that all workers have a sense of what is going on in the enterprise. They should know that one tenth of the material in the nappies comes from Ecuador; that, at any one time, some fifty of the firm's workers are on maternity leave; that one tenth of the aircraft are sold in India; *that the enterprise is serving other human beings.* Although the latter might be obvious, the sharing of such details will add to the workforce's feeling of social connectedness. Steiner clearly laid much store in this, in the companionship of human contact; in engagement replacing disfranchisement; in inclusion replacing isolation; in 'warmth' replacing alienation; in the workforce feeling part of something bigger, not just profit-fodder at the beck and call of their miserable line manager.

In conformity with a partnership principle, contracts between management and workers should not be wage contracts where one pays the other. Labour is not something to be bought and sold (Section 5.3.1). Instead, contracts should state who does what, and how the parties share the eventual proceeds. As such, what Steiner calls a voluntary or free partnership arises, that is to say, not one where a master / servant wage dependency exists. (One could also argue *neither* is free, perhaps, since both manager and worker depend on each other!)

> No matter how favourably we view labour contracts, so long as they establish wage relationships, workers will not be satisfied. A humanly worthy existence for all will result only when contractual agreements govern the joint output of supervisors and workers but not labour itself. Then the worker-supervisor relationship will be one of voluntary partnership. (CW333, p. 11)

How co-workers in an organisation are paid is considered in Sections 7.3.4 ('Remuneration—Part 1') and 7.4.14 ('Remuneration—Part 2').

In the words of Charles Waterman: 'The man who merely hires his labour-power to an enterprise (which is what the wage system means) is not related to it as a full human being. His work (except insofar as skill and craftsmanship relieve it) is a dull grind: a section cut out of his life and rendered meaningless. He cannot habitually put his heart or mind into it so long as he is being used as a tool, and thinks of the management as "they".'[213]

In summary:

- Partnership ethos ideally replaces the principle of worker being dependent on 'work giver'.
- Old system of capital and wages to give way to a system of reciprocal services, 'justly exchanged'.

---

[213] Charles Waterman, *A Middle Way for Britain* (Shrewsbury: Christian Community, 1948), p. 5.

- Contract between blue collar and white collar to reflect what each does and how they might share the proceeds, not how one buys the labour of the other.
- Command-and-control hierarchy is generally practical (at least for larger concerns).
- Regular discussion between management and workers is important so that workers have stronger sense of the whole, and therefore stronger sense of participation, inclusion, self-worth, connectedness.

7.4.7 Division of labour / specialisation

Although Steiner's comments regarding the division of labour do not amount to recommendations as such, they are of passing interest since, by touching on the downsides as well as the obvious advantages of the division of labour, they add context for subsequent considerations. (They also very quickly put to bed any notion anyone might have had that Steiner was an advocate of self-sufficiency.)

We can all see the common sense behind the division of labour, behind different people specialising in different things instead of everyone trying to do everything themselves. If, each time you wanted a pineapple, you had to travel to the Dominican Republic—in a boat you had built yourself—with tools you had made yourself—out of iron you had mined yourself, life would be a challenge. And you certainly wouldn't be able to do it for £1.50—the typical cost of a pineapple. On the other hand, if you were to specialise and bring back a thousand pineapples, it wouldn't take much more time than bringing back just one. Economies of scale would arise. You could sell the pineapples and pay someone else to do all that mining!

> ... we must of course remember that there is no sense nowadays in studying economic processes other than those which stand entirely under the sign of the division of labour; for it is these with which we are in fact concerned. (CW340, p. 129)
>
> Everyone who to-day makes a coat for himself or who supplies himself with his own food grown on his own land, actually sustains himself too expensively, because when there is division of labour, every product will be cheaper than it can be when one produces it for oneself. (CW79, 30 November 1921)

By specialising in one field, we become faster, more efficient, and this applies just as much *within* an enterprise as it does *between* enterprises. My enterprise as a sole trader might be to sell pineapples while you work for a firm making ships. But the manufacture of ships within your company will involve different people with different skills, working at different processes. Tasks will be subdivided such that each worker becomes specialised and efficient in a small handful of processes and perhaps never even has to put down a tool in order to pick up a different one (if, that is, automation has not taken over completely).

Whilst acknowledging—celebrating even—the phenomenon of the division of labour and how this underpins civilisation and creates surplus value which frees people up for leisure, for cultural pursuits, for work on rights, and for further innovation in the economic realm, Steiner (like many others) also highlights the shortcomings that accompany it. A number of his comments in this regard were aired in Chapter 2—'What's the Problem?'.

One problem is that, under the division of labour, management is needed for the sake of overview and co-ordination of all the diverse roles, and this management can end up abusing its power and working its subordinates to the bone for little pay. We shall leave this complaint to one side in this section of the book. Whilst it may be *related* to the division of labour, it is not, in itself, a *direct result* of it; management can behave more equitably, after all. Exploitation of workers is addressed at length in other sections.

But two significant downsides that *can* be a direct result of the division of labour, at least under much of that division of labour seen in mass production from the industrial revolution onwards, are those problems of alienation that have already been considered: workers lose not only (a) the gratifying human connection with their customers that in previous centuries would have existed among craftsmen etc. but also (b) a gratifying connection to the end product. If you are just turning one or two screws, pressing one or two buttons, or soldering wires to capacitors all day long, you are less likely to experience that satisfaction and 'pride' in your work that craftspeople once had. You may rarely even see the end product.

Problem (a)—no human connection with your customer—might not have applied to specialisation in its more basic form of olden times—where one person grew cabbages while another made boots.

Here people might have come together once a week at the market. Division of labour at this level does bring people together. But as it increases, as workers in factories busy themselves from dawn until dusk on the shop floor without ever getting near a customer, people are then driven apart, and Steiner deems this (as do others) a significant social problem. The absence of this human element can make work miserable and ungratifying. The problem is of course ameliorated to some degree by workers having each other for company in the factory ('That is one of the reasons why girls prefer working in weaving sheds in a deafening din to sitting lonely in a kitchen', remarked Bernard Shaw).[214] But seeing the same handful of fellow workers, month in, month out, is socially very different to seeing many different customers at market every week.

Problem (b)—no gratifying connection to the end product is certainly stark in many factories. At worst, the worker uses so few of their capacities that they become little more than automatons at work, repeating the same few processes for hour after mind-numbing hour.

> ... *after all, vast sections of mankind today are employed in such a way that their work cannot conceivably interest them. (CW83, p. 152)*

Of course, the division of labour—even on a grand scale—existed long before the Industrial Revolution. At their height in the 13th century, Venetian boat builders could assemble an entire naval galley in a single day![215] Such vessels might not have had the six million parts that a jumbo jet has today, but that is still quite a feat. And the great pyramids in Egypt demonstrate very ably that the division of labour was also around long before medieval times.

> ... *the unprejudiced observer cannot help looking at, say, ancient Egypt or ancient Babylon, and observing that these states contained cities of an enormous size, and that these achievements,*

---

[214] Bernard Shaw, *The Intelligent Woman's Guide to Socialism and Capitalism* (Edinburgh:R&R Clark Ltd, 1929), p. 80.
[215] See Wikipedia: Venetian Arsenal.

too, were only made possible by a division of labour. [...] I must point out that division of labour, too, which in modern times has rightly been seen as the central social problem, was also found in earlier epochs of human development; it was in fact what made the Oriental social systems possible, and these in turn have since affected Europe. In Europe, division of labour, after being less common at first, gradually evolved. I would say: division of labour in itself is a repetition of something that also occurred in earlier times; but in the Oriental civilisations it bore the stamp of a society in which individuality was still dormant. The modern division of labour, which makes its appearance along with technology, on the other hand, impinges on a society of men who are now seeking to expand their individuality to the full. Once again, then, the same phenomenon turns out to have a quite different significance in different ages. (CW83, p. 140)

So the contention is that, whilst in earlier times the division of labour was much less of an affront to the individual, in recent centuries people feel more burdened by spending their lives engaged in monotonous, repetitive work.

In relation to all this, a point worth remembering is that mutuality—in the sense of mutual interdependence—continues to grow when people specialise. People may be driven apart by specialisation, but they also become more dependent on one another.

Also, it is recognised that not every case of manufacture involves out-and-out division of labour. Whilst the norm may be mass production, there is also a place for one-offs, especially when commodities become artistic and involve individual initiative, craftsmanship, and creativity. Concerning fashion goods, for example, Steiner observed:

It can be that the division of labour should not be applied into every corner of life, as this could restrict cultural life. There is a price on aesthetics, of course, but I do not want you to think that I am fanatical about the cheapening effects of the division of labour. (CW341, p. 203)

In summary:

- Whilst being a cornerstone of economic progress, the division of labour can …
- lead to company structures that exploit labour;
- separate workers from their customers and so make their life ungratifying and dull;
- separate workers from the end product and so make work ungratifying and dull;
- mean repetitive, soul-destroying work.
- This has been more of a problem in recent centuries since people's sense of individuality has grown.
- The division of labour need not apply to every last corner of economic life.

Reflections in relation to the present

The ever-increasing technological advances since Steiner's day, with their concomitant division of labour, have brought with them the possibility for an ever growing proportion of society to benefit from an ever widening range of goods. A new Range Rover now rolls off the production line every 86 seconds, but when the old Land Rover Defenders were phased out in 2016, the interval between each vehicle emerging from the factory was a pathetic 4 minutes!

In somewhere like the UK, however, where extensive *de*-industrialisation has come to pass in recent decades, as well as ever increasing levels of automation, highly repetitive, soul-destroying work has reduced enormously. Estimates regarding the increasing effects of automation on future employment prospects vary between 'significant' and 'cataclysmic'. But if boring, repetitive work can be mechanised, if goods can be produced with far less of the toil needed than hitherto, this is surely to be welcomed. However, the problem can then shift from ungratifying, dull work to an ungratifying, dull life devoid of any work at all. And all the while, income shifts away from workers and towards capital (those who own those automated factories), creating ever greater social divides (as if the fact that the 26 richest people in the world owning as much wealth as the 3.8 billion people who make up the poorer half of the world's entire human population wasn't obscene enough already).[216]

Also, whilst in more developed parts of the world, automation may be increasing, further afield the old problems of mind-numbing mass production have not disappeared by any means. A nose around some of the factories in Calcutta or Zhengzhou making your t-shirts and laptops would doubtless be a sobering experience. Indeed Chinese billionaire businessman Jack Ma recently hailed the '996' system (working from 9am until 9pm, 6 days a week) as a 'blessing' and those against it as 'slackers'.[217] It is hard to imagine that those who are enslaved by such an ethos have much in the way of a fulfilling relationship to the end product, or to end customers, or to life in general. Although anyone required to work more than 44 hours per week is supposed to be paid overtime, this, apparently, 'has not been well enforced'.[218]

Oh, and we also have those armies of unfortunates, in their battery-hen cubicles, employed as cold callers to phone unsuspecting victims and sell them things they didn't know they wanted. Fulfilling relationship to end product? Fulfilling relationship to the customer? Joyful work? I don't think so.

7.4.8   Motivation for work

Notwithstanding Steiner's advice that management keep workers fully in the loop, fully informed about the whole business in order to maintain a level of connectedness and meaning for the worker, most of his comments regarding motivation for work amount less to suggestions for the economic realm per se and more to how a threefold articulation of public life as a whole can be of assistance.

Naturally, he does not propose abandoning mass production and returning to an un-division of labour, or to the craftsmanship of former times, in order to counteract the worker's demotivating alienation from customer and end product:

---

[216] Larry Elliott, 'World's 26 richest people own as much as poorest 50%, says Oxfam', *The Guardian,* 20 January 2019.
[217] https://www.bbc.co.uk/news/business-47934513.
[218] https://www.bbc.co.uk/news/world-asia-china-58381538.

The division of labour and of social function that has become necessary in modern times separates the labourer from the recipient of the product of his work. There is no changing this fact without undermining the conditions of modern civilisation; nor is there any way of escaping its consequence—the weakening of one's immediate interest in one's work. The loss of this interest must be accepted as a result of modern life. Yet we must not allow this interest to disappear without finding other kinds to take its place, for human beings cannot live and work indifferently in the community. (CW24, p. 42)

Steiner sees Marxism as being of little help in this regard:

The owner [of the means of production] has goods produced because they bring him profits; the worker produces them because he is obliged to earn a living. A personal satisfaction in the finished product itself is felt by neither. In fact, one touches a very essential part of the social question when pointing to the lack of any personal relationship between the producers and the goods produced in the modern industrial system. However one must also be clear that this lack of a personal relationship is a necessary consequence of modern technology and the attendant mechanisation of labour. It cannot be removed from the economic life itself. Goods produced by extensive division of labour in large industries cannot possibly be as closely associated with the producer as were the products of the medieval craftsman. One will have to accept the fact that, regarding a large part of human labour, the kind of interest that previously existed is past and gone. However, one should also be clear that without interest, a man cannot work; if life compels him to do so, he feels his whole existence to be dreary and unsatisfying.

Whoever is honestly disposed towards the social movement must think of finding some other interest to replace the one that is gone. [...] An enormous economic conglomerate regulated according to the Marxist plan ... would make human life a torment because of the ensuing lack of interest in any sort of work. [...] while one can arouse a certain amount of enthusiasm for such an aim through the excitement of the struggle to attain it, the excitement ends as soon as this aim is realised, and people thus fitted into the wheels of an impersonal social machine are inevitably drained of everything resembling a will to live. (CW24, pp. 106-107)

But Steiner also dismisses the usual idea of monetary gain as being a healthy stimulus for work. As you may remember from his comments in 1905, long before he presented his threefold ideas to the world, he found the idea of people working simply in order to make a living most unwholesome. He remarked how important he felt it was that people should not just work out of self-interest, but that they find motivation for work in a feeling of mutuality and service to others. Seventeen years later, he reasserts this view:

> *How are we to eliminate from the economic process this principle of working for a living? Those who to this day are still mere wage earners—earners of a living for themselves—how are they to be placed in the whole economic process, no longer as such earners but as men who work because of social needs? Must this really be done? Assuredly it must. (CW340, p. 44)*

Similarly:

> *It is true that, within the social order which contemporary conditions have occasioned, the prospect of economic gain has attained enormous importance. But this fact is no less the cause of the conditions which are now being experienced. These conditions call urgently for the development of some other motivation for the actuation of individual abilities. (CW23, p. 87)*

> *It should be obvious that a new incentive to work must be created the moment there is any thought of eliminating the old incentive of egotistical gain. An economic management that does not include this profit motive among the forces at work within the economy cannot of itself exert any effect whatever upon the human will to work. [...]*

> *If the economic system is to be organized in a way that can have no effect on our will to work, then our will to work must be stimulated in some other way. The threefold social order recognizes that at the present stage of human evolution, the economic sphere must limit itself exclusively to economic processes. The administration of such an economic order will be able, through its various organs, to determine the extent of consumers' needs, how the produce may best be brought to the consumers, and the extent to which various articles should be produced. However it will have no way of calling forth the will to produce ... (CW24, pp. 80-82)*

In a way, this passage is puzzling. If the workings of the economic realm are not well placed to motivate people to work, does this imply that the 'association' which Steiner talks so much about in connection with the economy really only concerns the simple logistics of production / circulation / consumption, not with acting as motivator? If so, how would one reconcile this to such (previously-quoted) comments as:

> *Associations are the health bearers. Associations work towards the harmonizing of interests, so that the interests of the producers and the consumers are harmonized ... (CW79, 30 November 1921)*
>
> *... human co-operation in economic life must be based on the fraternity which is inherent in associations. (CW23, p. 81)*

The first of these two quotes perhaps need not bother us as it is just talking about production, distribution and consumption of commodities finding a healthy balance, not necessarily about motivation for work. But the second reminds us that he sees associations as underpinning—or even being the expression of—the fraternity on which the economic realm should be based. One would think this more comradely ethos should at least provide *some* degree of motivation for work.

Be that as it may, what is clear is that Steiner does not think it healthy when those with uninspiring jobs see their weekly or monthly pay packet as the main reason for their work, and he certainly does not consider the economic as the *only* realm from which an inspiration to work can come.

Instead, he maintains help can come from the two non-economy aspects of society—the cultural and rights realms—once these have had a threefold overhaul.

> *The effects of division of labour must be balanced by vital mutual relationships among people in the community. Division of labour separates people; the forces that come to them from the three spheres of social life, once these are made independent, will draw them together again. The division of society has reached its zenith. This is a fact of experience, and it gives our modern social life its stamp. Once we recognise it, we realise the*

imperative demand of the age: to find and follow the path that leads to reunion. (CW24, p. 49)

It is from the cultural and political spheres, as they are made independent, that the necessary new interests will arise. From these two independent spheres will come impulses involving viewpoints other than those of mere increase of capital or wages. (CW24, p. 42)

More specifically, from the cultural domain (firstly):

The threefold social order ... aims at establishing within an independent, self-sustaining cultural life a realm where one learns in a living way to understand this human society for which one is called upon to work; a realm where one learns to see what each single piece of work means for the combined fabric of the social order, to see it in such a light that one will learn to love it because of its value for the whole. It aims at creating in this free life of spirit the profounder principles that can replace the motive of personal gain. Only in a free spiritual life can a love for the human social order spring up that is comparable to the love an artist has for the creation of his works. If one is not prepared to consider fostering this kind of love within a free spiritual-cultural life, then one may as well renounce all striving for a new social order. Anyone who doubts that men and women are capable of being brought to this kind of love must also renounce all hope of eliminating personal profit from economic life. Anyone who fails to believe that a free spiritual life generates this kind of love is unaware that it is the dependence of spiritual and cultural life upon the state and the economy that creates desire for personal profit—this desire for profit is not a fundamental aspect of human nature. It is this mistake that makes people say constantly, 'to realise the threefold order, human beings must be different than they are now.' No! Through the threefold order, people will be educated in such a way that they will grow up to be different than they were previously under the economic state. (CW24, pp. 82-83)

A free spiritual-cultural life creates interests that dwell in the depths of the human being, and imbue one's work and all one's action with a living aim and meaning for social life. Developing and nurturing human faculties for the sake of their own inherent value, such a cultural life will call forth a consciousness that our talents and our place in life have real meaning. Moulded by individuals whose faculties have been developed in this spirit, society will continually adapt itself to the free expression of human abilities. The legal life and economic life will take on a form in keeping with the human abilities that have been allowed to develop.

The deep inner interests of individuals cannot unfold fully and freely within a cultural life that is regulated by politics, or that develops and uses human faculties merely according to their economic utility. (CW24, p. 42)

This motivation will have to be found in the social understanding *which issues from a healthy spiritual life. With the strength of free spiritual life, the schools, education, will equip the individual with impulses which, by virtue of this inherent understanding, will enable him to put his personal abilities into practice. (CW23, p. 87)*

Whereas formerly we looked at the product, we shall now look at the man who requires the product. Whereas formerly the product was loved, the love of man and the brotherhood of man will now be able to make their appearance in the soul that has developed, so that men will know the reason for their duties. (CW83, p. 146)

Commerce acquires a meaning only when it is seen to serve something in human life that extends beyond economics, something quite independent of all commerce. Work that gives no intrinsic satisfaction will acquire worth if performed by one of whom it can be said, when viewed from a higher spiritual standpoint, that he is striving toward ends of which his economic activity is only the means. This view of life from a spiritual standpoint can be acquired only within a self-subsistent spiritual-cultural branch of the social organism ...

The complicated form of modern industry, with its mechanisation of human labour, requires a free, self-subsistent spiritual-cultural life as a necessary counterbalance. [...] If human nature is not to succumb to this mechanisation, whenever human beings stand within the mechanised system of labour, their souls must always be able to rise freely ... [to an appreciation of higher things, as made possible by] a free spiritual-cultural life. (CW24, p. 108)

A liberated, alive, cultural life, entirely unconstrained by the state or business, means education and other forms of culture can evolve in such a way that they engender a love of humanity, greater meaning in people's lives, a better appreciation for our interdependence / the workings of 'the whole', constructive feelings that can counteract the repetitiveness and drudgery of uninspiring work. If the full spectrum of our human capacities can freely unfold, one enters life with greater verve.

And Steiner contends motivation for work can also come from the rights realm:

> ... the democratically ordered life of the legal sphere will provide the impulses for the will to work. Real relationships will grow up between people united in a social organism where each adult has a voice in government and is co-equal with every other adult: it is relationships such as these that are able to in enkindle the will to work 'for the community'. One must reflect that a truly communal feeling can grow only from such relationships, and that from this feeling, the will to work can grow. For in actual practice the consequence of such a state founded on democratic rights will be that each human being will take his place with vitality and full consciousness in the common field of work. Each will know what he or she is working for; and each will want to work within the working community ... (CW24, p. 83)

> In a social order based on division of labour, the work one performs, while affording no satisfaction for its own sake, may nevertheless satisfy through the interest one takes in those for whom one performs it. Such an interest must, however, be developed in living community. A legal system in which every individual stands as an equal among equals arouses one's interest in one's fellows. One works in such a system for the others because one gives to this relationship between oneself and others a living foundation. From the economic order one learns only what others demand of one. Within a vital legal and political life, the value one man has for the other springs from the depths of human nature itself, and goes beyond our merely needing each other in order to produce commodities meeting various needs. (CW24, p. 107)

> The old devotion, the immediate companionship with the thing he has made, exists no longer; yet it must be replaced by

something else. What can this be? It can only be replaced by enlarging men's horizon, by raising them to a level on which they can come together with their fellow men in one great circle, eventually with all their fellow men within the same social organism as themselves, in which they can develop an interest in man as man. It must come to pass that even the man who is working in the most remote corner at a single screw for some great machine need not put his whole self into the contemplation of the screw, but it must come about that he can carry into his workshop the feelings that he entertains for his fellow men, that when he leaves his workshop he finds the same feelings, that he has a living insight into his connection with human society, that he can work even without actual pleasure in his production because he feels he is a worthy member in the circle of his fellow men. Out of this impulse has sprung the modern demand for democracy and the new way of establishing public law on democratic lines ... The feeling must arise within us that the horizon of human beings must be enlarged, that men ought to be able to express their feelings with regard to their work in words somewhat like these: 'It is true, I have no idea how my work in making this screw will affect my fellow men, but I do know that, through the living ties that bind me to them by a common law, I am a worthy member in the social order, and have equal rights with other men.' This is the principle that must lie at the root of modern democracy, and it must work in the feelings of one man towards another as the fundamental principle of the modern public legal code. (CW332a, pp. 70-71)

An independent legal life will create mutual relationships between people living in a community. Through these relationships, they will have an incentive to work for one another, even when the individual is unable to have an immediate, creative interest in the product of his work. This interest becomes transformed into the interest that he can have in working for the human community whose legal life he helped build. Thus the part one plays in the independent legal life can become the basis for a special impulse to live and work apart from economic and cultural interests. One can look away from one's work and the product of one's work to the human community, where one stands in relation to one's fellows purely and simply as an adult human being, without regard to one's particular mental abilities, and without this relation being affected by one's particular station in economic life. When one considers how

> *it serves the community with which one has this direct and intimate human relationship, the product of one's work will appear valuable, and this value will extend to the work itself.*
>
> *Nothing but an independent legal and political life can bring about this intimate human relationship because it is only in this sphere that each human being can meet every other with equal and undivided interest. All the other spheres of social life must, by their very nature, create distinctions and divisions according to individual talents or kinds of work. This sphere bridges all differences. (CW24, p. 44)*

Today, these passages can at first sound a bit far-fetched. Can a state structure *really* result in a different attitude to one's tedious work (if tedious it be)? The answer to this question, however, is probably: Well, if properly democratic, then almost certainly yes. If the alternative is *lack* of democracy, is having no voice, is an absence of fair treatment and a feeling therefore of being downtrodden and exploited, then, instead of sounding far-fetched, the observation is perhaps obvious: a worker who feels powerless and downtrodden by society is hardly likely to enjoy any great willingness to work for society. In Steiner's day, the worker had good reason to believe that the state, run as it often was by the propertied classes, was not really on their side.

When a legislature is democratised such that all can engage with it, and feel included in it, the individual will clearly enjoy a greater feeling of inclusion in society, a feeling of community, a feeling of fairness, a feeling that his or her feelings and opinions are as valid as the next person's, a feeling of human worth, a feeling that on the level of rights we are all equals. With a legislature of this sort, workers feel closer to their neighbours; and this can provide some measure of balance to counteract the downsides of the division of labour, some compensatory comfort in the face of uninteresting and isolating work. If, in the political domain, we feel equal to everyone else, our inclination (motivation) to work for them—for the whole— will increase.

Further, if, as Steiner recommends (Sections 5.2 and 5.3.1), our concept of the rights domain is expanded to include all labour matters, then this is also likely to have a significant additional impact on the will to work. If labour is entirely removed from the economic system such that it can no longer be purchased with a wage, workers—who have then become more like partners—are bound to enjoy greater motivation because of the enhanced feelings of inclusion and worth that ensue.

> *Today it is stressed on many sides, and rightly so, that the salvation of the world economy has to come from a heightened will to work, a will that has been diminished by the war. Anyone who understands human nature knows that this commitment to work can only come when people are convinced that in the future their work will be done under social conditions that guarantee them a dignified human existence. (CW24, p. 23)*

Concerning the motivation to work for others, one wonders with the following comments whether Steiner might have been having a dig at the wealthy, non-working theosophists / anthroposophists in his audience!

> *... we do not begin to have an interest in our fellow men until ... we hold the picture in our minds of a certain number of persons working for a certain number of hours in order that I may live within the social structure. It is of no importance to give ourselves a comfortable feeling by saying, 'I love people.' No-one loves people if he supposes that he is living on his money and does not in the least conceive how people work for him in order to produce even the minimum necessary for his life.*
>
> *But the thought that a certain number of persons labour in order that we may possess the minimum necessities of life is inseparable from another. It is the thought that we must recompense society, not with money but with work in exchange for the work that has been done for us. We feel an interest in our fellow men only when we are lead to feel obligated to recompense in some form of labour the amount of labour that has been performed for us... The feeling of obligation to the society in which we live is the beginning of the interest that is required for a sound social order. (CW186, pp. 55-57)*

In summary:

- Motivation for work can suffer when performing monotonous tasks under the division of labour. This is an unavoidable aspect of modern life.
- The prospect of personal gain is not the healthiest motivator for work.
- A different motivation for work is the ideal: love for one's fellow humans who will benefit from one's work.
- An independent, free, cultural life can cultivate (via education, etc.) this love for the human community.
- Motivation for work can also grow out of a properly democratic rights realm—wherein all adults have an equal voice, wherein exploitation is reduced, wherein greater inclusion results.
- When this rights realm also includes labour relations, labour's treatment as an economic concern—as a commodity to be purchased with a wage—is replaced by the worker being seen more as a partner. This brings greater fairness and feelings of self-worth, further enhancing motivation for work.
- Ideally, people should feel they must recompense, with their own work, what others have done for them in meeting their needs.

Reflections in relation to the present

To try and comment with any accuracy on how these observations might relate to the present day seems particularly challenging; the factors involved are so hard to assess and quantify.

We know that the factories of old, employing tens of thousands, are now much less common in the 'developed world', and that many repetitive, soul-destroying tasks within manufacturing have now been automated.

We know that the cultural realm—education in particular—was very enmeshed within the German state machinery when Steiner was talking, and that today it is more independent—although not *fully* independent.

We know that, in somewhere like the UK, our rights life with its universal suffrage enjoys a greater measure of democracy today. This greater democratic engagement has brought us significantly closer to the equality Steiner referred to, to the respect that he insisted was due to each adult, to safer working conditions, to a more reasonable working week, and so on.

But to what extent is our democratic process contaminated, for example, by the economic realm in the form of neo-liberal media, typically owned by billionaires, who are prone to ridiculing higher taxation or other rights realm matters that are detrimental to *them*? To what extent is our (in particular, the USA's) legislative process contaminated by corporate funding—where wealth trumps the one-person-one-vote basis of democracy? (These things are explored further in section 8.1.6.)

Also, our democratic legislatures of today still don't go as far as Steiner had in mind. Yes, they have doubtless improved since Steiner's day, and certainly since the days of Dickens' Bob Cratchit. Yes, amongst most advanced democracies, universal suffrage crucially became a permanent feature of the political landscape within a few years of Steiner being engaged in these matters. But our political institutions still include, and also exclude, various aspects of public life he advised they shouldn't. Of particular relevance here are his recommendations that, as well as labour relations (including how one approaches remuneration), control of capital (land and means of production) should also ideally be seen more as a matter concerning the rights realm. When left to the economy, varying power levels—and thence exploitation—ensue. As was seen in Sections 7.3.4 and 7.3.7, for example, Steiner recommends these factors of production be treated less as aspects of the economic realm and more as ones of the political. Much exploitation can then be replaced by something more equitable.

With the continuation of wages, we have a continuation of an employer / employee relationship that is frequently exploitative and resented. In the knowledge that workers often have to accept low wages (since to refuse a job offer can mean no unemployment benefit), employers frequently have the power over employees to profit handsomely from their cheap labour. On the other hand, the profit-sharing, *rights* approach that Steiner recommends would significantly enhance worker inclusion, engagement, satisfaction, sense of fairness, motivation (as well, no doubt, as appealing to their self-interest in procuring a higher income).

And when real-life games of Monopoly are prevented (because land and the finished means of production can no longer be purchased, but are instead only *granted* to proprietors in accordance with what is just, in accordance with the furtherance of the common good), then, once again, a more equitable society will result, and the motivation to work for it will therefore grow.

We know, also, that many will see the idea of working for the good of society as just some old starry-eyed idealism. For them, the idea of being motivated by anything other than earning money for themselves might seem ludicrous. On the other hand, we also know there are many who feel compelled to 'give back'. Amongst the younger generation, for example, one often sees a particularly mature love of humanity, concern for the planet, and mindfulness of ethical considerations. And given how many *non*-profit-maximising endeavours (charities, co-ops, etc.) already run very successfully, and in many cases have done for decades, perhaps it is in order to lay one's inner cynic aside and be open to the possibility that a meaningfulness—joy even—can be felt in seeing one's work less as a means to an income and more as something that is providing for one's fellows. As Rudolf Isler observes: 'We wish to accomplish our work because humanity needs it. If we suspect or even perceive that this is not so, our work becomes an inner burden to us.'[219] If we are asked to do something that seems pointless, this can be a very depressing experience. Naturally, though, it is much easier to turn one's attention to service—to providing for others—if one's own needs are properly met. If one is penniless, then looking after 'number one', understandably, usually becomes the priority.

We know, also, there are very many retirees—as well as others—who don't (financially) *need* to work but who nonetheless do voluntary work or engage productively in some way or other as they like to feel useful, to feel they are contributing. Experiencing meaningfulness in making a contribution is far from rare. Again, it may be true that such people might tend to be those who have had a fulfilling working life, who have set themselves up with an agreeable place to live in, and so on. Those in less comfortable circumstances may be

---

[219] Rudolf Isler, *Sustainable Society: Making Business, Government and Money Work Again* (Edinburgh: Floris Books, 2014), p. 62.

less likely to be motivated to go out and work for the sake of others. And there are also, of course, plenty of retirees and others of 'independent means' who are quite happy to spend their days working in the garden or playing golf.

But to try and determine exactly what factors may or may not have affected motivation for work over the decades since Steiner was speaking, and to what extent, seems almost futile.

In the 1980s, when all remaining UK coal mines were closed or mothballed, the affected miners (and others) raged against Prime Minister, Margaret Thatcher, who was considered ultimately responsible. But was the feeling of self-worth that these laid-off miners were losing based on a love of their work's contribution to society, or was their fury simply about loss of livelihood? Probably both. *Any* meaningful work can give one some feelings of achievement and self-worth, surely, compared to no work at all?

One might argue that today, because of the greatly improved standard of living in many countries since Steiner's day, many people with relatively lowly jobs (although certainly not all) can nonetheless experience considerable contentment and satisfaction in their lives. At the end of the working day—even a tiring and uninspiring working day—they can go home to a reasonably warm, dry house, eat some reasonable food, avail themselves of all manner of cultural delights on TV, Netflix, and so on. TV is one expression of a liberated cultural realm that is accessible to almost all (in many cultures), and is surely a significant contributing factor to that feeling of inclusion in society that Steiner deemed so important. Notwithstanding its shortcomings (poor taste or quality in many programmes, for example), there is frequently something of interest on offer for everyone: from sport or comedy at one end of the spectrum, through music and drama, to well-researched documentary at the other, more educational end of the spectrum. With dozens of TV channels, a factory worker doing uninspiring work can find a great many points of contact with a humanity they might have previously felt alienated from. One can imagine this aspect of cultural life indeed acting as a significant motivator for work, albeit a somewhat subconscious one. Via these nourishing points of contact with humanity, one might well feel more at peace with the world than in the days when almost all of one's waking hours were spent providing. In addition, numerous group activities and evening classes abound giving those with less-than-inspiring work further scope for human / cultural engagement. Such cultural endeavours are typically 'free' in Steiner's sense, i.e. independent from rights-realm or economic-realm interference.

7.4.9   Value

Although Steiner's comments concerning economic value do not amount to recommendations for social reform as such (which is essentially what this book is about), they relate to what he has to say about prices, and prices relate to certain of his recommendations. So his comments on value will now be considered briefly.

When it comes to what determines the value of a commodity, there are, broadly speaking, two schools of thought: on the one side there are the Intrinsic Value theories, such as the Labour Theory of Value, and on the other side there are the Subjective Theories of Value.

The Labour Theory of Value says the value of a commodity is determined by the amount of work needed to make / deliver it. So if it took eight hours to produce a commodity, one could say its value was equivalent to eight units. If, over time, part of the production process becomes mechanised, then this will, on the one hand, reduce the number of hours needed to produce the item, and this has a reducing effect on its value. On the other hand, the number of hours of work that were needed to create the machine (and its power source) get taken into account, and these have an increasing effect on the item's value. So, if the machine is considered good for 10,000 such commodities, then one ten thousandth of the work-hours needed to create it is added to the value of the commodity. The hours taken to create the machinery—hours, so to speak, stored up in the machinery—are known as 'finished labour' or 'dead labour', and the hours expended on the production of the commodity are known as 'living labour'.

This theory has been subject to modifications over time. Marx, for example, elaborates as follows: the value of a commodity is in fact determined by what he calls the amount of *socially necessary* work needed to produce it. By this is meant not the literal number of hours the person takes to produce the item, but rather the number of hours needed to feed, clothe and house the person while they produce the item. An issue, however, with this is that a good made by someone working 80 hours per week would be considered to have half the value of an identical good made by someone working 40 hours per week, all else being equal. This is because our 80-hour producer would be producing twice as many items in a week whilst nonetheless consuming the same amount of food, electricity, etc. as a 40-hours producer.

Another factor included in the 'socially necessary' Labour Theory of Value is the cost of the producer's education. If producing the item in question involves highly skilled / educated work, then the extra hours of work needed—for tuition—would also be included as part of the commodity's value. Nowadays, in the 'developed world', it would doubtless also be considered 'socially necessary' to include something for things like holidays and savings towards a pension and so on.

That is the Labour Theory of Value in a nutshell, and there are various criticisms of it. For example, if someone is a slow worker, their product will, under this theory, be 'more valuable' than an equivalent product made by someone who is a quick worker. So the theory has to assume an average productivity. And, crucially, the theory takes no account of the purchaser's subjective desire for the good. Someone might go to great lengths making something no one wants; then the Labour Theory of Value falls apart. Carl Menger (founder of the Austrian School of economics) observes in 1871: 'Whether a diamond was found accidentally or was obtained from a diamond pit with the employment of a thousand days of labour is completely irrelevant for its value. In general, no one in practical life asks for the history or the origin of a good in estimating its value, but considers solely the services that the good will render him ... The quantities of labour or of other means of production applied to its production cannot, therefore, be the determining factor in the value of a good.'[220] Basically, a calculator will have greater value in a bookkeeper's office than at the bottom of the Grand Canyon. That both goods were produced with the same amount of work is of little relevance.

From Menger and others, therefore, comes the assertion that value is based on the needs and desires of the buying public, on the utility which a commodity affords them. One person will have a stronger desire for a cruise around the Caribbean than another, so for the first person its value will be higher. Value is in the eye of the beholder

---

[220] Carl Menger, *Principles of Economics* (1871).

(or purchaser). Thus we have Subjective Theories of Value, based on the extent to which someone wants something, on their subjective desire. The most common of the Subjective Theories is Marginalism which, amongst other things, takes into account the 'marginal utility' of things, that is to say, takes into account the fact that, if you have just bought a car or a bag of chips, you probably won't want to do so again for a while.

Criticisms of these Subjective Theories of Value include the observation that the theory is somewhat tautological, circular. It says the value of a thing depends on how much someone values it. Whilst perhaps true, this is not really saying very much. It can't give any starting point on which to base price. It simply says: observe the price(s) at which the thing is changing hands, observe the price(s) at which producers are prepared to supply it, and observe the price(s) at which people demand it. It's a bit like having a theory to predict tomorrow's weather that says: when you wake up tomorrow, look out of the window. A further criticism is expressed well by Dutch Marxist, Ernest Mandel: '… it is, moreover, unable to explain how, from the clash of millions of different individual "needs" there emerge not only uniform prices, but prices which remain stable over long periods, even under perfect conditions of free competition'.[221] Significantly, critics also point out that, unlike the Labour Theory of Value, Subjective Theories can't be used to observe or analyse expropriation and exploitation. They ignore the production process, labour, and the distribution of takings, and assume profit simply arises in the market place rather than something created by work.

So, value depends on a range of factors which are constantly varying, and indeed Steiner considers as futile any attempt to come up with a general definition of it:

> … there can be no question of arriving at a definition of economic value. Once more you need only consider on how many circumstances—on the cleverness or stupidity of how many different people—the modification of labour by the spirit in any given instance will depend. There is every kind of fluctuating condition. (CW340, p. 32)

---

[221] https://en.m.wikipedia.org>wiki>marginalism.

For him, it is a case of firstly understanding that economic value is *created* in only one of two ways:

> Value arises only in connection with working on nature or improving work by inventiveness. (CW341, p. 208)

This is not so far away from the Labour Theory of Value since, in that theory, the term 'labour' includes not only physical labour but also time taken on mental effort. But Steiner makes a point of splitting the two things out: value is created either when nature is modified by labour, or labour is modified by 'spirit'.

> Through the spirit—by intelligence, reflection, perhaps even speculation—labour is given a certain direction ... (CW340, p. 32)

And the 'finished labour' that the Labour Theory of Value says is stored up in a factory's plant and machinery is covered by the following.

> These are the two essential poles of the economic process. There are indeed no other ways in which economic values are created. Either nature is modified by labour, or labour is modified by spirit. The outer expression of the spirit, in this connection, is in the manifold formations of capital. (CW340, p. 32)

The spirit / mental work behind the creation of a commodity can take a number of forms: it designs the product, it organises labour in an intelligent way, it designs plant and machinery to mechanise production. And the money capital used for making the plant and machinery will have been there in the first place because of profits from other enterprises that will have involved intelligence, ingenuity, 'spirit'.

Note, however, two words in the above quote. Firstly 'economic' as in 'economic value'. Steiner is not talking about value in general. An area of uncultivated, fertile land, or a shoal of fish in the sea, or a good wind, or simply the sunshine may be something of great value. But until the fish are caught, they have no *economic* value in his definition. And as we know, virgin land does not fall within Steiner's definition of the economy; it is not considered a commodity for purchase / sale.

And until the wind is harnessed to generate electricity or to propel a boat, no *economic* value arises. And we can benefit from the sunshine in all manner of ways without anyone having to work to bring it down to us. So this, too, has no *economic* value under his definition.

Note, secondly, the word 'created'. Economic values are only created by (a) nature being modified by labour, or (b) labour being modified by spirit. But this is not to say that value is *always* created whenever either of these two poles of activity get to work. Our hypothetical gardener who digs holes all day and then fills them up again may expend a great deal of labour but create no economic value. So, whilst in Steiner's definition, economic value can only be created by (a) or (b) or both, that does not mean (a) or (b) *necessarily* create economic value. What makes the difference between these two types of activity either creating or not creating economic value is what the resultant goods or services actually *are*, and the customer's desire to have them. Usefulness and desirability *determine* economic value. That human requirement has its part to play in determining economic value is the basis of the Subjective Theories of Value, mentioned above.

> *Where does the economic value arise? It does not arise where human labour accumulates, or becomes crystallised in the goods [...] the economic value must be sought within a kind of tension, and we can describe this economic value by saying: on the one hand, we have the goods, the wares; then we must consider their different qualities and also the place where they can be consumed. [...]. On the other hand we have the human requirements, ... interest which people have in the goods. [...] This tension, and nothing else, gives rise to the true economic value. The true economic value does not contain the idea of labour. (CW188(v), 26 January 1919)*
>
> *The economic value at any given moment is determined, on the one hand, by the demand, or the requirement, and on the other hand, by the definite, qualified goods which exist at a given time. This constitutes the true economic value of a merchandise ... (CW188(v), 26 January 1919)*
>
> *... a commodity has not merely the value we attach to it through our requirements and the personal importance we give to these*

> *requirements, which is then transferred to the commodity; it has also an objective value in itself. It has an objective value to the degree that it is durable or the reverse, lasting or perishable; to the degree that by its nature it is more or less serviceable, plentiful, or scarce. All these things condition an objective, actual economic value, the determination of which demands an objective, expert knowledge, and the production of which requires an objective technical capacity. (CW332a, p. 106)*

For Steiner, value is determined by the interplay between the nature of the goods themselves and people's desire for them. The effort put into making something does not determine value. If I, as a customer, am looking at two identical chairs, then they are of the same value to me even if one of them was made by a slow joiner who took twice as long as the joiner who made the other.

> *The corresponding demand may determine that goods which entailed a great amount of work must, under certain conditions, be sold cheaply [an intricately woven but ultimately unattractive rug, perhaps, RM]; and, within a sound economic process, the demand may determine that a product involving little work obtains a higher price [the stumbled-upon diamond, say]. Consequently the work involved can never be the decisive factor. (CW188(v), 26 January 1919)*

One could perhaps argue that, in the determination of value, even the inherent, objective attributes of a commodity (usefulness, durability, etc.) will ultimately be trumped by whether someone wants it or not. A cheese grater may be very useful and durable. But if everybody already has one in their kitchen, then they won't value another one. (All the same, sooner or later someone's six-year-old will have the bright idea that the cheese grater would make the perfect tool for rasping down a tree stump in the garden, quickly rendering it useless. Then a surplus grater, originally consigned to valuelessness, because no one wanted it, is found to have value after all—by the six-year-old's parents.) Steiner seemingly acknowledges the primacy of simple desirability when, three years after the above observations, he recalls how, in his youth, he had befriended a family who had discovered that a painting which had lain discarded in their attic for decades was now found to be worth a lot:

> What did the value depend on in this case? Purely and simply on the opinion men formed of the picture. [...] in no case does it depend on what a thing immediately 'is'. (CW340, p. 21)

But these observations (earlier quotes) that value is in part also determined by the objective attributes of the commodity (e.g. lasting or perishable), and not only by the desire of the customer, would be borne out if the two chairs in front of me *looked* identical, but weren't. If they were painted, wooden chairs, and the paint concealed the fact that one was badly made and would last only half as long as the other, then clearly they couldn't have equal value (in an objective sense), even though I, as purchaser, might place equal value on them after inspecting them superficially.

Matters could perhaps be described as follows: Ultimately, value depends on the extent to which someone desires the commodity (as per Subjective Value Theory). But the objective facts relating to the commodity (durability, etc.) will *influence* how desirable they find it.

So, on the one hand manufacturers are 'pushing' the commodity into existence via their physical and mental exertion; on the other, customers are 'pulling' on account of their need / desire for it. There are thus both intrinsic and subjective factors behind value. Effort *creates* value, but only by a combination of the end result and human requirement does the value become *determined*.

In summary:

- Economic value is *created* either by nature being modified by labour or by labour being modified by 'spirit'.
- But it is *determined* by the needs and wants of the consumer (influenced, as these are, by what and where the product *is*—how durable, how plentiful, how useful).

7.4.10 Price

Although price might in general be a reflection of economic value, it is by no means always so. It is quite possible to find two different outlets near to one another selling the same kind of muffin. Although these muffins will be of equal value to me, one shop may be charging a different price to the other. One value, two prices.

Steiner regards price as a central concern—even *the* central concern—of economic life:

> ... *the cardinal question of economics—namely, that of prices.* (CW340, p. 184)
>
> *In the last resort all the most important economic considerations really merge in this question of price. All the impulses and forces that are at work in economics culminate at length in price.* (CW340, p. 24)
>
> ... *directly one sees that the price question is one of such importance, that questions of capital or wages really fade into the background, then one has a sound thinking place to go upon.* (CW337a, 15 September 1920)

This last statement can seem somewhat extraordinary and, read in isolation, it perhaps is. Today, in the main, prices may be a bit low or a bit high here and there, but on the whole, apart from a few notable exceptions (e.g. housing) they don't seem very wide of the mark. On the other hand, extreme disparity of earnings abounds, and the ubiquitous—and increasing—rewarding of capital ownership over work is seen by a large portion of the population as highly problematic. However, Steiner was not simply focusing on price because prices *at the time* were such a big issue (hyperinflation was just months away). He is pointing to the fact that prices are the central station, if you like, to which the railways of such major things as wages or ownership of capital are connected. If the profit-maximising, private ownership of capital was not so excessive, for example, then prices might be different.

He qualifies this centrality of price as follows:

> *The cardinal question is the question of price. We must observe prices as we observe the degrees of the thermometer, and then look for the underlying conditions.* (CW340, p. 45)

> *... the price—the public price so to speak—which eventually emerges on the market, or in the circulation of goods, is really of far less economic importance than that which lies behind the forming of prices and of which price formation and price fluctuation are merely the final results. (CW340, p. 149)*

These may seem slightly contradictory remarks to the earlier ones; but the point is, prices are the end result of many key factors, they tell an overarching story that one needs to get to the bottom of. To have a healthy station, one needs to have healthy railways.

Above, Steiner talks of *observing* prices; but the following passages go rather further, suggesting that associative working ascertain the relative value of things and thence take action to *influence* price.

> *Economic judgments cannot be built on theory; they must be built on living association, where the sensitive judgments of people are real and effective; for it will then be possible to determine out of the association—out of the immediate experiences of those concerned—what the value of any given thing can be. Strange as it may sound, it is not possible to determine theoretically wherein the value of a product may consist. We can only say: a product enters into the economic life as a whole through the several parts of the economic process; and its value at a given place must be judged and estimated by association. (CW340, p. 131)*

> *Today we are absolutely convinced that the means of production and land are matters belonging to economic life. The impulse of the threefold order requires that only the reciprocal values of [commodities] shall come under the economic administration, and that prices shall approximate values, so that ultimately what finally proceeds from the economic administration is merely the determination of price. (CW332a, p. 120)*

'The determination of price'!
  Further,

> *The associations themselves, however, will belong entirely to the economic sphere and deal only with economic affairs, i.e. with the consumption, circulation, and production of goods and with the related process of price setting. (CW338(ii), p. 109)*

'Price setting'! And:

> I have often pointed out that this question of price adjustment is a
> cardinal one; that the fact of the matter is simply that, in the eco-
> nomic process, there are of course other questions, but that even
> such questions as wages and the like are not the primary ones to
> be settled; but that these also must be settled on the basis of the
> price question; that a quite definite price for any particular article is
> the only state of things which can be regarded as a healthy one in
> economic life. (CW337, 9 June 1920)

'Price adjustment'! And:

> In the sphere of economic life, therefore—in the associations—
> goods alone will have a part to play. This will, in turn, have an
> important consequence: we shall cease entirely to have any fixed
> notions of the price and value of an article. Instead, we shall say:
> the price and value of an article is something that changes with
> the surrounding circumstances. Price and value will be set by the
> collective judgment of the associations. (CW82, p. 179)

'Price and value will be set'! Also:

> Then there will remain to be regulated by the economic system
> only the valuation of commodities and of the service that one per-
> son should receive from another in exchange for his own service.
> For this purpose, certain persons will withdraw from the associa-
> tions composed of producers of various things, or of producers and
> consumers, and so on. These people will occupy themselves with
> the fixing of prices. (CW332a, p. 43)

Finally, ' … the fixing of prices'!

These comments can be slightly unsettling. On the one hand we
have: 'we shall cease entirely to have any fixed notions of the price
and value of an article' and on the other hand: 'a quite definite price
for any particular article is the only state of things which can be
regarded as a healthy one in economic life'. Again, such comments
appear, at first, to be at odds with one another. But the point Steiner

is making is that, whilst (a) an article should be seen as warranting a definite price *in a given situation* (e.g. when delivered to a particular location, in a particular year, with a particular harvest, say), (b) such a definite price cannot be regarded as fixed / applicable to all such articles in all situations regardless of where / when / by whom they were manufactured. A ton of wheat, in isolation, cannot be thought of as warranting a definite price; but in a given location and at a given point in time it can.

One can feel somewhat discouraged when trying to imagine how anyone could become interested in taking such a ponderous approach to pricing when, in the market we currently have, prices are able to find somewhere to settle with minimal effort. When Margaret Thatcher opined 'You can't buck the market!' wasn't she at least right about that?[222] We shall come on to what Steiner has in mind presently.

Also to be emphasised is that the expression 'fixing of prices' is not the best translation of the original German. It makes it sound as though Steiner is imagining that a 'correct' price—a Recommended Retail Price perhaps—would be imposed by some associational decree, by some edict from price setters. But this is not what he has in mind, as we shall see in the next two sections of the book. The German is *'Preisbildung'* and, elsewhere in the same lecture, *'Preisgestaltung'*. Rather than 'fixing of prices' these instead simply mean 'pricing' or 'price formation'. The following elucidate further:

> ... *determinations of economic value will arise out of the coalition of these associations, and in the central administrative body that will emerge from these economic interests. (CW24, p. 10)*

> ... *how do such negotiations come about that concern the mutual values of goods? Never within a uniform organisation, never between like and like, but only through associations. How can you find out what relationship the price of a shoe should have to the price of a hat if you do not let the hat maker cooperate in an associative way with the shoemaker, if association does not take place, if associations are not formed? [...] But that which is the origin—I do not say determination, but creation—of the right price, that can*

---

[222] Chris Giles, 'Thatcher's quest left "lasting scar" on the economy', *Financial Times*, 8 April 2013.

> *only develop through an associative life which goes between one industry and the next ... (CW337b, 10 October 1920)*
>
> *... prices would only be determined by associations between different industries. (CW337b, 12 October 1920)*
>
> *For what do these associations have for a task? They have the task ... to arrive at economically justifiable prices. When association and association exchange their experiences ... so can the price problem be solved practically. There is no theory to solve the price problem ... this cannot be done with numbers, this must be done by having a group of people who have experience in one industry, another group that has had experience in another industry, a third with a third industry, and so on, and that these groups bring their experiences together. The thing is not as complicated as you might think, and you can be quite sure that fewer people will be needed to set up associations in such a way that they can solve the price problem than are needed by certain states for their militarism and their policing! (CW337b, 10 October 1920)*

We have read of 'price creation', 'price adjustment', 'price formation', etc. And we have read that, ideally, this would be attended to either by 'the associations themselves' or by 'the collective judgement of the associations' or 'certain persons will withdraw from the associations ...' or by 'the coalition of these associations' or in 'the central administrative body that will emerge from these economic interests'. That is, somewhere within the associative structure or the central economic administration there would be specialists concerning themselves with price formation.

This prompts the following two questions: (a) on what basis would a suitable price be determined? And (b) once determined, how would such price take effect, how would it be adjusted / maintained? Answers to these questions are given in the next two sections of the book: 'Fair price' and 'Price adjustment by output adjustment'.

Steiner acknowledges that the factors underlying price are by no means straightforward.

> *... we cannot simply ask: what is the value of a commodity? The value is different according as the commodity is lying in a shop, or is transported to this place or that. (CW340, p. 20)*

> *... there can be no such thing as a general definition stating how the price of the thing is composed; that is an impossibility. (CW340, p. 25)*
>
> *It is wrong to try to consider price in any other way than by envisaging the interplay of values. Value set against value gives you price. And if, as we saw, value itself is a fluctuating thing, incapable of definition, may we not say that when you exchange value for value, price which arises in the process of exchange is a fluctuating thing raised to the second power? (CW340, p. 33)*

Intriguingly, though, in addition to the baker and publisher examples he gives of what a very simple economic association can look like, he gives the following *even simpler* picture which enables one to begin with very modest concepts:

> *... take the simplest economy: for someone doing business in the simplest economy, it also comes down to finding the correct prices for him in the end too. And the right prices are arrived at from the conditions specific to him. He determines the right prices from two concrete components: firstly, from what he would like to get for his products, and secondly, from what he gets. That is to say, even though still rather vague, he enters into an association with consumers. Association is always there, even when not formally concluded. (CW337b, 10 October 1920)*

That is to say, wherever producer and customer negotiate, even if this is between you and your window cleaner, one already has a very simple form of association. And out of this dialogue comes a price that both producer and consumer are content with. After reading this, though, one might be left wondering what is so very different between an associative approach, and the normal market approach that we are used to (and that Steiner is so dissatisfied with). Isn't the sole trader, characterised above, simply pricing his services according to what the market can bear? Aren't we simply back at supply and demand? The next sections of the book attempt to address these questions.

One thing this passage reminds us is that the association that Steiner suggests should underpin economic life, and which acts as the vehicle for the guiding principle of fraternity, need not be based on anything especially lovey-dovey or empathetic. It can simply amount to the parties involved somehow meeting one another and experiencing their inter-dependence, with all the conflicting interests that that may entail. By entering into dialogue with other parties, the tendency to only have oneself in mind is softened. The nature of this fraternity might well resemble that between two siblings who initially have to knock the corners off one another!

In summary:

- Price is the central phenomenon in economics—a phenomenon in which all other economic questions converge.
- By looking at the underlying conditions that lead to price one can get to the essence of economic life.
- Steiner suggests experts from associations (of different industries), or from the central economic administration, concentrate on establishing what the 'right', 'economically justifiable' prices for commodities are, and thence take action to encourage prices in the right direction (see following two sections).

7.4.11 Fair price

In Steiner's day, if an employer wanted to make widgets but knew the demand for them was such that production would only be viable if he (and it probably *was* a he) paid his workers a pittance, then he would pay them a pittance. And they would, in all likelihood, still turn up to work in order to avoid going hungry. If enough of them were affected, and affected badly enough, then their grievances might be expressed in strike action.

The arrival of minimum wage and living wage principles since then has no doubt helped. But if, as Steiner suggests, one were to do away with wages altogether, then how would one ensure that people were earning enough to live a decent existence? If there is no wage, then neither can there be a minimum nor living wage. But one might still want a minimum / living remuneration, or, better still, a decent remuneration.

As we have seen, Steiner places stewardship of labour conditions / labour relations within the rights realm. The economic realm simply has to accept any rules governing working hours and conditions as a given, in much the same way as it has to acccept the natural resources within this or that region are a given. In some European countries, the 40-hour week had already been introduced a decade or two before Steiner was concerning himself with the subject, so these ideas of the state taking care of labour were not new. In the USA, however, the 40-hour week did not become standard until 1940.

If a rights state decides that a certain level of remuneration should be a right for anyone working full-time, then the economic organism has to factor this in to its calculations. Any restrictions on the working week or any minimum remuneration threshold will have a bearing on price:

> *An economic organism which does not lay claim to human labour according to the needs of the various branches of production, but which has to operate in accordance with what the law allows, will determine the worth of commodities according to the work-performance of the men who produce them. Commodity values, which are unrelated to human welfare and dignity, will not determine work-performance. (CW23, p. 115)*

Steiner goes on to give a general formula for what he calls 'fair price'[223] which, whilst quite basic, he considers exhaustive for all circumstances:

> *Each working person must receive for a product an amount sufficient to completely satisfy his and his dependants' needs until he has again produced an object requiring the same amount of labour. Such a price relation cannot be officially established, but must result from co-operation between the associations active in the social organism. (CW23, p. 119)*

The first sentence in the quote defines 'fair price'. The second— concerning whether such price can be officially established or imposed—hints at the answer to the question raised in the previous

---

[223] Steiner uses the German adjectives '*gerecht*' (just, fair), '*richtig*' (right, correct), and occasionally '*wahr*' (true).

section, namely, once determined, how would such price take effect, how would it be maintained?

In similar words:

> A pair of shoes must have as much value as all the other products—be they physical or spiritual—that the shoemaker needs until he has made another pair of shoes. (CW337b, 12 October 1920)
>
> ... [a product's] value must equal the value of all other goods needed by the producer to fulfil his own requirements, until the time when he can again produce a similar piece of goods. ... Herein must be included, for instance, the needs of his children and what he must contribute for the support of persons incapable of working, etc. (CW24, p. 12)

As well as his depandants, this last sentence refers to what is generally covered by tax and National Insurance. We all need to produce a bit extra to care for those unable to produce, such as children, the elderly, the sick.

The word 'value' in these last two quotes should perhaps be replaced by 'price'. Otherwise we are back to Marx's notion of a value equalling the value of everything needed to sustain the worker during production—something Steiner questions when he states value is really determined by the consumer's desire for a good, determined by the extent to which the customer values it!

Aiming for 'fair price' was to be a matter for those working collaboratively in associations:

> Consumers, producers, and professionals [Berufsständen = professions] will form co-operatives and associations; corporate entities that will serve functions now left to chance in the marketplace. Today, production is governed by supply and demand, which are totally inaccessible to human thinking and human judgment. In the future, these new corporate bodies will decide which factors in commerce will determine price structures—that is, the value of goods. This is the only way that each individual's production will be exactly comparable in value to everything he or she needs until the next round of production. Economic activity will become equitable; the prices of certain goods will not be out of proportion to the prices of other types of goods. (CW333, p. 14)

> *The following example is rough, amateurish, and superficial, but it will have to do for today: if I make a pair of boots, the mutually agreed-upon sale price must allow me to purchase everything I need to meet my needs until I have made another pair. Of course society will have to establish organisations to ensure that the needs of widows, orphans, and the sick and disabled are met, and to provide for education and the like. The setting of equitable and realistic prices, however, which is exclusively the jurisdiction of the socially responsible economy, will depend on the formation of corporate bodies for that purpose, whether elected or appointed by joint producer-consumer associations. (CW333, p. 58)*

In this passage, education is included too; that is, the extra we all need to generate must also cover the running of schools, universities, etc. In addition, a company might well want to retain a certain amount of surplus to fund research and development. So, a 'fair price' might perhaps also need to include an element for this. The mention of associations electing or appointing those whose job it would be to concern themselves with price also serves to underscore how important Steiner sees this specialist task of pricing within associative life.

The differences between a 'fair price' approach and a living wage would include (a) for Steiner, the ideal is to move away from a wage where employer pays employee, (b) 'fair price' ideally covers *all* one's needs (not just basic ones), and (c) Steiner *could* be interpreted as implying that the 'fair price' received by senior executives should not be so different from that received by unskilled workers in the same organisation.

> *It cannot be a matter of any random determination of remuneration for work but the determination of mutual prices. Of course everything that relates to support for invalidity, sickness, child rearing/education etc. has to be taken into consideration too. (CW332a(ii), p. 73)*

The reader may have spotted that there is an element of circularity in this 'fair price' formula—similar to when spreadsheet users are scolded with the dreaded 'circular reference' error message! What I need to live on to make a window frame may include loaves of bread. But the baker of the loaves of bread will need windows. Wouldn't this leave those occupying themselves with price in an almighty tangle? The answer is probably: not necessarily, since Steiner's concern essentially seems to be about *relative* values / prices. If the baker can made a thousand loaves of bread in the time it takes me to make a window frame, then the price of this window frame needs to be about a thousand times that of a loaf of bread, all else being equal (i.e. assuming both of these artisans have identical needs, and the cost of the raw materials for a window frame approximately equates to the raw material cost for a thousand loaves of bread).

Of course, what might or might not be included in a person's needs will always be a question, and an intriguing one, at that. But it is a question to be resolved by those pricing experts in the discussions that are entered into within the collaborative working of the relevant associations. No doubt, in very hard times, such needs might be accepted as being little more than the basic needs of food, warmth, clothing, shelter. But as conditions improved, so would the range of things increase that were considered to be reasonably included in a person's list of needs: things that might bring greater comfort, enjoyment, inspiration, labour-saving, leisure, meaning. In an 'undeveloped' country with no electricity, a washing machine will be of no use, whereas in the 'developed world', such things would undoubtedly be regarded as a need.

In a region producing significant surpluses, funds over and above those required to cover the full needs of workers and those unable to work (including their healthcare, education, etc.) could be utilised in different ways. All could be allotted a similar amount which they could then spend on their chosen recreation. Or more could be paid for imports where suppliers from overseas were being paid substantially less than at home. Or more could be spent on education, public art or foreign aid. Or the rights realm might decide to reduce the working week, as proposed, for example, by the New Economics Foundation.[224]

---

[224] Miatta Fahnbulleh, 'How can we make the shorter working week a reality in the UK?', 5 November 2019, https://neweconomics.org.

Note also that the 'fair price' formula talks about what the producer needs in order to make the *next* similar item, not the one being sold. A small point, perhaps, but necessary. What I receive for the widget I have just made needs to keep me going until I have made the next one.

Notwithstanding these various considerations, Steiner accepts that, put as it is, the formula is very general and simplistic:

> *... just as we have to introduce into the theorem of Pythagoras the varying proportions of the sides, so shall we have to introduce many, very many more variables into this formula. Economic science is precisely an understanding of how the whole economic process can be included in this formula. (CW340, p. 72)*

As we saw in Section 7.4.9, Steiner identifies four phenomena that relate to value: (a) labour working on nature, (b) intelligence organising labour, (c) objective qualities relating to the product (usefulness, etc.), and (d) the extent to which a buyer has need or desire of it. The first two, if well applied, *create* value and accord with Intrinsic Value Theories such as the Labour Theory of Value. The third and fourth *determine* value and accord with Subjective Value Theory. However, for the purposes of 'fair price' (i.e. *price* as opposed to value) only the first two—(a) and (b)—are operative. That is to say, the price is ideally such that the physical and mental work needed to produce the commodity are factored in. Or, more exactly, my *outgoings* during the period of my (physical and mental) work are factored in (which is not dissimilar to Marx's 'socially necessary' approach to value, mentioned earlier). Need / desire / demand for the commodity is simply assumed.

As should always be borne in mind, Steiner emphasises he has no wish to promulgate anything resembling fanaticism or absolutism. He was offering *pointers* to help with the civilising of society. Whilst his 'fair price' could probably never apply in every last context, it is a general principle to be aimed for. Subjective Value Theory / value creating tension / the desire of the purchaser will still always be phenomena to be reckoned with, too. In the classic example of someone inadvertently stumbling across a large diamond whilst on a short walk out in nature, the eventual price will exceed the precious stone's 'fair price' by a long way. Yes, the discoverer might spend the rest of his or her life going on thousands of walks without stumbling across a similar gem; but the price they get for the first one may well exceed what they need to see them out until their dying day in any case.

Interestingly, there is some conflict between the 'fair price' concept and the following comment made in connection with the placing of capital (means of production) at the disposal of those with the most appropriate skills so that the common good is best served.

> *The only thing personally owned by the individual who operates an enterprise should be what he draws in accordance with the terms agreed to when he takes over responsibility for production, and which he feels are appropriate to his individual abilities; and which, furthermore, seem justified by the confidence of others in granting him the use of capital.* Should the capital be increased through the activities of this individual, then he would be entitled to a portion of the increase ... [my emphasis, RM] (CW23, p. 102)

Under such an approach, if a factory was made more efficient, those responsible would receive some of the increased profit. But under a 'fair price' approach, the staff would in theory already have been in receipt of all they needed for a decent livelihood. So, if 'fair price' were being applied to the nth degree, the greater efficiency in the enterprise might simply lead to a reduction in the sale price, or profit being allocated elsewhere; the staff would not need to receive more. This seeming inconsistency only serves to reaffirm what has just been mentioned: that Steiner was giving pointers, rather than laying down inflexible principles. He obviously saw some merit in rewarding people for more efficient work. After all, this benefits all. And in any case, people generally always like to have an additional treat or two. Remember, though, that whilst increased profit arising from increased efficiencies / productivity might merit higher remuneration, increased profit arising by management simply paying workers less, or cutting corners, or increasing product prices would not (see Section 7.4.14). And one imagines that, where greater efficiencies and higher profit *did* justify higher remuneration, then all co-workers might (repeat, *might*) be due a slice of the cake, in keeping with the principle of all co-workers sharing the proceeds of the particular concern they are part of.

A further, interesting aspect of all this is that, in the economic realm where fraternity is supposed to hold sway instead of equality, the 'fair price' idea (which, incidentally, was not only Steiner's[225]), in leading to all having their needs met, contains an equality *of sorts*. That is, to the extent that our needs for food, clothing, shelter, leisure, etc. are similar, an equality of remuneration is implicit in 'fair price'. But unlike in the rights realm where we should all be identically subject to the same laws, and identically responsible for political voting, our economic contributions and our economic needs are rarely identical. One person may have dependants, another not, and so on.

Two things that 'fair price' would *not* include (in a more threefold world) would be (a) any element of profit / dividends for external shareholders (although interest to lenders is acceptable, as is interest to the original entrepreneur, if retired but still living—see Section 7.3.7), and (b) rent. Ultimately, land and the means of production would be subject to the ownership models already discussed (i.e. passed on, as if by gift, from one expert to the next without financial consideration). There would be no absent owners in a position to demand a return; work would be rewarded, but not ownership. If people bake bread for me, then I must sing arias for them (OK, bad example!). Society is protected from prices containing economic rent.

> ... *true relationships are again and again being diverted, by falsified processes, into a mode of operation which introduces constant disturbances into the economic process. Continually to smooth out and compensate for the disturbances is one of the essential tasks of economics. People keep on saying that we ought to get rid of the evils of economic life; and they are inclined to have at the back of their minds the notion: 'Then everything will be all right and the earthly paradise will begin.' But that is just as though you were to say: 'I should like, once and for all, to eat so much that I need never eat any more.' I cannot do that, for I am a living organism wherein ascending and descending processes must constantly be taking place. Such ascending and descending processes must equally be present in the economic life; there must be the tendency on the one hand to falsify prices by the forming of rent [...] These tendencies are present all the time, and we must understand them in order to obtain, as far as possible, those prices which represent a minimum of falsification. (CW340, p. 94)*

---

[225] As well as Marx, Thomas Aquinas and others had similar ideas.

If economic rent is removed from the picture, one can then have:

> *... a social order in which services should ensure just reciprocal services, in which men shall work for men, not merely every man for himself ... (CW330(ii), 31 May 1919)*

When Steiner says prices are a more central issue in economics than capital or wages, one can imagine he may be thinking: a 'fair price' ensures these other issues are taken care of since (a) it does not include any rent / dividend element (that is, it would cover the manager's needs but not reward absent owners, bar possibly the original entrepreneur if they had built up the original enterprise without using capital built up by others—see Section 7.3.7), and (b) it would properly cover workers' needs too. The issue of price thus contains capital or wage issues within it. It is that central station to which the railways of capital, wages, and other economic issues are all connected.

Steiner suggests that the overcoming of competition is another of these 'railways' connected to price:

> *In economic life, fair prices must prevail. Then not everything will be predicated on the competition between capital and wages or on the competition between individual companies. For this, however, it is necessary to replace competition which finds its peak in the interplay between supply and demand, with sensible decisions and contracts ... (CW331, p. 24 June 1919)*
>
> *... what disappears as a result? Think it through: what disappears is competition. If one can thus determine price, if one can really determine price by industries coming together, then competition stops. It is only necessary to support this end of competition in a particular way. And one can support it in that way. (CW337b, 12 October 1920)*

If brotherly, collaborative dialogue within associations results in a particular price being agreed as 'just' by all concerned, then all the cat-and-mouse games of producers trying to undercut one another can stop.

'Fair price' perhaps sounds terribly idealistic. But why should it? If everyone were to get their full, respective needs covered in return for a 37.5-hour week (or whatever), this would doubtless engender a tremendous feeling of fairness (not equality, which is different) among the population. People would not be looking for promotion simply in order to get more take-home pay for themselves. With a 'fair price' approach, one can imagine an increased sense of camaraderie amongst the population arising—a sense of inclusion, a sense of 'we're all in this together'. Feelings of exploitation and alienation would be replaced by ones of inclusivity and respect.

However, to think in terms of some universal 'fair price' utopia is not what this is about, and the following from 1921 reminds us once again of Steiner's non-absolutist approach to these things:

> ... the associations will primarily have to further the tendency towards the correct price out of immediate life, so that everyone actually can purchase what he needs for his maintenance out of his own producing. I have once tried to bring into a formula what such a just price would look like. That does not mean of course that it should be determined abstractly. It is determined out of real life as I have indicated. But I have said: Such a price for any product in social life—that is, for merchandize—is this, that it makes it possible for a person to provide his keep and all his needs for himself and his family until he has produced the same product again. I don't state this as a dogma. I don't say this must be so, because one would never be able to implement this, as one cannot implant such theories into reality, I only say that that which will appear as the correct price through the associative working together will tend towards this direction. [...] when the associations work in the right way and out of the experiences of life without dogmatically saying the just price has to be such or such, this price will appear through the associative working. (CW79, 30 November 1921)

As Nye Bevan once said, 'We have a right to say ... it is better to have slightly dearer coal than cheaper colliers'.[226]

In summary:

- 'Fair price' is an ideal to be aimed for, even if only in approximate terms.

---

[226] Edmund Dell, *A Strange Eventful History: Democratic Socialism in Britain* (London: Harper Collins, 1999), p. 84.

- This ideal sees all receive enough for a piece of work to cover their needs and those of their dependants until they again produce a similar piece of work.
- The needs of those unable to work must also be covered, as should the needs of educational establishments.
- Some leeway between 'fair price' and the idea of producers receiving more (or less) income if they increase (reduce) profit on account of greater (lower) efficiency / productivity.
- 'Fair price' does not include an element for non-working owners (save, possibly, the original entrepreneur if they built the enterprises up without capital built up by others).
- 'Falsification' of prices as a result of economic rent is thereby reduced.

Reflections in relation to the present

In the economic landscape we are used to, prices can be above 'fair price' for a number of reasons, including: (a) shareholders expecting a return; (b) ground rent; (c) senior executives being paid inordinately large salaries or bonuses which cover their needs dozens or even hundreds of times over; (d) underproduction (demand for the product outstrips supply, and producers or distributors notice that some consumers of the product are prepared to pay more for it instead of go without); or (e) monopolistic behaviour, where little or no competition exists that might undercut prices. Not all industrialists try to milk their customers to the limit, of course. In Steiner's time, Henry Ford suggested that 'people throw overboard the idea of pricing on what the traffic will bear and instead go on the common sense basis of pricing on what it costs to manufacture'.[227]

Prices can also stray below 'fair price' for a number of reasons, including: (a) ruthless competition; (b) a producer cross-subsidising a product with surpluses made on a different product; (c) overproduction (supply outstrips demand, and sellers drop prices in an attempt to interest new buyers); (d) work is outsourced to a country where a starvation wage can be paid (as there is no minimum wage); or (e) the domestic minimum wage is not enough to lift workers out of squalor

---

[227] Henry Ford, *My Life and Work* (Hawthorne, CA: BN Publishing, 2008), p. 36.

and cover their full needs. The latter problem can lead to the strange anomaly of the state subsidising the producer (or, more accurately perhaps, its customers) by paying workers in-work benefits. US presidential hopeful, senator Bernie Sanders summed up matters thus: 'I don't believe it is a terribly radical idea to say that someone who works 40 hours a week should not be living in poverty.'[228]

Notwithstanding the above circumstances which can move prices away from 'fair price', prices may also settle close to 'fair price', even under the usual competitive paradigm with its supply and demand, if, that is, the enterprise is able to pay reasonable wages. But whilst, for some, something like a 'living wage' may be sufficient, for others it may only prevent the worker from going hungry and un-housed, but not enable them to enjoy a reasonable living and dignified existence. Sadly, minimum wage and living wage are one-size-fits-all concepts that do not allow for different people having different needs—on account of different numbers of dependants, for example (although this can be ameliorated to some degree with things like Child Benefit). Similarly, employment laws stipulating that all equivalent positions in a firm should be remunerated at the same rate have their shortcomings, too. Yes, they can certainly (and importantly) help guard against discrimination. But, if I have inherited a house and my peer has a mortgage or rent to pay, the rationale for me taking home less remuneration is persuasive. Seen from this point of view, such laws are perhaps rather unsophisticated. This takes us back to Steiner's proposal that work and income be separated. Income should ideally be related more to needs, not to what work you are doing. 'Fair price' embodies this principle.

My first job after university serves as an example of a company paying more conscious attention to the needs of staff. It was with a small banking institution—Mercury Provident—that had been set up by anthroposophists.[229] Remuneration was such that the reasonable needs of staff were covered. For me as a young, idealistic graduate, it simply felt good and equitable to know that staff with children received greater remuneration than I who, at that time, had none. But I knew that, if in future I might have children, the resultant increase in

---

[228] @BernieSanders, 13 February 2016.
[229] Mercury Provident plc later became the UK branch of Triodos Bank—a Dutch institution with similar ideals.

needs would be taken into consideration. In addition, the most senior executives received remuneration that was very modest compared to what one is used to hearing about in the financial world.

Two of the examples of associative practice cited in Section 7.4.2 ('Associations'), namely, Community Supported Agriculture and Fair Trade—are also good examples of Steiner's idea of 'fair price'. In both cases, producers, distributors and consumers associate, and prices are aimed for that take the producer's needs into consideration.

7.4.12 Price adjustment by output adjustment

As we know, prices in a conventional, market economy settle, in theory, at an equilibrium level where producers undercut each other until a point is reached where further undercutting would result in a loss to the producer. So, in theory, the consumer buys the commodity at the lowest possible price, beyond which production would not be viable. This could be seen as a 'fair price' *of sorts* inasmuch as it may be the lowest possible price, below which producers may not feel their needs are being met. However, producers may deny some of their needs (or, more to the point, deny some of their employees' needs) in order to remain competitive, and the price can thus slip below 'fair price'. Conversely, prices may rise above 'fair price' when, for example, producers (or retailers) take advantage of little competition and a somewhat helpless customer base, or when profits are paid to absent shareholders.

Steiner's approach to price adjustment is different. He recommends replacing what he sees as the haphazard (in his day, at least) production levels of a conventional economy with an altogether more conscious approach. That is, by monitoring economic activity, needs and prices, specialists seconded from economic associations would not only see how close to an equitable 'fair price' goods were selling for, but also how well needs were being met by production, i.e. whether there was overproduction or underproduction in any sector (Section 7.4.3). He saw this as a rational basis on which workers could be directed to this or that sector as needs varied.

When a product shows a tendency to become too dear, that is a sign that there are too few workers engaged on it. Negotiations must then be carried on with other branches of production to transfer workers from one branch to another where the need lies, in order that more of the lacking products may be supplied.[230] If a commodity tends to become too cheap, that is to say, to earn too little profit,[231] arrangements must be made to employ fewer workers on that particular product. This means that in the future the satisfaction of the needs of the community will depend on the way in which men are employed in industry. The price of a product is conditional on the number of persons engaged in its production. [...] human reason will take the place of chance, that as a result of the arrangements that will come into existence the price will express the arrangements arrived at, the contracts entered into. Thus we shall see a revolution of the market accomplished by the substitution of reason for the chances of the market now prevailing. (CW332a, p. 46)

... if at any place a certain kind of commodity becomes too cheap or too dear, those concerned must be able truly to observe this fact [...] ... when through experiences which can only grow out of the concerted counsels of the associations, they are able to say, as a result of such experiences: 'five units of money for so and so much salt are too little or too much, the price is too low or too high'—then and only then will they be in a position to take the necessary steps.

If the price of a commodity becomes too cheap [low], so that those who produce it can no longer receive sufficient remuneration for their excessively cheap services and their excessively cheap products, it will be necessary to assign fewer workers to this particular commodity. Workers will therefore have to be diverted to another piece of work. If, on the other hand, a commodity becomes too dear, workers will have to be lead over into this branch of production. Thus the associations will always be concerned with a proper employment of men in the several branches of the economic life. (CW340, p. 70)

Notable is that Steiner still appears to be assuming certain supply-and-demand behaviours continue under his model. He is not suggesting prices be in any way fixed, but that their levels and fluctuations in the marketplace be observed. He appears to be anticipating that shops

---

[230] More workers would not only increase overall output, but would in all likelihood also lead to greater economies of scale (with increased division of labour and efficiency), and thus lower prices.

[231] That is, too little to sustain co-workers properly. It is doubtful profit is here meant in its normal sense of the surplus available *after* staff remuneration.

would still increase the price of items they kept running out of and reduce prices of things they were struggling to shift. But the underlying production levels would be monitored and adjusted, via the redistribution of workers, in order to encourage prices in the direction of 'fair price'. Through associations, industry-wide co-operation would lead to such adjustment of production levels being agreed.

In response to this, one could argue that the usual market approach corrects production levels in any case: manufacturers employ or lay off workers as demand dictates. But in Steiner's day, with no real-time information to hand on sales and stock levels, it would have been much harder to maintain production levels that were sensitive to demand. And, as discussed above: under the usual supply-and-demand market approach, prices may settle some distance away from 'fair price', for example while companies desperately try to out-compete with one another. Then some of their underpaid workers' needs go unsated.

Also, under the more associative approach, instead of part of the workforce being thrown to the wind by an over-producer, they could instead be redirected elsewhere—to an under-producer—without having to undergo the uncertainty of unemployment in the interim. The transition could be a single, seamless manoeuvre, instead of: redundancy, unemployment, job-search, job applications, etc. As Charles Waterman says: 'It makes a great difference to an unemployed man whether his affairs are handled by his own organisation or by an agency with which he comes into contact only when he has entered the category of unfortunates who are out of work.'[232]

Managing the workforce in this way, associations would encourage prices in the direction of 'fair price'.

> *We must see to it that the worker is not restricted to one sole application throughout his life, but he is able to turn his hand to other things. (CW340, pp. 70-71)*
>
> *The task of the associations will be to arrange production in such a way that when too many people are working in any sphere they can be transferred to some other work. (CW340, p. 82)*

---

[232] Charles Waterman, *The Three Spheres of Society* (London: Faber and Faber, 1946), p. 86.

As everyone knows, an item of merchandize in economic circulation becomes too cheap if a great number of people produce the same thing, when there is overproduction. And everyone knows, that an item of merchandize becomes too expensive when it is produced by too few people. Through this we have a measure where the objective mean is of which I have spoken. This mean, the objective value, this objective price cannot be fixed as such. But when associations come into being which see their activity in practically getting to know economic life, to study it in every moment, in every present time, then the main observation can be how prices rise, how prices fall. And because associations occupy themselves with this rising and falling of prices, it can be accomplished by negotiations that a large enough number of people can be formed for an economic entity, a large enough number of people is active in a branch of production, that through negotiation one can bring the right number of people into a branch of production. This cannot be worked out theoretically, this can only be determined by people being in their appropriate place, so that these things are determined by human experience. Therefore one cannot say: this or that is the objective value. But when associations work in economic life in such a way that they make it one of their tasks gradually to eliminate businesses which make the prices too cheap as is customary, and to inaugurate others in their place which produce something else, then enough people will take part in the various branches of production. This can only be accomplished by a truly associative life. And then the price for a certain product will become closer to the objective price. So that we can never say: Because of such and such conditions the objective price must be this or that, but we can only say: When the right human association comes about, then by its work in the immediate life of the social organism the correct price can gradually emerge. The point is not to state how institutions should be that the socially right thing happens, but to bring people into such a social connection that from the collaboration of the people the social question can gradually be solved. (CW79, 30 November 1921)

This passage, and the following, also remind us that, whilst Steiner advocates a more conscious and rational approach to production, he is categoric that the organising of this be done by people close to the action, people directly concerned with economic life, and not through any state (rights realm) involvement.

> *To try to regulate these things bureaucratically, through the state, would be the worst form of tyranny; but to regulate it by free [of state interference, RM] associations which arise within the social sphere, where everyone can see what is going on—either as a member or because his representative sits on the association, or he is told what is going on, or he sees it for himself and realises what is required—this is what we must aim at. (CW340, p. 71)*

The levels of transparency referred to here seem especially pertinent to the more conscious approach to production that Steiner considers healthy. Associations would be effective when everyone who was affected and / or interested could see what was going on.

Were such an associational structure fully up and running in the economy, then one imagines the movement of workers from one factory to the next would largely be a case of fine tuning each month or quarter. But initially, the altering of production levels might be more substantial and require the closure of whole businesses and the setting up of others:

> *... if, for example, we lived in a transitional period where a particular article was being manufactured by too many businesses, if the article was being produced to excess, one would have to shut down individual businesses and conclude contracts with the workers of these establishments to continue working in a different industry. (CW331, 24 June 1919)*

> *... let's suppose that certain manufactured items tend to become too expensive which means that too few of them are being produced. When this happens, contractual agreements must direct workers to the branches of industry that can produce these articles. Conversely, if an item becomes too cheap, some of the factories producing it must be idled, and their workers redirected into other branches of production. Those who reject this process as too difficult, preferring to stick with small improvements in social conditions, cannot expect real change. (CW333, p. 58)*

Under normal supply and demand a new producer might decide to try their luck and enter a market that is already saturated with a certain product, only to discover, after a stretch of time, that it was not such a good idea after all: the products in question are not selling fast enough. After some delay (and heartache, no doubt), either this new producer, or perhaps a different one, will go out of business. If, on the other hand, the sector in question has its own professional body that sits within associations monitoring production and consumption of the product(s) in question, such things could be pre-empted. Bankruptcies, waste and heartache would be greatly reduced.

In summary:

- Associations to facilitate movement of workforce such that ...
- production levels are encouraged in a direction that engenders 'fair price'.

Reflections in relation to the present

Again, all this can sound very impractical to a person of today. With our global trade and millions of different products, often many thousands in a single shop or internet outlet—the idea of having associations or their seconded experts constantly observing economic processes and prices, and then arbitrating on production levels and employment levels can sound rather far-fetched. Indeed, Steiner himself was not oblivious to the layers of intricacy in such matters:

> *... the further the division of labour extends, and new needs arise in the process, the more does the differentiation of products increase, and the difficulties connected with price formation accumulate. (CW340, p. 90)*

We are so used to letting the forces of supply and demand determine a price that, more or less, suits buyer and seller. If someone starts up a business, surely the simplest is to let them work out what they think is a reasonable selling price to start with, and then they can tweak it up or down as the market becomes clear? To discuss the matter in association with others sounds like a layer of bureaucracy that businesses could do without, a constraint that might even slow the economic process down and thereby make products more expensive.

But when one considers the overlap, duplication, marketing battles and business failures involved in war-of-all-against-all competition, not to mention, in many cases, the sheer mean-spiritedness, and when one thinks about the extent of exploitation of the economically weak, especially those in less developed countries, one can then begin to imagine how these suggestions of Steiner's might have application— in some sectors and contexts more than others, no doubt (as discussed in Sections 7.4.2 and 7.4.3—'Associations' and 'Production according to need').

A simple, current application of these output-adjusting ideas might, for example, be found in fair trade. A co-operative of fair-trade banana growers, say, could be growing so many bananas that they were unable to sell them all unless they accepted a price that was too low to meet their needs. In such an instance, they could, in association with each other and consumer representatives in the importing country (e.g. the Fair Trade Association), decide to reduce banana output and start growing some other crop in lieu. They might then find they could get a more realistic price for their bananas. Although such an outcome might (eventually) also be achieved by conventional supply-and-demand behaviour, the difference here is that everything proceeds in an orderly manner. No growers are sent to the wall desperately and belligerently trying to compete with their neighbours. All parties agree (a) that diversification into another crop seems sensible, and (b) how to go about this such that everyone's needs are better met. They *associate*.

Steiner was fully cognisant of—and enthusiastic about—the development of world trade. But it is important to remember he was speaking on the subject during and shortly after the Great War when economic life in Central Europe, just like much of its population, was badly wounded, and inflation was about to become apoplectic. Making sure everyone's basic needs were taken care of would have been a high priority, and consciously adjusting production levels of essential commodities in order to pursue 'fair prices' and ensure affordability would have had particular relevance. As already alluded to, the more basic economic conditions that existed at the time would doubtless have been considerably more receptive to the associative approach than what we have today in somewhere like the UK. That said, if an associative, fair-price-pursuing economy was in full swing today, it would be interesting to see to what extent those otherwise building un-needed office blocks or luxury yachts, say, would instead be building houses to provide for those currently living in rotting housing stock on threatening, vermin-infested sink estates! And so on and so forth.

Concerning the idea of helping workers relocate from shrinking industries to expanding ones, a number of current authors and activists arguing for the introduction of a Green New Deal to combat climate breakdown propose similar measures. In particular, they propose that those working in fossil fuel industries be given direct transfers, where possible, to employment in renewables.[233]

7.4.13 Profit / profit maximisation

There is profit and there is profit. Just like Austrian economist Carl Menger some fifty years earlier, Steiner points out that, on one level, both parties to a transaction profit by the exchange. If I buy a doughnut, this means I am happier to have the doughnut than the money; the doughnut is of more value to me than the money. Conversely, the baker is happier to have the money than the doughnut. Both parties gain by the transaction.

> *We have therefore this peculiar phenomenon: two people make an exchange, and—at any rate in the normal process of purchase and sale—each one of them must make a profit. (CW340, p. 123)*

But what about what we normally think of as profit: the excess a producer or distributor receives over and above their costs? What role would *this* play in a world where production was predicated more on observed need, and where 'fair price' was aimed for such that it covered producers' needs but did not result in significant excesses over and above this?

---

[233] See, for example, Noam Chomsky and Robert Pollin, *Climate Crisis and the Global Green New Deal,* (London: Verso, 2020), Introduction.

> *Reducing everything to an interest in profit, rather than in the thing being made, is basically what poisons our entire economic life. (CW337b, 10 October 1920)*

This poison is ameliorated in large part by Steiner's suggestions that (a) external owners (requiring, as they generally do, maximum returns) be superseded by removing the means of production from the economic domain, where possible, so that these cannot be bought and sold, and (b) sensible remuneration levels being agreed when a new manager takes over the means of production.

However:

> *Profits may represent what they will in ethical terms; in conventional economic terms, they represent an indicator for the need to produce an article.*

Note: 'in *conventional* economic terms'.

> *(cont.) The further evolution of economics does require the elimination of profits, but for the following reason: because they make the production of articles dependent on accidents of the market, which the spirit of the age demands be abolished. One clouds one's judgement if one argues against profit because of its egotistical nature. [...]*

That is, production only for the sake of profit (maximisation) comes with hit-and-miss, competitive behaviour rather than enterprise based on collaboratively investigated needs.

> *(cont.) What is necessary for economic life is that profits as indicators should be replaced by groups tasked with establishing a rational correspondence between production and consumption that will abolish accidents of the market. The change from profits-indicator to a rational co-ordination of production and consumption, if correctly understood, will result in the elimination of the motives that have hitherto clouded judgement on this issue by removing them to the legal and cultural spheres. (CW24, p. 97)*

> *... in such an economic life as this there will be a return to a condition that has now almost ceased to exist because of the financial system in which money itself has become an object of economic business, a condition in which economic life will be re-established on its natural and worthy foundation. It will not be possible in future to carry on business by means of money, and for money, because economic institutions will have to deal with the respective values of commodities. That is to say, society will again return to goodness of quality, excellence of workmanship, and the capacity of the worker. (CW332a, p. 47)*

If production is tailored to levels that meet consumer needs, and a 'just price' is aimed for that meets producers' and distributors' needs, then producers can focus on efficiency and product quality without obsessing about how to wring those few extra dollars out of the system for themselves and their shareholders, and without obsessing about how to avoid loss of market share to rivals, or indeed how to steal it.

> *Anyone who thinks the capitalist orientation a mere intruder into modern economic life will demand its removal. However, he who sees that division of labour and social function are the essence of modern life, will only consider how best to exclude from social life the disadvantages that arise as a by-product of this capitalist tendency. He will clearly perceive that the capitalist method of production is a consequence of modern life, and that its disadvantages can make themselves felt only as long as increase of capital is made the sole criterion of economic value.*
>
> *The ideal is to work towards a social structure in which the criterion of capital increase will no longer be the only power to which production is subjected ... increase of capital should rather serve as an indicator that the economic life ... is correctly formed and organized. [...]*
>
> *If the object is to gain an increase in capital or a rise in wages, it is immaterial through what branch of production the result is achieved. The natural and sensible relation of people to what they produce is thereby undermined. (CW24, pp. 40-41)*
>
> *Under the influence of the threefold idea, the operation of social life will in a sense be reversed. Presently, one must look to the*

*increase of one's capital or wages as a sign that one is playing a
satisfactory part in the life of the community. In the threefold social
order, the greatest possible efficiency of common work will result
because individual faculties [cultural realm, RM] work in harmony
with the human relationships founded in the legal sphere [rights
realm, RM], and with the production, circulation and consumption
regulated by the economic associations [economic realm, RM].
Increase of capital, and a proper adjustment of work and the return
upon work, shall appear as a final consequence of these social
institutions and their activities. (CW24, pp. 48-49)*

Steiner's concern is less about removing profit entirely, and more that it
should not be the *raison d'être* of business. And indeed, in cases where
business ownership in the normal sense ceases, the lust for profit is
bound to abate.

Any profit that *is* made, over and above that distributed to the workforce, would be available to reinvest in the business, or for gifting to
cultural realm institutions (see Section 7.4.17), or even for subsidising
other struggling but worthwhile production (see Section 7.4.16).

In summary:

- Business not to be carried on by and for money. Profit maximis-
  ation is superseded (as shareholding is superseded).
- Efficiently meeting needs with quality goods is the aim, not profit.
- Profit might *result* from this.

Reflections in relation to the present

Our current, profit-maximising ways may have brought goods things,
but they have also brought cost-cutting by the owners of Grenfell
Tower,[234] deception by VW's emissions testers,[235] a former employee

---

[234] A block of flats in London which burned down in 2017, resulting in 74 deaths. It
had recently been fitted with low quality cladding which turned out to be inflammable.
[235] Graham Ruddick and Sean Farrell, 'CO2 findings may cost VW billions more',
The Guardian, 5 November 2015. VW was found to have rigged emission and fuel
consumption tests, a discovery which wiped over €30 billion (some 40%) off the
value of the company.

of 'big pharma' revealing how they were trained to misinform,[236] Apple deliberately slowing down people's older iPhones,[237] plastic recycling waste from UK households being dumped in the Turkish countryside,[238] Advanz Pharma and its affiliates inflating thyroid drug prices by 6,000% over an 8-year period (paying shareholders and directors £400m over the same period whilst avoiding tax in some of those years),[239] and Nestlé's erstwhile practice—exposed in the 1970s—of pushing their baby formula onto struggling African mothers in lieu of nutritionally superior breast milk.[240] The list goes on and on and demonstrates that under a profit-maximising capitalist system, a moral wasteland can so easily ensue where unscrupulous individuals all too frequently find their way to the top of organisations. George Monbiot, describing how bosses of private care companies have found they can get away with paying care workers less than the minimum wage (as they don't have to remunerate for the time spent travelling between clients) observes: 'The more costs and corners they cut, the more profitable their businesses will be. In other words, the less they care, the better they will do. The perfect chief executive, from the point of view of shareholders, is a fully fledged sociopath. Such people will soon become very rich. They will be praised by the government as wealth creators. If they donate enough money to party funds, they have a high chance of becoming peers of the realm. Gushing profiles in the press will commend their entrepreneurial chutzpah and flair. [...] Care workers function as a human loom, shuttling from one home to another, stitching the social fabric back together while many of their employers and shareholders, and government ministers, slash blindly at the cloth, downsizing, outsourcing and deregulating in the cause of profit. [...] One of the most painful lessons a young adult learns is that the wrong traits are rewarded.

---

[236] Jeffrey Roberts, '"We are trained to misinform"—Ex-big pharma sales rep speaks out about the deception in the pharmaceutical industry', 18 March 2015, www.collective-evolution.com.

[237] https://www.bbc.co.uk/news/technology-51413724.

[238] Will Humphries, 'Britain's plastic household waste dumped in Turkey', *The Times*, 17 May 2021.

[239] Rob Davies, 'Drug firm that raised prices by 6,000% paid shareholders £400m', *The Guardian*, 31 July 2021.

[240] Mike Muller, 'Nestlé baby milk scandal has grown up but not gone away', *The Guardian*, 13 February 2013.

[…] A study testing British senior managers and chief executives found that on certain indicators of psychopathy their scores exceeded those of patients diagnosed with psychopathic personality disorders in the Broadmoor special hospital.'[241]

Observing such phenomena, one can very easily worry that we might have lost our way as a human race. As Nelson Mandela said: 'We are, in this modern globalised world, each the keeper of our brother and sister. We have too often failed that moral calling.'

All the same, the many thousands or even millions of examples of not-for-profit enterprise that have been operating for decades in so-called advanced economies are cause for great encouragement. All manner of charities, social enterprise, co-operatives[242], environmental initiatives, community benefit societies, ethical businesses, as well as state-run social services and healthcare, already form a well-established—if minority—part of our economic landscape. They are well loved by those involved with them, and indeed, as already alluded to, the pride and love the British have for their National Health Service demonstrates just how people can value the idea of a service existing in order to meet a need rather than to make money.

Is this so outrageous? Smaller scale examples of not-for-profit enterprise would also include the likes of Community Supported Agriculture where the aim is to provide good quality produce, not to cut every corner possible (harming people, the environment and animal welfare) in order to maximise profit. CSA schemes don't, for example, surreptitiously try to increase the subscriptions of existing members whilst at the same time entice new members in with lower subscriptions, in the way that a number of duplicitous, profit-maximising utility companies have been exposed as doing. Business is fair, above board, and based on a simple, honest wish to provide a decent service and cover costs.

7.4.14 Remuneration—Part 2

As you may recall from 'Remuneration—Part 1' (Section 7.3.4), Steiner is emphatic that labour per se should not be seen as a commodity, and

---

[241] George Monbiot, '"Wealth creators" are robbing our most productive people', *The Guardian*, 31 March 2015.

[242] Especially those which are not set up purely out of the self-interest of the members.

so should not itself be bought with a wage. Involving relationships of power between two or more co-workers in an enterprise, labour is seen as a rights matter, is something to be protected and regulated in the rights domain, not the economic. Such protections should cover not only workplace hazards, working time limits, sickness arrangements, and so on, but also protection from exploitation, and so include the right of all workers to share in company proceeds, to share what they have produced together.

But if labour is to be entirely removed from the economic realm and never purchased with a wage, and if income is to come from a *right* to company proceeds, then why are we now considering income under the operational suggestions for the *economic* realm? This is because company proceeds come from the sale of commodities, and commodities are part of the economy. A right to a share of company proceeds amounts to a distribution of commodities—or sale proceeds, which represent commodities. Income is from sales of commodities (economic domain) not from labour (rights domain). Labour and income are thus separate. Furthermore, in relation to remuneration, Steiner advocates a 'division on economic principles', as we shall see.

The following comments further establish the sharing principle:

> *Before workers enter the factory, they will know how much and how long they need to work [this having been established, democratically, in the rights domain, RM] ... They will only need to discuss distribution of what is produced in collaboration with the employer. [...] Contracts will only govern distribution of what has been produced, not labour itself. (CW330(iii), p. 64)*
>
> *I have often pointed out that in modern times labour has become a commodity. Ordinary work contracts are based on this; they are based on the amount of work the labourer does for his employer. A healthy relationship cannot arise if the contract is settled in terms of so much labour, for labour must be treated as a rights question, settled by the political state, on the basis of the goods that are produced being divided between those who do the physical work and those who do the intellectual work. The contract can be made solely on the goods produced and not on the relationship of labourer and employer. This is the only way to put the matter on a healthy footing.*

But people ask: where do the social evils associated with capitalism come from? They say they come from the capitalist economic system. But no evils can arise from an economic system. They arise in the first place because we have no real labour laws to protect labour, and secondly because we fail to notice that the way the workers are denied their due share amounts to a living lie. But why have they been deprived? Not because of the economic system but because the social order itself allows the possibility of the individual capacities of the employer to be unjustly rewarded at the expense of the workers. The division of the proceeds ought to be made in terms of goods, for these are the joint product of the intellectual workers and the labourers. But if by virtue of your individual capacities you take something from someone which you have no right to take, what are you doing? You are cheating him, taking advantage of him! You have only to look these circumstances straight in the face to realise that the trouble does not lie in capitalism but in the misuse of intellectual i.e. spiritual capacities. Here you have the connection with the spiritual world. If you start by making the spiritual organisation healthy, so that spiritual, intellectual capacities are no longer permitted to take advantage of those who have to labour, then you will be bringing health into the social organism as a whole. (CW193, pp. 84-85)

When blue collar and white collar workers meet with each other, they need only consider economic issues because legal matters will be dealt with separately under the state's jurisdiction. The blue collar worker can associate freely with the manager of the business, because only the division, on economic principles of that which they have earned together will be allowed; there will be no economic compulsion resulting from the greater economic resources of the manager. The associative structuring of the economic body will place the blue collar worker's contractual relationship to the business manager in a totally different light. Up to now, he has been forced to fight against the interests of the business manager, but in his new associative role he will share in the fruits of production. Through the heightened awareness he has gained as a consumer, he will cultivate and profit by—rather than oppose—the same interest in production as the manager. (CW24, p. 10)

If productivity is increased, for example, this is not just something that will lead to more profit for business leaders; it will lead to a larger cake for *all* workers to share.

> *Human labour can only be freed from its commodity character—and it must be so freed—if the only type of contract that is possible between employer and employee does not relate to the work performed but instead to what properly serves a healthy organism, namely, to the distribution of the goods and services jointly produced. This is the demand that hides behind the Marxist theory of surplus value. And this is the way one must go beyond Marxist thinking. The question must be asked: how should the wage relationship end? How should the employment contract be replaced by a goods distribution contract? (CW329, 17 March 1919)*

If, instead of labour being purchased, if, instead of wages, all involved in a company have the right to a share of the profits / proceeds, then wasteful strike action becomes unlikely. The resentful feeling the worker once had of a compulsion to work, possibly for degrading levels of pay, is removed. Instead the worker enters freely into work in the sense that there is no master-servant dynamic. You are not working for me and in return I give you some money (employment contract). We work together and share the proceeds. Profit sharing prevents management from paying ever lower wages in order to increase profit and / or their own income, and so workers no longer need harbour the suspicion that management is exploiting them, profiting from the value added by the workers. Also, profit sharing engenders the realisation, by all working in an enterprise, that personal income can only be available if (a) products are made, and (b) people buy them; it emphasises this simple economic reality. No sales, no income. Instead of people 'working for a living', instead of them expecting to be paid for simply turning up to work, a collaborative, sharing paradigm encourages all to do a good job to meet the needs of customers. Personal income will then ensue.

> *People think so strongly in terms of today's societal makeup that they are simply not aware how, in reality, wages as such are a social untruth. In reality, the situation is such that the so-called wage earner collaborates with the head of an enterprise, and what takes place*

> *is really a debate as to how to distribute the proceeds—only this is concealed behind all sorts of deceptive circumstances, mostly behind power relationships and the like. Talking somewhat paradoxically, one could say that, even today, wages don't in fact exist, only the distribution of profit exists; except that normally he who is the economically weaker party feels short-changed by the distribution. That's all there is to it. One ought not simply superimpose onto a reality something that is based on a social error. As soon as the social structure is such as I have presented it ... it becomes obvious how a collaboration / co-working exists between the so-called employer and so-called employee, and how these terms then no longer apply, but instead how a distribution relationship exists. Then the whole wage phenomenon basically loses its meaning. (CW332a(ii), p. 73)*

One might wonder: would exploitation *really* be prevented by management and workers entering into contracts to share company proceeds? Couldn't management simply say to a worker: 'We will share as follows—for each rouble that you receive, we will receive two (or two hundred!)'? However, since Steiner emphasises all come to the table as free and equal collaborators, not as workers and work givers, then workers might have to agree to management's share just as much as management would have to agree that of workers. Until agreement has been reached by *all* sides, and contracts signed, no one gets anything. Powerful stuff! This interpretation is perhaps supported by the following where he says that remuneration arising from ...

> *... the use of capital and individual human abilities must derive, as is the case with all spiritual effort, from the free initiative of the doer on one side, and the free appreciation of those others who require his efforts on the other. The determination of the amount of these proceeds must be in agreement with the doer's own free insight into what is suitable, taking into consideration his preparation, expenditures, and so forth. His claims in this respect will be satisfied only when his efforts are met with appreciation.*
>
> *Through the kind of social arrangements described here, the ground can be prepared for a truly free contractual relation between manager and worker. This does not mean an exchange of commodities, i.e. money, for labour power, but an agreement as to the share each of the persons who jointly produce the product is to receive. (CW23, p. 89)*

The management will only receive the remuneration they are hoping to receive if their efforts are 'met with appreciation'. In theory, then, all in the organisation must agree to how the cake is to be divided. All need to discuss, collaborate, *associate*. It is not a case of management simply dishing out remunerational fait accomplis to workers. The following remarks also convey how the association principle of the economic domain ideally finds expression, first of all, within the microcosm of a single enterprise.

> *Associations work towards the harmonizing of interests, so that ... the interests between employers and workers are harmonized. Today we see how out of a diseased economic body the opposite of associative life is created, we see how passive resistance, locking out, sabotage and even revolutions come about. No-one with a healthy mind can deny that all this works in the opposite direction of the associative principle and that all this: sabotage, lock-outs, revolution and so on are symptoms of disease of the social organism that must be overcome through that which works in a harmonizing way. (CW79, 30 November 1921)*
>
> *The old misguided ways need to be abandoned where entrepreneurs sit up on high and, at best, behave paternalistically, while on the other side there are workers organized into trade unions ... This gap must first be bridged, and this cannot be done otherwise than by preparing real associations, real associations which consist in associating people from one side—from the entrepreneurial side, the management side, the spiritual worker side—and from the other side, the workers. In the first instance, an economic, a really social, economic association which embodies co-operation between consumers and producers cannot be formed. (CW337b, 11 October 1920)*

Such ideas are radical for many with a Western mindset, especially those unfamiliar with the likes of worker co-ops. The partnership business model is common enough; but that it should ideally be applied to every kind of enterprise, and in each case *include every worker*? That is certainly novel! To the extent that such an arrangement improves the lot of the lower-paid, one might be tempted to think of it as left-wing. But it must be remembered that Steiner had no time for socialism's ideas of community-run or state-run enterprise; the political system should only concern itself with laws.

The above quotes also confirm that a sharing of company proceeds need not mean that all have an *equal* share. Saying 'an agreement as to the share each of the persons who jointly produce the product is to receive' does not imply equal shares. Equality may be the guiding principle for the rights sphere. In the rights sphere there is a universality that says health and safety in work, for instance, applies to *all*; or holiday entitlement applies to *all*; or all have a right to a just share of company proceeds along *economic lines*:

> ... only the division, on economic principles of that which they have earned together will be allowed; there will be no economic compulsion resulting from the greater economic resources of the manager. (CW24, p. 10)

Division 'on economic principles' does not mean division into equal segments; it means division according to consumption needs— ascertained in brotherly association wherein the respective needs of the parties are taken into account.

The following comments remind us of the sorts of factors Steiner would see as justifying differing remuneration levels, as considered in Section 7.3.4 ('Remuneration—Part 1').

> ... the working head of a family will have a higher income than a single person. (CW23, p. 115)
>
> For example, the father of a family will stand quite differently within the social organism than a single person because, if the rights state really does develop as I propose, then every child will have the right to education, then the situation will not be that the father of the family has to distribute his meagre earnings over a large family, whilst a single person can consume everything for himself. The situation will be completely different. (CW331, 22 May 1919)

The right to a share is a rights-life matter; an associatively structured economic system can take care of distribution arrangements in each individual case, however. The meeting of needs is accomplished not by the rights realm but by the economic:

> *The right to necessities is a given. That is assured by an economic process that is real. Anyone who produces something will simply have the opportunity through the economic process to procure goods, which is much safer than an abstract right to do so. (CW331, 22 May 1919)*

> *... what today is called a minimum wage is thought of in terms of the wage relationship. [...] This question will have to be settled in economic life. The question then comes down to: whoever produces something will have to, in return, receive enough to meet his own and his dependants needs until he has again produced a like product. (CW337a, 30 May 1919)*

Of course, 'to each according to his needs' is not something that originates with Steiner and his 'fair price'; indeed, it predates Marx. But Steiner lays out particular tools for steering remuneration in this more equitable direction: (a) the rights domain confers the right to a share of company proceeds, (b) associative dialogue between workers and management arrives at a distribution they are content with ('an agreement as to the share each of the persons who jointly produced the product is to receive'), and (c) associative dialogue between the enterprise and its customers, with a view to aiming for 'fair price'. Where an enterprise employed tens of thousands, then workers would presumably need to elect representatives to voice their interests when associative discussion took place. Although somewhat akin to a trade union, such representation would operate within a more collaborative context than the adversarial ones of which Steiner despairs.

One can imagine that in some work scenarios people might still want to consider increased remuneration as compensation for more exacting work. For example, for anyone having to do night shifts (e.g. a midwife), it might be agreed that those enduring such unsocial sleep patterns should be due a slightly higher share than others, or possibly more holiday entitlement.

Management, too, might be thought of by their workforce as deserving extra remuneration if their position necessitated them taking stressful responsibilities home with them at night. They might be deemed to be allowed more comfort (e.g. to eat out more often) than others who could leave their work at work. But how do you measure this worry? Often management positions are in fact more enjoyable than more menial positions. There might at least be a general consensus within a firm that a degree of unequal sharing be acceptable provided no one's remuneration ever exceeds four times anyone else's. Or six times. Or whatever. Those with greater experience or responsibility, those who have to 'take the job home with them', could perhaps have a higher share for their additional troubles, in addition to those with higher needs. It would be down to all co-workers to agree these things.

Steiner's contemporary, the industrialist Henry Ford (who I seem to like quoting!), made an interesting observation regarding people's reluctance to take on additional responsibility in his factory employing tens of thousands of workers: 'Scarcely more than five per cent of those who work for wages, while they have the desire to receive more money, have also the willingness to accept the additional responsibility and the additional work which goes with the higher places ... The vast majority of men want to stay put. They want to be led. They want to have everything done for them and have no responsibility. Therefore, in spite of the great mass of men, the difficulty is not to discover men to advance, but men who are willing to be advanced.'[243] To what extent this applies today, I don't know. But it does suggest that additional pay might be in order for those with additional responsibility, expertise or worry. It can represent something of a luxury to be able to go home and switch off, and not have to engage in extra training, etc.

However, an issue with higher remuneration for more exacting work is that it then takes one away from the decoupling of work from income which Steiner sees as so important. Perhaps one could simply say: the more that any sharing arrangement observed his decoupling ideal, the healthier it would be in his eyes. Or, conversely, the more different seniority levels in a firm came with differing levels of pay, the less healthy this would be. And then just leave it at that. These are, after all, *suggestions*.

---

[243] Henry Ford, *My Life and Work* (Hawthorne, CA: BN Publishing, 2008), p. 70.

Further confirmation that Steiner is not necessarily talking about *equal* shares for all co-workers is contained in the following:

> ... in place of the so-called employment contract, a distribution contract between the spiritual worker and the physical worker can take place. Of course, former entrepreneurs with practical knowledge can also be included among the spiritual workers, if they get involved. In essence, the joint work of the manual and spiritual workers will underlie the contract, nothing else. They work together on some product and this product has a certain price. Taking into account respective circumstances and possibilities, this price must now be contractually distributed between managers and workers. Labour will no longer somehow be paid for; rather, when you produce goods, or direct such production, then you receive the appropriate share as per the distribution contract. But this can only be implemented when everything that constitutes labour law has been established. (CW331, 23 July 1919)

Presumably, 'taking into account respective circumstances' includes taking into account different needs (number of dependants, etc.). But exactly what is meant by 'and possibilities' is not explicit. Does it mean: good managers in our industry earn such and such, so our only chance of getting a good manager in our own business will be if we can offer at least such and such? But again, this would be marrying a particular level of remuneration to a particular job; it might also be straying from 'fair price'. Whatever Steiner means here, one thing would appear to be clear: that he advocates all within the organisation ideally agree how the cake be divided.

But even *this* conclusion is brought into question in 1920 when an audience member asks: 'Is the distribution of profit share only set within the organisation?' Steiner's response:

> That is not the point at all. In an economic region, individual needs will depend on the whole economic region. And the detail raised—the distribution of profit ['Gewinnanteil'] within the enterprise—does not arise in reality, because this has to come out of association. When someone does this or that work, they must receive this or that for their work product. It simply cannot be a question of setting the profit share within the business, but the whole structure of economic life should determine that one receives one's corresponding profit share. (CW337b, October 1920)

The last sentence is hard to reconcile with '[workers] will only need to discuss distribution of what is produced in collaboration with the employer' (see first quote in this section of the book) or co-workers having 'an agreement as to the share each of the persons who jointly produce the product is to receive'. I am tempted to think that 'It simply cannot be a question of setting the profit share within the business ...' applies more to an economy whose associative nature is advanced, whereas the other two comments (where profit share *is* set within a firm) can apply to any single enterprise in isolation, regardless of the general economic climate. But I concede this interpretation may be open to improvement. Nearly all of Steiner's lectures were taken down in shorthand and then published without him checking the results. So one also has to allow for occasional errors by stenographers. Whatever discrepancies there may be between the above statements, one thing seems certain: in his view, consideration of people's respective needs ought to be the driver behind the determination of remuneration. And this brings us back to the 'fair price' aim where commodity prices are such that producers receive sufficient to cover their (and their dependants') full spectrum of needs—needs that will vary depending on where you live in the world, etc.

So far we have been talking about organisations, about concerns with multiple co-workers. But what about a one-man-band? How would you pay a gardener to cut the hedge, if not by a wage? Steiner would presumably say that, even if you are paying him or her an hourly rate, you are still not paying a wage, you are not paying for the gardener's labour; otherwise you might as well also pay him or her to dig those rhetorical holes and then fill them up again. No, in reality you are paying for the 'cuttedness' of the hedge. Ideally you might pay the gardener on the 'fair price' principle. Indeed, with an hourly rate, you probably do something close to this already, if, that is, the gardener feels they are getting enough to cover what they feel are their reasonable needs (not just their basic needs). In the absence of colleagues or management, an hourly rate agreed between you and your gardener needn't be thought of as constituting the problematic wage relationship, in any case. No one 'above' the gardener is profiting by keeping their hourly rate low. The sole practitioner is not so exploitable if there can be no transfer of Marx's / Engels' surplus value in the direction of management or shareholders.

Steiner confirms the 'fair price' principle would ideally apply in all circumstances:

> *... this cornerstone of economic life—that a man must satisfy his needs until he again produces a like product—applies to all branches of spiritual and material life. (CW337a, 30 May 1919)*

However, for anyone whose work is within the independent cultural domain:

> *Everything necessary for the maintenance of the spiritual organisation, including remuneration, will come to it through the free appreciation of the individuals who participate in the social organism. The sound basis for the spiritual organisation will result from free competition among the individuals capable of spiritual work. (CW23, p. 114)*

> *What someone practices in the field of spiritual life is his own affair. What he is able to contribute to the social organism, however, will be recompensed by those who have need of his spiritual contribution. Whoever is not able to support himself within the spiritual organisation from such compensation will have to transfer his activities to the political or economic section. (CW23, p. 79)*

And as we have seen already in connection with a 'cultural worker' working in the economic realm (e.g. a CEO):

> *The proceeds from the use of capital and individual human abilities must derive, as is the case with all spiritual effort, from the free initiative of the doer on one side, and the free appreciation of those others who require his efforts on the other. The determination of the amount of these proceeds must be in agreement with the doer's own free insight into what is suitable, taking into consideration his preparation, expenditures, and so forth. His claims in this respect will be satisfied only when his efforts are met with appreciation. (CW23, p. 89)*

According to this approach, if a new CEO were recruited for a business, he or she might state what their needs were, remuneration-wise. If those requiring the new CEO's efforts (e.g. the custodians of the capital wishing to appoint, or the workforce, or both) were in agreement, then the new appointment would go ahead.

In addition to *needs* influencing remuneration, Steiner does suggest performance could also be a factor in someone's income going up or down:

> The only thing personally owned by the individual who operates an enterprise should be what he draws in accordance with the terms agreed to when he takes over responsibility for production, and which he feels are appropriate to his individual abilities; and which, furthermore, seem justified by the confidence of others in granting him the use of capital. Should the capital be increased through the activities of this individual, then he would be entitled to a portion of the increase ... (CW23, p. 102)

> The manager and sub-managers of an enterprise will have the means of production to thank for the fact that their abilities can provide them with the income they require. They will not fail to make production as efficient as possible, for an increase in production, although not bringing them the full profit, does provide them with a portion of the proceeds. [...] It is also in the spirit of what is presented here that when production falls off the producer's income is to diminish in the same measure as it increases with an expansion of production. (CW23, p. 113)

To some extent these passages could be seen to be in conflict with the idea of moving away from profit maximisation. This can seem puzzling, considering how disillusioned Steiner was about the ubiquitous pursuit of profit. But he is not proposing to reward *any* increase in profitability, only that arising from improved efficiency / productivity (i.e. not from raised prices, or the cutting of workers' pay, or cutting corners, or outsourcing production to a country where one can get away with paying one's workforce starvation wages). An increase in *productivity* means everyone in society benefits, after all, because greater output is achieved with the same effort (or the same amount of commodities can be produced with less effort, giving people more leisure time to pursue other interests).

These passages could also be seen to be in conflict with the idea of 'fair price', although perhaps only to a small degree. If remuneration as per 'fair price' is supposed to cover one's needs, then in theory this renders bonuses superfluous. But in reality, of course, even when people's needs are fully covered, they are usually happy to have a bit extra, and Steiner seems content with this bit extra where the common good has been served by increased productivity.

One imagines that the remuneration increases / reductions Steiner proposes here—for management—might also apply to their colleagues. That is, if manager remuneration rose on account of increased efficiency, then so too would workers' remuneration. But this is not explicit, and the following reiterates that Steiner does not necessarily envisage uniform remuneration patterns across the workforce:

> *If one person appears to have more income than another, this will only be because this 'more' benefits the community due to his individual abilities. (CW23, p. 114)*

And again in the following, he seems to acknowledge that some people will always end up with more than they need:

> *... whatever a person earns over and above his needs shall be constantly channelled into the spiritual / cultural system. It returns again to the spiritual / cultural sphere.*
>
> *Nowadays this arrangement applies only in the realm of intellectual property, where nobody finds it strange. The person cannot keep his intellectual property for his descendants for more than a certain period—30 years after his death at most—then it becomes public property. We ought to think of this as a possible model for the channelling back of surplus profits into the social organism, even if it is the result of individual effort ... (CW193, p. 83)*
>
> *... a person's surplus performance, made possible by his individual abilities, will be passed on to the community just as the legitimate support for the deficit performance of the less capable will be drawn from the same community. 'Surplus value' will not be created for the enjoyment of individuals, but for the increased supply of intellectual or material wealth to the social organism; and for the cultivation of what is produced within this organism but which is not of immediate use to it. (CW23, p. 116)*

So, after death, the deceased's capital would ideally be put at the disposal of people's capacities so as to serve the common good.

To reiterate, Steiner is at pains to emphasise that all these details are suggestions / illustrations / ideas and, as such, are secondary to his main principle of the threefold articulation of public life. He stresses there is little merit in trying to work everything out in detail, as the social organism must be allowed to 'live'. But, naturally, if one feels his general approach has merit, then trying to understand some of the potential implications, in more detail, might also have merit, even if there are gaps in the picture!

In summary:

- Labour is not a commodity and should not be bought with a wage; work and income are separated.
- Workers and management are collaborators / co-operators / partners, not employees / employers.
- Personal income for sole traders comes from selling their services or wares.
- In organisations, personal income comes from a contractual sharing, between all co-workers, of the proceeds arising from selling goods and services as an enterprise.
- All co-workers to agree the sharing ratios (although on at least one occasion Steiner does also suggest that such ratios could be determined within the 'fair price' formulations of a whole region).
- Those with more dependants or other greater needs receive more income than those with fewer.
- If productivity goes up or down (through increased / reduced efficiencies), the personal income of those concerned can go up or down, but possibly not to the same extent.
- Some (albeit minor) tension exists between this and 'fair price'.
- Some (albeit minor) tension between this and the idea of superseding profit maximisation.
- 'Cultural workers' procure personal income through free appreciation of those in need of their work.
- A person's surpluses are ideally returned to the community (after death), just as the deficit performance of the less capable person is supported by the community.

Reflections in relation to the present

With little prospect of any political party in any Western-style democracy advocating that wage contracts be replaced, across the board, by partnership contracts; and with little prospect of the whole economy and prices becoming associatively managed any time soon, then it must be down to individual enterprises to take a more sharing approach to remuneration unilaterally, if they so wish.

That said, the increasing awareness at UK government level of the extraordinary pay ratios between highest and lowest paid within some organisations is not only cause for modest encouragement but has also lead to one or two—albeit extremely tentative—measures to address the issue. In the UK's 2017 General Election, the Labour Party's manifesto included a commitment that no firms would be appointed for public sector work if the ratio between the lowest and highest paid exceeded 1:20. Expressing each co-worker's remuneration in relation to everyone else's would perhaps represent a small step in the direction of Steiner's sharing principle. Labour's 1:20 proposal would certainly sideline companies whose CEOs earn 100 or 200 times the lowest paid, which most people find excruciating. In the Mondragon Group in Spain, for example, the highest earners earn no more than 9 times the lowest.[244]

The UK's pay ratio legislation[245] that came into force in 2019 is, of course, still about *salaries* rather than the sharing of company proceeds, and it only requires companies to *publish* ratios, not curtail them. But still, this move was made by a Conservative government, which is perhaps noteworthy.

One can imagine these things slowly evolving, with different political parties in the future arguing for different maximum sharing ratios: one saying the highest earner should never take home more than four times the lowest, another party pegging the ratio at forty times, and so on. Such ideas, whilst possibly common sense to many, would

---

[244] A corporation of co-operatives that employs some 75,000 and which, with an annual turnover of about £10bn, is the largest company group in the Basque region of Spain.

[245] UK companies with more than 250 employees are required to publish the ratio between their CEO's pay package and that of their average worker.

undoubtedly be challenging for those of a neo-liberal mindset. But it would seem generally true that the less extreme the ratio, the better. The findings of Richard Wilkinson and Kate Pickett in *The Spirit Level* are clear: in high-income countries, social welfare is more affected by inequality than by wealth! The more unequal a country, the more likely is teenage pregnancy, drug use, obesity, mental illness, school drop-out, community breakdown, lower status for women, lower life expectancy, lack of trust, and imprisonment.[246] To this list one can also add poorer environmental protection. Citing studies confirming this, Kate Raworth observes: 'inequality erodes social capital—built on community connections, trust and norms—that underpins the collective action needed to demand, enact and enforce environmental legislation'.[247]

Concerning more sharing approaches to remuneration which individual enterprises can take and which go—to some extent—in the direction Steiner recommends, we do have various examples of this in 'the West'.

Bonuses and profit sharing are a start, although (a) these usually exist as a supplement to a wage / salary, (b) they are generally seen in companies which also pay dividends to outside shareholders, (c) they usually occur in companies that are profit maximisers, and (d) wage / salary levels almost always correspond to job types. So, any connection to Steiner's more needs-based, sharing suggestions is rather limited.

A number of co-operatives (in the UK, these employ some 225,000 people and turn over £35bn per year)[248] follow a much more equitable approach to remuneration, with some worker co-operatives in the wholefood sector, for example, paying either equal rates for all jobs, or equal rates with increases only relating to length of service.[249] Whilst Steiner might not have advocated equal remuneration for all co-workers, this would seem a far more just approach than one where

[246] Wilkinson, R. and Pickett, K. *The Spirit Level* (London: Penguin, 2009).

[247] Kate Raworth, *Doughnut Economics: Seven Ways to Think Like a 21st-Century Economist* (London: Random House, 2018), p. 172.

[248] www.uk.coop.

[249] Kate Whittle, 'Co-operatives myth: pay is equal for all members', *The Guardian*, 20 June 2013.

management earns remuneration dozens of times that earned by the lowest paid. All the same, when, in 2016, the boss of the Co-op Group asked for his salary to be reduced from £1.25m to £750k because the job had got easier (they were now in calmer waters), one did wonder, despite this being a welcome gesture, to what extent the admirable principle of co-operation lived in the sector.

Partnerships are common in certain types of business, and these are also more in keeping with Steiner's suggestions. But typically these are seen in 'the professions' and, more often than not, partners profit from the work of non-partners. The professions aside, a number of innovative examples exist where a business is owned by a Trust that partly belongs to staff, and where profits are shared amongst all co-workers. The John Lewis Partnership, is one such example. Yes, employees earn a wage, but this is a base remuneration that is paid until the profit is known. Generally, with partnerships, if partner A's remuneration goes up or down by 5%, then so does partner B's. This is a considerable improvement on the employment model where a boss's remuneration typically goes up when a worker's goes down. All the same, at John Lewis, the CEO still earns around £1m per annum— fifty times that of the lowest paid cashier.

Expressing pay grades in terms of percentages would be one way of realising a contractual sharing system. The most basic type of work could be a base against which all remuneration is pegged. The next level up might lead to remuneration of 105% of the base, and the next higher level after that, 110% etc. Under such a sharing system one might nonetheless want to limit the CEO's remuneration to five or ten times the income of the lowest paid, say (although don't forget Steiner's recommendation that any agreement to remuneration claims by 'cultural workers'—including business leaders—be left to those in need of their services (e.g. the others in the business), according to whether or not they appreciate such cultural workers). In a company restricted by Labour's proposed 1:20 policy, a CEO could still receive a 2000% premium as against the base worker. Naturally, for such remuneration principles to work effectively, the organization concerned would have to prevent management being tempted to supply their services through separate companies in order to take higher remuneration. Loopholes of this sort would need to be ironed out if the approach was going to be meaningful.

Under a sharing approach of this sort, however, we are back to remuneration that relates to a particular *job* as opposed remuneration that relates to needs; the separation of work and income that Steiner recommends does not apply.

A further measure proposed by the UK Labour Party (at their 2018 conference)—one that embodied the principle of workers sharing in company proceeds (which they have helped create, lest we forget)—was their proposal that workers receive dividends.[250] In a similar vein, Nick Clegg also had plans to offer companies incentives to make workers shareholders when he was Deputy Prime Minister.[251]

Although, seen from one point of view, it may be attractive to the Exchequer if higher earners bag most of company profits since they can all be taxed at the higher rates of income tax, more money in the pocket of a lower paid worker stimulates demand for goods and services which also generates revenue for the Exchequer (whereas more money in the pockets of multi-millionaires—who already have all the commodities they need—increases the price of real estate etc. as they look for something to buy with their money). Also, when the lowest paid can afford more of those things that make life more agreeable, then the need reduces for policing, youth services, prison services, health interventions, drug rehabilitation and so on, all of which are a drain on the public purse.

Economist Stuart Lansley observes: 'The two most damaging crises of the last century[252]—the Great Depression of the 1930s and the Great Crash of 2008—were both *preceded* by sharp rises in inequality. In contrast, the most prolonged period of economic success and stability—the post-war era to the mid-1970s, a period dubbed the "great levelling"—was one in which the proceeds of growth were evenly shared, between wages and profits and across earnings groups. [...] The central lesson of the last 30 years is that an economic model that allows the richest members of society to accumulate a larger and larger share of the cake brings a dangerous mix of demand deflation,

---

[250] Richard Vaughan, 'Workers would be given dividends by the employer', the *i* newspaper, 24 September 2018.

[251] John Elkington, 'Rediscovering the John Lewis economy', *The Guardian*, 9 March 2012.

[252] Meaning, no doubt, the two most damaging *financial* crises.

asset appreciation and a long squeeze on the productive economy that
will end in prolonged economic turmoil ... To escape today's era of
slow and intermittent growth and prolonged instability requires the
great concentrations of income and wealth to be broken up—just as
they were in the 1930s. Instead, across the globe, the great wealth
divide has continued to grow ... There needs to be wider recognition
that we have been backing the wrong theory on the impact of inequality, with disastrous consequences. A model of capitalism that fails to
share the proceeds of growth more fairly is not sustainable.'[253]

These comments echo the OECD's findings: 'The West's leading
economic thinktank ... dismissed the concept of trickle-down economics as it found that the UK economy would have been more than
20% bigger had the gap between rich and poor not widened since the
1980s ... Trickle-down economics was a central policy for Margaret
Thatcher and Ronald Reagan in the 1980s, with the Conservatives
in the UK and the Republicans in the U.S. confident that all groups
would benefit from policies designed to weaken trade unions and
encourage wealth creation.'[254]

Just how well—not!—'all groups' benefited from such policies
is demonstrated by a whole sea of damning statistics like the ones
cited by Stan Sorscher of the Economic Opportunity Institute (USA)
who charts how, between 1950 and 1975, the income of workers at
least keeps up with productivity growth. But in the mid-70s there is
a decoupling: productivity continues to grow, but workers no longer
share in this. And so those unedifying power dynamics continue to
worsen.[255]

In view of the above, Steiner's sharing approach to remuneration,
as well as greatly furthering social justice, also seems entirely consistent with the wish for a robust economy.

As discussed previously, the idea of different pay grades only for
different levels of task or responsibility is not consistent with his suggestion that remuneration levels should accord more with a person's

---

[253] Stewart Lansley, https://www.opendemocracy.net/openeconomy/stewart-lans-
ley/tackling-inequality-new-role-for-state, 19 March 2012.
[254] Larry Elliott, 'Revealed: how the wealth gap holds back economic growth', *The
Guardian*, 8 December, 2014.
[255] www.eoionline.org/blog/x-marks-the-spot-where-inequality-took-root-dig-here/.

needs. Someone with more dependants needs to buy more carrots! If sharing ratios were based on (or at the very least, influenced by) things like numbers of dependants, rather than on different types of work, then greater progress would be made towards what Steiner would regard as healthy. When I joined social bank Mercury Provident plc[256] in the 1980s, I distinctly remember the nice 'warm' feeling I got about the fact that colleagues with more dependants had a higher income than those with fewer (even though I had none). However, any organisation wishing to consider such an approach needs to be mindful of any 'equal pay for equal work' or 'equal pay for work of equal value' regulations that apply within their respective jurisdiction. Such rules can safeguard important principles of gender equality in work, for example, and any organisation wishing to pay more according to co-workers' needs would have to satisfy themselves that this could be done within prevailing employment rules.[257]

Concerning Steiner's principle of a person's surplus performance being returned to the community: our system of progressive income tax—where anything one earns above a certain limit is taxed at a higher rate—achieves this to *a small* extent. However, if someone has a stratospheric income, they still keep a good half of it, even if this half could be considered many times what would be needed to cover even the most lavish needs. Steiner's suggestion that capital / savings be allocated to the common good after death is also addressed by inheritance tax—but only in part, since he proposes all of a person's estate (including large personal gifts made during the benefactor's life) be returned to the community so many years after death, not just 40%—or whatever your country's inheritance tax rate might be.

7.4.15 Savings and loans

Notwithstanding the 'fair price' ideal—where prices are such that personal income is enough to cover the full set of one's needs until

---

[256] A bank founded by UK anthrosophists that later become the UK branch of Triodos Bank.

[257] In the UK, for example (or England, at least), we have the Equal Pay Act 1970 as amended by the Equal Value Regulations 1983 and the Sex Discrimination Acts of 1975 and 1986, which were superseded by the Equality Act 2010.

one has again produced a like item, Steiner did not preclude personal savings from his analysis, even though savings could (repeat, *could*) suggest income that is over and above needs. However, we all need to replace our car now and then, for example, and savings make this possible. As do loans, of course. If my car packs up, I will either have to buy a new one with savings, or if I don't have savings, I will need to borrow in order to make the purchase. I might borrow from my bank or I might buy in instalments, effectively borrowing from the car seller or some related third party. It would seem impractical if the remuneration of a 'fair price' worker would have to suddenly go up every so many years in order to cover a large, infrequent purchase such as a car. If I were to work at a particular firm for just a year, say, and my old car reached the end of its life during this time, to burden this firm (and its customers) with the full cost of my new car needs would raise more than trifling issues. A house purchase[258] would be even more problematic in this respect.

One must also remember that 'fair price' is something Steiner suggests one *aims for*; it will rarely—if ever—be some easy-to-work-out, exact figure that can be arrived at without further ado. For those needing a car, 'fair-price' remuneration would need to include an element for workers to either (a) put in their piggy bank for the next vehicle purchase, or (b) to repay the loan relating to the previous car purchase. In light of this, even in a highly threefold context, there will always be people earning over and above what they need to cover their immediate day-to-day expenses, and thus there will always be people with savings (in a region with a thriving economy, at least).

Another consideration in connection with savings is whether 'fair price' remuneration would feature a pension element for your

---

[258] Although the threefold approach does not view land as a commodity to be bought and sold, but as something over which *rights* of use are *granted*, a house (as opposed to the land on which it sits) is different. As nature modified by labour to form a consumer good, a house *is* part of the economic realm. It would naturally need to come with the automatic right to live on the plot of land on which it sat. As a rights matter, the right to occupy the piece of land where one's dwelling is sited is a matter for the democratic process. The democratic process is unlikely to deny citizens the right to live somewhere, i.e. the right to occupy a plot of building land, or at least a part thereof!

eventual retirement. If one momentarily 'thinks away' money, then it is clear that, in reality, it is people of working age who provide for retirees. They bake their bread, make their clothes, and work in the power stations that generate their electricity. Indeed, even if you 'think money back again', one's current pension contributions—certainly in the case of a state pension—could be thought of as maintaining current retirees, not as something being saved for one's own future.

The traditional view, of course, is that, if one invests for one's retirement, the investment enables companies to procure plant and equipment which results in future productivity. Future income arises, in part, thanks to our investment, so we should be due some of it. As you may recall, though, external ownership of the means of production does not fit well with threefolding. The finished means of production are not goods for consumption. Ideally, they are excluded from the buying / selling paradigm of the economy. Lending, however, is clearly acceptable in Steiner's eyes. Apart from his general comments about 'fair price' being such that the needs of dependants and those unable to work (which could include pensioners) should be covered, over and above the needs of the earner / worker, I am not aware of any specific comments he makes about pensions, about what mechanism he would see as the most healthy for covering the needs of retirees. But his suggestion, for example, that widows should have the *right* to a decent maintenance confirms that such things also have a rights-realm dimension (where things are decided democratically) as well as an economic-realm dimension.

Particularly unconventional, although not unique, is Steiner's idea that money should ideally depreciate, have a fixed lifespan, a 'use-by date'. This is covered later in Section 7.4.20 ('Dying money'), but insofar as it relates to savings:

There is something extremely unnatural today in the social order. This consists in the fact that money increases when a person simply possesses it. It is put in a bank and interest is paid on it. This is the most unnatural thing that could possibly exist. It is really utterly nonsensical. The person does nothing whatever. He simply banks the money, which he may not even have acquired by labour but may have inherited, and he receives interest on it. This is utter nonsense. But it will become a matter of necessity ... that money shall be used when it exists ... It must be used. It must be put into circulation and the actual affect will be that money does not increase but that it diminishes. If at the present time a person possesses a certain sum of money, he will have approximately twice that amount in fourteen years under a normal rate of interest, and he will have done nothing except merely had to wait. (CW186, p. 62)

Monetary investment must become subject to the fate of all other goods. Our current economy expects capital investment to double over a period of time. In a healthy economy, however, invested funds would vanish over that same time period, simply ceasing to exist. Today people are horrified by the suggestion that their monetary investment will not double in 15 years but will simply vanish because it is consumed or depreciated along with the goods it is used to purchase. Of course certain types of savings could be exempt from this rule. (CW333, p. 13)

One wonders what might have been in the back of Steiner's mind when he says certain types of savings could be exempt. Is he thinking about savings up to a certain level? Savings for a pension? Savings arising from work but not from ownership or inheritance? This is not clear. But the idea of making money simply by owning money is problematic.

There cannot be any 'interest on interest'. (CW23, p. 120)

... what amounts to interest on interest is strictly rejected ... So the capital growth that we see today, where capital can double in fifteen years, is impossible ... I'm talking about a legitimate interest rate. (CW331, 24 June 1919)

With share ownership being opposed (since, under threefolding, only commodities should be bought and sold, not the finished means of production), then receiving a return (dividend) *as well as* capital appreciation is out. Kate Raworth takes a somewhat similar view, inviting us to imagine if: 'enterprises raised finance not by issuing shares to outside investors but by issuing bonds, promising their stakeholder-investors not a slice of ownership but a fair fixed return'.[259]

Although shareholding is problematic, Steiner recognises that savings have a positive role to play. But without shares (or derivatives) being available, the options open to people with savings which they wanted to keep (i.e. not spend or give away), and who didn't want to set up their own business, would be to either (a) make loans directly to borrowers, (b) deposit their savings in a bank or some other lending institution, or (c) put them under the proverbial mattress.

> *Whoever has accumulated savings has surely also rendered services which entitle him to claim reciprocal services in the form of commodities, just as present day efforts give claim to reciprocal efforts; but these claims are subject to limits ... (CW23, p. 120)*
>
> *... earnings, acquisitions and savings which result from the individual's own work will remain in his personal possession until his death, or in his descendants' possession until a later date. Until this date, interest (the amount of which is to be determined from rights awareness and set by the rights-state) will be paid by whoever receives such savings for the procurement of means of production ... What someone saves and makes available for production serves the general interest, for it makes the management of production through individual human abilities possible in the first place. (CW23, p. 104)*

That is, savings generate loan capital that can be used to build factories, etc. What is curious, though, is that some of the above comments make mention of savings lasting beyond an individual's death, and others make mention of savings disappearing after fifteen years or so—with possible exemptions. One way to reconcile these two viewpoints could be to interpret them as meaning: those savings that are exempt from depreciation could last up to or beyond the individual's death. Another interpretation might be that the depreciation of savings is an ideal, but that the reality is such that a certain level of savings is both unavoidable as well as beneficial to society, and so savings need to be allowed to have their place.

---

[259] Kate Raworth, *Doughnut Economics: Seven Ways to Think Like a 21st-Century Economist* (London: Random House, 2018), p. 190.

Notwithstanding the useful role that savings can play, Steiner is clear that those lending into industry should only receive what he terms 'legitimate interest' but not bag all the profits (see Section 7.4.20). Profits / 'capital increase' exist, after all, thanks to the overall social organism, not least: the workers in the operation, the customers, the workers who designed or made the means of production, those who educated the designers, those who fed these people, and so on. Profits should not all accrue to me simply because I put up the funding at the beginning. Indeed, my ability to invest may in any case not have been entirely down to my own efforts. I may have 'earned' it thanks to others who laboured for me in some other enterprise. (I may have even inherited it because my great-grandfather was an imperialist parasite!)

Steiner sees associations within the economic realm as being best placed to guide lending decisions such that investment is made in those activities that society most needs:

In the old natural economy, one individual depended on another. Men were forced to work together, to bear with one another. They had to agree on certain arrangements, otherwise the economic life could not go on. Under the financial system the capitalist is, of course, also dependent on those who work, but he is quite a stranger to these workers. How close was the tie between consumer and producer in the old natural economy in which actual commodities were dealt with! How remote is the person who transacts business in money from those who work in order that his money may yield interest! A deep gulf has opened up between one human being and another. They do not get near to each other under the financial system of economy. This is one of the first things to be considered if we wish to understand how the masses of workers (no matter whether they are intellectual or manual workers) can again be brought together with those who also make business possible by lending capital. This, however, can only be done through the principle of association, by which men will again unite with each other as men. The principle of association is a demand of social life, but a demand such as I have described it, not one resembling those that often figure in socialistic programmes. (CW332a, p. 40)

Take the case of one who has money to lend. You will not let him lend in a senseless way; you will bring him into connection with his association. The association will act as a mediator. The association will provide him with the most sensible way in which to lend, or again, with the most sensible way in which to give ... The important thing is to bring about sensibly and in accordance with reason the things which happen in any case in the economic process but behind a mask. (CW340, p. 159)

The economic life in a threefold social order is built up by the co-operation of associations arising out of the needs of producers and the interests of consumers. These associations will have to decide on the giving and taking of credit. In their mutual dealings the impulses and perspectives that enter economic life from the cultural and legal spheres will play a decisive part. These associations will not be bound to a purely capitalist point of view. One association will deal directly with another; thus the one-sided interests of one branch of production will be regulated and balanced by those of another.

Responsibility for the giving and taking of credit will thus be left to the associations. This will not impair the scope and activity of individuals with special faculties; on the contrary, only this method will give individual faculties full scope. The individual is responsible to his or her associations for achieving the best possible results. The association is responsible to other associations for making good use of these individual abilities. Such a division of responsibility will ensure that the whole activity of production is guided by complementary and mutually corrective points of view. The individual's desire for profit will no longer impose production on the life of the community; production will be regulated by the community's needs, which will make themselves felt in a real and objective way. The need one association establishes will be occasion for the granting of credit by another. (CW24, p. 47)

Thus, within the context of associations, a banking / lending / investment-directing function would operate, acting as intermediary between saver and enterprise.

Given that, elsewhere, we have seen how Steiner advocates that bodies within the *cultural* domain ultimately be responsible for ensuring capital / the means of production are placed at the disposal of those individuals most capable of managing them for the benefit of all, it might at first seem inconsistent that here he is suggesting associations (i.e. facilities within the *economic* realm, not the cultural) would be instrumental in directing capital towards this or that producer. But the difference is simply this. Those working for associations in the *economic* realm would be involved in directing funds to this or that industrial concern; and those *cultural* realm bodies ultimately responsible for the means of production would be involved in ensuring the right *individuals* would *manage* the industrial concern (if a departing CEO did not wish or was not able to make this choice). Associations would have the best sense of where the need lay for expanded or new production, and thus where the need lay for finance.

Further:

> In the long run, credit cannot work in a healthy way unless the giver of credit feels himself responsible for all that is brought about thereby. [...] Theoretically, no one will want to deny that a larger sense of responsibility is necessary in the present-day world of business and economic affairs. To this end, associations must be created that will work to confront individuals with the wider social aspects of all their actions. (CW24, p. 50)

In this connection, the idea of ethical investment and of being conscious of the ramifications of one's investment decisions has grown considerably in many parts of the world over the course of the last four decades or so. Indeed, ethical investment is now a multi-billion pound 'industry'.

For Steiner (amongst others), one of the most damaging uses of capital is land-banking—where, simply as a means to preserve wealth, one either buys land, or lends to someone else, against mortgage, so that they can buy land. In his view, the best use of capital / savings (other than giving them away to further independent cultural life such as education) is that they are used as loans to enable production, to enable enterprise.

> Take the case of credit on land. In a healthy social life, an individual or a group possessing the necessary abilities may be given credit on land, enabling them to develop it by establishing some kind of production. It must be a development that seems justified on that land in light of all the cultural conditions involved. If credit

> *is given on land from the purely capitalist viewpoint, in the effort to give it a commodity value corresponding to the credit provided, use of the land which would otherwise be the most desirable is possibly prevented. (CW24, p. 46)*
>
> *In a healthy economic process we must not and cannot give 'real credit'—credit based on the security of land—even to a person working on the land. He too should only receive personal credit— that is to say, credit which will enable him to turn the capital to good account … It is one of the worst possible congestions in the economic process when capital is simply united with nature … (CW340, p. 65)*
>
> *… the evil damming up of capital on the land by capital investment, which is so ruinous for the economic life. (CW340, p. 154)*

By 'personal credit' Steiner does not here mean a loan to buy a car or washing machine; he means a loan to enable the borrower to apply their personal capacities in production, in enterprise, in service.

In a country that had fully taken threefolding to heart, the purchase and sale of land would be avoided, as has been established. Someone wanting to build a factory would instead be *allocated* an appropriate piece of land by the rights realm, on recommendation perhaps from the economic realm that this would meet a clear need, and on recommendation from the relevant capital-stewarding (and capacity-assessing) body within the cultural realm that this person had the requisite skills. Finance to build this factory, however, would not be secured on the *land*, since the land would have no value—in the sense that it would not be sellable.

In the climate we are used to, though, where land is bought and sold, any loan would ideally still not be *based on* the security of the land. That is, whilst the loan might be necessary to buy the land, the decision to lend would need to be on the strength of future productivity (which can also include delivery of cultural services) for it to be a healthy decision in Steiner's eyes. Whether this implies that land should not even be used as security when a loan *is* financing productivity is open to debate. Indeed, Steiner has even been interpreted by some as implying *no* form of security (not even personal guarantees, for example) should *ever* be taken, which, to my knowledge, he never said. This could certainly deter some people with savings from making loans if there was a possibility to make secured loans elsewhere (or deposit in a bank which made secured loans). Whichever interpretation one takes, what is clear is that, in Steiner's view, it is unhealthy to make loans to unproductive people, i.e. to enable land purchase such that the only point of the purchase is that the land will act as a store of value, of wealth. Loans should not be made simply because the value of the asset being purchased will be able to repay the loan. Loans should only be made to enable productivity. As we know, when land is bought as a store of value this can also increase land prices generally, because the very act of purchasing it promotes its scarcity.

In summary:

- With share ownership not being consistent with the threefold approach, loans have an important role in business start-up and expansion.
- The rights realm to set the interest rate from time to time (possibly with guidance from the economic).
- Lenders to have no share in profits beyond what Steiner terms 'legitimate interest'.
- Credit to be advanced for productivity, not simply to buy land with no intention to produce (i.e. 'personal credit' is fine but not 'real credit').
- Associations to perform an intermediary function, guiding the giving and taking of credit.
- Associations to encourage greater social responsibility by confronting individuals with the wider social effects of their actions.
- Investments ideally decrease in value over time, not increase. Some savings, however, could be exempt.

Reflections in relation to the present

Although, sadly, it is by no means the case that all savers are confronted with the wider implications of their investment decisions, the sizeable increase in ethical investment in recent decades means those who wish to save ethically can find a range of investment possibilities to suit. Much ethical investment exists within the share-holding, profit-maximising world, of course, where 'negative screening' (*avoiding* certain sectors) enables savers to at least steer clear of certain industries that are blatantly bad for people, like tobacco or armaments. An organisation like Vigeo Eiris provides research and rating services in this area, canvassing investors as to their ethical preferences, and screening investment opportunities accordingly. Whilst ownership of the means of production by those not active in the business is something Steiner cautions against, having some appreciation of the consequences of one's investment decisions is, at least, a start.

In addition to those ethical investment advisers who provide 'negative screening' services, other institutions offer 'positive screening', where only enterprise that actively promotes social and environmental health is financed. Triodos Bank, for example, not only lends exclusively into such sectors, but also publishes a complete list of its borrowers so that those depositors wishing to make a positive impact with their savings are able to do so in a very informed way. A level of transparency is maintained where all can see what is going on.

If Steiner's associative approach was common and widespread, however, then the savings-and-loans process would entail even greater overview of the economy as a whole. Those working within associations or the central economic administration, who were in a position to see the areas of greatest economic need, would convey to savers and banks that there was a need, say, for more housing or hospital beds, and that there were already more than enough office blocks. Lending would thence be encouraged into the construction of dwellings and hospitals, not offices. An institution like Triodos Bank does fulfil this function to *some* extent as it does try to closely consider the needs of society.

In relation to this, and also to Steiner's concern that loans be given to *producers* rather than to enable non-producers to buy land (which only encourages landlordism), it is interesting to note that George Monbiot et al, in their 2019 *Land for the Many* proposals proffered to the UK Labour Party, suggested the Bank of England 'should use credit guidance and other macroprudential tools to encourage a shift in bank lending away from real estate and towards more strategically useful sectors of the economy'.[260] Along similar lines, economist and socialist author Grace Blakeley recommends the creation of a public banking system that 'should be used to direct investment into socially desirable areas' (into ventures furthering Green New Deal principles, for example).[261] Although such proposals may be more closely linked to the rights state than Steiner's threefold analysis would recommend, there is nonetheless significant overlap here with his suggestions. Such proposals share the aim of steering finance in a more responsible direction, a direction where social and ecological needs are the driving force, not the desires of wealthy investors for profit maximisation.

In some cultures, the concern Steiner has about making money with money is addressed full on. Most—if not all—Islamic banks, for example, have a tradition of avoiding the payment of interest on deposits.

Where any substantial moves in the direction of threefolding coexisted alongside conventional models, one can imagine some conflict might arise with two types of enterprise competing for investment. If conventional models were offering investors the traditional stake in the business, namely, part-ownership of the means of production (shares) plus part of the profit (dividends), or were offering depositors (or their banks) security in the form of (sellable) land / means of production, then new ventures built along more threefold lines might struggle to obtain sufficient levels of loan capital if their business proposition carried even a modicum of uncertainty. If your average saver is going to take risk, they will generally also want the possibility of reward to accompany that risk. So, as long as share ownership and asset-backed loans exist, then the majority of savers will rather plump for these than make risky loans at low interest. Yes, some ethical savers, especially those who are financially comfortable, will take a different view; but the prospects of both types of investment opportunity existing side by side to any meaningful extent could potentially come with challenges. Risky lending along threefold lines could conceivably attract investors in this scenario if the interest rate were high. But the very fact of the need to meet high interest payments might only increase the likelihood of project failure. Notable

---

[260] https://landforthemany.uk.
[261] Grace Blakeley, *Stolen: How to Save the World from Financialisation* (London: Repeater Books, 2019), pp. 235–242.

in relation to this, however, is Steiner's suggestion that, in an associative environment, enterprise would only proceed if it was responding to a pre-investigated, concrete need. That is, with a ready market in the background, possibly even backed up by contracts (advance orders), proposed new enterprise would, in theory, actually be low-risk.

The emergence and increasing popularity, since around 2005, of crowd-lending sites / peer-to-peer lending does suggest there is a growing appetite for more transparent lending, and also a riskier type of lending if the interest rate is higher than otherwise. Although regulated by the Financial Conduct Authority (since 2014), peer-to-peer lending firms are unable to offer the peace of mind that banks can with their £85,000-per-depositor government protection. However, a peer-to-peer 'deposit' can still be lent to a wide range of borrowers, spreading the risk.[262] One can also imagine, in a context where three-folding had indeed been adopted widely in a particular region over an extended period, that associative financial institutions might also collaborate to spread your deposit across their entire lending portfolio, evening out the risk to depositors.

7.4.16 Cross-subsidy

What Steiner says about profitable businesses possibly subsidising loss-making business is, in a way, a rather small point. On the other hand, it serves as a good illustration of just how collaborative he imagines enterprise could become in a healthy economy. It also serves as a further example of how the meeting of needs should take precedence over the pursuit of profit.

> For example, should a company which is fulfilling a need not be in a position to pay its creditors the interest due them on their savings, other companies, in free agreement with all concerned, could make up what is lacking. (CW23, p. 114)

Note that the company deemed deserving of assistance is one that is 'meeting a need'. Note, also, that this comment addresses a problem that came up in the previous section: the problem of business uncertainty

---

[262] http://www.moneysavingsexpert.com/savings/peer-to-peer-lending.

deterring lenders from lending. If cross-subsidy is a possibility, then a business meeting a need that is nonetheless marginal in terms of profitability might still be able to attract adequate inward investment.

The following portrays how subsidy from profitable ventures could also reduce the cost of an expensive import, where necessary:

> *In the same way, the excessively high price of an imported product can be balanced by contributions from businesses that are able to yield returns higher than the requirements of those they employ. (CW24, p. 63)*

If fresh fruit, say, became so expensive that the health of the public was put at risk, the cost of this could be subsidised by firms in other sectors making profits over and above what they needed to cover their own costs.

In summary:

- Steiner sees cross-subsidy between businesses as a valid way to support the meeting of needs, if this cannot be done within the normal course of trade.

Reflections in relation to the present

Whilst the very idea of cross-subsidisation might have most free-marketeers shifting in their seats, one by no means has to look to socialist governments to find the general idea of subsidisation alive and well. Subsidisation of the kind Steiner is talking about might be rare—where a business voluntarily subsidises another business. But, as we know, *government* subsidy, using tax revenues, is an entirely familiar concept. (Of course, ultimately, it is always the economic realm that provides the basis from which tax is collected to make government subsidy possible in the first place.) Government subsidy is often made to protect this or that flagship industry of national importance. Or the intention might be to nudge the population towards more socially or environmentally desirable behaviour. For example, railways or loft insulation might be subsidised in order to reduce pollution. Or new, complex medical equipment or fledgling renewable energy technologies might be supported until these have become mature enough to stand on their own feet. To the horror of many, nuclear energy continues to be subsidised many decades after its introduction.[263]

En passant, it is also interesting to note that those on the neo-liberal, neo-conservative end of the political spectrum seem to have little problem with the idea of taxpayers subsidising *their* industry. Many seem quite content to let the state (taxpayers) bale out banks if there is a banking crisis, for example.

Steiner's cross-subsidy proposals—that bypass the state—would be unrealistic, of course, where producers were pure profit maximisers; these would only laugh at another company asking for a leg-up. But if some of his other recommendations were in place (e.g. (a) an absence of shareholders, (b) sensible formulae for executive remuneration, (c) the resultant departure from profit maximising, (d) collaborative working responding to need), such things would be entirely feasible. Naturally, that's a big 'if'. However, in answer to Margaret Thatcher's 'You can't buck the market!', one might observe: But what you *can* do is create a more conscious and collaborative economy built on association that puts people and planet before profit and so begins to address the extensive and unacceptable suffering that the market paradigm seems poorly equipped to correct. Not quite as snappy, perhaps!

Today there will undoubtedly be members of the co-operative movement, for example, who, if they had surpluses to spare, would be happy to support an ailing fellow co-op in a brotherly way if they felt it was providing a valuable service. And one can certainly imagine, in the fanciful shipwreck example mused over in Section 7.4.3 ('Production according to need'—where the passengers with a conveniently wide range of skills had to start a new society from scratch), that these unintentional pioneers would be quite content to work according to need, transferring excess in one area of work to support another area that was struggling, but nonetheless needed.

---

[263] Damian Carrington, 'Government finally admits it is subsidising nuclear—while cutting help for renewables', *The Guardian*, 22 October 2015.

Indeed, even if a more associative approach was only in its infancy, one can imagine small-scale, localised instances of cross-support between businesses still being quite possible .

One could argue, of course, that in some 'perfect', threefold world, successful enterprises would all be charging a 'fair price' and so excessive profits (over and above those needed for business expansion or funding of cultural realm activity—see next section) would not be available with which to subsidise struggling firms. Two responses to this could be as follows. Firstly, one could say that Steiner mentioning cross-subsidisation only serves to underscore his frequently-made point that a threefold analysis amounts essentially to a set of pointers, a road map, a direction to aim in, and not some seamless and absolute utopian programme wherein the perfect 'fair price' would obtain everywhere. Secondly, one could argue that in the developed world, with its high degree of ingenuity, productivity, automation and the like, there will *always* be extensive surpluses—we will always be able to produce far more than we actually need; and so there will always be surpluses to be found, languishing in this firm or that, that could be directed towards financially precarious business that was fulfilling a need, instead of being channelled to the already wealthy to purchase real estate or hide in offshore tax havens.

Whatever the circumstances, one can imagine that any subsidising enterprise, prior to imparting its largesse, would want reassurance that the need for subsidy had not simply arisen because the struggling firm had abandoned discipline and efficiency, and instead become complacent, flabby, entitled, or even 'too big to fail'!

7.4.17 Gift to education

Far more frequent than Steiner's comments about excess profits being used for cross-subsidisation were his recommendations that such profits be given to freedom-endowed, cultural-realm activity, most notably education.

In Section 7.3.6 ('Taxation') we noted the observations he made in 1919 to the effect that (a) determining education funding levels would necessitate co-operation between the three autonomous realms of society, and (b) personal choice ('free appreciation') is vital at all times in such cultural matters. Education vouchers were then cited as one potential way in which Steiner's proposed criteria could be met.

In 1922, though, when talking to economics students, he approaches the subject from a different angle:

> *But suppose there is too much capital. The several owners of capital will become painfully aware of the fact; they will not be able to start anything with their capital. This is indeed the case if you look into the matter historically. In actual fact, too much capital did arise, and the only way out which it could find was to conserve itself in nature. Thus we witnessed in the economic process the so-called rise in the value of land. (CW340, p. 66)*

The rise in the value of land !

Industrialisation had brought with it tremendous surpluses, at least for some, and in the absence of new investment opportunities, those holding such surpluses could buy land as a means to preserve their wealth and gain rental income, or they could deposit in banks which would lend to others to buy land. This in turn started the relentless increase in land prices which Steiner, and a good many others, argued was unhealthy. Surpluses, he argued, if not used for business expansion, should either be *lent* for enterprise / production (Section 7.4.15) or *given* to aid capacity building—education and other endeavours in the independent cultural life which uplift and enrich all aspects of humanity (including, ultimately, the economy—fertilising it with increased inventiveness).

> *It is a matter of sheer necessity for the capital to be used up ... in order that it may not unite with nature and so become unliving—a petrified deposit, as it were, in the economic process. For capitalised land is in fact an impossible deposit in the economic process. Let me expressly state that there can be no question here of any sort of political agitation. I simply unfold these matters as they take shape ... (CW340, p. 68)*

As we have seen, Steiner advised that, ideally, land would not be bought and sold like a commodity at all.

> *The excess of capital which has been acquired must not be allowed to flow into the land where it would become dammed up. Provision must be made for the elimination of the excess capital. The capital*

> *must not be allowed to become congested in the land. That is to*
> *say, at an earlier stage in the process, the congestion must be pre-*
> *vented by the free gift to spiritual institutions of the excess which*
> *has been acquired. Only what I described as a kind of 'seed' must*
> *be allowed to pass on. It is here that the concept of 'free gift' con-*
> *fronts us inevitably; there must be free gifts. [...] What would oth-*
> *erwise become dammed up in the land must vanish into spiritual*
> *institutions. I say once more, it must somehow vanish into the spir-*
> *itual institutions. It must take effect as a free gift. (CW340, p. 147)*

'Elimination' of excess capital is advocated; it should 'vanish'. A portion of corporate profits might well be used for business expansion if there were a need for more of the products in question. This could be seen as one sort of 'seed'—leading to new production. But the profit used for this is perhaps not *excess* profit. *Excess* profit would presumably be what is left over once enough had been reinvested for business expansion, and all co-workers had been properly paid. This excess, Steiner recommends, should be given to 'spiritual institutions'. In particular, this includes education in the form of schools, universities, research establishments:

> *... the sphere of the completely free spiritual life. In this sphere we*
> *find, above all things, teaching and education. Those who have*
> *to teach and educate stand undoubtedly within the sphere of the*
> *completely free spiritual life. (CW340, p. 77)*

Such education can consume the capital (e.g. by educators being remunerated in order to buy the provisions they need). By honing people's faculties, this education can be seen as another sort of seed—a very potent one which will grow and, sooner or later, bring fresh contributions to society.

Vocational training is mentioned in this connection, too:

> *You can use up the surplus capital [...] to instruct and educate the*
> *workers in one thing or another, so as to be able to transplant them*
> *into other callings. (CW340, p. 71)*

With such an approach, it is argued, harmful land price inflation can be lessened.

In an associatively structured economy, the associations would have a part to play in this process:

> ... the capital which presses to be invested, the capital which tends to march into mortgages and stay there, must be given an outlet into free spiritual institutions. That is the practical aspect. Let the associations see to it that the money which tends to get tied up in mortgages finds its way into free spiritual institutions. There you have the connection of the associative life with the general social life. Only when you try to penetrate the realities of economic life does it begin to dawn on you what must be done in the one case or the other. I do not by any means wish to agitate that this or that must be done. I only wish to point out what is. And this is undoubtedly true: what we can never attain by legislative measures—namely, to keep the excess capital away from nature—we can attain by the life and system of associations, diverting the capital into free spiritual institutions. I only say: if the one thing happens, the other will happen too. (CW340, p. 82)

Although a slight digression from the topic in hand (i.e. gift to cultural institutions), the words 'what we can never attain by legislative measures' are highly noteworthy. Despite Steiner's insistence that land is a rights realm concern, not something to be bought and sold like a commodity (economic realm), he appears to concede here—in 1922—that to hope the rights state might come to *prohibit* its purchase and sale might be unrealistic. This only serves to underscore the role of more micro ways of moving land from the economic system to the rights system, such as via the Land Trust model discussed in Section 7.3.7.

One way, then, of preventing excess profits from increasing land purchase and landlordism is by diverting / gifting such profits, as they arise in economic enterprise, to the cultural domain. In this way, less money ends up chasing a finite land mass.

Another way can be via Steiner's suggestions around inheritance—where, so many years after death, the estate of someone with significant capital is repeatedly gifted onwards to productive people,[264] instead of remaining something which rentier heirs can enjoy ad infinitum.

A third way is by ...

> ... transmitting as much nature-property as possible in the shape of free gifts to those who are spiritually productive. (CW340, p. 82)

That is, land (as opposed to money capital) can be removed from the economic realm (without actually legislating against its purchase and sale) by simply encouraging its gift to the 'spiritually productive' in furtherance of the common good. Again, such land can be held in trust—e.g. a Land Trust—in perpetuity for the benefit of society in such a way that any right to buy and sell it, and extract economic rent from it, is removed. (Here, the rights realm is involved simply inasmuch as ownership of the land becomes a matter of right, not purchase. Such rights can be enshrined in a trust deed, without any blanket legislation coming into force, across the realm, against the sale and purchase of all land.)

As should be clear by now, Steiner was certainly not proposing some sort of revolution or dictatorial coup that would reverse all historical rights, countermand people's land, and appropriate this for 'the new method'! He makes this very clear already in 1917:

> What is here described should not be imagined as a utopian programme; it is not intended to eliminate historical rights and legal structures. To anyone who examines it closely, it represents something that with full awareness of all historical rights and by recognition of factual circumstances can grow without any concerns out of the present state structures. (CW24(ii), p. 100)

His threefold approach was something that could facilitate a gradual movement away from land ownership that comes with rights of *sale*, to something which just comes with rights of *use*.

---

[264] Under direction from specially constituted bodies within the cultural realm, if the deceased's Will does not specify to whom the capital should be entrusted—see Section 7.3.7.

But in relation to the topic in hand (the gift of surplus money to education and other 'free' cultural endeavours that nurture / fertilise / vitalise the cultural / mental / moral / skills life of mankind), one can observe how this transaction plays itself out over time. On the one hand, the teacher is providing a service—a commodity—and so must be paid (see Section 5.3—'Definition of Economic Aspect'). If looked at only from a limited perspective, however, education can appear to involve rather more consumption than production, i.e. teachers and pupils eat, but it is less clear what economic values come back out of the classroom—what this service really amounts to. The pupil may not have even enjoyed it! But as Steiner points out—and as is more or less universally accepted—in the long run such cultural activity is highly productive, in economic terms too:

> *Suppose we have a teacher who is a skilful, well-rounded man. He teaches very young children, primary school children. And assume for the sake of simplicity ... that all the children he teaches become shoemakers. And through his skill, by developing the capabilities of his children so that they becomes smart thinkers and approach their occupation as shoemakers intelligently, and through his practical guidance using all sorts of educational means he makes his children more skilful so that they now become shoemakers who can produce as many boots in ten days, say, as others can in fifteen days ... (CW338, 15 February 2021)*

Although the extra output by all of his pupils is more or less down to the teacher, Steiner defines the *payment* for the initial education, the payment for the teacher's upkeep, not as one of purchase / sale, but as one of gift. This is considered further in Section 7.4.19 ('Three types of money'). There is no quantifiable result at the end of a school lesson; the full economic consequences may only arise years later, or indeed there may be little value to show at all if the lesson was poor or the child inattentive.

> *With a gift, the value disappears, economically speaking, to reappear later elsewhere. (CW341, p. 208)*

Even though the economic value disappears—is consumed—there is generally a very definite, *eventual* benefit to society.

> ... *follow especially those portions of available capital which go into foundations, scholarships and other spiritual or cultural 'goods' which in the course of time act to fertilise the whole process of spiritual production and enterprise of every kind. You will perceive that free gifts are the most fruitful thing of all in the whole economic process. (CW340, p. 112)*

Or, as Benjamin Franklin put it: 'An investment in knowledge pays the best interest.' (Rather than 'knowledge', Steiner might have said 'capacities'.) In a similar vein, Karl Marx observed that the productivity of machines / technology was 'out of all proportion to the direct labour time spent on their production, but depends rather on the general state of science and on the progress of technology, or the application of this science to production'.[265] Tony Blair also appreciated these things and announced that his three priorities as Prime Minister would be 'education, education, education'. The expansion of capacities is funded by gift money, and so gift money is the most fruitful thing of all ....

One could also observe that, with a wholesome, nourishing education, people are not only likely to be more productive in their work life, they are also *less* likely to be an economic drain on others, since fewer police and prison services will be needed, fewer health services will be needed, and less ecological destruction will occur.

In the previous section of the book ('Cross-subsidy') we saw how Steiner suggests that financial support for loss-making enterprise might come from profitable enterprise—if the loss-making enterprise was meeting a real need. But in the case of gift to the 'free' cultural realm, he also appears to see *individuals* as having a role to play, as well as organisations (organisations, in any case, only amounting to groups of individuals):

> *We cannot arrive at a healthy economic process unless, in the first place, it is made possible for people to have something to give and, in the second place, they have the good will and intelligence to give what they have. (CW340, p. 112)*

---

[265] Karl Marx, *Grundrisse der Kritik der Politischen Ökonomie* (1857-8).

This is interesting: it suggests that 'fair price' would ideally be such that it would furnish people with funds over and above what they needed for their and their dependants' immediate livelihood. It implies people's needs be *fully* met such that they are not choosing between a holiday, say, and making a donation to a research establishment or some awareness-raising campaign about the plight of the jungle in Borneo, or whatever. Rather, the holiday is perhaps a 'given', and there is still enough left over for gifting.[266] On another occasion (reference mislaid) Steiner also suggests the management of a highly profitable business might discuss and agree with workers the total remuneration to be distributed amongst all colleagues, and, separate to that, an amount of gift from the business to support education.

It is possibly slightly surprising that he suggests experts within associations (i.e. the *economic* realm) could be on hand to advise where gift could be directed, that is, to which institutions in the *cultural* realm:

> *The association will act as a mediator. The association will provide him with the most sensible way in which to lend, or again, with the most sensible way in which to give… [my emphasis, RM]. The important thing is to bring about sensibly and in accordance with reason the things which happen in any case in the economic process but behind a mask. (CW340, p. 159)*

But remember, even cultural endeavours have their economic dimension and, as such, will also need to be part of the associative life.

And what might this mask be, behind which, he notes, such funding transactions currently happen?

> *As things are now you do give, but the gift is absorbed into the general pool of taxation. It vanishes into a vague economic fog and you do not observe what happens. (CW340, p. 159)*

---

[266] Steiner's comment that it is important for people to have the goodwill and intelligence to want to give suggests he also sees an important role for the cultural domain in educating people into appreciating the universal benefit to humanity when people's capacities are expanded.

Is it not strange that Steiner, with one hand, (a) returns independence to education by reducing the importance of state funding (and thus state influence), but then, with the other hand, (b) appears to take independence away again by suggesting *economic* associations could be on hand to guide funding decisions? But the latter need not compromise cultural freedom. When the funding comes from tax, the bureaucracy of the rights state can—and often does—decide where to deploy it, and what the conditions of this funding are. With the above suggestions, however, economic associations only *advise* benefactors where the needs are. (These needs would reveal themselves when educational, or research, or awareness-raising bodies conveyed to the economic domain their inability to meet the demand for their services unless further funding was secured. Experts within associations would thus be the ones to have an overview of where the economic needs lay within society.)

Whatever particular mechanism enabled surpluses in the economy to fund cultural life, proper threefold separation would always be paramount in order to avoid those conflicts of interest where one or another industry sponsors scientific research, for example, which then—surprise, surprise—finds in favour of the industry in question!

In summary:

- Excess capital ideally given to 'free' cultural life, most notably education.
- By being attuned to the needs across society, economic associations can play a role in helping with such gifting decisions.
- By enhancing people's capabilities, free gift is seen as 'the most fruitful thing of all in the whole economic process'.
- It has the added advantage that it reduces the amount of capital wealth available that people otherwise strain to preserve by buying land, which increases land scarcity and therefore price. (Such investment in land, Steiner suggests, is unlikely to be prevented by legislation.)
- Land can also be removed from the economic process by its repeated onward gifting to those who are productive (making rent-free land available for the common good, in perpetuity).

- A parallel exists between the gifting of *money* capital to 'free' cultural life (e.g. cultural life that *enhances* people's capacities, such as education) and the periodic, onward gifting of *means-of-production* capital to the 'half-free' cultural domain (i.e. where individual capacities are *applied* in the service of economic production, e.g. business management).

Reflections in relation to the present

In relation to the funding of education, it is interesting to note Steiner's change of emphasis between 1919 and 1922. In Section 7.3.6 ('Taxation') it was noted how in 1919 he spoke of (a) dialogue between the three administrations to establish what levels of education were possible, and (b) the core principle that education then be freely chosen by learners / learners' parents. Education vouchers were cited as a possible current-day mechanism to achieve this.

But all bar one of the comments quoted in this ('Gift to education') section are from 1921—1922, i.e. after the threefold campaign had been significantly wound down. By now, it was probably apparent that cultural life (or its education part, at least) was not yet going to be granted the complete independence he emphasised was important. That is, the (rights) state was going to keep its mitts on most education provision (culture), and if you wanted anything different you were going to have to pay for it.

So, whilst the above comments on the one hand make the general point that excessive capital build-up is socially damaging and that, for a healthy society, it should be used up on things like education, there was also an immediate practical aspect to this vis-à-vis independent education. This was going to need independent sponsorship of the kind that the Waldorf-Astoria cigarette factory had already generously provided in order to establish the school Steiner had been asked to help found. This need for 'private' funding continues to apply today in most countries. In the UK, there are one or two *tax*-funded Steiner / Waldorf schools (whose pedagogical independence is affected thereby), but the other Waldorf schools in the country have endured decades of often existential financial struggle—not for lack of families wanting this sort of education, but because of the wish of schools to tread a particular path. This is a path that rejects, on the one hand, state funding (in order to keep state interference to a minimum), and, on the other, a path that embodies their desire to be socially inclusive instead of elitist. Typically, therefore, they charge nigh-on unworkably low fees.

The general point about the need for excess corporate profits to be used for funding cultural life / individual capacities is perhaps most harrowingly illustrated when one considers that billions of pounds in corporate profits are ushered away into offshore tax havens each year, and yet we are supposedly unable to afford the youth services so desperately needed in the middle of the most horrific knife crime epidemic.[267]

The sizeable donating culture we already have in better-off countries[268] perhaps illustrates that Steiner's ideas about gifting are not all that radical. And that extremely wealthy individuals often see the sense in giving to support education and research is demonstrated by countless examples. Take Azim Premji, Chairman of the Indian software firm Wipro who, in 2019, gave $7.5bn (yes, billion!) to improve education in rural and small-town India, taking his total given in support of education to over $20bn since 2001.[269]

In a more threefold world, one can imagine a more widespread gifting culture could occur very naturally. If upon retirement of a business manager, for example, the corresponding means of production were subject to onward gift to new management (a) without financial consideration, (b) without shareholders, (c) with executive pay subject to sensible formulae, (d) with the new management being formally bound to operate in the interests of societal need, then significant surpluses could soon accumulate over and above those needed for R&D or expansion. Some of these surpluses could be made available for co-workers to gift to 'free' cultural life.

---

[267] https://www.google.com/amp/s/www/independent.co.uk/news/uk/crime/knife-crime-stabbings-offences-england-wales-rise-latest-uk-a9159511.htm-1%3famp.

[268] E.g. via charity, crowd-funding, or corporate giving as seen, for example, in the Co-operative Group in the UK giving some 5% of its profits each year—the 'community dividend'—back to the communities where it trades.

[269] https://www.goodnewsnetwork.org/indias-largest-charity-donation-azim-premji/.

7.4.18 Validity of money

Some of the things Steiner says about money, per se, further illustrate his proposed threefold separation of function and, in particular, where he sees the dividing line falling between economy and state.

> *The legitimacy of money as a means of payment, for example, would no longer be the responsibility of the government, but would depend upon measures taken by the administrative bodies of the economic organization. (CW23, p. 117)*
>
> *No political state will ever solve the currency question in a satisfactory manner by making laws. Contemporary states will only solve it by renouncing their efforts at reaching a solution and leaving the necessary measures to an autonomous economic organism. (CW23, p. 120)*
>
> *Modern governments are asking what to do about the chaotic nature of currency values. The only answer to this question is this: for heaven's sake leave it all alone if you are political administrators, and cede the administration of currency and money to the economic organism. (CW189, p. 101)*
>
> *First and foremost, the entire regulation of the currency must be removed from the political state. Currency, money can no longer be something that is subject to the political state, but something that belongs in the economic body. (CW329, 2 April 1919)*

If one remembers the main characteristics of the three realms of society and, in particular, that the main function of the political / rights realm is to consider what is just and right, to provide a system that propagates—and upholds—laws / the rules we collectively wish to live by, then these remarks make full sense. The logistics of economic activity should be left to economic bodies, and whilst this, first and foremost, means the legislature (rights realm) should not concern itself with the running of industrial concerns, it also means other responsibilities that usually sit within the Exchequer or trade and industry portfolios of the state should instead be shouldered by the economic realm's central administration.

That's not to say the democratic process of the rights realm would be completely deprived of involvement in economic policy (see Section 9.3). Choices would still need to be made within the rights realm about aspects of tax-and-spend (e.g. what tax levels are advantageous, what a fair level of unemployment benefit might be, etc.). Naturally, any laws arrived at would then apply to all equally, as is appropriate for the rights domain.

In summary:

- Money per se would ideally be a concern of the central administration of the economic realm rather than the state.

Reflections in relation to the present

The two main tools in a typical political administration's monetary policy (which, in turn, forms one part of its economic policy) are the ability to influence interest rates and the ability to influence the money supply (e.g. through quantitative easing). If Steiner recommends that money-supply considerations fall to the economic administration, but that the setting of interest rates be a matter, at least in part, for the rights state (as mentioned earlier), where would this leave monetary policy? Section 9.3, later in the book, looks briefly at economic policy but, in short, it seems Steiner would advocate monetary policy falling largely to the economic administration since, even if the rights realm were to *set* interest rates, it is hard to imagine it doing so without very close dialogue with (or even direction from) those in the economic administration.

When in 1997 the UK's Chancellor Gordon Brown took monetary policy in a somewhat threefold direction by bestowing a level of independence on the Bank of England, this removed the ability of those working in the rights domain to tinker with interest rates for the sake of short-term, party-political manoeuvring—a spectacle as unhelpful for long-term, economic stability as it had been unseemly.

7.4.19 Three types of money

It does actually take place, ladies and gentlemen: in the economic process money undergoes metamorphoses; it acquires different qualities as it becomes loaned money or gift money. (CW340, p. 155)

> *In the social organism there is no such thing as 'money as such',
> there are only these three kinds of money. Moreover, each kind of
> money only becomes what it is at the moment when it is actually
> entering into the economic process or passing over from one form
> of economic process to another. (CW340, p. 161)*

When Steiner introduced his threefold approach to social reform, he
didn't talk a great deal about money, other than say that, as time goes
by, it should become seen more as the world's bookkeeping (see Section
7.4.22). But in 1922, when delivering the course of more specialised
lectures to economics students, he enumerated what he saw as three
types of money. This was not out of some abstract obsession with
threefoldness, obviously; he contended three types of money simply
exist.

The transaction types of (a) purchase and sale, (b) lending and borrowing, and (c) giving and receiving, which have been touched on
already, each have their own character, and Steiner argued that the
money itself, in a sense, changes character depending on which kind
of transaction it is subject to. Thus he talks of three kinds of money:
purchase money, loan money and gift money. He not only describes
their character and life cycle, but also how it would bring health to
the economic process if not only (a) people were more conscious of
the different phases money goes through, but also (b) if those col-
laborations within the economy—the associations—together with the
economic realm's central administration ultimately were to find ways
to more consciously regulate the relative levels of each type of money
within the economy in order to better maintain a balance that accords
with need.

The three types of money can be characterised as follows:

When making a purchase, I hand money to a seller in exchange
for a commodity. There is an immediate exchange. The value of the
money at this point is that it buys me the commodity I am purchasing.
Its value is reflected in the pizza I am buying, or the piano.

When an economy has developed such that surpluses are produced,
such that some people now have more than they need for immediate
purchases, these 'savings' can be made use of by others to become
economically productive. An entrepreneur / business can make use of

them to build up the means of production—to procure a tractor, say, or build a power station. When lending money, one is not expecting a commodity in return, but possibly repayment of the loan at a later date, or some interest, or both. There is no immediate exchange. Whilst, when handing over money to make a *purchase*, one is sizing up the value of the commodity being purchased, when making a loan, instead of looking to a commodity for value, you are instead considering the capability of the borrower to be productive so that capital or interest or both can come back to you at a later date. Steiner advises a decision to lend should ideally be based on the borrower's capacity to *produce*, not on the fact that they might simply be procuring some asset that can be sold again later in order to clear the loan. One is looking at the ability of the borrower to apply their spirit / intelligence in the wise use of the loan money for the building up of means of production, or for working capital, or for whatever else they may need in order to enter into production—production which will create economic values with which to serve society and which will also generate sufficient income to enable the borrower to repay the loan, or pay interest, or both.

> *The spirit which the man applies in turning the money to good account—giving it value—this alone will have economic value at this stage ... If a fool gets hold of it and 'scatters it all to the winds', it is an altogether different thing than if a clever man gets hold of it and starts a fruitful economic process with it. (CW340, p. 55)*
>
> *The moment loaned money comes into circulation the spirit of man seizes it. Human thinking sets to work and it is through this entry of human thinking into the process that loaned money receives its actual value. When a banknote is lent to a man who is about to undertake some business—at the moment he begins to use it, it would be far more important to write on the note whether the man is a genius or a fool in business. For the value of the loaned money in the whole economic process will henceforth depend upon the way he acts with it. (CW340, p. 154)*

Whether, given the above, one wants to think of *all* types of loan as 'loan money'—in Steiner's sense—is a question. If a loan is made to enable some domestic purchase like a washing machine, car or house this is not really about giving an entrepreneur the wherewithal to go into production; it is simply about enabling the consumer to spread the cost of a commodity purchase over time. If a house is going to last a lifetime it would seem reasonable to spread the cost of purchase over a number of years. But, assuming he or she does not work from home, the house no more sets the entrepreneur up for production than does their toothbrush. It is a consumer good, not an investment good.

Although investment *in shares* is problematic from a threefold point of view (as covered in Section 5.3.2), the funds involved could nonetheless be thought of as 'loan money' to the extent that they are not being used by the investor to procure commodities—consumer goods—for themselves, but, instead to enable the building up of means of production.

Concerning gift, Steiner points out how this is an integral part of economic life too. The very young, the very old, and the unemployed are given sustenance without producing commodities in return. Economically speaking, they are pure consumers. There is no (economic) return to the giver. More often than not, though, Steiner gives the term 'gift money' a particular slant, which distinguishes it from the mere redistribution involved when some of a productive person's output is made over to an unproductive person. 'Gift money', in Steiner's analysis, typically implies capacity building, education.

> *Gift-money, fundamentally speaking, is all that is spent on education. This plays an enormous part in the economic life. Gift-money, again, is all that is spent on endowments and the like—all that has the effect of preventing the evil damming up of capital on the land by capital investment, which is so ruinous for the economic life. (CW340, p. 154)*
>
> *All that we put into the educational system is a gift—notably when it is a question of a really free spiritual life. (CW340, p. 159)*

Not *all* spending on 'cultural activity' would imply gift money. Money spent on that 'half-free' cultural life operating in the economic realm (organising labour, say) would not be considered 'gift money'. And even though an artist, say, might be working in the 'free' cultural domain ('free' in the sense that the artist can work without interference from the economic or rights realms, or from anyone else working within the 'free' cultural domain, for that matter), when I buy a work of art or go to a concert, there is still an immediate return to me—a commodity—which disqualifies my payment from being 'gift money'. The distinctions become less clear, perhaps, when a philanthropist commissions a piece of public art or the composing of a symphony that will uplift humanity in the future, not just the sponsor.

Money given to scientific research on the other hand would indeed fall within the definition, since capacities (knowledge) are being furthered and there is no immediate payback to the giver. Indeed, the researcher might *never* make a single discovery. With education (especially of children), there is no definite 'result' or quantifiable value being purchased. When a school receives money to educate a 7-year-old, it is not at all clear what the end result will be, where the child's strengths will lie. One has little idea of the nature, extent or timing of any 'return' to society. It is just a case of expanding and developing a child's faculties. The child might end up becoming a brain surgeon or a bus driver. The end result is irrelevant. The point is to simply nurture the development of their capacities as fully as possible (an aim not unique to Steiner, of course). Such education will hopefully be rewarding for the individual concerned, but it should also be rewarding for society too, since whatever the individual can offer will be increased, will be offered with a clearer head, a more dexterous hand, and a good heart.

Naturally, that is not to say that education with a particular end in sight—a less 'free' piece of education—is somehow unworthy. Where an adult is being trained to be a dentist, the outcomes aimed for are largely predetermined: knowledge of root canals, dentures and so on. Funding such a training, however, would still be thought of as 'gift money'. Yes, the end result is more defined. That is, I, the trainee dentist give you, the trainer, money; and you the trainer give me the knowledge / skills I need to get to work as a dentist. There is a definite outcome—dentistry skills—being acquired (or at least sought). But the economic values that accrue from this lie largely in the future. With the education of a child, there is a *kind* of outcome—increased capacities—being acquired too. The point is that in both cases—dentist or child—capacities are being developed, the economic results of which only appear later, if at all, and Steiner considers the funding for this process as 'gift money'.

If you buy a package holiday for your ageing grandmother, on the other hand, or indeed a sandwich for someone begging in the street, it seems to be a question whether Steiner would see these as cases of 'gift money'. He would probably have seen this simply as a redistribution of 'purchase money'. It is less about capacity building and more about purchasing an immediate 'return', albeit a return for someone other than yourself.

The distinction between what he might or might not consider 'gift money' is also not so clear when one considers, let's say, a £1m donation to an environmental charity to remove plastic from the ocean. This is not about an individual purchasing an immediate return for themselves. The values will arise in the future, possibly even after the donor has passed away. But even though no repayment of this donation is required, might Steiner have seen it more as loan money than gift money since it enables the charity to buy equipment (means of production) and get on with its cleaning-up job—an activity where capacities will be *applied*, not developed? Or might he have seen it as gift money, after all, since the benefactor kisses the capital goodbye such that it will be used up in some activity, not simply bestowed on an heir who might perpetuate 'the evil damming up of capital on the land' by capital investment? Steiner is not explicit about this, as far as I am aware. But what he *is* explicit about is the funding of education and capacity building: this certainly entails 'gift money'.

> ... *follow especially those portions of available capital which go into foundations, scholarships and other spiritual or cultural 'goods' which in the course of time act to fertilise the whole process of spiritual production and enterprise of every kind. You will perceive that free gifts are the most fruitful thing of all in the whole economic process. (CW340, p. 112)*

Rudolf Isler notes in connection with loan and gift money: 'Lending and giving allow something to grow in the medium or long term. In both we are concerned with capacities, though in a quite different way in each case: loan money creates entrepreneurial capital and exists to enable capacities to be *applied* in commerce. Gift money on the other hand exists to create income so that capacities can *grow*.'[270]

---

[270] Rudolf Isler, *Sustainable Society: Making Business, Government and Money Work Again* (Edinburgh: Floris Books, 2014), p. 20.

This seems a good rule of thumb: purchase money procures commodities; loan money enables someone to apply their capacities in the production of commodities; gift money enables these capacities to be developed in the first place.

Steiner describes a life cycle through which one form of money metamorphoses into the next.[271] Purchase money builds up through trading under division of labour. This results, sooner or later, in surpluses / savings arising here and there. These savings are lent to others to build up other business, and further surpluses then arise. Savings then become extensive enough for a gift to be made to education and other cultural enrichment. A greater transparency of these metamorphoses, and management of the volumes of money moving from one phase to another (by the associations and central economic administration) are considered by Steiner as desirable.[272]

> If such associations can be achieved, commercial experience will enable something to arise that can indeed lead to a genuine social ordering, just as healthy human organism leads to a healthy life. There will be circulation in the economy of purchase, loan and gift money. There can be no social organism without these three. We may want to rail against gifts and donations, but they are a necessary part. You deceive yourself if you say that a healthy social organism should make gifts unnecessary. Yet you pay tax, and taxes are merely a roundabout way of making donations to schools and other facilities.
>
> People deserve to have a social order in which they can always see how things flow without having to make suppositions. When social life has been extricated from today's general muddle, in which everything is mixed up together, we shall begin to see ... how money circulates [...].
>
> People can only participate in social life as a whole through associations which make visible how the life of society flows. Then the social organism will be healthy. (CW305(ii), pp. 161-162)
>
> You will readily perceive that if you do not wish to leave the thing to chance—if you wish to bring reason into it—you simply must

---

[271] See, for example, CW340, p. 155.
[272] See, for example, CW340, pp. 159-161.

interpose the necessary associative bodies at the transition points between purchase-money, loaned money, gift-money and the renewal of money. [The 'renewal' of money is covered in the next section, RM] (CW340, p. 159)

In summary:

- There are three types of money: purchase, loan and gift money.
- Purchase money procures commodities; loan money enables someone to apply their capacities in the production of commodities; gift money enables these capacities to be developed in the first place.
- Purchase money builds up in society until some have more than they need; from this, loan money arises, and gift money becomes possible.
- The value of purchase money is what it can buy; the value of loan money—to the economy as a whole—depends on the capabilities of those who are borrowing it; gift money fertilises capabilities and is 'the most fruitful of all'.
- The more transparent this lifecycle is, the healthier society will be.
- Ideally, bodies within the economic realm regulate the lifecycle of money more consciously.

Reflections in relation to the present

To some extent, we are already used to the relative levels of these three types of money being centrally regulated. Principally in order to control inflation, the Bank of England's Monetary Policy Committee will raise interest rates to stimulate saving / depress spending (i.e. stimulate the conversion of purchase money to loan money), or vice versa to achieve the reverse. And via taxation the government raises 'compulsory gift' for education and other public services.

Steiner's recommendation that the rights administration's involvement in these logistics be reduced in favour of involvement by the economic administration has to a very small extent been addressed in the UK by the fact that the Bank of England (albeit a state-owned organisation) has, since 1997, made monetary policy decisions independently of politicians. Responsibility for balancing purchase money / loan money is at something of a remove from the rights realm. But the rights realm is still closely involved in procuring gift money (via taxation) for education. To remove / reduce its involvement, and thus remove / reduce the compulsory nature of the 'gift' in favour of something altogether freer, raises the questions around underfunding of education which were looked at briefly in Section 7.4.17—where an alternative mechanism was considered for generating gift money such that citizens (either individually or collectively as businesses) themselves chose, out of their 'free appreciation', which educational establishments to support. The funding of such cultural activity, with particular reference to education vouchers, is considered further in Section 7.5.1.

7.4.20 Dying money

Money will wear out, just as commodities wear out. (CW23, p. 120)

The idea of dying money is a further instance of a suggestion Steiner makes that need not be thought of as integral to the threefold reforms he proposes. This, too, he introduces more as a topic for research which, like many of his other operational suggestions, is entirely subsidiary to his main treatise—that the institutions representing the rights realm limit themselves to rights realm matters, and similarly for the other two realms. As repeated a number of times, he did not regard his proposals as a programme, prescriptive down to every last detail, and he did not insist his ideas could only be effective if adopted hook, line and sinker. So, budding threefold reformers need not read sections such as this one and promptly throw in the towel!

Steiner recommends it would be best if money were to always represent commodities—goods and services:

... commodity production, the only means through which the possessor of money will have been able to attain it [unless they are a dependant or on welfare, or in receipt of some other gift, RM], will back every coin and banknote. (CW23, p. 119)

And he points out that, inasmuch as money should represent the value of goods exchanged, over the course of time it doesn't entirely reflect the reality of the situation, the reality of value decay. Whilst goods— both consumer goods and investment goods (those going to make up the means of production) decay at varying rates, money retains its nominal / face value indefinitely. Purchasing power might in certain contexts reduce on account of inflation, but the nominal value will still endure, in theory forever.

So he suggests that, in order to better reflect reality, money should either depreciate over time or at least be issued with an expiry date after which it ceases to be valid tender. He suggests the lifespan could be calculated as the approximate average lifespan seen across all goods, from goods which can last centuries at one end of the spectrum—such as houses etc.—to perishable foodstuffs or services at the other, which might not even last a day. On different occasions, he suggests such an average might lie somewhere between 15 and 30 years.

... apart from a few exceptional goods of very long duration, we always have to do with goods which pass away in time. They lose their value, and after a certain lapse of time are no longer there.[273] The one exception, strange to say, in our whole economic life is money. Although it occupies a position of perfect equivalence to the other elements of economic life, money does not wear out ... Now if it were in a true relation of equivalence to the goods that are produced, money, too, would have to wear out, like other goods. That is to say, if the body economic contains money which is incapable of being used up—money which does not wear out—we may well be giving money the advantage over goods, which do wear out. This is a most important point ... (CW340, p. 143)

Everything that is a genuine object of use or consumption is subject to decay. Now, when for the purposes of pure exchange we use money as an equivalent, we must admit that, as against articles which decay, money is an unfair competitor. (CW340, p. 153)

---

[273] As explained previously, Steiner does not consider unelaborated land as belonging to the economic system.

If, instead of lasting forever, money were to wear out in order to reflect its relation to commodities, this would discourage people from hoarding it:

> Due to the nature of these relations, arrangements will have to be made whereby money loses value for its possessor once it has lost its significance. Property in the form of money passes on to the community after a certain length of time. In order to prevent money which is not working in productive enterprises being retained through evasion of the economic organization's measures, a new printing could take place from time to time. (CW23, p. 119)

Such wearing out can also (along with other measures) partly address the thorny issue of ownership being rewarded at the expense of work—the often-criticised feature of our current system.

> ... think, on the other hand, how little an individual person has to do if he possesses £20[274] in money today and wishes to possess double that amount in 15 years' time. He need do nothing at all; he can withdraw his entire labour power from the social organism and let other people work. All he need do is to lend his money and let other people do the work. Unless he himself in the meantime sees to it that the money is spent, the money need not be used up. This is the very thing which brings into the body social so much of what is afterwards felt—shall we say—as a social anomaly, as an injustice. (CW340, p. 144)
>
> Monetary investment must become subject to the fate of all other goods. Our current economy expects capital investment to double over a period of time. In a healthy economy, however, invested funds would vanish over that same time period, simply ceasing to exist. Today people are horrified by the suggestion that their monetary investment will not double in 15 years but will simply vanish because it is consumed or depreciated along with the goods it is used to purchase. Of course certain types of savings could be exempt from this rule. (CW333, p. 13)

---

[274] 500 Swiss francs in the original German.

Under 'Savings and loans' (Section 7.4.15), we wondered what exemptions Steiner might have had in mind in this last sentence. Pensions perhaps? Or savings up to a certain limit?

A further, novel aspect of Steiner's approach is that money that is about to 'die' can be given away to the 'free' cultural realm, most notably education, at which point it would be given a new date stamp by the economic administration and the process would start again.

> *If you are thinking in a true economic sense, then, where it is a question of free gifts, you will use old money—money that loses its value as soon as possible after the gift is made ... At this point, needless to say, there must be some rejuvenating process. The money, in fact, must have a successor. (CW340, p. 159)*
>
> *... gift money, which is the oldest, must be handed over to an association which will bring the valueless money back again into the whole economic process ... (CW340, p. 160)*

Of course, old, dying money is going to be of little use to some recipient working in the cultural domain if the supermarket won't accept it on account of its near-death state. So bringing the money back to life again for a new term is necessary. However, since Steiner has pointed out the lack of reality in money lasting indefinitely, one might well ask to what extent this magical new lease of life itself reflects reality!

Think of it like this. If I have a lot of bananas and other perishable produce in the house which I cannot possibly consume by the end of the week, then these things are going to go bad and get thrown away. That is, economic values will die. On the other hand, I could coax my neighbour out of retirement to give some children in the township a couple of extra maths lessons in return for being fed for the week. The values in the produce will have then been transferred to someone else before being scattered to the winds (i.e. the compost heap). Yes, by the end of the week, the produce that was going to die, has still died. It may have been eaten rather than thrown away, but the economic values have still died. The difference, though, is that a new commodity has now been generated—maths lessons. It surely goes without saying that when someone gets to work and produces goods and services, they *create* value; the economy is not all a one-way street of decay! Values are constantly being created by people, too, and maths lessons are no different. Education may be a classic example of cultural life, but it still has an economic dimension to it (Section 5.3—'Definition of Economic Aspect'). A maths lesson is also a service and thus has a commodity aspect. And since a commodity (the maths lesson) has arisen, as it were, out of thin air, the money that was about to die can rejuvenate. If the bananas had simply been thrown away, values would have died, and that would have been the end of the story. But when used to feed a teacher, new values have come to life (maths lessons), and to reflect these new values, the money can be reborn. If money is to mirror the appearance / disappearance cycle of commodities, it needs to be born as well as devalue. (With respect to the maths lessons, yet further values may of course arise in the future when some of the children go on to apply their maths in work situations, but that's a whole other story.)

And how did Steiner imagine that the dying of money could take effect in practice?

As purchase money it keeps its value until the end. The question is more a technical one of circulation, and of how this happens. It is not easy to form a picture of money's gradual [my emphasis, RM] loss of value. To do so would require an extraordinarily bureaucratic apparatus. I would like to stress that I do not wish to agitate, only to say what the reality is. [...]

This necessitates the ageing of money. It is merely a question of how to do this. Now one can only give outer effect to the gradual [my emphasis, RM] devaluation of money by stamping money, the fully stamped notes being processed by officials. But this necessitates a very complicated bureaucracy. So it is not a question of outer devaluation, but of guiding money through the real course of economic events. This can be done by first giving all types of money the form of a bill, that is, with an expiry date. Such a date cannot be abstractly chosen, of course, but has to be estimated out of the facts of the time of issue ... (CW341, p. 220)

Here, Steiner appears to be saying (a) ideally, money *should* gradually depreciate (e.g. a £10 note becomes worth £9.99 next week, £9.98 the following week, and so on until it 'dies' perhaps 1,000 weeks / 20 years later), (b) to achieve this would be too much of an administrative headache as, at regular intervals, one would have to take notes to some bureaucrat who would stamp them with updated values, (c) the solution, therefore, would be to issue money with an expiry date and let it be nominally worth £10 for its full lifespan ('As purchase money it keeps its value until the end') and then 'die' at maturity, (d) in which case, its gradual depreciation would take effect by 'guiding money through the real course of economic events'. This is where things start to get very involved! For example, of older money:

> In real economic circulation such money would have a lower use-value, (but not purchasing value). The older it becomes the less its use-value, and this would convert it into gift money, to be reissued as young—that is, 'new'—money again. [...] (CW341, p. 221)

Or:

> If an enterprise is set up with the young money it can be planned over a long term. With old money it cannot be. (CW341, p. 221)

Comments like these can very quickly make one feel out of one's depth; they certainly seem to pose more questions than they answer. The following, however, makes it easier to allow oneself to admit that anything beyond a cursory introduction to this is really beyond the pretentions of this book:

> I am only sorry that we cannot go on for months detailing instances where we can see that the facts are as I have stated, with regard to the valuation and devaluation of money. This, however, should really be our task. All that can be said in the present lectures should be taken as a basis for further researches in economics. (CW340, p. 155)

In summary:

- As against goods, money that does not wear out is an 'unfair competitor'.
- As something that mediates exchange, it is a representative of goods and would ideally wear out *gradually* to reflect the fact that goods wear out.

- It would wear out over a term that approximated the average lifespan of all goods—possibly somewhere between 15 and 30 years.
- For administrative reasons, Steiner suggests a *gradual* wearing out would be impracticable and that, instead, it could be stamped with a 'use-by' date.
- Dying money would reduce the ability to make money by owning money; it would also discourage hoarding.
- If donated for work in the independent cultural realm just before expiry, such date-stamped money would be given a new lease of life, i.e. a further 15-30 year term.

Reflections in relation to the present

As money consisted largely of notes and coins a hundred years ago, to reflect any *gradual* wearing out would, as Steiner says, have been very difficult. Hence his proposal that currency could be date-stamped.

But wouldn't there be a problem with this too? If someone was sitting on £10m of savings they didn't need, but knew that it was going to expire in a few months' time, what would they do? If they were of an altruistic turn of mind, they might make the donations to education and research that Steiner suggests would trigger a new date stamp for the currency—so that its life cycle would start afresh. But might they instead decide to buy a yacht or a Rembrandt or something else that only wore out very slowly, knowing that they would be able to sell these later if they wished? At first sight, this might appear as a flaw in the use-by date approach; but the thing is: dealers in yachts and Rembrandts would be unlikely to have much interest in money that was soon to die. So, whilst the money might amount to £10m nominally, in practice it might be worth very much less. In other words, where money carried a use-by date, people would continually need to be jumping through all sorts of mental hoops to arrive at an estimate of real value that was at all useful. Commercial life would have to take on a whole new complication, with some shops perhaps only accepting tender that had four years left to run, others perhaps insisting on five. Although mental gymnastics are not a bad thing in themselves, one can imagine people would find getting used to this new way of thinking—one that was constantly having to make mental adjustments to the value of their currency—something of a challenge! Can one therefore seriously imagine any region of the world having sufficient belief in the health-giving effect of a depreciating currency—a currency that matched the reality of commodity depreciation—and then, on account of this belief, adopting this new approach to currency in earnest? The chances of such a change of direction would certainly seem slim.

A straight-line, *gradual* depreciation, on the other hand, would be much easier for the public-at-large to grasp. Under such an approach, complicated discounting algorithms would not need to embed themselves in the national psyche. And with the possibility we now have of having cashless money systems, a gradual wearing out would be relatively easy to implement. Computer-based tender could very easily be made subject to algorithms that reduced £10 to £9.99 next week, £9.98 the following week, and so on.

To realise the principle of dying money getting a new lease of life, upon expiry, if given to education and research, everyone could, for example, have two accounts: a current account and a restricted, capacity-building account. The owner of £10 would see this reduced to £9.99 a week later, and the 1p of value that had been removed could be credited to the capacity-building account. From this, they would be able to make gifts in support of education and research, etc.

Clearly, as Steiner says, this is more a topic for research than one for any immediate attempt at implementation. All manner of implications follow on from such an idea, not least the temptation savers would have to swap such tender for any foreign currency not subject to ageing, or, on inheriting £10m of younger money, say, to go and buy a yacht or a Rembrandt rather than see the inheritance gradually disappear (at a rate of what might be £10,000 per week). Would there really be any point in discouraging hoarding if, instead, you were encouraging profligacy?

Another question one could ask is: is there a conflict between Steiner's idea of dying money, where people's capital savings would slowly reduce, and his comments, covered in Section 7.4.15 ('Savings and loans'), supporting the payment of modest interest to savers who lend to enable economic production? If people can get a modest interest, then savings generate earnings; but if capital slowly depreciates, then they generate 'losings'!

As we have seen, Steiner has no time for the idea of capital growth:

> ... what amounts to interest on interest is strictly rejected ... If the reality I described ... really came about then growth of capital that we see today, where capital can double in 15 years, would be out of the question. I was not speaking of such things but of legitimate interest. [...] there must be the possibility for previous work to be used for later productivity. However, the only way that this can happen, the only way ... for me to have a certain benefit from this ... is by means of legitimate interest, as I call it ... (CW331, 24 June 1919))

There are different ways of interpreting this. If your capital attracts interest at 5%, then it will double in fifteen years. So, one interpretation would be that Steiner rejects interest of 5%. Maybe even 4% or 3%. For him, a 'legitimate rate' might be 2% or even 1%. Another interpretation could be that he is relaxed about interest (even at 5%, say) but rejects such interest being paid *in addition to* capital growth (as with shares, where you may see capital growth *as well as* dividends). However, if all your money (including interest earned) generates interest at 5%, it *will* double in 15 years! Another interpretation could be that interest of 5% is fine, but you don't get your capital back—ever. This would fit with ...

> Money lent for production does not return, it stays there. But we insist on selling the means of production ... However, if one imagines the means of production as something one does not sell, then the money stays in ... (CW341, p. 221)

A further interpretation of a 'legitimate rate' could be that, an interest rate of say 5% is fine, but that the capital should depreciate in accordance with the dying money ideas under consideration. The wearing out of savings and the earning of interest are in fact not mutually exclusive. Interest could even be set such that it exactly offsets the wearing out—in which case the lender would nominally have the same amount of money at the end of the loan as they did at the beginning. Udo Herrmannstorfer calls this 'dynamically sustained monetary stability'.[275] Or interest could be above or below this figure.

As pointed out already, Steiner suggests the rights realm would set the prevailing rate of interest, although this would presumably be in close consultation with the economic realm whose associative bodies and central administration would have a good sense of the need to stimulate or dissuade saving, that is to say, stimulate or dissuade the conversion of purchase money to loan money.

Steiner is by no means alone in advocating the ageing of money. His contemporary, the economist Silvio Gesell,[276] devised a concept he called Freigeld which required periodic payments for stamps to keep currency valid—in effect a negative interest rate. This would have been administratively burdensome, no doubt. But as noted above, with the possibility nowadays for computer-based currency, a gradual depreciation could be applied with relative ease. Heavyweight economist John Maynard Keynes concurred with Gesell, referring to him as that 'strange, unduly neglected prophet, whose work contains flashes of deep insight', adding 'The idea behind stamped money is sound'.[277]

Contemporary economist Kate Raworth points out that the negative interest rates used since 2014 by Japan, Sweden, Denmark, Switzerland and the European Central Bank amount to much the same thing as dying money. In parallel with Steiner, she notes money's 'most unusual feature: it runs counter to the fundamental dynamic of our world. Given time, tractors rust, crops rot, smart phones break, and buildings crumble. But money? Money is cumulative for ever, thanks to interest'.[278] Accordingly, she posits that a 'demurrage-bearing' currency could be used not only to correct this anomaly, but designed in such a way so as to steer investment decisions that ensured long-term sustainability (e.g. capital invested in renewable energy, say, could be excused from dying for the time being).

---

[275] U Herrmannstorfer, 'Pseudo Market: economy, labour, land, capital and the globalization of the economy' (Stuttgart: Institut für soziale Gegenwartsfragen, 1997), p.104 [as pdf from www.threefolding.net].

[276] In 1919, Gesell was appointed People's Representative for Finances within the Bavarian Soviet Republic, but the latter came to a violent end just seven days later.

[277] John Maynard Keynes, *The General Theory of Employment, Interest, and Money* (London: Macmillan, 1936), p. 353.

[278] Kate Raworth, *Doughnut Economics: Seven Ways to Think Like a 21st-Century Economist* (London: Random House, 2018), p. 273.

Notwithstanding the complex and far-reaching implications of the above, one can of course always allow any superfluous capital one might have to lessen—by donating to education and research, or to projects working for ecological enrichment and so on.

7.4.21 Nature-based currency

We shall find that our currency ... will have to be inscribed, let us say: 'Wheat producible over a given number of acres', and this will then be equated to other things. The different products of the soil are the easiest things to equate. So you see where it is we must start from—our figures must mean something. It simply leads away from reality if money has inscribed on it: 'So much gold'. It leads towards reality if he has inscribed on it: 'This represents so much labour upon such and such a product of nature'. For we shall then have this result: Say there is written on the money 'x wheat', all money will be stamped 'x of wheat, y of wheat, z of wheat'. The real origin of the whole economic life will then be made evident. Our currency will be referred to the usable means of production upon which bodily work is done—the means of production of the given economic region. (CW340, p. 181)

Each one in every moment will then have his connection with nature, even in the money. It is just this which makes our present-day relations so unsound: they have become so far remote from nature—the connection with nature is no longer there. If we can bring it about (and it is only a question of evolving the nec- essary techniques in the associative life) that we really have the nature-value recorded on our paper money in place of the indefin- able gold value, then we shall see directly—in every-day business and intercourse—how much a given spiritual service is worth. For I shall know, when I paint a picture, that for me to have painted this picture so many workers on the land, for example, have to work for so many months or years on wheat or oats, etc. Think how transparent the economic process would become ... Yes, and that is just what we need. For by this means true economic conditions will be brought about. (CW340, p. 182)

... all the labour that can be done must come from the given pop- ulation and, on the other hand, all that this labour can unite with must come from the given land. Everyone needs what this labour

brings about and, as to those who can save themselves [i.e. be spared, RM] the labour on account of their spiritual services, the others must perform it for them in addition to their own. Thus we arrive at the actual basis of economic life.

Looking at things in this way, we shall admit that even in our present highly complicated economic life, that which was universal in the most primitive conditions—where the simple exchange of goods, shall we say, was the essential thing—still plays its part. The difference is that we are no longer able to see the connection clearly everywhere. But we shall have it before us always, when the connection with nature is expressed in our currency notes. Whatever we may do, the connection with nature is always there. Do not let us forget it! It is reality. (CW340, p. 184)

Being reasonably self-explanatory, these passages need little by way of elucidation. Remember, though, how *unelaborated* nature has no economic value in Steiner's definition. So, the proposal here is currency values which relate to nature *products*, to nature modified by labour.

Interestingly, in the summer of 1923 when hyperinflation was at its worst (by the autumn, one US dollar was worth over four *trillion* German marks—that is four thousand billion marks!) economist and erstwhile German Treasury Secretary Karl Helfferich proposed creating a new currency—the '*Roggenmark*'—pegged against the value of rye. However, on account of the greatly fluctuating price of rye at the time, this was rejected and gold was used as the reference instead. Thereafter, twelve zeros were removed from prices!

In summary:

- For the sake of healthy economic transparency, Steiner recommends currency be based on simple products of nature.
- To effect this, he makes various suggestions: 'Wheat producible over a given number of acres' or 'So much labour upon such and such a product of nature' or 'X of wheat, y of wheat, z of wheat' or 'So many workers on the land … have to work for so many months or years on wheat or oats'.

Reflections in relation to the present

What a single farmer can produce today, of course, with the impressive machinery at his or her fingertips, far exceeds what could be produced in 1922. But one could nonetheless apply the same principle today as Steiner broached back then: money could be related to basic crops. What is not clear is whether, within the time needed to produce a kilogram of wheat or rye (or whatever), Steiner would also have included the time spent caring for the workhorses, harvesting the hay to feed them through the winter, making the plough, scythe and flail, mining and transporting the iron that went into these tools, and all the rest of it. If he would, then the complexity in calculating a total man-hour figure could today be multiplied many times over on account of the fact that farm equipment is now what it is, with sophisticated tractors and combine harvesters comprising components manufactured in many countries, and containing materials from the world over. One way of circumventing this issue might be to take a product of nature, the cultivation of which is labour intensive and uses little machinery—such as grapes, perhaps.

Whilst notes and coins—even those with use-by dates—could be inscribed with 'x of wheat', 'y of wheat', it would also be possible for a gradually depreciating, computer-based currency to reflect some nature value. A money balance could equate to a reducing weight of grain or grapes or whatever. For example, instead of £10 reducing to £9.99 after one week, the currency could be 10kg of grapes reducing to 9.99kg of grapes after one week.

The issue of nature-related currency is perhaps not a big one, not something Steiner referred to on many occasions, unlike the general threefold articulation of society which he campaigned for quite vigorously over an extended period.

7.4.22 Bookkeeping as money

A currency concept that Steiner referred to somewhat more than he did nature-based currency was the concept of money being a case of simple accounting.

> One needs to think of money more as a form of bookkeeping [...]
> All forms of money transactions are bookkeeping. It's just that
> money changes hands, instead of entries changing from debit to
> credit columns. (CW341, p. 223)

> *... the characteristic money has currently acquired—of being a commodity—will fall away. The monetary system will consist only of a kind of adaptable accounting system to record the exchange of goods between those who belong to each economic area. There will be a kind of credit recording system when someone procures something he needs. Thus the monetary system will be a kind of accounting system ... (CW337a(ii), p. 30)*

So, not a commodity itself but only something that mediates the exchange of commodities.

> *In the threefold social organism, money will exist as a means of circulation only—in the sense that it will be a kind of flexible book-keeping ... In the economic life of the future everything will be based on service and reciprocal service. For a service one will receive a docket, as it were, that means nothing other than: on the active side [of a ledger, RM] sits all that corresponds to my performance, and which is available to me to exchange for whatever meets my needs ... (CW331, 2 July 1919)*
>
> *In the circulation of money we have in effect the world's bookkeeping. And this is, as everyone can really see for himself, what should be aimed at. For in this way we give back to money the only quality which it can properly have—that of being the external medium of exchange. Look into the depths of economic life, and you will see: money can be nothing else that this. (CW340, p. 176)*

Traditionally, in addition to it being a medium of exchange, money is also considered to have the attribute of being a store of value. But Steiner reasons it should lose value, as we have seen. For him, being a means of exchange is 'the only quality which it can properly have'.

Moreover, the type of exchange it should facilitate should only be *commodity* exchange, that is to say not the purchase of land, nor finished means of production; just goods and services:

> *Money, in a healthy social organism, can be nothing other than a draft on commodities produced by others, which the holder may claim from the overall social organism because he has himself produced and delivered commodities to this sector. (CW23, p. 117)*

> ... *commodity production, the only means through which the possessor of money will have been able to attain it ... [unless, presumably, they are a dependant or on welfare, or are in receipt of loan or gift money, RM] (CW23, p. 119)*

If money can only be used to mediate *commodity* exchange, then the rentier element in the economy falls away. That is, if money can only be used to buy commodities, but not land or the finished means of production, then ultimately neither will it be used to pay rent for land or dividends to owners of the means of production. People get money from producing, not ownership.

Also, if money can only mediate commodity exchange, then it can no longer be used to pay for labour—to pay a wage:

> ... *money itself is made a commodity, and thus the money, which in truth may not be a commodity, can become completely independent in economic life. But that is the basis of capitalism [...] power over labour is created by capital [...] One gets the possibility of procuring manpower by releasing the money as an independent commodity from the economic process, while the money should in fact simply be a valueless abstraction with which only commodities can be traded. But through this independence of money, labour has become the servant of power / capital. (CW331, 22 May 1919)*

> *If the piece of paper I have in my wallet is really nothing more than something for procuring goods, then basically there can be no compulsion to work. The piece of paper should always somehow relate to output accomplished. (CW331, 22 May 1919)*

Such an approach certainly has its attractions. Money being returned to its original purpose of facilitating commodity exchange, of being a token of exchange instead of something that allows armies of currency traders around the globe to waste their lives speculating and betting against this currency or that, and being 100% unproductive in the process—adding precious little to the total of available values in the world. Any profits they make can only arise as the result of someone else's loss. What a sorry state of affairs we are in when these activities are considered respectable!

Whilst Steiner advocates an accounting form of currency that can only mediate exchange of commodities, it should be noted (from other comments we have considered) that giving, lending and taxing are quite acceptable within his analysis.

In summary:

- Ideally, currency ceases to be regarded as a store of value, as something to be traded, as a commodity in itself.
- Instead, it is only regarded as a medium of commodity exchange.
- It should just be a way of recording sales and purchases of goods and services—a simple accounting technique, a unit of account for recording the transfer of commodity values.
- These economic values exclude labour, land, the means of production, ground rent.
- Such values can also be lent, given and taxed, however.

Reflections in relation to the present

In *Sustainable Society*, Rudolf Isler draws attention to the similarities between, on the one hand, the alternative money systems in existence today such as LETS (Local Exchange Trading Systems) and CES (Community Exchange Systems) and, on the other, Steiner's vision of money representing, in essence, an accounting system recording products and services either purchased or rendered, instead of being a thing taking on a life of its own.

LETS took off in the 1980s; its Internet-based CES cousin is more recent. 'Credit is recorded on the account of a member who sells goods or services to another, and a debt of equal amount is lodged on the account of the purchaser ... Thus every account fluctuates around a zero point between debit and credit. This is similar to the way we ordinarily cover our monthly expenses with our monthly wage, so that during the month our current account fluctuates around an average level. No one should accrue more debts than they can regularly pay off. [...] It is therefore necessary for every account to have a lower debt limit [...] The words "credit" or "asset" should not mislead us into thinking it is something one "owns". It would be better described as a claim or right to goods and services; and instead of debts, one could speak of an "obligation to perform" …'.[279]

Although a tiny movement relative to all the currency values in circulation, there are now thousands of LETS / CES systems in existence around the world, operating with varying degrees of success. Each separate system tends to be valid only in one smallish geographical area—often, for example, being limited to a single town—making it rather homespun. Those who wish to take part in one of these systems usually register, in the first instance, with a declaration of whatever goods or services they can provide. They are given an account with a zero balance and an 'overdraft facility'. They can then trade with one another and each time they make a sale, their balance goes up, and each time they buy, it goes down. Members are generally given credit and debit limits, and their balances are published, often along with a list of their 'offers' and 'wants'. Typically, someone's debit / credit limits can be increased / reduced by the administrators of the system, depending on the individual's sale and purchase levels. In some schemes, the unit of currency is an hour of work, elsewhere it is pegged to the national currency; sometimes it is something else.

There are advantages and disadvantages to these schemes. A significant advantage is that it enables people in a particularly run-down area to trade with one another, even if they do not have much normal currency to spare. So for example, Mr Gates can babysit for Ms Kardashian who can clean windows for Mr Beckham who can make jam for Mr Gates, and so on! With euros harder to come by in Greece in recent years, for example, these alternative currencies have become more popular there.

A significant disadvantage, with LETS / CES systems, at least at the stage they have reached thus far, is that one can rarely satisfy every need. Shoes or a car, say, may be out of reach if these commodities have been made two or three countries away. This is not an insurmountable problem that is inherent in the system, but exists only because these currency systems are localised and relatively undeveloped (which does safeguard against fraud, it has to be said). Another problem experienced with some schemes is that take-up can be poor

---

[279] Rudolf Isler, *Sustainable Society: Making Business, Government and Money Work Again* (Edinburgh: Floris Books, 2014), pp. 31-32.

which can deter newcomers who might not be confident that they will be able to spend what they have earned. Again, this is not an *inherent* problem of such a system.

Sometimes, LETS / CES currencies run beneath the radar of the respective country's taxation system, which can create unfairness of tax burden on those not participating. One might argue that, since these systems have so far been taken up in mainly un-affluent quarters, this problem is, to all intents and purposes, academic, since those participating would largely fall below taxation thresholds in any case. But were a LETS system to be seriously developed, then it would be proper that those involved were subject to tax in order to avoid a disproportionately high tax burden falling on everyone else.

The relevance of LETS to Steiner's accounting approach is not that he was necessarily advocating an alternative money system to compete with hard currency. His ideal, it seems, would be that the prevailing currency itself become more accounting-like, more LETS-like, and so lose its ability to be seen as a commodity in itself, lose its ability to be the subject of currency speculation, lose its ability to enable the wielding of shareholder power that forces anti-social, unecological, profit-maximisation-at-all-costs behaviour on producers, lose its ability to drive rentier economies that reward ownership at the expense of work, lose its ability to facilitate payment for (and exploitation of) work, lose its ability to underpin the finance economy run by money and for money which, as Marx observed, leads 'to the purest and most colossal form of gambling and swindling, and to reduce more and more the number of the few who exploit the social wealth'.[280] In this connection, it is interesting to note that US *financial* sector profit exceeded 40% of all business profit between 2001 and 2003, having been around the 20% mark from 1960—1985![281] This is an extraordinary thing considering the financial sector does not really produce very much.

---

[280] Karl Marx, *A Contribution to the Critique of Political Economy* (Moscow, 1977), Preface, https://www.marxists.org/archive/marx/works/1859/critique-pol-economy/preface-abs.htm.

[281] Paul Mason, *Postcapitalism: A Guide to Our Future* (London: Allen Lane, 2015), p. 99.

As Isler points out, not only does the experience to date of LETS systems help one envisage the accounting nature of money that Steiner felt was important to promote, but also the more recent emergence of Internet banking makes it a lot easier to imagine such an approach than would have been the case in Steiner's day—when the money supply was based on banknotes, coins and the gold standard.

With conventional currency, (a) anyone without money cannot trade, and (b) if the population increases / reduces or people become busier / idler, and the money supply (the amount of money in circulation) is not increased / reduced to reflect this economic growth / shrinkage, then one has inflationary / deflationary pressures to contend with, as the fixed amount of available money has to now be used to facilitate more / less exchange. With a LETS / CES / accounting approach, the number of IOUs (i.e. money!) in circulation increases / reduces depending on output. That is, the money supply pulsates as people are more or less busy; and the sort of inflation / deflation caused by an inadequate money supply is addressed. (Naturally, inflation / deflation based on under / over-production will still arise. If the number of cars being produced halves, their price will go up. There will always be the prospect of product-specific inflation when demand outstrips supply.)

From the following, it seems parallel currency systems were already being tried when Steiner was talking:

> ... *money circulation will become a flexible bookkeeping in the economic organism. The beginnings of such things actually exist already. As you know, a kind of credit already exists in certain areas that can be transferred without money changing hands ... (CW331, 2 July 1919)*

Although a number of logistical considerations might accompany the accounting approach to currency, LETS / CES well illustrate some basic principles. They also illustrate how currency need not be controlled by the rights realm at all, but can instead largely remain a concern of economic life (notwithstanding the rights realm's involvement in matters of taxation or, for that matter, fraud).

Advances in computer cryptography, most notably as seen in so-called block-chain technology, have led to the emergence of a-national crypto currencies, the most famous being Bitcoin. Such developments further illustrate how the internet can be harnessed for secure, cross-border, transactional purposes. However, currencies like Bitcoin, which initially come into circulation by people applying scarcely believable amounts of processing power[282] to basically solve puzzles (i.e. not by them doing any useful work) seem rather remote from the reality of commodity production that Steiner felt a currency should reflect.

* * *

Having looked at a good number of Steiner's observations, suggestions and innovations concerning operational matters in both the political and economic realms, we will now look at some of his operational suggestions for the cultural realm. But before proceeding, it should perhaps be emphasised yet again that a number of the economy-related comments just considered—especially those concerning currency and the like—were ideas he presented more as topics for research than as essential components of his threefold proposals. When reading some of these more radical ideas, the temptation can rather easily be to think: these ideas are so unusual … it is completely unrealistic to think they might be implemented any time soon … I will therefore not waste any further time on them. In this way his main thesis of threefold articulation, which would seem not only more implementable in quite a number of areas but also, in some instances, quite pressing, can easily be passed by.

7.5 Operational Remarks—Cultural Realm

As established previously, the cultural dimension of the threefold view of society includes not only the great cultural institutions of science, learning, the arts, divine worship but also everything that comes from the individual and interfaces with society, including what comes from

---

[282] Needing, according to Wikipedia, the same amount of electricity as that consumed by the entire country of Ecuador, or, according to the BBC News on 13 April 2021, half of that consumed within the UK!

individuals and feeds into the other two realms—the political and the economic. It is concerned with:

> ... everything which must blossom forth from each human individuality and be integrated into the social organism. (CW23, p. 59)
>
> ... everything which is created out of the single human individuality and needing to be incorporated into the social organism. (CW328(ii), 5 February 1919)
>
> ... everything flowing into the social organism which depends on the natural gift of individuals, the natural spiritual and physical talents coming from single individuals. (CW328(ii), 5 February 1919)

... everything that bursts forth from individuals and enters society!

And, as was also established previously, Steiner asserts that, within the cultural domain, freedom should be paramount, that all must be entirely free to develop and apply their various capacities, that educators be free to strive for the best ways of assisting this, that students (or parents) be free to choose their educators, that religion be an affair of choice, that art and science be left to evolve of their own accord, uncontaminated by political or economic interests, that freedom of thought and expression be celebrated, and so on. The individual should be free to go in whatever direction they find most fitting. Personal liberty is key. Naturally, an individual's freedom can only apply to the extent that it does not impinge on anyone else's.

> Cultural or spiritual life must really be free, not just in theory but in a real, living way. The human being standing within it must feel this freedom. (CW339(iii), 14 October 1921)
>
> ... the vital element of this member of the social organism must have its centre in the free unfolding of the physical and spiritual arrangement of the human being. Everything needs to be based on the sphere of the individuality. Everything flowing into this must come from the centre of the human individuality, and the physical and spiritual faculties must have free, evolutionary possibilities ... (CW328(iii), 10 February 1919)

With freedom being the leitmotif, Steiner unsurprisingly makes only a small handful of suggestions as to the *organisation* of the cultural realm.

On the other hand, he offered numerous suggestions—indeed a colossal body of work—as to how some of the activities within this realm could be developed healthily, especially education. But the key word here is 'offered'. In keeping with the freedom he 'preached', he encouraged all to take or leave, as they saw fit, what he or anyone else had to say regarding cultural matters; he was always at pains to stress that people should use their powers of unbiased, critical thinking at all times.

As well as suggestions that relate to the *organisation* of the cultural domain, some of his suggestions that relate to the *content* of activities within this realm will also be touched on briefly, where these seem relevant to societal health. Both sorts of consideration—ones regarding *organisation* and ones regarding *content*—feature in the coming pages of operational suggestions for the cultural domain.

7.5.1 Funding

How cultural realm activity is funded is not entirely straightforward.

We know that institutions 'belonging' to the economic domain receive income from sales. And we know that institutions 'belonging' to the rights domain receive income via taxation.

We also established in Section 5.4 ('Definition of Cultural Aspect'), that any input into these two systems that comes from individual capacities is, in fact, a contribution from the cultural domain:

> *The technical ideas that derive from spiritual life ... derive from spiritual life even when they come directly from members of the state or economic sectors. All organisational ideas and forces which fecundate the economic and state sectors originate in spiritual life. Compensation [remuneration] for this input to both social sectors will come either through the free appreciation of the beneficiaries, or through laws determined by the political state. (CW23, p. 80)*

Thus, funding of *this* sort of cultural life—the cultural life that feeds into the other two domains—will come either from sales or tax. On one occasion, Steiner refers to this type of cultural life as the 'half-free' cultural life: people applying their capacities in institutions 'belonging' to the economic or rights realms do not do so in a context of complete freedom. In the economic realm their work will occur, to a greater or lesser extent, in association—in dialogue—with the wishes of interested parties (consumers and distributors). In the rights realm, it will occur in dialogue with the populace at large.

But what of the *'free'* cultural life? What of those great cultural institutions of the arts, sciences, learning and religion which Steiner advises should operate entirely independently?

Here, Steiner considers the guiding principle of personal liberty—freedom—to be central. Funding of the 'free' cultural life is to come via the 'free appreciation' of individuals.

> As the payment of taxes must be compulsory even in a healthy social organism, what on the other hand is given to the spiritual life can be a matter of free will alone; for the spiritual life must be built wholly upon the spirit of man and be completely emancipated from anything else. (CW189(iii), 2 March 1919)

Further:

> Everything necessary for the maintenance of the spiritual organ-isation, including remuneration, will come to it through the free appreciation of the individuals who participate in the social organ-ism. The sound basis for the spiritual organisation will result from free competition among the individuals capable of spiritual work. (CW23, p. 114)

> What someone practises in the field of spiritual life is his own affair. What he is able to contribute to the social organism however, will be recompensed by those who have need of his spiritual contri-bution. Whoever is not able to support himself within the spiritual organisation from such compensation will have to transfer his activities to the political or economic section. (CW23, p. 79)

The leitmotif of freedom that applies to the cultural component of society necessarily comes with its twin: competition. If no one likes the contribution I am making with my capacities, then: tough! I will have to do something else. If I think I can sing nicely, but no one agrees, then I can't make a living singing. Steiner recommends that the 'free appreciation' that sponsors cultural activity should come direct from individuals, from the cultural realm itself, and not from some state bureaucracy, not by committee.

In one sense, his comments regarding 'free appreciation' and competition apply regardless of to which realm someone's workplace predominantly 'belongs'. A bricklayer or a chief executive of a multinational will be such because they are good at what they do. Competition of this kind—competition in the cultural aspect—applies just as much in 'half-free' cultural life (where capacities are applied in the economic or rights domains) as in more 'free' cultural life—where practitioners are at liberty to 'follow their star'. Note, however, we are not here talking about competition in the *economic* realm, about competition in the sense of producers trying to undercut each other or engage in whatever other subterfuge they can in order to steal a march on their rivals, but competition of the sort where the person better at laying bricks, lays bricks; i.e. competition in the cultural realm—the realm concerned with individual capacities.

In the cultural realm that is 'free', however, (i.e. where activity is independent of the other two realms, as well as free of interference even from others operating predominantly within the cultural domain itself), practitioners are not doing anyone's bidding; they are individuals who act purely from out of their own faculties. If a philosopher is battling with questions of morality, say, or an artist is painting a picture, then, provided they are not looking over their shoulder out of eagerness to please a patron, they will work in complete freedom. Turner did not paint *Rain, Steam, and Speed* as a result of some political process, nor following associative discussions with interested parties; and rightly so!

So, Steiner opines that, ideally, independent cultural domain activity should be funded entirely out of 'free will alone'. That is, in freedom, the artist paints a picture or the vicar gives a sermon, and then you decide for yourself whether to buy the painting or donate to the church. If you like what you see, you can let your 'free appreciation' express itself in financial support. It is not appropriate for a state department to make such decisions on your behalf. And this applies in particular to those institutions of the cultural realm that Steiner singles out as those which are not only *based on* capacities but also *cultivate* these capacities: i.e. schools, universities, research establishments, training facilities, awareness-raising campaigns and other places of learning. With these, he recommends that they be decoupled from the rights state (where the majority decides how to proceed) and instead be maintained by free appreciation, the free choice of the individual. Thus, innovation, diversity and vibrancy replace plain-vanilla uniformity—a uniformity that can rather too easily become tyrannical.

Despite this general principle of personal choice or 'free appreciation', personal income in the 'free' cultural domain might nonetheless arise via different mechanisms. The income a philosopher working in a university receives would amount to the 'gift money' mentioned in Section 7.4.19 ('Three types of money'). Although such income might come via taxation (i.e. 'compulsory gift'), it is not provided in exchange for a defined and quantifiable commodity. It is given to enhance personal capacities. And even where there *is* a more defined commodity being paid for, such as a work of art, payment to the artist might still come via taxation if it is a piece of public art. (With a more threefold delineation in place, public art might be more a matter for the cultural administration than the rights state, however.)

Where a work of art is purchased, the transaction cannot readily be thought of as one of gift. It amounts to the purchase of a consumer good (the different realms continuously overlap, remember!). All the same, this commodity purchase does not mean the artist will be producing pictures based on associatively arrived-at contracts; he or she can still (unless prescriptively commissioned) paint in complete freedom. Whilst an art *poster* might have been manufactured in a repetitive system that feeds into a network of retail outlets that have a supply contract with a printer, say, the artist will not be part of associative, pre-agreed arrangements that respond to predetermined needs, that respond to customers saying they wish their souls to be touched in this specific way or that! No, generally the artist will first paint the picture in complete freedom, and it will then be bought out of 'free appreciation'. Yes, dining chairs or winter coats will be purchased on the same basis, but only because they have a design (i.e. an artistic, cultural, individual) element to them, unlike, say, petrol or sultanas which can be purchased purely on the basis of utilitarian need.

To us today, it may seem obvious that anything with an artistic aspect to it will be created by free initiative, and purchased out of free appreciation. But in emphasizing these things, Steiner will almost certainly have been, at least in part, countering the arguments of some of those communists whose slogans had won over many a mind at the time.

Inasmuch as both he and communist thought proposed production be based on pre-identified need where possible, then there could be said to be some small measure of overlap between the two schools of thought. But, as we have seen, Steiner's threefold approach is quite unlike communism in that he emphasises the state should have no part in economic production. And further, he is emphatic that the human spark of the cultural domain should be left entirely free to flourish as it will. Under no circumstances should the state be allowed to tyrannise the spark of individuals—individual initiative, individual choice, etc. As Paul Mason observes when discussing the 'cyber-Stalinism' of two planned-economy theorisers (Paul Cockshott and Allin Cottrell) and the shortcomings of their IT-based approach: 'A computerised plan … might tell the shoe industry to produce shoes, but it could not tell Beyoncé to produce a surprise album marketed only via social media, as she did in 2013'.[283]

One other point of contact with communist thought is Steiner's proposal that the means of production should not be there simply to be enjoyed by non-working individuals—e.g. absent shareholders or extractive descendants of the original entrepreneur. But again, his approach is entirely different to what one saw East of the Iron Curtain. He insists it is not for the state to determine how such capital be used. Again, it is about enabling the capabilities of *individuals* (cultural domain) to be productive for the community—see Section 7.3.7 ('Land and the means of production').

And in Section 7.4.17 ('Gift to education') the principle was established of using excess financial capital arising from economic activity to enrich those capabilities, i.e. the principle of channelling such surpluses, by gift, into education, training, research. The following reinforces this.

> *Endeavour to work towards dividing the social organism into its three spheres, … and the kind of socialisation will then occur which, in accordance with certain legal concepts, will see to it that whatever a person earns over and above his needs shall be constantly channelled into the spiritual / cultural system. It returns again to the spiritual / cultural sphere.*

---

[283] Paul Mason, *Postcapitalism: A Guide to Our Future* (London: Allen Lane, 2015), p. 234.

> *Nowadays this arrangement applies only in the realm of intellec-*
> *tual property, where nobody finds it strange. The person cannot*
> *keep his intellectual property for his descendants for more than a*
> *certain period—30 years after his death at most—then it becomes*
> *public property. We ought to think of this as a possible model for*
> *the channelling back of surplus profits into the social organism,*
> *even if it is the result of individual effort, and also channelling back*
> *what is covered by the capitalist system. The only question is, into*
> *which areas? Into that area which can take care of the individual*
> *capacities of people, whether spiritual or otherwise; into the spiri-*
> *tual / cultural realm. Things will be managed this way when people*
> *take their rightful place in the social organism. This is what this way*
> *of thinking will lead to. (CW193, p. 83)*

If surpluses arising in the economy are made available for funding education and so on, the question then becomes: which *particular* institutions are to benefit? Again, the 'free appreciation' principle Steiner advocates is sovereign. If the parents of 800 children like the look of school A, and the parents of 400 other children like the look of school B, then school A will need roughly twice as much money as school B to cover materials, staffing and building needs. As established in 'Gift to education' (Section 7.4.17), associations or the central economic administration could establish the demand for different educational establishments and thence facilitate a logical distribution of funding.

And, as Steiner points out, even differing geographic boundaries for the economic and cultural administrations need not act as any hindrance to such mutual engagement:

> *How is the cultural life to draw necessary support from the eco-*
> *nomic life if the administrative boundaries of their two spheres*
> *do not coincide? To find the answer one need only reflect that a*
> *self-governing cultural life confronts the independent economic life*
> *as an economic corporation. As an economic corporation, it can*
> *enter into agreements for its economic support with the economic*
> *administrative bodies of its regions, regardless of any larger eco-*
> *nomic region to which these administrative regions may belong.*
> *Anyone whose concepts of what is possible in practice are limited*
> *to what he has already seen, will look upon these proposals as*

'grey theory'. He will think, too, that the necessary arrangements will prove too complicated to work. Whether the arrangements prove complicated or not will depend entirely on the skill of the particular people who arrange them. However, no one should oppose measures demanded by the present-day necessities of the world for fear of supposed complications. (CW24, p.60)

The words 'a self-governing cultural life confronts the independent economic life as an economic corporation' remind one that even cultural endeavour has an economic *dimension* to it. A university may 'belong' to the cultural domain but it still also provides *services* for which it needs to be paid. Such overlap between the realms is looked at further in the next chapter.

Naturally, in the absence of the sort of economy implicit in the above quote (that is, an economy that is both associative as well as entirely independent of the state), then other funding mechanisms for independent education are needed which can uphold the threefold principle of cultural independence.

Fee-paying schools are a start, but they are not the best since attendance at these relies on the economic position of parents. The cultural and economic realms remain too closely joined (although pedagogical independence can indeed be maintained, to a degree).

In Section 7.3.6 ('Taxation'), education vouchers were considered as quite a good solution to the conundrum. To satisfy the requirement of cultural independence, though, these need to come, irrevocably, with no state strings attached vis-à-vis pedagogy.

Yet another approach was seen with the first Waldorf school, set up in Stuttgart in 1919. Here, funding came almost entirely from a single industry—the Waldorf-Astoria cigarette factory. It may have been a bespoke solution, but it enabled cultural (pedagogical) independence to prevail. Of course, any funding of this sort for cultural life—i.e. direct from business—would at all times need to be arranged such that a hygienic separation of the two realms was maintained and conflicts of interest avoided. For example, it would be important that a medical research facility was never funded by a pharmaceutical company. That said, if the latter was a business structured along threefold lines, motivated by service and brotherliness rather than profit, then the risk of conflict of interest would be significantly reduced, since the business would have little interest in suppressing the truth. Remember, associative industry would dispense with obsessions about profit maximisation, competition, share price, dividends, etc. and instead be concerned with service.

Whether education was funded by such gift, straight from industrial profits, or via a mechanism where those in need of the education for their children simply received sufficient remuneration to cover such cost (via 'fair price'—Section 7.4.11—and the profit-sharing rights established in Section 7.4.14), or whether some other mechanism were adopted is perhaps not so important. As with his other operational suggestions, Steiner is not proposing hard and fast rules, but advocating hygienic separation between the three independent administrations such that the guiding principle of freedom / personal liberty is respected in cultural matters. With education vouchers, for instance, parents would need to be entirely free to spend these at whatever school they wished, not only those overseen by a state bureaucracy.

Whilst education, in its rather unique position, might also come with a right of access enshrined by the rights domain, it is perhaps worth reminding oneself that certain other cultural matters would not. A right to so many religious services per annum would be strange. As such, funding for these remains via private patronage alone, that is to say, without the involvement of the economic or rights administrations.

In summary:

- 'Half-free' cultural life—work in the economic or rights domains—is funded by sales or tax.
- 'Free' cultural life should at all times be funded out of 'free appreciation' / personal choice.
- This might take the form of gift—where the funder does not receive a commodity in exchange for their money, but capacities are being enhanced.
- It might take the form of a purchase—where payment is made in exchange for, say, a painting.

- It might be via tax, but it is not deemed healthy if the state determines *to whom* the funding be paid. E.g. even if a university professor is paid out of tax, her original appointment to the post should have arisen out of 'free appreciation', as should the applications to her course of study.

Reflections in relation to the present

As noted previously, former UK Prime Minister, Margaret Thatcher, does seem to have held threefold instincts with respect to the freedom of education, being keen, as she was, on the idea of education vouchers (never introduced) where parents would be left entirely free to 'spend' them at whichever school they wished. Although these would have still been funded via taxation, they would have undoubtedly brought greater freedom and vitality to the education sector. They would have furthered the 'free appreciation' of which Steiner speaks.

Steiner's mention of the 'spiritual worker' being able to exist on account of other individuals freely appreciating what comes from the spiritual worker's capacities could be interpreted as a nod to those astronomic incomes enjoyed by certain musicians or sportspeople. Inasmuch as freedom and free appreciation apply in this realm, this interpretation is perhaps not incorrect. However, his general principle of needs being covered as expressed in 'fair price' would perhaps ideally take precedence over any idea of inordinately excessive levels of income. All the same, 'fair price' could, in theory perhaps, also include needs that the average person might think extravagant. It could also be interpreted as a minimum rather than a target (somewhat akin to a living wage, but one that properly covered all reasonable needs), although I'm not aware of Steiner ever having said this.

> ... this cornerstone of economic life—that a man must satisfy his needs until he again produces a like product—applies to all branches of spiritual and material life. *[my emphasis, RM]* (CW337a, 30 May 1919)

An example Steiner himself sets would seem instructive also: For some five years, he gave evening classes on a range of subjects at the Berlin Workers College founded by Marxist, Karl Liebknecht, eventually becoming the most popular speaker by a long way, with classes exceeding 200 print workers, metal workers, automotive assembly-line workers and the like. On account of his popularity, the college directors proposed paying Steiner in proportion to the audience he attracted, but he rejected this idea, suggesting that, instead, all lecturers be given equal increases if funds allowed. This suggestion was adopted—the increases being covered by the takings from Steiner's talks. (This anecdote was related some time later by someone who had attended the board meeting where this had come up.) It is possible Steiner was simply being modest, although this gesture also appears consistent with both the needs-based 'fair price' approach as well as (and perhaps even more so) with the 'fundamental social law' he observed back in 1905 ('The well-being of a total community of human beings working together becomes greater the less the individual demands the proceeds of his achievements for himself …'). Steiner was eventually dismissed by the college for refusing to toe the Marxist line—a doctrinaire take on life seeming more important to the college's socialist leadership than enjoyable self-betterment for proletarian workers.

7.5.2   Education

> *A time must come when it becomes clear to people already in school what they are through the social organism, and what they are therefore obliged to give back to the social organism … There will come a time when children will learn social understanding as school children. Because this has been neglected under the influence of modern technology and capitalism we have come to these present conditions, to a social organism in this diseased state. (CW329, 2 April 1919)*

As has already been established, Steiner saw education as a central—if not *the* central—activity existing within the cultural realm of society. Here we will consider both its organisation / co-ordination as a sector as well as recommendations he made regarding educational content and pedagogy (for children). Comments he made about the former— organisation / co-ordination—relate more directly to the threefoldness of the social organism. Comments about curriculum and pedagogy do not fall so directly under the 'threefold' banner, but since they have such a direct bearing on the general subject of this book, namely societal health, they are touched on too. Strictly speaking they should perhaps be covered outside the chapters on threefolding; but as they will only be considered briefly, a separate chapter seems scarcely warranted.

Organisation / co-ordination of the education sector

The following passages speak for themselves.

> The administration of education, from which all culture develops, must be turned over to the educators. Economic and political considerations should be entirely excluded from this administration. Each teacher should arrange his or her time so that he can also be an administrator in his field. He should be just as much at home tending to administrative matters as he is in the classroom. No-one should make decisions who is not directly engaged in the educational process. No parliament or congress, nor any individual who was perhaps once an educator, is to have anything to say. What is experienced in the teaching process would then flow naturally into the administration. By its very nature such a system would engender competence and objectivity. (CW23, p. 12)

> Even the schools which directly serve the state and the economy should be administered by the educators: law schools, trade schools, agriculture and industrial colleges, all should be administered by the representatives of a free spiritual life. (CW23, p. 13)

> ... the collective will [i.e. the public, via democracy, RM] cannot express what is to arise from individual human abilities; here institutions must function so as to allow the individual to achieve full expression. In a way, the human being might be compared to a natural landscape. One cannot cultivate and manage an expanse of land without considering its different aspects. The nature of each part must be studied so that one can learn what it might produce. Thus, in the realm of culture, individual initiative based on individual capabilities must become socially effective; cultural life may not be determined through the will of all. Within the realm of culture this universal will becomes antisocial because it deprives the community of the fruits that individual human capabilities can provide.

> Thus self-administration of the cultural life is the only way to promote individual abilities. Only through self-administration will conditions exist that give rise not to a universal will that suppresses the

fruitfulness of the individual for social life, but rather a condition in which individual human accomplishments can be taken up into the life of the whole for its benefit.

Certain criteria will be established from within such a self-governing spiritual-cultural life whereby the right people may be put into the right positions, and immediate, vital trust can take the place of laws and regulations. Educators will not look to laws and regulations for their educational aims; instead, they will become observers of life and seek to learn, by listening to life, what it is they have to inculcate. It will be possible within the cultural sphere to avail oneself of persons who, through years of experience in practical life, are well versed in the ways of law and economics. In the cultural sphere, they will in turn encounter people with whom they can, through lively intercourse, exchange and reshape their practical experience and bring it to educational fruition. On the other hand, administrators in the cultural sphere may occasionally feel the need to enter the arena of practical life in order to utilise and revitalise their own knowledge.

[...] a lively exchange can take place between the cultural organism and other branches of society. When tradition and public opinion is reshaped in the cultural life, the potential for vitality is far greater than in an inflexible system. (CW24, pp. 5-6)

The place and function of educators within society should depend solely on the authority of those engaged in this activity. The administration of the educational institutions, the organization of courses of instruction and their goals should be entirely in the hands of persons who themselves are simultaneously either teaching or otherwise productively engaged in cultural life. In each case, such persons would divide their time between actual teaching (or some other form of cultural productivity) and the administrative control of the educational system. It will be evident to anyone who can bring himself to an unbiased examination of cultural life that the peculiar vitality and energy of soul required for organizing and directing educational institutions will be called forth only in someone actively engaged in teaching or in some sort of cultural creativity. (CW24, p. 75)

... out of good instinct, modern social democracy has coined the phrase: religion must be a private matter. In the same way, strange as it may sound to a person of today, all spiritual life must be a private matter, based on the trust that those who wish to receive

> *it have for those who can offer it. Certainly, I know that many people today fear that if we can choose our own school, we—or our descendants—will all become illiterate. We will not. (CW329, 2 April 1919)*
>
> *The current antisocial state of affairs is the result of individuals entering society who lack social sensitivity because of their education. Socially sensitive individuals can only develop within an educational system which is conducted and administered by other socially sensitive individuals. No progress will be made towards solving the social question if we do not treat the question of education and spirit as an essential part of it. An antisocial situation is not merely the result of economic structures, it is also caused by the antisocial behaviour of individuals who are active in the structures. It is antisocial to allow youth to be educated by people who themselves have become strangers to reality because the conduct and content of their work has been dictated to them from without. (CW23, p. 14)*
>
> *The school must be self-managing; teachers cannot be civil servants. (CW298, p. 13)*
>
> *All juridical, pedagogical and spiritual concerns are in the free hands of the individual. In this domain the state only has the right to police, not the right to initiate. (CW24(ii), p. 80)*
>
> *A basic principle of ... a threefold social order is to work towards an independent school system, making it free of the State so that the State does not even inspect schools. The activity of self-administered schools should arise purely from cultural needs.*[284]

These passages are self-explanatory.

In summary:

- Self-administration of the education sector is advocated, free of any interference from the economic or rights realms.
- The administration of educational institutions should be undertaken by those who are also simultaneously educators (or at the very least working in the independent cultural domain).

---

[284] Quoted in Richard House, *Pushing Back to Ofsted: Safeguarding and the Legitimacy of Ofsted's Inspection Judgments—A Critical Case Study* (Stroud: InterActions, 2020), p. 23.

- Trust, personal choice, reputation replace laws and regulations (regarding educational content and method).
- Ideally, the state does not inspect schools, or, if it does, then it's involvement can only be one of 'policing'—e.g. safeguarding all from harm.

Reflections in relation to the present

It is an extraordinary thing that a politician with limited knowledge of education or child development can become responsible for the country's education. This state of affairs has seen the sector lurch from one crisis to the next in the UK in recent years as one Secretary of State's attempts to make their mark are then superseded by those of the next. This meddlesomeness has seen teacher morale drop to desperately low levels, and brought a crisis not very far from boiling point.[285]

A particularly worrying example of the absence of relevant skills at ministerial level has been witnessed in early years' education. Repeated evidence from abroad shows that delaying the introduction of formal learning until about age 7 results in greater wellbeing amongst children (compared to a shocking mental health problem among UK children, with even 9-year-olds talking about suicide),[286] as well as, frequently, higher eventual academic outcomes.[287] Estonia and Finland are each a case in point. Here formal schooling starts at 7. But compared to the UK's 13th position in the OECD's 2018 PISA rankings of academic outcomes (for what they are worth), Estonia and Finland ranked 5th and 7th respectively (or 1st and 2nd in Europe!).[288] After Ireland changed its early years' curriculum in 2008 (a change which raised the starting age for reading and writing to six), subsequent PISA statistics showed literacy had shot up in those children coming through after the change.[289] Children can be put off school

---

[285] Sally Weale, 'Third of new teachers quit within five years', *The Guardian*, 25 October 2016.

[286] Sally Weale, 'Mental health of pupils is "at crisis point", teachers warn', *The Guardian*, 16 April 2019.

[287] See, for example, David Whitebread of Cambridge University, https://www.cam.ac.uk/research/discussion/school-starting-age-the-evidence.

[288] https://www.teachertoolkit.co.uk/2019/12/03/pisa-2018/.

[289] Sue Palmer, https://nowwearesix.org.

entirely by being introduced to reading, writing and other types of abstract thinking before their cognitive makeup is suited to such things. As every gardener knows: you don't put your seedlings out too early! But children in the UK generally start formal schooling aged 5 (4 in Northern Ireland—the lowest in Europe).

Despite the fact that the ability to learn has been comprehensively demonstrated not to be a linear process, consecutive UK politicians have nonetheless decided they know best and approached education like filling a bath, drip by drip: the sooner you start filling, the more water you will have by bath time. Lamentable research is then referenced to back up this ignorance, like, for example, research that demonstrates that if you start teaching reading at 5, pupils will be better readers at 7 than if you start at age 6. Surprise, surprise! This is all irrelevant if you fail to look at 'A' level results or indeed whether children were so put off learning by premature cognitive grind (not to mention teacher- and parent-stressing tests) that they did not get anywhere near an 'A' level when the time came.

These follies are then perpetuated by an equally ignorant press. The front-page splash 'Parenting crisis: half of five-year-olds not ready for school' was particularly excruciating in this regard.[290] The even more startling front-cover headline in 2014: 'Ofsted chief: send children to school from the age of two' made the Ofsted[291] boss Sir Michael Wilshaw look particularly out of his depth.[292] Can he *remember* being two? Or even four? The story concerned the fact that children from the poorest backgrounds can be '19 months behind in reading and numeracy by the time they start compulsory schooling at five'.[293] Whilst it is undoubtedly the case that deprived children will on the whole be found to be 'behind' in their development, the article displayed little recognition that children from privileged backgrounds thrive because they live in peaceful, respectful, warm (in both senses) homes, share healthy meals around a table with loving,

[290] Charlie Cooper, 'Parenting crisis: half of five-year-olds not ready for school, research shows', *The Independent*, 23 September 2014.
[291] The UK schools inspectorate.
[292] Graham Paton, 'Ofsted chief: send children to school from the age of two', *The Telegraph*, 3 April 2014.
[293] Richard Garner, the *i* newspaper, 3 April 2014.

conversing family members, etc. In their youngest, most vulnerable years, these children are protected.

Thankfully, there are signs that these erroneous ways may be nearing their end in the UK, with even the National Union of Teachers calling, in 2015, for formal schooling to be delayed until 7, for example,[294] and, in 2019, the Labour Party proposing to abolish any testing of children in the younger years that reduces education to an inane exercise of teaching only to pass tests.

Our education would certainly benefit from being disentangled from the political realm altogether; the latter should be restricted to rights / legislation. Change is desperately overdue. Yes, the democratic process / the rights realm can enshrine each child's *right* to an education; but if equality (uniformity!) is applied to educational content and pedagogical approach, vitality, plurality, innovation and improvement get sucked out.

In relation to this, Charles Waterman noted in 1948: 'Our history since the close of the Middle Ages has a long record of strenuous battles for freedom of religious belief and practice, freedom of speech and writing, freedom of the Press. The whole Nonconformist movement, closely allied with political Liberalism, sprang from this source. In the eyes of the world the independent Englishman, with his home his castle, stood for this principle. State education, which runs counter to it, was not a native growth; the impulse for it came from Germany.'[295]

On the plus side, the range of educational opportunities for most school *leavers* is incredibly broad nowadays. One can do degrees in just about every conceivable subject, and even the imposition of tuition fees in the UK in recent years, despite being unpopular, is no ultimate hindrance to students from more modest backgrounds since repayment is contingent on earning above a certain level after graduation.[296]

---

[294] By Agency, 'NUT calls for primary school children to play in the classroom up to the age of 7', *The Telegraph*, 2 April 2015.

[295] Charles Waterman, *A Middle Way for Britain* (Shrewsbury: Christian Community, 1948), p. 4.

[296] See, for example, Martin Lewis, https://moneysavingexpert.com/students/student-loans-tuition-fees-changes.

Educational content and style (curriculum and pedagogy)

Steiner occasionally comments on university education, taking issue with this or that professor, approach or viewpoint, for example; but the educational ideas for which he has become widely known concern the education of children. In 1919, at the request of the boss of the Waldorf-Astoria cigarette factory in Stuttgart, he inaugurates a school for the children of the factory workers.[297] This is both a new school but also a new *type* of school that, over time, leads to the creation of many similar schools around the world.[298]

The pedagogical innovations in his approach are covered in a veritable wealth of books by both him and other authors, so there seems little merit in saying much about them here. But for those with a passing curiosity, a few distinguishing features are offered below. They are, after all, not only interesting in themselves but also relevant to social reform inasmuch as the providing of an uplifting space where social sensitivity within a child can be nurtured will have a direct bearing on the social qualities of society later.

Naturally, Steiner wanted the Waldorf School to be simply a good school. He would almost certainly have agreed with every single aim of the UK's most famous school, Eton College, for example, namely:

- promoting the best habits of independent thought and learning in the pursuit of excellence;
- providing a broadly-based education designed to enable all boys[299] to discover their strengths, and to make the most of their talents within Eton and beyond;
- engendering respect for individuality, difference, the importance of teamwork and the contribution that each boy makes to the life of the school and the community;

---

[297] We will leave to one side the irony that one of the most ardent and financially supportive admirers of Steiner's efforts in pursuit of the common good was the owner of a tobacco concern!

[298] Today there are over a thousand Steiner schools and some two thousand Steiner kindergartens in over sixty nations.

[299] The Waldorf School, however, took both boys and girls which was rare in 1919.

- supporting pastoral care that nurtures physical health, emotional maturity and spiritual richness;
- fostering self-confidence, enthusiasm, perseverance, tolerance and integrity.[300]

To what extent Eton College or a Steiner school achieve these aims is a separate question. But one thing one *can* say is that Steiner's way of getting there differed in many ways from convention.

The school in Stuttgart was novel for its time in that it not only catered for both girls and boys, but also, by teaching the children of both workers and management, it was the first school in Germany to bring children together from all socio-economic strata. One thing Steiner stressed was that the Waldorf School was not there to teach anthroposophy; it should not be a 'worldview school'.[301] Anthroposophy, he emphasised, was not for children but something adults could study out of complete freedom, if they so wished.

> In the Waldorf School in Stuttgart we have tried to found something as far as is possible in our time which is not built on programs but only flows out of pædagogy and didactics. The Free [i.e. independent] Waldorf School has a number of teachers. They would, if they met together, be able to think up ideal programs for the school, for which I would not particularly praise them. We don't need that. The people, the living human beings constitute the staff. And what they are able to do, the best that can be elicited from them, that should be developed. All ideal programs are dismissed, all prescriptions are dismissed, everything is placed into the immediate impulse of the individual ability. No prescription disturbs him who is to act—and that is just the task of the individual human being—out of pædagogy and didactic in a certain area of spiritual life. Of course to-day one can only realize such things up to a certain point. In practical life one can nowhere realise an ideal, but one must do what is possible in the circumstances of life. (CW79, 30 November 1921)
>
> In educating, what a teacher does can depend only slightly on anything he gets from a general, abstract pedagogy: it must rather be

---

[300] https://www.etoncollege.com/EtonsAims.aspx?nid=7228fed0-c26f-4dd6-ae1d-db79bdcsc748 (accessed 4 September 2018).
[301] Albert Schmelzer, *The Threefold Movement, 1919: A History* (Forest Row: Rudolf Steiner Press, 2017), p. 182.

newly born every moment from a live understanding of the young human being he or she is teaching. One may, of course, object that this lively kind of education and instruction breaks down in large classes. This objection is no doubt justified in a limited sense. Taken beyond those limits, however, the objection merely shows that the person who makes it proceeds from abstract educational norms, for a really living art of education based on a genuine knowledge of the human being carries with it a power that rouses the interest of every single pupil so that there is no need for direct 'individual' work in order to keep his attention on the subject. One can put forth the essence of one's teaching in such a form that each pupil assimilates it in his own individual way. This requires simply that whatever the teacher does should be sufficiently alive [e.g. not simply regurgitating notes or dryly passing on information, RM]. If anyone has a genuine sense for human nature, the developing human being becomes for him such an intense, living riddle that the very attempt to solve it awakens the pupil's living interest empathetically. (CW24, p. 113)

In a state school, everything is strictly defined ... everything is planned with exactitude. With us everything depends on the free individuality of each single teacher ... Classes are entrusted entirely to the individuality of the class teacher ... what we seek to achieve must be achieved in the most varied ways.[302]

The important thing is that we do not rob teachers of their strengths of personality by forcing them to work within the confines of government regulations.[303]

... in my Philosophy of Freedom *I described the moral impulse that is at the same time the most profound social impulse guiding the human being as 'moral intuition'. Something needs to come to fruition in us that can guide us even in the most concrete situations and tell us: this is what you must do now. [...] you have to look at the individuality of each human being with the presupposition that moral intuitions reside in his or her heart and soul. All education must be aimed at awakening these moral intuitions ... (CW305(ii), p. 149)*

---

[302] Quoted in Richard House, *Pushing Back to Ofsted: Safeguarding and the Legitimacy of Ofsted's Inspection Judgments—A Critical Case Study* (Stroud: InterActions, 2020), p. 23.

[303] Ibid., p. 24.

The above comments are quite general; the following cover some of the more specific—and unique—suggestions Steiner made concerning the education of children:

1. An emphasis on helping the child develop their unique individuality.

> A child's spiritual individuality is something completely sacred ... (CW83, p. 112)
>
> The question should not be: what does a human being need to know and be able to do for the social order that now exists, but rather: what capacities are latent in this human being, and what lies within that can be developed? Then it will be possible to bring ever new forces into the social order from the rising generations. The life of the social order will be what is made of it by a succession of fully developed human beings who take their place in the social order. The rising generation should not be moulded into what the existing social order chooses to make of it.
>
> A healthy relation exists between school and society only when society is kept constantly supplied with the new and individual potentials of persons whose educations have allowed them to develop unhampered. (CW24, pp. 71-72)
>
> Our function becomes that of an awakener of the child's soul and not a crammer of the soul.[304]

2. *How* one teaches (pedagogy) is as important as *what* one teaches (curriculum).

> Thus, what matters is not so much what the children in the Stuttgart Waldorf school are taught as how they are taught. (CW334, p. 121)
>
> For it can very well happen that owing to the nature of the staff and children in 1920, say, one will proceed in a manner quite different from one's procedure with the staff and children one has in 1924. For it may be that the staff has increased and so quite changed, and the children will certainly be quite different ... Experience gained day by day in the classroom is the only thing that counts. (CW305(iii), p. 3)

---

[304] Quoted in Richard House, *Pushing Back to Ofsted: Safeguarding and the Legitimacy of Ofsted's Inspection Judgments—A Critical Case Study* (Stroud: InterActions, 2020), p. 24.

3. Close consideration is given to children's constitutions. For example, Steiner points out that one of the four temperaments[305] usually predominates in each child and that paying attention to this provides one way of differentiating the ways to reach and engage children. He advises children of different temperaments are particularly receptive to different teaching approaches: phlegmatic children respond well when there is great enthusiasm in the teacher; melancholic children respond particularly sensitively when they hear about suffering, etc. From puberty onwards, the teacher takes further developmental influences into account.

4. In the younger years, physical development and co-ordination are considered paramount. Free play in the kindergarten builds healthy children with solid foundations (on which mental development can grow more easily later). In the early years of formal schooling, children do things like learn to knit, as this fosters sensory integration and greater dexterity which helps their ability to think later.

5. The start of formal schooling—writing and then reading (in that order), for example—are introduced around age 7 when (the change of teeth occurs and …) when the child's makeup is more suited to this type of focused thinking. From age 7/8, most children readily develop an interest in this and so learn it extremely efficiently. Teaching children reading and writing earlier, *before* their makeup is suited to this sort of thinking (a) takes their energy away from developing their physical strength and dexterity which can flourish when they play and are not having to strain mentally, (b) puts countless children off learning altogether, or can inappropriately and prematurely have them marked down as failures.

6. Recognition that, up to the change of teeth, the child develops essentially through imitation and *doing*, so KG teachers should be people who are worthy of imitation (i.e. kind, dignified, etc.). Not only the teacher's actions, but also their thoughts and feelings should be noble ones that are suitable for the child to imitate.

---

[305] Melancholic: introverted thinker; tendency to sadness; often bony-framed; Choleric: strong willed; tendency to anger; often smaller framed; Phlegmatic: stick to the task; tendency to plod and over-appreciate their food; Sanguine: sunny but scatty; physical lightness.

> *You cannot teach a child to be good merely by explanation ... What you actually are ... is the most essential thing of all for the child.*[306]
>
> *If you look at young children with some understanding, you will always find that they are imitative and do what 'big people' do. For young children, it is extremely important that the people around them do only what they should imitate. It is important that you think and feel only what children should imitate when you are in their presence. (CW296, 9 August 1919)*

From his rare insights into human development, Steiner makes the seemingly paradoxical observation that allowing children to imitate, sheep-like at this age (and not burden them, for example, with reflecting, or memorising, or reading and writing), greatly enhances their freedom in adult life, that is to say, strengthens their own *un*-sheep-like individuality later.

7. Recognition that, between the change of teeth and puberty, the child lives particularly in *feeling* and as such learns especially well in an artistic environment.

> *The children at first draw and paint the forms out of which they can then develop the letters. In other words, they start with the artistic and then proceed to the intellectual. To allow the inherent needs of the child to unfold properly in this developmental phase, all teaching must be based on this artistic approach. (CW334, p. 125)*

8. Recognition that, between the change of teeth and puberty, the child also lives particularly strongly in fantasy and imagination which, if nurtured properly, can be a powerful tool in the child's growth.

> *In the child between the change of teeth and puberty it is not the intellect but the fantasy that is predominantly active; we must constantly be thinking of the child's fantasy, and therefore, as I have often said, we must especially develop fantasy ourselves ... (CW311, p. 1)*

---

[306] Quoted in Richard House, *Pushing Back to Ofsted: Safeguarding and the Legitimacy of Ofsted's Inspection Judgments—A Critical Case Study* (Stroud: InterActions, 2020), p. 23.

For example, a less Waldorf approach to introducing children to good and bad is the more abstract, dry, factual approach via the child's intellect (e.g. saying to children: 'It's not very nice to do such and such, so we shouldn't do it')—which is more likely to leave the child feeling somewhat 'cold'. The Waldorf approach, on the other hand, would involve the telling of a story which portrayed good or bad deeds in vivid 'pictures' such that the child *experiences* the profound sense of injustice, or uprightness, or whatever in their *feelings*. Doing this, without analysing or summing up the moral of the story at the end, appeals to the child's pictorial way of thinking—which comes before 'thinking in words' in child development. According to Steiner, this is a far more effective way of teaching children such things.

9. Recognition that, between the change of teeth and puberty, the child also has a longing and a love for authority, and that it is therefore particularly important for their teachers to be people worthy of respect, whose wisdom they can reliably look up to and trust.

> Anyone who can look at life impartially would agree how fortunate it was for his inner harmony of soul throughout life if, at this age, he was able to look up to this or that person of authority with a proper respect. He did not now imitate this person; the relation was such that he felt: through this human individual is revealed to me what I myself ought to be and want to be ... (CW83, p. 107)
>
> Children experience a great uplifting if they can do everything because a person they look up to says it is the right thing to do. There is nothing worse for children than attempting to develop their judgment too early, before puberty. (CW296, 9 August 1919)

Again, Steiner makes a surprisingly counter-intuitive connection between this pedagogical element and the child's growth into adult life.

> What we implant during these years will form the basis for what adults within the social organism experience as equal rights for their fellow human beings. The feeling for equal rights for other human beings cannot exist in adults if a feeling for authority is not implanted in them during childhood. Otherwise, adults will never become mature enough to recognise the rights of others. (CW296, 9 August 1919)

10. Recognition that it is once puberty has arrived that the faculty of critical thinking can really begin to come into its own. At this age, young people start to live especially comfortably in the intellectual pursuit of ideas and ideals, and it is really only once they have reached this age that they should be educated to begin developing their own mature opinions and judgement.

11. Steiner recommends that in this last phase of childhood, integrated with immersion in academic disciplines proper, education should have a particular focus on arousing young people's powers of empathy and compassion for the experiences of others. This kindling of a love of humanity in youth can particularly arouse a feeling of brotherliness in adulthood.

The feeling of fraternity ... can never warm the relationships in economic life as history requires if we do not develop a love of humanity during these years. The kind of fraternity we must strive for in future economic life can exist in human souls only if we form education after the age of fifteen so that we work completely consciously toward a general love of humanity, and only when all questions regarding world views and all education ... are based upon a love of humanity or, more generally speaking, a love of the external world. (CW296, 9 August 1919)

12. Emphasis is also placed on young people of this age doing manual craft work to complement their academic learning.

13. Throughout the formal school years (age 7—18), subjects are introduced in 'main lessons' at ages which are particularly suitable. Steiner highlighted how the developmental steps of a growing child broadly follow the developmental steps taken by humanity throughout the epochs of history, and that it is enlivening for children to learn about particular subjects at particular stages of their childhood. These 'main lessons' generally take up the first two hours of each morning, and every three or so weeks, the subject will change.

... if one introduces into the child's world of concepts and feel-ings what coincides just at that period of life with the direction taken by his own developing powers, one then gives such added vigour to the growth of the whole person that it remains a source of strength throughout life. If in any period of life one works against the grain of these developing powers, one weakens the individual. (CW24, p. 114)

14. The arts, sciences, humanities, crafts and physical education are taught holistically in equal measure such that head, heart and hand are all honed together, with each discipline helping the maturing of the other two. So, in addition to academic learning, the 'heart' (emotional intelligence / morality / etc.) can also grow through the child experiencing beauty by receiving and creating pictures, music and other forms of art, and through hearing many stories, particularly in their younger years, stories that stir the heart. And the hand is educated through playing, initially, and later through the learning of different crafts.

15. Neither coercing children to learn through fear of punishment, nor appealing to their egoistic ambition, but instead aiming to engender in them inspiration and love for learning, for the sub-ject matter, and for their teachers. Education works best if based on love.

16. Leadership of the school is by a 'college of teachers' where no single individual is considered all-seeing and wise enough to 'rule' as a headteacher over all the other teachers, or to out-trump their opinions.

Instead of a school director or headmaster we have the college meetings, in which there is a common study and a common striv-ing towards further progress. There is therefore a spirit, a con-crete spirit living among the college of teachers which works freely, which is not tyrannical, which does not issue statements, rules or programmes, but has the will continually to progress, continually to make better and better arrangements, in meeting the teaching requirements. Today our teachers cannot know at all what will be good in the Waldorf School in five years' time, for in these five years they will have learned a great deal, and out of the knowledge they will have to judge anew what is good and what is not good … Educational matters cannot be thought out intellectually, they can only arise out of teaching experience. And it is this working out of experience which is the concern of the college of teachers. (CW310, p. 4)

The school, therefore, will have its own management run on a republican basis and will not be managed from above. We must not lean back and rest securely on the orders of a headmaster; we must be a republic of teachers and kindle in ourselves the strength that will enable us to do what we have to do with full responsibility. Each one of you, as an individual, has to be fully responsible. (CW300, p. 11)

… our college meetings in the Waldorf School which are the heart and soul of the whole teaching. In these meetings, each teacher speaks of what he himself has learned in his class and from all the children in it, so that each one learns from the other. No school is really alive where this is not the most important thing, this regular meeting of the teachers … This is the real purpose of the college meetings, to study human development so that a real knowledge of human nature is continually flowing through the school. The whole school is the concern of the teachers in their meetings, and all else that is needed will follow of itself. (CW311, p. 2)

17. Although not a concern in Steiner's day, the use of IT in learning is minimised until the children are in their teens. This ensures both a 'soul warmth' in the classroom arising from human-to-human contact; but also a rich experience of wonder and love for nature, particularly since natural materials are used wherever possible, especially in the kindergarten.

18. An endeavour to keep children of the same age together in a single class / form for most of their school career despite differences in ability (these differences are addressed through shorter-term differentiated teaching methods / groups). Through this, children can learn to appreciate the full range of the human condition, to help each other according to strengths and weaknesses, to grow in tolerance and appreciation for one another.

19. Aim to educate in such a way that this confers an ability to continue learning throughout life.

> *... the important thing is learning to learn. Learning to learn, so that, however old one is, one can remain, up to the very year of one's death, a student of life. Today even when people have taken their degree, as a rule they have exhausted their powers of learning by the time they are out of their twenties. They are unable to learn anything more from life; parrot-wise, they reel off what they have absorbed up to then. (CW192(iv), pp. 34-35)*

20. Taking the child's sleep into account and the part it plays in their psychology and learning.

21. The whole college of teachers will on occasion objectively, confidentially and respectfully carry out a 'child study' together—this alone has been found to bring about a beneficial effect on the child concerned.

> *In the teachers' meeting the individual child is spoken about in such a way that teachers try to grasp the nature of the human being as such in its special relationship to the child in question ... If we want to observe children in their real being we must acquire a psychological faculty of perception. (CW310, p. 6)*

22. Perhaps of less relevance today, but Steiner was keen for children of all faiths—and none—to be welcomed to the Waldorf School. Where religious instruction was concerned, he advised children be split up and receive lessons from representatives of their respective faiths. However, he also described the human warmth that should underlie the school as the universal spirit of love, as expressed in the New Testament:

> *... it is the spirit of Christianity that wafts through all our rooms, that comes from every teacher and goes out to every child, even when it seems that something very far from religion is being taught, such as arithmetic, for example. Here it is always the spirit of Christ that comes from the teacher and is to enter the hearts of the children— this spirit that is imbued with love, real human love. (CW298, p. 32)*

* * *

Whilst by no means a comprehensive list of the distinguishing features of Waldorf education, the above shows some of the innovation Steiner brought to the field. In different parts of the world, such suggestions are observed to a greater or lesser extent according to what circumstances allow.

7.5.3   The Arts

Organisation

Unlike a school teacher or university lecturer, an artist, composer or playwright needs no campus. They can get on with their work in blissful isolation in a quiet corner of their own home. Yes, an artist may need a gallery from time to time, and a composer or playwright will need a venue, but the organisation of these is generally left alone by the state. The freedom Steiner advocates is usually a given.

Content

Whilst Steiner's comments on art and design don't really fall under the heading of social reform, what he says about the social function of art is not entirely irrelevant.

> *It is a matter of great and social significance to men, that everything by which they are immediately surrounded in life should take on an artistic form. Every spoon, every glass, should have a form well adapted to its use, instead of a form chosen at random to serve the purpose. One should see at a glance, from its form, what service a thing performs in life, and at the same time recognize its beauty. Then for the first time large numbers of people will feel spiritual life to be a vital necessity, when spiritual life and practical life are brought into direct connection with each other. (CW332a, p. 94)*

The particular style of organic architecture seen in the buildings Steiner designed or inspired is quite unique, and one can certainly at times find oneself wondering how some of these designs reveal their purpose! He also founded an art of expressive movement which he called eurythmy, where gesture is used to portray sound and meaning. This is also used in educational, dramatic and therapeutic contexts.

In summary:

- Whilst form might follow function, it is conducive to social health when it also *expresses* function, and is also artistic.

Reflections in relation to the present

We have all seen that particular type of regimented housing with external spaces made up of random, disconnected oblongs devoid of any beauty. That those consigned to live in such oppressive developments can end up displaying increased levels of anti-social behaviour seems hardly surprising. Thankfully, at least *some* understanding of the connection between 'warm' physical surroundings and improved social attitudes seems to have become apparent, with a gradual move away from some of the more extreme forms of architectural brutalism.

7.5.4 Religion and spiritual teaching

> *Our disinclination to recognise ourselves as beings of soul and spirit must be overcome. A one-sided transformation of the economic life, a one-sided reconstruction of political institutions without nurturing a socially healthy and productive state of soul, is more likely to lull humanity with deceptive dreams than to fill it with a sense for reality. (CW24, p. 79)*

Whether or not there is a divine world is an age-old argument that shows no signs of being settled in a hurry.

Steiner wrote at length on religion, especially Christianity—which he felt he only came to fully understand in his 40s. In his autobiography, he movingly talks of eventually standing …

> *… before the Mystery of Golgotha in a solemn festival of knowledge. (CW28, p. 319)*

But the spiritual teaching and world-view contained in what he called anthroposophy is not about religious worship but about the spirituality that pervades everything, a spirituality he said every healthy human being can get closer to and even very slowly begin to apprehend—if regular soul exercises / meditation are practiced. He claimed we all have latent faculties to this end that can be developed. He also emphasised that anthroposophy as a path of spiritual growth was suitable for people of any religion or none. He repeatedly stressed, however, that, as with all spiritual / cultural matters, freedom to embrace, reject, or keep an open mind about such matters was paramount.

> We can only speak of human freedom when we compare it, not with the freedom of a ship on the sea, perfectly adapted to the forces of wind and weather, but when we compare it with the freedom of a ship that can stop and turn against wind and weather ... (CW332a, p. 84)

> We must find a spirituality that comes quite naturally from our own heart but also from the hearts of those, however lowly, with whom we speak. Just as the sun shines on all of us, so does genuine spirituality shine on every human being regardless of position or class and without concern for any kind of social class struggle. We have reached a momentous point in world history, for the demand now is that all human beings should be able to step onto the stage of history as individuals. (CW305(ii), p. 144)

> Since the middle of the fifteenth century human evolution has taken the line of development of the individuality, of personality. To expect of anyone today that he should attain a vision or an understanding of the higher worlds on authority, or in any other way than by the force of his own individuality or personality, is to expect of him something that is against his nature. (CW332a, p. 95)

Although Steiner regarded Christ as the central, towering figure in earth evolution, his anthroposophical approach to spiritual development is, in *one* sense, the exact opposite to that practiced in most Christian churches. Whereas in a Christian service the principle is that the Divine be 'brought down' by the celebrant to bless the congregation / individual, in anthroposophical self-development, the aim is for the individual to grow and refine their faculties of soul such that they ultimately 'raise themselves up' to apprehend the Divine. Very easily said! In this sense it has some congruence with Buddhism's striving for enlightenment.

Despite the centrality of Christ in Steiner's world-view, despite his writing and speaking at great length on Christianity (as well as other religions), and despite, for example, the painstaking advice he gave to Friedrich Rittelmeier—a Protestant theologian—regarding the founding of a movement for religious renewal which came to be known as The Christian Community, many within the traditional Christian Churches (with some notable exceptions[307]) have been very wary of Steiner.

> *Thus it has happened that the religious communities, having failed to develop their insight into the world of soul and spirit, and having preserved the old traditions, now see in the new methods of spiritual research, in the new paths of approach to the soul and spirit, an enemy to all religion, whereas they ought to recognise in these new methods the very best friends of religion. (CW332a, p. 82)*

To distil Steiner's comments on spiritual and religious matters into a couple of bullet points is of course ludicrous, but the following are general themes with a particular relation to social life:

- The spiritual in the world and in each individual is a reality that is objective, not subjective.
- The emerging importance of the individual over against the group means spiritual or religious teachings will less and less be accepted on authority.

Reflections in relation to the present

The increasing drift away from religion in the 'developed' world over the last century hardly needs pointing out. However, that people are increasingly taking their spiritual development into their own hands is also apparent. The House of Commons and the BBC headquarters in London, for example, each apparently now have their own meditation / mindfulness room. Heck, even war veterans in the US are being encouraged to meditate as treatment for PTSD![308]

---

[307] See, for example, *A Scientist of the Invisible* and *The Battle for The Spirit (The Church and Rudolf Steiner)*, both by Ven. AP Shepherd DD (1885—1968), former Archdeacon of Dudley and Canon of Worcester.

[308] Alex Mathews-King, 'Meditation helps forces veterans to tackle traumatic combat stress', the *i* newspaper, 16 November 2018.

7.5.5   The judiciary

As established in Section 6.2 ('Rights—Égalité—Democracy') rights and responsibilities—laws—are determined by the 'will of the people' via equality and democracy (be that direct or parliamentary). In the courts, however, establishing guilt and sentencing does not fall to the will of all. Instead, the capabilities of the individual judge and barristers must analyse the specific circumstances of each individual case. The will of the democratic process gives way to the skill of the individual; and thus the rationale is laid out for the judiciary's position within the cultural domain (the domain of individual capacities), not the political. Those institutions that concern themselves with the appointment of judges fall within the cultural domain.

> Those who administer[309] the cultural sphere will be called upon at the same time to appoint the judges [...] It will be important that no judge shall be nominated for political reasons. The reasons for his nomination will be like those that determine the nomination of the best teacher to a particular post. Becoming a judge will be something like becoming a teacher or an educator. Of course, in this way the judicial finding will differ from that laid down by the law arising from a democratic foundation. By the example of penal law ... we see how the personal disposition of the individual human being is outside the sphere of democracy and can only be judged in an individual way ... The decisions of justice grow beyond and above the limits of democracy. (CW332a, p. 72)

Individuals with the relevant skills are appointed as judges by individuals with the relevant skills. The whole matter takes place within the scope of *individuals* with the necessary capacities, i.e. within the cultural domain.

But what of the *content* of judicial work, as opposed to the *organisation* of the judiciary?

I am not aware of Steiner having said much in public about how to treat criminal behaviour. There is one occasion when he suggested criminal behaviour would be greatly reduced if everyone sang at

---

[309] The original translation is 'control', but 'administer' is truer to *'verwalten'*.

school! And on another occasion (references misplaced) he suggests that, in the future, a criminal will be seen more as someone who is ill and needs to be withdrawn from society to be healed rather than punished. Rehabilitation replaces retribution. This would accord with the following:

> *Let us suppose we have before us a criminal, a man whom we call especially immoral; on no account must we think that this unmoral man is devoid of moral impulses. They are in him and we shall find them if we delve down to the bottom of his soul. There is no human soul—with the exception of black magicians, with whom we are not now concerned—in which there is not the foundation of what is morally good. If a person is wicked, it is because that which has originated in the course of time as spiritual error overlies moral goodness. (CW155, 29 May 1912)*

In summary:

- Whilst legislation comes from the democratic political realm ...
- judicial decisions fall to *individuals,* i.e. fall within the cultural realm.
- Judges are appointed by a body that sits within the cultural realm.
- (As established in Section 5.4, however, the matter reverts to the political realm when it comes to the formality of *executing* sentences.)

Reflections in relation to the present

The above sentiments are not so far from what we have in somewhere like the UK. People are elected to Parliament by all, democratically, but judges are appointed by individual experts. In 1748, Montesquieu advocated a separation of powers based in part on the British constitutional system with its independent judiciary.[310] Judges cannot be arbitrarily sacked by Ministers. Indeed, with judicial review, they can even prevent government getting above itself.

---

[310] Charles-Louis de Secondat, Baron de la Brède et de Montequieu, *The Spirit of the Laws* (1748).

We shall leave to one side the detail of (albeit efficacious) case law where judges, rather than the political realm, refine legislation by interpreting it as it applies to individual circumstances.

In the USA, the appointment of Justices to the Supreme Court (nominated by the President and confirmed by the Senate) and Clerks (appointed by the Justices) contravenes Steiner's recommendation that no judge should be appointed for political reasons. The US Supreme Court's infamous intervention in the 2000 'hanging chads' presidential election, when George W Bush was effectively chosen instead of Al Gore, illustrates the extent to which this can be problematic.

President Erdoğan's recent mass dismissal of judges in Turkey is another example of state intrusion into juridical matters.[311]

7.5.6   Stewardship of land and the means of production

We saw in the definition of the economic realm (Section 5.3) that the finished means of production, whilst having an obvious relationship to economic life, do not themselves 'belong' to it, in Steiner's threefold analysis. They feed into the production process, but they are not themselves commodities and, ideally, would not be bought and sold. People—entrepreneurs / managers—have a *right* of disposition over them, and as such the means of production are a concern of the rights realm. On *which* people such rights are bestowed, however, comes down to individual judgement. Those with the relevant individual capacities appoint those with the relevant individual capacities.

In Section 7.3.7—when considering operational suggestions for the *rights* realm, a lifecycle for the circulation of the means of production was outlined. When an entrepreneur or manager retires, he or she either chooses a successor themselves or can leave this appointment to a facility within the cultural realm—made up of individuals with the capacities necessary for deciding on which new manager(s) to confer rights of disposition. In this respect, the means of production fall under the auspices of the cultural realm. The economic system (production / circulation / consumption of commodities) makes use of them, the legal realm (rights / responsibilities / law) stipulates and

---

[311] Paul Mason, *How to Stop Fascism: History—Ideology—Resistance* (London: Allen Lane, 2021), p. 62.

safeguards succession rights, but final arbitration over who administers them falls to bodies within the independent cultural realm. These adjudge which new managers are to be given the unfettered right to use the means of production in furtherance of the common good.

The socialistically-minded strive for the administration of the means of production by society. What is justified in their efforts can only be attained when this administration becomes the responsibility of the spiritual sector. The economic coercion which the capitalist exercises when he develops his activities from the forces of economic life will thereby become impossible. And the paralysing of individual human abilities, as is the case when these abilities are administered by the political state, cannot occur. (CW23, p. 89)

This healthy social organism must be arranged such that capital circulates between the intellectually capable. This circulation of capital means that, over time, what has to be administered capitalistically,[312] can also in fact be administered for the sake of the common good. (CW329, 9 April 1919)

When the capitalist can no longer put his own capacities into the administration of the capital, he must see—or if he should feel himself incapable of such a task, a corporation of the spiritual organisation must assume the responsibility of seeing that the management of the business shall pass to a highly capable successor, able to carry it on for the benefit of the community. That is to say that the transference of a business concern to any person or group of persons is not dependent on purchase or any other displacement of capital, but is determined by the capacity of the individuals themselves. It is a matter of transfer from the capable to the capable, from those who can work in the service of the community to those who can also work in the best way for the common good. On this kind of transference the social safety of the future depends. It will not be an economic transference, as is now the case; this transference will result from the impulses of the human being, received from the independent spiritual-intellectual life and from the independent legal-political life. There will even be corporations within the cultural organization, united with all other departments of the cultural life, on which the administration of capital will devolve.

---

[312] By which is meant: the means of production are in the hands of individuals, not in the hands of the state.

> *Thus, instead of handing over the means of production to the community, we transfer it from one capable person to another equally capable, that is, the means of production are circulated within the community. This circulation depends on the freedom of the cultural life by which it is effected and upheld. (CW332a, pp. 118-119)*

Falling under the auspices of the cultural domain, the means of production are run by individual capacities which can freely get to work without interference from profit-maximising shareholders and without bureaucratic state interference.

> *Take, for example, the case where someone is in a position to receive loaned capital on credit and is thus enabled to establish an undertaking or an institution and to produce by means of it. He goes on producing so long as his own personal faculties are united with the institution. Afterwards, the thing he has worked up will be handed on in the most intelligent way to some other individual who has the necessary faculties. It will be transferred by a gift—a gift, not from one man to another, but one that takes place through the whole course of economic life. We need only consider how such gifts will be able to be made in an intelligent way by the threefold social organism. Here the domain of economics borders on the social element in man, in the most comprehensive meaning of the term. It touches on that which needs to be conceived for the social organism as a whole. (CW340, p. 133)*

In connection with this onward gifting of capital such that it serves the common good, Edward Udell observes: 'For Steiner, there was nothing arbitrary about conceiving the matter in this way, because capital results not only from the genius of entrepreneurs, but in significant part through their collaboration with workers, consumers and many parts of society.'[313] Indeed, the work of Professor Mariana Mazzucato has shown how it is often taxpayer money which starts technological innovation: public money funds scientific research, the results of which are then

---

[313] Edward Udell in Martin Large and Steve Briault (Eds), *Free, Equal and Mutual: Rebalancing Society for the Common Good* (Stroud: Hawthorn Press, 2018), p. 87.

taken up by private capital. But private capital does not necessarily return the favour![314]

Again, Steiner is not talking about all means of production being transferred into the cultural realm's control overnight in some coup-like exercise in appropriation, but suggests a gradual passage from one realm to the other could come about if his advice were taken up:

> *Little by little the administration of capital will move of its own accord from the economic to the spiritual, cultural sphere. However much we may rail against capitalism there is nothing we can do about it, for we need it. What matters about capital and capitalism is not that they exist but what the social forces are that work in them. Capital has come into being through the intellectual ingenuity of human beings; it came into being out of the cultural, spiritual sphere through the division of labour and intellectual knowledge. Merely as a way of illustrating the possibilities, and not to make a utopian statement, I described ... how capital might stream towards the spiritual, cultural sphere of the social organism. Just as the copyright on books lapses after 30 years, so that the content becomes common property, so, I suggested, might someone—having amassed capital and had capital working for him while he was himself engaged in the work which his capital generated—transfer his capital to the common good after 30 years or so. I did not state this as a utopia but merely as a possibility of how, instead of stagnating everywhere, capital might begin to flow and enter the bloodstream of social life. All the things I wrote were illustrations, not dogmas or utopian ideas. I merely wanted to hint at what might be brought about by the associations. What actually happens may turn out to be something quite different. When one has brought life into one's thinking one does not set down dogmas to be adopted, one counts on human beings. Once they are embraced in the right way by the social organism they themselves will discover what is meaningful and useful socially in the environment in which they find themselves. In everything I say I count on people, not dogmas. (CW305(ii), pp. 158-159)*

---

[314] Ann Pettifor, *The Case For the Green New Deal* (Verso: London, 2019), p. 18.

In summary:

- Ideally, the means of production are neither held in state ownership, nor owned by shareholders not directly engaged in the enterprise.
- Instead, they are passed on, not by sale or inheritance, but as by gift from one entrepreneur / management group to the next, according to relevant capacities.
- The departing management chooses the successor, but if they are unwilling / unable, then ...
- a body within the cultural realm takes responsibility for this, such that the means of production are again used in the most efficacious manner for the common good.
- Steiner suggests such capital as amassed in the means of production could leave the original entrepreneur's estate within so many years of their retirement or death, much like intellectual property.

Reflections in relation to the present

Steiner's concerns about the means of production being managed by people unqualified for the job relate more to communism than capitalism. It is not so common for underperformers to last long in senior management positions under modern-day, capitalist scrutiny. A few glaring exceptions doubtless do exist: the scandal of certain bankers being able to reward themselves multi-million pound bonuses despite loss-making activity springs to mind! But whilst Steiner's concerns about the *management* of the means of production may seem less relevant in modern-day, capitalist industry, current *ownership* and ownership succession of such means of production is highly at odds with what he deems healthy. As we know, when the means of production are bought and sold by shareholders, these investors, whilst not managing the business, can nonetheless direct it. That is, they can force their profit-maximising, short-termist, corner-cutting, labour-exploiting, environment-trashing aims on the business, aims that might favour the shareholder at the expense of more or less everyone else and the planet.

Steiner's recommendation that the means of production cease to have saleable value, and instead are simply passed to new management—if necessary with the guidance of a body within the cultural sphere—addresses this problem head-on, and the interests of the common good are preserved. In relation to such considerations, economist Kate Raworth observes: 'In the midst of the industrial revolution— when industrialists issued shares to wealthy investors while hiring penniless workers at the factory gate—that was a fair assumption. But what determined each group's respective share of earnings? Economic theory says it is their relative productivity, but in practice it has largely turned out to be their relative power. The rise of shareholder capitalism entrenched the culture of shareholder primacy, with the belief that a company's primary obligation is to maximize returns to those who own its shares.

'There's a deep irony to this model. Employees who turn up for work day-in, day-out are essentially cast as outsiders: a production cost to be minimized, an input to be hired and fired as profitability requires. Shareholders, meanwhile, who probably never set foot on the company premises, are treated as the ultimate insiders: their narrow interests of maximising profits comes before all. No wonder that, under this set-up, the average worker has been losing out, especially since trade unions in many countries were stripped of their bargaining power from the 1980s onwards.'[315]

When Steiner's suggested lifecycle for the means of production was outlined in Section 7.3.7 (under operating suggestions for the rights realm), Land Trusts were cited as a good present-day example of how his principles can find expression. When a farmer retires from a farm that is held in a Land Trust, he or she may well be involved in finding a new farmer, but ultimately responsibility for this falls to the Trustees. Ensuring that the farm is passed on to someone with the best available capabilities, these Trustees are in effect a specially constituted body within the cultural domain of the sort Steiner describes. They ensure the means of production pass on to individuals with the right capacities, they safeguard optimal succession for the common good. The emergence of new legal forms in recent years (like Community Benefit Societies and Community Interest Companies in the UK, and

---

[315] Kate Raworth, *Doughnut Economics: Seven Ways to Think Like a 21st-Century Economist* (London: Random House, 2018), p. 189.

the new corporate charters in the US described by analyst Marjorie Kelly[316]) demonstrate an increasing interest in more innovative ownership models. One can feel greatly encouraged by this.

* * *

This marks the end of an extended section of the book (indeed, about half of the entire book!) that has looked at various operational details suggested by Steiner. Before moving on, it is important to reiterate (yet again!) his insistence that these operational suggestions are no more than that—suggestions!—and that his principal concern is that the threefold nature of society be recognised and the need for social structures conducive to each realm be respected. A newcomer to threefolding, dipping into this or that lecture or essay, or into secondary literature such as this, can easily gain an unbalanced view of his societal observations if they only happen to open a book where one of his more obscure suggestions is mentioned, and then read no further. Notwithstanding, it is hoped the perusal of these operational suggestions, at some length, will have helped flesh out an understanding of the more central principles Steiner enumerates.

---

[316] Kelly, M. *Owning our Future: The Emerging Ownership Revolution* (San Francisco: Berrett-Koehler, 2012).

8. Overlap

Having looked at (a) the definitions of society's three domains, (b) the guiding principles appropriate to each, and (c) a good number of the operational suggestions Steiner makes for each, attention will now be turned to the interface between one realm and the next.

> ... *so does one function of the social organism need to be kept in balance by another. (CW24, p. 92)*

As has become clear, the three realms of society are not neatly separated or spatially delineated. Yes, they are distinct; but *completely* independent from one another they are not. Rather than sectors they are perhaps better seen as *aspects*. And these aspects overlap, intermingle, interpenetrate. For example:

> ... *we need only glance at economic life itself in order to see how to the smallest details spiritual, political, and purely economic affairs overlap. (CW332a, p. 205)*

Professionally, the individual's work is certainly likely to predominate within one or the other realm. As a politician or baker or professor, the individual ...

> ... *will have a professional interest in the sector[317] which includes his occupation. (CW23, p. 126)*

But ...

> *Every person can for instance be active in all three realms if he has the strength for it — the social organism is not divided into classes. The point is not that this or that person is active in this or that realm, but that objectively, apart from man, these three realms are*

---

[317] The original German here is '*Glied*'—member.

> *administered independently out of their intrinsic conditions, so that a person can belong to all three or to two or to one, but administers each out of the principles of that realm. (CW79, 30 November 1921)*
>
> *... the same human beings who have a connection with the spiritual life, occupy a legal position, and carry on business. The measures the human being takes, the manner in which he associates with others, the way in which he transacts business, is all permeated with what he has developed in his spiritual life, and with the legal order he has established [...] They are the same men ... (CW332a, p. 113)*
>
> *The unity of the organism will not thereby be endangered in any way, for this unity is securely grounded in reality by the fact that each human being has interests within all three parts of the system, and that (notwithstanding their mutual independence) the central authorities at the head of each will be able to harmonise their various measures. (CW24, p. 57)*
>
> *In the human being, these three functions are united; in the course of life, one becomes involved in all three. (CW24, p. 84)*

The human being operates in all three realms. Each individual is subject to / protected by laws, and, if an adult, can also vote. We thus all operate within the rights realm. And we all need to eat and buy clothes, etc. and so, as consumers at the very least, we are all involved in economic life. And we all have an individuality and capacities that have been nurtured at school and that we then apply in society throughout life. As such we all function within the cultural domain too.

In our work life, we may operate predominantly in one realm, but we are nonetheless always citizens, so to speak, of all three. The teacher whose profession sits in the cultural realm will also buy food (economic life) and vote in elections (rights life). Someone working at the supermarket checkout (economic) will have once been to school (cultural) and will have the right not to be attacked in the street (rights). And a politician (rights) may go to a lecture (cultural) by bus (economic). And so on.

And just as an *individual's* work life might sit predominantly within one of the three realms, so do *organisations* generally 'belong' to this realm or that. A brick factory is predominantly an economic institution; a university is predominantly concerned with the cultural realm; a legislature is predominantly concerned with the rights realm. For this reason, it is easy to picture the realms as sectors and thence slip into the notion of clear delineation always existing between them. Moreover, Steiner recommends a separate, central administration for each realm which can further reinforce the idea of a clear, geographic delineation between them, as can his comment, for example, that if someone can't make a living in the cultural domain, they will have to transfer their efforts to the political or economic.

However, as individuals we have a relationship to all three realms even if our work might predominate in one. And similarly, an individual's work setting—indeed any organisation—will itself have a connection to all three realms even if it essentially 'belongs' to one. For example:

> ... no economic thought is real which does not reckon with what is done by spiritual work, if we may call it so, that is to say, fundamentally by thinking. [...] Spiritual work begins the moment work itself—that is to say, labour—is organized. (CW340, p. 76)

> ... even in picking blackberries... there is some spiritual work. If of two blackberry pickers, one is stupid and makes extra work for himself by picking where they are scarce ... (CW340, p. 167)

Or:

> When we refer to the purely economic elements in the economy we are referring to goods and commodities. But as soon as we refer to the developed economy, that is, the economy based on the division of labour [...] what flows into the actual economy ... as labour must be associated with the sphere of rights and the state ... (CW338(iii), p. 189)

> What [the spiritual and rights realms] produce within their own sectors [sic] are not commodities however; they only become such once they enter into the economic process. Their activities are not commercial within their own sectors; the economic organism's management carries on its commercial activities using the achievements of the other sectors. (CW23, p. 118)

So, a university lecture is cultural activity from the point of view of the cultural domain. From the point of view of the economic domain, the lecture is a service, and goods and services are commodities, i.e. economic. For delivering this service (commodity), lecturers are paid—enabling them to buy food and clothing.

> How will these spiritual workers economically endue their 'products'—their sermons for example (even these must be conceived in an economic sense) and their school lessons—with value? (CW340, p. 165)

Also:

> ... those who work in the spiritual domain need to eat, drink, dress; so they also need to form economic corporations which, as such, should be integrated within the economic body, which in the economic body associate themselves with those corporations that can, in turn, serve their interests. The same thing must happen with the co-operation of those people who work in the state life. (CW337a, 3 March 1920)

It was noted earlier in the book how Steiner uses the analogy of the human body to illustrate societal threefolding: just as the human body consists of (a) a rhythmic, cardio-pulmonary system centred in the heart / lungs, (b) a nerve-sense system centred in the head, and (c) a metabolic-muscle system based in the stomach / limbs, so too does the social organism have three aspects. And despite also being entirely distinct, these three aspects of society similarly work together:

> ... the impulse to establish the threefold social organism is not to bring about the separation of what belongs together, but actually the co-operation of factors that ought to work together. (CW332a, p. 113)
>
> The three members of the social organism must stand in the right relation to one another, so that they may work on one another in the right way. That was the real meaning of the threefold commonwealth—not the splitting into parts of the three members; the

> *spitting apart is always there. The point is rather to find how the*
> *three members can be brought together, so that they may really*
> *work in the social organism with inherent intelligence, just as the*
> *nerves-and-senses system, the heart-and-lungs system, and the*
> *metabolic system, for example, work together in the natural organ-*
> *ism of man. (CW340, p. 134)*

Indeed, the human body analogy can be taken a step further: just as each of the human body's three aspects has a direct relation to the other two (e.g. the energy-hungry nerve-sense system centred in the brain receives from the rhythmic, blood-circulating system, centred in the heart / lungs, nutrients that were prepared in the metabolic system), so too do society's three realms each have a direct relation to the other two. In a sense, then, each of the three societal realms is itself threefold. The economic system, for example, contains elements of the rights and cultural realms:

> *This leads us, in turn, to look for a threefold structure in the econ-*
> *omy itself. In other words, what flows into the actual economy—in*
> *which goods are produced, circulate and consumed—as labour*
> *must be associated with the sphere of rights and the state; and*
> *capital, which is actually the cultural element, must be associated*
> *with the cultural life. […] the transfer of capital, the circulation of*
> *capital must have a specific relationship to the cultural life. This is*
> *the key thing—that we learn to keep these three areas separate in*
> *the economy. (CW338(iii), p. 189)*

And Steiner points out that, just as in the human body an unhealthy state of affairs in one system can lead to an unhealthy state of affairs in another, so too can sickness in one *societal* realm adversely affect the other two. If, for example, your metabolism is overburdened from overeating, consequent imbalance in the blood can irritate your nerve / sense system and give you a headache. Similarly, problems in one societal realm cause problems in another (in addition to the inappropriate fusion of different realms being problematic in itself).

In summary:

- The three realms are not spatially delineated but interpenetrating aspects.
- Typically, the individual will work predominantly within one realm, but …
- … will always have a relation to all three realms.
- An organisation operating principally within one realm will also be closely related to the other two.
- Thus, each aspect is in itself threefold.
- The aim is not to keep the three realms completely apart, but rather to properly constitute each so they can work together in a healthy, hygienic way.

8.1   How one realm affects another

More detailed consideration will now be given to how each realm can healthily—or unhealthily—relate to the other two. Each of the three realms can either *appropriately serve* the other two, or *inappropriately influence*, dominate, manipulate or hinder the other two. As Steve Briault observes: 'Such invasion leads to social pathologies.'[318] If each realm, independently constituted in the manner inherently appropriate to each, does not overstep its remit, then they will work together more harmoniously for the overall good.

These various permutations of relationship between realms will now be considered, particularly bearing in mind the guiding principles that are fundamental to each realm, namely—*liberté, égalité, fraternité*. It is also a good moment to recall how decisions are arrived at in each realm: in the rights realm, decisions are arrived at by all; in the economic, they are arrived at within associations between interested parties; in the cultural, it is essentially down to the individual. This was summarised in the table introduced in Section 6.5:

---

[318] Steve Briault in Martin Large and Steve Briault (Eds), *Free, Equal and Mutual: Rebalancing Society for the Common Good* (Stroud: Hawthorn Press, 2018), p. 33.

	The realm concerning	More particularly	Decisions made by	Guiding principle
Cultural aspect	Human faculties …	their cultivation, expression and application in society	Individuals	Freedom
Political realm	Rights and responsibilities …	establishing and upholding these to protect society	All	Equality
Economic system	Goods and services …	their production, circulation and consumption	Interested parties in association	Brotherliness

8.1.1 Rights aspect appropriately serving cultural aspect

If the rights realm affects the cultural in any way, can the latter really be called free?

As we have seen, the cultural realm encompasses everything that comes from the individual's capacities and interfaces with society—the application of these capacities not only in traditional cultural realm matters, but also their application in economic and rights matters. With its particular role in enriching these capacities, education was singled out as a special case of cultural-realm activity.

If this cultural realm concerns what comes from individuals (their life of thought, feelings, beliefs, skills), then freedom in this sphere means freedom of thought, freedom of expression, freedom of choice, freedom of the individual to apply their capacities and follow a path of their choosing, to believe this creed or that, to indulge their individual tastes, to choose this education or that, to voice opinions without fear of persecution, to conduct scientific research without preset agendas, to vote left or right, to buy a cake instead of a book, and so on. Freedom in this sphere does *not* mean freedom of vicars to embezzle the church funds or teachers to beat their pupils. And the freedom to bully a colleague because they are disabled, or to stand on the street corner and scream racist ideology would not be attractive. The principle of individual freedom can only be meaningful to the extent that one person's freedom does not impinge on another's. It is the rights realm's job to establish rules of engagement, to ensure all have equal rights

and responsibilities, to ensure we all have a fair and safe space in
which to operate.

> *Only a superficial critic will say, 'What, then! Is the cultural life not
> to be bound in its pursuits by existing legal relations?' Certainly it
> must be bound by them. However, it is one matter if the people,
> who pursue the cultural life, are dependent on the legal life; and
> quite another matter if the pursuit of the cultural life rises on its own
> from the institutions of this legal sphere. (CW24, p. 124)*
>
> *All juridical, pedagogical and spiritual concerns are in the free
> hands of the individual. In this domain the state only has the right
> to police, not the right to initiate. (CW24(ii), p. 80)*

Cultural life—the flowering of the individual human spirit in society—
should not be *determined* by the state but rather be given free rein.
It should be allowed to emerge in whatever way it wishes. The state
simply protects. We all benefit from the security and rules we all,
democratically, choose to live by. We enjoy freedom from physical
attack in the street, and so on. The weak are protected.

Where, exactly, to draw the line between one person's freedom and
another's may not always be obvious. In liberal democracies it is generally recognised that freedom of expression should not be curbed
because of others desiring freedom from offence. If one tried to censor
everything such that no one was offended, this very censorship would
in any case offend a lot of people! Moreover, what progress would be
made without debate? If a religious person is offended by the opinions
of an atheist, or an atheist is offended by the opinions of a religious
person—too bad! They don't have to listen to one another. If someone
reads this book and afterwards wants to declare threefolding a load of
old rubbish, so they should! Or in the same way that someone who dis-
likes Damien Hirst's art does not have to look at it, so an atheist does
not have to read the Bible. Naturally, though, sensible restrictions are
generally placed on freedom of speech by the rights domain such that
people are protected as far as possible from personal hurt and untruths.
Thus we have laws against hate speech and libel. Here the rights domain
is *appropriately serving* the cultural realm by protecting a safe space
where one person's freedom does not encroach on another's.

George Orwell remarked that if liberty 'means anything at all, it means that everyone shall have the right to say and to print what he believes to be the truth, provided only that it does not harm the rest of the community in some quite unmistakable way' and, further: 'it means the right to tell people what they do not want to hear'.[319]

With respect to education, the rights realm can ensure children have a *right to* education, can ensure they are safe from harm, can ensure that the school is not defrauding parents, can ensure the school is not spreading hate, can ensure teachers are entitled to sick pay and time off at night to sleep! It provides an equitable, protective space within which individual / cultural freedom can flourish. It champions rights, rules, responsibilities that apply to all fairly, justly, equally. It should not step outside its rights remit, however. In cultural matters, it can 'police' but not initiate.

8.1.2 Rights aspect inappropriately influencing cultural aspect

Steiner asserts that, if those who focus on matters of equality—matters that apply to all—meddle in cultural life, they undermine its vitality. In the cultural realm, where capacities are all different, equality is meaningless. We do not want stultifying, plain vanilla across the board. Religion, science, art, education should have their guiding principle of freedom respected at all times.

Political and legal measures for the nurture of the spirit sap the strength of cultural life, while a cultural life that is left entirely to his own inherent interests and impulses will strengthen every aspect of social life. (CW24, p. 33)

In regard to political life, the state requires functionaries and even learned men to fill its appointments, and these have been educated according to the stereotyped pattern prescribed for them by the state [e.g. diplomats being quite at home in perpetrating and per-petuating imperialism, RM]. The state, in its appointments, wishes

---

[319] From a Preface proposed for his book *Animal Farm* in 1945, but first published by the *Times Literary Supplement* on 15 September 1972. See www.orwellfoundation.com.

and expects that qualities should be cultivated in individuals that can be used to its own advantage, but that brings about intellectual and spiritual enslavement even if a man imagines himself to be free. He is not aware of his dependence, does not see that he is confined within the limits of the stereotyped model held up to him. (CW332a, p. 108)

A rather extreme example of cultural life being inappropriately determined by the rights aspect was seen in the old Soviet bloc where books were censored, religion was outlawed, and even expressing one's opinion could attract severe punishment. You did what was expected of you. Although much has changed in Russia in recent decades, even today apparent state curtailment of free speech can still find painful expression: 'Dozens of security cameras monitor the streets around the Kremlin. None, it appears, was looking in the right place when four bullets were fired at the Russian opposition leader, Boris Nemtsov'.[320]

In Steiner's analysis, even a *healthy, democratic* rights domain should not determine matters in the cultural realm; but when these are determined by an undemocratic polity, as seen for example in Saudi Arabia or North Korea today, matters can become particularly problematic.

As we know, a favourite, culture-controlling step taken early on by tyrannical rights realms is to clamp down on press freedom. But before we look too far down our noses at certain foreign regimes where press freedom barely exists and newspapers / TV are barely disguised mouthpieces and propaganda merchants for the incumbent regime, it might be as well to remind ourselves of those times when our own BBC, once respected—revered even in some corners of the world—as an independent voice of truth, appears to fall short, too. That the Chairman of the BBC is appointed by the Queen on recommendation of the government is not ideal to start with. From a threefold point of view, the possibility for such influence ought not to exist in the first place. (In February 2021, for example, former donor to the Conservative Party Richard Sharp was appointed to the role. And that

---

[320] Allison Quinn, 'Kremlin's security cameras miss the street murder of Putin critic', The *i* newspaper, 3 March 2015.

was after a Conservative government had pushed for right-winger (as it happens) Charles Moore to be appointed.[321]) And then, at times, coverage of this or that foreign entanglement can seem rather more government-scripted than based on rigorous investigation of the truth. An exaggerated bias that vilifies a particular foreign regime here, the turning a virtual blind eye to the crimes of others there (e.g. Israel's contravention of international law in Palestine) appears designed simply to justify foreign policy or for the sake of diplomatic comfort. Heck, the USA are our sworn allies, so how can we possibly question their support of twisted wrongdoers? Heck, Saudi Arabia buys hangar-loads of our weapons, so we must pretend we haven't noticed their gender-based control-freakery. (The USA's own media, Gore Vidal despairs, 'is kept well nourished by disinformation from executive-controlled secret agencies like the CIA'.)[322] In 2021 senior journalist at the *Daily Mail*, David Rose ('the BBC has become, affectively, a propaganda arm of the government'), revealed the despotic ways UK governments (from Tony Blair's to Boris Johnson's) control the media, with threats of limiting access to press briefings, and so on.[323] Such influence was also painfully in evidence when Culture Secretary, Oliver Dowden, ousted two board members from TV broadcaster Channel 4 in 2021.[324]

Concerns about state interference in our own cultural realm are not helped by stories like the following: '… in 2002 the government launched a little-known television propaganda service that seems to mimic the US government's deceptive approach to fake news. The British Satellite News website says it is "a free television news and features service". It looks like an ordinary news website, though its lack of copyright protection might raise some questions in alert journalists. Broadcasters can put BSN material "directly into daily

---

[321] Dan Sabbagh, 'No 10 told Charles Moore appointment could put BBC's independence at risk', *The Guardian*, 27 September 2020.
[322] Gore Vidal, *Dreaming War: Blood for Oil and the Cheney-Bush Junta* (Forest Row: Clairview Books, 2003), p. 12.
[323] 'How the government controls the media. A Daily Mail journalist speaks out', 2 March 2021, https://gloria.tv/post/494JALBX8vLc6tiu3edk7xWtD.
[324] Polly Toynbee, 'Even in the NHS, Tory rule is being embedded', *The Guardian*, 8 June 2021.

news programmes". In fact, BSN is provided by World Television, a company that also makes corporate videos and fake news clips for corporations such as GlaxoSmithKline, BP and Nestlé [...] World Television produces the fake news, but its efforts are entirely funded by the Foreign Office, which spent £340m on propaganda activities in the UK alone in 2001'.[325] One might argue that there are occasions when fighting an information war can be excused if it prevents a shooting war. But one could also argue that by being truthful and noble we might gain greater international respect, set an example and be more trusted by those who value integrity. Besides, lies are rarely told with noble intent. Causing confusion, they provide no sound foundation on which to base international dialogue and progress, even if (supposedly) committed with good intentions.

Another example of overreach by the rights realm was evident during the Covid-19 phenomenon in 2020-21. Not only did the UK government encourage millions who were basically not at risk of succumbing to the disease (e.g. the under 20s with no prior medical conditions) to take a new *type* of gene therapy vaccine that came with no long-term safety data. It also, via Ofcom (which in 2017 was also given the power to regulate the BBC), to all intents and purposes shut down debate by threatening statutory sanctions on any media broadcasting 'medical or other advice which ... discourages the audience from following official rules and guidance'. It also advised media, in no uncertain terms, to strongly challenge any statements that 'undermine people's trust in the advice of mainstream sources of information about the disease'.[326] So, despite the obvious dangers in administering a new generation of untested drugs, and despite over 1,500 deaths having already resulted from these drugs in the UK alone (according to the government's own figures), counter-arguments were rarely heard in the mainstream media. Eminent academics and physicians would raise substantive concerns (e.g. that suckling infants were experiencing intestinal bleeding after their mothers had taken the jab),

---

[325] David Miller, 'The propaganda we pass off as news around the world', *The Guardian*, 15 February 2006.
[326] https//drive.google.com/file/d/1jCfzYCQGB0oHFrkSS0rBQLWix_qADSSI/ view?fbclid=IwAR2MVJfH9NYPsmSYRrnY2yg4Tf_wJ-dlvjRREOMVKq_ A4oLIMc-4ID2KDr8.

and then be summarily 'cancelled' and even warned by regulators to keep quiet.[327] Other professors would complain that their university administration had a policy of not saying anything counter to government policy or its medical advisers, and also that they had received veiled hints that government grants would dry up if they did.[328] It was blatant censorship. And these things occurred despite profound questions not only of medical ethics but also of glaring pragmatism. It was as though thalidomide had never happened! What if, in ten years' time, half of those billions of people around the world taking this completely new kind of gene therapy were to develop some terminal blood condition, or become infertile, or whatever? One would then be facing a global catastrophe of unprecedented proportions, making anything like Covid appear microscopic by comparison.

Another recent example of UK state activity in the cultural realm that is inconsistent with a threefold approach has been the government's attempt to meddle in heritage sector work and prevent museums from trying to give a more accurate portrayal of some of the more unsavoury aspects of Britain's past. 'Oliver Dowden, threatens cultural boards, vetoing the reappointment of an academic to the Royal Museums of Greenwich and causing the chair to resign in disgust', noted Polly Toynbee.[329] The Museums Association went so far as to express concern that a 'climate of fear has been created [by the UK government] amongst museums and museum staff'.[330]

A yet further instance of rights-realm trespass into cultural-realm activity is the UK government's involvement in schools, with the content and delivery of education. There have been some improvements in recent years, it is true. Whilst private schools may have always

---

[327] See for example viral immunologist Dr Byram Bridle of the University of Guelph (2021), https://odysee.com/@hugotalks:8/Doctor-'We've-Made-A-Big-Mistake-With-Vaccine'-Hugo-Talks-lockdown:q and also https://bitchute.com/video/MJz1yNUoWMJL/, and Dr Peter ('the most published cardiologist in the world') McCullough (2021), https://johnwaters.substack.com/p/covid-19-vaccines-renowned-physician?fbclid=lwAR35kzhdYR5f-P3lbhfeYe51LeKQX7ob-oCwxJ0nLwAjqoPek9uG6P3QZn5w.

[328] Reported by Dr Mike Yeadon, https://podbean.comea/pb-fxdut-ff643b.

[329] Polly Toynbee, 'Even in the NHS, Tory rule is being embedded', *The Guardian*, 8 June 2021.

[330] *Governance and Leadership*, March 2021, p. 6.

enjoyed relative freedom, there are now also greater freedoms within some British state schools as seen, for example, in so-called 'free schools' (although this can of course also be reversed by subsequent governments, sadly).

But repeated state meddling in UK education has not only led to a profoundly demoralised teaching profession over some decades, as mentioned in Section 7.5.2, but also to those incoherent education policies that fly in the face of the evidence that disproves the idea that an early start to formal education is a good thing.[331] Successive Education Secretaries with woeful understanding of child development have fashioned policies leading to swathes of UK youth ending up significantly behind those in many other countries in terms of both mental health and academic outcomes.

The cultural freedom deemed necessary under a threefold approach can be restored by the state relinquishing all influence over education, subject only to keeping watch over the rights of the matter (e.g. the right of each child to an education, and their right to remain free from harm). With a more threefold demarcation of function in society, the post of Education Secretary within government would, in all probability, not be needed at all. Ditto the Culture Secretary. Co-ordination of education and culture (to the extent that this is necessary) would be a matter for the *completely* independent cultural domain.

Of governments feeling the need, in the name of accountability, to closely control anything funded by taxation, Bertrand Russell observed: 'Every taxpayer feels that he has a right to object if, in any State-supported institution, anything is taught of which he personally disapproves ... "democracy" is interpreted as meaning that the majority knows best about everything. Are birds descended from fishes? Are there reasons for doubting whether Joshua made the sun stand still? Has the church ever been hostile to scientific doctrines subsequently accepted? Is Aristotle's doctrine of the syllogism capable of

---

[331] See for example: S. P. Suggate (2009) 'School entry age and reading achievement in the 2006 Programme for International Student Assessment (PISA)', *New international journal of educational research,* p. 48; or S.P. Suggate, 'Watering the garden before a rainstorm: the case of early reading' in S. P. Suggate & E. Reese (Eds), *Contemporary Debates in Child Development and Education* (London: Routledge, 2012), pp. 181-190.

improvement? The prevalent feeling in America, except among the highly educated minority, is that such questions should be decided, not by the opinions of those who have studied them, but by the prejudices of the ignorant majority. This makes the life of a teacher in a state institution somewhat hectic: at every moment he or she has to fear that the pupil will repeat something to his parents, they will repeat it to the priest or the pastor, and there will be the devil to pay'.[332]

As noted previously, Margaret Thatcher does seem to have had healthy, threefold instincts with respect to the freedom of education, being keen, as she was, on the idea of education vouchers (never introduced) where parents would have been free to 'spend' them at whichever sort of school they wished. Interestingly, such cultural liberty also addresses the problem highlighted by more socialistically minded author, Paul Mason, who bemoans 'the effort to turn public education systems into machines for producing obedience and quantifiable skill, not vigorously inquisitive and rebellious minds'.[333] For proper cultural freedom to obtain, the remit of any state-backed schools inspectorate also needs to be strictly limited to rights matters—like child safety—and have no connection with matters pedagogical.

For threefold hygiene to be maintained, rights realm practitioners stick to rights matters; they don't trespass into cultural ones. Whilst the realms overlap and interpenetrate, they nonetheless remain distinct.

8.1.3   Rights aspect appropriately serving economic aspect

Whenever one man tries to obtain a commodity from another, he touches in some way the other's rights to the commodity in question, so that economic life with its circulation of commodities is permeated throughout by all sorts of legal conditions. (CW332a, p. 106)

---

[332] From an article 'British and American Nationalism', contributed by Bertrand Russell to *Horizon* in January 1945.
[333] Paul Mason, *Clear Bright Future: A Radical Defence of the Human Being*, (UK: Allen Lane, 2019) p.188.

That laws and rules are needed within the economic realm is reasonably self-evident. Customers need protection from mis-selling, from being sold faulty goods, from products detrimental to health, etc. Sellers need protection from bouncing cheques and shoplifting. If someone signs a contract, there need to be rules that hold them to it. Rules—and what is just—are established in the rights domain.

Also, as we have seen, a significant factor in economic activity that is supported by the rights domain is that of co-worker relations. The rights realm safeguards workers' rights to minimise hazard, exploitation (ideally), etc.

> What results as just and equitable from the resolutions taken on the basis of the democratic state is introduced into the economic sphere by those who are occupied in industry, but it is not their work to ... make laws. They receive the law and carry it into operation in the economic life. (CW332a, p. 66)

The rights realm, independent of industrial interference, provides an equitable, fair context in which the economy can operate, a context that benefits all.

Steiner does not mince his words when emphasising the need, also, for a political system that keeps the corporate world in its place:

> ... reality will be created in the threefold social organism by the preparation of an independent basis for political life, reality from which, through human intercourse and human relationship, a strong impetus towards a system of law and equity arises, capable of keeping the economic life within its proper limits. (CW332a, p. 69)

> To perceive clearly the idea of the threefold order, one must be willing to understand that the economic life needs to have its own forces continually corrected from outside ... This necessary corrective will be supplied when there is an independent cultural life and corresponding independent legal sphere to make provision for it. (CW24, p. 105)

> A foundation must be sought for the necessary legal and political conditions for the state that must exist in order to be able to grapple with and dominate modern economic organizations. We ask how a state of rights, political impulses, can be attained that can meet the great demands of the problem. (CW332a, p. 17)

The word 'dominate' is a strong one. The original German is *'meistern'* which actually means master / cope with / deal with. Nonetheless, one might ask: doesn't this imply a rights realm that is straying outside 'serving' and into the realm of 'influencing'? But the economic system is about production and distribution of goods and services that meet the needs of consumers. Steiner is not proposing the rights realm should concern itself with *these* things. It should, however, provide a legal context to protect the vulnerable, protect the environment, protect workers, ensure product safety, etc. With laws, the rights realm serves the economic by keeping it within healthy, needs-meeting confines.

As things are at the moment, though, we see examples of big business marauding about the place and wreaking havoc in various corners of the globe, like messed-up 1970s rock stars trashing their hotel rooms. Stronger laws are needed to prevent such tragedy. Naturally, this applies more to some countries than others. In the USA, for example, agriculture is still allowed to use 72 pesticides that are banned in the UK.[334]

Formulating and policing legislation that applies internationally is of course difficult, as demonstrated by the painstaking efforts of the late barrister Polly Higgins—and now her successors—to enshrine a crime of 'ecocide' into international law.[335] When legislatures are inappropriately (from a threefold point of view) tied up with (or corrupted by) economic matters, they can be incredibly sluggish to get on top of these things, especially when, as Kate Raworth points out: 'For over 70 years economics has been fixated on GDP, or national output, as its primary measure of progress.' Basically, we have been aiming for a very questionable form of progress. 'That fixation has been used to justify extreme inequalities of income and wealth coupled with unprecedented destruction of the living world. [...] we have economies that need to grow, whether or not they make us thrive: what we need are economies that make us thrive, whether or not they grow'.[336] In relation to GDP, Professor Robert Pollin notes: 'there is

---

[334] George Monbiot, 'Sold Out', 15 June 2020, https://www.monbiot.com/2020/06/15/sold-out/.

[335] https://eradicatingecocide.com and also https://www.stopecocide.earth/.

[336] Kate Raworth, *Doughnut Economics: Seven Ways to Think Like a 21st-Century Economist* (London: Random House, 2018), pp. 25—30.

no disputing that it fails to account for the production of environmental bads as well as consumer goods. GDP also does not account for unpaid labour, most of which is performed by women. GDP per capita also tells us nothing about the distribution of income or wealth'.[337]

Laws frequently need updating in order to keep up with changing business practices. More recently, for example, laws across Europe have thankfully been introduced to reduce the irritating practices of tele-sales, cold calling and junk mail. (We could perhaps also do with legislation to prevent internet security firms sending e-mails trying to sell virus protection when you already have it installed on your computer—*their own version, what's more!* Yup—bitter experience!) Such practices lead to exploitation of the vulnerable and gullible.

In an equitable, meeting-of-needs, associative, brotherly / sisterly economy such scheming would undoubtedly be less of a problem. But, even where this existed, a completely independent rights realm, free from industrial pressures and conflicts of interest, would still always be best placed to provide the appropriate safeguards, prevent the citizen from being exploited, the planet from being damaged, the common good from being undermined.

8.1.4   Rights aspect inappropriately influencing economic aspect

As we now know, under a threefold approach, the government / legislature should concern itself with rights, responsibilities, laws, and that's more or less it. It should leave the economy, the provision of commodities to the economic system.

> ... *the political system will inevitably destroy the economy if it seeks to take it over ... (CW189, p. 10)*
>
> *If one were to harness economic life to the administration of the state, one would deprive it of its efficiency and freedom of movement. Those engaged in economic work must receive the law from somewhere outside of economic life, and only apply it ... (CW24, p. 92)*

---

[337] Noam Chomsky and Robert Pollin, *Climate Crisis and the Global Green New Deal* (London: Verso, 2020), p.116.

Again, an extreme form of the rights aspect occupying itself with the economic was seen in the former Soviet bloc—under that system which was a cause of profound concern to Steiner and which led to an economy riddled with inefficiencies, and shops often with precious little on the shelves. Production needs to be run by experts in their field, not state officials working for Gosplan.[338] The aim was to centrally plan the USSR's economy; the results for the population were dire.

> ... through the demands for the increase of political and legal power over the economic life, tyranny of the state, of the legal system over the economic system will arise. We see that the changes demanded for the recovery of economic life are not such as arise naturally out of the economic conditions themselves; rather, this demand arises out of the quest for political power, which aims to take possession of and dominate economic life. (CW332a, p. 110)

Ultimately, Steiner observes, political control of economic matters can become the basis of war. Shortly after the First World War, he noted:

> A large part of the war's causes must be sought in the fact that the nations exploited the economy to augment their power, or in the fact that people involved in economic pursuits sought to promote their own economic interests by means of politics. Individual economies served to disrupt a world economy striving for unity. The various nations sought to turn the economic gains that should have remained within the economy to political advantage. (CW24, p. 16)

And it is not just totalitarian governments that should refrain from trying to administer economic matters; even the most healthy, democratic legislatures should too.

Since the 1980s, the privatisation programme in the UK has seen the government divest itself of British Aerospace, British Airways, British Telecom, British Gas, British Rail, British Leyland, the Royal Mail and so on. Whilst this divesting is in keeping with a threefold

---

[338] Gosplan (1921—1991) was the Soviet Union's State Planning Committee responsible for central economic planning.

approach, the solution—ownership by profit-hungry, worker-exploiting, private capital—sadly is not. Tory instincts that industry should not be run by the state are consistent with threefolding. Labour's instincts that industry should be more community minded and not reward ownership at the expense of workers and customers are also consistent with threefolding. How such divestment could have been structured efficaciously for the common good is dealt with elsewhere in the book.

Notwithstanding the privatisation programme that began in the 1980s, there are other examples where the UK legislature is still involved with economic matters. Various functions within the government's Business, Innovation and Skills department, or the Treasury, or the Department for Transport spring to mind. And overseas Consulates engage in economic negotiation and even have trade targets.[339]

In France, the state owns most of energy firm EDF which produces about a quarter of the European Union's electricity; in Germany the state owns Deutsche Bahn—one of the biggest railway companies in the world. Whilst management of facilities in the economy is outside the state's function as a legislator, and therefore not consistent with threefolding, to place such facilities within a structure that *is* consistent with the threefold approach (e.g. into a trust in perpetuity for the collaborative meeting of needs instead of for the generation of profit for shareholders), would, however, be very much easier from a position of public (i.e. state) ownership than private ownership by shareholders. Policymakers with privatisation on their minds, take note!

Rights realm practitioners should stick to rights realm matters. If they try and run business, not only are they likely to do it badly (e.g. by having a bureaucratising, stultifying effect on it, or simply because they lack the skills), it will also compromise their ability to focus on their primary purpose:

When the rights-state manages the economy it loses the ability to regulate human rights. (CW23, p. 64)

---

[339] *Inside the Foreign Office*, BBC1, 22 November 2018.

8.1.5 Economic aspect appropriately serving rights aspect

Those who work within the institutions of the rights realm need to live. These include the politicians we choose to represent our views and who propose, discuss and enact legislation. They also include people working within the Civil Service, and those who are upholders of the rules such as the police and the (one prays, never needed) armed forces. They all need food, clothing and shelter; they need goods and services; they need the economic domain.

By generating more goods and services than are needed by those whose work sits predominantly in the economic system itself, the institutions of the economic system—business—make it possible for those working for the rights realm to live. Such 'surplus' goods are bestowed on the latter via taxation.

And apart from providing rights realm practitioners with their livelihood, the economic realm also provides the rights realm with its various tools of the trade: office space for politicians, police cars, pencil sharpeners ...

At the more macro level, the central administration of the economic realm will also provide costing information to feed into the law-making process. A country's rights realm might propose to maintain a right to housing, say, or right to further education free at the point of use, or a right to universal healthcare, or a right to a three-day weekend, and the financial dimension to such decisions would need to be clarified in dialogue with the central bodies of the economic domain.

Of course, these various ways in which the economic realm supports the political can—and do—take place without any appreciable, conscious threefold structure in place. We are here only concerned with clarifying how one realm healthily or unhealthily relates to another.

Steiner also makes the wider point that with a threefold demarcation in place, the economic domain can play a pacifying role between states:

> *In the future, the history of events leading up to this war will be written so that it will directly be shown how the war arose through the unfortunate reciprocal interference of these three areas of life in the intercourse between nations. By their separation, the forces of one area of life work outwardly to have a harmonising effect on the others; the forces of economic interests especially balance out conflicts that arise on political grounds ... (CW24(ii), p. 103)*

That is to say, if one state is in disagreement with another, an independent economic realm will nonetheless want to maintain good relations across the border in order to keep trading. If, on the other hand, industry is controlled by the state, the state may then be more tempted to flex its (more powerful) muscles. And conversely, if industrial relations break down between regions, state conflict is less likely to ensue if the state is not concerned with industry.

8.1.6   Economic aspect inappropriately influencing rights aspect

Economic experience cannot play itself out in the sphere where the rights due every adult should come to the fore ... Recognition given a person because of work in a special field of the economy cannot be expressed in the structure of the state, where only that which is valid for all persons equally prevails ... (CW24, p. 9)

... it is thought that those who administer economic affairs will also at the same time develop the laws [used in economic affairs, RM]. This assertion proves an absolute lack of understanding of real life. It is not the economic system, in which efficiency above all things is necessary to promote production, that can bring forth suitable legal conditions. (CW332a, p. 68)

If men carry over their economic interests into the legislation and administration of the rights-state, then the resulting rights will only be the expression of these economic interests. (CW23, p. 64)

If those focused on the economic realm attempt to wield influence in politics and thus undermine the rights realm's guiding principle of equality, as enshrined in one-person-one-vote democracy, then there is a problem. Indeed, the corruption of politics by economic interests is one of the world's most egregious problems, and it comes in several guises.

One such guise—which the USA suffers from in the extreme—consists of corporate lobbying accompanied either by 'dark money'[340] or overt donations to political parties and presidential campaigns. 'Donations' are made in the hope and expectation of legislation favourable

---

[340] 'Dark money' donations made by third party non-profit organizations that do not have to reveal who their donors are.

to the donor, as opposed to laws beneficial for the common good. Policy is more or less bought. Indeed, without such donations, it seems almost impossible for someone who isn't independently wealthy to mount a successful presidential campaign, as the cost of these can run to hundreds of millions of dollars. In 2012, more than $2.5 billion was spent during the Obama versus Romney presidential campaign.[341] Such payments to the political realm betray glaring conflicts of interest and surrender the principle of one person, one vote in favour of one dollar, one vote. The result can be one-sided tax breaks, lax environmental protection, misinformation surrounding the efficacy or dangers of pharmaceuticals, and so on.

In an 'advanced' country like the USA—with many millions of highly educated people, it seems almost absurd that the most basic problem of conflict of interest has *still* not been overcome. Indeed, with Michael Moore's page after jaw-dropping page of conflicts of interest around the time of the GW Bush administration, one can end up wondering whether corruption in the USA is so ingrained and widespread that a critical mass has been reached from which there is no return.[342] Steiner—and others—sometimes refer to the tendency that civilisations have of collapsing under the weight of their own decadence, and, when considering corruption of this sort, you wonder whether we are perhaps looking at the seeds of the USA's eventual downfall from world prominence. But then there were also those millions of Bernie Sanders supporters recently, pushing for something more equitable; so who knows? Here was a rare candidate running on an anti-corruption, anti-big money ticket who managed to raise enough to mount a presidential campaign without either personal wealth or substantial corporate sponsorship. Instead, millions of small donations supported him, and both in 2016 and 2020 he came second in his bid to be the Democratic Party nomination for President of the United States.

But when a report even comes out of Princeton University saying the USA is no longer a democracy, you know the system urgently needs an overhaul.[343]

---

[341] 'U.S. Supreme Court strikes down overall donor limits', BBC News 2 April 2014, http://www.bbc.co.uk/news/world-us-canada-26855657.

[342] Michael Moore, *Stupid White Men: And Other Sorry Excuses for the State of the Nation* (London: Penguin Books, 2002).

[343] https://www.bbc.co.uk/news/blogs-echochambers-27074746.

Citing the Centre for Responsive Politics,[344] Gary Lamb observes: 'There is no lack of statistics documenting the flow of money from tens of thousands of interest groups at the state and federal levels aimed at influencing elections and legislation. The federal government alone had 13,746 active registered interest groups that spent \$3.49 billion lobbying elected officials on behalf of their agendas. Industrial interest groups play a major role in lobbying and electing officials as well. For example, from 1990 to 2010 AT&T contributed over \$45 million to candidates, 45 per cent to Democrats and 55 per cent to Republicans. Individual candidates showed no restraint in collecting funds from as many industries as possible. Chuck Schumer (D-NY), for instance, collected over \$100 million from 12 of the 50 top U.S. industries contributing to the 11th Congress during the 2009-2010 election cycle. This flow of money has nothing to do with the democratic principles of individual equality and majority rule'.[345] That this acute problem could be addressed by election spending being limited in some way by statute is easy enough to see. But the inappropriate influence / conflict of interest suits both briber and bribed alike, and a captive media makes sure a sleepy public doesn't notice something's amiss.

Under Steiner's analysis, even a brotherly / sisterly, associative economic realm should not interfere with politics, with rights. But when it comes from an aggressive, self-seeking, crush-thy-neighbour, exploit-thy-customer-if-at-all-possible economic realm, this is doubly unfortunate. As Martin Large says: '… corporate lobbying and funding political parties secure benefits for the wealthy; it's socialism for the rich'.[346]

As a result of legislators buckling in the face of such corporate pressure, we see, for example, the licensing of pharmaceuticals that are less effective than existing treatments[347]; we see weak environmental protections; we see the non-labelling of GM foods.

[344] http://www.opensecrets.org.

[345] Gary Lamb, *Associative Economics: Spiritual Activity for the Common Good* (Ghent, NY: The Association of Waldorf Schools of North America, 2010), p. 128.

[346] Martin Large in Martin Large and Steve Briault (Eds), *Free, Equal and Mutual: Rebalancing Society for the Common Good* (Stroud: Hawthorn Press, 2018), p. 102.

[347] Richard Smith, 'Foregone conclusions', *The Guardian*, 14 January 2004.

(Happily, since 2020, GM foods have needed to be labelled in the USA.[348] One would, after all, expect it to be a basic right for people to know what is in the food they are buying. And to not want to buy GM food would seem the most natural thing, given that it poses a serious threat, because of cross-contamination, to the vitality of traditional crops which have proven their life-supporting qualities over tens of thousands of years. As the reader will probably know, under the pretence that only pesticide-intensive GM farming can feed the world, bio-tech companies have developed—and, of course, patented—a number of GM crops. But lest we forget, it was one or two of those same companies which, not so many years ago, were developing the 'terminator gene' to remove plant fertility. This would have meant that farmers and growers, instead of keeping (now useless) seed for the following year's crop, would have been forced to buy new seed every year from bio-tech patent holders.)

It is as well also to remember that the UK is not immune from the problem of inappropriate influence of the rights realm by the economic. Yes, it may be vastly less serious than in the USA, but a front page article in 2014 was telling. It revealed that Lord Levy, Tony Blair's chief fundraiser, had warned Labour leader Ed Miliband that he 'had to do more to win over business chiefs whose financial support the party needed'.[349]

Another way in which the corruption of politics by economic interests can manifest is seen when industrialists literally enter the employ of the legislature, or, coming out the other side of the revolving door, politicians (with those all-important connections) enter industry or financial institutions, 'gliding from a position of public responsibility into one of private gain'.[350] Personnel travel to and fro without, it seems, the necessary Chinese walls being erected to prevent conflict of interest. 'The movement of senators and congressmen and women from the house of representatives and the senate into the lobbying

---

[348] Amy Harmon, 'G.M.O. foods will soon require labels. What will the labels say?', *The New York Times*, 12 May 2018.

[349] Tim Shipman and Maria Woolf, 'Labour donors hammer "death wish" Miliband', *The Sunday Times,* 5 October 2014.

[350] Richard Brooks, 'The Greensill affair shows just how rotten system is', *The Guardian*, 16 April 2021.

firms on K Street further underlines this evident corruption of our political institutions, as do declining corporate tax rates and decreases in effective taxation on the rich'.[351]

Citing his childhood years, Steiner bemoaned how the Austrian Imperial Parliament comprised representatives from industry, from the Chambers of Commerce, significant landowners and the like.

> *When parliaments are composed of representatives of economic interest, majorities can always be found to pass resolutions effecting those interests and to make laws that have nothing whatever to do with that feeling of justice that exists between one man and another. (CW332a, p. 65)*

Today, the suspicion that the US establishment is rotten to the core isn't really helped when the Deputy Commissioner for Foods at the FDA[352] is a certain Michael R. Taylor, formerly of Monsanto.[353] Or when fossil-fuel-funded Scott Pruitt[354] is appointed to head up the Ministry for the Environment. The latter is possibly less surprising in that it occurred under President Trump (despite his promises to 'drain the swamp'), but the former appointment occurred under the supposedly cleaner President Obama. Or, as Naomi Klein lamented, 'In any other moment, the very fact that the CEO of Exxon Mobil is now the Secretary of State would be the central scandal. Here we have a situation where there is so much else to concern us it is barely a footnote'.[355] The 'so much else' of concern included all the chaos arising under President Trump, like his decision to withdraw the USA from the Paris Climate Accord—one of many actions that suggested an inappropriate influence of economic interests in those of rights.

On this side of the Atlantic, where we perhaps like to think we have more effective checks and balances, the extraordinarily sinister

---

[351] Christopher Schaefer in Martin Large and Steve Briault (Eds), *Free, Equal and Mutual: Rebalancing Society for the Common Good* (Stroud: Hawthorn Press, 2018), p. 120.

[352] Food and Drug Administration—responsible for protecting and promoting public health through control of foods, medicines, etc.

[353] https://en.m.wikipedia.org (accessed 26 August 2018).

[354] https://en.m.wikipedia.org (accessed 26 August 2018).

[355] Naomi Klein, 'Trump is an idiot, but don't underestimate how good he is at that', *The Guardian*, 11 June 2017.

investor / state settlement clauses of a proposed Transatlantic Trade and Investment Partnership (TTIP) deal survived several *years* of negotiation between the USA and the EU, during which MPs were not even allowed to see the proposals. The treaty fell eventually after the implications were spread far and wide across social media in 2013. All this suggested corporate power had also infiltrated the European Commission's negotiators. Otherwise, how could it have survived years of negotiation? As the reader may know, under the investor / state settlement clauses, corporations would have been able to sue whole countries for loss of profit had those countries ruled against accepting their products for any reason—such as on grounds of human health or environmental protection. Furthermore, the courts which were to arbitrate in such cases were to be secretive courts set up by corporations themselves! Such corporate capture of the rights realm makes a mockery of the rights realm's guiding principle of democracy. The same applied to the Transpacific Trade Partnership (TTP) until the USA withdrew in 2016, whereupon the remaining signatory nations altered some of the offending clauses in the successor agreement—the CPTPP (Comprehensive and Progressive Agreement for Trans-Pacific Partnership). Such overreaching corporate power represents the economic realm inappropriately influencing the rights realm, writ large. It is interesting to note, also, that some years earlier, the (unelected) European Commission had 'been trying to force GM crops into Europe over the heads of its member states'.[356] Further, after several countries in Europe and other parts of the world had instead followed the precautionary principle and adopted a moratorium on the importing and growing of GM foods, the judges of the WTO itself, despite in theory allowing product rejection on both health and environmental grounds, ruled in favour of the industry, saying the GM ban adopted by various countries broke WTO trade rules—a highly problematic declaration which was rightly criticised as 'an intervention into countries' freedom to establish the levels of environmental and human safety they deem appropriate'.[357] Even if, nowadays, the view is quite widespread that the push for GM amounts to an attempt to enslave much of the

---

[356] John Vidal, 'America's masterplan is to force GM food on the world', *The Guardian*, 13 February 2006.

[357] Sue Mayer, 'Cut and dried?', *The Guardian*, 15 February 2006.

world economically, one needs to be ever vigilant when there is no proper threefold demarcation to keep industrial interests away from legislation.

Or consider the Leaders Group elite dining club in the UK. In 2019 it was reported members have to donate £50,000 to the Conservative Party which entitles them to join the Prime Minister (when Tory), Cabinet ministers and other senior Tories at dinners, lunches and drinks receptions. In return for this access, they have given over £130 million to the Tories since 2010, £18 million of that from just five hedge fund backers. Indeed, sixty Leaders Group donors are collectively worth over £45 billion.[358] In 2021 we heard of similar shenanigans—clubbers this time labelled the 'Advisory Board'—and of Prime Minister Boris Johnson cosying up to the likes of Peter Cruddas, 'the online trading tycoon who gave the Tories £500,000 days after being elevated by Johnson to the House of Lords'.[359] One doesn't really need to be a threefold enthusiast to see that this blatant and shocking corruption of the rights domain by the economic needs to stop as a matter of some urgency. Perhaps donations to the Labour Party by trades unions need to stop too; but any argument that these are just as bad can be dismissed on account of the fact that they represent a sea of small donations from tens of thousands of members who are generally of very powerless and modest means—people who need the protection of the political realm the most.

If the economic domain starts to influence foreign policy aspects of the rights realm, matters can then become even more troubling. Arguably, the most pathological results of non-threefold practice are the barbarously cruel acts of war that are committed for the sake of commercial advantage, often justified with what can be the most devious of expressions, namely: 'in the national interest'. The real perpetrators generally cover their tracks sufficiently to avoid any invitation to attend the International Criminal Court.

[358] Peter Georghegan, Seth Thévoz, Jenna Corderoy, 'Revealed: The elite dining club behind £130m+ donations to the Tories', 22 November 2019, https://www.opendemocracy.net/en/dark-money-investigations/revealed-the-elite-dining-club-behind-130m-donations-to-the-tories/.
[359] George Parker, Sebastian Payne, Tom Burgis, Kadhim Shubber, Jim Pickard and Jasmine Cameron-Chileshe, 'Inside Boris Johnson's money network', *The Financial Times*, 30 July 2021.

Such scheming might involve surreptitiously sowing disquiet between rival camps in foreign lands in order to provoke civil war, with possibly Uncle Sam's military industrial complex 'helpfully' coming to the aid of one side by bombing the other back to pre-Industrial-Revolution helplessness, and in the process removing any alleged threat to U.S. supremacy (i.e. in the process, promoting its economic advancement). Henry Ford noted 'We ought not to forget that wars are a purely manufactured evil and are made according to a definite technique. A campaign for war is made upon as definite lines as a campaign for any other purpose. First, the people are worked upon. By clever tales the people's suspicions are aroused towards the nation against whom war is desired. Make the nation suspicious; make the other nation suspicious. All you need for this is a few agents with some cleverness and no conscience and a press whose interest is locked up with the interests that will be benefited by war. Then the "overt act" will soon appear. It is no trick at all to get an "overt act" once you work the hatred of two nations up to the proper pitch'.[360]

As Christopher Schaefer says: 'We say we support and promote democracy and yet in America we allow uncontrolled amounts of money to affect election outcomes, and as a country have financed and supported the overthrow of democratically elected governments in Chile, Iran, Egypt, the Ukraine and elsewhere'.[361]

When the US took the decision to invade Iraq in 2003 on the strength of seemingly fabricated evidence of that country developing weapons of mass destruction, it appeared there were people with close connections to the decision makers who had high stakes in US armaments production, i.e. people working for companies like Halliburton who stood to gain financially from the forthcoming death. (Hey, the more bombs we drop, the more money we make. Woohoo, it must be Christmas!) Such things can make the West's talk of 'rogue nations', 'axis of evil' and 'failed states' particularly hollow.

One might wonder why US citizens are not up in arms about their leaders (and those unelected puppet masters) wreaking havoc around

---

[360] Henry Ford, *My Life and Work* (Hawthorne, CA: BN Publishing, 2008), p. 162.
[361] Christopher Schaefer in Martin Large and Steve Briault (Eds), *Free, Equal and Mutual: Rebalancing Society for the Common Good* (Stroud: Hawthorn Press, 2018), p. 47.

the world, taking taxes from people barely able to afford them to fund exorbitant military campaigns abroad which then benefit the oil, gas and armaments interests of the 1% or 0.1%. Why is the public so asleep to the horrors of visiting heartbreak, blindness, limb loss, agony, lack of running water, and general human tragedy on the peoples of foreign lands when there appears little or no risk to the USA's security? Would the populace really stand by and do nothing if it were aware of these acts of sickening depravity and self-serving that were being committed in its name? But when truth is suppressed, too many citizens—in their comfort—will all too often believe that 'the powers that be' can be trusted to ensure everything is taken care of and anyone up to no good will be dealt with. Politically, millions of voters simply nod off, especially when a neo-liberal media is singing all the right lullabies! The pen might be mightier than the sword; but the neocons have stolen the pen! (The corporate world's capture of the news media is addressed in forthcoming Section 8.1.8.)

In just a few words, Paul Mason illustrates how little appreciation we in the West can have for the callousness of our acts: 'In Gaza, in August 2014, I spent ten days in a community being systematically destroyed by drone strikes, shelling and sniper fire. Fifteen hundred civilians were killed, one third of them children. In February 2015, I saw the US Congress give twenty-five standing ovations to the man who ordered the attacks'.[362] And Gore Vidal laments: 'Americans have no idea of the extent of their government's mischief. The number of military strikes we have made unprovoked against other countries since 1947-48 is more than 250. These are major strikes everywhere from Panama to Iran. And it isn't even a complete list. It doesn't include places like Chile, as that was a CIA operation. I was listing only military attacks.'[363] Noam Chomsky's brief account of just one example of this mischief—the USA's installing a 'murderous dictatorship' in Guatemala after a decade of progressive reform—is almost too unbearable to read.[364]

---

[362] Paul Mason, *Postcapitalism: A Guide to Our Future* (London: Allen Lane, 2015), p. xix.

[363] Gore Vidal, *Dreaming War: Blood for Oil and the Cheney-Bush Junta* (Forest Row: Clairview Books, 2003), p. 185.

[364] Noam Chomsky and Robert Pollin, *Climate Crisis and the Global Green New Deal* (London: Verso, 2020), p.131.

Whatever the reasons for all these things, this is not civilisation! James Bamford of Reuters observed: 'The list of wars the United States has entered with disastrous results continues to grow. Engaging Russia in endless cyber war based on questionable evidence will add to it. It's time to find better alternatives.'[365] One imagines (hopes) that a point will eventually come when these things will seem obvious to everybody, just as it seems obvious to us today that theft is wrong, slavery is barbaric, etc.

But lest we forget, the UK's 'ethical foreign policy' in the 1990s, led by the well-meaning Robin Cook, did not last long under New Labour's Tony Blair. Despite a million 'not in my name' protesters campaigning against the Iraq war in 2003, for example, and despite the 'dodgy dossier' of apparently fabricated 'evidence' of Iraqi weapons of mass destruction, the UK joined the US invasion of Iraq with seemingly little thought about the aftermath, and Blair (who now 'flits around the world giving speeches on democracy, while receiving huge cheques from despots')[366] went from being a popular politician to what many regard as someone with blood on his hands and a reputation damaged irretrievably. 'The main effect of our intervention has been to create an enormous terrorist threat that didn't previously exist', wrote David Clark in *The Guardian*.[367] Before a single child loses a parent, before a single parent sees their child crippled or blinded by shrapnel, before visiting heartbreaking agonies on the innocent, surely every other avenue should be meticulously exhausted first.

It is also as well for us Brits to remember that it was not so long ago that 'we', too, engaged in horrific atrocities in the name of empire. We may have been brought up to believe that ours is a country of fair play, cricket, tea on the lawn, and polite, gun-less policemen, but (NB: the following is upsetting in the extreme), '... the mass British theft of Kenyan land had prompted a backlash. Thousands of destitute Kenyans began to fight against the British. They responded by

---

[365] James Bamford, 'Commentary: Don't be so sure Russia hacked the Clinton emails', Reuters, 1 November 2016, https://www.google.com/amp/s/mobile.reuters.com/article/amp/idUSKBN12X075).

[366] Ian Birrell, 'Delusional, self-serving Blair is back', the *i* newspaper, 16 June 2014.

[367] David Clark, 'Blair's foreign policy is now a threat to national security', *The Guardian*, 25 August 2006.

herding more than 300,000 Kenyans into gulags to be whipped, cas-
trated and raped. Many had their eardrums burst with knives, others
were doused in paraffin and burnt alive. The soldiers were told they
could kill anyone they wanted "so long as he is black" and they slew
more than 50,000'.[368]

Or, '... far from building up India to make it capable of self-rule,
in reality the British destroyed it. When Clive of India arrived in
Calcutta, he described it—as all visitors did—as a place of such
"richness and abundance [that] neither war, pestilence nor oppression could destroy [it]". But he did his best. Within the first century
of British occupation, the population fell from 150,000 to 30,000
as its industries were wrecked. By the time the British left, it was
one of the poorest places in the world. Jawaharlal Nehru, the man
elected prime minister after [our] heroes finally left, explained:
"Those parts of India which have been longest under British rule are
poorest today..." [...] Or look at ... the British Empire's conscious
policy of mass starvation of Indians in the 1870s and 1890s. In reality, severe natural climate disruption hit India, and there was massive
crop failure. The British viceroy—Lord Lytton, appointed because he
was Queen Victoria's favourite poet—declared that grain shipments
to London must continue, by force if necessary. The institutions [pre-
sented] as Britain's glorious gift to India—the railways and telegraph
lines—were in fact used more efficiently to steal and ship out India's
food, so Londoners could enjoy them over breakfast. Some gift. And
even this was not enough. Lytton went further and declared all relief
efforts illegal. The result? One journalist noted that the train lines of
India were strewn with "bony remnants of human beings" begging
for grain. "Their very eyeballs were gone ... Their fleshless jaws and
skulls was supported on necks like those of plucked chickens. Their
bodies—they had none; only the framework was left." Some 29 million innocent people died ...'[369]

This is what can happen when the economic realm inappropriately
influences the rights realm.

---

[368] Johann Hari, 'There can be no defence for empire', *The Independent*, 12 June
2006.
[369] Ibid.

In the light of such atrocities, it is excruciating when someone like Prime Minister David Cameron, on an official trip to India in 2013 declares 'I think there is an enormous amount to be proud of in what the British empire did and was responsible for'.[370] Such declarations flag up gaping shortcomings in British education—even at the hallowed Eton College. Indeed, they undermine what genuine claims our culture might (and does) have to bringing truly good things to humanity. To his credit, as Labour leader, Jeremy Corbyn voiced a wish to correct these rose-tinted distortions of our past in the classroom. It may not be very threefold to have politicians (rights realm) interfere with education (cultural); but truth is surely better than lies!

So much for inappropriate corporate influence in foreign policy.

In a fascinating article, Paul Carline charts how certain US Presidents bemoaned the undermining of democracy by scheming financial interests. For example, Founding Father, Thomas Jefferson lamented: 'banking institutions are more dangerous to our liberties than standing armies', or in 1861 (the year of Steiner's birth, as it happens) Abraham Lincoln famously observed: 'The money powers prey upon the nation in times of peace and conspire against it in times of adversity. It [sic] is more despotic than a monarchy, more insolent than an autocracy, and more selfish than bureaucracy. It denounces as public enemy all who question its methods or throw light upon its crimes. I see in the near future a crisis approaching that unnerves me and causes me to tremble for the safety of my country. Corporations have been enthroned, an era of corruption in high places will follow, and the money power of the country will endeavour to prolong its reign by working on the prejudices of the people until wealth is aggregated in a few hands and the Republic is destroyed'.[371]

And after Woodrow Wilson had signed the Federal Reserve Act in 1913 (the Federal Reserve was set up by private bankers and has the power to print money and lend this to the government!), he declared three years later: 'I am a most unhappy man. I have unwittingly ruined my country. A great industrial nation is controlled by its system of

---

[370] Quoted in Yasmin Alibhai-Brown, 'Why Corbyn is Britain's true patriot', the *i* newspaper, 16 October 2018.

[371] Paul Carline, 'Democracy and "we, the people"', *New View*, 3rd quarter, summer 2010.

credit. Our system of credit is concentrated. The growth of the nation, therefore, and all our activities, are in the hands of a few men. We have come to be one of the worst ruled, one of the most completely controlled and dominated governments in the world; no longer a government of free opinion, no longer a government by conviction and vote of the majority, but a government by the opinion and duress of a small group of dominant men'.[372] And in his inaugural speech, Roosevelt vowed to get rid of the 'money changers' from the temple of US democracy.[373]

But Carline suggests the problem is more nuanced than this, pointing out how vested interests, rather than wanting to completely destroy democracy, in fact benefit from the calm and legitimacy it (or at any rate, a version of it) bestows on the status quo. Steiner appreciated this too:

> ... in 1910 someone [i.e. French journalist and economist Francis Delaisi] wrote that large-scale capitalism had succeeded in making democracy into the most marvellous, flexible and effective tool for exploiting the whole population. Financiers were usually imagined to be the enemies of democracy, the individual concerned wrote, but this was a fundamental error. On the contrary, they run democracy and encourage it, for it provides a screen behind which they can hide their method of exploitation ... For once, therefore, a man woke up and saw that what mattered was not to proclaim democracy but to see the full reality; not to follow slogans, but to see things as they really are. This would be particularly important today, for people would then realise that the events which reign with such blood and terror over the whole of humanity are guided and directed from just a few centres. [...] it is quite easy to lull people to sleep with abstract concepts and make them believe the opposite of what is true. (CW177)

Another aspect of corporate power undermining democracy—one that one rarely hears much about—is the often self-serving power wielded by certain secret societies. As Steiner cautioned a hundred years ago, Western society is bedevilled by secret societies many of which, one is

[372] Paul Carline, 'Democracy and "we, the people"', *New View*, 3rd quarter, summer 2010.
[373] Ann Pettifor, *The Case For the Green New Deal* (Verso: London, 2019), p. 48.

given to understand, harbour anything but a charitable attitude.[374] They can operate powerful networks, with members in senior industrial, political and media positions who then go on to appoint and promote younger members without others (i.e. non-members) realising what's going on. The power to set agendas and narratives and affect many aspects of society then ensues. At best, such lack of transparency is inconducive to societal health; at worst, it amounts to a psychopathic, mafia-like primitivism. Observing the level of cruelty that so many in the US establishment are capable of (e.g. ordering those overseas bombing raids with little justification from a defence point of view), one wonders whether, were the members and vows and decisions of certain secret societies to be made public, a good number of the most senior figures within the US political and corporate world would be imprisoned. They would do well to remember that it was not only hands-on henchmen who were given the severest sentences in Nuremburg, it was also those within whose power it was to stop the butchery, but yet failed to try.

That's not to say, by any means, that everyone in a secret society is a baddy. I have known a Freemason or two who I would regard as having only noble intent; and Steiner himself described at some length the force for good that Freemasons, in particular the earlier ones, brought into the world, and how the anonymity of their good deeds made them all the nobler.[375] Nonetheless ...

> Look at Anglo-American cultural life today [...] you have what are called the secret societies, which exercise more influence than people realise. They are proud to be custodians of ancient Egyptian and oriental culture, but this has become so filtered, so diluted, that it now consists of nothing more than symbols. (CW194, p. 46)
>
> ... those secret societies that are exercising a great deal of power in the English speaking world, the power of which the general public has

---

[374] See for example TH Meyer, *Ludwig Poltzer-Hoditz: A European,* (Forest Row: Temple Lodge, 2014), Chapter 24, and also Rudolf Steiner, *The Karma of Untruthfulness: Secret Societies, The Media, and Preparations for the Great War* (Forest Row: Rudolf Steiner Press, 2005).

[375] See for example Rudolf Steiner, 'Involution and Evolution as they are interpreted by Occult Societies', 23 December 1904.

no inkling. These secret societies gather together under the most sympathetic of external regulations, and they have gained more and more power […] Lodges of freemasons—in other words societies that make good tools in the hands of the secret societies … (CW196, p. 63)

It is interesting to note that Steiner talks of such secret societies operating behind the scenes of those societies one *has* heard of, like the Freemasons. It is also notable that another such society one has heard of—the Skull and Bones—had two members running against each other in the 2004 US presidential election—John Kerry for the Democrats and George W Bush for the Republicans. At least with authentic Freemasons, members are usually forbidden from discussing politics or religion, so on the face of it, such bodies might be innocuous from a political point of view. But the following was noted in the *i* newspaper in 2018: 'Two Freemason lodges for MPs and journalists are operating secretly in Westminster. The revelation has led to calls for politicians to be forced to register their membership'.[376] It is a tricky one. On the one hand, why shouldn't people be allowed private lives that are private? On the other hand, if they are engaged in public service with a private, un-transparent agenda, this can create 'invisible forces', Deep State, glaring conflicts of interest, the military-industrial complex, seemingly deranged levels of wealth stockpiling, and what former US President Bill Clinton referred to as 'secret government'[377], etc.—phenomena that may not apply to the Freemasons per se, but which may well apply to other organisations behind them.

Whilst in 'the West' we might have democracy after a fashion, it has a number of aspects in need of early, significant reform in order for the principle of equality in the political domain to be properly realised and the public's trust in the democratic process restored. One doesn't have to know about Steiner's ideas to see that contamination of the rights domain by the economic, especially an extreme neo-liberal one, can have devastating consequences.

---

[376] William McLennan, 'Freemasons operating secretly in Westminster', the *i* newspaper, 5 February 2018.
[377] Paul Carline, 'Democracy and "we, the people"', *New View*, 3rd quarter, summer 2010.

8.1.7   Economic aspect appropriately serving cultural aspect

Whether seen from a more personal perspective or a more institutional one, the economic realm provides a sustaining base for the cultural. For the individual, the consumption of commodities keeps us alive. Food, clothing and shelter from the economic realm provide sustenance such that one's faculties have a foundation on which to operate, grow, flourish and find expression in society. These treasures entering society from our talents constitute society's cultural domain; they are only possible because we also eat.

Seen from the point of view of institutions, and indeed society at large, the same applies. Those institutions that are essentially economic—businesses, the economic system—provide commodities that sustain those institutions falling under the cultural realm banner, such as places of learning, places of worship, etc. Institutions 'belonging' to the economic realm create more goods than they need to sustain just themselves, and this surplus of goods is used by institutions 'belonging' to the other two realms so they can also function. Such goods include both sustenance for those working in cultural realm organisations, as well as their tools of the trade, such as crayons and lecture halls.

The mechanisms via which such support might pass from the economic aspect to the cultural were addressed in Section 7.5.1—where the funding of the cultural domain was considered.

Another (albeit less frequent and less direct) way in which the economic domain can support the cultural is as follows:

> I once told an industrialist, an excellent man at his job, what was needed in order to bring things back to life: 'Suppose you have an employee who is fully integrated in the life of your factory. Then along comes a technical college and snaps this man up, not someone recently trained but someone who is fully immersed in the life of the factory. For five or ten years this man can talk to the youngsters about what the life of a factory really is. Then, when he gets a bit stale, he can return to the factory.' Well, such things will make life complicated, but they are what our time requires. There is no getting away from it. (CW305(ii), p. 163)

To keep the cultural realm ever practical, current, alive, relevant, down to earth, 'real', there is advantage to be had when people who predominately work in the other two realms now and then transfer into education. (On the other hand, transfers between the economic and political realms would need to be arranged with the utmost care in order to avoid those 'revolving-door' conflicts of interest mentioned earlier.)

8.1.8   Economic aspect inappropriately influencing cultural aspect

An economy that governs the rights of human beings, and educates them according to its own interests, reduces the person to a mere cog in the economic machinery. It stunts the human spirit which can develop freely only when it unfolds according to its own innate impulses. (CW24, p. 85)

Again, in a threefold system, not even a fraternal, associative, economic domain should influence the content of the 'free' cultural domain; but if an aggressively profit-maximising one does, the problems can be far greater. The guiding principle for the cultural domain is freedom; if the economy starts to determine its content, freedom is forfeited.

Naturally, in the case of the 'half-free' cultural realm where people are applying their capacities in industry, then the various aspects of production will determine the focus of this 'half-free' cultural life, the focus of such people's faculties as applied in work. But in the 'free' cultural realm (where ideas, culture, the mind, learning, skills, science, research, religion, art, literature, music, truth, morality, etc. sit), economic influence should have no place.

In the neo-liberal climate of the West, however, we have glaring instances where this is not so and harmful conflicts of interest arise:

- Corporations pay for scientific studies, and sometimes even manage to fund university departments who then may be reluctant to publish studies criticising the practices of their patrons. Science is thus compromised, progress is undermined, morality suffers, truth is lost. The revelations that not only did (a) Keele University cancel all aluminium research after scientists linked aluminium in vaccines to human health problems, but also that (b) this seemed to coincide with the university receiving money from the Bill & Melinda Gates Foundation was a case in point. This raised the question of what strange motives might be at work.[378] Or we have, for example, 'Internal Monsanto files obtained in litigation show multiple tactics were employed by the company and industry allies to manipulate scientific papers about its products'.[379] We also have oil companies and the like forming supposedly objective science groups that then go on to deny climate change. Even if you are one of those who look at the melting polar ice caps and still think climate change is the stuff of hippy doom-mongers, you might at least believe the Chief Executive of Lloyds of London: 'We are seeing a rise in both the frequency and severity of natural disasters'.[380] And even if you still contend climate change is nonsense, you might nonetheless concede it is problematic when ExxonMobil, Koch Industries and their peers spend over half a billion dollars on climate-change-denying lobby groups between 2003 and 2010.[381] Gift from the economic realm to culture may be a good thing; but for societal health to obtain, this needs to be structured such that cultural freedom at all times remains sacrosanct. If the benefactor is a brotherly economic concern, with a corporate structure to match (as discussed elsewhere), any corrupting influence would at least be minimised.

• In the UK, universities have sadly become businesses with a continual eye on profit. This can significantly compromise learning. Instead of a seminar consisting of a dozen or so students in conversation with a professor, for example, this can now mean a hundred students in a large room doing work assignments and putting their hand up if they need assistance from a tutor. Indeed, in 2013, the UK's (Conservative, note) Education

[378] UK Column News, 7 April 2021.
[379] Carey Gillam, 'Science shouldn't be for sale—we need reform to industry-funded studies to keep people safe', *The Guardian*, 18 Feb 2020.
[380] Dame Inga Beale, Chief Executive of Lloyds of London on the Andrew Marr Show, BBC1, 7 October 2018.
[381] Paul Mason, *Postcapitalism: A Guide to Our Future* (London: Allen Lane, 2015), p. 249, and also http://sams.scientificamerican.com/article/dark-money-funds-climate-change-denial-effort/.

Secretary, Michael Gove was caught proposing that academy and free schools become profit-making enterprises—an uncomfortable example of how entrenched the belief can be in the neo-liberal and slightly bizarre dogma that profit-seeking leads to best outcomes in every situation, that self-interest leads to an improved society.[382] Further, 'Grave concern has also been expressed in many circles that mass academization is nothing short of an asset-stripping exercise, where at some future date, a (right-wing) government will at a stroke sign over literally billions of pounds' worth of erstwhile public land to private-sector academies, thus essentially stealing what are the community's assets and giving them to private corporate interests, to capitalise and dispose of as they wish'.[383]

- We have TV adverts directed at children which (quite apart from distastefully interrupting children's programmes) make them think it is perfectly acceptable to have certain products or eat certain foods that are full of unhealthy ingredients like sugar and artificial additives. Such adverts rarely have the bests interests of the children or indeed society at heart, only the interests of the company trying to sell its wares, typically with little regard for any long-term consequences to health. But these adverts penetrate the child's psyche and can stay there a long time. They manipulate their minds, their capacities. They penetrate our culture.

'Schoolchildren are being told that foods high in fat or sugar are a necessary part of a balanced diet, under guidelines and teaching materials produced by an organisation partly funded by food manufacturers. The British Nutrition Foundation (BNF) which includes Coca Cola, Mars and British Sugar among its members, has helped write the "core competencies" on diet and health for school lessons on nutrition. The seven-page document makes no reference to obesity or the links between foods high in saturated fat and sugar and heart disease and diabetes. In the paper, the

---

[382] James Cusick, 'Cash for classrooms: Michael Gove plans to let firms run schools for profit', *The Independent*, 2 July 2013
[383] Richard House in Martin Large and Steve Briault (Eds), *Free, Equal and Mutual: Rebalancing Society for the Common Good* (Stroud: Hawthorn Press, 2018), p. 203.

BNF recommends the use of the government's "eatwell" plate—a pictorial representation of the foods that make up a healthy diet. One of the groups is "foods and drinks high in fat and /or sugar", such as cola, cake, crisps, sweets and biscuits. The government's own material makes clear that these "are not essential to a healthy diet, and should be consumed only in small amounts". However, a BNF presentation to support teaching on the eatwell plate did not make it clear that foods high in fat or sugar are not essential, describing all the different food groups shown on the plate as those "which are needed to make up a healthy, varied diet". Zoe Harcombe, a nutritionist, said it "beggared belief" that a can of cola was on the "eatwell" plate and that it was now being embedded in the national curriculum. She said: "advice on nutrition for children needs to be drawn up by experts who are independent of the food industry".'[384] Well, quite!

- We have the pharmaceutical industry leaning on or even infiltrating the FDA in the USA to approve new medicines that, yes, might be fractionally better than no medication at all, but which tests have shown are worse than other medication already in existence.[385] Why do they allow this? Because the licence period for the existing medication has run out, so there is no money to be made on it anymore. Such revelations strongly suggest there is an urgent need to remove anything to do with profit maximisation from anything to do with health and medical research.

The following—where all three societal realms were involved—provided a particularly stark illustration of the problem: 'Britain has spent £600m on a stockpile of influenza drugs that are no better than paracetamol in relieving flu symptoms and are next to useless in preventing a pandemic, according to a major study. The companies behind the two main anti-flu drugs, Tamiflu and Relenza, held back crucial information that would have shown just how ineffective their drugs were in clinical trials, according to the independent scientists who compiled the report. Their investigation found little or no evidence to support the

---

[384] Jon Ungoed-Thomas and Justin Stoneman, 'Pupils told can of cola is part of a healthy diet', *The Sunday Times*, 24 May 2015.

[385] Richard Smith, 'Foregone conclusions', *The Guardian*, 14 January 2004.

manufacturers' claims about the effectiveness of the two drugs and questioned the rationale for building up an emergency stockpile of 40 million doses. The scientists also criticised the drug-regulatory authorities for failing to ask for the full details of the clinical trials before giving their approval. The report is also a searing indictment of the opacity of the pharmaceuticals industry. It took more than four years of negotiations to convince the Swiss company Roche, which makes Tamiflu, and the British firm GlaxoSmithKline the manufacturers of Relenza, to release the full details of their 46 clinical trials. The main authors of the report, compiled by the respected Cochrane Collaboration of independent medical scientists, advised the Government not to buy any further stocks of Tamiflu or Relenza. Details held by the drug companies revealed that the only benefit of the anti-flu drugs was that they shortened the period of symptoms by about half a day'.[386]

Here the economic realm has inappropriately influenced the cultural realm by releasing misleading information in order to reduce instead of enhance knowledge (and this misleading information in the cultural realm has in turn gone on to inappropriately influence the rights realm). It is a wonder that those responsible within the two companies concerned are not in prison.

Inappropriate shareholding by those in positions of authority is another way the economic realm can corrupt the cultural (as well as the political). The BMJ noted this during the Covid-19 outbreak, when it observed the UK's response 'relies too heavily on scientists and other government appointees with worrying competing interests, including shareholdings in companies that manufacture Covid-19 diagnostic tests, treatments, and vaccines'.[387]

• Another example of inappropriate influence in the cultural realm by the economic has been seen in the UK where the income of the doctor's practice has been affected by how many tablets they prescribe, 'distracting doctors' attention from responding to the

---

[386] Steve Connor, 'Britain wasted £600m on "useless" flu drugs', the *i* newspaper, 10 April 2014.

[387] 'Covid-19: politicisation, "corruption" and suppression of science', *The BMJ*, 13 November 2020.

complex medical needs of their patients in favour of the mass prescription of these drugs on which their income so closely depends'.[388] Whilst what a doctor does may have an economic dimension to it inasmuch as they provide a service (i.e. a commodity), the service they provide is decidedly based on their individual capacities. Diagnosing an illness or prescribing a treatment should be based on individual judgement, on a cultural realm that is independent and uncontaminated by the economic. One upshot of this particular problem was the shocking revelation that 15% of pensioner hospital admissions were associated with medication-induced problems. ('Within weeks I went from being an active 65-year-old to a doddering old man'.)[389] When a review published in 2021 revealed 'As many as 110m medicines given out each year may be unnecessary and potentially harmful', there were tentative signs from the UK's Health Secretary that this would be addressed.[390]

• Another highly problematic instance of cultural realm contamination by the economic is seen in the news media which, in large part, are owned by oligarchs with wide-reaching corporate interests. A gullible and sleepy public is drip-fed what far too often amounts to propaganda and distortions that scoff at anything that does not perpetuate the status quo—a status quo which, for example, normalises tax regimes and off-shore loopholes which suit the 1%, not to mention the 0.1%. If share prices fall in the lead-up to an election, for example, because a more left-wing party starts doing well in the polls, it is striking how so many of the newspapers get away with portraying this as proof that left-wing policies are bad for the economy. The markets have fallen—what on earth are you stupid voters thinking?! Rarely pointed out, however, is that share prices fall because expectation of future returns falls, and expectation of future returns falls when (a) corporation tax is expected to rise (which can contribute to better public services), and (b)

---

[388] James le Fanu, 'The tablets that do more harm than good', *The Daily Telegraph*, 19 November 2012.

[389] Ibid.

[390] Andrew Gregory, 'Crackdown on doctors overprescribing drugs', *The Guardian*, 22 September 2021.

better laws are expected—laws which will prevent business cutting costs by exploiting workers or harming the environment. The economic realm is corrupting the cultural by limiting debate, limiting the dissemination of different points of view, undermining people's capacities. The revelation during the UK's 2017 general election that fully 80% of its media was owned by just 5 billionaires (Richard Desmond, Jonathan Harmsworth, David Barclay, Fred Barclay, and Rupert Murdoch) was of particular concern. The relentless barrage of slander in many of the newspapers against the leader of the Labour Party, Jeremy Corbyn, when he was proposing tax measures unfavourable to their non-domiciled, billionaire owners was as excruciating as it was blatant. Similarly, in the USA, one repeatedly sees a gullible readership being guided to believe and vote for the very policies that impoverish them and further enrich the ultra-wealthy. It could be seen as a mild form of brainwashing when most 'news' outlets lead readers / viewers to believe that the levels of indifference that right-wing politicians and other establishment figures have towards the misery and suffering of so many around them is normal and part of a civilised world. Or when you have the bizarre spectacle of millions of US voters turning a blind eye to the slaughter of thousands of families overseas for 'the cause' (whatever that cause may be) whilst at the same time screaming 'pro life' back home.

Noam Chomsky observed: 'The smart way to keep people passive and obedient is to strictly limit the spectrum of acceptable opinion, but allow very lively debate within that spectrum—even encourage the more critical and dissident views. That gives people the sense that there's free thinking going on, while all the time the presuppositions of the system are being reinforced by the limits put on the range of the debate'.[391]

And in 1949 none other than Albert Einstein warned that: 'under existing conditions, private capitalists inevitably control, directly or indirectly, the main sources of information ... It is thus extremely difficult, and indeed in most cases quite impossible, for the individual citizen to come to objective conclusions'.[392]

---

[391] Noam Chomsky, *The Common Good* (1998), p. 43.
[392] https://www.goodreads.com/quotes/8757490-private-capital-tends-to-become-concentrated-in-few-hands-partly.

A newspaper may be a commodity (economic realm), but its *content* arises from journalistic *capacities* and concerns the mind, the general life of thought, concerns the improvement or broadening of other people's knowledge / capacities and as such is very much part of the cultural domain. Now, you might say, if freedom is the cultural realm's guiding principle according to threefold analysis, billionaires should also be free to operate a newspaper. A threefold response to this would be: Yes, newspapers should enjoy cultural freedom (i.e. *content*-freedom / *editorial* independence from economic interests) at all times, and in order to improve the chances of this, there should be no non-working owners. The means of production—the business—are not themselves commodities and ideally would not be buyable / sellable. Furthermore, journalists and editors would ideally have no outside economic interests (shares) that could undermine their truth-telling. Conflicts of interest would then be greatly reduced. If there is a clear line like this between the economic and cultural realms, then debate within the media stands a much higher chance of comprising idea versus idea rather than one economic interest versus another economic interest.

The distortions of fact by the billionaire-owned media need not only apply in the lead-up to elections, of course. Gore Vidal's stateside complaint that he has to rely on the British, French and Italian press to find out what is going on in the Middle East reminded us of this.[393] Here in the UK, however, it is also a source of immense national shame when so many newspaper staff are prepared to see their employer poison the public life of thought with lies and yet still not resign from their posts, as happened after George Monbiot and others published *Land for the Many*. 'We showed how the billionaires and other oligarchs could be put back in their boxes. The result has been four extraordinary weeks of attacks in the Mail, Express, Sun, Times and Telegraph. Some of these reports peddle flat-out falsehoods'.[394] Has our society really become one in which it is acceptable to lie? It is particularly alarming that these newspapers continue to be bought

---

[393] Gore Vidal, *Dreaming War: Blood for Oil and the Cheney-Bush Junta* (Forest Row: Clairview Books, 2003), p. 193.

[394] George Monbiot, 'After urging land reform I now know the brute power of our billionaire press', *The Guardian*, 3 July 2019.

by a great many who would consider themselves people who value goodness of character. As George Orwell said of the British press: 'most of it is owned by wealthy men who have every incentive to be dishonest about certain important topics'.[395] And Bernard Shaw: 'the newspapers are owned by rich men. And they depend on the advertisements of other rich men. Editors and journalists who express opinions in print that are opposed to the interests of the rich are dismissed and replaced by subservient ones'.[396]

This contamination of the public life of thought (cultural realm) by vested interests (economic realm) would be greatly reduced if no one could become the proprietor of a newspaper or TV business through purchase. Full editorial independence could then rest with the editor, who, it could be arranged, would only be appointed so long as they had no conflicting interests that could profit from distortion of truth. Editors would be appointed solely for their intelligence, eloquence and commitment to truth-telling. Naturally, journalism includes analysis as well as the reporting of dry facts, so *opinion* will always need to have a place alongside complete impartiality. Press freedom is a nuanced subject.

But *The Guardian* and *The Observer*, for example, are owned by the Scott Trust which was created 'to secure the financial and editorial independence of the Guardian in perpetuity and to safeguard the journalistic freedom and liberal values of the Guardian free from commercial or political interference'.[397] With a more threefold structure such as this, they can print: 'Bring out the violins. The land reform programme announced by the Scottish government is the end of civilised life on earth, if you believe the corporate press. In a country where 432 people own half the private rural land, all change is Stalinism. The Telegraph has published a string of dire warnings, insisting, for example, that deer stalking and grouse shooting could come to an end if business rates are introduced for sporting estates. Moved to tears yet? Yes, sporting estates—where the richest people in Britain, or oil sheikhs and

---

[395] From a Preface proposed for *Animal Farm* in 1945—see www.orwellfoundation.com. First published by the *Times Literary Supplement* on 15 September 1972.
[396] Bernard Shaw, *The Intelligent Woman's Guide to Socialism and Capitalism* (Edinburgh:R&R Clark Ltd, 1929), p. 64.
[397] https://www.theguardian.com/the-scott-trust/2015/jul/26/the-scott-trust.

oligarchs from elsewhere, shoot grouse and stags—are exempt from business rates: a present from John Major's government in 1994. David Cameron has been just as generous with our money: as he cuts essential services for the poor, he has almost doubled the public subsidy for English grouse moors …'.[398] (Not that *The Guardian* is perfect. Their decision to ignore some highly irregular aspects of the Covid-19 phenomenon was a case in point and, to many, a big disappointment.)

A complete absence of financial influence in reporting would be the ideal. When George Osborne is given £85,000 for a *single speech* in the City (an average Brit would take around three years to earn this), he is unlikely to welcome articles critical of the City (London's financial centre) in the *Evening Standard* which he edits. Similarly, when unscrupulous journalists, without risk of prosecution, can make stories up in order simply to sell papers, this is inappropriate economic realm influence (a shameless push for sales) in the cultural realm. The media has an unedifying record as purveyor of half-truths and downright lies, and—for the sake of everyone's dignity, surely—there is an acute need to bring an end to this or, at the very least, reduce it in ways that do not amount to censorship. Striving for truth whilst maintaining press freedom is always an interesting challenge. Observing threefold principles by ensuring the independence of the three realms can play a substantial part, however.

The internet can (*can!*) bring with it a democratisation of narrative, a significant freeing of information and dialogue from the clutches of corporate interests (as well as state interests). Before *social* media, we just had the media—newspapers, radio, TV. And so, to challenge the status quo on issues of social justice, for example, seemed too tall an order for most young people, and on the whole they disengaged from the debate. To some extent this has been ameliorated by Facebook, Twitter, etc. where people can share with others the information that interests them. Many have become more engaged, politically, and don't have to swallow whatever passes as news in the mainstream media—which are then simply bypassed. They now realise that thousands of others share the same interests and ideals as they do. Frequently, stories concerning public life that demonstrate goodness of character, dignity and morality gain more traction than the

---

[398] George Monbiot, 'Breaking the silence', *The Guardian*, 3 December 2014.

childishness excreted by the gutter press. Petitions against various abuses of corporate power attract millions of signatures.

The ability of social media to allow wider debate showed itself in 2015 when the relatively un-slick left-winger Jeremy Corbyn was elected head of the UK Labour Party (whose membership grew to an unprecedented 500,000), and left-winger Bernie Sanders ended up as one of the two most likely people to become presidential nominee for the Democrats in the USA, something that would probably have been unthinkable twenty years earlier with only daily, often fraudulent character assassinations from the mainstream media. Here were two individuals voicing strong concerns about lack of social justice, and the vilification of whom in the mainstream media ranged from sniggering to brutal. On the internet, however, without the economic realm inappropriately influencing the cultural, their voice could be heard.

As we know, though, the freedom and ease with which one can disseminate information on the internet also means anyone with basic internet skills can, in effect, broadcast stuff that is made up (not just unscrupulous journalists!), means readers still have to use their discernment to decide whether or not something might be 'fake news'. Whereas before, consumers of mainstream media had to be on their guard to spot disingenuous reporting, internet users now need to be wary of a very sophisticated diet of propaganda. 'Troll farms, bots, dark ads, fake news ... are being used to change politics and crush dissent'.[399]

Also, as Paul Mason notes, 'For the first twelve years of the internet era (1995-2007), power was distributed downwards. By ending the stranglehold over the broadcast of information, formerly held by states and corporations, the internet famously "changed everything". [...] The rise of smart devices, alongside the monopolization of social media by giant corporations and the strict enforcement of copyright laws, reversed this trend, returning power over information back to the hands of corporations and states. [...] the algorithms deployed by Amazon, Apple, Google and Facebook are designed to influence our behaviour. [...] The switch from open to closed systems, from words to pictures, from public to private conversations happened because, for one brief moment, people gathered up all the dreams,

---

[399] Peter Pomerantsev, 'The new propaganda', *The Guardian Weekly*, 2 August 2019.

plans and connections they had assembled online, and took them onto the streets. [...] The networked revolutions of 2011-13 were so brief, and so unlike anything before in history that, once they were defeated, people quickly forgot how terrified the global elite had been. [...] I remember the words of my TV producer: "You can taste freedom".[400]

Another downside of social media is that users can get so used to only engaging with ideas they themselves subscribe to (the 'echo-chamber' phenomenon) that tolerance for other points of view can suffer. The spectrum of debate then becomes limited in a new way. But this particular problem is not a result of inappropriate influence from the economic realm.

8.1.9   Cultural aspect appropriately serving rights aspect

The cultural aspect concerns everything that sprouts from the capacities of individuals and enters society. This contribution from individuals serves the political / rights system principally in two ways. It comes in the form of the talents of those politicians and others who work in this domain; and it comes in the form of the insights we, the public, apply when voting for them. And via education at all levels, institutions of the cultural domain enrich these human capacities, foster mental, moral and even physical capabilities in all which raises the level of insight among those who can then serve the rights realm more ably as politicians; and it raises the level of insight amongst the general public who can then vote in the political process in a more discerning way.

Everybody is educated in that free spiritual life; our children are brought up in it; we find our immediate spiritual interests in it; we are united with it. The very people who are thus united with that spiritual life and draw their strength from it, are the very same people who live within the legal and political life, and determine the legal order governing their relations with one another. They establish that legal order by the help of the spiritual impulses that they take in from the spiritual life, and this legal order is the direct result of what has been acquired through contact with the spiritual life. (CW332a, p. 112)

---

[400] Paul Mason, *How to Stop Fascism: History—Ideology—Resistance* (London: Allen Lane, 2021), pp. 54-56.

It is not only formal education, of course, that enriches people's capacities—capacities which make them more able participants in the political process. It is other aspects of cultural life too, such as literature, for example, or awareness-raising campaigns.

And when a politician is interviewed on TV on a Sunday morning, this is not really an activity in the political realm. It is educational, it is informing, it contributes to the debate, to the realm of ideas, albeit political ideas. It is cultural-realm activity. The guiding principle of equality does not apply at this point, but freedom. The interviewer is free to ask whatever questions they deem appropriate. The interviewee is free to give their opinions, or toe the party line. The viewer is free to make up their own mind about this opinion, or, indeed, to turn off the telly. The same even goes for a parliamentary debate or a live TV debate between would-be political leaders. *Individuals* should be free to express their views as this helps find best policy solutions. Yes, these ideas and views then *feed into* the political process. But the political process itself concerns the actual creation of laws by *everyone* voting equally, albeit acting, as they generally do, through their democratically elected representatives. These representatives, in turn, vote to adopt or reject whatever laws are being proposed, the law of the land before which we are all equal, the rights and responsibilities that keep society fair and safe.

As Jeffrey Sachs reminded his audience in the Oxford Union: 'Without properly informed civil society, politics is impossible. Period!' [401]

8.1.10 Cultural aspect inappropriately influencing rights aspect

If the rights domain's guiding principle of equality (democracy) becomes violated by the cultural domain, this is unhealthy according to threefold analysis. Not even the institutions of a *free* cultural life should be allowed to undermine democracy. But in some parts of the world one sees totalitarian theocracies where policy is determined by Scripture, or an interpretation thereof; there is interference in the political domain from a cultural life that is arguably un-free.

As Steiner says, edicts from priest-kings may have been appropriate in Ancient Egypt or earlier, but not nowadays. He relates how,

---

[401] Jeffrey Sachs, Full Q&A, Oxford Union, https://youtu.be/eKjbF9Db6J8.

today, human beings carry significantly more evolved individualities and should all therefore have a say in the political process.

If unelected bishops sitting in a second chamber like our House of Lords act purely in a scrutinising, advising, revising capacity, then obviously this is not as serious as if they were to actually *determine* policy by sitting in the House of Commons—the sovereign chamber. That would amount to inappropriate influence if they had not been elected; the democratic principle would be undermined. However, if one of them, not from within the legislature but simply from their respective parish, were to write an open letter to the government, say, or to a newspaper to place a matter of conscience in the public domain for politicians (and their electors, the public) to mull over, to take or leave, this would be different. This would simply amount to an addition to healthy debate and as such would fall within the cultural domain. It would not be crossing the line into the political domain, into actually *determining* policy. Anyone can write such a letter.

In the USA, the 1791 First Amendment's stipulation that religion and government be kept separate ensured the country's legislature would enjoy a degree of independence from inappropriate cultural influence.

A very different way in which the cultural can inappropriately influence the rights domain is seen in monarchy, autocracy, or dictatorship. The cultural domain is about the individual, the genius of their mind (and other qualities), and in a dictatorship the voice of the single individual—the monarch or the dictator—drowns out that of the populace. The dictator rules rather than serves. The political realm's guiding principle of equality is replaced by the agency of a single individual—an individual, moreover, who is unlikely to be anywhere near all-seeing enough to do the job that a democracy can do.

Even where, say, the UK Prime Minister decides on their own, or perhaps just in their 'inner circle' (Blair) or 'kitchen cabinet' (Thatcher) to take a particular course of action and ignores agreed ways of working (e.g. Cabinet / Parliament), one could call such autocratic behaviour inappropriate cultural influence in the political realm. The principle of democracy is undermined.

The point is, wherever possible, the guiding principle of equality / democracy should be maintained in the rights domain, the rights system.

It is particularly inspiring when an autocracy comes to this conclusion without threat of revolution as did, for example, the much loved fourth King of Bhutan. Indeed, his son—the fifth king—walked great distances across his country to meet his people in remote villages etc. to explain the introduction of democracy (in 2007-8) and the responsibilities that would go with it.[402] This seemed a truly enlightened act in a country which, instead of promoting gross national product, promotes gross national happiness—which is measured not in terms of Hedonia (short-term pleasures) but by Eudaimonia—blessedness—meaning harmony with others, with nature and with our deepest aspirations and highest potential.[403]

8.1.11 Cultural aspect appropriately serving economic aspect

The cultural realm constantly serves the economic system. Individual human capacities (intelligence, know-how, skills, creativity / innovation, etc.) flow into product design, managerial acumen, production engineering, craftsmanship, and so on. These capacities give rise to value within the economy even though they themselves 'belong' to the cultural domain. These values may come in the form of 'mental commodities' (e.g. advice of some kind) or as contributing factors in the production of physical goods.

The technical ideas that derive from spiritual life flow into the economic sector [Wirtschaftsleben = economic life]. They derive from spiritual life even when they come directly from members of the state or economic sectors. All organisational ideas and forces which fecundate the economic and state sectors originate in spiritual life. (CW23, 80)

Enterprise is based on ideas; ideas come from the cultural realm—the realm of human faculties.

---

[402] http://www.legalserviceindia.com/article/1266-Monarchy-To-Democracy-In-Bhutan.html.
[403] Ha Vinh Tho, 'International day of happiness: what is true happiness?' (19 March 2019), http://havinhtho.blogspot.com/2019/03/international-day-of-happiness-2019.html?m=1.

One might observe: Surely every instance of production involves skills of one sort or another, so where, precisely, is the line that distinguishes between economic realm and cultural? Yes indeed! To the extent that all workers—even the most menial labourer—are using their capacities to some extent, then every co-worker is bringing cultural life to the economic. *There is overlap*, just as in the human body there is overlap—the circulatory heart-lung system constantly feeds the nerve-sense head system, for instance.

> *Production experts, however, come from the independent spiritual realm, for this encompasses all that flows into production through human abilities. (CW338, 16 February 1921)*

The technical know-how, skills, managerial and inventive ideas etc. that come from the cultural realm and feed into economic life, into commodity production, often continue to do so long after an individual has passed away. As Steiner points out, thanks to his invention of differential calculus, Leibnitz is still to this day helping to build all tunnels for road and rail. And a doctor might treat a poorly shoemaker such that the latter returns to work two weeks earlier than otherwise. On the day of the medical consultation, no extra shoes have been made; but going forward, two additional weeks of production are achieved, thanks to the doctor's capacities. Likewise with someone in R&D. During the period in which they are inventing, nothing will be produced. But, going forward, it might be a very different story.

Furthermore:

> *The administration of the spiritual and cultural life, placed on its own footing, will supply the economic life with the human spiritual impulses that can fructify it ever and again, so long as this [economic] administration keeps within its own province and controls only goods and lines of production. (CW24, p. 68)*

That is, it will not be to the economic realm's long-term advantage if it tries to interfere in the cultural realm.

As an aside—something alluded to also at the beginning of this book—Steiner himself made a significant contribution to agriculture and thus to the production of physical commodities in the economy.

In founding what is known as biodynamic agriculture he inaugurated an approach which, amongst other things, produces award-winning wines, and consistently outperforms both conventional and organic agriculture in long-term soil fertility tests[404]—something of critical concern when the UN has suggested there may only be sixty harvests left in conventionally-farmed soil.[405]

If an expert in production (of whatever sort) 'comes from' the cultural domain, one might then wonder what guiding principle he or she should be working under. Should freedom (and competition) be their guiding principle if what they are contributing—their skills, flair, etc.—stem from the cultural domain? Or should they be working with a fraternal, associative frame of mind, working, as they are, in the economic realm? The following pertains:

> ... *production, which requires knowledge about how to produce, how one works out of human capabilities, needs the human individual[406], but ... everything to do with merchandise, with the goods when they have been produced, is subject to the collective judgement. (CW79, 30 November 1921)*

While I am assembling a motorbike, I am using my individual skills; this is a cultural realm contribution. But the *system* that co-ordinates production and distribution with consumption—be that of motorbikes or cabbages—is very much the economic realm. Here, *individual* judgement is not decisive, but the interests of different parties in association with one another. In this associative system of needs being met, fraternity is operative. But in production as such, the individual's judgement is operative, individual capacities are what is important, albeit half-free ones—half-free because the individual is duty-bound to apply their abilities to the task in hand.

---

[404] See, for example, findings of 20-year field trials at https:www.fibl.org/en/Switzerland/research/soil-sciences/bw-projekte.dok-trial.html#c29084.

[405] Susan Cosier, 'The world needs topsoil to grow 95% of its food—but it's rapidly disappearing', *The Guardian*, 30 May 2019.

[406] A possibly better translation of '*das menschliche Individuum auf den Plan ruft*' is 'brings the human individual into the picture'.

*Imagine the free spiritual life in the social organism really freed
so that the individual faculties were always able to evolve to the
full. Then the free spiritual life will be able to exert an extremely
fertilising influence on the half-free spiritual life—i.e. on that spiritual life which enters into the process of material production.
(CW340, p. 81)*

As well as via individual capacities feeding into production, the cultural
realm also contributes to the economic as follows:

*The producer must be able, indirectly or directly, through insti-
tutions of which we have spoken [i.e. associations, RM], to see
what men need for their consumption. He must then devote
himself unselfishly and with understanding to some kind of
production for which he has the capability. It is only necessary to describe this, and people will be forced to see that the
real motive power of production is self-sacrificing love towards
human society.*

*Nothing constructive will ever be said regarding the actual solution
of the social problem until it is understood that production can only
be regulated in a social manner by the creation, through the spiritual and equity[407] organisations, of a source from which unselfish
love for the various branches of production can flow into the human
soul, because of the producers' interest in their fellow men and in
life. (CW332a, pp. 133-134)*

*... the old devotion, the immediate companionship with the thing
he has made, exists no longer; yet it must be replaced by something else. What can this be? It can only be replaced by enlarging
men's horizon, by raising them to a level on which they can come
together with their fellow men in one great circle, eventually with all
their fellow men within the same social organism as themselves, in
which they can develop an interest in man as man. It must come to
pass that even a man who is working in the most remote corner at*

---

[407] Although, in this section, we are concerned with the contribution made
by the *cultural* realm to the economic, this relates to Steiner's observation
that a well constituted *rights* realm can also increase motivation for work
(see Section 7.4.8).

a single screw for some great machine need not put his whole self into the contemplation of the screw, but it must come about that he can carry into his workshop the feelings that he entertains for his fellow men, that when he leaves his workshop he finds the same feelings, that he has a living insight into his connection with human society, that he can work even without actual pleasure in his production because he feels he is a worthy member in the circle of his fellow men. (CW332a, p. 70)

This feeling of belonging in brotherliness with other people is the chief thing we have to understand as being the spiritual part of economic life. (CW193, p. 34)

Those working within the independent cultural realm can, if sufficiently insightful, promote a healthy love of humanity and provide meaning for people from which a will to work can arise, a motivation to work that can otherwise be undermined by the monotony of the factory floor. Such promotion of a healthy love of humanity might begin with good parenting, but it can then take a significant step forward at school. A well-rounded education can make a person feel more part of the wider human family.

And then, upon leaving education and entering the workplace, there will be other motivating ways a person might feel culturally connected. Steiner is on record (no pun intended) as having found mass media distasteful. In respect of that great-grandfather of Spotify—the gramophone—he bemoaned the idea of culture being 'pressed into a machine'. However, it is probably also true to say that a factory worker who is doing highly repetitive work might feel more culturally connected and thus much happier by listening to the radio while working. Likewise, one can imagine that the array of drama, documentaries, comedy, etc. on offer on TV when they get home in the evening adds considerably to their cultural nourishment, their growing understanding of the world, their feelings of human connectedness, their 'inner capacities'. This could also be seen as a form of the cultural realm supporting the economic, albeit a rather indirect one.

With the ever increasing automation of factory processes, with robots able to replace ever more drudgery, these considerations are perhaps less relevant to what they were when Steiner was alive. But they are by no means irrelevant. If one were to go to India or China and watch tee shirts or laptops being made, this would doubtless be confirmed. And, no doubt, many of those performing this un-automated, repetitive work for long hours each day are unlikely even to have access to the music and drama that we in the 'developed' world have ready access to on radio or TV.

Steiner's recommendations concerning the stewardship of land and the means of production so that these serve the common good, are another example of the cultural realm supporting the economic:

It is impossible to reach a just determination of price as long as the means of production and land function as they now do within the economic system. The disposal of land, systematised in the laws relating to its ownership, and the disposal of the finished means of production (for example, a factory with its plant and equipment), should be no matter for the economic organisation. They must belong partly to the spiritual and partly to the legal. That is to say, the transfers of land from one person or group of persons to another must not be carried out by purchase or through inheritance, but by transference through legal means, on the principles of the spiritual organisation. The means of production through which something is manufactured—a process that lies at the basis of the creation of capital—can only be looked at from the point of view of its commodity costs while it is being built up. Once it is ready for operation, the creator of it takes over the management because he understands it best. He has charge of it as long as he can personally use his capacities. But the finished means of production is no longer a commodity to be bought and sold. It can only be transferred by one person or group of persons to another person or group of persons by law, or rather, by spiritual decisions confirmed by law. Thus, what at present forms part of the economic life, such as the laws relating to the disposal of property, to the sale of land, and to the right of disposal of the means of production, will be placed on the basis of the independent legal organisation working in conjunction with independent spiritual organisation. These ideas may appear strange and unfamiliar today, but this fact is just what is so sad and bitter. Only when these things find entrance into the minds and souls and hearts of men, so that the human being orders his social life accordingly, only then can be fulfilled what so many try to bring about in other ways but always without success. (CW332a, pp. 120-121)

The rights realm can provide a legal framework for ownership succession of the means of production which enshrines the principle that these are passed on, without financial consideration, to those most able to manage them for the common good. Certain types of corporate legal form are more suited to this than others. And Steiner recommends that, if the departing proprietors cannot choose a successor, then appropriately constituted facilities within the cultural sphere (an arms-length Trustee body, perhaps, or some other panel of experts) select the most able 'inheritee' to continue production. Here too, then, the cultural realm can support the economic.

Finally, capital itself (either in the form of means of production or in the form of loan money—which enables the means of production to be built up in the first place) is a prime example of the cultural working in the economic. This might sound odd, but the logic is as follows: the loan money will have arisen as surplus in some other economic concern. This economic concern will only have been able to generate these profits thanks to the intelligence of those organising labour, etc, thanks, that is, to human faculties, to the cultural realm.

> *What aspect of the spirit is rightly present in economic life? [...]*
> *Capital is the spirit of economic life. And a great amount of harm*
> *existing in our day arises from the fact that the administration of*
> *capital, its fertilisation and fruitfulness as it were, is withdrawn*
> *from the life of spirit [e.g. is invested for rental income rather than*
> *invested in productive abilities, RM]. (CW189, p. 102)*
>
> *... capital essentially belongs to that relationship in the economic*
> *life which supports the economy culturally. Capital is what creates*
> *the economic centres, the enterprises. It is the cultural element in*
> *the economic life. But under modern materialism such cultural life*
> *in the economy has assumed a materialistic character. However, it*
> *is nevertheless the cultural life in the economy. The capitalist ele-*
> *ment is the spirit in the economic life. (CW338(iii), p. 189)*

8.1.12 Cultural aspect inappropriately influencing economic aspect

For Steiner, decisions in the economy are ideally made associatively, in the meeting of producer, distributor and consumer, in the dialogue between inter-dependent needs. The corollary to this is that he sees decisions taken by individuals in isolation as unhealthy—when, that is, these decisions concern the economic system itself, the merry-go-round of production, distribution, consumption. Individual decisions *at each end* of this process are not a problem: consumers decide for themselves what they want to buy; producers, with their expertise, decide for themselves the best, most efficient way of producing something. But *what* to produce, and *in what quantity*, is ideally arrived at out of association, out of a mechanism whereby the wishes of consumers are in dialogue with production capabilities, and, out of this, the needs of consumers are met with a rational response from industry. For Steiner, the idea of someone, on their own, speculatively deciding to manufacture some new widget and then trying to sell it without first making efforts to ascertain need is an inferior approach. Naturally, to think in terms of absolutes here is not realistic. There will always be some business start-ups which simply cannot gauge need until potential customers have inspected the merchandise, run the new widget through their fingers, and perhaps then got their wallets out. In relation to this, I remember how in the early 1990s it seemed most of the population could simply not see the point of this new 'internet' thing. Why on earth is anyone going to spend a lot of money on a home computer to look up something about this or that songbird, or this or that hotel, when there are perfectly good ways (so we thought) of doing this already?

When the individual predominates in economic matters, when unrestrained freedom of the individual takes priority over any recognition of our economic interdependence, then a healthy, *cultural* liberalism can turn into *economic* neo-liberalism. Then, instead of the economy's guiding principle of fraternity, one sees the cultural realm's guiding principle of freedom become freedom to exploit others, to ruin competitors, to foist substandard goods on the vulnerable, etc. The cultural is inappropriately influencing the economic, and we then have a problem.

At the other end of the spectrum, instead of *too much* freedom passing from its appropriate domain of the cultural realm to that of the economic, one can see an economic realm dominated by a cultural realm wherein *too little* freedom prevails. This might be seen where some totalitarian theocracy bans certain products and generally tyrannises the satisfaction of what individuals see as their needs.

* * *

In summary, there is both positive and negative overlap between the three societal realms:

- The cultural realm serves the other two realms by providing them with human capabilities.
- The political realm serves the other two realms by providing them with a just and safe environment in which to operate.
- The economic realm serves the other two realms by providing them with goods and services.
- The cultural realm undermines the other two realms if, with its focus on the individual, it compromises their guiding principles of equality (rights realm) or brotherliness (economic).
- At the other extreme, entrenched cultural dogma can tyrannise the rights and economic domains.
- The political administration undermines the other two realms if it steps outside its own sphere of rights, as this can have a stultifying, bureaucratising effect on them.
- The economic realm undermines the other two realms if it compromises their guiding principles by getting involved. By stepping outside its own sphere of economics, business can have a corrupting effect on both liberty (cultural domain) and equality (rights domain).
- In general, when the institutions of one realm try to operate outside of that realm, when they step beyond their proper function and meddle with the other two realms, this is detrimental to society's health.

8.2   Some obvious institutional examples

The previous section showed how the three broad aspects of the social organism can affect one another in both healthy and unhealthy ways. In this section, a few different types of institution will be considered to clarify how the three aspects overlap and interpenetrate in specific fields of work.

It should be emphasised that the overlaps that occur within institutions are there regardless of whether the institutions are endeavouring to operate in a threefold manner. The other thing to remember is that every *individual* continually lives within all three realms, regardless of which type of institution they might work in. We are all subject to laws and can vote, and thus live in the rights realm. We all eat food and wear clothes provided by others and are thus economic actors. And we all have our individual capacities and have received education and other forms of inner enrichment; we are therefore also actors within the cultural domain.

Firstly, three simple examples are considered where just one of the realms very obviously predominates in the organisation.

8.2.1 Example 1—a factory manufacturing roof tiles

The main thrust of this operation is clearly economic in that it is all about producing commodities—roof tiles—to meet the requirements of those who need them. It sits squarely within the economic realm (as, indeed, do the shops selling the tiles, since these are part of the distribution process—which is also part of the economic realm). The guiding threefold principle relevant to this factory would therefore be *fraternité*; the main thrust of its business would be determined by the dialogue between itself and its customers, i.e. in association with others.

Within this organisation, however, the rights realm will feature too. Labour laws will protect co-workers: the relationships between staff will be subject not only to contractually agreed ways of working but also to national laws relating to working hours, health and safety, etc. And the organisation, together with its suppliers, distributors and customers would all have the right not to be defrauded or physically attacked, for example, and to expect all parties to any contract to adhere to its terms, and so on. Also, the organisation—or its management at least—will have the right to operate the means of production. Rights and responsibilities, as enshrined by the prevailing legislature, will be ever present in the organisation (as well as in society generally, providing a safe and stable context in which economic activity can proceed).

The cultural realm within this company is represented by the co-workers' capacities, especially the organising intelligence within management. Roof tiles being very low tech, there might be little by way of product design (which is also part of the cultural realm), but the production knowhow of *all* concerned still amounts to human faculties and so comes from the cultural realm. Also, the machinery involved in the production process—the means of production—will have been invented and built thanks to the ingenuity coming from individuals, from the cultural domain. And the capital used to procure such machinery in the first place will have been generated thanks to ingenuity and enterprise elsewhere.

So, all three realms overlap in the factory. If the factory was operating along conventional lines but wished to operate in a more threefold way, then it could observe some of the principles outlined previously. For example, the factory would ideally not be owned / purchased by outside shareholders. And, rather than operating in a competitive, profit-maximising way, it would work in a collaborative, associative way, discussing customer needs, distribution possibilities, production techniques with interested parties, and where possible enter into contract with them as suppliers (of tiles), and as consumers (of raw materials).

The appointment of the CEO would be based on their capacities—a competitive process would ensure that the best person for the job got the job, rather than, say, the half-interested offspring of the previous owner or a new proprietor who was able to simply buy the business. This would ensure the greatest efficacy / productivity for the common good.

The factory might also want to consider some of Steiner's other suggestions, bearing in mind at all times that these were suggestions and not prescriptive instructions. For example they might want to look into whether their pricing could be moved (up or down) more in the direction of 'fair price'. And the remuneration of workers could be structured such that there was a partnership sharing of the overall business proceeds instead of wage contracts. Naturally, any measures adopted would have to comply with the prevailing laws governing work.

But notwithstanding the presence of all three realms, the factory is predominantly an economic concern and so, in a threefold world, its focus would be associatively meeting the needs of consumers. The other two realms support this activity.

8.2.2   Example 2—a university

Such an institution functions predominantly within the cultural domain. Not only is the teaching—being based on capacities—a contribution from the cultural domain, but also this teaching liberates, nurtures, enriches the minds, the capacities, the inner 'tools' of others. As far as the education is concerned, the university's prevailing leitmotif ought, according to threefolding, to be freedom. The other two realms should play no part in the *content* of this cultural life. It falls to professors how best to cultivate ideas and knowledge. This is not determined by the political administration (save, perhaps, in order to prevent hate speech or incitement to violence), and the economic realm too would have no leverage. It would be impossible for corporate beneficence to 'steer' research in a direction that was convenient to the donor. The corrupting effects of this, illustrated in Sections 8.1.2 and 8.1.8, demonstrate the importance of the threefold independence Steiner recommends. In addition, university education in a threefold context is freely available to those who can make best use of it; not simply to those whose parents have the *economic* wherewithal to buy it.

However, in the university the rights realm *will* apply in such things as legal protection from physical attack, or in sickness benefit and holiday entitlement for all staff. And the university will have a right to occupy the land it sits on.

And the economic realm will also feature. Lecturers need to eat, need commodities. To procure these, they need remuneration for their services—services which also have a commodity nature to them, an economic dimension in addition to the obvious cultural dimension. Even though such remuneration might come from what Steiner termed gift money, this gift money will enable lecturers to purchase commodities in the economic realm. (As mentioned previously, institutions 'belonging' to the economic realm produce more commodities than are required for their own needs, and some of this excess passes over to the independent cultural life.)

And when the university buys basketballs, computers or lecture halls, it will again be functioning within the economic sphere: it will be purchasing commodities. Ideally, it would do so associatively.

A more indirect way in which the university will overlap with economic life arises from the fact that, on account of the education provided, the capacities of students become enhanced, and these enriched capacities then go on to fecundate the economic life in the future. Being more indirect, however, this cannot really be considered part of the day-to-day engagement of the university in the economic realm.

Being predominantly a cultural organisation, though, the university would 'belong' to the cultural realm and probably be registered

with some umbrella body within the cultural domain's central administration—for the sake of coordination purposes. If it was considering
offering a new degree in geology, say, it might first want to talk with
such central administration to understand what the demand might be
for this. If the existing geology courses in the country were never
more than 75% full, then it might want to think twice before offering another one. But it would still be free to do so if it wished, if it
thought its new course would be a superior one, say, and attract the
'free appreciation' of sufficient applicants.

8.2.3   Example 3 — a police force

In such an organisation, the rights realm is predominant inasmuch as
the job of the police is to uphold the rights, obligations, rules which
society has elected to adopt. The police are part of the rights-state
apparatus. As such, how they proceed is fundamentally determined not
fraternally (e.g. in association with the suspects they accost!), nor by
free individual decisions (let's arrest this suspect but not that one), but
rather is determined by all *equally*. That is to say by all voters acting
equally through the democratic process.

Again, though, the economic realm will also feature. Officers have
to live, have to be remunerated, and the force also needs to buy police
cars, etc. This is enabled by some of the surplus production from institutions 'belonging' in the economic realm (i.e. business) being made
available to the force, via the mechanism of taxation.

The cultural realm will also feature in the minds and capacities of
the police officers, in their ability to think on their feet, interact cor-
dially with the public, investigate crime and so on.

In a society structured along threefold lines, the police would
operate under the protocols that we should be familiar with in the
West, namely, they would uphold the rights that had been democratically decided on by all those within the state; and they would treat
each member of the public equally without discrimination and so on.
Equality would be the watchword.

It should be noted, though, that the guiding principle of equality /
democracy that applies to the rights realm (wherein the police force
sits) would only apply at the more macro level, not the micro. That
is, it would not necessarily apply *within* institutions falling under the

auspices of the state. The one-person-one-vote guiding principle of the legal realm applies to the state-wide making and 'suffering' of laws. It does not necessarily apply to the day-to-day running of each organisation within the legal realm. For a police force to be effective it would in most instances be important that a hierarchy and line of command be maintained. As alluded to earlier in the book: if, during some episode of riot control, events were to take an unexpected turn for the worse, it would be inadvisable for the officers on duty to promptly all sit down and have a meeting to democratically decide amongst themselves how best to proceed!

There are one or two ways in which a police force could be more threefold or less threefold. It could perhaps, as purchaser of commodities and thus as an actor within economic life, be part of a confederation with other police forces, through which it purchased its supplies. To be associative, this joining with others would not be with the sole aim of attracting bulk discounts on account of the large orders made co-operatively by several forces at once. Instead, it could, in association with producers, give them greater stability by guaranteeing a certain level of repeat orders, enabling these producers to plan in advance for a certain level of sales—and thus production—rather than leaving them in the usual produce-and-hope paradigm. Such practice may well happen already.

And our police force could also consider paying its personnel less according to rank and more according to their needs, the number of their dependants, etc.

On the cultural level, the police would promote officers according to people's abilities (as is hopefully always the case), not because they are friends with the incumbent ruler of the land, or in the same Masonic Lodge.

Being predominantly a rights realm operator, however, the police force would fall under the auspices of the rights realm's central administration, i.e. the state.

8.3 Some less obvious institutional examples

Having looked at three types of organisation that sit reasonably squarely within one or the other of the three societal realms, some different organisations will now be considered where the focus is less obvious.

8.3.1 Example 4—a hospital

Is a hospital predominately working in the cultural, economic or rights realm?

Given that the rights realm is about establishing and upholding rights, we have to rule this realm out. Acting together as an electorate, we may have decided that a National Health Service is a desirable thing to have. And, representing us, the rights state may well then have enacted legislation that says everyone—who is able—is obliged to contribute to a national health insurance scheme, and that all then have a right to treatment, free at the point of use, when they fall ill. To the extent that we all might have an *obligation* to contribute, and a *right* of access to care, the rights realm is in evidence, and the principle of equality applies. The rights realm also then needs to ensure that the necessary real estate is made available. These rights will be established and 'policed' through the political process. But that does not mean it is the rights realm which also then co-ordinates and delivers the medical care. The state *might* indeed be doing this, but it is then acting outside the rights realm.

Inasmuch as all, or certainly most, of the work done in a hospital is based on people's capacities—their intelligence, their empathy, their surgical skills and so on, the work that goes on belongs to the cultural domain (just as those aspects of work in a factory that require use of the individual's capacities also 'belong' to the cultural realm). Nurses are rarely mere cogs in a machine of care. And, happily, the principle of equality is not relevant when someone is appointed as a brain surgeon! People will have trained as surgeons etc. via the free competition—appropriate in the cultural domain—that ensures only those most suited can do so. Thus the cultural domain is very much in evidence in our hospital.

Thirdly, a hospital is very much an economic body providing services. We go to hospital because we want our broken leg or our cholera fixing, which in a way is not so different from having our boiler fixed when it breaks down. There is a simple transaction: we have a need and the service provider meets that need. The patient goes into hospital for a very definite good: the 'mendedness' of their leg, the cure of the cholera. As such, hospitals operate in the economic realm.

In view of this, it makes good sense for hospitals to associate with 'consumers' (patients) to ascertain the prevalence of different illnesses and accidents needing treatment across the region, and to collaborate with one another in order to collectively work out the most efficient way of providing the necessary treatments. One hospital, on account of its size and location, might be deemed suitable to cover just one town; another might be able to cover two. Such association can be seen within the UK's National Health Service—one of the most popular institutions in the country. The various health providers collaborate to address the health needs around the regions; their work is based on addressing needs, not on trying to make profits. Having said that, there are those times when the NHS will, for the sake of cost-cutting, take an unpopular decision (to close a local maternity ward, for example), and patients—or their representatives—have had to make a particularly concerted effort to get their side of the story taken into account, their side of the association acknowledged. Naturally, the association in something like the NHS has to take on a particular colouring. It is not a case of 'customers' contracting to come in with a broken leg once per annum!

Whilst, in the 'free' cultural domain, it is appropriate for someone such as an artist to freely compete with other artists for the soul needs of the public, it would make little sense for hospitals to spring up all over the place to compete for patients. Speculative competition and duplication like this—in the economic domain—would be wasteful. *Individual* health practitioners, on the other hand, are a somewhat different matter. Doctors, as well as osteopaths and reflexologists, work out of highly individualised capacities and, as such, are best left free to compete with one another to be taken on. Individual patients should be at liberty to choose this or that practitioner out of their 'free appreciation'. General practitioners in primary care often work on this basis. That is, out of 'free appreciation' you can choose to go to this doctor or that, according to which one you think understands your situation better. Whilst in theory the NHS could offer alternative therapies based on associative dialogue with patients wishing for such (in addition to homeopathy which is already offered to a small extent), it is perhaps unrealistic to expect a currently very stretched NHS to move towards this any time soon. Even much of dentistry is provided outside of the NHS. However, without great loss to the NHS, even the more fringe therapies could be included if practitioners were only paid when used, i.e. when their services 'met with appreciation'. With around ten anthroposophical hospitals in Germany (which are complementary rather than alternative), things seem considerably more advanced there than in the UK as far as responding to need is concerned.

To summarise: To the extent that hospitals are economic units—providing services—they ideally collaborate with one another and associate with 'customers' (patients, or their representatives) to meet needs. Such collaboration would ideally also apply between hospitals and their suppliers (of beds, bandages, etc.). To the extent that hospitals utilise human faculties—e.g. the skill of doctors—then freedom (and competition) apply. Those most able in medical matters are taken on as doctors, out of 'free appreciation'. To the extent that the rights realm features in the hospital (e.g. right to treatment, labour laws, working time regulations, etc.), then the principle of equality applies.

8.3.2   Example 5—a golf club

If the rights realm is about the creation and the upholding of the rules by which we all choose to live and interrelate, does a golf club fall into this domain? Club members certainly have a right to use the golf course, after all. However, since a golf club is not about legislating and upholding that legislation, it is not an institution 'belonging to' the rights realm.

The cultural realm concerns what enters society from the individual, from their capacities, and also what is given to the individual to grow those capacities. The person running the golf club might be considered a cultural worker in much the same way as the person running the tile factory. And, when playing golf, a club member will be using their capacities—and perhaps even trying to improve them. So could the club therefore be thought of as part of the cultural domain?

And the economic domain, as we know, is about the production, circulation and consumption of commodities—of goods and services. Predominantly, the club concerns the meeting of its members' need for a golfing amenity. The members pay a club subscription which funds the services offered by those running the club: the club house is kept in good repair, the fairways and greens are mown, etc. Thus the club is *predominantly* an economic affair. There is association between those running the club and its members (customers).

The other realms nonetheless feature, though. If the rights-state in which the golf club exists were arranged in a completely threefold manner, then the land used for the golf club would not have been *bought*; it might not even have been possible to buy it. The rights realm would confer the right of use, guided in all probability by recommendations from the other domains. Before the golf course was set up, the economic domain might first ascertain that people's basic needs for food and shelter were being met, that the agricultural sector already had access to plenty of fertile land to grow the food required, and so on. It (the economic domain) might also ascertain that there were no other golf courses nearby and that there was sufficient interest in golf to justify the creation of a new golf course. And the cultural realm (represented, say, in some golf club advisory panel) might even ascertain that the person or group wanting to set up the golf course knew what they were doing. Perhaps only once these matters had been confirmed would a licence be granted by the rights realm for the golf course to use the land in question. The land would not be *bought*, and so membership might be considerably cheaper than otherwise.

Given that a golf course takes up a significant amount of land and therefore can affect a large number of people (depending on where it is sited), the local political process itself (e.g. the local authority / council), might invite broader debate to ensure the democratic principle was maintained within the granting of planning permission. If people want to buy rocking chairs and place them in their living rooms, that is of no concern to the public / the democratic process. But if people want to take up a swathe of land, this is a different matter. If the proposed golf course was to be sited on a piece of land no one had much interest in, this would be a different matter than if it was to be sited in an area of particular beauty used by thousands of ramblers each year, or on a highly fertile stretch of land that could be used for growing those cabbages.

8.3.3   Example 6—a hunger relief charity

A hunger relief charity set up in response to a famine overseas is not about the state apparatus of law-making. The state may well have an overseas aid budget or a crisis relief policy, but let's assume our charity has been set up because these mechanisms have proven too unresponsive or inadequate to deal with the plight in question.

But to which of the other two realms does it 'belong'?

To the extent that is about getting food to the relevant corners of the earth as quickly and efficiently as possible, it is an economic entity. It is concerning itself with the distribution of commodities to meet needs, albeit outwith the normal process of sale and purchase. Inasmuch as it is focusing entirely on need and not on profit, it is already in keeping with certain of Steiner's associative, brotherly suggestions.

However, if the charity also focuses on awareness-raising it is educational and thus part of the independent cultural domain. As such it might also have the hope—and mission—to influence the political process with the aim, for example, of getting the overseas aid budget increased or explaining the broader, collateral impact of famine, say. But this is still activity within the cultural domain: it is about broadening people's (both the public's and politicians') consciousness and pricking their consciences in the hope of influencing policy; it is not directly legislating. (Similarly, a human rights charity like Amnesty International, whilst concerning itself very definitely with rights, is nonetheless not really part of the legislative realm. It is not legislating; it is awareness-raising, educating.)

8.3.4   Example 7—a bank

In which domain does a bank sit? Let's assume the bank is of the old-fashioned variety and just provides two services: (a) bank accounts (current and savings), and (b) loans. (Trading on the capital markets is in any case precluded under threefold analysis.)

Such an institution is clearly not about determining or upholding rights and laws, so that's one realm ruled out—the rights realm. The rights realm, law, will of course *feature* in aspects of the bank: from the relationships between staff, to the obligation to give a depositor their money back in a timely manner if they ask for it.

If not principally rights-realm members, are banks instead concerned with what emanates from individual capacities, or are they more concerned with the economic system, the production, circulation and consumption of commodities?

Inasmuch as they provide a *service* that facilitates the commodity circulation process, the buying and selling process, i.e. a stewardship and clearing system for purchase money, a bank is predominately at work in the economic realm.

Remember:

> *... commodity production, the only means through which the possessor of money will have been able to attain it,*[408] *will back every coin and banknote. (CW23, p. 119)*

Comments like this, and those others where Steiner describes money as essentially representing an accounting system that records the exchange of commodities (Section 7.4.22), support the idea of a bank being very much an agent in the economic domain.

However, as far as the lending side of a bank is concerned—especially commercial lending—there is also close affinity with the cultural domain. We have seen how Steiner recommends that the means of production would ideally be lifted out of the purchase-and-sale mechanism of the economic realm, as they are not commodities for personal use but, rather, are factors of production to be taken hold of by the human spirit in the most advantageous manner. He proposes facilities within the cultural realm should ultimately be responsible for allocating these means of production, when the previous proprietor is unable.

But when making a decision about to whom to lend, a bank requires just those individual capacities for discerning the suitability of someone to run a factory or some other enterprise, for discerning whether a prospective borrower has the relevant capacities to make a success of their enterprise. This discernment is much the same as the discernment required to intelligently pass the means of production on from one manager to a successor. There is thus a significant manifestation of the cultural aspect within the lending function of a bank, as it necessitates this individual discernment. That said, Steiner advises that responsibility for lending should ultimately lie with the associations of the economic realm, although he does also acknowledge 'the impulses

---

[408] Unless they are a dependent on welfare, or in receipt of loan or gift money.

and perspectives that enter economic life from the cultural and legal spheres will play a decisive part' (see below—my emphasis):

> *The economic life in a threefold social order is built up by the co-operation of associations arising out of the needs of producers and the interests of consumers. These associations will have to decide on the giving and taking of credit. In their mutual dealings the impulses and perspectives that enter economic life from the cultural and legal spheres will play a decisive part. These associations will not be bound to a purely capitalist point of view. One association will deal directly with another; thus the one-sided interests of one branch of production will be regulated and balanced by those of another.*
>
> *Responsibility for the giving and taking of credit will thus be left to the associations. This will not impair the scope and activity of individuals with special faculties; on the contrary, only this method will give individual faculties full scope. The individual is responsible to his or her association for achieving the best possible results. The association is responsible to other associations for making good use of these individual abilities. Such a division of responsibility will ensure that the whole activity of production is guided by complementary and mutually corrective points of view. (CW24, p. 47)*

As we know, under a threefold approach, economic life is associative, and production is focused on meeting need, not making profit. And since the associative bodies Steiner describes have their ear to the ground as regards prevailing needs, it seems natural that these bodies would be instrumental in the lending process. They would be best placed to identify those industries most able to respond to need, and therefore best placed to identify the most 'deserving' recipients of loan capital.

As a rule of thumb, one could say that identifying the most needed industries is an economic-realm matter, and identifying the best people to run these industries is a cultural-realm matter.

For two reasons, then, a bank can be seen as part of the economic domain: (a) by providing current account services, it acts as a significant agent in the commodity exchange process, and (b) by allocating loan money, it acts as an agent in enabling that production that most meets needs.

As such, a bank in a threefold world would be very much linked into associative life. Yes, by providing loan capital, it is also enabling the entrepreneur—human faculties—to go into production, and so there is a significant connection with the cultural domain. But this nonetheless occurs within the broader context of meeting needs.

Of course, all bank workers (not just those assessing loan applications) are using their intelligence throughout the day in any case, so banks—like any other organisation in the economic domain—benefit from the cultural realm continually. To this extent the guiding principle of freedom applies; it is via free competition that people are appointed to bring their skills to the workplace.

8.3.5   Example 8—a dinner party at someone's house

Although all three realms will be 'guests' at such a party, as a private affair the party will not, of course, be a concern of any of the three societal administrations. Yes, all friends present will be subject to laws preventing physical attack. As such the rights domain will be in evidence. Yes, conversation and conviviality will flow thanks to people's capacities. The cultural realm will therefore be ever present too. And yes, people will consume food and drink and thus be active economically.

But this consumption of food and drink is not really the main point of the party. These friends, after all, would have eaten elsewhere, had they not got together. One could perhaps (somewhat tenuously) argue that the eating and drinking is not even the main *economic* aspect of the party. The main point of the party is to have an enjoyable time with friends. We have a *need* for social contact, and our friends meet this need. But since we meet the same need in them, the arrangement is reciprocal. They give us an enjoyable experience; we give them an enjoyable experience. Whilst these enjoyable experiences are based on the capacities of all present (cultural realm), they could also be regarded as reciprocal *services*. Although undoubtedly a bit perverse to think of the party in such transactional terms, it can nonetheless help one see how the realms continually overlap!

Compare with going to see a play: the main point of this is not the refreshments in the interval, but the enjoyable experience. Yes, what the playwright and actors do comes from their capacities (cultural domain). But they are also providing the audience with a service. There is an economic *dimension* to the matter, and so we pay for our seats. At a dinner party, however, all guests are both 'producers' and 'consumers' (of enjoyable experiences), and so payment doesn't even cross our minds. In a way, the guests even associate before getting together—by choosing a time agreeable to all, etc. Naturally, though, the whole thing is an entirely informal affair. No contracts are drawn up for this exchange of enjoyable experiences!

The meaning people find in bonds of friendship—and in human connection generally—is based on what 'bursts forth' from human capacities, from the human spirit; it is based on the cultural realm. Indeed, this meaning is arguably among the most significant drivers in our lives. Thus, our dinner party—indeed all forms of celebration— are very much part of cultural life. As such, the principle of freedom is sovereign. Thankfully, so much so that the party (unlike, say, universities) won't have any connection with any central administration that might happen to exist within the cultural domain. It is a private affair that has little bearing on public life or social reform.

8.3.6   Example 9—a Local Authority / County Council

Whilst the cultural realm will be in evidence in a District Council inasmuch as people's individual capacities will be at play (as with any other organisation), the organisation is clearly not predominantly about cultural life, about the flourishing of individual capacities.

The focus of a District Council is essentially the other two realms. To the extent that it is providing housing, bin emptying and highway services, it is an actor within the economy, it is providing goods and services—commodities—to meet needs. To the extent that it is establishing local by-laws via local elections (legislating for environment-protecting measures perhaps, or new cycle lanes, or granting planning permission), it is working in the rights realm.

If one wished to maintain the threefold 'hygiene' of not trying to establish and uphold rights and responsibilities whilst at the same time providing goods and services, one might want to separate the two functions into two separate bodies. One—the district *rights* council—would take care of the legislative aspect of the above functions, would concern itself with what is right and just. The other—the district *services* council (i.e. an economic association)—could take care of public services. The guiding principle active in the former would be equality as expressed through democracy; in the latter it would be fraternity as expressed through associative working— through consultation with end users. Its *raison d'être* would not be to pursue profit, but to meet needs.

However, it should be noted that most of what local authorities provide by way of services will be done in an associative way already. Refuse collection, for example, if it is not outsourced, will operate on a needs-based, collaborative model without a fixation on making profit. The refuse collection departments of local authorities up and down the country will, in all likelihood, also be collaborating with each other to compare notes on the best waste bin types, the most efficient waste collection lorries, approaches to recycling, incineration issues, and so on.

This mixing of rights and services in County Councils seems unproblematic in a number of instances and, in any case, consistent with Steiner's remark that ...

> What we need, however, is for government to retain the initiative only in the centre—that is, to retain oversight of security services, public hygiene, and the like ... (CW333, p. 20)

Things like collecting rubbish are a matter of public hygiene, after all. And when this is not outsourced to profit maximisers but, instead, the means of production (e.g. those waste collection lorries) are held and managed in such a way to serve the common good, etc. then one can see a number of healthy, associative principles being observed.

8.3.7   Example 10—a newspaper

Newspaper publication is another aspect of life that is not so straightforward to pigeon-hole. Ignoring advertising, newspapers generally do two things: they report on events ('the news') and they report opinion—which can also be buried, or not so buried, within the tone of the reporting of events.

These newspapers are then sold as commodities in the hope of making a profit, unless, that is, they are owned by a not-for-profit trust or by a wealthy proprietor who may be less interested in making a profit and more interested in peddling a point of view and trying to influence opinion.

As has already been established, to the extent that production of even the most rudimentary physical item relies to some extent on individual skill, this production relies on cultural-realm activity. Skills come from the cultural-realm. So, clearly, the writing of articles—which requires a gift for writing—is cultural-realm activity. A smaller amount of skill might be required where it is simply a case of rather mechanically regurgitating facts: train derailed in Berwick; 15 injured. And more will be required where a highly analytical mind is required, one that is able to assimilate extensive amounts of information in order to explain the complex series of events occurring, say, in a politically volatile corner of the earth. And the writer of opinion is perhaps even more decisively operating within the cultural realm since what they write comes from inside their individual, inner nature. Journalism is also adding to the general life of thought, provoking the thought life of the reader to grow in understanding, to become aware of tangential political implications, or whatever. Such a writer is much the same as the author of a novel or painter of a picture whose work cannot really be based on associative response to economic need; it needs to be received (or rejected) by the free appreciation (or lack thereof) of the reader. The book or newspaper *publisher* may be active in the economic system of production and circulation of commodities; but the author—or artist—is working in a realm characterised not by collaboration and association, but ideally by individual freedom, free expression.

> ... in the newspaper industry, all three modes of human activity essentially flow together ... On the one hand, we have the publisher, the one who has to see to it that the newspaper is printed, that it is distributed in the right way, and so on. That is a purely economic task. On the other hand, we have those who write the newspaper ... Newspaper writers and the editorial team belong to spiritual life. And since on both sides, both in the economic part of the industry and in the spiritual part one is dealing with people who, in turn, stand in relation to other people, not only to their subscribers but also to the public at large, one is dealing with the relationship between one person and another, that is to say, with rights relationships. (CW337a, 30 May 1919)

During the lecture from which this passage is taken, Steiner goes on to describe how the corporate world can control the narrative and enslave the media which should be there to enlighten humanity. He consequently explains the need for a measure of threefold separation *within* the newspaper business:

> In the future one should aim for the newspaper publisher, the printer ... to exist inside the economic organism. The editorial staff will not be present in the economic organism, but will be entirely subject to the self-administration of spiritual life ... This will give the journalist great independence from the economic interests of the newspaper publisher. (CW337a, 30 May 1919)

Thus, editorial independence would not be compromised by a proprietor with their own agenda, with shady links, say, to the armaments industry such that pressure was put on the editor to sell the case for an unjustifiable war. This editorial independence ideally would also exist in relation to advertisers, so that journalists were not deterred from writing articles inconvenient to these income sources.

8.3.8   Example 11 — a home for adults with learning disabilities

This is another example where the economic realm and cultural can both be prominent.

The focus in such an institution will in large part be economic. It will provide housing and a daily cooked meal which are commodities. There are likely to be carers ensuring that the residents remain safe, and are given a regular bath. But giving someone a bath is not so very different to a hairdresser giving them a haircut or a cobbler mending their shoes. It is an economic service, albeit one that is appropriately served by the bath-giver's caring skills, by the cultural domain. Indeed, the cultural, human-faculties aspect will be particularly strong where there is interaction with the residents, as this requires highly individual decisions and is, one could say, in some ways like an art. However, it is not like an art to such an extent that the carer freely decides how to deliver their care, and the service user freely takes it or leaves it, depending on the 'free appreciation' they feel for the carer's care. No, the carer provides the care the service user would like.

To use current parlance, the care is 'person centred'. As such, the care is a service, a commodity, a consumer good.

Further, the provision of such care is also likely to require a high degree of association both with individual service users (to ascertain individual needs) as well as across a geographical region—to ascertain the numbers of people in need of such facilities, generally, both now as well as in the future; to ascertain the various aspects of care needed and in what proportion. Also, a single home is likely to be a member of some central confederation (a providers' umbrella body) that can co-ordinate activity such that the right level of provision ensues.

Notwithstanding the above, where there is therapeutic or educational input, or even simply song and mirth, with the aim of helping to develop the capacities of the resident and provide soul enrichment generally, this is more directly part of the cultural realm. Unlike a bath or a haircut which are services with a definite result at the end, nurturing the capacities of an individual is an open-ended and highly individualised affair, and it falls under Steiner's definition of the cultural domain.

As with the other institutional examples given, such a home will also be appropriately served by the rights realm at all times, too, of course. Laws will be there to adjudicate on conduct, to protect service users, to regulate employment relations, and so on.

* * *

As well as individuals existing in all three aspects of the social organism, the above examples demonstrate that organisations, too, even those which very clearly 'belong' to one particular realm, will always have direct connections to the other two.

These organisational examples have been given simply to demonstrate this fact—the interpenetration of the three realms in society. With the exception, possibly, of the newspaper example, they serve less well as illustrations of the more serious problems which arise from a lack of threefold independence, i.e. those problems considered in Section 8.1 ('How one realm affects another'). The grave, macro problem of corporate corruption of state integrity, for example, is not illustrated by these micro, organisational circumstances.

9. Related Considerations

The threefold social organism has now been looked at from a number of angles; but before moving to the concluding stages of the book, a few unexplored tangents will briefly be considered.

9.1   More on egoism and altruism

Steiner points out that in one sense egoism is to be expected; it need not necessarily come with negative connotations. There is a difference between self-interest and selfishness.

> ... we may ask what element of human nature lies at the root of requirement, of consumption. Egoism is at their root. It is important that this fact should be properly understood. If it is understood, no one will feel impelled to ask with regard to the economic life: how can we overcome egoism? But rather: how is it possible for altruism to meet the just demands of egoism? (CW332a, p. 133)

One could perhaps ask whether, in the case of *basic* necessities, consumption might rather be at the root of egoism instead of egoism being at the root of consumption. Be that as it may, Steiner notes how, in cultural life, egoism is especially present:

> Where our spiritual / cultural life is concerned, what is the dom-inating impulse? Fundamentally it is personal interest which, although it is on a soul level, is egoistic. What people want from religion is that it 'saves' their souls; they want education to develop their talents, and they want either to enjoy whatever they choose to indulge in by way of artistic presentations or to gain an increase of life forces. It is always the case that what leads a person to the life of the spiritual sphere is egoism, of a grosser or a more refined sort. This is perfectly understandable. (CW193, p. 51)

He also notes that even altruistic deeds can come from egoism!

> *In speaking of egoism, we should recognise that it starts with the bodily needs of the human being. We cannot understand what arises from the bodily needs of the human being lest we regard it as belonging to the sphere of egoism. The needs of the human being proceed from egoism. Now we must believe that it is possible to ennoble the feeling of egoism and, therefore, it is not a good thing to form one's opinions from the phrases current on this subject. To say that egoism must be overcome by love does not help us much to understand egoism. For the point is, that he who meets his fellow men with a purely human interest and understanding acts differently from one whose interests are narrow, and who gives no thought to all that fills the hearts and souls of his fellow creatures, and who is without interest for his surroundings. On this account, the former, who is truly interested in his fellow men, need not be less egoistic in life than the other because his egoism may be precisely his desire to serve human beings. It may call forth in him a feeling of inner wellbeing, of inner bliss, even of ecstasy, to devote himself to the service of his fellow men. Then, as far as the outer life is concerned, deeds that are absolutely altruistic to all appearance may proceed from egoism; in the life of feeling they cannot be appraised otherwise than as egoism. (CW332a, pp. 129-130)*

> *Much of what we carry out in common with other men is absolutely founded on egoism, and still may be credited to the noblest human virtues. If we contemplate maternal love, we find that it is absolutely founded on the egotism of the mother; yet it manifests itself most nobly in the common life of humanity. (CW332a, p. 131)*

There are notable parallels between the above and what sociologist Anthony Giddens observes in 1998: 'The "me" generation is a misleading description of the new individualism, which does not signal a process of moral decay. Rather to the contrary, surveys show that younger generations today are sensitised to a greater range of moral concerns than previous generations were. [...] Many leftish critics have a reserved attitude towards the new individualism. Self-fulfilment, the fulfilment of potential: aren't these just forms of therapy-talk, or the self-indulgence of the affluent? Obviously they may be, but to regard them as nothing more is to miss a sea change in people's attitudes and aspirations'.[409]

Apart from egoism and altruism in their normal, psychological sense, Steiner also at times uses these terms with a quite different, *economic* meaning in connection with production. When he does, he explains they carry no moral undertones, no connection to the soul or emotion; he simply means producing things for oneself (in the case of *economic* egoism) and producing things for others (*economic* altruism). Whilst his economic egoism may simply mean the objective act of producing for oneself, it is nonetheless problematic since the division of labour (which basically amounts to producing for others) is a far more efficient and efficacious way of going about production.

> ... the further the division of labour has progressed, the less the individual person can work for himself, economically speaking. I am talking about an economic principle that I have been trying to popularise since 1904, but humanity does not want to understand this principle. Whether one likes it or not, in a social organism in which there is division of labour—and this is the case with every social organism in the modern civilised world—in such a social organism, one cannot work egoistically, economically speaking [my emphasis, RM]. All of an individual's work must go towards the totality. [...] This has become a fundamental economic principle: that man cannot work for himself in a social organism where the division of labour prevails, that he can only work for others. Whatever happens, this economic altruism prevails. If one sins against it, that is, if upon these naturally occurring foundations one places a superstructure whereby one acquires for oneself in an egotistical way the fruits, which in a true social process actually flow to the whole, then one introduces into the world what I would like to call a real lie. The egoism of today's economic order is nothing more than a sum of real lies, of sins against what actually happens below the surface and what amounts to a law of economic altruism. (CW329, 9 April 1919)
>
> ... with the rise of the modern division of labour, the economic life as such depends on egoism being extirpated ... I beg you to

---

[409] Anthony Giddens, *The Third Way: The Renewal of Social Democracy* (Cambridge: Polity Press, 2008), p. 35, also citing Helen Wilkinson and Geoff Mulgan, *Freedom's Children* (London: Demos, 1995).

take this remark not in an ethical but in a purely economic sense. Economically speaking, egoism is impossible. I can no longer do anything for myself; the more the division of labour advances, the more must I do everything for others. The summons to altruism has, in fact, come far more quickly through purely outward circumstances in the economic sphere than it has been answered on the ethical and religious side. (CW340, pp. 42-43)

That is, altruism in the normal sense, has not really kept up with what we do as producers—*economic* altruism, i.e. serving others. He continues:

In this lecture I'm speaking neither idealistically nor ethically, but from an economic point of view. What I have just said is intended in a purely economic sense. It is neither a God, nor a moral law, nor an instinct that calls for altruism in modern economic life—altruism in work, altruism in the production of goods. It is the modern division of labour—a purely economic category that requires it. [...] as economic systems expanded into a world economy, it became more and more needful to be altruistic, to organize the various social institutions altruistically; while, in their way of thinking, men had not yet been able to get beyond egoism and therefore kept on interfering in a clumsy, selfish way. (CW340, p. 43)

We all specialise in one or two types of production and so do not really produce for ourselves; instead we all produce for one another. But the widespread reluctance of people to also develop an altruistic mentality in the normal, non-economic sense creates a disconnect between their soul life and the simple reality of economic altruism, of producing for others.

9.2   Can an organisation be threefold on its own ?

As we have seen, threefolding is about allowing each of the three aspects of society to enjoy an appropriate measure of independence, free of inappropriate influence from the other two realms, such that each can operate according to its respective guiding principle—the three guiding principles being those that inspired the masses during the French Revolution.

Notwithstanding that this approach is ultimately put forward as a way of structuring society *overall* in a healthy way, one can also pose the question: can a single organisation—in isolation—be more (or less) threefold, regardless of society's general makeup?

The answer to this will generally be 'yes'.

Just as the three realms coexist in society overall, so too, as we have seen, do they coexist in each organisation. So, whilst a manufacturer, for example, will be occupied with economic realm matters, it will also consist of co-workers who are subject to laws made in the rights realm, and it will also benefit from their capabilities, capabilities which 'belong' to the cultural realm. And so on and so forth. The three systems are intermingled, as was illustrated in Chapter 8 ('Overlap').

If a lone organisation sees merit in the threefold approach and wishes to make itself more consistent with these ideals, it needs to (a) identify where the three aspects feature in its operation, (b) ascertain whether each is free of inappropriate contamination by the other two realms, and (c) ascertain whether each is operating according to its respective guiding principle.

It could start, for example, by considering what commodities (goods and services) it is providing and what commodities it is consuming. It could then consider whether its relationships with customers and / or suppliers could be more associative, could employ better dialogue, could be more brotherly, could promote greater business certainty, etc.

Having looked at those aspects of the operation that fall within the economic system—the system of getting commodities to where they are needed, the organisation could then look at those aspects that fall under the rights system (e.g. co-worker rights, or ownership of the means of production). It could consider whether the rights-realm aspects within the organisation could be more just; it could consider whether its wage system could be replaced by a right of co-workers to a share of company proceeds, etc. Since the rights realm ultimately concerns the prevailing legislation in the state, built on the equality inherent in democracy, those in a single organisation ought not do anything unilaterally to corrupt this principle. It is all of voting age who take equal responsibility for this process. It is vital no financial incentives (bribes) are given by the organisation to political parties etc. in order to influence policy over the heads of the electorate.

And where individual faculties, individual expression, individual initiative were concerned (cultural realm), it would be beneficial to ensure that those faculties had adequate freedom in which to flourish.

And it would be beneficial that the appointment and promotion of co-workers was based on free competition, as allowed, for example, in equal opportunities practice.

In the previous chapter ('Overlap') some more specific examples were given as to what sort of measures particular organisations could take to become 'more threefold'. A research facility (cultural) or a presidential campaign (rights) could shun those corporate bribes (economic), say. And Steiner's example, given earlier, of a newspaper publisher teasing its three aspects apart is also instructive. He is by no means dismissive of more isolated efforts to bring health into societal matters. As another example:

> The state-owned schools and economic enterprises do not have to be eliminated overnight; but the gradual dismantling of the state educational and economic apparatus could well develop from small beginnings. (CW23, p. 108)

At the same time, the following comment he makes to economics students in 1922 shows he is also keen for at least some people to be mindful of the bigger picture, certainly when it comes to economic matters.

> The economic process does indeed consist in an infinite number of interdependent factors. The single phenomenon is the outcome of an untold number of factors, all of which work into one another. To understand it, it simply will not do to think—if I may put it so—so very near at hand. All your thinking on economics will lead to disaster if you let your thoughts be guided only by what lies in the immediate neighbourhood of the single persons who are engaged in it. You will never get to grips with the economic process in this way. You must learn to envisage the social organism in its totality. (CW340, p. 48)

As we have seen a number of times, though, Steiner is entirely averse to being prescriptive:

> There is no point in answering theoretical questions such as: 'What attitudes must employer and employee adopt? How should a factory be socially structured?' Proper associations, groups of actual people must be established. From these the answers will come in due time. (CW305(ii), p. 132)

9.3   Economic policy

If, under threefolding, the state should not try and manage economic matters, where does this leave economic *policy*? During elections, one is often prompted to consider: is this or that party trusted on the economy? Would Bill Clinton's 'It's the economy, stupid!' even be relevant in a threefold social organism, or would politicians in fact be completely relieved of all things economic?

Broadly speaking, economic policy falls into two categories: (a) monetary policy, which concerns interest rates and the controlling of the money supply (the amount of money in circulation), and (b) fiscal policy which concerns state spending, taxation and state borrowing. Let us very briefly consider these main components of economic policy:

- Concerning control of the money supply, Steiner's comments about the validity of money being a matter ultimately for the economic realm (Section 7.4.18) suggest he would see the money supply as a matter for this realm too. The money supply has little to do with rights, after all, and a lot to do with ensuring appropriate levels of currency exist in the economic system to facilitate the efficient circulation of goods and services to meet needs.
- Concerning interest rates, however, he does suggest this could be partly a matter for the political realm (Section 7.4.15). Every now and then the state (in close consultation with the economic domain, one must surely presume) would establish the *right* of lenders to interest at a particular level. The simplistic-ness of this—a single interest rate—will no doubt have many cringing. But the aim here is just to ascertain basic principles. Also, as has often been stressed, Steiner's threefold proposals by no means constituted an all-or-nothing set of measures, but rather an approach that could be taken in different directions. Interestingly, Gordon Brown as UK Prime Minister devolved on the Bank of England the decision to independently (of government) set interest rates, with a view to meeting inflation targets. This was largely in order to prevent any government that was seeking re-election from taking

interest rate decisions purely for short-term electoral reasons rather than for the long-term good of the economy. One cannot help feeling Steiner would have approved of this. I suspect he would have said: let the central administration of the economic realm (or perhaps the Bank of England) propose the rate, and the rights realm will then enshrine it in law.

- Thus, with money supply and interest rate decisions falling largely to the economic domain, the state in a threefold setting is, in large part, relieved of monetary policy concerns.
- The more political aspect of economic policy is fiscal policy—especially taxation and public spending. At the extreme right-hand end of the spectrum there is the laissez-faire, dog-eat-dog, social Darwinist view that thinks everyone should fend for themselves and the government should keep out of it. At the extreme left there is the out-and-out Commie who thinks the government should run everything and see to it that everyone has exactly the same to spend at the end of the month. Somewhere in between sit the political parties we are used to. Lower taxes, benefits and public services cry the Conservatives; higher taxes, benefits and public services cry Labour. Although this is all about where commodities end up and in what proportion (that is, all about economics), it is also highly political, about *how* we should divide up what we have, about the rights of the matter, about what is just. Should unemployment benefit include an element enabling the claimant to go away on holiday twice a year? Should prisoners have to work for their food? Should all have free access to libraries? Should benefits only be funded by the very wealthiest, or should everyone in paid work contribute something? Should all co-workers in a company have a right to a share of the proceeds (see Sections 7.3.4 and 7.4.14 on remuneration)? And so on and so forth. These questions concern rights and responsibilities, and are thus decided by society as a whole—within the political domain. But remember, Steiner proposes an uber-senate wherein areas of overlap between realms can be discussed and co-ordinated. Rights to benefits and the like can only be established once it is known what can be afforded, and this information

will be known by the economic domain. The uber-senate provides a space for dialogue where dialogue is needed:

> *A kind of senate—elected from the three bodies that have the task*
> *of ordering the political / military, the economic, the judicial-edu-*
> *cational affairs—looks after the common interests, including, for*
> *example, the joint finances. (CW24(ii), p. 81)*

- Within 'tax and spend', there are also those large projects that
  central governments invariably get involved with. Should Cardiff Bay be redeveloped? Should we have a new, high-speed rail
  link from London to the North? Should we subsidise renewable
  energy while the technology matures? Should we build a wall
  on the Mexican border? Whilst erecting a state boundary might
  fall under the remit of the legislature (even in a threefold world),
  building a railway or sponsoring regional regeneration or renewable energy are less clear-cut. Yes, urban regeneration and new
  railways might both involve the rights realm on account of the
  likely need, in both cases, for legislation to evict citizens from
  their homes and pass on the *right* of use of the land to those managing the projects. And yes, renewable energy might concern the
  rights realm on account of an obligation passed into legislation
  to leave a less polluting world for future generations. But apart
  from that, urban regeneration, new railways, and sponsoring
  renewables are about meeting needs (for decent buildings, travel
  possibilities, and electricity). Such projects are less about rules
  and more about the production of commodities. From a threefold
  point of view, therefore, they fall in large part under the auspices
  of the economic realm. Thus, both realms are involved, and the
  uber-senate of which Steiner speaks would no doubt have a role.
  But what about the funding channels? If the legislature takes
  responsibility for overseeing these things, as it might at the
  moment, it can use tax revenues to fund them. And if it decides
  to do something wasteful like send a flock of sheep to the moon
  (give it a couple of years!), we can vote them out and replace them
  with another lot who will use our tax money for more important
  things. There is accountability. But what if financing the rede-
  velopment of a derelict corner of some city were to fall to the

economic administration in a broadly threefold setting? Steiner does not, as far as I'm aware, suggest the economic administration have tax-raising powers, so where would they get the money? Well, if one imagines a threefold approach in full swing, with Steiner's suggestions having been adopted to the point where the means of production are no longer seen as private playthings for wealthy predators, where production is collaborative, where prices are 'fair prices', where silly salaries for executives are rare, where rentier elements have largely fallen away, etc.—then the various economic associations would be able to call on very significant surpluses for allocating in the direction of arising needs. Presumably also, there would always be scope to agree funding approaches in the uber-senate in any case.

- As discussed in Section 7.3.6 ('Taxation'), whenever it was considered desirable to nudge consumer behaviour in one direction or another with financial incentives, rather than via education or laws, then this could be achieved using tiered pricing based on a graduated purchase tax. This could be used to prevent car washing and lawn watering where water was scarce, for instance, without penalising modest use for drinking, cooking and washing. With tax being a matter of law, however, the rights realm would still have its part to play. The following demonstrates Steiner is not averse to the rights domain playing a part in economic matters (presumably via the uber-senate) where the economic realm alone is unable to achieve a desired outcome:

In healthy economic life, with its separation from the other spheres of the social organism, it might become apparent that it costs more to grow wheat, say, in one region than another due to soil conditions. And it may be that associative life alone cannot compensate for this difference. But it can be corrected entirely through the life of rights [note!], and in such a case it could come about entirely by itself that those who purchase wheat at a cheaper price, and thus spend less, must pay a higher tax than those who have to pay more for the wheat, and must thus spend more. (CW189, p. 85)

It seems clear from this that Steiner regards the rights domain in general, and taxation in particular, as acceptable agents to support the meeting-of-needs process, where this proves necessary.

The traditional aims of economic policy—to boost the economy and curb inflation and unemployment (the latter, less so since Thatcher)—are not so much about rights and responsibilities, but more about the logistics of the economic processes. As regards unemployment, Steiner talks about economic associations being responsible for shepherding laid-off workers into new roles. And as regards inflation, he advises, for example (a) associations arrange production to meet needs as far as possible (if supply meets demand, then inflation is unlikely), and (b) the economic realm should also be responsible for ensuring that there is the right amount of currency in the system. Thus, from a threefold point of view, the promotion of full employment and the control of inflation would perhaps fall largely to institutions of the economic domain. As discussed previously, however (Section 7.3.3), if automation advanced to such an extent that all the necessary work in a region / state could be achieved by people working just three days per week, the rights realm, following inter-realm consultations within the uber-senate, could enshrine in law that the working week go down to three days. The economic realm could then see to it that prices, work and income were adjusted accordingly. The rights domain would establish what was just and equitable; the economic system would need to see to the logistics.

Other aspects of economic life where the state typically gets involved, but which do not form part of economic policy, include:

- Trade policy (tariffs, foreign trade agreements), which Steiner proposes fall largely to the economic realm (Section 7.3.6). As he points out, a problem with states running industry can be that, if the state does not get its way, commercially, this can, in the worst case, lead to armed conflict. With a threefold separation, however, the state does not run enterprise and so the likelihood of war is much reduced. However, where an embargo / sanction is imposed, not for reasons of self-interest, but for reasons of human rights within the excluded state (like the one against

South Africa in the 1980s, for example, that was supported by
130 countries on account of apartheid), then this might presumably be seen as a justifiable intrusion of political life into economic life. Naturally, with such situations, it is important the
embargo does not simply end up hurting the very citizens one is
trying to protect.

- Regulations covering things like product safety should ultimately fall under the remit of the state / the rights realm, and
trade agreements / imported goods (previous bullet point) need
to be subject to such rules just as much as domestic goods. Consumers have a *right* not to be harmed; producers have a *responsibility* not to pollute, etc. As covered in Sections 8.1.6 and 9.4.5,
Investor-State Dispute Settlement clauses, as exposed in the
once-proposed TTIP trade deal, represent a gross violation of
this principle. (Standardisation—as opposed to regulation—is a
different matter. If it seems practical for all light bulbs to have
the same fitting, then that is a matter for the economic realm; it
is not a question of rights or responsibilities. It is a question of
self-regulation, not of law.)

- Another regulatory activity in the economic domain concerns
monopolies and mergers—tempering behaviour by business that is
exploitative. In a comprehensively threefold setting with a widely
associative economy this would be the concern of the associations
between producers and consumers in their quest for 'fair price' and
meeting needs. In a less threefold / less associative setting, however,
it might best remain—at least in part—within the rights realm as it
is about rules, law; regulation, that is, rather than standardisation.
Even if enacted by the rights realm, however, such anti-monopoly
/ antitrust regulation would have to involve close dialogue with the
economic domain which would have the relevant facts at its fingertips.

Economic policy—and the other ways in which the state might
play a part in the economy—is a very broad subject, and the scraps
offered above can only act as the scantest starting point for further
thought. What seems clear, though, given just how much time a
typical political administration spends on economic matters, is that
Steiner envisages a greatly reduced role for the 'government' where

threefolding is taken up in earnest. A comment like the following confirms this (my emphasis):

> *The right to education could be arranged in that* the economic organization's administration, in accordance with general economic situation, calculates the amount of educational income possible, *while the rights state, in consultation with the spiritual organisation, determines the rights of the individual in this respect. Once again, this indication is meant as an example of the direction in which arrangements can be made. It is quite possible that quite different arrangements would be appropriate in specific cases. However they can only be found through the purposeful co-operation of the three autonomous members of the social organism. (CW23, p. 115)*

That is, if institutions in the rights domain need to talk to institutions in the economic domain to ascertain basic macroeconomic metrics, then clearly a substantial separation of the economic system from the political is implied. 'For most economists this leads into a world that is altogether too unfamiliar to contemplate', Arthur Edwards notes![410]

Naturally, with the implications being so far reaching, any movement of Treasury / Exchequer functions from rights state to central economic body could only evolve in a thoroughly measured and pragmatic manner if societal health were going to be optimised. This is arguably one of threefolding's most significant questions: how to peel away stewardship of economic matters from the rights state, and transfer it to an independent *economic* administration in a way that ensures an increase in society's economic health. Remember, Steiner ultimately advises that such an economic administration would carry legitimacy and accountability not via *general* elections, but via representation of—and negotiation between—the various consumer and producer interests within a structure of greater and lesser associations. The approach is plural rather than public. Wherever the economic administration needed rights-state collaboration in order to introduce some economic measure, though, this could always be thrashed out in uber-senate discussion.

---

[410] Arthur Edwards, *'Three kinds of money'* (Masters Degree Thesis, 2008).

9.4   International dimension

9.4.1   Similarities and differences between peoples

Within the cultural realm's life of thought, one thing with a particularly international dimension is science since it concerns the pursuit of truths that are universal—truths that don't vary from country to country. However:

> *Science was not able to pour into the human soul international impulses deep enough to resist the terrible influences of these last years … Intellectuality is not powerful enough to work creatively in life. (CW332a, p. 139)*

Steiner does, however, suggest that what he calls *spiritual*[411] science or anthroposophy—that is, spiritual knowledge from self-development through sustained meditative practice etc.—is well suited for the fostering of understanding between peoples. This is because it not only brings one closer to an appreciation of the spiritual within oneself, it can also lead one to appreciate the spiritual in 'the other' and an all-pervading divine intelligence in the cosmos. And since, at its deepest core, the spiritual in oneself is from the same place as the spiritual in someone else, such self-development can become a force for understanding and brotherhood between different peoples. Genuine spiritual perception, he says, can ultimately take one beyond the subjective experiences of the soul to an apprehension of objective spirit which …

> *… is one and the same in the experience of all human beings all over the earth if it is only sought deeply enough. [...] The roots from which things spring are in various places. The final source of all results is the same over the whole earth. […] When the spirit is understood, it is found to be something that does not separate, but unites men, because it can be traced back to the inmost being of man, and because one human being brings forth the same as another, and because he fully understands that other. […] Then,*

---

[411] Spiritual now in the profounder sense, not in the threefold sense (as in the spiritual / cultural realm of society).

over the whole earth, people will find it possible to tolerate the different national peculiarities ... there will be no need for an abstract uniformity everywhere [...] Then in the individual peoples will appear ... interest in the production and consumption carried on by other peoples. Then through the spiritual life, the legal and judicial life of the peoples, one nation will really be able to develop an understanding of other nations and peoples over the whole earth. (CW332a, pp. 140-141)

The internationality of the spirit must furnish the understanding, must permeate with love that understanding of other nationalities, and must be able to expand that love to internationalism ... (CW332a, p. 144)

Just as every single person, if he wishes to share in the work of the community, must take an interest in production and consumption wherever it is carried on, just as every member of the community must be interested in the whole sphere of economy, consumption, production and distribution, so in every country in the world impulses must prevail that would lead to a genuine interest in every other country. Thus nothing resembling the chance conditions of the present market could prevail among the peoples of the earth, but a real inner understanding would prevail among them. Here we come to the deeper sources of what is being sought through the abstract ideals of the so-called League of Nations ... (CW332a, p. 138)

At its core, spirit—like science—is also something that is universal throughout the world. But it touches one more deeply than 'cold' science and can thus act as common bond, as something that can be at the root of international understanding, empathy and respect.

Moreover ...

... it is also true that the needs of human consumption all over the earth are not affected by variations in nationality. Human wants are international, only they are the opposite pole of what is spiritually international. The internationality of the spirit must furnish the understanding, must permeate with love that understanding of other nationalities, and must be able to expand that love to internationalism ... Egoism is equally international. Internationalism will

> *only be able to establish a connection with world production when*
> *the latter springs from a common spiritual understanding, from a*
> *common spiritual conception of unity. Never out of the egoism of*
> *the peoples will understanding of universal consumption arise.*
> *From a universal spiritual perception alone can that develop that*
> *proceeds not from egoism, but from love, and that, therefore, can*
> *govern production. (CW332a, pp. 143-144)*

There is a universality of economic wants in the world. We all need food, we all need clothes. There is also, if one looks deep enough, a common humanity, a universality of spirit. A proper understanding of the latter can kindle the love needed to address the former.

But notwithstanding these archetypal phenomena we share with other peoples, Steiner is naturally not suggesting that all cultures are essentially the same. Different nationalities clearly have different peculiarities, different strengths and weaknesses, different instincts, different makeup to their psyches:

> *... we must not give ourselves up to the simple belief that the social*
> *impulses are to be conceived in a uniform way over the whole*
> *world. It will cloud and mislead all our thoughts and judgements*
> *about the social question if we do not take into account that human*
> *communities throughout the civilised world are differentiated. We*
> *must avoid the error into which we fall when we say of the social*
> *question that this or that holds good; human society must be*
> *ordered thus and thus. (CW186(ii), p. 116)*

Steiner characterised different national colourings in numerous lectures. For example, in *The Challenge of the Times*, different traits between Western, Central and Eastern Europe are addressed, that is, even within an area that is relatively small, globally speaking.[412] Referring to the shortcomings of the Communist ideal of a programme applicable globally, he observed (what is perhaps rather obvious):

> *People are simply not identical in their natures over the whole*
> *earth, as Trotsky imagines ... (CW186, p. 218)*

---

[412] CW186, pp. 1-41.

And ...

> *Utterly unreal thoughts are expressed by one, therefore, who sup-*
> *poses that it is possible to proceed socially in the same way in Rus-*
> *sia, China, South America, Germany or France. (CW186, p. 83)*

Whilst various strains of self-development through meditative discipline, if they are esoterically sound, might slowly be able to help bring peoples around the world closer to one another (inasmuch as they can help bring people closer to the spiritual essence shared by humanity as a whole), within the threefold approach to societal betterment, a flexibility exists that makes it suitable for all shades of culture, that allows different peoples to arrive at different results in their pursuit of social health. This flexibility consists in the simple fact that, in the political domain, the *people* within each state decide for themselves how they want to proceed, rights-wise (democracy); in the economic domain, groups of *people* in each region talk to one another in—and between—associations (brotherliness / sisterliness); and in the cultural domain, *people* are left entirely free in any case (liberty).

> *We must not imagine that people are the same all over the world,*
> *or that the social question can be solved in the same way all over*
> *the world. We must know that the social question has to be solved*
> *in different ways. Out of the impulses in the different peoples it is*
> *seeking to solve itself in different ways. But this, my dear friends, is*
> *only possible on a foundation such as is provided here ...*
>
> *[...] threefolding will make it possible to reckon once more with*
> *the differentiation of humankind. [...] this threefold structure*
> *contains inherent universality. For the social structure of the*
> *West will take shape in such a way that administration, the con-*
> *stitution, the general regulation of public life, public security in*
> *the widest sense, will preponderate. [N.B. Steiner was speak-*
> *ing in 1919]. The other two will be to some extent subordinate,*
> *dependent on this one. In other regions of the world it will be*
> *different again. Once again one of the three will predominate and*
> *the other two will be more or less subordinate. Within a threefold*
> *conception you have the possibility to find, in your own view of*
> *things, the differentiation of realities ... Thus what you find as*

> *the ideal of the social structure will be differentiated over the whole of the earth. This is the fundamental difference of view here presented ... from other views. This view is applicable to realities from the very outset because it can be differentiated within itself and applied in a differentiated way to the realities of life. Such is the difference between an abstract and a concrete view of things. An abstract theory consists of so many concepts of which one believes that they will bring happiness. A concrete view is one of which one knows: its nature is such that something can grow and develop in the one case, something else in another, and a third in a different case again ... This is what distinguishes a view of realities from all dogmatism. Dogmatism swears by dogmas, and dogmas can only maintain their sway by tyrannising realities. A conception of reality is like the reality itself; it is inherently a living thing. Like the human or any other organism, it is mobile and alive, not fixed and rigid. In the same way a real conception inherently lives, grows or develops, now in one direction now in another. (CW186(ii), pp. 127-130)*

With these words, Steiner counters the arguments of those Socialist and Communist thinkers who thought their approach should / could be successfully introduced the world over. He regards this as abstract fantasy. Instead, the threefold approach he proposes allows for wide differentiation of practice, whilst at the same time always making it easier for social disease to be tackled and social health, promoted. Today, the risk of 'tyrannising realities' with dogma stems less from communism, perhaps, and more from those who think economic neo-liberalism should be imposed wherever possible, regardless of regional appetite. Under Steiner's analysis, if a region's people wish to engage in protectionism, or whatever else, then so they should.

9.4.2 International conflict

Steiner regarded the entanglement of cultural, economic and political concerns within single state administrations as a chief factor behind the First World War, the horrors of which were still very raw in people's psyches—especially in Europe—when he was speaking on the subject.

His efforts to convince the politically active of the health-giving effects of a threefold approach were concentrated in the two or three years around the time of the armistice.

> *The vital necessities of modern humanity dictate that any further amalgamation of the spiritual, legal and economic spheres is an impossibility. That it is impossible was shown by the catastrophe of the world war: economic and cultural conflicts became conflicts between states that were then obliged to resolve themselves in a way that is impossible when cultural life opposes only cultural life and economic interest opposes only economic interest. (CW24, p. 61)*
>
> *Each of the three sectors ['Gebiet' = area] will have an independent relation to the corresponding sector of another social organism. Economic relations between countries will exist without being directly influenced by the relations between their respective rights-states. Conversely, the relations between rights-states will develop, within certain limits, completely independently of economic relations. Through this independence of development, the relations will act upon each other in a conciliatory way in cases of conflict. [...] The spiritual organizations of the various countries will be able to enter into mutual relations which derive exclusively from the common spiritual life of mankind. The self-sustaining spiritual sector ['Geistesleben = cultural life], independent of the state, will develop conditions which are impossible to attain when recognition of spiritual activities is dependent on the rights-state instead of the spiritual organism's administration. In this respect there is no difference between scientific activities, which are obviously international, and other spiritual activities. A people's own language and everything related to it also constitute a spiritual area. National awareness itself belongs to this area. The people of one language-region do not come into unnatural conflict with the people of another if political organizations and economic power are not used to assert their cultures. (CW23, pp. 127-128)*

These observations were especially relevant to the ethnic tensions in and around the Austro-Hungarian Empire prior to the war. If the state is removed from cultural concerns—and Steiner includes ethnic interests within the cultural domain—then the ability of ethnic concerns to assert themselves militarily is removed. Similarly, if the state is only concerned with legislation, with what is just, with upholding the law, it will not become dragged into economic tussles.

> The Austro-Hungarian state structure had been in need of a reorganisation for more than half a century. Its spiritual life, with roots in a multiplicity of ethnic communities, required the development of a form for which the obsolete uniform state was a hindrance. (CW23, p. 132)

> Conflicts that stem from one sphere of life will thus be balanced through another sphere. Nations or alliances that lie in economic conflict drag the cultural and legal interests into the conflict if they are unitary states whose governments combine the administration of cultural, legal and economic concerns. However, in a social organism where each of these three spheres has a separate administration, economic interests will, for example, have a balancing effect on opposing cultural interests. (CW24, p. 17)

> If the social organism is divided into three, conflicts can no longer arise at the borders because the one thing does not interfere in the other ... state conflicts due to economic conflicts do not arise so quickly when everything is not mixed up. (CW331, 22 May 1919)

> Economic and intellectual / cultural conflicts that assumed the form of national enmities have unnecessarily produced outcomes that would be impossible if, on the international level, cultural affairs dealt only with cultural affairs and economic interests with other economic interests. (CW24(iii), p. 54)

Business in one state will talk to business in another state, cultural endeavours will engage with cultural endeavours, one rights realm will talk to another rights realm. Indeed, Steiner points out, the geographical extent of an economic or cultural area need not even sit within a single state:

> Within the national boundaries that have arisen historically, cultural, political and economic interests will not necessarily coincide. (CW24, p. 16)

9.4.3 The special role of economic activity in international relations

Steiner had no problem with globalisation in its more benign sense; indeed he saw the development of a world economy as entirely natural:

> *Economic life tends to evolve into a uniform world economy without considering the given national boundaries. Humanity as a whole is striving to become one single economic community. (CW24, p. 15)*

The question is not so much about whether a world economy is a good thing; it is more about what *sort* of world economy is a good thing.

> *... the very first step towards the improvement of international relations is to be able to carry on commerce across frontiers, but on different principles from those on which the present system of exchange is based. (CW332a, p. 137)*

And on what principles were 'the present system of exchange' based? For one ...

> *... national governments determine international relations in areas where it would be more natural for the economic groups directly concerned to do so. An industrial concern that needs the raw materials of a foreign nation ought to be able to obtain them by negotiating directly with the owners; everything pertaining to this arrangement should remain entirely within the economic cycle. It is plain to see that recently economic life has assumed forms tending towards this kind of self-contained functioning, and in this self-contained cycle of economic life (which is gradually tending to become a worldwide unity) the intervention of national interests represents a disturbing element. [...]*
>
> *This internationalism of the economy indicates that in the future the various regions of the world economy will need to enter into relations independent of the relations that various people may have through life interests outside the economic sphere. The states will need to leave the establishment of economic relations to those persons or groups engaged in economic activity. (CW24, pp. 58-59)*

That is, economic globalization is beneficial, but the rights sphere should not be involved in its management (although if economic activities start to go in directions that the public deems unhealthy, unwelcome or risky then the rights sphere might step in with corrective *laws*—to stop land grabs, for example, or the import of GM crops, or timber from forests that are not sustainably managed). By and large, nowadays, state-run industry hardly features in the UK, or even Germany—where the unitary state model had been so problematic, in Steiner's view.

As we have seen, he took a particularly dim view of traditional social-ism, as it would kill off economic initiative and innovation. He also noted how problematic it would be when it came to international trade:

> *An economic super-co-operative forced into the framework of a present-day national government could not develop economically profitable relations with the private capitalist economies of foreign countries. When centrally administered, economic operations are hampered in their free unfolding, which is required in relationships with foreign countries. Free initiative and speed, so important for decision-making within such relationships, can only be attained when commerce between industry and foreign markets (as well as commerce between foreign industry and domestic markets) is direct and handled solely by those immediately involved. (CW24, p. 19)*

A 'world economy' has certainly progressed at pace in recent decades. But it seems forever to be bedevilled not by socialistic principles, but by ones that are exploitative, profit-maximising, rent-seeking, extractive, selfish. In this connection, Paul Mason suggests: 'we save globalization by ditching neoliberalism'.[413]

In relation to his threefold proposals, Steiner notes:

> *... the peoples of the earth have not yet reached the point of ennobling their national egoisms sufficiently to enable a collective economy of the whole earth to arise out of the economic values they individually create. One nation tries to outdo the other in matters of economic advantage. Unreal points of view thus arise among the peoples, whereas the new instincts of mankind call out for a common economic life of the whole earth—in effect an Earth economy. (CW335(ii), 10 March 1920)*

---

[413] Paul Mason, *Postcapitalism: A Guide to Our Future* (London: Allen Lane, 2015), p. xi.

Also …

> … in the threefold social order the profits of foreign trade raise the standard of living of the entire population, while in the capitalist community the profits will benefit only a few. That the threefold social organism apportions it differently among the populace will not affect the balance of trade itself. (CW24, p. 64)

9.4.4 A threefold state in isolation

> Of course the objection can be made … that this can only come to pass when all states make a beginning. No! One single so-called state can make a beginning; it is indeed so, one single state can begin. And when it has, it will have done something for all mankind. (CW189(v), 15 February 1919)

> Of special significance is the fact that the social goals described here, although valid for humanity in general, can be realized by each individual social organism regardless of other countries' initial attitudes. Should a social organism form itself according to the three natural sectors, the representatives of each sector could enter into international relations with others, even if these others have not yet adopted the same forms. (CW23, p. 129)

Steiner also asserts it is not only entirely feasible for a state to follow a threefold approach regardless of what its neighbours are up to, but also that such a state can become a beacon to those without a threefold structure:

> … the individual nation's progress toward establishing a threefold order will be highly exemplary for other states. The effect will make itself felt not only morally, through the social character of the way of life the inhabitants of the threefold organism enjoy, but also through the awakening of purely economic interests. (CW24, p. 22)

> Through organising its labour force rationally to make certain products attractive to foreign countries, the threefold organism can assure that the disturbances it causes among unitary states will not lead to boycott of its economy. An oasis within the area it shares

with the national economies, the threefold nation will prove that the changeover to threefolding indeed represents economic progress and, in general, a step forward for humanity. (CW24, pp. 22-23)

There is no doubt that the economic conditions of any single country under the threefold social order cannot fail to act as a model for foreign countries. The circles concerned about a socially just distribution of wealth will strive to bring about the threefold system in their own country when they see how expediently it works for others. (CW24, p. 65)

Notwithstanding the feasibility of a lone country adopting threefold principles, Steiner also opines that domestic protections and other price-adjusting measures can have their place in international trade, even though free trade might be the ideal:

Within a unified world economy, free trade offers the best way of guaranteeing that production in separate parts of the world is neither too expensive nor too cheap. A social body with independent economic management that is not surrounded by threefold organisms will, of course, be forced to protect certain branches of production from economically unfeasible price reduction by raising tariffs. The management of these tariffs will then be entrusted to associations for the public's benefit. (CW24, p. 22)

A management responsible for export will be able to act completely out of its own free initiative in its commercial dealings with foreign countries; and domestically it will maintain relations with those associations that will help the most with the supply of raw materials and the like, to satisfy foreign demands. The same will be possible for import management.

It will be necessary, however, that in trade with foreign countries no products will be imported whose production costs or purchase price will impair the population's lifestyle. Nor should relationships with foreign countries cause domestic production branches to be destroyed because the lower cost of foreign products makes continuation of domestic production unprofitable. Yet all this can be effectively prevented through a system of associations. Should a firm or a trading corporation conduct its business to the detriment of domestic production, they could be prevented from doing so by those respective associations from which they cannot exclude themselves without making their working situation impossible.

The necessity can arise, however, that the cost is too high for certain products that must be purchased from abroad for various reasons. Faced with such a necessity ... An administration that occupies itself solely with economic processes will be able to bring about adjustments that show themselves within these economic processes to be necessary. [...] the excessive cost of a foreign good can be offset through subsidies from concerns whose earnings surpass the needs of its workers.

In addition to all such preventative steps that a threefold social organism can take to counteract the damage it sustains through commerce with states averse to the threefold idea, it may become necessary to resort to additional measures that are similar to the principle of tariff. It is easy to see that autonomy of economic life dictates different premises for such measures than those needed when treatment of import and export depends upon majority rule within groups of people united by political and cultural interests. Economic organizations that combine their efforts for practical reasons have as their goal a price structuring that has a social affect; such endeavours could never arise out of individual groups' desire for profit. That is why the economic life of threefold social organisms strives toward the ideal of free trade. (CW24, pp. 20-22)

... dealings with foreign countries should not lead to the producing or importing of goods whose production cost or selling price might injure the standard of living of the native population. Workers producing goods for export must receive what is required to maintain their standard of living as compensation for what they produce. Products that come from abroad must, generally speaking, be available at prices that allow the native worker who needs them to purchase them. (CW24, p. 63)

The caution behind Steiner's otherwise general support for free trade would certainly seem to have considerable relevance to those poorer countries which can be (and have been) short-changed by the rest of us in our current neo-liberal climate. As Larry Elliott observed in 2005:

The Harvard economist Dani Rodrik is one trade sceptic. Take Mexico and Vietnam, he says. One has a long border with the richest country in the world and has had a free trade agreement with its neighbour across the Rio Grande. It receives oodles of inward investment and sends workers across the border in droves. It is fully plugged into the global economy. The other was the subject of a U.S. trade embargo until 1994 and suffered from trade restrictions for years after that. Unlike Mexico, Vietnam is not even a member of the WTO.

So which of the two has the better recent economic record? The question should be a no-brainer if all the free trade theories are right—Mexico should be streets ahead of Vietnam. In fact, the opposite is true. Since Mexico signed the Nafta (North American Free Trade Agreement) deal with the U.S. and Canada in 1992, its annual per capita growth rate has barely been above 1%. Vietnam has grown by around 5% a year for the past two decades. Poverty in Vietnam has come down dramatically: real wages in Mexico have fallen.

Rodrik doesn't buy the argument that the key to rapid development for poor countries is their willingness to liberalize trade. Nor, for that matter, does he think boosting aid makes much difference either. Looking around the world, he looks in vain for the success stories of three decades of neo-liberal orthodoxy: nations that have really made it after taking the advice— willingly or not—of the IMF and World Bank.

Rather, the countries that have achieved rapid economic take off in the past 50 years have done so as a result of policies tailored to their own domestic needs. Vietnam shows that what you do at home is far more important than access to foreign markets. There is little evidence that trade barriers are an impediment to growth for those countries following the right domestic policies.

Those policies have often been the diametric opposite of the orthodoxy. South Korea and Taiwan focused their economies on exports, but combined that outward orientation with high levels of tariffs and other forms of protection, state ownership, domestic-content requirements for industry, directed credit and limits to capital flows.[414]

Or as Ann Pettifor simply states: 'Africa is not poor, it is impoverished ... it has been made poor, mainly by free trade, liberalisation and privatisation, all of which exacerbate the massive losses, extraction and slavery associated with colonial exploitation'.[415]

---

[414] Larry Elliott, 'Two countries, one booming, one struggling: which one followed the free-trade route?', *The Guardian*, 12 December 2005.
[415] Ann Pettifor, *The Case For the Green New Deal* (Verso: London, 2019), p. 77.

These examples support the assertion that, despite the general superiority of free trade, domestic protections can have their place in maintaining a robust economy at home. This is also echoed by Kate Raworth who, citing Ha-Joon Chang's *23 Things They Don't Tell You About Capitalism*[416], notes how today's high-income countries like the UK and USA have been encouraging less developed countries to adopt free trade policies that we ourselves rejected when building our own formidable economies, opting instead for tariffs, industrial subsidies and state ownership when it suited us.[417]

Leaving to one side the now-widespread argument for leaving fossil fuels in the ground in order to tackle global warming, the slow, painful death of the UK coal mining industry well illustrates some of the issues in the free-trade-versus-protectionism debate. On 18 December 2015 the last productive coal mine in the UK was closed. In Russia, the cost of extracting a ton of coal was £30, in the UK it was £43. UK users of coal—power stations, for example—therefore chose to import, as it was cheaper. However, one could take the view, especially if there were still decades' or centuries' worth of known coal reserves beneath our feet, plus high unemployment, that subsidising production from a more profitable sector within the economy (merchant banking perhaps?) would make sense because the country's overall productivity would improve. That is, a number of UK residents who would otherwise be doing nothing would instead be productive—extracting coal. The idea of such cross-subsidy may well make the free-market ideologue wince. Nonetheless, the industry had been heavily subsidised both in the UK and in most of Europe for decades: if you keep people productive who would otherwise be doing nothing, this helps your balance of trade.

Looked at from a world-economy perspective, however, one could argue as follows: in Russia they have coal seams that are far richer and more accessible than those in the UK and, as a result, it takes a significantly lower number of work hours to extract a ton of coal over there than it does over here. So, from a world-economy point of view

---

[416] Chang, H-J, *23 Things They Don't Tell You About Capitalism* (London: Allen Lane, 2010).

[417] Kate Raworth, *Doughnut Economics: Seven Ways to Think Like a 21st-Century Economist* (London: Random House, 2018), p. 90.

rather than a UK point of view, it might make sense (economically, at least) for Russians to mine coal instead of Brits, as they can get more out, quicker. Overall productivity for humanity in general might then increase. It makes sense to pick blackberries where they are abundant rather than scarce!

A further question to ask when looking at the matter from a world-economy / overall productivity point of view would be: if UK mines stay open (thanks to subsidy), is there then something productive for those unused Russians to do? And, alternatively, if UK mines close, is there something else productive that the now-redundant UK miners can do?

An additional question to ask, if looking at the matter from a purely UK point of view, would be (this is less applicable to coal which can also be sourced from Argentina, Australia, etc.): by stopping domestic production and letting the relevant skills die out, are we leaving ourselves vulnerable to shortage in the event of discontinuities in supply?

Notwithstanding these various tangents, the main point of this section has been to convey Steiner's assertion that a country can successfully pursue threefold principles whether or not its neighbours are interested in same.

9.4.5 The European Union

The EU is an interesting example of an international project addressing the social arrangements between peoples. Although free trade amongst European countries was already being advocated by Keynes in 1920, it was not until after WWII that more formal connections grew, ostensibly out of a wish to overcome the nationalism that had stoked the two cataclysmic world wars centred in Europe. The Council of Europe was founded in 1949 as a 'forum where sovereign governments could choose to work together with no supra-national authority'.[418] This body focused on human rights and democracy. As such, it focused largely on rights-realm matters. In 1957 the EEC (the 'Common Market') was inaugurated, establishing an *economic* customs union initially between

---

[418] See Wikipedia: European Union.

six countries. Since then, integration between member states has been expanded and cemented by various treaties, and the number of members has risen to 28.

In 2016, the UK held a referendum on whether or not to remain in the EU. 52% of the electorate voted to leave, and 48% voted to remain. This threw up a number of anxieties about a 'divided nation'. Passionately held views were exchanged between friends, workmates, family members and politicians—often including colleagues within the same political party. In England and Wales more voted to leave than remain. In Northern Ireland and Scotland, more voted to remain than leave.

Arguments in the Leave ('Brexit') camp included: (a) if the UK leaves, it will no longer be forced to accept unlimited EU immigration—net immigration (albeit from around the whole world) having increased to a million people every three years, with concern that this was starting to put appreciable strain on infrastructure (the equivalent for the USA, if calibrated by land area, would be net immigration of over forty million every three years); (b) the EU's huge bureaucracy is very expensive to maintain—costing the UK alone £148m net, every week, between 2014 and 2018 (or more / less, depending on what you include / exclude)[419]; and (c) despite a stated wish to be so, the EU is not entirely democratic since, even though members of both the European Parliament and European Council are elected, members of the European Commission are *appointed* (albeit by the Parliament and Council), and it is only *this* body which may propose legislation. This tends to have the effect that only policies are put forward that lead to ever closer political union. Thus, it is an exercise in ratcheting, leading ultimately to a United States of Europe. And if a decision in a United States of Europe is taken that turns out to be a bad one, the entire region will be affected. So, for example, if an EU edict deemed GM food acceptable, but it then turned out such crops were contaminating hitherto far more robust, traditional crops that had stood the test of time over tens of thousands of years, the problem would be a massive one rather than one limited only to those countries that had welcomed GM. A particularly alarming surrender of democracy (arguably one of the biggest in the UK in my lifetime) was threatened by the European

---

[419] https://commonslibrary.parliament.uk/research-briefings/cbp-7886/.

Commission's long-running TTIP (Transatlantic Trade and Investment Partnership) negotiations with the USA. A leak in Germany's *Die Zeit* in 2014 revealed that, within the proposed treaty, there were Investor-State Dispute Settlement clauses that would have given *companies* the right to sue *governments* banning products on account even of health or environmental damage! This triggered uproar and led to an EU-wide consultation which showed that fully 97% of respondents were against the offending provisions.[420] Further, a petition in 2015 against TTIP altogether, gathered over three million signatures.[421] But for the leak, such issues might not have come to light in time. In the end, with little enthusiasm from the USA's President Trump, negotiations stopped in 2019.

Another issue in the sovereignty / democratic-deficit argument against the European Union was that, if any country wishes to change something within its borders (e.g. put a stop to unlimited immigration), it can't, unless it persuades the 27 other member states (each of which has power of veto) that it is worthwhile.

Although not completely insurmountable, a yet further factor in the democratic-deficit argument went something like the following: The political process involves a conversation between citizens, and it is very hard for ordinary citizens to be part of this conversation when (a) it involves a plethora of different languages, and (b) the reportage / media feedback loop between Brussels and the UK is so minimal. When *domestic* politicians appear in the media, you can keep an eye on them and vote them out if you are unimpressed. But, before the referendum, few had any idea what the EU was up to. As I say, this was not an insurmountable problem and could have been addressed with better reportage.

Arguments in the Remain camp included (a) borderless trading with the other member states avoids a layer of bureaucracy (and therefore costs and 'friction'), is extremely valuable, and to lose this will affect the UK's economy far more adversely than will be countered by an increased ability to trade with countries further afield; (b) tackling some of the world's big problems—such as environmental

---

[420] www.europarl.europa.eu/doceo/document/E-8-2015-009564_EN.html.
[421] Lee Williams, 'TTIP: Three million people sign petition to scrap controversial trade deal', *The Independent*, 5 October 2015.

destruction—can only really be done when countries co-operate closely; (c) acting 'as one' provides security in the face of a perceived threat from Russia; and perhaps most persuasively (d) acting 'as one' prevents those dreadful armed conflicts the region had experienced in the previous century. An appreciable factor behind the 'Remain' vote also seemed to be (e) that people simply wanted to feel 'connected', 'part of something bigger', to express international friendship, to engage in grown-up collaboration and dialogue, and disown what they saw as bigoted, xenophobic, jingoistic small-mindedness.

With seemingly valid arguments on both sides of the fence, this turned out to be a knotty problem with no simple solution. In all likelihood, however, the whole thing would have been far less contentious and much easier to manage had threefold principles obtained.

As it is currently, rights and economics are combined within the one body; the EU doesn't dabble so much in cultural affairs. Yes, there are *separate departments* within the EU to deal with legislative considerations on the one hand, and economic ones on the other. And, no, the EU does not try to actually run industry (although does have a central bank to oversee currency, maintain price stability, etc.). But the two aspects—economic and political—are nonetheless closely joined. As a result, the EU is able to say to its members: you cannot have access to the single market (an economic consideration) unless you allow free movement of people (a rights consideration).

Without wishing to be over simplistic, one can imagine the UK's torment about whether to be 'in' or 'out' would have been greatly alleviated if, instead of one body (the EU), there were two, each with an appropriate level of independence as per threefold principles. If there were, on the one hand, a common market (the EEC) wherein production, circulation and consumption of goods and services were allowed to proceed as efficiently as possible, without trade barriers, the UK would in all likelihood be 'in', as would those others who are currently 'out': Iceland, Norway and Switzerland. Indeed, in a threefold world, trade matters might not be decided by democratic vote in any case. The decision whether or not to be in the EEC could simply fall to economic bodies and their central administrations, according to what was practical. People wouldn't get to vote 'in', and they wouldn't get to vote 'out'. They would simply express needs via their buying patterns or in associative dialogue. The extent of collaboration between home and abroad would rest on what smaller or larger groups of producers, distributors and consumers saw as the most efficacious way to proceed.

And if, separate to a common market, there was a *political* forum (like the Council of Europe) for political *co-operation* on matters of collective concern, such as environmental degradation, these countries (including the UK) would probably be 'in' too. If, on the other hand, this entailed ever closer political integration along the lines that appear to be heading towards a United States of Europe, then they would probably stay 'out'. This continual wish for full political union appeared to be confirmed in 2019 when, despite the UK's vote to leave, and despite increasing right-wing unease against the EU having risen in the likes of France, Austria, Hungary, Sweden and the Netherlands, the person appointed (note) to replace Jean Claude Junker as President of the European Commission was Ursula von der Leyen—apparently someone committed to ever closer political union. So, the agenda seems clear: business as usual and closer integration, rather than try to understand what the issues are and then work on areas that appear problematic—like free movement of people which, it seems, may be unpopular in a number of member states.

As far as free movement of people is concerned, the UK has perhaps been a special case. Since so many continentals have only English as a second language, they have aimed for the UK when they have had itchy feet. For the sake of non-Brits reading this book it would perhaps be as well to mention that, barring a handful of bigots, the vast majority of those who articulated a concern about the *rate* of net immigration (i.e. not about immigration itself) seemed to have had doubts about the country's ability to adequately assimilate the newcomers at the speed at which they were arriving. That is, their concerns were not based on small-minded intolerance. One only wonders whether, with seemingly so many within the EU administration being wedded to the idea of slowly leading the EU into single state-hood, it may well be that the EU risks becoming the architect of its own disintegration. Winston Churchill also fancied political union—a United States of Europe—but it seems an open question whether this attitude might only provoke the very nationalism he fought against.

* * *

9.4.6   International dimension summarised:

- The realisation that the same divine spirit lives in all peoples around the world can become a force for understanding and brotherhood / sisterhood between peoples.
- There is also a universality of basic needs / wants throughout the world.
- However, different cultures will always have different 'flavours' and will therefore find different solutions to social issues.
- With their inherent flexibility, threefold principles can be fruitfully applied in any part of the world.
- Representatives of the economic realm in one region communicate with representatives of the economic in another. Likewise administrators of one rights realm can talk to those of another rights realm; and the cultural will talk to the cultural.
- A country following a threefold approach can function well alongside others that don't.
- A country following a threefold approach can become a beacon for those that don't. It is likely to set a good example of how to organise society such that greater social health prevails.
- A world economy of free trade with minimal state involvement is best (the ideal being trade that is associative).
- Where necessary, however, the economic realm can use tariffs or other measures to ensure international trade does not inappropriately threaten domestic production or the quality of life of importer or exporter.
- Where a good needs to be imported that cannot be afforded by those who need it, consideration can be given to subsidy from firms whose profits exceed what they need to cover costs.
- A threefold approach can ultimately prevent war since an issue arising within one societal realm cannot so easily drag the other two realms into the dispute.

9.5   Universal Basic Income / Citizen's Income

A Universal Basic Income (UBI) or Citizen's Income is a non-means-tested means of survival that all adults would receive—non-earners and earners alike. Although radical, the idea has its supporters to both left and right. Those to the left argue it is a way of giving all a stake in society, a slice of the very big cake which is otherwise only shared between those with the good fortune to take part, and which disproportionately goes to those who are already wealthy. Advocates to the right, Milton Friedman[422] among them, argue it removes the colossal bureaucracy that is otherwise needed to vet applicants for unemployment benefits, disability benefits, student finance, etc.

A number of economists—like author and former Greek finance minister Yanis Varoufakis—point out that the technologies in, say, an iPhone have arisen thanks to research sponsored by numerous government grants which were enabled by our taxes.[423] Instead of being held in common, however, these technologies become appropriated by private capital. Varoufakis argues a UBI could be seen as a dividend to society from such intellectual property. He acknowledges that a UBI involves giving money to 'the undeserving'—to beach bums and the rich, for example. But he also argues—like Friedman—this is preferable to spending money on a whole bureaucracy to separate the deserving from the undeserving. He suggests that a UBI is a *foundation on which to stand*, not a safety net. It is like a trust fund that gives all our children freedom of action, not just Paris Hilton.

One or two of the things Steiner says in 1905 (a dozen or so years before he enumerates threefolding) could well lead one to think he would have approved of a UBI. For example:

> ... the course of evolution is in the direction of completely volun-
> tary[424] work. This path no one will change or reject. Just as the
> Greek labourer did his work under the compulsion of his master
> and a present labourer works under the compulsion of wages, sim-
> ilarly in the future only freedom will obtain. Labour and compensa-
> tion [i.e. remuneration] will in future be completely separated.
>
> [...] And what is the labour of the present time? It is based on
> self-interest, on the compulsion that egoism exerts on us. Because

---

[422] Adviser to both UK Prime Minister Margaret Thatcher and U.S. President Ronald Reagan.

[423] https://yanisvaroufakis.eu/2016/05/12/technical–change-turns-basic-income-into-a-necessity/.

[424] '*zur völlig freien Arbeit hin*'—in the direction of completely free work (e.g. not as servant to a master).

> *we want to exist, we want labour to be paid for. We work for our own sake, for the sake of our pay. In the future we will work for our fellow human beings, because they need what we can provide. That is what we will work for. We will clothe our fellow human beings, we will give them what they need—in completely free activity. Compensation [remuneration] must be completely separated from this. Labour in the past was tribute, in the future it will be sacrifice. It has nothing to do with self-interest, nothing to do with compensation [remuneration]. If I base my labour on consumer demand with regard to what humanity needs, I stand in a free relation to labour and my work is a sacrifice for humanity. Then I will work with all my powers, because I love humanity and want to place my capacities at its disposal. That has to be possible, and is possible only when one's livelihood is separated from one's labour. And that is going to happen in the future ... People must be educated for voluntary[425] work, one for all and all for one. (CW88, pp. 60-61)*

At first sight, these comments would seem to support the idea of a UBI. 'Labour and compensation will in future be completely separated' and 'In the future we will work for our fellow human beings, because they need what we can provide' can seem wholly in keeping. But they are not *entirely* in keeping. Under UBI, the assumption is that anyone who works will still be paid for their work as well, which (a) is not consistent with Steiner's separation of work and income, and (b) does not necessarily imply his ideal that we will work for our fellows and not for the sake of ourselves (i.e. we might still work simply to increase our income). Under UBI, no one would be forced to do grotty jobs, but—so the theory goes—they would get done because people might be able to double their income by doing them. Also, Steiner saying 'one for all and all for one' suggests everyone does their bit, which is rather different to saying: you don't have to work if you don't want to—which is implicit in a UBI.

It is also during this (pre-threefold) talk that Steiner suggests people could start to separate work and income by forming the income communities mentioned at the start of the book. As far as I am aware, however, he does not mention this idea in public again. Thirteen years

---

[425] The German is *'frei'*—free.

later, when he has begun to talk about the threefold approach, he observes:

> Everything that a person acquires in such a way that it is received in exchange for his work within the social system has an unwholesome effect. A wholesome condition results within the social system only when a human being has to support his life, not by his own work, but from other sources within society ...
>
> The goal towards which we must work—of course, in a rational and not Bolshevistic way—must be that of separating work from the provisions of the means of existence. [...] When no one is any longer recompensed for his work, then money will lose its value as a means for acquiring power over work. There is no other means for overcoming the misuse that has been perpetuated with mere money than by forming the social structure in such a way that no one be recompensed for his work, and that the provision of the means of existence shall be achieved from an entirely different source. It will then naturally be impossible to use money for the purpose of compelling anyone to work ... Money must never in future be the equivalent for human labour, but only for inanimate commodities. (CW186, p. 59)

Again, such comments can at first appear to support the idea of a UBI. But, as was covered at some length earlier in the book: once Steiner is in full threefold swing, his proposals regarding separation of work and income do not resemble anything close to a UBI. Instead, he advocates replacing wage relationships with profit-sharing ones and so on. In this way, remuneration does not come from one's *labour* (thus, labour and income are separated) but from the sale of the commodities one has had a part in manufacturing. I don't pay you for your work (a master / servant relationship); instead we work in partnership, making things for other people, and share whatever proceeds arise from sales. (See for example Sections 7.3.4 and 7.4.14—where remuneration is covered.)

An issue with UBI, of course, is that it is hard to cost because you don't know how many people would simply stop working if UBI came on stream. To give 50 million UK adults a UBI of £15,000 each would cost £750 billion per annum. In the fiscal year ending 2019, the UK's *total* public spending was £818 billion, of which some £222 billion went on welfare and pensions—which a UBI could replace. So you would still need to wring another half a trillion pounds of tax (£750bn—£222bn) out of the economy to fund such a UBI. Would this be at all feasible? Would many producers, on account of higher tax rates, simply move overseas, resulting in lower tax *revenues* instead of higher ones? In the UK's 2019 general election, the Green Party pledged to introduce a UBI of at least £4,628 per annum by 2025. But this would not even cover housing costs, so one would still need a whole bureaucracy to assess need for extra benefits.

The various pilot studies that have been done around the world in an attempt to ascertain how people's behaviour would be affected by a Basic Income have been very inconclusive. One in Finland only involved 2,000 *unemployed* people and was discontinued in 2019 seemingly with few useful findings. Surely, one thing you need to ascertain is the extent to which *employed* people in unattractive jobs will decide enough is enough if you pay them to stay at home. Would the standard of living in the country sink badly as many people decided they would rather play computer games or titivate their gardens than continue in that unpleasant or stressful job? The pilot study in Utrecht in the Netherlands was only applied to a *subset of one city* and reminded one of Steiner's comments about it being no good when little enclaves are supported by the rest:

> … *or whether someone founds a little settlement like an economic parasite which can only exist because the rest of the world is there around it, which can only exist so long as it can maintain itself as a parasite on the commercial world and then perishes. (CW305(ii), p. 109)*

> *Many years ago, when Oppenheimer was already a housing man, he said: 'Now I have the capital, we can found a new cultural colony.' I replied: 'Doctor, let's talk about this project when it has perished.' For it has to perish. It is not possible to create a little area within the general economy, based on privileges derived from something different, without its becoming a parasite within the economic life as a whole. Such enterprises are always parasites. They last until they have taken enough from others; but then they perish. (CW341, p. 181)*

Paul Mason and others argue that, with ever-increasing automation, there is simply not enough work to go round, and so a UBI makes sense.[426] But when, in the UK, (a) massive benefit *cuts* have been deemed necessary (albeit by tax-averse Conservatives) under the 'austerity' programme, (b) the pension age has had to creep up to 67 because pensioners are otherwise deemed too expensive to support, (c) the NHS is suffering from a huge shortage of staff, (d) the roads are full of potholes, (e) police numbers are so low that thousands—even millions—of crimes (particularly against women) go un-investigated, and (f) we are struggling to maintain a decent level of care for the elderly, and so on and so forth, such claims do not seem entirely convincing. If we can't even give 65- and 66-year-olds a UBI, one wonders how we might afford to give it to everyone. Would it really be feasible to raise tax receipts to the extent necessary? Perhaps; it would be interesting to see the costings! (And it is acknowledged one could similarly ask: would it really be feasible to interest people in 'fair price', the removal of wage contracts, and other threefold measures? These, however, can be introduced incrementally by those who are interested— see Chapter 13.)

The difficulties behind getting a reduced workforce (reduced on account of some stopping work once in receipt of a UBI) to provide for an increased non-working contingent would presumably be more problematic in those countries like Japan that have experienced both a large drop in fertility rates (so, fewer young people) and simultaneous rises in life expectancy (so, more old people). Where this happens, the productivity of those of working age needs to increase, not reduce, if such a country wants to stand still from a standard of living point of view (which, admittedly, is not the same as a quality of life point of view—something we all too often forget. Even Simon Kuznets who devised the concept of Gross National Product in the 1930s noted: 'the welfare of a nation can scarcely be inferred from a measure of national income').[427] In 10 years' time, the UK is forecast to have 1 million more people over 75 also.

---

[426] Paul Mason, *Postcapitalism: A Guide to Our Future* (London: Allen Lane, 2015), pp. 278-286.

[427] Kuznets, S. (1934) *National Income 1929-1932*, 73rd US Congress, 2nd session, Senate document no. 124 (7).

Of course, in Steiner's day, industrial life was very different. Most of the processes that are now automated were carried out by people either standing at machines or wielding hand tools. A lot more work *had* to be done if all were to get their basic needs met. So one could surmise that he would not necessarily have been against a UBI on principle, for all time. Comments like …

> … *of course, everyone is compelled to work by social circumstances; the choice is: either work or starve. (CW337a, 30 May 1919)*
>
> *If he is to contribute his share, as he certainly must … (CW332a, p. 17)*

… perhaps do not rule out a UBI in the event of widespread automation. But they certainly ruled it out at the time. As did:

> *Just as children have the right to an education, the elderly, infirm and widows have the right to a decent maintenance. (CW23, p. 116)*

If *everyone* was to be in receipt of a decent maintenance, as with a UBI, then he would not have felt the need to single out the elderly or infirm. And the following, where he firmly links remuneration with the production of goods and services, further confirm that a UBI was not what he had in mind:

> … *commodity production, the only means through which the possessor of money will have been able to attain it … (CW23, p. 119)*
>
> *Now to the questions of Pastor Heisler: how to get an apartment, etc. […] In the threefold social organism, a man will not only have to look for a place to live, he will also do something else! He will be something, a factory director, carpenter, or whatever. One can live by being a factory director or carpenter; for this you will be remunerated. […] you must not imagine: I am a human being and therefore must have an apartment. Instead you have to assume: I'm not just a human being, but I also have something to do somewhere, and, under normal social conditions, having a place to live is among the things that come to me in return. (CW337a, 16 June 1920)*

Earlier in the book (Section 7.4.11), we also examined the importance Steiner laid on 'fair prices'—where all should receive enough for their output as enables them to live until they have again produced like output. This too asserts his connecting, at all times, remuneration with production of goods and services. If someone was *already* in receipt of enough to live on (a UBI), then talking about 'fair price' for commodities would be meaningless.

An argument sometimes put forward for UBI is that it frees people up to 'find themselves', to find self-fulfilment, to contribute what they *like* doing, to 'follow their star'. But Steiner appears to have little time for such sentiments:

> *What someone practices in the field of spiritual life is his own affair. What he is able to contribute to the social organism however, will be recompensed by those who have need of his spiritual contribution. Whoever is not able to support himself within the spiritual organisation from such compensation will have to transfer his activities to the political or economic section. (CW23, p. 79)*

> *A young man was once asked by his professor to write his thesis on the commas in Homer ... This, of course, is work that does not contribute to the social process in the least ... From an economic point of view, one must bear in mind that this young man needs one and a half years to complete the task. During this time he has to eat, drink, and dress. In order that he can do that, it is necessary for however many people to work to provide his food and drink. But he squanders his productive power, he does nothing for society. He becomes a parasite of social life ... (CW331, 22 May 1919)*

> *... as regards the present day, one might indeed venture to say that if 99 per cent fewer books were produced, it would probably be very much to the happiness of mankind. Just think of the mounds of lyrical poems (always emanating, of course, from unrecognised geniuses!) that come out in batches of three to five hundred, but of which fifty are sold at most: how much unnecessary work is carried out there. (CW337a, 15 September 1920)*

Whilst Steiner may frown on *unnecessary* work, he nonetheless seems clear: people still need to work, to contribute; and work should respond to the needs of others.

But what about the vastly more automated world of production that we have today, or the even more automated world of tomorrow? If the amount of work needed to sustain a community falls, then the hours that each worker needs to contribute fall too. It seems clear from the following that Steiner would have been sympathetic to work being shared around such that all could enjoy a four or three day week, or whatever, if the total needs of the community were still being met. Each could then have a similar amount of leisure time, instead of some slaving for sixty hours per week, while others work only ten.

> *If every human being performed his share of manual work every-where on the earth—well not absolutely everyone but this is an ideal we can get close to—then no one would need to do more than three to four hours manual work a day, at most ... More than three to four hours of manual labour are not necessitated by fac-tors at work in humanity's evolution but instead—and we can say this quite calmly, without any emotion, as a fully objective fact—by the countless idlers and people taking advantage of social bene-fits. These things must be considered in a completely clear-eyed and honest way. (CW192(v), p. 207)*
>
> *If things were thought through sensibly in economic terms, people would need to work much less than at present. (CW341, p. 196)*

It should be noted that amongst the 'idlers' Steiner mentions in the first of these two quotes, he would have included anyone living off their investments or their estate, without working. A year or two after Steiner died, Bernard Shaw also noted: 'If we each took our turn and did our bit in peace as we had to do during the war, all the necessary feeding and clothing and housing and lighting could be done handsomely by less than half our present day's work, leaving the other half free for art and science and learning and playing and roaming and experimenting and recreation of all sorts'.[428]

But before getting too carried away with the idea of an increased automation allowing us to do next to no work, it is also surely import-ant to remember the sweatshops in Bangladesh and Cambodia, the

---

[428] Bernard Shaw, *The Intelligent Woman's Guide to Socialism and Capitalism* (Edinburgh: R&R Clark Ltd, 1929), p. 39.

millions of people in distant lands sewing our pyjamas and harvesting our coffee beans in return for the slimmest of income. An investigation in 2006 by War on Want, for example, found people in Bangladesh working up to 80-hour weeks for 5p an hour—with one day off per fortnight. And if any worker leaves or complains, there are plenty of others to take their place.[429] Would a UBI, in part, stimulate a parasitic mindset that allowed those closer to home to contribute nothing if they wished, whilst distant, brown people had to slave away on our behalf?

Steiner is clear: he argues all, who can, should make a contribution; not a financial contribution, but a contribution of work:

> ... the thought that a certain number of persons labour in order that we may possess the minimum necessities of life is inseparable from another. It is the thought that we must recompense society, not with money but with work in exchange for the work that has been done for us. We feel an interest in our fellow men only when we are led to feel obligated to recompense in some form of labour the amount of labour that has been performed for us. [...] The feeling of obligation to the society in which we live is the beginning of the interest that is required for a sound social order. (CW186, pp. 56-57)

> It is true to say that, in the future, production should not be for the sake of profit, but for the sake of consumption. That is quite correct, as it is important that everyone gets what they need. But this still doesn't create a healthy community. That only arises when a service is met with a reciprocal service, that is, when the individual is inclined to produce a service of like value in return for what others produce and deliver to him. [...] isn't it the case that if people want to live in a human community, they need to work, perform a service. By doing so, they produce something that has a meaning for others. (CW331, 24 June 1919)

> The beneficial social structure will ... put a stop to the attempts of those who strive only for capital assets, but shirk participation in the economic process ... The harmfulness of the nonworking

---

[429] Randeep Ramesh, 'An 80-hour week for 5p an hour: the real price of high-street fashion', *The Guardian*, 8 December 2006.

recipient of dividends is not that to a small degree they diminish the working man's earnings, but that the sheer possibility of someone being able to have an income without working for it lends an anti-social aspect to the whole economic body. (CW24, p. 11)

Even within our own circle [i.e. the anthroposophical movement, RM], where this could so easily be understood, people do not always reflect that everything we receive obliges us to return an equivalent to society and not simply enjoy. (CW186, p. 58)

... an awareness will develop ... of the socially harmful results of transferring capital to unproductive persons. (CW23, p. 107)

These comments would seem to further confirm that Steiner was not advocating anything resembling a UBI.

Ultimately, as we know, Steiner regards labour considerations / worker rights as a matter for the rights realm. So, if at some rather distant point in the future, we were to have robots which could build our roads and satisfactorily operate our hospitals (I don't personally share the view some people have that more or less everything can become automated!), then the threefold approach ultimately leaves it to voters to decide if a three-day working week or some other measure should be introduced.

... the number of hours individuals must work to support themselves will be determined on a purely democratic basis. (CW333, p. 57)

Ultimately, then, it is also down to the electorate whether a UBI is desirable; the democratic process, in the end, trumps any recommendations any individual might make.

In my own view, though, it would seem impractical for a country to go from no Basic Income to a Universal one, overnight. Surely the place to start—if any country deemed it affordable and desirable— would be to give it to 65- and 66-year-olds first, and possibly those up to the age of 25, enabling young adults to either (a) study without building up student debt, or (b) save up for a deposit on a house, (c) travel, (d) generally find their feet, etc. Such a measure could even dissuade anyone (if such women really exist) who is tempted to get pregnant for no other reason than simply because it will lead to single-parent benefits for however so many years.

As a general point, rights usually come with responsibilities. If I have a right not to be attacked in the street, I also have a responsibility not to attack anyone in the street. If I have a right to clean air, then I have a responsibility not to pollute. But does a right to receive goods made by others, without having to recompense them, one-sidedly allow rights to trump responsibilities? At present there seems to be plenty of work to do. There is a pressing need to care for the sick and elderly, protect victims of crime (via prevention as much as prosecution), and care for our public spaces: graffiti adorns urban walls, weeds grow out of cracks, grass verges are infested with litter, brambles hang over pavements, roads are full of potholes, concrete signposts are crumbling at bus stops. One could even muse whether those in receipt of unemployment benefit should be given a day or two of work per week. Might giving the long-term unemployed simple tasks like collecting litter even restore their faith in themselves when they found they could take pride in doing things that society appreciates? Possibly not; I am no psychologist.

Two further comments that suggest it is doubtful Steiner would have supported UBI are:

Money, in a healthy social organism, can be nothing other than a draft on commodities produced by others, which the holder may claim from the overall social organism because he has himself produced and delivered commodities ... (CW23, p. 117)

In the economic life of the future everything will be based on service and reciprocal service. For a service one will receive a docket, as it were, that means nothing other than: on the active side [of a ledger, RM] sits all that corresponds to my performance, and which is available to me to exchange for whatever meets my needs ... (CW331, 2 July 1919)

10. The Threefold Approach Summarised

The threefold view of society has now been looked at from a number of angles and in some detail, and before moving on, it perhaps makes sense to briefly take stock and reassert an overview.

In its essence, threefolding constitutes an extremely simple set of principles which, if observed, can prevent deep conflicts of interests and far-reaching societal problems. It notes there are three broad aspects of society that are fundamentally different in nature, and that these are best administered separately.

A cultural domain concerns what 'bursts forth' from individuals, what enters society from the whole spectrum of people's capacities. A political domain concerns rights and responsibilities, legislation, the rules we all choose to live by. An economic domain concerns the production circulation and consumption of commodities—concerns, basically, getting things to where they are needed.

In a self-determining domain of cultural and intellectual affairs, individual capacities must develop on the basis of freedom. In the sphere of rights, which includes employer-employee relationships [Arbeitsverhältnis], the prevailing principle must be the inherent equality of all human individuals. And the economy must be governed by the true sister-and-brotherliness that can flourish only in co-operative associations ... Liberty, equality, and fraternity will each be able to prevail in one of the members of the threefold body social. Liberty will thrive in cultural and intellectual affairs, equality in a democratic sphere of rights, and fraternity in economic activity. (CW333, p. 17)

The whole of social life thus falls into three distinct fields. In that of spiritual life, it is for the individual to speak. In the democratic sphere of law, it is for all men to speak, since what matters here is the relationship of man to man on the basis of simple humanity—where any human being can express a view. In the sphere of economic life, neither the judgment of the individual, nor that which flows from the unsifted judgments of all men, is possible. In this sphere, the individual contributes to the whole, expert knowledge and experience in his own particular field; and then, from associations, a collective judgment can emerge in the proper manner. It can do so only if the legitimate judgments of individuals can rub shoulders with one another. For this, however, the associations must be so constituted as to contain views that can rub shoulders and then produce a collective judgment. The whole of social life, therefore, falls into these three areas. This is not deduced from some utopian notion, but from a realistic observation of life. (CW83, p. 172)

One man can never set up a social programme, for inner individual life goes in quite a different direction from the setting up of social programmes. One can only say: thus and thus must men stand, thus must men be orientated in the field of the spiritual life, thus in the political field, and thus in respect to the economic life. Then what is necessary will result. [...] The essential thing therefore is this, that one find the tendencies, the inherent structure of the social organism.

It is not a matter of setting up programmes, but of finding the way in which men must live together in order to discover what social impulses they may have. [...] How often in the last few weeks have I had said to me: 'Yes, this man and that man are presenting definite programmes that regulate the social life in every single point'. But that is of no avail; people have always done that. Just look how countless the Utopias are. But there should be no Utopias, there should be something that is rooted in practical life. (CW192, 21 April 1919)

In summary:

- Society has a threefold nature with a cultural (individual capacities) aspect, a political (rights) aspect and an economic (commodities) aspect.
- Each aspect has an affinity with *liberté, égalité, fraternité* respectively.
- The ideal of equality is fostered via the mechanism of democracy in political life. The ideal of fraternity is fostered via the mechanism of association in economic life. The ideal of freedom is fostered via the absence of any mechanism in cultural life.
- Social disease arises when these three realms are tangled together in their administration.
- Conversely, societal health increases when the three realms have an independence such that the relationship between them amounts to 'appropriately serving' but not contaminating. At its most basic, this 'appropriately serving' can be seen in: how the

rights realm protects society; the economic realm feeds society; the cultural realm inspires and quickens society.

- In the rights domain, decisions are made by all; in the cultural domain, decisions are made by the individual; in the economic domain, they are made by interested parties in dialogue, in association.

At the end of Chapter 6, this was summarised in tabular form as follows:

	The realm concerning	More particularly	Decisions made by	Guiding principle
Cultural aspect	Human faculties ...	their cultivation, expression and application in society	Individuals	Freedom
Political realm	Rights and responsibilities ...	establishing and upholding these to protect society	All	Equality
Economic system	Goods and services ...	their production, circulation and consumption	Interested parties in association	Brotherliness

And diagrammatically:

The *definitions* of the three societal realms may not be quite what one expects, and to clarify this has been one of the aims of this book (Chapter 5). Another aim has been to clarify how the realms intermingle and overlap (Chapter 8). Indeed, they overlap such that the three great (but potentially conflicting) principles of *liberté, égalité, fraternité* can coexist.

> ... three great ideas ... have arisen in human development. One idea is that of liberalism, another that of democracy, the third is that of socialism. If one is honest about these three ideas, one will not be able to mix all three together in confusion, or eliminate one by the other, but one will have to say to oneself: from the independent cultural life something must stream out ... which surges into the whole organism. That is free human development, that is the liberal element. In the political state, in the rights life, something must live wherein all human beings are equal. That is the democratic element. And in the economic life the brotherly element must prevail. (CW329(ii), p. 71)
>
> ... liberty in spiritual matters; equality in the state if that is what people want to continue calling this third; and fraternity in relation to the economic life. I know well written books which rightly emphasize that the three ideals of liberty, equality and fraternity contradict one another. It is true, equality decidedly contradicts liberty. [...] If we muddle everything together these things contradict one another. (CW186(ii), p. 146)

Liberté, égalité, fraternité can find their fullest expression when uncompromised by over-closeness of the three domains. 'The slogan, in fact, needs to be amplified to read: spiritual liberty, political equality, economic fraternity. Then, although it remains revolutionary, its practical meaning is made clear'.[430]

With the appropriate level of independence between the realms, certain fundamental tensions in public life are resolved—like the one between *liberté* / individualism on the one hand and *fraternité* / social caring on the other. A threefold approach respects both the individualism craved by most as well as the acute need for a more responsible,

---

[430] Charles Waterman, *The Three Spheres of Society* (London: Faber and Faber, 1946), p. 269.

socially focused and environment-restoring economy. The following, highly simplistic table shows under what conditions these two sentiments—liberty and socialness—can best manifest.

	Feudalism	Traditional Capitalism	Traditional Socialism	Threefolding
Liberty	☹	☺	☹	☺
Socialness	☹	☹	☺ (in theory)	☺

It is admitted, of course, that most left-of-centre social democracies also aim to be in the right-hand, double-smiley column! And it is worth repeating that threefolding by no means claims to be a quick fix, and overnight route to social bliss!

Somewhat less prosaically, Rudolf Steiner expressed the importance of both liberalness and socialness in the following words he wrote inside a book he gave his colleague Edith Maryon:

> *The healthy social life is found / When in the mirror of each human soul / The whole community finds its reflection / And when in the community / The strength of each one is living (this is the motto of the social ethic).*[431] *(Verses and Meditations, p.117)*

That is: social health arises if the individual carries society in their consciousness, and if the potential of each individual can flourish.

The noble slogan of many a socialist (a slogan predating Marx, although made popular by him in 1875): 'From each according to his ability, to each according to his needs' is also encapsulated within the threefold approach. However, there are key differences between state socialism and threefolding when it comes to how to try and achieve this. Regarding abilities, capacities, Steiner is emphatic that these be given completely free rein, not prevented from full expression by a meddlesome state bureaucracy (Soviet or other). Regarding needs,

---

[431] In German: '*Heilsam is nur, wenn / Im Spiegel der Menschenseele / Sich bildet die ganze Gemeinschaft / Und in der Gemeinschaft / Lebet der Enzelseele Kraft*'. The original translation has '*Kraft*' down as 'virtue', which is not accurate.

he is of course also keen to see these met for all as far as possible. But, again, his approach is very different to that advocated by state socialism. He regards the nationalisation of industry, the running of industry by the state as something to be avoided. Ditto the running of industry by the 'proletariat'. Industry is to be run by experts in production who, via associative working, endeavour to meet needs in the most efficacious way possible. The political realm should just concern itself with rights and responsibilities.

But traditional capitalism, dominated as it is by profit maximisation, competition, self-interest, gross inequality, a rentier mindset and a financial economy—run by money, for money—is completely rejected, too.

From a threefold standpoint, one could take the view that right-of-centre minds have a healthy instinct that industry should not be part of the legislature; but they lack any feeling for how it should be run in a way to optimise societal health. Left-wing minds, on the other hand, appreciate that industry should be run socially for the purpose of providing for everyone's needs; but they come to the wrong conclusion as to what to do with it, and put it back under the government umbrella.

Threefolding is neither 'more state' nor 'more market'. It suggests alternative approaches that are unfamiliar to both.

The usual way in which the centrist tries to accommodate both ideals (socialness and liberalness) is by letting capitalism run wild, and then taxing it in an attempt to clean up the mess (social and otherwise). The term 'third way', which was already used in varying degrees in different countries some decades before being used to describe Tony Blair's New Labour politics, has, in the main, been associated with a social democratic position, a market socialism, a balance between liberty and equality, a path somewhere between the extremes of state socialism and laissez-faire neo-liberalism. As Jack Straw said: 'It turns its back on the first and second ways—the free market individualism of the 1980s and the statism that went before it and to which it was an extreme reaction.'[432]

---

[432] Jack Straw to the Nexus Conference, London, 3 July 1998 (quoted by Terry Boardman in 'The third way of 1998 and the new politics of today—some observations', *New View*, 3rd Quarter, Summer 2010).

Anthony Giddens—allegedly Tony Blair's favourite intellectual—states: 'A huge task lies before us: to create a form of responsible capitalism in which wealth creation is reconciled with social needs, including environmental ones.'[433] In his book *The Third Way*, he sketches out a rather different 'political middle' to Steiner:

> Classical social democracy thought of wealth creation as almost incidental to its basic concerns with economic security and redistribution. The neoliberals place competitiveness and the generating of wealth much more to the forefront. Third way politics also gives very strong emphasis to these qualities, which have an urgent importance given the nature of the global marketplace. They will not be developed, however, if individuals are abandoned to sink or swim in an economic whirlpool. Government has an essential role to play in investing in the human resources and infrastructure needed to develop an entrepreneurial culture.
>
> Third way politics, it could be suggested, advocates a *new mixed economy*. Two different versions of the old mixed economy existed. One involved a separation between state and private sectors, but with a good deal of industry in public hands. The other was and is the social market. In each of these, markets are kept largely subordinate to government. The new mixed economy looks instead for a synergy between public and private sectors, utilising the dynamism of markets but with the public interest in mind. It involves a balance between regulation and deregulation, on transnational as well as national and local levels; and a balance between the economic and the non-economic in the life of the society. The second of these is at least as important as the first, but attained in some part through it.
>
> A high rate of business formation and dissolution is characteristic of a dynamic economy. This flux is not compatible with a society where taken-for-granted habits dominate, including those generated by welfare systems. Social democrats have to shift the relationship between *risk* and *security* involved in the welfare state, to develop a society of 'responsible risk takers' in the sphere of government, business enterprise and labour markets. People

---

[433] Interview with Labinot Kunushevci on 23 May 2016, https://www.google.com/amp/s/economicsociology.org/2017/11/15/giddens-we-are-suffering-from-cosmopolitan-overload-and-a-huge-task-lies-before-us-to-create-responsible-capitalism/amp/.

need protection when things go wrong, but also the material and moral capabilities to move through major periods of transition in their lives.

> The issue of equality needs to be thought through carefully. Equality and individual liberty can come into conflict, and it is no good pretending that equality, pluralism and economic dynamism are always compatible ....[434]

Although not suggesting the state actually *runs* enterprise like it did in the old unitary state models disapproved of by Steiner, Giddens' sentiments do make the economy a key concern of the state. He opines the state, as though stirring a big tasty soup lest any elements get stuck on the bottom of the pan, has a role in maintaining a vibrancy and adaptability among the populace (via, perhaps, attractive retraining possibilities and the like) such that the economy remains productive. Nothing wrong with that, perhaps. In a threefold context, also, the state might concern itself with *rights* to retraining possibilities in the event of unemployment. Yes, a threefold polity might arrive at the necessary laws in uber-senate dialogue with the economic and cultural administrations, but, nonetheless, it would still be involved.

The key difference, perhaps, between Giddens' (New Labour's) third way and Steiner's is that, whilst Steiner advocates a more collaborative, associative, brotherly economy, the Giddens'—and Blairite—approach embraced the juggernaut of private capital, free markets and competition to the point of neo-liberalism, as epitomised by New Labour's Peter Mandelson being 'intensely relaxed about people getting filthy rich'.[435]

The result? More social pain. And more environmental destruction.

Yes, the economy may have remained dynamic, but the approach proved very weak at addressing gaping inequalities. 'Trickle down' provided no more than a trickle.

By contrast, Steiner offers some basic principles to support an acutely needed (and longed-for-by-many) change of direction—that

---

[434] Anthony Giddens, *The Third Way: The Renewal of Social Democracy* (Cambridge: Polity Press, 2008), p. 99.

[435] Some years later, he admitted these remarks were 'spontaneous and unthoughtful' and that 'People simply do not want to live in a world that puts abstract economic efficiency or "liquidity" in financial markets above their personal sense of economic security for themselves and their families. It is hard to argue that they are wrong.' See: https://www.google.com/amp/s/amp.theguardian.com/politics/2012/jan/26/mandelson-people-getting-filthy-rich.

all-important system change which economist Kate Raworth calls both 'distributive and regenerative by design' (i.e. where wealth is spread out more equitably, and environmental vitality is promoted).[436]

---

[436] Kate Raworth, *Doughnut Economics: Seven Ways to Think Like a 21st-Century Economist* (London: Random House, 2018), p. 156.

11. Post-threefold Comments

A century has passed since Steiner's spell of political campaigning, and, as we know: even a week is a long time in politics! The following two comments act as an almost comedic reminder of one aspect of life that has changed since those days:

> *The Germans have never understood the first thing about economics, and they have absolutely no talent for it. (CW196, p. 226)*
>
> *It does not matter whether we copy machines from the West—we will never build them as exactly as the West—or whether we imitate false teeth from the West, we will never make them as elegant. It does not really matter what it is! If we simply imitate we will never cope with the West because it does not need to take what we produce. (CW338(iii), p. 182)*

Given that, before WWI, Germany had the most advanced chemical industry in the world and was producing half of the world's electrical equipment, these are quite intriguing observations.[437]

Be that as it may, a year or two after Steiner has wound down the threefold campaign he observes:

> *You must remember when the Threefold Commonwealth was first mentioned, we did not yet stand face to face with the monetary difficulties of today [hyper-inflation, RM]. On the contrary, if the threefold commonwealth had been understood at that time, these difficulties could never have occurred. Yet once again we were faced by the inability of human beings to understand such a thing as this in a really practical sense. When we tried to bring the threefold commonwealth home to them, people would come and say: 'Yes, all that is excellent, we see it perfectly. But, after all, the first thing needful is to counteract the depreciation of the currency.' Ladies and gentlemen, all that one could answer was: 'That is contained*

---

[437] Thayer Watkins, *The Economic History of Germany*, https://www.sjsu.edu/faculty/watkins/germany.htm.

in the threefold order. Set to work with the threefold order. That is the only means of counteracting the depreciation of the currency.' People were asking how to do the very thing which the threefold commonwealth was meant to do. They did not understand it, however often they declared that they did.

And now the position is such that if we are to speak once more today to people such as you, we can no longer speak in the same forms as we did then. Today another language is necessary, and that is what I want to give you in the present lectures. (CW340, pp. 15-16)

The lectures he is referring to are his lectures on economics—given largely to students of economics. Much of the material in those particular lectures has not been covered in this book. As well as very challenging in places, they are also, in large part, about economic theory, whilst this book is more about Steiner's suggestions for *action*.

A week later, when referring to the threefold campaign, he notes:

I very carefully tried only to give guidelines, examples, illustrations. I wanted to evoke a consciousness of what can be achieved if someone is responsible for the means of production only for as long as he is able to be, at which point it is transferred to someone else. I can readily imagine that what is thereby achieved could be done in different ways, but I only wanted to give indications. I wanted to show that one finds alternatives if the threefold nature of social life is given true effect—that is to say, if one really frees the cultural life, places the life of rights on a democratic basis, and allows the economic life to be represented by associations. I am certain that in this way the economy will take its right course—that the right things will take place in the economic life. I want to rely on people finding the right course of action. (CW341, p. 182)

These comments are made in Switzerland in July 1922. In Oxford the following month, he observes:

At a very significant moment in history between the end of the war and the Versailles attempt at a peace settlement I endeavoured to sketch out a way of developing an organic structure for our present

social organism in accordance with the three parts of social life ...
(CW305(ii), p. 125)

I wrote my book Towards Social Renewal *at the request of friends in Stuttgart in the southern part of Germany, and this book deals with the specific period of spring 1919 and the specific place, southern Germany. I imagined that if people were to find the will to do something, then at that time and in that place this will would be such that there would be an understanding for the things suggested by this book not so much as points in a political programme but as directions of will.*

The question dealt with in the book is different for the eastern part of the civilised world, for Russia and Asia; it is different for Central Europe, and different again for the western world for England and America. You can reach this conclusion if you think realistically. (CW305(ii), p. 126)

Right until the middle of the 19ᵗʰ century Germany remained essentially agrarian, a country in which agriculture dominated. What modern industry there was ... was more or less the function of the state and tended to become more and more absorbed by the state structure and integrated in it.

Make a realistic comparison between pre-war Central Europe and pre-war Western Europe. In Western Europe the economic sphere of commerce and industry managed to remain separate from the state, as did the cultural life to an even greater degree in the way it retained its independence from the other two strands.

In Central Europe there was a compact amalgam of cultural life, legal-political life and economic life. So in Germany there was a need to tease the three strands apart before they could be brought to work together in an organic way; they needed to be side by side for collaboration to be possible and so that the links between them could be established.

Here in the West the three strands sit side by side, clearly separated from one another. Even spatially the cultural life is separated off to such an extent that you can get the feeling, for example here in Oxford, that culture and learning lead a life of their own in splendid isolation from any state or economic life going on elsewhere. Consequently there is also a sense of this isolated cultural life no longer having the strength to work outwards into the other two strands. It seems to live within itself and have no organic links through which to interweave with the other two.

In Germany you feel that cultural life is so interwoven with the life of the state that it will need a good deal of help before being able to stand on its own feet. Here in England, on the other hand, cultural life is so independent that it takes no notice at all of the other two strands. If you think realistically about the whole social aspect today and the fundamental impulses that sustain it, you will find that such differences give the situation in each country its own quite distinct colouring.

I therefore find it quite natural that my book Towards Social Renewal, *which was widely read in Germany in 1919, should now be almost, although perhaps not quite, forgotten there. The moment in time when the suggestions made in it might have been realized has now passed as far as Central Europe is concerned. (CW305(ii), pp. 127-128)*

I therefore believe that Towards Social Renewal *should in future be read more in the West and in Russia, for in Germany there seems to be no possibility of putting any of the suggestions it makes into practice. In the West, for instance, people will find there is much that can be learnt from the book. Without being utopian it clearly describes how the three strands ought to run side by side and yet interweave with one another. In the West the point in time is irrelevant for here, too, there remains much to be done with regard to the proper interlinking of the three strands of cultural life, economic life and the political-legal life of the state.*

Above all we shall have to learn to think in a really modern way so as to achieve the capacity to form judgments about social matters that are relevant to modern times. Please do not take this superficially. What I mean is that we need to acquire social judgments that are relevant today, and we can only do this if we look into the depths that lie beneath the surface of social phenomena. In this connection we are faced with a remarkable fact. It is impossible for an individual alone, however intelligent or idealistic or practical—and I should like to underline 'practical' three times!— to arrive at a social judgment at all. It is a social mystery that any social judgement reached by someone in isolation is wrong. (CW305(ii), p. 127)

Once the threefold campaign in Southern Germany has failed to reach a critical mass, Steiner clearly sees little merit in flogging dead horses, and so turns his energy mostly to other matters. At the same time, though, as illustrated by the above comments from 1922, his conviction in the on-going validity and vitality of the threefold approach does not change. Despite Britain's societal landscape being very much more threefold than Germany's, in the sense that the unitary-state entanglements of the three realms seen in Germany are far less in evidence once Steiner sets foot in Dover, he nonetheless stresses the British can learn much by taking the threefold nature of social life into account (not least because, although not being tangled up, the three realms hardly take any notice of each other; they are not appropriately serving each other to keep things in a healthy relation. There is an absence of 'proper interlinking', as he puts it).

12. Relevant to Now ?

In March 1919, Steiner observes:

> *... threefolding is not an arbitrary invention but simply what we can observe when we study the deeper forces at work in human evolution, which have become active today and will, whether or not we prefer otherwise, be realised in the next ten, twenty or thirty years.* *(CW189, p. 86)*

The next ten, twenty or thirty years? By 1950 at the latest? This statement can at first seem very wide of the mark. To what extent this prediction might have been borne out by events in all the various corners of the Earth is beyond my limited knowledge. But if in 'most western countries, mainly in Europe, the great age of nationalization and successful public enterprise was the three decades following the great depression' (so, 1929—1959), it seems clear that, in a good number of countries, state involvement in industry, for one, *grew* before it shrank.[438]

Two events in Germany in 1949, however, have some bearing on the matter. In May of that year West Germany's *Grundgesetz* constitution was enacted. This stressed human dignity, individual freedom, and, in Article 7, Paragraphs 4 and 5, guaranteed the right to set up independent schools.[439] And then in August of the same year, the first Bundestag election was held. In this, the Social Democratic Party (SPD) which advocated a traditional socialist approach (with extensive public ownership of industry and central planning of much of the economy) was narrowly beaten by parties favouring a social market economy (i.e. a market economy with a welfare state and redistribution).

Whilst a social market economy might at times seem rather more market than social, this election heralded a rejection of state-run enterprise. And whilst the guaranteed right to set up independent schools did not lead to any wholesale rejection of state education (today about

---

[438] Pier Angelo Toninelli, *The Rise and Fall of State-Owned Enterprise in the Western World* (New York: Cambridge University Press, 2008), p. 14.

[439] Christoph Fuhr, 'The German Education System since 1945: outlines and problems', 1997, https://files.eric.ed.gov.

9% of schools in Germany are independent), the assertion simply of the constitutional right also signalled a decoupling of the three societal realms along threefold lines. The Bundestag vote in favour of social market loosened the state's mandate to run industry. The *Grundgesetz* constitution loosened state influence in cultural matters. (It perhaps goes without saying that during the recently overcome Nazi period, the state had held a wide-ranging stranglehold over both the economic and cultural domains.) So, in Germany at least, thirty years after the above remark by Steiner, threefold principles had indeed started to replace the old unitary state model he considered so problematic. And it is interesting to note how, with less entanglement between state and economy, Germany managed to decidedly move on from having 'absolutely no talent' for economics!

However, at the end of WW2, Britain, if anything, went in a less threefold direction for a time. Not only was Clement Attlee's Labour Party elected (in 1945) on an explicitly socialist manifesto, but it beat war hero Winston Churchill's Conservatives by a thumping majority. Nationalisation of some key industries followed over the next five years: the Bank of England, coal, civil airlines, rail, water, electricity, gas, iron and steel.[440] In his in-depth assessment of British socialism, though, Edmund Dell concludes that: 'By 1956 it was perfectly clear that, if labour ever came to power again, it would attempt to run a capitalist market economy. It might nationalize a bit for old time's sake [some might argue it was a bit more than a bit, RM] or even to save a bankrupt industry from liquidation. But there would be nothing like the extensively nationalized, centrally controlled economy to which [some] had looked forward in 1940'.[441] All the same, it wasn't really until the 1980s that state involvement in industry met fulsome rejection in Britain (amongst other countries). Although the typical market privatisations that followed under Thatcher's watch lacked key social features suggested by Steiner, the withdrawal of the state from the management of industry was itself in keeping with the threefold idea of independent administrations for the different domains.

---

[440] Pier Angelo Toninelli, *The Rise and Fall of State-Owned Enterprise in the Western World* (New York: Cambridge University Press, 2008), p. 18.
[441] Edmund Dell, *A Strange Eventful History: Democratic Socialism in Britain* (London: Harper Collins, 1999), p. 277

Similar privatisations occurred in other countries. And in 1989, the tentative freeing of the three realms from their mutual entanglement in the Soviet Union found iconic expression in the fall of the Berlin Wall. In the same year, Britain's Labour Party under Neil Kinnock more or less retired the goal of extensive nationalisation. In the 1990s, even China began accommodating certain types of capitalism.

To varying degrees across Western Europe, then, the state reduces its involvement in religion (less so, in education) and largely withdraws from trying to run industry[442]—that key component of the socialist model Steiner vigorously denounced. Today, industry largely does its own thing, and we have reasonably extensive cultural freedoms. So, threefold 'forces' indeed established themselves as Steiner expected, although perhaps not as quickly as he seems to have envisaged, and, it is true to say, not very thoroughly.

Yes, in the UK, the state no longer gets bogged down by its responsibility for British Telecom, British Airways, British Leyland and other businesses that politicians should not have been expected to have the expertise to oversee. But in general, separation of the three realms has only been partial, and all sorts of cross contamination still exists. And whereas it might have once been the state that pulled all sorts of societal strings, it now seems to be the economic realm that is the main interloper throwing its weight around. And an unhealthily constituted economic realm, at that! Had threefold principles been more closely observed when German or the aforementioned UK industries were denationalised, for example, they would not have ended up as cash cows for remotely owned, private capital. The means of production would not have been sold (into the economic realm of purchase and sale) but would have been placed under the auspices of the cultural domain, from whence they would have then fed into the economic system to serve the common good, as has been discussed at some length in previous chapters.

In relation to the present, one can ask in what ways might Steiner's analysis be remotely relevant anymore, bearing in mind that other huge societal changes have occurred since his time—in addition to significant threefold disentanglement at macro level. These other

---

[442] Not completely, however, as Norwegian postal services, Swiss trains, French electricity and German savings banks demonstrate, for example.

changes include: a steep decline in the blue collar working class; the entry of women into the workforce, complicating the concept of full employment (and resulting, in part, from the arrival of the contraceptive pill in 1960); ease of travel (widespread holidays abroad—albeit interrupted by the Covid-19 phenomenon, teenagers owning cars, etc.); an increase in university education (in the 1960s, 10% of women had degrees; today it is nigh-on 50%)[443]; increased global pollution followed by increased concern for ecology; a marked increase in the standard of living (cramped, cold, vermin-ridden, damp houses give way to council houses, washing machines, a good variety of foodstuffs, etc.); improved hygiene; improved medication (the discovery of antibiotics being key); a resultant increase in life expectancy (the number of people over the age of 85 has grown twenty-fold)[444]; an increase in 'post-materialist' values (where quality of life becomes less associated with the maximising of economic reward and more with meaningful or enjoyable work, care for the environment, altruistic causes, self-expression, the propensity for experiences—like travel—over physical goods)[445]; greater personal freedoms; a sharp increase in single parent families; widespread access to learning and entertainment from radio, TV and, latterly, the further unshackling of information brought on by the internet.

And whereas, in Steiner's day, machines often made the life of the proletarian a dull and repetitive existence, today artificial intelligence and robots are taking a growing number of jobs away from people entirely. In the 1930s you could find 100,000 people working in a single shipyard on the Clyde. No longer. Along with lack of employment comes a lack of purpose, closely followed by a lack of positive outlook and a lack of good mental health. The upside is that more of our needs are taken care of by machines. People don't have to work so hard (especially in dull, repetitive, strenuous work); they can pursue other interests. No doubt many a worker—although by no means *all* workers—would bite your hand off if you offered them lack of

---

[443] Barra Roantree and Kartik Vira, 'The rise and rise of women's employment in the UK', IFS Briefing Note 234 (London: 2018), p. 2.

[444] Anthony Giddens, *The Third Way: The Renewal of Social Democracy* (Cambridge: Polity Press, 2008), pp. 120-121.

[445] Ibid., pp. 19-21.

purpose in lieu of their 40 hours of hard, dirty grind per week! But when this is accompanied by a sizeable drop in disposable income, the picture is not so straightforward.

Social conditions can change remarkably quickly over short periods of time. That one can be overtaken by events rather quickly was illustrated when the Chairman of Shell had to ingest humble pie in 1998 and exclaim, in connection with environmental and consumer groups: 'We were somewhat slow in understanding that these groups were tending to acquire authority. We underestimated the extent of these changes—we failed to engage in a serious dialogue with these new groups. [...] simply put, the institutions of global society are being reinvented as technology redefines relationships between individuals and organisations'.[446] In 2015, this slowness to appreciate change was on display, for example, when the Westminster bubble, big business and a fairly 'captured' media seemed to be so busy scratching each other's backs that the popularity of a rather un-slick left-winger, Jeremy Corbyn, took them completely by surprise. Shocked disbelief was widespread. Similar phenomena were seen in the USA with the rise of left-wing presidential hopeful, Bernie Sanders.

The answer to how Steiner's recommendations might be relevant today will of course vary depending on which country you are in. But what about in an average Western democracy like the UK? Our economy is hugely complex, as well as international, and becomes more so by the year. Would it be at all realistic—or desirable—to think one could further tweak public life in the direction Steiner saw fitting? Habits are deeply ingrained and vested interests entrenched. On the other hand there is also great intellectual flexibility, resourcefulness and plurality which can relish innovation. There is also growing appreciation that 'we can't go on like this'.

And what about an assessment of the extent to which threefold principles have already been adopted at the more *micro* level? To write a summary of the recommendations Steiner made, one 'only' has to acquaint oneself with the fifteen or so English books that feature his offerings in this regard, and the fifty or so lectures / seminars not yet available in English. But to give a survey of the innovative businesses

---

[446] Cor Herkstroter quoted in Anthony Giddens, *The Third Way: The Renewal of Social Democracy* (Cambridge: Polity Press, 2008), pp. 49-50.

or political movements that are in keeping with the threefold idea—
be that intentionally in keeping, or simply by accident—requires a
knowledge I lack; and I can only apologise to anyone whose work is
highly relevant to all this, but of which I am ignorant.

There are undoubtedly many thousands of examples of these threefold principles at work around the world, though. These principles
are, after all, often a matter of common sense. Wherever the state
withdraws from interference in the cultural realm (including education and religion) and leaves it free to proceed as it will, that is a
threefold principle. Wherever the state does not try and run industry
(including natural monopolies), that embodies a threefold principle.
Wherever businesses are set up with mutuality / fraternity at their
core, that embodies a threefold principle, particularly if the means
of production are safeguarded from predation, in a way that these are
passed from one management to the next, in an ownership structure
for the benefit of the common good in perpetuity. Wherever businesses
are placed in trusts with no external, profit-extracting owners, as with
Land Trusts, these demonstrate a good fit with Steiner's analysis,
since the means of production are then not treated as belonging to the
economic domain. When Elizabeth Warren pledges in her 2020 presidential campaign to remove the corruption of corporate cash from
U.S. politics, that embodies a threefold principle.[447] When politics are
properly democratic, that is a threefold principle. When individuals
are free to express themselves as they wish, or indeed when industry is
run, not by ineffectual heirs or state bureaucrats, but by those who, on
the strength of their skills, have freely risen to the top, that embodies a
threefold principle. When Kate Raworth enthuses about policymakers
following a dashboard of non-financial metrics, this relates directly
to fundamental threefold principles: human and planetary welfare are
not seen in terms of money (economics) but in terms of rights and
responsibilities.[448] And so on.

The USA's First Amendment came with the foresight, already in
1791, to keep religion and the state separate. But, sadly, corporate

---

[447] Sheelah Kolhatkar, 'Elizabeth Warren's crusade against corruption', *The New
Yorker*, 17 September 2019.
[448] Interview with Kate Raworth at Trees as Infrastructure Workshop, https://
vimeo.com/377023491.

interests were not excluded from the state at the same time. Indeed, none of the 27 ratified amendments address this. Is it perhaps time for a 28th Amendment to solve this highly toxic issue and restore the one-person-one-vote principle of democracy—where all individuals have an equal say? Vested corporate interests would undoubtedly have something to say about this!

Probably one of the biggest examples of threefolding being consciously attempted at a more formal, macro level is in the Philippines: 'The most advanced of these efforts in conscious threefolding is taking place in Bayawan City, Negros Oriental, with over 120,000 residents. The city has just allocated over P1 billion pesos ($20 million) of its budget to fund programmes and projects identified in a societal threefolding process involving key sectors of business, government and civil society. The leadership of the government itself convened and facilitated the threefolding initiative, including the City Mayor and his top aides, assisted by a formal, legally mandated threefold council.

'This initiative is by no means perfect, but it is a very promising beginning. Already, dozens of mayors of towns and cities have expressed their interest in undertaking societal threefolding processes in order to craft their sustainable integrated area development (SIAD) plans. The Philippine Development Plan (2017-2022), the official medium-term strategic plan of the entire government, explicitly mentions threefolding and (SIAD). And an entire government agency of the Philippine government, the Department of Environment and Natural Resources (DENR), has adopted SIAD and threefolding as its strategy for achieving environmental protection and sustainable development'.[449]

To what extent the cultural realm is left completely free and independent of government in this city, I don't know. To what extent business interests are kept out of the legislation process, I don't know. To what extent business in the area is associative, I don't know. To what extent there is a good understanding in the region of what does, and does not, constitute each realm (as defined by Steiner), I also don't

---

[449] Nicanor Perlas (recipient of the alternative Nobel Prize) in Martin Large and Steve Briault (Eds), *Free, Equal and Mutual: Rebalancing Society for the Common Good* (Stroud: Hawthorn Press, 2018), p. 7.

know. But the point is, not only is there a formal recognition that a threefold nature of society exists, there is also an attempt to bring such considerations into policy.

In Chapter 8 ('Overlap'), we looked at multiple examples of how the three realms can inappropriately influence one another in the absence of proper threefold disentanglement. The starting point was specific types of overlap between the realms, and then examples were given. But the analysis can of course be in the opposite direction: one can start with a particular social issue, and then consider what factors might be at play. This is done, very non-exhaustively, in the following brief sections. A few of our more pressing societal challenges are the starting point, and consideration is then given to what sorts of inappropriate overlap might be in evidence. Being brief, these sections will likely make little sense unless the foregoing chapters of the book have first been digested.

12.1 Environmental destruction

'*The Guardian* believes that the problems we face on the climate crisis are symptomatic and that fundamental societal change is needed'.[450]

Our current, capitalist system generally rewards not only those who mistreat their workers the most but also those who mistreat the environment the most. Loss of soil fertility, deforestation, global warming, bee colony collapse, drought, over-fishing and a host of other ecological matters of acute concern are exacerbated by the imprudent short-termism of irresponsible corporate behaviour and the propensity of many countries to ignore the precautionary principle (of erring on the side of ecological caution, even if cause and effect is circumstantial rather than proven).

With a threefold demarcation of function in place, a strong, independent legislature, not subject to inappropriate lobbying (bullying) from industry would arrive at laws to protect the environment far more easily than a legislature also worrying about the economy and, in particular, getting funding (bribes) for political campaigns. The legislature under a threefold structure would only be concerned with what the rights of the matter might be, with what was just. From this, more sound regulation would follow.

---

[450] Editorial, *The Guardian*, 21 October 2019.

Similarly, if scientific research was part of a completely independent cultural domain and could not be captured by corporate interests (e.g. by corporate sponsorship of research or university departments), such interests would be much less able to withhold findings inconvenient to their own industry, much less able to sow doubt in people's minds about the dangers of this or that pollution, say, when there might otherwise be consensus.[451]

Similarly, if *complete* cultural freedom existed in the media, then billionaire media moguls would be much less able to introduce falsehoods into the narrative.

In addition, if manufacturers were not driven by profit maximisation and outside shareholders (who would not exist if the means of production were decoupled from the economic realm as Steiner suggests), but instead were driven by the principle of brotherliness, of mutual service, they would not seek to cut corners at every opportunity, they would not be prone to engaging in environmentally damaging practices in order to boost profit. The obsessions with profits, share price and capital growth would no longer be 'a thing'.

So, without spending long on this, we already have four clear examples where inappropriate economic influence can lead to environmental destruction: (a) economic capture of the means of production (e.g. via share purchase by profit-maximisers) whereas, under threefolding, these would be a matter for the rights and cultural domains, (b) economic capture of the political process itself, via corporate funding of political campaigns, (c) economic capture of culture, via corporate funding of research, and (d) economic capture of culture via corporate influence in the media.

12.2 Housing shortages

At the time of writing, we have a pressing housing shortage in the UK with an estimated 4,000 individuals sleeping rough and 70,000 households living in temporary accommodation. It was heartbreaking TV viewing seeing some of these latter families trying to make do in the

---

[451] See for example http://sams.scientificamerican.com/article/dark-money-funds-climate-change-denial-effort/ or Phoebe Keane, 'How the oil industry made us doubt climate change', BBC News, 19 September 2020.

run-up to Christmas, living out of a few bags either in bed and breakfast accommodation (if they were lucky—and at high cost to the taxpayer) or in extremely unpleasant and precarious quarters with no furniture, no roots, and no lasting friendships for the children on account of frequently missing school or changing schools multiple times. At the same time, for example, there were recently 13 *empty homes* for every homeless adult in Dublin, and 85 in County Cork![452]

The shortage of housing has also lead to rocketing house prices making life extremely difficult for first-time buyers as well as renters who frequently find themselves with little left at the end of the month, once they have paid for the roof over their head.

If, as Steiner (amongst others) suggests, land were treated as a rights-realm matter instead of being part of the economic realm where it can be bought and sold, then it would be a matter of right as to who could use it. A right to occupy land would be bestowed on those who had need of it—such as those needing somewhere to live, or those producing commodities. Builders would perhaps not be allowed to sit on 600,000 building plots up and down the country, only to build on these as and when the fancy takes them.[453] These plots could be allocated to builders with the proviso that they complete construction within some time frame—18 months, say—and then immediately release them into the market—a market that would ideally not include any land element in the price.

Other laws could be enacted that limited a person's right to multiple housing plots. The rights realm (ultimately, all of us, via democracy) could cap this at one, or two, or three housing plots, say. The quota could be periodically adjusted to make sure there was sufficient housing for everyone wanting to buy, everyone wanting to rent, and, after that, those wanting holiday quarters, and so on.

Some progress has been seen in this area more recently with, for example, over 80% in a Cornwall Council referendum backing a ban on the building of second homes in St Ives.[454] Further afield, New Zealand is considering restrictions on non-resident property investors,

---

[452] Pat Doyle, 'In Dublin there are 13 empty homes for every adult in homelessness', www.thejournal.ie, 22 February 2017.

[453] Graham Ruddick, 'Revealed: house builders sitting on 600,000 plots of land'; *The Guardian,* 31 December 2015.

[454] http://www.bbc.co.uk/news/uk-england-cornwall-36204795.

Singapore and Hong Kong impose extra taxes on foreign buyers, and Switzerland has had restrictions on foreigner-owned homes since the 1960s.[455]

According to threefold analysis, land is a rights-realm matter. It is not produced, circulated, consumed, i.e. ideally it is not part of the buying-and-selling paradigm of the economic realm. If it was properly treated as a rights-realm matter instead of always being available to the highest bidder, a more equitable distribution would ensue.

12.3 Poverty / wealth disparity

' ... nothing will satisfy your greed. You work generations of us to death until you have each of you more than a hundred of us could eat or spend; and yet you go on forcing us to work harder and harder and longer and longer for less and less food and clothing. You do not know what enough means for yourselves, or less than enough for us. You are forever grumbling because we have no money to buy the goods you trade in; and your only remedy is to give us less money. This must be because you serve false gods. You are heathens and savages. You know neither how to live nor let others live'.[456]

Those who follow the news in media owned by billionaires are perhaps called on less often to worry about these things. But the more left-of-centre news follower will be familiar with headlines that provoke feelings ranging from 'something ain't quite right here' to feelings of profound sadness, or even anger.

Steiner noted in 1919 how five working class families could live for six months for the price of a pearl necklace.[457] Now, it may be true that, in the 'developed world' today, the poor are generally less poor than in those days. But in the USA today, under 500 families own almost half the nation's wealth,[458] and according to Oxfam, not only does the richest 1% of the world's population own as much as the remaining 99%, but

---

[455] https://www.bbc.co.uk/news/business-42964656.

[456] George Bernard Shaw, *The Adventures of the Black Girl in her Search for God* (1932).

[457] CW332a, p. 115.

[458] Christopher Schaefer in Martin Large and Steve Briault (Eds), *Free, Equal and Mutual: Rebalancing Society for the Common Good* (Stroud: Hawthorn Press, 2018), p. 184.

also the 26 richest people in the world have as much wealth as the 3.8 billion people who make up the poorer half of the world's entire population.[459] Further, 'A global super-rich elite had at least $21 trillion hidden in secret tax havens by the end of 2010, according to a major study. The figure is equivalent to the size of the U.S. and Japanese economies combined'.[460] Add to this the fact that, often, the poor pay taxes whilst the richest avoid them, and the picture is truly shocking.

Of course, there are a few notable, principled exceptions where a few of the ultra-wealthy campaign for higher taxes for themselves. But in the USA, CEOs of Fortune 500 companies made 20 times that of the average worker in 1950. In 1980, it was 42 times. In 2000, it was 120 times. In 2013, it was 204 times.[461] The worst offenders pay themselves nearly 5,000 times that of the average worker.[462] In the UK it was 60 times as much in the 1990s; in 2015 it was 180 times.[463] And so on. Hedge fund manager Sir (services to philanthropy!) Chris Hohn paid himself £270m, 1,800 times the Prime Minister's salary. And hedge funds don't even produce anything![464] In 2020 it was revealed that, on average (!), FTSE 100 bosses would have earned the same amount after three working days—i.e. by January 4th—as their average workers would earn in the whole year.[465]

When it came to light in 2013 that the CEO of the Royal Bank of Scotland (which had been rescued by the state!) Stephen Hester had received almost £8m, he insisted he would not give up his bonus, saying: 'We have done huge things to rescue the company for society and for its stakeholders. It is entirely proper for me to be assessed on what we have done'.[466] Thank you, Mr Hester; and the geriatric nurse working night shifts?

---

[459] Larry Elliott, 'World's 26 richest people own as much as poorest 50%, says Oxfam', *The Guardian,* 20 January 2019.

[460] http://www.bbc.co.uk/news/business-18944097.

[461] https://m.huffpost.com/us/entry/3184623?guccounter=1.

[462] https://www.marketwatch.com/amp/story/guid/C1FDA00-592A-11E8-BA56-A2BAFA7BOBAC.

[463] George Monbiot, '"Wealth creators" are robbing our most productive people', *The Guardian*, 31 March 2015.

[464] https://www.theguardian.com/business/2017/dec/07hedge-fund-boss-pays-himself-270m-despite-hedge-fund-only-making-200m.

[465] https://www.bbc.co.uk/news/business- 51000217.

[466] James Moore, '£8 million a year? That's modest, says RBS chief', the *i* newspaper, 12 February 2013.

Of those taking home absurd remuneration packages, only the most delusional think they are really worth it. In relation to this, Vince Cable (former Business Secretary and leader of the Liberal Democrats) once shared: 'I have asked one or two of the more sympathetic bankers to explain it to me. The response has been: "It's not that I need the money, it is because others get it so I should, too." That is a ludicrous mind-set'.[467]

At the other end of the spectrum it was found, in 2014 for example, that *two thirds* of jobs taken during the course of a year paid below the living wage.[468] And 200,000 more children in the UK fell into poverty between 2013 and 2017, taking the total to some 4 million! *In the UK!* Even those in reasonably paid jobs are typically having to slave like crazy just to pay the rent.

'Children growing up in poverty constantly move home, make long journeys to school and have to stay indoors in unsafe neighbourhoods, a report has revealed. The Children's Society said it discovered some "heart-breaking" stories, including one about a nine year old who had moved house eight times and attended four different schools. Interviews with scores of children found problems worsened in older years'.[469] The term 'precariat' is a good one, if harrowing!

And we have all seen the news reports of far profounder hardships further afield. Some 30% of the world's population lives on the equivalent of one US dollar a day.[470] Many are less fortunate even than that.

Economist Thomas Piketty charts how and why, under the sort of capitalism we are used to, inequality is not only self-perpetuating but self-*increasing*.[471] And unless we act, wealth disparities will only increase even further as automation increases. The automation of production processes, whilst boosting productivity (on one level, helpful, as it frees people from having to perform repetitive drudgery), is likely to lead to fewer in work, and therefore more living in poverty,

---

[467] Stefano Hatfield, 'My boyish plan for economic equality? Could work ...', the *i* newspaper, 17 March 2014.

[468] Gwyn Topham, 'Record poverty among working families', *The Guardian,* 24 November 2014.

[469] Alan Jones, 'Poor Children move too often', the *i* newspaper, 27 March 2017.

[470] Anthony Giddens, *The Third Way: The Renewal of Social Democracy* (Cambridge: Polity Press, 2008), p. 152.

[471] Thomas Picketty, *Capital in the Twenty-First Century* (Cambridge, MA: Harvard University Press, 2014).

whilst profit flows will increasingly favour the providers of the capital that funds the automation. As we know, ever-widening prosperity levels between the haves and have-nots leads to ghettos, ever-worsening gross national happiness and, ultimately, social unrest.

If, on the other hand, Steiner's suggestions had been adopted when he made them a century ago, then one can imagine that, by now, there would be demonstrably less of such inequity in somewhere like the UK.

If land had been treated as a rights matter, if succession rights had been such that land was always passed on to those who need it (for production or housing), not to those with capital, this would have helped.

If industry had been structured such that the means of production were increasingly moved out of the economic system, that would have helped. Without the means of production being buyable or sellable, the *right* of use would pass from one management to the next to use in furtherance of the common good. Shares and dividends would not be part of the setup. Ownership would not be rewarded at the expense of work.

'Fair price' would have helped—whereby, ultimately, everyone receives for their output sufficient to lead a decent life.

If working relationships had been moved from the economic realm (the realm of purchase and sale, i.e. wages) to the rights realm, that would have helped. Then, remuneration in the form of sharing the partnership proceeds would have greatly reduced worker exploitation, as would executive remuneration according to pre-agreed formulae when new management were granted possession of capital / the means of production.

An economy focused on the associative meeting of needs, as opposed to profit maximisation, would have helped.

A cultural domain independent of economic or political influences would also have meant greatly reduced contamination of journalism, rather than a billionaire-owned media constantly normalising tax regimes favourable to the mega-rich.

And, especially in somewhere like the USA, a rights domain independent of the economic domain would have put a stop to corporate lobbying (bribes). The latter, with money often trumping the people, has led to a badly corrupted democracy, and, at times, even the bizarre spectacle of wealthy elites paying lower rates of tax than those on low incomes.

12.4 Health issues

We are living far longer than a century ago or even half a century ago, so that is something to be celebrated. Health improvements have been achieved in different ways: via medical advance, better nutrition, less smoking, dryer houses with better sanitation, etc. However wanting it may be, societal progress still happens!

All the same, far too many food producers are more interested in profit than in the health of their own customers. If business was associatively directed towards need instead of towards wringing as much profit out of the customer as possible, would bottles of orange-coloured, orange-flavoured water, brimming with artificial additives and refined sugar (and contributing to widespread obesity and diabetes in the process) adorn supermarket shelves, or would actual orange juice be more widespread— and more affordable on account of people's income conforming more to 'fair price' principles? In England alone, hospital admissions for obesity-related treatment are exceeding one million per annum![472]

And if the political administration stopped meddling in the cultural realm, would a resultant reduction in obsessive testing and box-ticking 'administrationalism' in schools lead to children being allowed to be children, with a resultant improvement in their mental health, instead of nearly 20,000 UK children arriving at Accident and Emergency departments (!) in one year for want of appropriate mental health services being available after 5pm?[473]

> *Illnesses that appear in later life are often only the result of educational errors made in the very earliest years of childhood.*[474]

And if the cultural realm was properly independent of the economic, we would not see research into new drugs skewed to make them look more effective than they in fact are; we would not see Coca-Cola paying

---

[472] Sophie Hutchinson, 'Over a million hospital admissions for obesity', BBC News, 18 May 2021.

[473] Daniel Boffey, 'A&Es hit by children's mental health crisis', *The Guardian*, 26 December 2015.

[474] Quoted in Richard House, *Pushing Back to Ofsted: Safeguarding and the Legitimacy of Ofsted's Inspection Judgments—A Critical Case Study* (Stroud: InterActions, 2020), p. 23.

scientists to downplay the role of sugary drinks in the obesity crisis;[475] and we would not see training courses in journalism that were directly funded by big pharma such that conflicts of interest could take root and breed.[476] The efficacy of medicines and therapies in relation to long-term health outcomes could be subject to far more objective assessment.

And if profit maximisation was not the objective of the pharmaceutical industry, and if the rights realm in somewhere like the USA was not horrendously contaminated by the economic (via big pharma donations), would new medicines be licensed that are actually less effective than existing (patent-expired!) ones?[477]

And if agribusiness took long-term husbandry, long-term stewardship, and long-term *need* to heart instead of virtually drip-feeding herds and flocks with antibiotics for the sake of a fast buck, would we be witnessing the emergence of antibiotic-resistant superbugs potentially threatening to send medical practices back to the Middle Ages?

And so on and so forth.

12.5 Selfish foreign policy

Causing strife and hardship overseas for the sake of one's own advantage is an issue below the radar of many citizens, no doubt. Out of sight, out of mind! As discussed previously, the phrase 'in the national interest', whilst sounding ever so reasonable, can conceal the most psychopathic of behaviours. In the final analysis, we are talking here about people in the West who are prepared to countenance others dying if it furthers their own agenda.

And, if not actually dying … 'During the post-war boom, capitalism suppressed the development of the global south. The means by which it did so are clear and well documented. Unequal trade relationships forced much of Latin America, all of Africa and most of Asia to adopt development models that led to super-profits for Western companies and poverty at home. Countries that tried to reject these models,

---

[475] Mary Kekatus, 'Coca-cola "paid scientists to downplay how sugary beverages fuelled the obesity crisis between 2013—2015"', medical journal study finds', *The Daily Mail*, 3 August 2020.

[476] Gary Schwitzer, 'Drug company influence in journalism', *HealthNewsReview*, 2 August 2020.

[477] Richard Smith, 'Foregone conclusions', *The Guardian*, 14 January 2004.

such as Chile or Guyana, had their governments overthrown by CIA coups or, as with Grenada, by invasion. Many found their economies destroyed by debt and by the "structural adjustment programmes" the IMF dictated in return for debt write-offs. With little domestic industry, their growth models relied on the export of raw materials, and the incomes of the poor stagnated'.[478]

But are we not all in some way guilty if we perpetuate the establishment that allows such agendas to prevail? To his credit, even the seemingly small-minded President Trump could, on at least one occasion, see the wood for the trees, stopping, as he allegedly did, a bombing mission in the Middle East because he learned around 150 people would die.[479] Of course, any claims to conscience he might have had are perhaps not very credible when one considers his whole 'body of work', when, for example, no efforts were made to stop Israel's flouting of international law. To bulldoze a helpless Palestinian family's house down, and their olive grove, and tell them to leave the place they have called home since childhood, all in order to expand your own territory, requires a particular strain of cruelty (not to mention an indifference to stirring up Arab rage). Allowing such inconsistent interpretations of international law betrays a deeply sinister and primitive aspect to the manoeuvrings of certain countries in the so-called developed world. Oh, and most other Presidents in recent US history have seemingly not been any better. In 2016 alone, the USA dropped, on average, three overseas bombs per hour, 24/7, *over the entire year* under President Obama.[480] Perhaps there are shady characters in the military-industrial-banking-complex that make sure a steady trickle of assassination threats are brought to the attention of any President who starts talking about international law instead of 'the national interest'. But if the country's security agencies are not able to keep on top of such threats, then is the country any better than any of those other mafia-type setups the USA delights in deriding as failed states?

---

[478] Paul Mason, *Postcapitalism: A Guide to Our Future* (London: Allen Lane, 2015), p. 102.

[479] Jimmy McCloskey, 'Donald Trump stopped attack on Iran after being warned 150 would die', *Metro*, 21 June 2019.

[480] Madea Benjamin, 'America dropped 26,171 bombs in 2016. What a bloody end to Obama's reign', *The Guardian*, 9 January 2017.

When the UK keeps quiet about these things, because of our so-called special relationship with the USA, well, we are (in theory) pursuing the national interest at the expense of the global interest and the furtherance of human dignity. Too many British politicians seem more concerned about allies and allegiances than about what is *right*. Prime Minister Boris Johnson saying the UK government is against an International Criminal Court investigation into Israel's settlement building in the West Bank (amongst other things) because it 'gives the impression of being a partial and prejudicial attack on a friend and ally of the UK's' is just one deplorable example.[481] Mistreating foreigners not only carries with it the immediate impoverishment and struggles of the exploited (which can lead over into regional civil wars over farmland etc.) but it can ultimately come back to bite the oppressor as the latter is faced with refugee problems, long-term festering resentment, hatred or even terrorism. If the West, over the last century, had shown its best side, behaved in an upright way, set a good example and not fought wars for oil and greedy influence, one does wonder whether the hatred directed at 'us' by certain extremists would have quite the venom that it has today. The British reputation for fair play, however precarious and tenuous (undeserved?), would certainly have been something worth trying to live up to.

But when certain circles in already wealthy countries perpetrate horrific wars in pursuance of further domination of other nations, it becomes clear we have a lot to do. And, of course, awareness of the effects of one's own country's deeds is not helped by poor reporting. The majority of those in the media seem less interested in getting to the bottom of things, less interested in the truth, less interested in their consciences, less interested in the health of the world and 'the good', and more interested in their own comfort zones, keeping their noses in the News Corp trough, watching (and scratching) their backs, or their hush-hush allegiances, or their grubby self-interest agendas. There are a few notable exceptions, of course. And to be fair to (some of) the media, many of the secretive, strategic manoeuvrings we are talking about, with their long-term, geopolitical objectives that seems barely believable, are kept so opaque that reporting on them accurately is truly problematic.

---

[481] Oliver Holmes, 'Palestine condemns Johnson for opposing court's Israel inquiry', *The Guardian*, 16 April 2021.

Wealthy countries rampaging around in 'undeveloped' countries generally betrays inappropriate influence of the economic realm in the political. Billionaire-owned media turning a blind eye to same, generally betrays inappropriate influence of the economic realm in the cultural.

There is nothing new about all this, of course. In Steiner's day, the great industrialist Henry Ford wrote: 'We ought to wish for every nation as large a degree of self-support as possible. Instead of wishing to keep them dependent on us for what we manufacture, we should wish them to learn to manufacture themselves and build up a solidly founded civilisation. When every nation learns to produce the things which it can produce, we shall be able to get down to the basis of serving each other along those special lines in which there can be no competition. The North Temperate Zone will never be able to compete with the tropics in the special products of the tropics. Our country will never be a competitor with the Orient in the production of tea, nor with the South in the production of rubber. A large proportion of our foreign trade is based on the backwardness of our foreign customers. Selfishness is a motive that would preserve that backwardness. Humanity is a motive that would help the backward nations to a self-supporting basis. Take Mexico, for example. We have heard a great deal about the "development" of Mexico. Exploitation is the word that ought instead to be used. When its rich natural resources are exploited for the increase of the private fortunes of foreign capitalists, that is not development, it is ravishment. You can never develop Mexico until you develop the Mexican. And yet how much of the "development" of Mexico by foreign exploiters ever took account of the development of its people. The Mexican peon has been regarded as mere fuel for the foreign money-makers. Foreign trade has been his degradation'.[482]

Various threefold recommendations, if observed, would reduce some of these problems. Treating land as a rights matter, not a buying-and-selling, economic matter would prevent land grabs and ensure respect for indigenous peoples. 'Fair price' and associative business (e.g. Fair Trade) would respect indigenous peoples. A media that told the truth, uncontaminated by commercial or state interests (i.e. a cultural

---

[482] Henry Ford, *My Life and Work* (Hawthorne, CA: BN Publishing, 2008), p. 163.

realm independent of the economic and political) would wake people up to what is going on. The absence of profit-maximising, external shareholders (by removal of the means of production from the economic realm) would greatly reduce plunder. It would also prevent people benefiting from war on account of, say, their Halliburton interests.

If the state is just concerned, as Steiner recommends, with establishing and upholding rights and responsibilities, and not with either the economic realm nor the cultural, then the impetus for conflict is greatly reduced. His recommendations can be a blueprint for a more peaceful and respectful world.

> *In the beginning such a development will have to be limited by territorial boundaries. Yet it contains the possibility of settling national and global antagonisms by peaceful means. National and other agitators would be completely deprived of influence. (CW24(ii), p. 80)*
>
> *What is valid for Central Europe ... is a parliamentarianism in which the political, the economic and the general human relations can unfold independently of one another ... and thereby support one another instead of entangling themselves in their outward effects and creating conflicts. Central Europe frees itself and the world from such conflicts when it excludes such mutual interference of the three human realms in life from its state structures. (CW24(ii), p. 99)*

12.6 Crimes against the person

The dreadful epidemic of serious assault that we have been experiencing is one societal problem where it is not so easy to identify any particular facet of threefolding as one that might contribute to a solution; at least, not directly. But being such a harrowing and urgent issue, it would seem remiss not to refer to it.

When reading that not only has a gang of youths attacked a random passer-by, including, for example, stamping on their head, but also that one of the girls (!) has filmed the attack on her mobile phone, one can feel completely overwhelmed by the depth and complexity of the issues revealing themselves.[483] Where does one start when faced with a cruelty or lack of empathy so complete that it can amount to

---

[483] www.mirror.co.uk/news/uk-news/teen-girl-punched-head-stamped-9604939.amp.

indifference towards the agonies of a completely innocent passer-by, unknown to the attackers?

Crime figures show that, for all our impressive GDP, we have got something desperately wrong as a society. In 2018, the USA had over 2 million in prison—nearly 0.7% of the entire population.[484] In 2012, they had more prison guards than high-school teachers. In England and Wales, 44,000 incidents involving a blade or sharp object were committed in the year to June 2019; that is one, on average, every 12 minutes.[485] In 2017 it was reported that even some 6-year-olds in London were carrying knives!

And then we also read front page headlines declaring 'Burglary victims forgotten by police' or 'Half of those reporting a crime do not get a response from investigating officers' or 'Fears that many property offences are effectively being decriminalised' which further remind us of the urgent need to take a long, hard look at the way we organise ourselves as a society. It seems unlikely that such problems are going to be solved with increased automation and robotics!

The complex mixture of factors behind crimes of this seriousness can include: (1) poverty, especially when this sits side-by-side with affluence, (2) a lack of respect and love received by the perpetrator in childhood, (3) drug and alcohol abuse, and (4) alienation from / lack of engagement in society.[486] A typical example of the latter is lack of meaningful employment opportunities: '… unemployment was under a million and the police recorded 2.5 million crimes. In 1993, nearly three million were unemployed and 5.5 million crimes were recorded. When unemployment fell in 1987 and 1988, so did crime. When unemployment rose in 1990 and 1991, crime followed suit'.[487] Other factors affecting crime (and the factors are often interrelated, of course) include: peer pressure, school exclusions, poor social services, poor housing, closure of youth services, low police numbers, poor community dialogue and cohesion, etc.

---

[484] Wikipedia: Incarceration in the United States.

[485] https://www.google.com/amp/s/www.independent.co.uk/news/uk/crime/knife-crime-stabbings-offences-england-wales-rise-latest-uk-a9159511.html%3famp.

[486] D. Weatherburn, 'What Causes Crime?', NSW Bureau of Crime Statistics and Research, https://www.bocsar.nsw.gov.au/Publications/CJB/cjb54.pdf.

[487] Nick Cohen, 'What Causes Crime?', The Independent, 4 June 1995.

Ways in which a threefold approach could help in some small way seem rather tenuous and indirect. But taking the first four factors, one at a time:

1. Poverty: Ways in which threefolding can reduce poverty were looked at above—in Section 12.3.
2. Damaged childhood: The most cruel forms of crime are arguably those where the perpetrator uses physical violence against the victim or torments them with a traumatic fear, and perpetrators of such crimes are likely to have had traumatic childhoods. Yes, they might have had food, clothing and shelter—of sorts—but been born into an 'underclass' in some neighbourhood where they heard about or witnessed frightening experiences outside involving gangs, etc. Perhaps there was no upright role model within the family either, or they were even in fear of their own family members. With little or no experience of peace, beauty, goodness, love, trustworthiness; with no evidence that any other way of living is possible, it would hardly seem surprising if a child lacked the tools to act in a civilised way. They might be entirely devoured by an overwhelming sense of hostility and dread and then, with few experiences of goodness to draw on, no trust in the world, grow into a teenager with sociopathic traits. If there are only one or two such teenagers in an area, the problem may be containable. But it may not take many more for a critical mass to be reached whereby even those who might otherwise have been happy to lead upright lives now become so afraid of not fitting in, or so afraid of another gang, that they will get sucked into the desperate state of affairs themselves. Soon, some of these youths may become far-from-ideal parents themselves, and the vicious cycle continues.

Those with a more retributive, right-wing turn of mind are likely to favour the 'law approach' instead of the 'public health approach': criminals are criminals and so should be punished, and thereby deterred (in theory). End of story. It's all terribly simple. But if any of us law-abiding worthies had had to experience the tormented childhoods that some individuals have had to endure, one wonders just what a mess we ourselves might be. But for the grace of God!

How to break this cycle is surely one of society's biggest questions, and, again, it is hard to point to any particular threefold tenet and declare this part of the solution.

One can imagine that the more equitable approaches to work, to remuneration, to land ownership, considered earlier in the book, could help, little by little, over longer periods of time. People might become better parents if, instead of being burdened by feelings of resentment and exploitation, they experienced self-worth and respect from society.

Although not so related to threefolding, the following observation of Steiner's tallies with a respectful approach to imprisonment being tried in Norway—an approach that has demonstrated substantially greater rehabilitation and reduced rates of reoffending compared to when you treat criminals like dirt.[488]

> *Let us suppose we have before us a criminal, a man whom we call especially immoral; on no account must we think that this unmoral man is devoid of moral impulses. They are in him and we shall find them if we delve down to the bottom of his soul. (CW155, 29 May 1912)*

Again, not so directly related to threefolding, but one can also imagine that some measure of help could come from a wider availability of Steiner's Waldorf kindergartens and schools. These provide a highly child-oriented, gentle and reverent approach that is sensitive to the vulnerabilities of the younger years. In kindergarten, toddlers: bake bread and paint in natural, homely surroundings; are given plenty of time for free play—both indoors and out; and on most days are also told fairy tales which frequently contain lasting moral pictures—where mischief-makers get their comeuppance etc. As there is little at this stage to tax the undeveloped intellect, or to make youngsters feel results are expected of them, or feel failures, they can just 'be children' and feel safe and free of unnecessary pressure. This reassuring and strengthening experience is further enhanced when the kindergarten leader is a model

---

[488] See Emma Jane Kirby, 'How Norway turns criminals into good neighbours', BBC News, 6 July 2019 and Erwin James, 'The Norwegian prison where inmates are treated like people', *The Guardian*, 25 February 2013.

of goodness, deep caring, uprightness and love, as is always hoped for within Waldorf settings. People so often forget just how vulnerable young children feel—even those from loving homes—when they are so unworldly and still trying to make sense of their surroundings. This oversight seems especially prevalent amongst many who don't have small children in their lives—like a number of bureaucrats within the Department for Education, one suspects! A highly caring kindergarten experience certainly won't undo the suffering of a child living under frightening conditions at home; but it could help.

The independence of the cultural realm advocated in the threefold approach would prevent meddlesome politicians, with little knowledge of child development, insisting on ever earlier drumming-in of the three Rs, and so on. This would certainly remove inappropriate pressure from young children whose natural cognitive development has not yet reached a stage where it can readily assimilate these things. In particular, it would bring some peace to those children with a problematic home life—those who will be the least able to concentrate on premature 'head work'. State intervention in kindergartens too often seems to come with a box-ticking sterility when what young children need in order to become inwardly and outwardly strong, later on, are things like beauty, reassurance from caring, trustworthy adults, etc.

Steiner made an intriguing comment concerning crime which was that, if all children sang together regularly throughout their school career, crime would drop markedly. Also, whenever he visited the Waldorf School in Stuttgart, he was always keen to ascertain that the children loved their teachers. He recommended education be based neither on fear (of punishment) nor appeals to egotism ('if you wanna be rich—etc.'), but on love (love for the subject, love for the teachers, love for the school experience generally). His aim was for children to come to school joyfully.

Of course, such an educational approach can only offer partial solutions alongside the work of social services, youth services, etc. in combating any cycle of damaged childhood—a cycle that might well have built up over generations.

3. Drug / alcohol abuse: The two potential crime-provoking effects of this are (a) lowered feelings of responsibility and sensitivity towards others, which can (not will) increase the likelihood of

crimes against others, and (b) someone addicted to a drug may struggle to hold down a job, and so steal in order to be able to afford the next fix. Those who are relatively well adjusted may be unlikely to become dangerous if intoxicated, and, conversely, there are plenty of examples of cruel inhumanity carried out by strict abstainers—as seen for example amongst some Islamist fanatics. Whilst intoxication can frequently be problematic and result in hooliganism etc, it is usually when combined with other factors that it starts to become more threatening.

Again, whether any aspect of threefolding could be pointed to as a direct solution to such things is a question. However, it would appear that drug addiction may occur more often in people for whom the world is experienced as a cold, sterile, loveless, isolating place. Ways of preventing such feelings in the first place could include (a) nourishing, holistic, loving, caring childhood experiences at school, and (b) a collaborative rather than a dog-eat-dog economy, a world that didn't feel 'rigged'.

4. Alienation/unemployment: It is surely partly as a result of bad organisation how some have to live a treadmill, nose-to-the-grindstone, exhausting existence in order to keep the wolf from the door, whilst others must endure the emptiness of unemployment. Surely, everyone would be happier if the treadmillers could reduce their workload to say four days a week, and the otherwise unemployed could pick up the rest. Obviously one would not want to prohibit people from working more than four days a week. Many people are fortunate enough to love their work, and such a ruling would adversely affect productivity, would reduce the overall meeting of needs. For those feeling ground down by laborious or stressful work, however, a 'fair price' approach that said all should be able to afford to live a decent life if they did four days of productive work per week might result in a population far more at peace with itself. Those otherwise alienated by unemployment would gain in self-belief.

As covered in Sections 7.3.4 and 7.4.14, Steiner recommends wages be superseded by an approach to remuneration where all co-workers would have a right to a *share* of company proceeds. Naturally, this would bring increased feelings of inclusion in society. But even with the continuance of wages, greater observance of other threefold principles would make it easier to raise the minimum wage such that even the lowest paid could fully support themselves when doing four days' work per week, say, instead of five. A minimum wage increase of this sort would almost certainly be resisted by business leaders. But with threefold safeguards in place—ones that prevented the economic realm from contaminating the rights realm—these more fortunate members of society would be less able to inappropriately influence rights-realm decisions. Politicians would not be so eager to please business leaders (often the wealthiest in society) if large donations to political parties and presidential campaigns were no longer a feature of public life (the economic corrupting the political). They would be able to focus exclusively on rights and responsibilities—on what is just—and not be continually worrying about inconveniencing some of the most privileged people in society. Also, if (as per Section 5.3.2, for example) outside shareholding was superseded, and the means of production, instead of being buyable / sellable, were a matter for the rights and cultural realms, and only came with rights of *use,* not rights of sale (because, not being consumer goods, they were no longer considered part of the economic domain), then dividends to outside owners would stop, and obsessions with profit maximisation would greatly reduce. This would also reduce resistance to an increased minimum wage.

And if the media—e.g. TV and newspapers—could also not be bought and sold but, instead, the *right* to operate them was simply transferred from one skilled proprietor to the next, then the ability of ultra-rich moguls to control the media—and the narrative—would be greatly reduced, too. Their dislike of tax, or any other measures that reduced their profits, would no longer be normalised in the media, and thence in the minds of the unwary, voting public.

Even if the four-day-week was not yet thought affordable, the unemployed could still be given all manner of useful work in a more organised economy—as those much needed carers for the sick and elderly, for example, or as carers of our very run-down public spaces. As a way to prevent unemployment, Steiner suggests bodies within the associative economic domain could be tasked with ensuring anyone being laid off would be found alternative work (Section 7.4.12).

So much for the first four of the factors, mentioned above, behind crimes against the person. Other suggestions made by Steiner would have relevance to other factors. For example, his proposal that excess economic profits be used particularly to fund education (Section 7.4.17) would mean more money would be available for desperately needed, inner-city youth services—money that might otherwise only be funding an ever increasing kingdom of luxuries for non-working shareholders.

Being typically structural in nature, Steiner's suggestions would in most instances only represent very indirect contributions to the task of reducing crime. But they could arguably be significant in the longer term.

Before moving on, it should perhaps also be acknowledged that another particularly harrowing type of crime against the person is seen where children are subject to sexual attack. Once again, it is hard to see any direct ways in which threefolding could help. But in the UK, for example, the scale—the prevalence—of these issues is so distressing it would also seem wrong not to refer to them among the more serious problems of the day.

Whether it's the NSPCC (National Society for the Prevention of Cruelty to Children) appeal that revealed a child in distress phones them every 25 seconds, or whether it's the front page headline that tells us 'Two million children are referred to social services' (in a 12-month period), the acute need for these organisations reveals a shocking state of affairs.[489] In 2019 the NSPCC revealed that over 75,000 sexual offences against children had been committed in one year in the UK (with *The Guardian* having reported in 2016 there were over 10,000 victims under the age of 10)—a shattering and bewildering statistic that is testament to a society which surely has to urgently reflect on the way it goes about things.[490] And these were just the known cases! According to the NSPCC, their figures represented a 30% increase compared with the previous year. One can only speculate as to what might have been behind the increase. Better detection? More widespread reporting (making offenders increasingly

---

[489] Emily Dugan, 'Two million children are referred to social services', *The Guardian*, 29 October 2014.

[490] https://www.nspcc.org.uk/what-we-do/news-opinion.

feel such crimes are just ordinary)? A poorly policed internet (also making offenders increasingly feel their crimes are more normal)? Disturbing revelations about 1970s celebrities (also making offenders increasingly feel such crimes are more normal)? Reduced fear amongst offenders of the consequences? (Not that one would condone vigilantism, but in the 1970s, such offenders would live in fear of physical violence, both inside prison and out.) In relation to all this, it is perhaps also worth noting that it is only thanks to the more recent appointment of Pope Francis that many people have been able to consider that the Catholic Church might not, in fact, be rotten to the core.

Again, although one would only want to make such a claim *extremely* tentatively, it is arguable that Steiner's approach to education could make a difference in some small way, since it aims not only to nurture the intellect but also the emotional intelligence, such that people eventually mature into upright and empathetic citizens, citizens who will not become perpetrators against the vulnerable. Other educational approaches would doubtless claim to do this too; and how successful these all are in relation to each other, I don't know. As mentioned in Section 7.5.2, though, a Waldorf school, instead of trying to educate the child to be good by feeding dry facts to their undeveloped analytical abilities, young children are told fairy tales, and the like, that touch their souls and sink in to a level of experience that has enduring meaning. There is no box-ticking, there is no checking to see if the child can repeat, parrot-fashion the lessons learned—which in any case is no proof they have 'got it'. They are given stories where they *feel* right and wrong. A Waldorf teacher I was once talking to put it very beautifully (in relation to six-year-olds): 'We don't expect much back at this age. We are just planting seeds.'

But these seeds go deep. The painful instances of injustice in Grimms' fairy tales, for example, are images a child *experiences* as unjust; they are not just dry facts that don't touch him or her. They stimulate moral feelings which contribute to a moral education. The principle is that this leads to upright adults later. But, thanks in large part to seemingly ignorant ministers, we have the ever earlier start to formal learning, i.e. education policy that can only be described as incoherent. Such policy is based on the misguided belief that child development is a linear thing, and the sooner you start with the 'three Rs', the further children will get. The rights realm is inappropriately interfering with the cultural. A healthy instinct for the specialness of childhood can sometimes seem very far away indeed. (*En passant*: a few years ago, this lack of healthy instinct even found expression in a high street chain selling clothes *for toddlers* emblazoned with large skulls!)

Once again, it is acknowledged that it is rather speculative to muse that more Steiner education, by eventually leading to more upright citizens, could make much difference to the grave problem of adults mistreating children. But it has a role, perhaps. Even if it does have some small role, though, this is only related to threefolding inasmuch as it highlights an example of inter-realm trespass, i.e. the rights realm inappropriately interfering with the cultural realm, by encouraging education practice which is out of kilter with child development. (The state certainly has a child protection / safeguarding role in society. But that is not an educational, cultural matter. That is the rights realm properly concerning itself with rights-realm matters.)

* * *

The previous few pages have taken a very fleeting and non-exhaustive look at some of the ways in which Steiner's ideas could help with *some* of our more pressing social ills. Read in isolation, they will only portray a very sketchy impression of his recommendations. But in combination with the examples given in earlier chapters to illustrate this or that principle, they perhaps support the idea that certain threefold ideas have significant and on-going relevance. And particularly so, I would argue, in countries where daily struggle for survival is widespread.

There are rarely quick fixes to entrenched social issues, and Steiner's recommendations are no exception. These come more in the form of *structural* measures that are preventative in the long term. If they had been adopted a hundred years ago, when he made them, or even fifty years ago, one can certainly imagine we might now be looking at a society considerably more at peace with itself.

13. Further implementation

A number of the reforms that Steiner advocates, then, would seem to have on-going relevance, but what prospect might there be of realising them further?

The UK's two most popular newspapers are *The Sun* (circulation in 2019: 1.41 million) and the *Daily Mail,* (1.25 million)[491], and one wouldn't necessarily single out either of these as leading standard-bearers for questioning the status quo. So one could feel that attempts at improving the world are always going to be something of an uphill struggle. Wouldn't a more threefold arrangement of public life only be received by more of the same cynicism that meets many other constructive attempts to improve societal health? But then one also learns that Russell Brand, for example, in a very different corner of the political universe, has almost 12 million Twitter followers, and it becomes clear there is in fact a great openness (longing, even) for fresh, innovative and more equitable ideas.[492]

Indeed, when, in opinion polls, it transpires a full 90% of German citizens think we need a different type of economy, then improvements of one sort or another would seem more possible.[493] After all, even in that lobbyist-addled polity that is the USA, someone as conscientious as Bernie Sanders—who has spent a lifetime fighting for social justice—very nearly became Democrat nominee for President. Twice! And consider once again how a single Swedish schoolgirl with Asperger's and concerns for the planet can have more influence than a great many career sociopaths and ecopaths with snouts in the neo-liberal trough!

Integral to the on-going relevance of Steiner's suggestions is his own insistence that they should not be taken as anything fixed. His central argument of maintaining the integrity of the three societal

---

[491] Wikipedia: List of newspapers in the UK by circulation.

[492] https://www.socialbakers.com (accessed 27 August 2017).

[493] Gerald Häfner in Martin Large and Steve Briault (Eds), *Free, Equal and Mutual: Rebalancing Society for the Common Good* (Stroud: Hawthorn Press, 2018), p. 132.

realms certainly can be seen as continually valid. But anyone—be they producer, consumer, adviser, activist, artisan, policymaker, business leader, environmentalist, citizen—who feels there may be some merit in adapting and adopting some of Steiner's ideas can decide for themselves which of these seem more relevant to their work and the social context they are in.

> The intention of the specific examples mentioned here is to better illustrate the indicated direction. A productive goal can still be attained as long as movements coincide with the direction given. (CW23, p. 106)
>
> ... because I want to see reality grasped as reality, it is not important to me that all my suggestions are carried out to every last detail. If at any point you start work along the lines I have indicated today, something completely different may result, but it will be something that is justified in the face of real life. (CW329, 11 March 1919)
>
> Of course to-day one can only realize such things up to a certain point. In practical life one can nowhere realize an ideal, but one must do what is possible in the circumstances of life. [...] I do not give actual proposals how this or that institution should be but turn directly to human beings and say: When human beings work together in the right way and in the right way find the aspects from which they have to view the social question, then the best which can come about will come about. (CW79, 30 November 1921)

Steiner offers great encouragement by suggesting people crack on with efforts *approximately* along threefold lines rather than dogmatically getting hung up about archetypes and perfection.

> ... we have to be clear that what we fail to develop until tomorrow, be it ever so good, may well be worse than what we develop today even if it is not quite as good. (CW338(iii), p. 194)
>
> ... if we wish to root ourselves in reality we have to relate to actual contemporary conditions, to what exists, and not build castles in the air. (CW189, p. 5)

Building on what is there already is entirely acceptable in his eyes. For example, in relation to the economic realm (the economic realm *in his day*, at least):

> *Institutions already in existence—consumers, producers, the entre-preneur—everything already in existence needs to come together in associations. (CW305(ii), p. 161)*
>
> *People who depend on their accustomed lines of thought will say: 'These are very fine ideas, but how are we to make the transition from pres-ent conditions to the threefold system?' It is important to see that what has been proposed here can be put into practice without delay. One need only begin by forming such associations. Surely no one who has a healthy sense of reality can deny this is immediately possible. Associa-tions based on the idea of the threefold social order can be formed just as readily as companies and consortia were formed along the old lines. Moreover, all kinds of dealings and transactions are possible between the new associations and the old forms of business. There is no ques-tion of the old having to be destroyed and replaced artificially by the new. The new simply takes its place beside the old; the new will then have to justify itself and prove its inherent power ... (CW24, p. 47)*

A good example of Steiner's complete willingness to build on what is there already was shown by his close discussions with—and encouragement of—the Works Councils in Southern Germany in 1919. Amongst other things, these were pressing for worker direction of companies—something contrary to the threefold principle of freedom and competition in the cultural realm of capacities, where the best person for the job gets the job (that is, the person with the most suitable capabilities on account of their intrinsic talents, their experience and expertise). But Steiner has faith that the workers will recognise and appreciate that good managers prevent work becoming chaotic. In the factories where Works Councils were present, he encouraged all workers—both blue collar and white—to *elect* management (which would then be subject to intermittent re-election). He thus endeavours to respond to the social forces emerging through the proletariat of the day striving to take matters in hand themselves. Steiner's discussions with Works Councils are described in detail by Albert Schmelzer.[494]

---

[494] Albert Schmelzer, *The Threefold Movement, 1919: A History* (Forest Row: Rudolf Steiner Press, 2017), pp. 127–130.

Flexibility and 'aliveness' are key:

> You should not imagine everything according to Swiss conditions. Life is becoming more and more international. In Germany, something completely different is necessary today than, for example, a few years ago. You can continue working from any starting point; it will just be a question of building further. [...] be it in a cooperative, in a union, in any party ... wherever one sits, one can arrange things in such a way that these three parts come out ... (CW329, 19 March 1919)

> ... one could think up all sorts of ideas of how the social organism should be structured. But that can never be the question. The question can only be this: How is it possible to structure it? How must its members work together, not that it is the best, but the one which through its own strengths is the possible one, which will have the least of the indicated disease symptoms and can develop in the most healthy way possible? (CW79, 30 November 1921)

> It is self-evident that what has been presented here cannot consider the details. Such details reveal themselves in true practical impulses only in the execution. Only a utopian could invent the details. (CW23, p. 100)

> The worst misunderstanding connected with this book with its social intentions was that people read it in the wrong way; and they continue to do so. They do not want to adapt their thoughts to life; they want life to adapt to their thoughts. This, however, is not at all the precondition for social arrangements with which we are dealing here. (CW305(ii), p. 154)

As well as broad-brush, Steiner's approach is incrementalist rather than absolutist, pragmatic rather than revolutionary. Even following the upheaval of the Great War, he suggests any greater respect for the threefold makeup of society can only be expected to manifest in a gradual way:

> It is only necessary to decide once and for all that the rights-state must gradually relinquish its control over spiritual life and the economy, and not to offer resistance when what should happen really happens: that private educational institutions arise and the economy

> *becomes self-sustaining. The state-owned schools and economic enterprises do not have to be eliminated overnight; but the gradual dismantling of the state educational and economic apparatus could well develop from small beginnings [...] The essential element of the ideas developed here is that ... the realisation of such ideas is to come about by building upon what already exists. Through this building, the dismantling of the unhealthy elements is induced. ... what absolutely must be attained: a course in which the value of what has hitherto been produced, and the abilities which have been acquired, are not simply thrown overboard, but are preserved. (CW23, p. 108)*

> *... the essential thing in our present time is to strive for a kind of structural classification within the social organism. I always say 'strive for', for there is no question of wanting to effect a revolutionary change overnight. (CW193, p. 44)*

> *The threefold idea is not a program or system for society as a whole, requiring the old system to cease suddenly and everything to be 'set up' anew. The threefold idea can make a start with individual undertakings in society. The transformation of the whole will then follow through the ever-widening life of these individual institutions. Because it is able to work in this way, the threefold idea is not utopian. It is a force adequate to the realities of modern life. (CW24, p. 47)*

> *... when we strive after the gradual realization of the above-mentioned threefold structure it can only be realized little by little; we do not aim at sudden reforms or revolutions, but merely indicate a new direction; single measures in keeping with this new direction can be introduced, indeed, everything which calls for reform today can in all details be done in such a way as to follow these guiding lines, this new direction ... (CW188(v), 26 January 1919)*

Of course, some incremental steps in a threefold direction are likely to have (and have had) less impact than others. For example, if within a single institution just one aspect of Steiner's advice were adopted, this might not make a huge difference. Denationalising a utility company, say, only to sell it to profit-maximising, private capital will solve some problems only to create others.

All the same, he sees great merit in small beginnings since, if the steps one takes prove themselves as health giving, they will be emulated.

> *... one does not mean that one wants to revolutionise the whole world, but that one can begin in a certain area. Then I do think it will be very contagious if conditions come about in an area that are really healing; that will be thoroughly contagious. This will contribute to internationalisation. (CW331, 22 May 1919)*

And even though adopting threefold ideas might not always be straightforward, the following serves as one reminder about the potential consequences of complacency or apathy:

> *It should not be rejected ... because its realisation might be found difficult. If one stops making progress in real developments in the face of such difficulties, then one creates entanglements that later discharge violently. (CW24(ii), p. 83)*

Whether it is violent discharge, environmental destruction, profound inequity or whatever else, it seems obvious that sticking to our current ways will only increase the likelihood of such tragedies. As economics commentator Grace Blakely observed in her inimitable way: 'The question is whether or not we are able to build something new before it all goes to shit'.[495]

---

[495] Grace Blakely, 'How to save the world from financialisation', interview with Michael Walker of Novara Media (novaramedia.com) live streamed on 10 September 2019.

14. Concluding Remarks

A fair amount of material has been covered since 'income communities' and the other things Steiner was talking about to a smallish audience in 1905. As we have seen, these more niche ideas give way, at the end of the Great War, to his observations about the threefold nature of society—a nature that is no abstraction but simply exists. These observations lead to a substantive approach to reform that reaches a wide audience across the social spectrum—from the proletariat at one end to political figures and royalty at the other. Interestingly, some amongst the latter show a keen interest while many of those with arguably the most to gain—the proletariat—struggle to get their heads round it or their weight behind it. Little wonder, perhaps: it is considerably more nuanced and not as easy to understand as the sound bites of their socialist, communist and trade union leaders (who also use 'threats of party discipline and appeals to party loyalty' to undermine worker interest in Steiner's approach).[496] Steiner's ideas were quite different to what people were used to hearing. And if it's any consolation to a still-befuddled reader of this book, had I tried to understand *everything* Steiner said about social matters before writing it, it would never have been written!

Naturally, the hope is that, in these pages, threefold ideas have been described sufficiently well to be grasped. In a few places I felt a bit out of my depth, so no doubt some parts will have been more helpful than others. And without any doubt at all, a good many questions have been left unanswered. Some of these will perhaps be addressed by bears with bigger brains. Others, perhaps, can only meaningfully be addressed, in the moment, by those on the ground.

By and large, the suggestions Steiner makes for social *action* have been covered; less attention has been given to any theory or background observations on which those suggestions might be based. And how the various features of threefolding may or may not overlap with the vast array of documented political ideologies—of which there are over three hundred—is largely beyond my knowledge and so has

---

[496] George Kaufmann quoted in Joanna Scott, *Death in Europe—Why?* (London: Simpkin Marshall, 1941), p. 21.

barely been touched on. And, again, I must apologise to the thousands of initiatives that doubtless exist which are structured along similar lines to what has been presented, but of which I am ignorant. Some readers may feel that much of what has been presented coincides with what they already think of as common sense—which I would think is a good thing.

The main premise of threefolding—the idea of a hygienic level of independence between different aspects of society, such that each plays to its strengths without contamination by either of the other two—is perhaps not so difficult to grasp. What are more radical, however, are some of the more detailed suggestions Steiner makes as to how this approach could take shape, *and in particular how he defines the three realms* and includes certain things within the definitions that might come as a surprise (e.g. the means of production not belonging to the economic realm).

Of course, what is—and isn't—radical is frequently a matter of personal taste. It is noteworthy how in certain democracies the labels of 'radical' or 'extreme' seem more generally to be levelled against the 'loony left' than against Vince Cable's 'right-wing nutters'.[497] Little wonder, though, when places like the USA have a polity *and media* largely doing the bidding of the super-rich who are content to normalise and perpetuate the status quo (as it happens!). But an 'elite' getting away with wrecking the planet or poisoning their own customers or paying less tax than relative paupers—simply because they have paid money to political parties? *That* is extremism.

Whilst what Steiner enumerated might amount to a genuine third way between state socialism and rapacious capitalism, the question has been posed towards the end of the book: is there *really* any point engaging with his ideas considering he made them 100 years ago when the social landscape was very different to what we have today; when, for example, there were over a million men working down coal mines in the UK? After all, most of us can now, after a few mouse clicks, have a new washing machine arrive on our doorstep within a couple of days. Things are pretty good, and they have most certainly improved enormously in many corners of the globe since Steiner's day.

---

[497] Former leader of the UK's Liberal Democrats, when referring to the politics of the USA.

But as we know, we—the human community—are battling with a desperate situation, with ecosystems in peril, with heart-crushing despair still suffered by millions near and far, whilst, for example, the 26 richest people in the world, like medieval monarchs, have as much wealth as the poorer half of the globe's entire population (all 3.8 billion of them), or whilst cocooned hedge fund managers continue to siphon vast wealth out of the system without really producing very much, and without paying much tax either, thanks to their off-shore arrangements.[498] We—humanity—seem to constantly go round in circles making the same mistakes over and over again, groping in the dark for a more dignified, noble direction, and semi-paralysed, it seems, in the face of political powers beset with corrupt influences.

Nowhere is this more true, perhaps, than in the English-speaking world where, if we are not careful, we could well end up in some decadent backwater with our greed, ecocide, guns, stupidity, corruption and pain whilst, elsewhere, civilisation marches forward. Twenty-eight years after writing *Earth in the Balance: Ecology and the Human Spirit*, former US vice president Al Gore recently despaired: 'Incremental improvements to address these challenges are no longer enough; our economic system requires a fundamental upgrade to sustainability'.[499] And Prince Charles, with a lifetime of acute concern for the earth, has urged a 'paradigm shift, one that inspires action at revolutionary levels and pace'.[500]

I would venture to suggest that Steiner provides some of the incisive ideas needed to focus this upgrade, this paradigm shift, notwithstanding his insistence that incremental efforts *do* have merit. An appreciation of the threefold nature of the social organism can, I would argue, help even the most forward-thinking policymaker get their bearings when working for a future that Kate Raworth terms 'distributive and regenerative by design'.[501] It can inform the societal structure wherein 'the ideology

[498] Larry Elliott, 'World's 26 richest people own as much as poorest 50%, says Oxfam', *The Guardian,* 20 January 2019.
[499] Jillian Ambrose, 'Gore: urgent economic overhaul needed to tackle climate crisis', *The Guardian*, 26 June 2019.
[500] Mark Thompson and Max Foster, 'Prince Charles: we need a new economic model or the planet will burn', CNN Business, 22 January 2020.
[501] Kate Raworth, *Doughnut Economics: Seven Ways to Think Like a 21st-Century Economist* (London: Random House, 2018), p. 156.

of extreme individualism and competition [can be overturned by] the uniquely human qualities of altruism, empathy and collective action'—the hopes of Ann Pettifor in *The Case for the Green New Deal*.[502]

Prince Charles made the above comments in Davos when attending the 50th annual meeting of the World Economic Forum—a body whose stated aims include a number of ostensibly welcome features, like encouraging companies to: ditch neo-liberalism; discard short termism; pay their fair share of taxes; root out corruption; respect the needs of mother earth; improve employee wellbeing; and respect human rights throughout their supply chains. To this end, WEF's founder Klaus Schwab brought out *Stakeholder Capitalism* in 2021—a book wherein he proposes companies report on social and environmental performance as well as financial. Such measures, he argues, will bring change. But whether this would be any more successful in reforming companies than the 'triple bottom line' approach that has also been around since the 1990s is hard to say. The WEF has at least engaged the 'big four' accounting firms in devising the metrics. But what is advocated still largely boils down to a reporting exercise in what otherwise remains a highly competitive, profit-maximising form of capitalism. In addition, deep scepticism about the WEF remains widespread; it is seen as a club where elites meet. The biggest concern, it seems, is the organisation's apparent lack of attention to what are, after all, basic threefold principles. Political leaders cosy up with leaders of big business (WEF's funding typically comes from global enterprises with an annual turnover in excess of five billion US dollars), and so suspicions are rife that unelected representatives from Big Tech, Big Pharma, Big Profit-maximiser have leverage in areas they shouldn't. In 2019, 'more than 400 civil society organisations and 40 international networks heavily criticised a partnership agreement between WEF and the United Nations and called on the UN Secretary General to end it'. Such agreement, they argued, amounts to 'disturbing corporate capture of the UN, which moved the world dangerously towards privatised global governance'.[503]

As we have seen, Steiner's approach allows for proper societal hygiene by keeping the different realms at their rightful arm's length, protecting the integrity of each.

---

[502] Ann Pettifor, *The Case For the Green New Deal* (Verso: London, 2019), p. 67.
[503] Wikipedia: World Economic Forum (accessed 20 October 2021).

Complete freedom in culture—i.e. in the development and expression of the individual's faculties; a more brotherly economy; and *proper* equality both before the law, and in establishing the law: the observance of these basic ideals is surely central to creating a healthier world. As has been shown, it can help society benefit from some of the intended advantages of more socialistic approaches (e.g. a more equitable distribution of wealth) without losing the boisterous entrepreneurship and adaptable economy found in capitalism. It can thwart corrupting influences in the media that wish to downplay exploitation at home or even imperial slaughter abroad. It can help ensure that the door is not left open for large concentrations of power and control freakery which can ultimately manifest in the most sinister forms of tyranny—something we are potentially at risk from if we let unelected elites sway debate and control narratives. And so on.

Citing various studies that demonstrate people are, in general, naturally compassionate, and that selfish behaviour only results from the actions of a relative few preaching 'greed is good', Owen Jones notes: 'If we can build a society that encourages greed and sentiments which justify inequality, then we can also build a society nurturing solidarity, compassion and equality. It has proven all too useful for defenders of our bankrupt order to portray it as the rational expression of humanity. But the opposing evidence is there, and it is stark. In a world where prosperity exists alongside such misery, it should give hope to those who believe there really is another way'.[504]

In a similar vein, Steiner notes in 1908:

> ... human beings have created conditions of misery purely out of wrong-headed thoughts. [...] How can joy and love become impulses of daily work again? [...] Remember only what mothers do if they work out of love for the child. Remember what the human being is capable of if he does anything because of love for other human beings. Love for the product of one's work is not necessary; there needs to be connection between human being and human being ... what the future must bring back is an all-embracing understanding and love between human being and human being ... Not until he is able to work because of love for his fellow men is it possible to

---

[504] Owen Jones, 'Grotesque inequality is not a natural part of being human', *The Guardian*, 24 November 2014.

create real impulses for a future development of human welfare. [...]
if human beings need my work, that is an impulse for work that can
induce me 'to a merry song'. (CW56, 12 March 1908)

A decade later, with his descriptions of a threefold approach well under
way, he observes:

Again and again you may find in books on ethical life ideas relating
to benevolence, tolerance, love—love is a very favourite subject—
and similar things. But the way in which they are dealt with does
not enable them to exercise any influence upon human beings.
The moral concepts which are advanced in such an abstract way
have no moral force and contain no moral impulses. [...] do you
find in the words or writings of modern men, belonging to the so
called intellectual circles, anything which can influence humanity
in such a way that ethical requirements become at the same time
socio-economic requirements? The most essential point which
should be borne in mind today is that a straight path must lead
from the field of ethics, religion and spirituality to the most com-
mon, daily questions of economic life, of national economic and
social life. (CW188(vi), 2 February 1919)

It seems highly likely that, had Steiner's approach to social democracy
been adopted in a few countries when he proposed them 100 years ago,
we would now be looking at a far more satisfactory state of affairs in
those regions: not perfect, perhaps; but more equitable, more responsible,
more peaceful, more content, more joyful. It also seems clear that a
number of his ideas continue to have relevance to the on-going debate
about better ways of organising ourselves.

Such a deep longing of the heart
when behind it stands the concentrated power of thinking
of a seer and initiate like Asita
carries in itself the seed of its fulfilment.

Hermann Beckh [505]

---

[505] Hermann Beckh, *From Buddha to Christ* (1925).

Acknowledgements

Phew, we got there!

On completing this book, I would like to thank the following for being prepared to look at it (or parts of it) in draft, jumbled form and for providing invaluable feedback (and, on occasion, much-needed encouragement!): Josie Allwyn, Michael Balcombe, Simon Blaxland-de-Lange, Richard Bunzl, Carol Elloway, Richard House, Christopher Hudson, Margaret Jonas, Deborah Leah, Veronica Tapp, Jenny Vowles. Thank you also to Sibylle Eichstaedt for help with translating some tricky bits of German, and for occasionally letting me write in a quiet corner of her house when I needed somewhere else to be that was free of distractions. Thank you, too, to former colleague Stuart Field whose comments, ten or more years ago, acted as something of a trigger to my eventually embarking on the project. I am also hugely indebted to the late Eve and Anthony Kaye who, a while back, pointed out how a certain type of 'Celtic knot' could serve as a useful illustration of threefolding. Thank you also to Cameron Masters for helping to create the related diagram used in Chapters 6 and 10.

It would be nice also to have a list of people to blame for the book's undoubted shortcomings; but alas! The book is of course long; very long. But perhaps the spadework it contains can act as a resource to enable one of those 'bears of bigger brain' to write something snappier and better in due course.

Finally, thank you, reader, for buying the book! I hope you find some of it useful.

Bibliography

Works by Rudolf Steiner referenced in this book

CW ref.	Source
4	*The Philosophy of Spiritual Activity* (New York: Anthroposophic Press, 1986)
23	*Towards Social Renewal* (London: Rudolf Steiner Press, 1977)
24	*The Renewal of the Social Organism* (New York: Anthroposophic Press, 1985)
24 (ii)	'Memoranda of 1917' published in *Social and Political Science* (Forest Row: Sophia Books, 2003)
24 (iii)	Quoted in Peter Selg, *The Fundamental Social Law: Rudolf Steiner on the Work of the Individual and the Spirit of Community* (Great Barrington, MA: Steiner Books, 2011)
28	*The Course of My Life* (New York: Anthroposophic Press, 1977)
30	'The Social Question', published in *Social and Political Science* (Forest Row: Sophia Books, 2003)
34	'The Science of the Spirit and the Social Question', https://wn.rsarchive.org/GA/GA0034/SocQue_index.html
54	*Brotherhood and the Struggle for Existence* (New York: Mercury Press, 1980)
54 (ii)	'Brotherhood and the Fight for Survival', https://wn.rsarchive.org/GA/GA0054/19080302p01.html
56	'Occupation and Earnings', https://wn.rsarchive.org/Lectures/GA056/English/eLib2015/19080312p01.html
56 (ii)	Quoted in Peter Selg, *The Fundamental Social Law: Rudolf Steiner on the Work of the Individual and the Spirit of Community* (Great Barrington, MA: Steiner Books, 2011)
79	'The Central Question of Economic Life', https://wn.rsarchive.org/Lectures/GA079/English/eLib2019/19211130p01.html
83	*The Tension between East and West* (New York: Anthroposophic Press, 1983)
88	'The Social Question and Theosophy' published in *Social and Political Science* (Forest Row: Sophia Books, 2003)

155	'The Spiritual Foundation of Morality', https://wn.rsarchive.org/GA/GA0155/19120530p01.html
172	*Das Karma des Berufes des Menschen in Anknüpfung an Goethes Leben* ['The karma of human vocation in relation to Goethe's life'] quoted in Peter Selg, *The Fundamental Social Law: Rudolf Steiner on the Work of the Individual and the Spirit of Community* (Great Barrington, MA: Steiner Books, 2011)
177	'Into the Future', https://wn.rsarchive.org/Lectures/GA177/English/RSP1993/19171028p01.html
186	*The Challenge of the Times* (New York: Anthroposophic Press, 1941)
186 (ii)	'The Metamorphosis of Intelligence' published in *Social and Political Science* (Forest Row: Sophia Books, 2003)
188	'Human Science and Social Science'
188 (ii)	https://wn.rsarchive.org/GA/GA0188/19190201p01.html
188 (iii)	https://wn.rsarchive.org/GA/GA0188/19190124p01.html
188 (iv)	https://wn.rsarchive.org/GA/GA0188/19190131p01.html
188 (v)	https://wn.rsarchive.org/GA/GA0188/19190126p01.html
188 (vi)	https://wn.rsarchive.org/GA/GA0188/19190202p01.html
189	*Conscious Society* (Forest Row: Rudolf Steiner Press, 2018)
189 (ii)	https://wn.rsarchive.org/GA/GA0189/19190307p01.html
189 (iii)	https://wn.rsarchive.org/GA/GA0189/19190302p01.html
189 (iv)	https://wn.rsarchive.org/GA/GA0189/19190315p01.html
189 (v)	https://wn.rsarchive.org/GA/GA0189/19190215p01.html
190	*Vergangenheits und Zukunftsimpulse im sozialen Geschehen* ['Past and future impulses of social occurrences'] quoted in Peter Selg, *The Fundamental Social Law: Rudolf Steiner on the Work of the Individual and the Spirit of Community* (Great Barrington, MA: Steiner Books, 2011)
192	'Prelude to the Threefold Commonwealth', https://wn.rsarchive.org/GA/GA0192/19190421p01.html
192 (ii)	Quoted in Peter Selg, *The Fundamental Social Law: Rudolf Steiner on the Work of the Individual and the Spirit of Community* (Great Barrington, MA: Steiner Books, 2011)
192 (iii)	'Pedagogy from the Standpoint of the History of Culture', https://wn.rsarchive.org/GA/GA0192/19190608p01.html
192 (iv)	Quoted in Francis Gladstone, *Republican Academies* (Forest Row: Steiner Schools Fellowship Publications, 2001)

192 (v)   Quoted in Rudolf Isler, *Sustainable Society: Making Business, Government and Money Work Again* (Edinburgh: Floris Books, 2014)

193   *The Esoteric Aspect of the Social Question* (London: Rudolf Steiner Press, 2001)

194   *Ideas for a New Europe* (Sussex: Rudolf Steiner Press, 1992)

196   *Ideas for a New Europe* (Sussex: Rudolf Steiner Press, 1992)

196 (ii)   *What is Necessary in these Urgent Times* (Great Barrington, MA: SteinerBooks, 2010)

197   *Polarities in the Evolution of Mankind* (New York: Anthroposophic Press, 1987)

296   'Historical Requirements of the Present Time', https://wn.rsarchive.org/Lectures/GA296/English/AP1969/19190809p01.html

298   *Rudolf Steiner in the Waldorf School*, quoted in Francis Gladstone, *Republican Academies* (Forest Row: Steiner Schools Fellowship Publications, 2001)

300   *Conferences with Teachers*, quoted in Francis Gladstone, *Republican Academies* (Forest Row: Steiner Schools Fellowship Publications, 2001)

305   *Threefold the Social Order* (Canterbury: New Economy Publications, 1996)

305 (ii)   *Rudolf Steiner Speaks to the British* (London: Rudolf Steiner Press, 1998)

305 (iii)   Quoted in Francis Gladstone, *Republican Academies* (Forest Row: Steiner Schools Fellowship Publications, 2001)

310   *Human Values in Education*, quoted in Francis Gladstone, *Republican Academies* (Forest Row: Steiner Schools Fellowship Publications, 2001)

311   *The Kingdom of Childhood*, quoted in Francis Gladstone, *Republican Academies* (Forest Row: Steiner Schools Fellowship Publications, 2001)

328   *The Social Question* (Fremont, MI: Rudolf Steiner Archive and e.Lib, 2017)

328 (ii)   https://wn.rsarchive.org/GA/GA0328/19190205p01.html
328 (iii)   https://wn.rsarchive.org/GA/GA0328/19190210p01.html
328 (iv)   https://wn.rsarchive.org/GA/GA0328/19190308p01.html
328 (v)   https://wn.rsarchive.org/GA/GA0328/19190203p01.html

329   'Die Befreiung des Menschenwesens als Grundlage fur eine soziale Negestaltung' ['The liberation of the human being as the basis for social transformation'], https://anthrowiki.at/GA_329 [Translations by RM]

329 (ii)   Quoted in Albert Schmelzer, *The Threefolding Movement, 1919: A History* (Forest Row: Rudolf Steiner Press, 2017)

330   *Neugestaltung des socialen Organismus* ['Redesign of the social organism'] Quoted in Peter Selg, *The Fundamental Social Law: Rudolf Steiner on the Work of the Individual and the Spirit of Community* (Great Barrington, MA: Steiner Books, 2011)

330 (ii)   'The Impulse toward the Threefold Social Order', https://wn.rsarchive.org/GA/GA0330/19190531p01.html

330 (iii)   Quoted in Rudolf Isler, *Sustainable Society: Making Business, Government and Money Work Again* (Edinburgh: Floris Books, 2014)

331   'Betriebsräte und Sozialisierung' ['Works councils and socialisation'], https://anthrowiki.at/GA_331 [Translations by RM]

332a   *The Social Future* (New York: Anthroposophic Press, 1972)

332a (ii)   *Soziale Zukunft* (Dornach: Rudolf Steiner Verlag, 1977) [Translations by RM]

333   *Freedom of Thought and Societal Forces* (Great Barrington, MA: SteinerBooks, 2008)

333 (ii)   Quoted in Peter Selg, *The Fundamental Social Law: Rudolf Steiner on the Work of the Individual and the Spirit of Community* (Great Barrington, MA: Steiner Books, 2011)

334   *Social Issues: Meditative Thinking and the Threefold Social Order* (New York: Anthroposophic Press, 1991)

334 (ii)   Quoted in Rudolf Isler, *Sustainable Society: Making Business, Government and Money Work Again* (Edinburgh: Floris Books, 2014)

335   'The Threefold Order of the Body Social—Study Series II', https://wn.rsarchive.org/GA/GA0335/19200915p01.html

335 (ii)   'The Peoples of the Earth in the Light of Anthroposophy', https://wn.rsarchive.org/Lectures/19200310p01.html

337   'On Propaganda of the Threefold Social Order', https://wn.rsarchive.org/GA/GA0337/19200609p01.html

337a	'Soziale Ideen. Soziale Wirklichkeit. Soziale Praxis. Band 1' ['Social ideas, social reality, social practice. Part 1'], https://anthrowiki.at/GA_337a [Translations by RM]
337a (ii)	Quoted in Rudolf Isler, *Sustainable Society: Making Business, Government and Money Work Again* (Edinburgh: Floris Books, 2014)
337b	'Soziale Ideen. Soziale Wirklichkeit. Soziale Praxis. Band 2' ['Social ideas, social reality, social practice. Part 2'], https://anthrowiki.at/GA_337b [Translations by RM]
338	*Wie Wirkt Man für den Impuls der Dreigliederung des Sozialen Organismus?* ['How does one work for the impulse of the threefold social organism?'], https://anthrowiki.at/GA_40 [Translations by RM]
338 (ii)	Quoted in Peter Selg, *The Fundamental Social Law: Rudolf Steiner on the Work of the Individual and the Spirit of Community* (Great Barrington, MA: Steiner Books, 2011)
338 (iii)	Published in *Social and Political Science* (Forest Row: Sophia Books, 2003)
339	'The Art of Lecturing', https://wn.rsarchive.org/GA/GA0339/19211013p02.html
339 (ii)	https://wn.rsarchive.org/GA/GA0339/19211012p01.html
339 (iii)	https://wn.rsarchive.org/GA/GA0339/19211014v02.html
340	*World Economy* (London: Rudolf Steiner Press, 1977)
340 (ii)	*Economics: The World As One Economy* (West Hoathly: New
341	Economy Publications, 1993)
V&M	*Verses and Meditations* (Bristol: Rudolf Steiner Press, 1993)